engage

COLLEGE READING

IVAN G. DOLE
North Lake College

LESLIE TAGGART

WADSWORTH
CENGAGE Learning·

Australia • Brazil • Japan • Korea • Mexico • Singapore • Spain • United Kingdom • United States

Engage: College Reading
Ivan G. Dole, Leslie Taggart

Senior Publisher: Lyn Uhl

Director of Developmental Studies:
Annie Todd

Executive Editor: Shani Fisher

Development Editor: Marita Sermolins

Assistant Editor: Beth Rice

Editorial Assistant: Matt Conte

Media Editor: Amy Gibbons

Marketing Coordinator: Brittany Blais

Marketing Communications Manager:
Linda Yip

Content Project Manager: Corinna
Dibble

Senior Art Director: Cate Rickard Barr

Senior Print Buyer: Betsy Donaghey

Rights Acquisition Specialist: Don
Schlotman

Production Service: Lachina Publishing
Services

Text Designer: Lachina Publishing
Services

Cover Designer: Nancy Goulet

Cover Images: iPad image:
www.gettyimages.com; Wii image:
www.fotosearch.com; iPhone image:
www.shutterstock.com; Computer
image: www.shutterstock.com

Compositor: Lachina Publishing Services

For product information and technology assistance, contact us at
Cengage Learning Customer & Sales Support, 1-800-354-9706

For permission to use material from this text or product,
submit all requests online at **www.cengage.com/permissions**.
Further permissions questions can be emailed to
permissionrequest@cengage.com.

Library of Congress Control Number: 2011933493

Student Edition:
ISBN-13: 978-1-4130-3317-5
ISBN-10: 1-4130-3317-2

Wadsworth
20 Channel Center Street
Boston, MA 02210
USA

Cengage Learning is a leading provider of customized learning solutions with office locations around the globe, including Singapore, the United Kingdom, Australia, Mexico, Brazil, and Japan. Locate your local office at **international.cengage.com/region**

Cengage Learning products are represented in Canada by Nelson Education, Ltd.

For your course and learning solutions, visit **www.cengage.com**.

Purchase any of our products at your local college store or at our preferred online store **www.cengagebrain.com**.

Instructors: Please visit **login.cengage.com** and log in to access instructor-specific resources.

Printed in the United States of America
3 4 5 6 7 15 14

Contents

Preface   x

Plan for Success   xxvii

PART 1   Reading and Study Strategies   3

CHAPTER 1   Engaging with Reading   4

PREVIEWING THE CHAPTER   4

Why Is Reading Important?   5

    Getting Motivated to Read   6

    The Power of Visualizing Your Future   8

Watching Videos, Reading Articles, and Talking with Classmates   12

Read and Talk   *The Power of Choice* (College Success Textbook)   *12*

Reading Is an Interaction   15

    Before You View or Read   17

    While You Are Viewing or Reading   21

    After You View or Read   24

Increasing Your Reading Rate   29

    Your Reading Rate Is Based on Your Reason for Reading   33

CHAPTER SUMMARY ACTIVITY   35

ENGAGE YOUR SKILLS   36

MASTER YOUR SKILLS   39

Focus on Communications

    College Communications App:
    Celebrity Endorsements (Advertising Textbook)   *45*

    Career Communications App:
    Today's Generations Face New Communication Gaps (Magazine
    Website)   *56*

Image: © iStockphoto.com/Terry Morris

CHAPTER 2 Expanding Your Vocabulary 66

PREVIEWING THE CHAPTER 66

Read and Talk *CNN Reporter Sanjay Gupta Becomes Part of the Story in Haiti* (Online Newspaper) 67

Vocabulary Strategies 71

Define Words As You Read Using Context Clues 71

Find Context Clues While Reading 72

Recognize Four Kinds of Context Clues 73

Create EASY Note Cards to Study Words 87

Understand the Connotations of Some Words 91

Study Vocabulary Systematically Using Word Parts 93

Roots Carry the Basic Meaning 94

Prefixes Add Information to the Meaning 95

Suffixes Show How Words Act in Sentences 97

Using Your Knowledge of Word Parts to Make Meaning 100

Word Parts Glossary 103

Understand the Vocabulary of College 106

Focus: How Textbooks Show Which Words Are Important 108

Focus: Learning Vocabulary via Diagrams 109

CHAPTER SUMMARY ACTIVITY 111

ENGAGE YOUR SKILLS 113

MASTER YOUR SKILLS 116

Focus on Health

College Health App:
How Can I Change a Bad Health Habit? (Health Textbook) 124

Career Health App:
Join Our Fight Against AIDS (Website) 132

CHAPTER 3 Identifying Topics and Main Ideas 139

PREVIEWING THE CHAPTER 139

Read and Talk *Breaking Out: One School System's Success with Autistic Children* (Magazine) 140

MAPPS: A Reading Plan 143

Marking the Answers to Your Questions 144

What Is the Reading About? The Topic 145

Image: © James Steidl/Shutterstock.com

What Is the Point of the Reading? The Main Idea   154

Location of the Topic Sentence: Anywhere   163

Thesis Statements in Textbook Sections   169

CHAPTER SUMMARY ACTIVITY   175

ENGAGE YOUR SKILLS   177

MASTER YOUR SKILLS   179

Focus on Education

College Education App:
Technology and Learning (Education Textbook)   *185*

Career Education App:
School Texts :(: Educators Differ on How to Handle Cell Phones in Classrooms (Online Newspaper)   *196*

CHAPTER 4 Noticing Patterns of Supporting Details   **205**

PREVIEWING THE CHAPTER   205

Read and Talk *Gunfire on Campus: Lesson Learned* (Criminal Justice Textbook)   *206*

What Is the Proof? The Supporting Details   208

Major versus Minor Details   212

Patterns that Organize Supporting Details   219

Types of Organizational Patterns   222

     Classification: What Kinds Are There?   222

     Comparison and Contrast: How Are These the Same? How Do They Differ?   224

     Definition: What Is This? What Does It Mean?   227

     Examples: What Are Examples of This General Idea?   228

     Cause and Effect: What Made This Happen? What Does This Lead To?   230

     Time Order: When Did That Happen? What Steps Does It Take?   232

     Space Order: Where Are Things Located?   235

     Each Pattern Answers a Question   236

CHAPTER SUMMARY ACTIVITY   244

ENGAGE YOUR SKILLS   246

MASTER YOUR SKILLS   249

Focus on Criminal Justice

College Criminal Justice App:
Home Confinement and Electronic Monitoring (Criminal Justice Textbook)   *257*

Career Criminal Justice App:
Dogs Trained to Smell Cell Phones Will Fight Prison Drug Crimes (Website)   *266*

Images: Brand X Pictures/Jupiter Images; © Rambleon/Shutterstock.com

CHAPTER 5 Applying Reading Comprehension Skills through Note Taking 275

PREVIEWING THE CHAPTER 275

Ask Questions and Mark the Answers 276

Turn Titles, Headings, and Subtitles into Questions 276
Read to Answer the Question, Then Mark the Answer, and Repeat 279
Mark Only the Most Important Ideas 284
Should You Highlight or Annotate? 284
Turning Highlights and Annotations into an Outline 288

Use Cornell Notes to Record Ideas 303

Paraphrase to Recall Ideas 312

Switch It, Flip It, Tweak It 312
Flesh It Out 316

CHAPTER SUMMARY ACTIVITY 319

PART 2 Critical Reading Strategies 323

CHAPTER 6 Asking Critical Thinking Questions 324

PREVIEWING THE CHAPTER 324

Read and Talk *Lone Survivor* (Memoir) *325*

Critical Thinking Is a Learning Process 327

Level 1: Remembering 329
Level 2: Understanding 329
Level 3: Applying 329
Level 4: Analyzing 329
Level 5: Evaluating 330
Level 6: Creating 330

Using Critical Thinking to Determine Hierarchy 335

Using Critical Thinking to Analyze Test Questions 340

Applying Critical Thinking to Reading Passages 345

CHAPTER SUMMARY ACTIVITY 352

ENGAGE YOUR SKILLS 354

MASTER YOUR SKILLS 356

Focus on Visual Arts

College Visual Arts App:
Paleolithic Cave Painting (Art Textbook)   *364*

Career Visual Arts App:
Every Child Needs the Arts (Online Education Journal)   *377*

CHAPTER 7 Inferring Meaning from Details   388

PREVIEWING THE CHAPTER   388

Read and Talk *Illegal Fireworks Likely Cause of Massive Arkansas Blackbird Deaths* (Magazine)   *389*

The Process of Making Inferences   392
Inferences that Fit All the Details   394
The Role of Prior Knowledge in Making Inferences   397
Generalizing by Identifying Patterns among Ideas   405
Inferring Implied Main Ideas   413
   Inferring the Topic Sentence of a Paragraph   413
   Inferring the Thesis Statement of a Longer Selection   420
CHAPTER SUMMARY ACTIVITY   425
ENGAGE YOUR SKILLS   427
MASTER YOUR SKILLS   431

Focus on Environmental Science

College Environmental Science App:
Easter Island: Some Revisions in a Popular Environmental Story (Ecology Textbook)   *437*

Career Environmental Science App:
A New World (Nonfiction Book)   *446*

CHAPTER 8 Evaluating the Author's Purpose and Tone   460

PREVIEWING THE CHAPTER   460

Read and Talk *Now What Was My Password? . . .* (Textbook)   *461*

Three Main Purposes (PIE Review)   463
Distinguishing Between Denotation and Connotation   470
   Connotations Suggest a Subjective Tone   474
   Lack of Connotations Suggests an Objective Tone   475

Considering a Word's Degree of Intensity 478

Learning to Use More Specific Tone Words 480

Understanding the Different Tones of Literal and Figurative Language 485

A Simile Is Like a Metaphor, but a Metaphor Is Not a Simile 485
Personification 487
Hyperbole 488
Understanding Irony 490

Understanding How Tone Supports the Author's Purpose 495
CHAPTER SUMMARY ACTIVITY 503
ENGAGE YOUR SKILLS 504
MASTER YOUR SKILLS 508

Focus on Computer and Information Sciences

College Computer and Information Sciences App:
The Hacker (Computer Science Textbook) 516

Career Computer and Information Sciences App:
Social Media and Politics: Truthiness and Astroturfing (Social Technology Blog) 527

CHAPTER 9 Evaluating Points of View 538
PREVIEWING THE CHAPTER 538

Read and Talk   *The Potential Lover: Is This Person Attracted to Me?* (Online Magazine) 539

Fact, Opinion, and Bias 542

Facts Can Be Verified 543

Opinions Are Subjective 545

Words That Can Express Opinions 549

Adjectives 549
Qualifiers 553
Comparatives and Superlatives 556

Sources of Information 560

Expert Opinion 561
Informed Opinion 562
People on the Street 562

Bias for a Viewpoint 567

CHAPTER SUMMARY ACTIVITY   575

ENGAGE YOUR SKILLS   577

MASTER YOUR SKILLS   581

Focus on Psychology

College Psychology App:
Improving Everyday Memory (Psychology Textbook)   *587*

Career Psychology App:
Domestic Drama: On-Again, Off-Again (Website)   *597*

CHAPTER 10 Applying Critical Thinking Skills to Visuals   607

PREVIEWING THE CHAPTER   607

Textbook Visuals   608

Interpreting Visuals   608

Interpret Tables   609

Interpret Pie Charts   614

Interpret Line Graphs   617

Interpret Bar Graphs   620

Interpret Flowcharts   623

Interpret Photographs   625

CHAPTER SUMMARY ACTIVITY   628

PART 3   **Reading Across the Disciplines   631**

Reading A: Health   632

Stress on Campus   *633*

Reading B: Business Communication   653

Communicating in a Diverse Environment   *654*

Reading C: Sociology   674

Overcoming the Factors of Poverty: The Big Five   *675*

Credits   697

Index   702

Image: © iStockphoto.com/Marcello Bortolino

Engage: College Reading is the third book in a series designed to motivate students by focusing on the strengths they have already developed and the knowledge they have already gained through their life experiences, while at the same time sharing with them new reading strategies that increase their chance for reading success in college. Like *Activate: College Reading* and *Connect: College Reading, Engage* teaches methodical approaches to common reading tasks and then provides plenty of practice to help students internalize them. All three books go beyond the multiple-choice format for reading comprehension and ask students to explain their answers. This simple step has profound implications for how much students learn to think about their reading.

The three books address three different levels of college readers as well as different approaches to reading selections. *Activate* is for students reading at the 6th to 9th grade reading levels. *Activate*'s end-of-part application readings give students the opportunity to transfer skill-based practices into holistic reading applications from academic and real-world readings. There is also a dedicated part with theme-based reading at the end of *Activate*. *Connect* is for students reading at the 9th to 12th grade reading levels. *Connect*'s chapter-end readings take a thematic approach. *Engage* is for students reading at the 10th to 12th grade reading levels. The chapter-end readings in *Engage* take an across-the-disciplines approach. All three books, however, start where students start: with a love of media.

A Book Designed to Engage the YouTube Generation

As you enthusiastically greet your class each semester, you know that your students may not bring many formal reading strategies with them to the college reading classroom, but they do bring a wealth of life experience. And if students haven't had certain experiences themselves, they have probably lived them vicariously through the media. Because many students have enjoyed using multimedia such as television, movies, and the Internet more than they have print materials, *Engage: College Reading* draws on these media experiences to help students learn reading strategies and stay engaged in reading.

- **Viewing Media Is Linked to the Reading Process.** Chapter 1 shows students how they use a "before, during, and after" process when watching a television program (or movie) and then demonstrates how to apply the same process to reading. Media is also used as a means to help students gain knowledge before reading a text selection.

- **Videos Bolster Prior Knowledge.** For each reading at the beginning and end of Chapters 1–4 and 6–9, and for all three readings in Part 3, students can view a video on a closely related topic. They can then approach the reading with this prior knowledge, increasing the likelihood that they will comprehend the reading. The videos are online at the Reading CourseMate for *Engage: College Reading,* accessed via CengageBrain.com.

- **Audio Makes Reading More Engaging.** Your students can also find two kinds of audio files on the Reading CourseMate for *Engage: College Reading* that help make reading a more engaging experience and aid students who have auditory learning preferences.

  - Each "Read and Talk" reading (at the beginning of each of Chapters 1–4 and 6–9) is read aloud so students can listen to as well as read them.

  - Each red vocabulary word in every reading has a corresponding audio file so students can hear how the word is pronounced. These audio files help students gain confidence using the new vocabulary in conversation.

**Videos Related
to Readings**

**Vocab Words
on Audio**

**Read and Talk
on Demand**

Critical Thinking Required!

A byword of the Dole/Taggart reading series is critical thinking. *Engage: College Reading* prepares students to succeed in their college courses and their careers by

- guiding them to apply reading comprehension skills,

- analyzing an author's purpose, tone, and use of ideas,

- inferring meaning from details,

- and evaluating points of view for credibility.

This is just one side of the coin, however. Throughout, *Engage* also emphasizes that in college, students need to be able to summarize their reading and explain their analyses to others.

- **The "Why?" question** is asked after every multiple-choice question in the book. Students are asked to explain their thinking in writing after they have selected an answer by going back into the reading selection and finding information to support their answer. This allows students to practice analysis and learn to provide evidence for their ideas, a skill they will use in every college course. Students' answers can also provide instructors with valuable feedback about what students are noticing or ignoring as they read.

_____ 1. Which of the following is the best topic sentence for paragraph 2?

    a. For Bethany, texting has become a form of addiction, she said.

    b. Averaging 13,000 texts a month, she said she has memorized the keypad to send messages undetected in class by pecking away from the safety of her bulky Carhartt jacket pocket.

    c. At least, she did until Friday.

    d. That's when a teacher noticed her looking at the screen and confiscated it for the first time, adding her device to the nearly 15 others housed at the front desk until the end of the day, when students are allowed to retrieve them.

WHY? What information in the selection leads you to give that answer? _____

_____

_____

- **Part 2 focuses on critical reading strategies.**
  - Chapter 6 introduces the updated Bloom's taxonomy, discusses how to use the taxonomy to figure out what kinds of responses are being asked for on tests, and teaches students how to ask questions as they read.

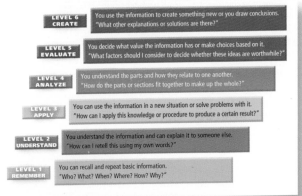

LEVEL 6 CREATE — You use the information to create something new or you draw conclusions. "What other explanations or solutions are there?"

LEVEL 5 EVALUATE — You decide what value the information has or make choices based on it. "What factors should I consider to decide whether these ideas are worthwhile?"

LEVEL 4 ANALYZE — You understand the parts and how they relate to one another. "How do the parts or sections fit together to make up the whole?"

LEVEL 3 APPLY — You can use the information in a new situation or solve problems with it. "How can I apply this knowledge or procedure to produce a certain result?"

LEVEL 2 UNDERSTAND — You understand the information and can explain it to someone else. "How can I retell this using my own words?"

LEVEL 1 REMEMBER — You can recall and repeat basic information. "Who? What? When? Where? How? Why?"

  - Chapter 7 is a detailed approach to drawing inferences, both cause-and-effect inferences and detail-to-generalization inferences.
  - Chapter 8 takes a thorough look at purpose and tone; it emphasizes particular categories of words for students to notice and question.
  - Chapter 9, on evaluating points of view, helps students distinguish among fact, opinion, and bias and includes a unique system for evaluating facts given by a source and the expertise of the source to determine its credibility.
  - Chapter 10 asks students to apply their critical thinking strategies to viewing the kinds of graphic and visual information they will find often in textbooks.

- **Critical thinking underlies vocabulary questions** that appear after the chapter-end "College App" and "Career App" readings and after the three readings in Part 3. Instead of providing students with a list of vocabulary words and definitions before a reading, *Engage* points to context clues and word part clues during reading so that students can figure out the meanings of words. (See the margin of page 45 for an example.) This critical thinking process is true to how experienced readers figure out word meanings on the fly. In addition, the "Language in Use" activities that accompany each chapter-end reading require students to use vocabulary words in new contexts.

Access the Reading CourseMate via www.cengagebrain.com to hear vocabulary words from this selection and view a video about this topic.

Domestic Drama: On-Again, Off-Again

Elizabeth Svoboda

Reading Journal

1 For Laura, a 35-year-old corporate recruiter from New York City, dating had always felt like a Ferris wheel ride. When a relationship started to feel wrong, she'd leave to get a new **vantage** point on things, but as the pain of singleness set in, she retreated to her former partner for comfort, ending up back where she started. She'd repeat the cycle several times before breaking things off permanently. "It became this crazy pattern," she says. "They weren't good guys at all, but whenever something in my life was difficult, I would go back."

vantage Use your prior knowledge to think of what a *vantage* point might be when you leave a relationship.

○ Why did Laura go back?

● Language in Use

> vantage embarking fervent fleeting hiatus
>
> estrangement panacea elucidate acquiesced

1. Life is _____, but sometimes we get a second chance. Such was the case for Maurice Hamonneau, a soldier in the French Foreign Legion during World War I.

2. He was wounded, which forced him to take a _____ from consciousness for several hours. When he awoke, he realized that the book he had in his breast pocket had saved his life.

3. The book was *Kim* by Rudyard Kipling; it had stopped a bullet. As you can imagine, he became a more _____ fan of Kipling than ever before.

4. When he heard that Kipling was mourning the loss of his own son, Maurice wrote a letter offering him not a _____, but the book that had saved his life (bullet still embedded), as well as a medal he had been given.

5. The gesture moved Kipling greatly. He _____ on the condition that the book and medal be returned if Maurice had a son. When Maurice did indeed have a son, Kipling returned the book and medal with a letter to the son, containing the advice that he should always carry a book of at least 350 pages in his left breast pocket for protection!

Reading for College

- **Varied Readings from Across the Disciplines.** *Engage: College Reading* includes a very diverse selection of readings from college textbooks across the disciplines, including

  - marketing
  - biology
  - advertising
  - history
  - sociology
  - anthropology
  - psychology
  - education
  - American government
  - graphic communication

  - anatomy and physiology
  - business ethics
  - human development
  - policing
  - criminology
  - health
  - abnormal psychology
  - population studies

  - music appreciation
  - culinary studies
  - composition
  - environmental science
  - business management
  - economics

  Part 3, titled "Reading Across the Disciplines," adds three longer readings to the mix, representing the fields of health, business, and sociology. *Engage* provides college textbook reading selections both for brief, targeted reading practice and for longer, more sustained reading.

- **Reading Skills Prepare Students for Academic Reading.** Part 1 of *Engage: College Reading* focuses on foundational skills that students need in order to successfully read their college textbooks.

  - Chapter 1 introduces the reading process.

  - A comprehensive review of vocabulary strategies is provided in Chapter 2, including some brief material intended to demystify the language of the college curriculum and information on vocabulary patterns found in textbooks.

  - Chapter 3 focuses on identifying topics and main ideas by introducing a system called MAPPS, which is a device for remembering the structure of text and relationships among ideas. Throughout the book after MAPPS is introduced in Chapter 3, students are asked to create these visual outlines and summaries after chapter-end readings to help them internalize the heuristics on which MAPPS is based.

Mark = Mark the answers to your questions.

About = Topic: What is the reading about?

Point = Main idea: What is the point?

Proof = Supporting detail: What is the proof?

Summary = A combination of the topic, point, and proof.

- Chapter 4 covers patterns of supporting details by focusing on the connections between familiar questions people ask and the patterns that answer them.

- Chapter 5, "Applying Reading Comprehension Skills through Note Taking," is a short chapter provided to apply the processes and strategies of Part 1 to a learning task that students will use in every college course: taking notes and summarizing material so that they don't have to constantly reread in order to study for a test. The Cornell note-taking system is explained, and two methods for paraphrasing ideas in order to review them are introduced.

Moving Beyond College to Careers

Many students attend college to improve their professional prospects, and *Engage: College Reading* focuses on this desire as a way to help students become and stay motivated to read.

- **Creating Motivated Readers.** Chapter 1 opens with a section called "Why Is Reading Important?" that discusses how college reading is needed to enter certain career fields. That section also asks students to investigate the income potential of careers they are considering. This realistic appraisal will, we believe, help students develop a longer-term motivation. In addition, we have found that many developmental students don't understand the motivational power of visualizing their futures, so Chapter 1 also includes an interaction that guides them in developing a vision and a plan for making that vision a reality.

- **Exploring Available Careers.** More than motivation is needed for career success; knowledge of options is also important. The two readings at the end of Chapters 1–4 and 6–9 both relate to a particular discipline. They focus on:

- communications (Chapter 1)
- health (Chapter 2)
- education (Chapter 3)
- criminal justice (Chapter 4)
- visual arts (Chapter 6)
- environmental science (Chapter 7)
- computer and information sciences (Chapter 8)
- psychology (Chapter 9)

Before each "College App," which is a reading from a college textbook, a graphic shows students several disciplines that the reading relates to. It then names some of the fields of work that the discipline prepares a student to enter. We hope for two results from these figures:

1. That students will start to understand that in, say, a psychology textbook, they will also find interesting connections to other fields. They can search for these connections to stave off boredom when reading in an area that is not of particular interest to them.

2. That students will become aware of career fields they probably haven't considered because they didn't know that they exist.

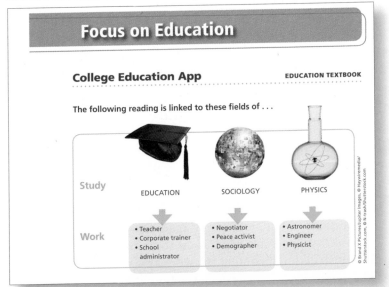

Focus on Education

College Education App   EDUCATION TEXTBOOK

The following reading is linked to these fields of . . .

Study	EDUCATION	SOCIOLOGY	PHYSICS
Work	• Teacher • Corporate trainer • School administrator	• Negotiator • Peace activist • Demographer	• Astronomer • Engineer • Physicist

© Brand X Pictures/Jupiter Images, © Haywiremedia/Shutterstock.com, © N-trash/Shutterstock.com

bluestocking/iStockphoto.com (pens/pencils)

- **Enjoying Reading Relevant to Careers.** The second chapter-end reading is called a "Career App." Students may not be ready to read technical material from a career not yet started, but they can read about interesting current events and controversies linked to the fields they may enter later. Generational approaches to on-the-job communications, teachers' responses to having cell phones in the classroom, criminal justice's training of dogs to halt drug deals prisoners make on prohibited cell phones, how the arts express intelligence—all provide glimpses into possible careers and the joys and challenges students will face as workers.

A Progression of Skills Within a Holistic Framework

- **Progressive Practice Allows Students to Integrate Skills.** *Engage: College Reading* focuses students' attention on one skill at a time to give them the best opportunity to fully integrate each skill before moving on.

  - **Interactions Provide Targeted Practice.** The first four chapters in each of the first two parts of the book include targeted activities ("Interactions") for immediate practice, as well as two more comprehensive activities—"Engage Your Skills" and "Master Your Skills"—that not only give students additional practice but can also be used to test individual skills.

  - **College and Career Apps Supply Practice Readings.** Two major readings at chapter's end are the "College App," a selection from a college textbook, and the "Career App," a non-text-book reading from the same discipline. These two readings are accompanied by questions on all the major reading skills.

  - **Part 3 Features Longer Readings.** In addition, three readings in Part 3, "Reading Across the Disciplines," are arranged by length, at about 1,350 to 1,520 to 2,200 words, respectively. Each of these readings is accompanied by fifty questions, allowing them to be used as practice tests as well as being a significant additional source of reading practice.

- **Students Engage with Visual Summaries.** Along with all these questions about third-party readings that appear throughout the book, students are also asked to summarize their understanding of instructional content in two ways.

- **Section Reviews.** At the end of each section of a chapter, students fill in graphics with the key ideas from the section. Doing this gives them an opportunity to pause and reflect on what they have just learned and, if necessary, to review the main points.

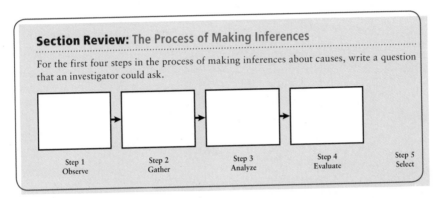

Section Review: The Process of Making Inferences

For the first four steps in the process of making inferences about causes, write a question that an investigator could ask.

| Step 1 Observe | Step 2 Gather | Step 3 Analyze | Step 4 Evaluate | Step 5 Select |

- **Chapter Summary Activities.** At the end of the chapter, a Chapter Summary Activity requires a retrospective look at the whole chapter; the result is a reading guide for the skill under discussion that the student can use as a review later in the course or whenever it's needed.

**Chapter Summary Activity:
Engaging with Reading**

Chapter 1 has discussed how to read as an active process, showing you strategies you can use before, during, and after you read to increase your reading comprehension. Fill in the following Reading Guide by completing each idea on the left with information from Chapter 1 on the right. You can return to this guide throughout the course as a reminder of how to use the reading process to your advantage.

Reading Guide to Engaging with Reading

Complete this idea	with information from Chapter 1.
Reading is important because it can help you achieve two goals:	1. _____ 2. _____
Before you read, you should do four things:	3. _____ 4. _____ 5. _____ 6. _____
While surveying, pay attention to these parts of a reading selection:	7. _____ 8. _____ 9. _____ 10. _____ 11. _____
The author always has a purpose. The three general purposes the author may have are these:	12. _____ 13. _____ 14. _____

- **Emphasis on an Active Reading Process throughout *Engage*.** The framework for all this skill development is the active reading process introduced in Chapter 1 and then revisited in all the major readings. Students practice a full reading process in every end-of-chapter reading and all the readings in Part 3.

Before they read, students:

- survey the reading,
- guess its purpose,
- predict the content,
- and activate their prior knowledge.

While they read, students:

- answer clarifying questions and
- use context clues to understand unknown words.

After they read, students

- respond to questions about:
  - main idea,
  - supporting details,
  - author's purpose,
  - relationships,
  - and fact, opinion, and inference,
  - map or outline the reading (once the relevant concepts are introduced),
  - and respond to questions at the Apply, Analyze, and Evaluate levels of (the updated version of) Bloom's taxonomy (once the relevant concepts are introduced).

● Pre-Reading the Selection

The excerpt that begins on page 45 comes from the textbook *Creative Strategy in Advertising.* The excerpt is titled "Celebrity Endorsements."

Surveying the Reading

Survey the textbook selection that follows. Then check the elements that are included in this reading.

_____ Title

_____ Headings

_____ First sentences of paragraphs

_____ Words in bold or italic type

_____ Images and captions

Guessing the Purpose

Based on the source and the title of the reading selection, do you think the authors' purpose is mostly to persuade, inform, or express? _____

● Comprehension Questions

Write the letter of the answer on the line. Then explain your thinking.

Main Idea

_____ 1. Which of the following best states the main idea of paragraph 3?

    a. Before they reach the stage where they can and do take action to change, most people go through a process comparable to religious conversion.

    b. First, they reach a level of accumulated unhappiness that makes them ready for change.

    c. One pregnant woman, for instance, felt her unborn baby quiver when she drank a beer and swore never to drink again.

    d. As people change their behavior, they change their lifestyles and identities as well.

WHY? What information in the selection leads you to give that answer? _____

_____

_____

Supplements

Instructor's Manual and Test Bank

Written by Ellen Zimmerli of Lehigh Carbon Community College, this Instructor's Manual and Test Bank features chapter summaries and a wide variety of activities and handouts to use in the classroom. Each chapter includes quizzes on content and vocabulary in addition to full chapter tests, a midterm, and a final. You can also access the Instructor Companion Site for *Engage: College Reading* at **login.cengage.com** and download an electronic version of the Instructor's Manual and Test Bank, in addition to interactive PowerPoint® slides for each chapter, sample syllabi, and ExamView® test bank files.

CourseMate Reading CourseMate

Cengage Learning's Reading CourseMate brings course concepts to life with interactive learning, study, and exam preparation tools that support the printed textbook. Watch student comprehension soar as your class works with the printed textbook and the textbook-specific website. Reading CourseMate goes beyond the book to deliver what you need!

Reading CourseMate includes:

- An interactive eBook
- Interactive teaching and learning tools, including
  - Quizzes
  - Flashcards
  - Videos
  - Additional Practice Readings Accompanied by Comprehension and Vocabulary Quizzes
  - Timed Reading
- Engagement Tracker, a first-of-its-kind tool that monitors student engagement in the course. Tailored for *Engage: College Reading*, Reading CourseMate also provides audio versions of "Read and Talk" readings with embedded videos on topics

pertinent to the readings included in *Engage*. The videos give students the prior knowledge they might be lacking and increase their cultural literacy. Look for this icon in the text, which denotes resources available within CourseMate, and access them via **login.cengage.com**.

aplia Aplia for *Engage: College Reading*

Aplia for *Engage: College Reading*, an online reading and learning solution, uses compelling material, interactive assignments, and detailed explanations to give students the structure and motivation to become better readers. With Aplia for *Engage*, students practice identifying main points and supporting details, honing critical thinking skills, reviewing vocabulary, and improving comprehension.

Each lesson assignment begins with an engagement page that features an interactive multimedia application to spark students' interest. The engagement page also includes a quote, introduction to the lesson, and comprehension questions that correspond to the multimedia feature.

The core concepts page covers the main objectives of the textbook, such as strategies to increase a student's reading comprehension, surveying and identifying the purpose, main idea, and supporting details of a reading, and identifying word parts such as suffixes and prefixes. The material uses multiple choice, check box, scenario, identification, and comprehension questions.

Compelling readings provide questions of varying difficulty with detailed explanations that let students try a problem again if they get it wrong the first time. Students can also interact with the text by using built-in tools that allow them to annotate, underline, and highlight. The in-text vocabulary review uses ten new and challenging words taken from the readings and reviews. The reading page also includes reviews of the synonyms and antonyms of each vocabulary word.

To learn more about Aplia for *Engage: College Reading*, visit **www.aplia.com/ developmentalenglish**.

Acknowledgments

We would like to thank the superb editorial, production, and marketing teams at Cengage Learning who have collaborated with us in making *Engage: College Reading* a textbook we can be proud of. Annie Todd, Director of Developmental English and College Success, has been an inspiring leader and steadfast supporter through all three books in the series. Marita Sermolins, Development Editor, has also been our partner from the first book to the last, reading and clarifying our work and keeping us on track as we made decisions about content and organization. Corinna Dibble, Content Project Manager, shepherded our baby through copyediting and page proofs until her own baby arrived—congratulations, Corinna! Elizabeth Rice, Assistant Editor, directed the development of the Course-Mate website and the Instructor's Manual that accompanies this book with wisdom and good cheer.

We would also like to say a heartfelt "Thank you!" to all the reading instructors from across the country who read drafts of these chapters and patiently answered hundreds of questions about every aspect of the book. Their dedication to their students and to their profession shines through their comments. We mulled over every one of them and incorporated every suggestion that we could from these experienced and thoughtful teachers. Thank you to the following generous readers:

Charlene Aldrich, Trident Technical College

Melissa Barrett, Portland Community College

Carla Bell, Henry Ford Community College

Nancy Bertoglio, American River College

Gail Bradstreet, Cincinnati State Technical and Community College

Beth Bynum, Guilford Technical Community College

Kathleen Carlson, Brevard Community College

Teresa Carrillo, Joliet Junior College

Charlyn Cassady, The Community College of Baltimore County

Sharon Cellemme, South Piedmont Community College

Richard Conway, Molloy College

Cynthia Crable, Allegany College of Maryland

Michelle Cristiani, Portland Community College

Leah Deasy, SUNY-Jefferson

Joan Dillon, Bloomsburg University

Desiree Dumas, Greenville Technical College

Marie Eckstrom, Rio Hondo College

Debbie Felton, Cleveland State Community College

Sandra Frank, Mt. Hood Community College

Suzanne Franklin, Johnson County Community College

Deborah Freckleton, Bethune-Cookman University

Genice Gilreath, Santa Anna College

Carey Goyette, Clinton Community College

Brent Green, Salt Lake Community College

Angela Hebert, Hudson County Community College

Patricia Hill-Miller, Central Piedmont Community College

Charles Hunter, San Jose City College

Judith Isonhood, Hinds Community College

Julie Jackson-Coe, Genesee Community College

Mahalia Johnson, Greenville Technical College

Susie Johnston, Tyler Junior College

Patricia Jones-Lewis, Hudson County Community College

Miriam Kinard, Trident Technical College

Monique Mannering, Brookhaven College

Donna Mayes, Blue Ridge Community College

Eldon McMurray, Mt. Hood Community College

Julie Monroe, Madison Area Technical College

Roxanne Morgan, American River College

Norma Pravec, Bloomfield College

Susan Reynolds, Seminole State College of Florida

Richard Richards, St. Petersburg College

Natalie Russell, Truckee Meadows Community College

Adnan Salhi, Henry Ford Community College

Susan Silva, El Paso Community College

Patti Smith, Jones County Junior College

Stanley Snelson, University of Texas at Brownsville

Deborah Spradlin, Tyler Junior College

Lynn Strong, University of Arkansas at Little Rock

Kendra Vaglienti, Brookhaven College

Michelle Van de Sande, Arapahoe Community College

Danhua Wang, Indiana University of Pennsylvania

Patricia Windon, St. Petersburg College

Ellen Zimmerli, Lehigh Carbon Community College

Leslie would like to thank Ivan for being a true writing partner and excellent friend. From start to finish, Ivan has been productive, persistent, and profound in his thinking about how to teach and inspire students to achieve. Leslie would also like to thank Chuck King for his excellent food and his insistent puns, both absolutely necessary ingredients to this entire series. And to my children, Sara, Harmony, and Phoenix, a hug, a smile, or an e-mail from you can keep me writing for a day and a night! Thank you for your constant support and love over these past five years.

Ivan would like to thank Leslie for being AWEsome. You truly are a gifted author, editor, and friend. Your insight and instinct are spot on, and I thank you for being willing to share this journey with me. Ivan would also like to thank Deneé for being patient, supportive, and willing to allow me to take on this adventure. You have sometimes been my inspiration, motivation, and distraction, but you always have my admiration and affection. To my twins, Bella and Lilli, Daddy loves you with all his heart, and I am proud of the troupers you have been, the good readers you are, and the young ladies you are becoming. Lastly, to my new little one on the way . . . hurry up and get here, would ya!

Plan for Success

In order to plan for success, you need to know a few things. First, you need to know who your instructor is and how to contact him or her. Second, you need to make a connection with some of your classmates, so you can get homework if you are absent or discuss assignments or talk through any questions you may have. Next, you need to be aware of the syllabus guidelines, especially as they relate to grading policies. You also need to think about and clarify any short- and long-term goals that you are working toward. Finally, having specific steps in your plan for success is essential. We wish you the best as you begin.

Find Out About Your Instructor

What is your instructor's name? _____

What is your instructor's e-mail address? _____

What is your instructor's office phone number? _____

What are your instructor's office hours? _____

Get to Know Your Classmates

Write down the name and contact information of at least two students in your class whom you can call or e-mail for any work you miss or have questions about. This list can be adapted as you make friends with your classmates.

1. _____

2. _____

3. _____

Read and Understand Your Class Schedule or Syllabus

What are three important goals for this course? _____

_____

_____

_____

What is the course policy on attendance? _____

How is your grade determined? _____

What is your instructor's drop policy? _____

Circle yes or no to indicate whether a certain kind of information is on your class schedule or syllabus.

1. The name of a required textbook	Yes	No
2. Student learning outcomes or objectives	Yes	No
3. The date of the midterm exam	Yes	No
4. A grading scale	Yes	No
5. The date of the final exam	Yes	No
6. Holidays	Yes	No
7. A lab requirement	Yes	No
8. A weekly reading assignment	Yes	No
9. A weekly vocabulary assignment	Yes	No
10. Information about Student Services	Yes	No

Write down other important dates or requirements your class schedule or syllabus includes:

- _____
- _____
- _____
- _____
- _____

Ask questions on anything you are unsure of.

What Are Your Short-Term and Long-Term Goals?

Goals generally fall into one of five different categories:

1. Mental—learning, reading, studying

2. Physical—health, diet, exercise, sleep

3. Relational—family, friends

4. Financial—save, budget, make more money

5. Spiritual—grow in faith, explore your beliefs

We will define short-term goals as any goal that you can accomplish within the next year. Please write down one short-term goal you have for each category. We will help you with the first one!

1. Mental: <u>To pass this class with an A.</u> _____

   _____

2. Physical: _____

   _____

3. Relational: _____

   _____

4. Financial: _____

   _____

5. Spiritual: _____

   _____

We will define long-term goals as any goal that you can accomplish within the next two to five years. Please write down one long-term goal you have for each category. We will help you with the first one!

6. Mental: <u>To graduate with a certificate or degree in</u> _____

   _____

7. Physical: _____

   _____

8. Relational: _____

   _____

9. Financial: _____

   _____

10. Spiritual: _____

   _____

Investigating What Makes Students Successful

Life as a student is busy. You may be trying to balance school, a part- or full-time job, your family, perhaps even young children. The demands on you are great. However, you have enrolled in college for a purpose. You have a goal in mind. You want to earn a degree, get a better job, or maybe make more money to provide a comfortable life for you and your family. Whatever your reason, you have chosen to improve yourself through education, and that is a wonderful goal.

Understand that the main purpose of school is learning. No matter how many roles you are juggling, school will demand your attention. You will have to choose priorities in order to be successful in school—just enrolling will not be enough.

Being in school is like running a marathon. Unlike a sprinter, who races all out for a short distance, marathon runners must pace themselves so they can go the whole distance. As a student, you are signing up for a whole semester, and you must pace yourself from beginning to end in order to be successful.

Your goal in this and every course you take is to earn an A, right? OF COURSE! Here are some strategies to help you achieve your short-term goal of getting an A and your long-term goal of graduating.

1. **Believe in yourself.** Belief in oneself is not a magic formula for automatic success. However, do not underestimate the power of belief. It affects your emotions, thoughts, assumptions, and behavior. **Write one specific way that you can believe in yourself.**

   _____

2. **Know what motivates you.** Remember why you are here. What is your goal? What are you working for? Keep your short- and long-term goals in mind. Reward yourself for jobs well done. It can be a small reward—watching your favorite TV show after completing homework. Or it can be a bigger reward—going out with your friends, or anything else that will motivate you to make a short-term sacrifice to achieve your academic goal. **Write one thing that you can use to motivate yourself to do well in this class.**

   _____

3. **Be organized.** Make sure you have a folder for important documents from each of your classes. Know assignment due dates. Turn assignments in on time and in the format your instructor has requested. Buy a planner or use your smartphone. Enter study times in your planner or calendar so that you make time to do your work. Have an organized place where you do your homework. Make a commitment to create a weekly schedule for schoolwork, and stick to it. **Write down when you will be doing the homework for this class each week.**

   _____

4. **Prioritize.** Make to-do lists and order them.

   1—for the most important items that need to be done today

   2—for items that are important but not as urgent as the number 1's

   3—for things that are least urgent but still need to be done soon

   Write down a specific plan for how you will prioritize your schoolwork.

   _____

5. **Be active.** Participate actively in class. Ask questions and be prepared to discuss ideas with classmates. If you do not understand something, ask your instructor. Chances are someone else has the same question. Also, be present as you are studying. Do not passively read, but actively engage your mind so you do not waste your time or energy by just going through the motions. **Write one specific way you will be active in class.**

   _____

6. **Don't procrastinate.** Do homework the day it is assigned rather than the night before it is due. You will be a much more effective student if you study a little each day rather than try to cram it all in at the last minute. Also, when you procrastinate, you tend to have emergencies. By planning, prioritizing, and organizing, you can avoid a lot of stress because you have a game plan and are following it. **Write down an idea of how you can avoid procrastination.**

   _____

7. **Network.** Who can you use to your advantage to help you in your academic success? Are your parents a good resource? Are your friends encouraging you or distracting you from school? Are you utilizing your instructors? Have you identified the good students in your classes with whom you can form study groups? Do you know what resources your school offers, such as labs, advising, counseling, career services, and so forth? **Write down one person and one resource you can use to become a more accountable student.**

   _____

8. **Keep your health in mind.** Do not underestimate the power of a good night's sleep, a healthy diet, and exercise. All of these will help you manage stress, stay focused on your studies, and keep a positive attitude. **Write down one way you can maintain or improve your health.**

   _____

9. **Take the initiative.** Read ahead. Ask questions. Make connections. If you are absent, come to the next class with any missed work done. Review your material a few minutes each day in order to be better prepared for class discussions, quizzes, and tests. Make the effort to talk to your instructor and develop a rapport with him or her. **Write down one strategy that will help you take the initiative.**

_____

10. **Always do your best.** If you always do your best, then you are a success, even if you do not get the highest grade. Be honest. Do not cheat, which actually leads to failure. Treat others the way you wish to be treated and chances are they will return the gesture. **Write down something that gets in the way of you doing your best. Then write down one idea for how to overcome this temptation.**

_____

Discuss the ten items from the preceding list with a partner. Talk about how each of you can be a successful student this semester. See how your ideas are similar to a classmate's or if one of you has thought of a different idea that may be motivating to others.

engage

COLLEGE READING

PART 1

Reading and Study Strategies

In the 2010 remake of *The Karate Kid,* Dre Parker (Jaden Smith) tells his kung fu teacher, Mr. Han (Jackie Chan), that he wants to learn how to control other people by using his chi (inner energy). Han tells him that will take a lifetime of practice and focus. Dre claims he already has great focus, but Han dangles him over a river and shows him that he doesn't. Mr. Han tells him, "Your focus needs more focus!"

Often, we are like Dre. We want to get the reward without doing the work—we want the return without the investment. But life doesn't work that way. Dre learned that winning requires effort, sweat, and sometimes even pain. Success will not come to you, but you can find success if you go looking for it, and if you do the work required to earn it.

Your job in this course is to get from here to there. Where "there" is depends on you. You can do well—even better than you think you can. But you will have to focus and make an investment of time and effort.

. . . .

Share Your Prior Knowledge
Share with a classmate three things that help you focus.

1. _____

2. _____

3. _____

Now share three things that disrupt your focus.

1. _____

2. _____

3. _____

1 Engaging with Reading

Previewing the Chapter

Flip through the pages of Chapter 1, and read all the headings that are printed like this:

Why Is Reading Important?

Write one question you have about one of the headings in Chapter 1.

_____

_____

Write one statement you believe is true about one of the headings.

_____

_____

Plan to come back and comment on your question and statement when you have finished working through the chapter.

_____

_____

 To access additional course materials for *Engage,* including quizzes, videos, and more, please visit www.cengagebrain.com. At the CengageBrain.com home page, search for the ISBN of *Engage* (from the back cover of your book) using the search box at the top of the page. This will take you to the product page where these resources can be found.

 Videos Related to Readings   **Vocab Words on Audio**   **Read and Talk on Demand**

Why Is Reading Important?

Reading fluently is the most important skill you can develop to help you succeed in college. You will do a tremendous amount of reading in your college classes. No matter what courses you take, you will read textbooks and other materials as a primary way to gain new knowledge and to give you new perspectives on knowledge you already have. Here are a few examples:

- To get an associate's degree in nursing, a student reads textbooks in anatomy, physiology, pharmacology, microbiology, chemistry, nutrition, and psychology.

- To earn a degree in hospitality management, a student reads in the fields of accounting, finance, law, human resources, management, and marketing.

- To become a bilingual education teacher, a student reads about child growth and development, classroom management, the history of education, methods of teaching particular subjects, and language acquisition.

- To earn a degree in forensic science, a student reads textbooks in biology, chemistry, physics, and anthropology.

Taking a class in any of these subjects will require reading the course textbook and related books and articles. To complete your degree requirements, you'll need to learn an effective reading and thinking process to understand these materials. This book will help you do that. But keep in mind this book is not teaching you how to read. You already know how to do that. Rather, this book will equip you with a process for reading that you can apply in each class you take. In addition, it will teach you how to think critically about new ideas and concepts—in other words, how to analyze and evaluate what you read.

| INTERACTION 1–1 | What Do You Want to Do When You Get Out of School? |

With a classmate or as a class, discuss the following questions.

1. What career are you thinking of pursuing? _____

_____

2. Why do you want to earn this degree, or what interests you about this career? (If you are not sure exactly what degree you want to get, that's okay! Just discuss

what you think you might want to do). _____

_____

3. What is the minimum degree requirement to be competitive in this field? _____

_____

4. Name some specific classes or types of classes that are needed to pursue this career/degree. _____

_____

Getting Motivated to Read

Imagine you are on a classic TV game show. You have just won, and you have ten seconds to decide which of these two ways you want to receive your prize money:

1. Twenty thousand dollars per day for thirty days.

2. A single penny that doubles every day for thirty days.

Which did you choose?

At the end of thirty days, choice 1 would give you a not-too-shabby $600,000. Sounds pretty good, huh? But what about choice 2? At the end of the same thirty days, choice 2 would add up to an astonishing $5,368,709.12!

This illustrates the concept of compound interest; you probably didn't think a penny would add up to very much, but a little can add up to a lot over time.

So how does this apply to school, you ask? Well, people who earn a college degree usually increase their income potential, earning more than people without a degree. The U.S. Census Bureau estimates that a person with a bachelor's degree will earn an average of $1 million more during his or her lifetime than a person who has only a high school diploma. So the sooner you earn your degree, the sooner you can start earning that extra million dollars. As Mark Twain said, "The secret to getting ahead is getting started."

According to the College Board's *Education Pays 2010* report and the Bureau of Labor Statistics, the average annual earnings for workers age 25 and over increase with more education. Here is a chart from 2008 data showing this trend.

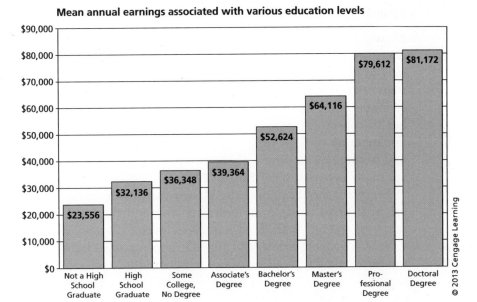

Mean annual earnings associated with various education levels

Chart data:
- Not a High School Graduate: $23,556
- High School Graduate: $32,136
- Some College, No Degree: $36,348
- Associate's Degree: $39,364
- Bachelor's Degree: $52,624
- Master's Degree: $64,116
- Professional Degree: $79,612
- Doctoral Degree: $81,172

Figure 1.1 The More You Learn, the More You Earn

Source: Bureau of Labor Statistics, Current Population Survey

Data: 2008 annual averages for persons age 25 and over; earnings for full-time wage and salary workers.

INTERACTION 1–2	Find Out the Income Potential of a Career You Are Interested In

Do an Internet search for a career you are interested in. Type "Occupational Outlook Handbook" in your search bar and then search for your career at the Bureau of Labor Statistics site: www.bls.gov/oco. If you have not chosen a specific career, then search for any career you think you might want to have. Find the following information and bring it to the next class:

1. What is the starting salary for the career you are interested in? _____

_____

2. What is the median income for a person after five to ten years of experience in this career? _____

3. What is the top earning potential of someone in this field? How many years does it take to reach this level? _____

The Power of Visualizing Your Future

Money may not be the main reason why you have chosen to get an education. You probably want a better future, and money is only one part of that. Research has shown that education benefits not only your finances but also your health and your family life, as well as society at large. For example, people with higher education tend to be more health-conscious, have children who are better prepared academically, donate more of their time or money to express their social conscience, and become more politically involved as active voters.[1] In short, there are many benefits to earning an education beyond finances.

Everyone should dream about their future while they are preparing for it. It helps to keep us motivated through the hard times. In fact, many of today's household names—Oprah Winfrey, Will Smith, Jim Carrey, Michael Jordan, and Suze Orman—made a habit of visualizing the future they wanted before they achieved it. Apparently, Jim Carrey wrote himself a check for $10 million in 1990. On the check he wrote for "acting services rendered." He postdated the check for November 1995 and kept it in his wallet. In 1990, he was still basically unknown. But by 1994, he had achieved phenomenal success with his roles in *Ace Ventura: Pet Detective* and *The Mask*. Based on this success, Jim Carrey was paid $7 million for the lead role in *Dumb and Dumber*. By 1995, he was well on his way to being on the A-list of Hollywood stars and earning $20 million per film.

Did the act of writing the $10 million check make Jim Carrey become successful? No! (Wouldn't it be nice if life were that easy?) But he could see himself earning millions, so he had a plan and made decisions that would take him in that direction. Then he worked hard, using his talents and abilities, to overcome difficulties and learn new skills to reach his goal. As Dave Ramsey, a popular and successful financial advisor with a nationally syndicated show, likes to say, "The difference between a dream and a goal is a *plan*."

| INTERACTION 1–3 | Visualize Your Future |

Take a few minutes to visualize your future, as you would like it to be.

- Take this exercise seriously.
- Dream big.
- Include as many details as possible.

1. College Board Advocacy & Policy Center. (2010). *Education Pays 2010*. Accessed at: http://trends.collegeboard.org/education_pays.

1. **Imagine your life.** What will your life be like in five to ten years when you have achieved what you are working toward today? To visualize the details of your future life, walk yourself through one of your days five or ten years from now:

   - It is morning and you have just woken up. What time is it? What do you see? Who do you see?

   - Roll out of bed and go to your closet to get dressed. What's in your closet? What type of clothes will you wear to work today?

   - It is now time to eat breakfast. What do you see? What are you eating? Who are you eating with?

   - It is now time to leave for work. Where do you work? How will you get there?

   - What type of work do you do? How do you feel about your work?

   - It is now lunchtime. How long do you take for lunch? Are you eating with anyone?

   - It is now the close of your workday. What are you doing? What time is it?

   - What will you do now that work is over?

   - How does your day end?

2. **Answers about your future.** Take a few minutes and record your thoughts for the following questions:*

   a. What were my most important feelings about this day? _____

   _____

   _____

   _____

   b. What type of work did I choose for myself? Why? _____

   _____

   _____

   _____

   c. Did I work with people, ideas, or things? _____

   _____

   _____

   _____

*Adapted from WGBH, "Teachers' Guide: Visualize Your Future," *They Made America* at www.pbs.org/wgbh/theymade america/tguide/resources_visual.html

d. Did I use interests/hobbies/skills that I am developing now? _____

_____

_____

e. Did I work for someone else, or was I in charge of the business? _____

_____

_____

f. Was I satisfied with the job I chose? Why or why not? _____

_____

_____

g. What did I learn about myself in this activity? _____

_____

_____

3. **Make that future happen.** Now that you've developed a sense for where you want to be a few years from now, answer this question: What can I do to make that future happen? Only list things that you yourself can do—don't include any actions that other people would have to take.

I can make this future happen by . . .

• EXAMPLE: Take the prerequisite classes needed to get accepted in an RN (registered nurse) program.

• _____

• _____

• _____

• _____

4. **Consider the value of reading.** Now use your imagination to consider the value of reading more effectively. How does reading at the college level fit into the picture you have just painted of your future? For each of the following life contexts, name at least one benefit of knowing how to read more effectively. After you have responded as well as you can on your own, get into small groups and discuss your answers together. Add new ideas from your discussion to your list.

Life context	Reading benefits this context by . . .
Home and family (or attractiveness as a date or potential partner)	
Career and earning ability	
Self-confidence and self-esteem	
Health and well-being	
Other contexts that matter to you (name them here)	

Watching Videos, Reading Articles, and Talking with Classmates

In college, reading is just one aspect of how you will share new ideas with others in your class. So the first reading in each chapter of this book is meant to give you the chance to talk about reading. Read the article, and then use the four discussion questions to talk about your ideas with your classmates and your instructor.

There is also an accompanying video that your instructor may choose to show in class or that you can access at the Reading Course-Mate website for this book at www.cengagebrain.com. In addition, vocabulary words printed in red give you practice in defining words as you read.

Read and Talk   COLLEGE SUCCESS TEXTBOOK

Access the Reading CourseMate via **www.cengagebrain.com** to hear a reading of this selection and view a video about this topic.

The Power of Choice

1   The main ingredient in all success is wise choices. That's because the quality of our lives is determined by the quality of the choices we make on a daily basis. Successful people stay on course to their destinations by wisely choosing their beliefs and behaviors.

© Bettmann/CORBIS

2   Do beliefs cause behaviors, or do behaviors lead to beliefs? Like the chicken and egg, it's hard to say which came first. This much is clear: Once you choose a positive belief or an effective behavior, you usually find yourself in a cycle of success. Positive beliefs lead to effective behaviors. Effective behaviors lead to success. And success reinforces the positive beliefs.

3   Here's an example showing how the choice of beliefs and behaviors determines results. Until 1954, most track-and-field experts believed it was impossible for a person to run a mile in less than four minutes. On May 6, 1954, however, Roger Bannister ran a mile in the world record time of 3:59.4. Once Bannister had proven that running a four-minute mile was possible, within months, many other runners also broke the four-minute **barrier**. In other words, once runners chose a new belief (a person can run a mile in less than four minutes), they pushed their physical abilities, and suddenly the impossible became possible. By the way, the present world's record, set in 1999 by Hicham El Guerrouj of Morocco, is an amazing 3:43.13. So much for limiting beliefs!

barrier Given that the four-minute mile was considered impossible, what is the likely meaning of *barrier*?

4   Consider another example. After a disappointing test score, a struggling student thinks, "I knew I couldn't do college math!" This belief will likely lead the student to miss classes and **neglect** assignments. These self-defeating behaviors will lead to even lower test scores, reinforcing the negative beliefs. This student, caught in a cycle of failure, is now in **grave** danger of failing math.

neglect Given the context, what does *neglect* mean here?

grave What does *grave* mean here?

5   In that same class, however, someone with no better math ability is passing the course because this student believes she can pass math. Consequently, she chooses positive behaviors such as attending every class, completing all of her assignments, getting a tutor, and asking the instructor for help. Her grades go up, confirming her **empowering** belief. The cycle of success has this student on course to passing math.

empowering Consider the word parts *em-* + *power* + *-ing*. What does this word mean?

6   Someone once said, "If you keep doing what you've been doing, you'll keep getting what you've been getting." That's why if you want to improve your life (and why else would you attend college?), you'll need to change some of your beliefs and behaviors. **Conscious** experimentation will teach you which ones are already working well for you and which ones need revision. Once these new beliefs and behaviors become habit, you'll find yourself in the cycle of success, on course to creating your dreams in college and in life.

conscious Think about this word's opposite, "unconscious." What does *conscious* mean?

—From DOWNING. *On Course: Strategies for Creating Success in College and in Life* (pp. 3–4) Copyright © 2011 Cengage Learning.

Talking About Reading

Respond in writing to the questions below and then discuss your answers with your classmates.

1. In the reading, running a mile in under four minutes is an example of how an accomplishment changed the belief that something couldn't be done. Can you think of another example of something that used to be considered impossible but is now commonplace?

   _____

   _____

   _____

2. Think of a time when you first thought you couldn't do something but then later accomplished it. What allowed you to succeed?

   _____

   _____

   _____

3. Can you think of someone you know who has been successful because of positive thinking and effective behaviors? How about someone who has been a failure because of negative thinking and ineffective behaviors?

   _____

   _____

   _____

4. The article says, "If you want to improve your life (and why else would you attend college?), you'll need to change some of your beliefs and behaviors." Which of your beliefs and behaviors do you need to change in order to have a better chance at success?

   _____

   _____

   _____

Reading Is an Interaction

> The harder Tom tried to fasten his mind on his book, the more his mind wandered. So at last with a sigh and a yawn, he gave it up.
>
> —Mark Twain, *The Adventures of Tom Sawyer*

Do you ever feel like Tom in this quotation from Twain's classic book? What do you do to keep your mind from wandering when you read?

_____

_____

_____

The simple answer is that you need to become engaged in what you are reading. Reading is an active process. You cannot be passive when you read and expect to be successful. There are several basic ways you can interact with what you read.

Use your imagination. Using your imagination while you read is one way to actively participate in the interaction of reading. Interactivity is the ability of two (or more) things or people to act on one another and affect one another. When you read, you have a better chance of understanding the text if you interact with it. Let what you are reading affect you. Place yourself within the text. Form a mental picture of what the author is saying. Involve your senses: see, smell, feel, touch, and hear what you are reading. Your imagination is powerful. In fact, Albert Einstein said imagination is more important than knowledge because it takes you beyond the limits of knowledge.

Use your body. Another way to interact with your reading is to use your body. This doesn't mean hitting your head against the book in frustration! Rather, when you read, keep your pencil in your hand. This automatically puts you in a different frame of mind than if you are just sitting there like stone, moving only your eyes. And use the pencil! Mark the important parts while you read. When you get to a point in the text you don't understand, underline it and scribble your question in the margin. When you disagree with the author, write "No way!" and then add your own explanation. When you read something completely new, try to figure out how it fits into your prior knowledge.

Let's apply the principle of interactivity to something you probably do every day, or at least a couple of times a week—watch TV. Applying an interactive approach to watching TV will help you transfer this principle over to reading. (If you don't watch TV, you can take the exact same steps in relation to movies.) In both watching TV and reading, you can have interactions before you view or read, while you view or read, and after you view or read.

INTERACTION 1–4   **What Do You Do When You View?**

Talk with a classmate about the interactions you have in the following situations.

1. What do you do *before* you watch a movie or TV show?

   - _____
   - _____
   - _____
   - _____

2. What do you do *while* you watch a movie or TV show?

   - _____
   - _____
   - _____
   - _____

3. What do you do *after* you watch a movie or TV show?

   - _____
   - _____
   - _____
   - _____

Before You View or Read

> A habit cannot be tossed out the window. It must be coaxed
> down the stairs a step at a time.
>
> —Mark Twain

The skill of reading well requires changing bad reading habits and developing good reading habits, and only you can change your habits. Becoming an effective reader does not happen overnight; it takes time and practice. A place to start is with the processes you use before you view a movie or TV show. You can use these simple strategies before you read, and they will dramatically improve your comprehension:

- Guess the purpose of the reading selection.
- Survey it to get an overview of what will be coming.
- Predict what's going to happen.
- Think about your prior knowledge of the subject matter.

We will discuss each skill one at a time.

Figuring Out the Purpose

Every author, like every director of a TV show or movie, starts out with a general purpose for the work they are going to create. Identifying that purpose is the first step in effective reading as well as viewing.

Three General Purposes That Authors Have

Persuade: Attempt to change the reader's or viewer's thoughts, attitudes, or behaviors.
Inform: Attempt to teach the reader or viewer about key information, usually factual.
Express: Attempt to express an emotion or to cause readers or viewers to feel emotions, such as amusement, sadness, horror, and so on, often by using stories.

To remember these general purposes, use the word PIE (the first letter of each category).

INTERACTION 1–5	What Is the Purpose of That Show You Watch?

TV shows and movies all have a purpose or, at times, more than one purpose. In the table below, give examples of TV shows that persuade, inform, or express.

Name of program	Type of program	Purpose of program
Bodies in Motion	Exercise	Persuade
MythBusters	Science show	Inform
The Office	Comedy	Express
_____	_____	Persuade
_____	_____	Inform
_____	_____	Express
_____	_____	Persuade
_____	_____	Inform
_____	_____	Express

You can see that different types of programs, called **genres,** have different purposes. The same is true for different kinds of reading material. For example, *Time* magazine has the main purpose of informing readers about current events. What about *Cosmopolitan* magazine? The articles in *Cosmo* do inform readers about various topics, but why? To entertain readers, and thus their main purpose is to be expressive. College textbooks have the main purpose of teaching students—their purpose is to inform. But some books might set out to persuade you. For example, the book *The Tipping Point: How Little Things Can Make a Big Difference* attempts to persuade readers that sometimes, a single, small event can change the course of history. Even though author Malcolm Gladwell shares a lot of facts with readers along the way, his main purpose is persuasion. And other books have an expressive purpose, like the *Twilight* series, *Of Mice and Men, Beloved,* or *The Notebook.*

Before you start reading, you have two basic ways to predict the author's purpose. Sometimes you can tell just from the title of a reading selection what its purpose is. For example, an article called "BP Should Be Repentant" is a persuasive reading; the word *should* shows that the writer wants readers to believe that BP (British Petroleum) did something wrong. The article is not simply reporting information. (An informative title might state "BP Is Repentant.")

Other times, you can make an educated guess based on where the reading selection appears—if it's in a newspaper, for example, whether it is in the news section, on the opinion page, part of the want ads, or a comic strip. When an article is printed in the letters-to-the-editor section, the writer's main purpose is to persuade readers. The publishing context can reveal a lot about the author's purpose.

INTERACTION 1–6	Determine the Main Purpose of a Reading

For each of the following examples of reading material, decide whether the main purpose is likely to be persuasive, informative, or expressive. Consider both the **title** and the publishing **context** (source). Mark each selection with P, I, or E, and discuss the reasons for your answer with your classmates.

P = Persuade: to cause readers to change how they think, feel, or act.
I = Inform: to teach readers about key information, usually factual.
E = Express: to express an emotion or to cause readers to feel emotions like amusement, sadness, horror, and so on, often by using stories.

_____ 1. An article from cbsnews.com called "Fierce Winter Storm Sweeps across Midwest."

_____ 2. A section in a marketing textbook called "Identify Market Segments."

_____ 3. An editorial in the *Dallas Morning News* called "The Glaring Weaknesses of Our Governor."

_____ 4. A graphic novel entitled *The Spirit: Femmes Fatale* by Will Eisner.

_____ 5. An article about the exhibit "The World of Khubilai Khan: Chinese Art in the Yuan Dynasty" at the Metropolitan Museum of Art's website.

_____ 6. An article in the *New York Times* online called "Women Earning More Doctoral Degrees Than Men in U.S."

_____ 7. A self-help book by Gary Chapman entitled *The 5 Love Languages: The Secret to Love That Lasts.*

_____ 8. A feature article from *Rolling Stone* entitled "Eminem and Lil Wayne's New Video Tackles Bullying."

_____ 9. The book *The Wave: In Pursuit of the Rogues, Freaks and Giants of the Ocean* by Susan Casey.

_____ 10. A book about pregnancy by Heidi Eisenberg Murkoff, *What to Expect When You're Expecting,* 4th edition.

More than One Purpose

An author can have more than one purpose. As an example, writing intended to persuade readers will often contain informative facts or an emotional story. An article, book, advertisement, TV show, or movie can have elements of each purpose, but there is usually a main purpose. To give an illustration, let's look at item 9 in Interaction 1–6: a book called *The Wave: In Pursuit of the Rogues, Freaks and Giants of the Ocean* by Susan Casey. The book's main purpose is to inform readers about the hugest waves ever seen, like the wall of water 1,740 feet tall that hit the Alaskan coast in 1958. But readers are fascinated by stories of the waves that have crumbled shorelines and the surfers who have been killed trying to ride them—and so the book also has a second purpose: to be expressive.

Surveying a Reading Is Like Watching a Preview

When you go to a movie, often you have already seen the preview for it several times. The preview shows you some of the highlights of the movie. You often know who the main characters are (and which actors play them); you've viewed some of the scenery and settings; and you have a sense of the film's genre—you know whether the movie is going to be a fast-paced action adventure, a romantic comedy, or a horror flick. Similarly, if you take a few moments to survey or preview a reading selection, you will tremendously improve your chances of comprehending the reading selection. When you preview, you do not read the whole selection, you examine only a few parts.

The parts you should look at are shown on the next page in an article from *Rolling Stone* magazine. These parts are the title, the subtitle, the first sentence of each paragraph, the photos and their captions, and headings.

When you survey or preview a reading, you become able to make predictions about it. Making predictions (an interactive process, as you have seen) allows you to access your prior knowledge about the material covered in the reading.

You Already Know Something About This

When you sit down to watch your favorite TV show, you already know about it from previous episodes. When you survey a reading, you've already learned something from the title, the images, the captions, and the headings. Aside from these obvious pieces of information, though, it's quite likely you know more.

For example, you may have seen *Glee* or heard something about it from a friend or family member, the news, or a magazine. So when you see an article about *Glee*, you probably already know something about the show. All of this knowledge that you bring to your viewing or reading is called your **prior knowledge**. (*Prior* means "before.") You want to activate, or set in motion, your prior knowledge as much as you can before you start reading. Doing this takes advantage of a natural pattern of learning for people: fitting what they are learning into what they already know.

While You Are Viewing or Reading

Have you ever gone to a movie like *Twilight* with a hard-core fan? This person has read the book three times already, knows all the characters, all the actors who portray the characters, where the film was made, and all the gossip surrounding the stars, the film, and the author. Or have you ever gone to a professional sporting event or watched a game

Headings: This brief article does not include headings, but many longer articles and textbook chapters certainly will. Read each heading and think about it for moment.

TELEVISION

Glee's Unstoppable Roll

How the hit show, with its brilliant second season, filled the void left by MTV and became a pop-culture juggernaut By Rob Sheffield

Photos and captions: What information can you gather from this photograph?

Title: What do these words reveal about the subject?

Subtitle or sentence in large type: What do you learn from reading this sentence?

First sentences of paragraphs: Read the first sentence of each paragraph quickly.

MANY PEOPLE PREdicted *Glee* would run out of gas after the novelty wore off. But these people turned out to be totally wrong, because the Fox musical juggernaut is on a historic run. This season just keeps getting stronger – every episode makes you wonder how they'll top it next week. The Britney

Glee
Tuesdays, 8 p.m., Fox

and *Rocky Horror* episodes aren't merely the show's funniest moments ever – they prove how *Glee* has taken its place at the heart of pop culture, where radio and MTV used to rule supreme. It's where music and dancing and high school and drama and sex all go to intersect – no TV show has really held that position before.

When Bob Dylan went rock & roll in 1965, he famously declared, "The only place where it's happening is on the radio and records. That's where the people hang out." In 2010, there might not be much left of records or the radio. But *Glee* has embraced that vision of pop music as the place where the people hang out. Part of its greatness is its sincere nut-case enthusiasm for every style of music under the sun. Nothing is off-limits on *Glee*: They'll sing Color Me Badd, Syreeta, Aerosmith or Lady Gaga, coasting from show tunes to trash-rock oldies to hip-hop to Vegas razzle-dazzle. Like MTV in its prime, *Glee* will devour anything and turn it into pure spectacle. It's almost like the kids of New Directions are the last real pop stars, the only ones who have the *cajones* to embrace the strangeness of the American pop pageant.

Really, the key to this whole season is that amazing Britney episode, where Rachel says, "Let's face it, Finn, this relationship is only going to work if we're both losers." That sums up *Glee*, and that's also its message to America. Nobody at William McKinley High School listens to music for the sake of coolness – they're *all* loser underdogs, and they love music because it embodies that same underdog spirit.

So there's something incredibly generous and affectionate about the way *Glee* treats the most godforsaken corners of pop music. *Glee* creator Ryan Murphy clearly loves to rescue forgotten obscurities, just as he loves to bring new resonance to famous tunes you thought were played out. Every episode seems to dig up at least one song you thought you'd never hear again – hell, in a lot of cases, they're songs you *hoped* you'd never hear again. But that boldly eclectic embrace is what gives *Glee* its kick. And that's why nothing

THE WATCH LIST

The League
Thursdays, 10:30 p.m., FX
The second season of this comedy is as pungent as the first – a hilarious look at fantasy-football-league dudes who make one another's life crises infinitely more agonizing.

Bored to Death
Sundays, 10 p.m., HBO
The detective sendup keeps getting more twisted as Jason Schwartzman brings the neurosis, Ted Danson brings the pain and Zach Galifianakis constantly finds ways to humiliate himself. **R.S.**

else on TV can touch its ambition or impact.

This season has been a huge leap for *Glee* in terms of warmth. *Glee* is still full of magnificently bitchy dialogue, especially when Santana Lopez is around: You gotta love how she tells Brittany, "I'm making out with you because I'm like a lizard. If I don't have something warm beneath me, I can't digest my food." But it's gotten more expansive emotionally as well as musically. The characters have become much more likable and humane, and that emotional growth has allowed *Glee* to avoid the disastrous missteps that have hobbled so many high school series, like *The O.C.* and *Gossip Girl*. The earliest episodes had a petulant edge, as if *Glee* arrived with a chip on its shoulder, but success has made *Glee* sweeter, and that's only made it more adventurous. The instant-classic Britney episode only worked because everyone was incredibly respectful to both the music and the girl, right down to her high-five with Artie. *Glee* couldn't have pulled that off last year.

Some people complain that this season contains less plot, but that just proves people really need something to complain about. Increasingly, *Glee* trusts the music to tell the story, and that's why it's hopping from one high to another. Brittany singing Britney's "I'm a Slave 4 U" wasn't just more entertaining than Season One's teen-mom subplot, it was more interesting and profound.

The *Rocky Horror* episode was a strange triumph, directed by *Hairspray*'s Adam Shankman. When Will Schuester is trying to explain this Seventies glam-rock musical to the students, he says, "It was for outcasts, people on the fringes who had no place left to go but were searching for someplace, anyplace, where they felt like they belonged." That's exactly the turf *Glee* has claimed, with an audacious spirit that the rest of the pop world seems to have abandoned. Yet that's the spirit that has made *Glee* a one-of-a-kind creative phenomenon. And that's why America loves *Glee* the way Britney loves pizza with ranch dressing. ◎

with a hard-core fan? This person knows all the players, the history of each of them and the team, the coach, and the strengths or weaknesses of everyone involved! Or maybe you have gone to a concert with a die-hard fan of Taylor Swift or Bon Jovi or Eminem or Lady Antebellum. They know all the words to all the songs on every album the singer or group has made. (Maybe *you* are one of these dedicated people!) If so, you'll understand that there are differences between what a casual viewer sees and what a dedicated viewer knows and sees.

One of the differences is that the casual viewer might get caught up emotionally in the moment-by-moment movie scenes, but the dedicated viewer retains a broader, more critical perspective on what is happening. Or a casual spectator might get wrapped up in what looks like a bad plan by the coach, but the die-hard fan knows it is all part of the bigger strategy. Due partly to their greater experience and partly to their intense curiosity, dedicated fans know more about the movie director's or coach's options, and thus, they are in a better position to know why a particular choice was made and whether the choice was a good one.

The same kinds of differences are true for casual and dedicated readers. While the casual reader may be reading one sentence at a time and thinking about its meaning, the dedicated reader is not only doing that but is also staying interactive by asking the types of questions shown in Table 1.1.

Table 1.1 Learning Tasks to Accomplish While Reading

To accomplish these learning tasks while reading . . .	the interactive reader asks these questions:
The reader tries to understand what the author is saying.	• What does it mean when the author says this? • Can I explain this using my own words?
The reader monitors (tracks) whether he or she is comprehending the material and applies strategies to aid comprehension. You may be losing comprehension • if you have to slow your reading considerably, • if you go back to reread a section several times, or • if you can't tell what is important and what is not.	• I don't understand. If I keep reading, will this become clearer? • I don't know this word. Can I figure it out from the surrounding words? If not, I'll use the dictionary. • I have read this same paragraph three times already and I don't get it. What is the main idea here?

continued

To accomplish these learning tasks while reading . . .	the interactive reader asks these questions:
The reader searches for the relevance of the reading to his or her own life and to other ideas and situations.	• How does this connect to what I already know? • What examples of this have I experienced or do I know about?
The reader is open to learning something new that doesn't necessarily fit easily into known information.	• How is this different from what I thought was true?
The reader searches for the significance of the ideas.	• Why is this important? • What effects do these ideas have? What are the consequences?

After You View or Read

What you do after you watch a TV show, a movie, or a YouTube video depends partly on your purpose for watching it to begin with. If you were watching *The Simpsons*, you may just laugh a final laugh and turn the channel. But if you were watching a presidential candidate debate, you would probably spend some time afterward thinking about what each person had said and whether you wanted to vote for him or her. Similarly, after you read a selection that is meant to be persuasive, you might ask yourself if the writer has convinced you of his or her point and why. After you read a textbook chapter or other informative reading material, you might ask yourself what you just learned—and why it matters.

In college, you will be expected to carry on conversations about the information you read. And even if you don't speak up in class, you will still probably be required to take at least one test on the information you have read. So you need effective strategies that will help you learn, study, and remember the information. You are probably already familiar with the reading strategies of highlighting and note taking. Reviewing the passages you have highlighted and annotated after you read will help you remember the most important information. Chapter 5 in this book will help you develop a strong connection between your during- and after-reading strategies.

INTERACTION 1–7   Choose an Informative Article

Here are four guidelines for choosing an informative article for the activities that follow.

1. The topic or subject must interest you.

2. The article must have an informative purpose.

3. The article should have at least *ten* paragraphs.

4. You are going to use the article for five activities, so you need to have a copy of it.

To find your article, look in your campus library's periodicals section (either onsite or online); visit your local bookstore, newsstand, pharmacy, or grocery store; or simply go online with your favorite search engine. (*Hint:* Numerous special-interest magazines exist. You may want to think about subjects you care about and then see if you can find magazines about any of these subjects. If you already subscribe to one, it'll be easy.)

INTERACTION 1–8   The Title, the Purpose, Your Interest

Don't read the article yet! First, survey it based on the strategies discussed on pages 17–21.

1. What is the title of the article? _____

_____

2. What is the source of the article? _____

_____

3. What led you to believe the purpose of the article is informative? _____

_____

4. What is your reason for choosing this article (why were you interested)? _____

_____

INTERACTION 1–9   Survey Your Informative Article

1. You noted the title of your article in Interaction 1–8. What information do the words in the title suggest will be discussed? _____

_____

2. Does your article include any headings, sentences in large type, or subtitles? If so, read them and then list what you learned about the article from them. _____

_____

_____

_____

3. How many photos, illustrations, or other images appear throughout the article?

_____

a. How many of these have captions? _____

b. What additional information about the article do you gain from the images and the captions? _____

_____

_____

4. Preview the first sentence of each paragraph. What content do they seem to indicate the article will discuss? _____

_____

_____

INTERACTION 1–10   Activate Your Prior Knowledge

Reread what you wrote in Interaction 1–9 about the subjects that your informative article probably discusses. For each item you wrote, think of at least one piece of prior knowledge that you hold about that subject—even if that knowledge is vague. List five of these pieces of prior knowledge here.

- _____

- _____

- _____

- _____

- _____

INTERACTION 1–11 **Monitor Your Comprehension**

Finally! Now, you can read your informative article! As you read, jot down very brief notes in the margins of the article using these guidelines:

1. Put a √ next to a paragraph if you understand most of it.

2. Put an **X** next to a paragraph if you don't understand most of it.

3. Circle words you don't know if they seem important to know in order to understand the article.

4. After you read, compare the paragraphs that have √'s and those that have **X**'s. What made some paragraphs easy to understand and other paragraphs hard to understand? List your ideas, and then share them with a classmate to get more ideas.

- _____

- _____

- _____

5. Look up in a dictionary the meanings of the words you circled, and write the words and definitions here.

- _____

- _____

- _____

6. Reread the parts of the article where the words appeared. Did looking up the definitions help you understand those parts? Why or why not?

_____

_____

INTERACTION 1–12	Think About What You Learned, Its Relevance, and Its Significance

Review what you said in Interaction 1–8 on page 25 about your purpose for selecting your article, and then answer the following questions.

1. What did you learn from the article? List at least three ideas or pieces of information.

   • _____

   • _____

   • _____

2. What are the main points you want to remember? Why are these important?

   • _____

   • _____

   • _____

3. Was the article as relevant as you expected it to be when you selected it? Why or why not?

   _____

   _____

4. What did you find significant about the article? What was important about it to you?

   _____

   _____

5. Who else might find this article relevant, and why?

   _____

   _____

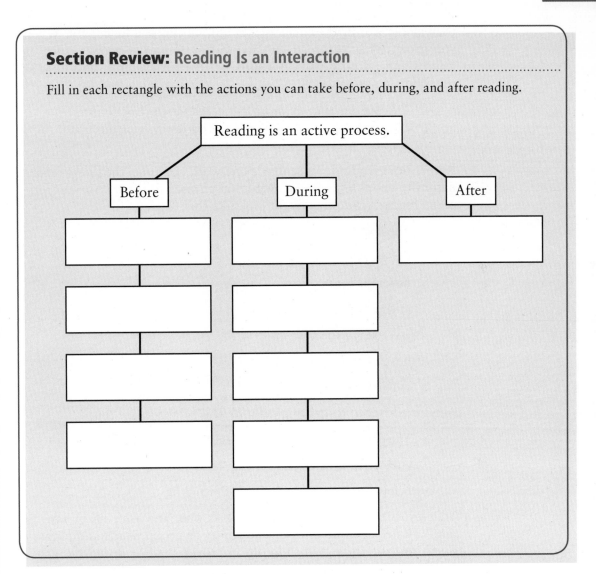

Section Review: Reading Is an Interaction

Fill in each rectangle with the actions you can take before, during, and after reading.

Reading is an active process.

Before   During   After

Increasing Your Reading Rate

You will read so much in college that it is worthwhile to learn how to read more quickly. One strategy for increasing your reading rate is chunking. **Chunking** is an act of grouping. You can chunk phonetic sounds in words. For example, when you were in elementary school and learning to read the word *chunk*, you broke it into two phonetic parts: *ch* + *unk*. Once you learned the word, you said it as one unit. Even though you are reading long and complicated passages rather than single words, the concept of chunking can still be helpful. When you group what you read into natural grammatical groups, such as clauses and phrases, you are chunking. For an example, let's look at the following sentence:

> The dog ran quickly down the beach, attempting to catch every seagull he saw before they flew away, scolding him angrily.

Rather than reading this sentence one word at a time, the fluent reader naturally chunks groups of words or phrases together. An inexperienced reader's chunking might look like this:

> The dog
>
> ran quickly
>
> down the beach,
>
> attempting to catch
>
> every seagull he saw
>
> before they flew away,
>
> scolding him angrily.

A more advanced reader might chunk this sentence like this:

> The dog ran quickly down the beach
>
> attempting to catch every seagull he saw
>
> before they flew away, scolding him angrily.

Your eyes read each chunked phrase as one, and your brain assigns meaning to the entire phrase. The ability to group words and phrases based on grammar tremendously improves reading speed. In addition to improved reading speed, chunking also helps the reader better understand how the words he or she is reading work together to create meaning. The entire phrase *The dog ran quickly down the beach* gives a whole picture compared to reading one lonely word at a time:

> The   dog   ran   quickly   down   the   beach

It is much harder to be a fluent reader if you just read one word at a time. It is also more difficult to comprehend what you are reading because you have to work harder to put single words together. You want to work smarter, not harder.

The best way to incorporate a chunking strategy into your reading is to consciously group words and phrases together while you read.

When you first start, you might only chunk a few words, but as you work on mastering this process, you should be able to widen your chunking to include word groups that convey more meaning.

INTERACTION 1–13	Practice Chunking

Read the following passage. The beginning is highlighted to show chunking. The chunking will vary through the reading. As you read try to read each chunked part, note if you are losing comprehension, and see how many words you are able to chunk while maintaining comprehension. Then you will have a baseline and can improve from there!

Using the Right Keywords in Your Job Search

Anthony Balderrama

1   The right words make all the difference in life. Try asking "Wanna get hitched?" instead of "Will you marry me?" for proof.

2   Even in a job interview, you wouldn't say, "Hey, dude." You'd probably say, "Nice to meet you." And your résumé wouldn't include slang, either. You know all this. At least, I hope you do.

3   But the need for well-chosen words starts when you search job postings. From the job title to the list of requirements, knowing how to tweak your words to yield the best results is vital to getting your job hunt started off right.

4   Here are a few ways to make sure you're using the right keywords:

Be a Copycat

5   In your résumé and interviews, you want to let your best qualities and unique point of view shine through. But to get to those stages, you first have to find the right job. That means you have to do something that's unacceptable in every other circumstance: plagiarize.

6   Go to an online job board and search for jobs that you think you're a great match for. Then study the language they use to perform your own searches. For example, if you find a listing for a project coordinator position that sounds ideal, you should apply for it, of course, and then pull out key phrases to search other jobs. If they use the phrase "method calibrations," plug that into the search field to see what other positions come up. Employers might use different job titles or you might find other positions that are good fits but you didn't know they existed.

—Anthony Balderrama, "Using the Right Keywords in Your Job Search." Used with permission from Careerbuilder. www.careerbuilder.com

Now practice chunking without any highlighting, and see how you do.

Don't Get Stuck on Titles

7   When you have defined goals for your career and subsequently your salary, you can find yourself fixated on having a certain job title. Although your ambitions are admirable and beneficial to your career, don't forget that not all titles are created equal. Every company has its own culture and often its own lingo. One employer's vice president is another's senior associate. Search for the job title you want, but remember to dig deeper for other title ideas.

8   Look to the responsibilities and skills detailed in a job posting for a more accurate gauge of its duties. You'll still find the jobs you're looking for if you search by responsibility instead of title, except you'll be working backward. If, for example, you want a retail manager position, you should search for related terms, such as "supervisor" or "customer relations." Filter through the results to find good matches. You might find that you're a perfect fit for a "team leader" position that you wouldn't have otherwise found.

Treat It Like a Search Engine

9   When you're looking online for something that interests you—say, a new apartment—you suddenly become a master of the Internet query. You're trying different keywords, searching by ZIP code one moment and neighborhood nickname the next. If there's an available property in a two-mile radius, you'll find it. You know how to work a search engine without a second thought.

10   Take that mentality to your job search. One of the simplest ways to broaden or narrow your search is to use quotation marks. Searching for a phrase without quotation marks (i.e., dental assistant) will find you jobs with either word in the description. However, enclosing the entire phrase (i.e., "dental assistant") in quotes will only return jobs with those words together in that exact order. If you find your searches are returning too many hits or too few, play with quotes. You can also use the advanced-search options to tailor your searches or use other shortcuts, such as minus signs to exclude words from results.

—Anthony Balderrama, "Using the Right Keywords in Your Job Search."
Used with permission from Careerbuilder. www.careerbuilder.com

1. How many words were you able to chunk comfortably? _____

_____

2. Did you find it easier to chunk when parts were highlighted, or when you were chunking naturally on your own? _____

_____

If you found chunking annoying or frustrating, don't give up yet. Give it some time. This strategy can improve your reading speed and comprehension. However, it takes a while to change behavior, and you have to want to change or improve.

Your Reading Rate Is Based on Your Reason for Reading

Your reading rate will vary as you read, depending on the content, your prior knowledge, your interest, and your purpose for reading. As a student, you need to be aware when you need to vary your reading rate. Your rate depends on what you are reading and what your reading purpose is. Reading rates also vary greatly from person to person.

Learning reading rate	100–200 words per minute
Average reading rate	200–350 words per minute
Casual reading rate	350–600 words per minute

Good readers adjust their speed to the material they are reading. An analogy to consider is a daily commute. Sometimes you fly along, and other times—due to traffic or lights or turns—you have to slow down. The same is true for reading. Sometimes you have to slow down, and sometimes you can speed up. This adjustment is determined by four main factors:

1. Your reading purpose (skimming is faster than studying)

2. The complexity of the material (some subjects are more dense)

3. Your prior knowledge (you know more about some subjects)

4. Your interest in the material (some subjects are more interesting to you)

The following list describes readings rates from slowest to fastest, according to your reading purpose:

- Long-term learning

- Short-term recall

- Basic understanding—the average reading rate

- Skimming—surveying to get an overview

- Scanning—searching for specific info

In general, readings that are difficult for you will cause you to slow down. There are several reasons for difficulty:

- You come across vocabulary that you do not understand.

- The sentences are long and complex and require you to slow down to understand the relationships of the words, phrases, and clauses.

- The ideas are confusing, theoretical, or abstract, like those in a philosophy or religion class, or the ideas involve complex processes such as those in science classes.

Familiarity with the content will speed up your reading, and lack of prior knowledge will slow you down. The more you know, the faster you'll go. Conversely, the less you know, the slower you'll go.

Finally, if you find the material boring, it will be much harder for you to stay focused. Although this is common, it is not a valid excuse for not reading or for not slowing down your reading. The trick to reading boring material is twofold:

1. Practice the strategies for reading already discussed in this chapter.

2. Develop some discipline.

You should be more motivated to learn an effective reading strategy now. The reason is simple: to save time. The more effective your reading strategy is, the quicker you can get through the boring material with comprehension so you can move on to the "fun stuff."

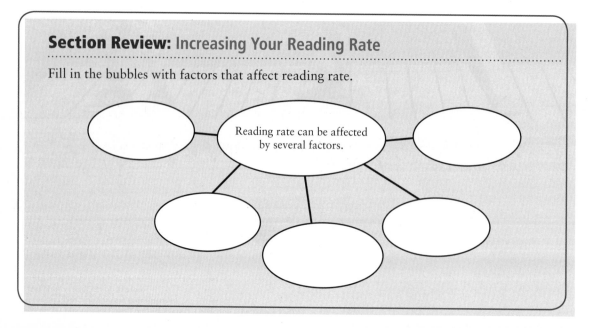

Section Review: Increasing Your Reading Rate

Fill in the bubbles with factors that affect reading rate.

Reading rate can be affected by several factors.

Chapter Summary Activity: Engaging with Reading

Chapter 1 has discussed how to read as an active process, showing you strategies you can use before, during, and after you read to increase your reading comprehension. Fill in the following Reading Guide by completing each idea on the left with information from Chapter 1 on the right. You can return to this guide throughout the course as a reminder of how to use the reading process to your advantage.

Reading Guide to Engaging with Reading

Complete this idea	with information from Chapter 1.
Reading is important because it can help you achieve two goals:	1. _____ 2. _____
Before you read, you should do four things:	3. _____ 4. _____ 5. _____ 6. _____
While surveying, pay attention to these parts of a reading selection:	7. _____ 8. _____ 9. _____ 10. _____ 11. _____
The author always has a purpose. The three general purposes the author may have are these:	12. _____ 13. _____ 14. _____
Prior knowledge is knowledge that you have _____ you read.	15. _____
As you read, stay active and focused. You can use six strategies to help you while you read:	16. _____ 17. _____ 18. _____ 19. _____ 20. _____ 21. _____

Complete this idea	with information from Chapter 1.
To monitor your comprehension, ask yourself "Am I losing comprehension?" "Am I rereading?" and	22. _____
After reading, review and rehearse the information you read in three ways:	23. _____ 24. _____ 25. _____
Chunking can improve your reading speed. Chunking can be defined as:	26. _____ _____
Your reading rate is determined by four other things:	27. _____ 28. _____ 29. _____ 30. _____

31. Compared to interactive reading strategies you used before you read this chapter, what is one thing you will do differently because you find it more effective? Write your thoughts.

_____

_____

_____

ENGAGE YOUR SKILLS
Engaging with Reading

Before you read the following article, survey it, ask questions, predict its purpose, and check your prior knowledge. Then read and annotate it. Finally, answer the questions that follow.

Wahlberg, Ensemble Provide a Win in *Fighter*

Linda Cook

1   If Mark Wahlberg stars as an interesting character, the movie has a fighting chance at the box office.

2   In this case, it packs quite a wallop. *The Fighter,* based on the true story of "Irish" Micky Ward, features an outstanding cast in a fascinating story. With a recession still upon us, it's a nice rags-to-riches, real-life tale—this year's *Cinderella Man,* you could say—and brings with it a welcome message of hope.

3   Wahlberg stars in the title role, and we first see him in the early 1990s in his hometown of Lowell, Mass. Micky's older brother, Dicky Eklund (Christian Bale), is being followed by a camera crew from HBO. Dicky tells everyone they are filming him because of his boxing career.

4   But Dicky, despite all his bravado and ring smarts, is a drug addict who can't be trusted to arrive at the gym on time for his brother's training sessions. Dicky works with his mother, Alice (Melissa Leo), to arrange fights for Micky, who ends up in a bout with a fighter with 20 pounds on him. Micky gets the daylights beaten out of him.

5   Micky takes a hard stance with the help of his new girlfriend Charlene (Amy Adams): He starts over with a new team, including his father, George (Jack McGee), Charlene and trainer (Mickey O'Keefe). He begins to be taken more seriously as a fighter, but his personal life remains a struggle with his brother running afoul of the law.

6   Additionally, Micky's mother refuses to accept Charlene, who will not be bossed around by her and her tough bunch of daughters.

7   In a sense, *The Fighter* parallels another (fictional) movie that opened locally this week. Both the ballerina in *Black Swan* and Ward have to make tough decisions about where their loyalties and passions lie.

8   Wahlberg is superb as the man who fights at every turn, whether it's in the ring or with his family members. Bale simply shines as Dicky. In fact, we meet the real Dicky toward the end of the film and realize just how masterful Bale's performance is. He spent hours and hours with the real Dicky, and every minute of that paid off.

9   You won't have to be a sports fan to appreciate the challenges Ward faced or to appreciate the ensemble that provides a solid win in this riveting movie.

Use the material you highlighted or underlined to answer the following questions about the movie review.

1. What movie is this review about? _____

2. What kind of movie is it? _____

3–4. What other movies of this kind have you seen?

- _____

- _____

5. What do movies of this kind have in common? _____

_____

_____

6. After you surveyed the review, did you predict that the writer would suggest readers go see the movie?

       Yes   No   Maybe

7. Why did you give that answer? _____

_____

_____

8–13. Who are six characters in the movie, and which actors play them?

- _____

- _____

- _____

- _____

- _____

- _____

14–15. Have you seen any of these actors in other movies? If so, name the actor and the movie.

- _____

- _____

16–17. What are the author's purposes in this movie review? Circle any that apply.

       Persuade   Inform   Express

18–20. What are three words the author uses to describe Wahlberg and this movie?

- _____

- _____

- _____

MASTER YOUR SKILLS
Engaging with Reading

A. Before you read the following article, survey it, ask questions, predict its purpose, and check your prior knowledge. Then read and annotate it. Finally, answer the questions that follow.

When the Lungs Break Down

1. Turn this title into a question. _____

_____

Underline or highlight the answers to your question in the paragraph below.

1   In large cities, in certain workplaces, and even in the cloud around a cigarette smoker, airborne particles and gases are present in abnormally high concentrations. They put extra workloads on the respiratory system.

Bronchitis and Emphysema

2. Turn this heading into a question. _____

_____

Underline or highlight the answers to your question in the paragraphs below.

2   Ciliated and mucus-secreting epithelial cells line the walls of your bronchioles. This is one of the defenses that protect you from respiratory infections. Cigarette smoke and other airborne pollutants harm this lining. Smoking may contribute to bronchitis. Epithelial cells lining the airways become irritated and they secrete too much mucus, which accumulates. Tiny particles get stuck in the mucus and bacteria begin to grow in it. Coughing brings up some of this gunk, but if irritation persists, so does the coughing.

3   Initial attacks of bronchitis are usually treated with antibiotics, which help to keep bacteria in check. But if irritation caused by smoking continues, bronchioles are chronically inflamed. Bacteria, chemical agents, or both degrade the bronchiole walls, ciliated cells die off, and mucus-secreting cells multiply. Scar tissue forms and narrows or obstructs the airways.

4   In chronic bronchitis, thick mucus clogs the airways. Tissue-destroying bacterial enzymes go to work on the thin, stretchable walls of the alveoli. As walls crumble, inelastic fibrous tissue forms around them. Alveoli are enlarged, and fewer exchange gases. In time, the lungs become distended and inelastic. It becomes difficult to run, to walk, and even to exhale. These problems are among the symptoms of emphysema, a chronic ailment that affects over a million people in the United States.

5   A few people are genetically predisposed to develop emphysema. They do not have a workable gene for the enzyme antitrypsin, which can inhibit bacterial attack on alveoli. Poor diet and persistent or recurring colds and other respiratory infections also invite emphysema later in life. However, smoking is the major cause of the disease. Emphysema may develop slowly, over twenty or thirty years. Once this damage has occurred, lung tissues cannot be repaired.

Smoking's Impact

3. Turn this heading into a question. _____

   Underline or highlight the answers to your question in the paragraphs below.

6   Tobacco use kills 4 million people annually around the world. The number will probably rise to 10 million by 2030. It is estimated that each year in the United States, the direct medical costs of treating tobacco-induced respiratory disorders drain 22 billion dollars from the economy. As C. H. Brundtland, the former director of the World Health Organization, once put it, tobacco remains the only legal consumer product that kills half of its regular users.

7   Increasingly, laws are being passed to prohibit any smoking in public buildings, workplaces, restaurants, airports, and similar enclosed spaces. Such regulations currently provide smokefree areas to a little more than a third of the population of the United States.

8   Worldwide, tobacco companies continue to expand their sales. Developing countries hold about 85 percent of the more than 1 billion current smokers. Women and children are increasingly among them. Mark Palmer, a former U.S. ambassador, argues that exporting tobacco is the single worst thing we do to the rest of the world.

Topham Picturepoint TopFoto.co.uk

A child in Mexico City already proficient at smoking cigarettes, a behavior that ultimately will endanger her capacity to breathe.

9   Smoking marijuana (Cannabis) can also damage the respiratory system. Marijuana cigarettes are unfiltered and contain more tar than tobacco cigarettes. Smoke is inhaled more
deeply and "joints" are smoked down to their very ends, where tar is the most concentrated.
In addition to psychological effects, use of marijuana can cause or worsen asthma, bronchitis,
and emphysema.

—From STARR. *Biology: Today and Tomorrow,* 8e (pp. 378–379)
Copyright © 2008 Cengage Learning.

Based on the material you highlighted or underlined, answer the following questions
about this article.

4.   What is one reason lungs break down? _____

5.   What causes bronchitis? _____

_____

6–7.   What are two causes of emphysema?

●   _____

●   _____

8–10.   What are three ways marijuana can damage the respiratory system?

●   _____

●   _____

●   _____

B.   For each of the following types of reading material, decide whether the main purpose
is likely to be to persuade, inform, or express. Consider both the **title** and the publishing **context** (source). Feel free to add a secondary purpose if applicable.

P = Persuade: to change the reader's thoughts, attitudes, or behaviors.
I = Inform: to teach the reader about key information, usually factual.
E = Express: to express an emotion or to cause readers to feel emotions, such as amuse-
ment, sadness, horror, and so on, often by using stories.

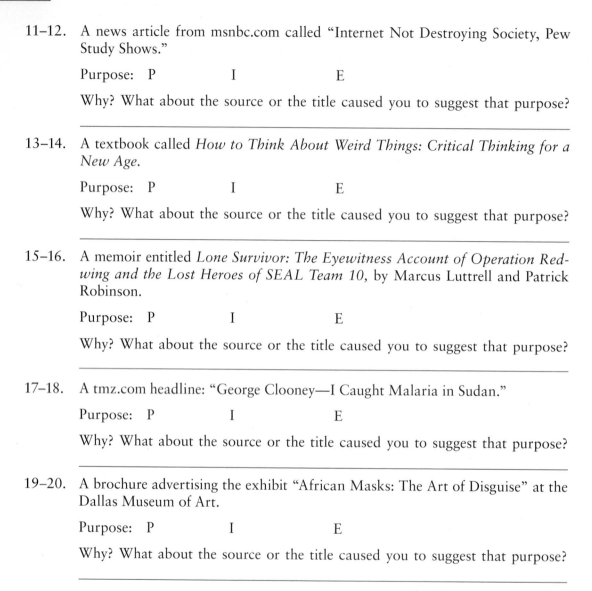

11–12. A news article from msnbc.com called "Internet Not Destroying Society, Pew Study Shows."

Purpose: P   I   E

Why? What about the source or the title caused you to suggest that purpose?

_____

13–14. A textbook called *How to Think About Weird Things: Critical Thinking for a New Age.*

Purpose: P   I   E

Why? What about the source or the title caused you to suggest that purpose?

_____

15–16. A memoir entitled *Lone Survivor: The Eyewitness Account of Operation Redwing and the Lost Heroes of SEAL Team 10,* by Marcus Luttrell and Patrick Robinson.

Purpose: P   I   E

Why? What about the source or the title caused you to suggest that purpose?

_____

17–18. A tmz.com headline: "George Clooney—I Caught Malaria in Sudan."

Purpose: P   I   E

Why? What about the source or the title caused you to suggest that purpose?

_____

19–20. A brochure advertising the exhibit "African Masks: The Art of Disguise" at the Dallas Museum of Art.

Purpose: P   I   E

Why? What about the source or the title caused you to suggest that purpose?

_____

Focus on Communications

College Communications App

The following reading is linked to these fields of . . .

Study

| ADVERTISING/ MARKETING | PERFORMING ARTS | PROFESSIONAL SPORTS |

Work

- Brand manager
- Advertising copy writer
- Advertising account executive
- TV cameraperson
- TV producer
- Ad salesperson

- Musician, singer
- Actor in TV and movies, on stage
- Dancer
- Performance artist
- Comedian

- Football player
- Basketball player
- Figure skater
- Soccer player
- Tennis player

● Pre-Reading the Selection

The excerpt that begins on page 45 comes from the textbook *Creative Strategy in Advertising.* The excerpt is titled "Celebrity Endorsements."

Surveying the Reading

Survey the textbook selection that follows. Then check the elements that are included in this reading.

_____ Title

_____ Headings

_____ First sentences of paragraphs

_____ Words in bold or italic type

_____ Images and captions

Guessing the Purpose

Based on the source and the title of the reading selection, do you think the authors' purpose is mostly to persuade, inform, or express? _____

Predicting the Content

Based on your survey, what are three things you expect the reading selection to discuss?

- _____

- _____

- _____

Activating Your Knowledge

Think about the commercials you see on television. What celebrities have you recently seen in commercials? Write down two or three celebrities and the products you've seen them advertising in a television commercial.

- _____

- _____

- _____

● Reading with Pen in Hand

Students who annotate as they read are more successful than students who do not annotate. That's why you will annotate each reading in *Engage* as you read. In the reading that follows, use the following symbols:

★ or ⟨Point⟩   to indicate a main idea

① ② ③   to indicate major details

Access the Reading CourseMate via **www.cengagebrain.com** to hear vocabulary words from this selection and view a video about this topic.

Reading Journal

● Have you ever seen any of the commercials mentioned in paragraph 1?

refrained Notice the contrast in this sentence. What does *refrained* probably mean?

Celebrity Endorsements

1   Some of the most popular commercials feature a Who's Who of pop culture. The *Wall Street Journal* credits the late Michael Jackson for helping usher in a new age of celebrity advertising when he signed a $5 million sponsorship deal in 1984 with PepsiCo. Celebrities and musicians had appeared in ads before, but the biggest stars had **refrained** out of fear of hurting their reputation. "Once reluctant stars and musicians began to say, 'If the King of Pop can do it, maybe it's OK,'" explained Josh Rabinowitz, senior vice president of music at WPP's Grey New York. Pepsi ads have gone on to feature a Who's Who of pop stars, including Madonna, Michael J. Fox, Ray Charles, Cindy Crawford, and Britney Spears. Other brands have followed Pepsi's success with celebrity endorsers.

©Steve Allen/Getty Images

2   There are numerous advantages to using celebrities, including the following:

3   *They have stopping power.* Celebrities attract attention and help cut through the clutter of other ads. The "Got Milk?" print campaign makes milk seem cool by showing hundreds of celebrities—from sports figures to political leaders to cartoon characters—sporting milk mustaches.

● Can you think of a celebrity from a "Got Milk?" commercial?

4   *Fans idolize celebrities.* Advertisers hope the admiration for the celebrity will be transferred to the brand. The trick is to make sure the celebrity doesn't overshadow the brand. The commercial that won the CBS poll for "Best Super Bowl Commercial of All Time" features a little boy befriending his idol, Pittsburgh Steelers lineman Mean Joe Greene. It opens on Greene **hobbling** down the players' tunnel, on his way to the locker room. It's quite apparent that the Steelers game wasn't going well and the defensive lineman was through for the day. An awestruck boy meets Greene in the tunnel and asks, "Ya . . . ya need any help?" The mean linebacker snarls back, "Naw." The boy tries to comfort the defeated lineman: "I just want you to know that . . . that you're the greatest." Greene mumbles, "Yeah, sure," trying to ignore the boy. But the boy insists on making Greene feel better, so he asks, "Want my Coke?" Greene waves him off but the boy **persists**, "Really, you can have it." Reluctantly, Greene accepts the offer and guzzles the 16-ounce bottle of Coke in one gulp. The Coca-Cola jingle starts playing, "A Coke and a smile, makes me feel good, makes me feel nice. . . ." The boy, looking dejected because he thinks he has failed to impress his hero, starts to walk away. Greene stops him and tosses his football jersey to him as a token of his appreciation. The delighted boy utters, "Wow! Thanks, Mean Joe!" and the jingle continues, "That's the way it should be and I'd like the whole world smiling at me. . . . Have a Coke and a smile." This endearing message, which ran in the 1980 Super Bowl, still resonates with viewers. And it makes the product, not the celebrity, the true star of the ad.

● Visualize this commercial as you read paragraph 4.

hobbling *Hobbling* is a verb. The next sentence gives a clue. What does *hobbling* mean?

persists The boy's action gives the clue. What does *persists* mean?

5   *People are fascinated about the personal lives of celebrities.* Sometimes even the **foibles** of celebrities can inspire ideas for persuasive messages. Willie Nelson, who got into trouble with the Internal Revenue Service (IRS), appeared in a commercial for H&R Block. In the commercial, he's forced to be the spokesperson for a fictitious shaving cream company as a way to payoff his back

foibles The clue to *foibles* rests in what Willie Nelson did. What does *foibles* mean?

● Did you find it interesting that Willie Nelson got into trouble with the IRS?

● Can you picture the bigger and smaller computer sizes?

relevant The example that follows explains this word. What does *relevant* mean?

● How much do you think celebrities get paid to sponsor a product?

● What celebrities can you think of who are no longer in fashion?

● Picture MC Hammer doing his dance in front of his mansion.

taxes. In real life, he released an album to pay his debt. Even if you don't know this little tidbit about the folksinger, the commercial makes sense. More important, there was a relevant connection to the advertiser. The commercial closes with this message: "Don't get bad advice. Let H&R Block double-check your taxes free. We'll find what others miss."

6 *Their unique characteristics can help communicate the selling idea.* Seven-foot five-inch basketball star Yao Ming appeared with Verne Troyer ("Mini-Me") in ads promoting Apple's 12- and 17-inch laptops. Yao is shown with the smaller screen, and Verne has the big screen. The two celebrities help further the selling idea—size—in a dramatic way.

7 *They're perceived as experts in their fields.* The trick is to make a **relevant** connection between a celebrity's expertise and the brand being advertised. An athlete is a natural spokesperson for sporting goods but doesn't seem credible when promoting junk food that's high in fat and calories.

8 Before you think a celebrity is the answer, consider these drawbacks:

9 *They're expensive.* Many top athletes, actors, and musicians command contracts in the millions of dollars. Smaller companies shouldn't even dream of spending this type of money, nor should companies trying to promote their low prices. Even large companies should think twice before plopping down millions of dollars for a celebrity, especially in a bad economy. High-priced celebrity endorsers may give consumers, stockholders, and employees the impression that a company is wasting money.

10 *They're often a quick fix, not a long-term strategy.* Celebrities go in and out of fashion, and as their popularity level shifts, so does their persuasiveness. Look at a *People* magazine from a decade or two ago. How many of the former superstars are still super popular?

11 Rapper MC Hammer made it big in the 1980s and spent money as if his star power would last forever. Soon he was out of the limelight and in debt, which prompted an idea for a Nationwide Insurance ad. The commercial opens with Hammer dancing to "U Can't Touch This" in front of a mansion with a gigantic, glittering "H" over the doorway (bling for a mansion). The commercial cuts to "5 minutes later" and shows Hammer sitting in front of his mansion, which has a foreclosure sign. The message: "Life comes at you

fast and when it does, Nationwide can help." The **self-deprecating** humor helps further the message that life is filled with uncertainty. Likewise, a 2009 Super Bowl commercial for Cash4Gold shows Hammer touting, "I can get cash for this gold medallion of me wearing a gold medallion!" In both ads, the has-been celebrity works better than someone who's widely popular.

12   *They may lack credibility.* Even though the Federal Trade Commission requires celebrities to actually use the products they endorse, 63 percent of respondents in a study published in *Advertising Age* said that celebrities are "just doing it for the money," and 43 percent believed celebrities "don't even use the product."

credibility Did the viewers think that the celebrities used the products they endorsed? What does *credibility* mean?

● Have you ever thought that the celebrity "doesn't even use the product?"

13   *They may endorse so many products that it confuses people.* Tiger Woods got into hot water for bouncing a Titleist golf ball on the wedge of a Titleist golf club while shooting a Nike commercial.

14   *They can overshadow the message.* Although a celebrity may draw attention to an ad, some consumers focus their attention on the celebrity and fail to note what's being promoted. In one spot, Yao Ming tries to pay for a souvenir from New York City by writing a check. The cashier responds, "Yo," pointing to a sign that says "no checks." Yao corrects her, "Yao." They go back and forth with the Yo, Yao routine and the spot closes with a brief pitch for Visa's check card. The commercial is a clever spin on the "who's on first" routine. The audience will likely remember Yao's name, but it's not as certain they'll remember which credit card company paid for the ad. The Visa brand name could easily have been made dominant if the cashier had asked the Chinese athlete to show his visa and passport and he presented his Visa check card instead.

● Have you seen this commercial, or did you imagine Yao in this verbal exchange?

15   *They may disparage your brand when they think no one's listening.* Executives from Adidas AG weren't amused when they read a blog from their star endorser, Gilbert Arenas. The Washington Wizards guard blogged about a signature Adidas shoe that had not yet been revealed to the public: "I'm sitting there looking at the shoe like 'I hope you guys aren't serious. Because I'm not going to wear this shoe. . . . Nobody is going to wear this shoe.'" He went on to say it reminded him of something a ballerina would wear. An Adidas spokesman told the *Wall Street Journal* that in the end the company benefited from the commentary. Adidas reworked the design and Arenas blogged "I think people are going to like the colors, but they're also going to like the shoe."

disparage What do Gilbert Arenas's actions show about his feelings toward the shoe? What does *disparage* mean?

● Can you imagine how people at Adidas felt when they first heard of Gilbert Arenas's comments?

16   *Bad press about the celebrity can hurt the sponsor.* The Kellogg Co. didn't renew Michael Phelps's contract after a British tabloid published a photo of the Olympic champion smoking pot at a campus party. Nike suspended its contract with NFL star Michael Vick after the NFL star was linked with an illegal dog-fighting ring. Kmart canceled its contract with golfing veteran Fuzzy Zoeller after he joked about Tiger Woods eating fried chicken and collard greens. And O. J. Simpson, once one of the most popular endorsers, probably won't be asked to appear in any commercials in the future.

> ● Do you know what O. J. Simpson did to not be asked to do any more endorsements?

17   "Having a highly paid, highly visible celebrity endorser is like having an expensive beach home on the Florida coast. It's swell, if you don't mind lying awake all night worrying about approaching storms," says Bob Garfield, ad critic at *Advertising Age*.

—Adapted from DREWNIANY/JEWLER. *Creative Strategy in Advertising*, 10e (pp. 12–16) Copyright © 2011 Cengage Learning.

● Check Your Skills While Continuing to Learn

The questions that follow will check your understanding (comprehension) of the reading selection. They address all the skills you will learn throughout the book. Here in Chapter 1, each skill is first described briefly. Then a sample question, an answer, and a reason for the answer are given. You can use these questions to see which skills you need to practice carefully.

A Suggested Learning Process

- Read and think about the skill.

- Study all three parts of the example: the question, the answer, and the explanation.

- Look back at the reading selection so you can understand the example.

- Answer the practice question as a check for yourself of how well you can already apply this skill.

- Note that you can keep track of your progress in applying the different skills by filling in the chart in the inside back cover of the book.

● Comprehension Questions

Write the letter of the answer on the line. Then explain your thinking.

Main Idea

Think of the main idea as the point of the paragraph or passage. To find the main idea, notice which sentence explains the author's most important point about the subject. The other sentences in the paragraph should offer explanations, examples, and details about the main idea. The details are more specific than the main idea.

Example

_b_ 1. What is the best statement of the main idea of paragraph 1?

   a. Some of the most popular commercials feature a Who's Who of pop culture.

   b. The *Wall Street Journal* credits the late Michael Jackson for helping usher in a new age of celebrity advertising when he signed a $5 million sponsorship deal in 1984 with PepsiCo.

   c. Celebrities and musicians had appeared in ads before, but the biggest stars had refrained out of fear of hurting their reputation.

   d. "Once reluctant stars and musicians began to say, 'If the King of Pop can do it, maybe it's OK,'" explained Josh Rabinowitz, senior vice president of music at WPP's Grey New York.

WHY? What information in the selection leads you to give that answer? Answer A introduces the topic. Answer B gives the main point of this paragraph, which describes the effect of Michael Jackson accepting a product endorsement. The other answers each give details about how Michael Jackson opened the way for other top celebrity endorsements.

Practice

_____ 2. What is the best statement of the main idea of the overall passage?

   a. There are numerous advantages to using celebrities.

   b. There are advantages and disadvantages to celebrity endorsements.

   c. Fans idolize celebrities.

   d. Before you think a celebrity is the answer, consider several drawbacks.

WHY? What information in the selection leads you to give that answer? _____

_____

_____

_____

Supporting Details

Think of the supporting details as the proof for the main idea. To locate the supporting details, find the main idea and then look for the information the author uses to explain it in more detail. Sometimes, if a main idea covers more than one paragraph, you will find the supporting details in several paragraphs.

Example

_c_   3. Which of the following details does *not* directly support this main idea from the last two paragraphs? *Bad press about the celebrity can hurt the sponsor.*

   a. The Kellogg Co. didn't renew Michael Phelps's contract after a British tabloid published a photo of the Olympic champion smoking pot at a campus party.

   b. Nike suspended its contract with NFL star Michael Vick after the NFL star was linked with an illegal dog-fighting ring.

   c. Having a highly paid, highly visible celebrity endorser is like having an expensive beach home on the Florida coast.

   d. Kmart canceled its contract with golfing veteran Fuzzy Zoeller after he joked about Tiger Woods eating fried chicken and collard greens.

WHY? What information in the selection leads you to give that answer? Answers A, B, and D give direct examples of sponsors dropping a celebrity due to bad press. These are major details in the paragraph. Answer C is a minor detail and not a direct support.

Practice

____   4. The main idea of paragraph 14 is this: *Celebrities may overshadow the message.* Which sentence below is the only one that directly supports this statement?

   a. Although a celebrity may draw attention to an ad, some consumers focus their attention on the celebrity and fail to note what's being promoted.

   b. In one spot, Yao Ming tries to pay for a souvenir from New York City by writing a check.

   c. The cashier responds, "Yo," pointing to a sign that says "no checks."

   d. Yao corrects her, "Yao."

WHY? What information in the selection leads you to give that answer? _____

Author's Purpose

The author's general purpose may be to persuade (change the reader's mind or behavior), inform (share information with the reader), or express (share feelings or make the reader feel a certain way, often through stories), or the author may have more than one purpose. At specific points in a text, an author may use a variety of methods to achieve the general purpose. You should always assume that the author has a particular reason for what he or she wrote.

Example

_c_   5. What is the authors' purpose in paragraph 1?

    a. To persuade readers that celebrities should be in commercials.

    b. To be expressive to readers by helping them enjoy popular commercials.

    c. To inform readers how popular stars became endorsers in product commercials.

    d. To persuade readers that Michael Jackson was the King of Pop.

WHY? What information in the selection leads you to give that answer? The authors don't use any words to suggest they are trying to persuade readers of anything, so Answers A and D are incorrect. Rather, they are stating facts: what happened that allowed stars to feel all right about endorsing products. The purpose is informative, as in Answer C.

Practice

    6. What is the author's purpose overall?

    a. To express emotion to readers through the sharing of endearing commercials.

    b. To persuade readers that their lives are being manipulated by commercials with celebrity endorsements.

    c. To persuade readers that celebrities are always trying to sell them something.

    d. To inform readers about the pros and cons of the use of celebrities to endorse products.

WHY? What information in the selection leads you to give that answer? _____

_____

_____

_____

Relationships

The ideas in a reading selection are related to one another in different ways. For instance, one sentence might discuss the causes of an event mentioned in a different sentence. Some relationships have to do with time, space, comparisons and contrasts, causes and effects, and so on. You may see the relationships between the ideas in different parts of one sentence, in different sentences, or even in different paragraphs. Many times, these relationships are indicated with signal words or transitions such as *but, and, however, for example,* and so on.

Example

__b__   7. What pattern is used to organize the description of the commercial in paragraph 4?

    a. Space order

    b. Time order

    c. Comparison

    d. Definition

WHY? What information in the selection leads you to give that answer? The words that first signal time order in paragraph 4 are *It opens.* Then the commercial is told from start to finish. This is time order.

Practice

_____   8. In the following sentence from paragraph 7, what is the relationship? *An athlete is a natural spokesperson for sporting goods but doesn't seem credible when promoting junk food that's high in fat and calories.*

    a. Time order

    b. Cause and effect

    c. Definition

    d. Contrast

WHY? What information in the selection leads you to give that answer? _____

Fact, Opinion, and Inference

A fact is a true statement that can be verified by using another source of information: *It is 85 degrees outside.* An opinion is a person's personal reaction: *It's too hot to play baseball.* An inference is an idea the reader gets from the other ideas that the author has stated: *That person must not like the heat.* To be valid, an inference must be a logical extension of what the author has written.

Example

<u> c </u>   9. Which statement is an opinion?

   a. Many top athletes, actors, and musicians command contracts in the millions of dollars.

   b. The commercial that won the CBS poll for "Best Super Bowl Commercial of All Time" features a little boy befriending his idol, Pittsburgh Steelers lineman Mean Joe Greene.

   c. In both ads, the has-been celebrity works better than someone who's widely popular.

   d. Fans idolize celebrities.

WHY? What leads you to give that answer? The word *better* is an indication that Answer C is an opinion. Some people might disagree with this opinion. Answers A and B are facts that many people know and can be checked; they are verifiable. Answer D is well known and is supported by fact.

Practice

____   10. Which of the following statements is a fact?

   a. The mean linebacker snarls back, "Naw."

   b. This endearing message, which ran in the 1980 Super Bowl, still resonates with viewers.

   c. "I'm sitting there looking at the shoe like 'I hope you guys aren't serious. Because I'm not going to wear this shoe. . . . Nobody is going to wear this shoe.'"

   d. Nike suspended its contract with NFL star Michael Vick after the NFL star was linked with an illegal dog-fighting ring.

WHY? What information in the selection leads you to give that answer? _____

_____

_____

_____

● Language in Use

The following words (or forms of them) were used in "Celebrity Endorsements." Now you can use them in different contexts. Put a word from the box into the blank lines in the following numbered sentences.

refraining	hobbling	persisted	foibles
relevant	self-deprecating	credibility	disparage

1. Having _____ means others believe in you, probably because you have been honest in the past.

2. It does not mean being perfect—after all, everyone has their _____ .

3. But it does mean _____ from telling lies.

4. In addition to lying, another trait people have that may cause others to _____ them is slanting a story to make themselves look better. It's not exactly lying, but it is manipulative.

5. These kinds of character traits are _____ not only in a person's personal relationships but also when others, such as previous employers, are asked to vouch for a person's reputation when they are seeking a new job or opportunity.

Career Communications App   MAGAZINE WEBSITE

● Pre-Reading the Selection

The excerpt that begins on page 56 comes from USAToday.com. The excerpt is titled "Today's Generations Face New Communication Gaps."

Surveying the Reading

Survey the selection that follows. Then check the elements that are included in this reading.

_____ Title

_____ Headings

_____ First sentences of paragraphs

_____ Words in bold or italic type

_____ Images and captions

Guessing the Purpose

Based on the source and the title of the reading selection, do you think the author's purpose is mostly to persuade, inform, or express?_____

Predicting the Content

Based on your survey, what are three things you expect the reading selection to discuss?

- _____

- _____

- _____

Activating Your Knowledge

Think about the communication style you and others of your generation have. What communication problems arise when you communicate with older generations (maybe with your parents or grandparents) or younger generations (kids)?

- _____
- _____
- _____

● Reading with Pen in Hand

Students who annotate as they read are more successful than students who do not annotate. That's why you will annotate each reading in *Engage* as you read. In the reading that follows, use the following symbols:

★ or (Point)   to indicate a main idea

① ② ③   to indicate major details

Access the Reading CourseMate via www.cengagebrain.com to hear vocabulary words from this selection and view a video about this topic.

Today's Generations Face New Communication Gaps

Denise Kersten

1   A surprising number of career books crossing my desk in recent months address the generation gap—or rather gaps—which has caused me to wonder: Why the sudden preoccupation with generational disconnect? The generation gap is not a new phenomenon; rebellious baby boomers coined the term in the late 1960s. But some experts say the **disparities** today are deeper and more complex, making it harder for workers of various ages to communicate.

2   "There are more pronounced differences between the generations today than there ever has been before," says Claire Raines, co-author of *Generations at Work*. "That's simply because our world has changed so much in the last 50 to 80 years." Plus, as older employees defer retirement and new ranks of workers come of age, more generations are **melding** into the workforce. "For the first time in history we have four distinct generations on the job," says David Stillman, co-author of *When Generations Collide*. Each

Reading Journal

● Predict what might be making it harder for workers of various ages to communicate.

disparities The following sentence gives a synonym. What does *disparities* mean?

● Visualize some of the changes that have happened in the world in the last fifty to eighty years.

melding If more than one generation is *melding* into the workforce, what does *melding* mean?

generation "uses a different language," says Paul Storfer, president of HR Technologies, a firm that develops workforce management software.

© Thomas Northcut/Digital Vision/Jupiter Images

- Think about what the term "communication skills" means to you.

savvy A synonym is given in the first sentence of the paragraph. What does *savvy* mean?

3   The term "communication skills," for example, might mean formal writing and speaking abilities to an older worker. But it might mean e-mail and instant-messenger savvy to a twentysomething. Being aware of generational differences can help you anticipate miscommunications and tailor your message for maximum effect—whether you're applying for a job, pitching a new idea to your boss or leading a team.

4   Of course, a person's age is just one factor shaping the way he or she communicates. Birth year alone doesn't necessarily dictate generational outlook. "There's not a magic age when you become a member of a generation," Stillman says. A tech-savvy and young-at-heart baby boomer, for example, might fit the Generation X profile, while a conservative Xer could think more like a traditionalist. But experts say you should keep these general patterns in mind when communicating across generations:

Traditionalists (born 1922–1943)*

- Who do you know that is a traditionalist?

5   The Great Depression and World War II were critical events shaping the mindset of the "Greatest Generation." These workers place a high premium on formality and the top-down chain of command. A traditionalist, for instance, is more likely to write a memo than shout across the room, and he might be offended by the more direct, immediate approach of Generation X.

6   Respect is also important. A study by Randstad in 2001 shows that respect is the traditionalists' top psychological need. Younger

*These years vary according to different demographic models.

workers might be accustomed to a flat corporate structure, but they can earn points with these colleagues by using formal titles instead of first names or scheduling a meeting rather than dropping in. Putting things in historical perspective also can help sell traditionalists on your message, Raines says, because they prefer to make decisions based on what worked in the past.

● Do you know someone who wants you to call them Mr. or Mrs.?

Baby Boomers (born 1943–1960)

7   "Boomers are people who work to live," says Connie Fuller, co-author of *Bridging the Boomer-Xer Gap*. Growing up with 80 million peers has made this generation a highly competitive one, and boomers are generally willing to sacrifice for success.

● Who do you know that is a boomer?

8   Recognition is important to boomers, according to the Randstad study, and Raines says they favor a personable style of communication that aims to build **rapport**. Like the traditionalists, baby boomers tend to favor a top-down approach and value respect. But they also can be credited with reshaping corporate culture with casual dress codes and flexible schedules.

● Does your workplace have a casual dress code or flexible schedule?

rapport What would a personable style of communication make possible with another person? What does *rapport* mean?

Generation X (born 1960–1980)

9   A higher divorce rate combined with an increase in working mothers meant many Xers grew up as "latch-key kids," frequently left to their own devices. They saw how much their baby boomer parents gave up for their careers; then they saw many of them laid off in the 1980s recession. As a result, Xers tend to be **skeptical**, highly individual workers who value a work/life balance. Most would rather be rewarded with extra time off than a step up the corporate ladder. If they need to work extra hours, they want to know why.

● Who do you know who is a Gen Xer?

skeptical If the Xers saw their parents taken advantage of or laid off, how might they feel toward businesses? What does *skeptical* mean?

10   Generation X was shaped by a culture of instant results—from remote controls to the birth of the Internet—so they value efficiency and directness. "When we've wanted information—boom—we've been able to get it," Stillman says. "Expectations are immediate and instantaneous." Older workers can communicate best with Gen Xers by cutting to the chase and avoiding unnecessary meetings.

● What's your favorite device that brings instant results?

Millennials (born 1980–2002)

11   Raised by young boomers and older Xers, the first members of this group are just entering the workforce.* "A lot of people are

● Who do you know who is a Millennial?

* This article was written in 2002. As of 2011, the age of Millennials would range from 31 down to 9.

collaborative There is no clue in paragraph 11, but the first sentence of paragraph 12 gives an example. What does *collaborative* mean?

leisure What type of activities do families often do together? What does *leisure* mean?

● Did you ever get to choose your family's leisure activities?

attribute Use the example given to understand what *attribute* means.

● Can you recall any of the generational trends mentioned in the previous paragraphs?

thinking that they're just like Generation Xers, only younger—and they're not," Raines says. Unlike the Xers, Millennials are highly **collaborative** and optimistic. They do, however, share Xers' emphasis on work/life balance and comfort with technology.

12   They've been taught to "put feelings on the table," Stillman says, and have had significant influence in how their families are run. These youngsters, for instance, make 74% of their families' **leisure** decisions, according to a study by Stillman and his co-author, Lynne Lancaster. It will be important to allow them a voice in the office and to present messages from a positive standpoint for these can-do young people, though we'll have to wait and see what effect they have on the corporate scene.

13   Looking at generational trends is one way to begin anticipating others' preferences and seeing differences on a less personal level. A baby boomer manager who knows that Generation X tends to value work/life balance, for example, might be less likely to **attribute** a worker's resistance to overtime as laziness. The two will be better able to work out a compromise. "Good business is based on good communication," Raines says. "We oftentimes think we know the one right way to communicate, and in business that just isn't the case."

—Denise Kersten, "Today's Generations Face New Communication Gaps." Copyright © 2002 by USA Today. Reprinted by permission.

● Check Your Skills While Continuing to Learn

The questions that follow will check your understanding (comprehension) of the reading selection. They address all the skills you will learn throughout the book. Here in Chapter 1, each skill is first described briefly. Then a sample question, an answer, and a reason for the answer are given. You can use these questions to see which skills you need to practice carefully.

A Suggested Learning Process

- Read and think about the skill.

- Study all three parts of the example: the question, the answer, and the explanation.

- Look back at the reading selection so you can understand the example.

- Answer the practice question as a check for yourself of how well you can already apply this skill.

- Note that you can keep track of your progress in applying the different skills by filling in the chart in the inside back cover of the book.

● Comprehension Questions

Write the letter of the answer on the line. Then explain your thinking.

Main Idea

Think of the main idea as the point of the paragraph or passage. To find the main idea, notice which sentence explains the author's most important point about the subject. The other sentences in the paragraph should offer explanations, examples, and details about the main idea. The details are more specific than the main idea.

Example

__d__ 1. Which of the following is the best statement of the main idea for the entire passage?

    a. The generation gap is not a new phenomenon; rebellious baby boomers coined the term in the late 1960s.

    b. The term "communication skills," for example, might mean formal writing and speaking abilities to an older worker.

    c. The Great Depression and World War II were critical events shaping the mindset of the "Greatest Generation."

    d. But experts say you should keep these general patterns in mind when communicating across generations.

WHY? What information in the selection leads you to give that answer? Answer D is the main point of this reading, which discusses communication gaps between four generations. Answer A is a general introductory idea, B is an example, and C is only about the traditionalists.

Practice

_____ 2. What is the best statement of the main idea of paragraph 6?

    a. Respect is also important.

    b. A study by Randstad in 2001 shows that respect is the traditionalists' top psychological need.

  c. Younger workers might be accustomed to a flat corporate structure, but they can earn points with these colleagues by using formal titles instead of first names or scheduling a meeting rather than dropping in.

  d. Putting things in historical perspective also can help sell traditionalists on your message, Raines says, because they prefer to make decisions based on what worked in the past.

WHY? What information in the selection leads you to give that answer? _____

_____

_____

_____

Supporting Details

Think of the supporting details as the proof for the main idea. To locate the supporting details, find the main idea and then look for the information the author uses to explain it in more detail. Sometimes, if a main idea covers more than one paragraph, you will find the supporting details in several paragraphs.

Example

  _d_   3. Which of the following details describes a person from Generation X?

  a. Is highly collaborative.

  b. Needs recognition.

  c. Finds climbing the corporate ladder motivating.

  d. Is distrustful of the establishment.

WHY? What information in the selection leads you to give that answer? Answer A describes the Millennials; Answer B describes the boomers; Answer C is the opposite of what is stated about Gen Xers; Answer D is supported by the word *skeptical* in paragraph 9.

_____

_____

Practice

  _____   4. Which of the following details is *not* supported by the text?

  a. Family and/or leisure time is important to Gen Xers.

  b. Millennials are having a mostly positive impact on the corporate culture.

  c. Traditionalists are typically conservative.

  d. Boomers are relationally driven.

WHY? What information in the selection leads you to give that answer? _____

_____

_____

_____

Author's Purpose

The author's general purpose may be to persuade (change the reader's mind or behavior), inform (share information with the reader), or be expressive (make the reader feel a certain way, often through stories), or the author may have more than one purpose. At specific points in a text, an author may use a variety of methods to achieve the general purpose. You should always assume that the author has a particular reason for what he or she wrote.

Example

 a 5. What is the author's overall purpose in this reading?

a. To inform readers of four distinct generations and general patterns for communicating with them.

b. To entertain readers by expressing the author's sarcastic perspective about the four different generations in the workforce today.

c. To entertain readers by giving anecdotes of each generation in the workplace.

d. To persuade readers that traditionalists are the "Greatest Generation."

WHY? What information in the selection leads you to give that answer? Answer A is supported by the details. The author names and describes four generations, communication issues they may have with one another, and ways to overcome them.

_____

Practice

_____ 6. What is the author's purpose in the section entitled "Millennials"?

a. To be expressive and entertain readers with endearing examples of how Millennials grew up.

b. To persuade readers that Millennials are spoiled and will probably cause many problems in the workplace.

c. To inform readers that Millennials are better at collaboration than the other categories of generations.

d. To inform readers of the general communication patterns that the Millennials have.

WHY? What information in the selection leads you to give that answer? _____

_____

_____

_____

Relationships

The ideas in a reading selection are related to one another in different ways. For instance, one sentence might discuss the causes of an event mentioned in a different sentence. Some relationships have to do with time, space, comparisons and contrasts, causes and effects, and so on. You may see the relationships between the ideas in different parts of one sentence, in different sentences, or even in different paragraphs. Many times, these relationships are indicated with signal words or transitions such as *but, and, however, for example,* and so on.

Example

__c__   7. What pattern is used to organize the supporting details in paragraph 2?

      a. Space order

      b. Time order

      c. Contrast

      d. Definition

WHY? What information in the selection leads you to give that answer? Words that signal contrast here are *differences, distinct, different.*

_____

Practice

_____   8. What two patterns are found in the following sentences? *Unlike the Xers, Millennials are highly collaborative and optimistic. They do, however, share Xers' emphasis on work/life balance and comfort with technology.*

      a. Cause and effect

      b. Time and space order

      c. Classification and example

      d. Comparison and contrast

> **WHY?** What information in the selection leads you to give that answer? _____

_____

_____

_____

Fact, Opinion, and Inference

A fact is a true statement that can be verified by using another source of information: *It is 85 degrees outside.* An opinion is a person's personal reaction: *It's too hot to play baseball.* An inference is an idea the reader gets from the other ideas that the author has stated: *That person must not like the heat.* To be valid, an inference must be a logical extension of what the author has written.

Example

_c_   9. Which statement below is an opinion?

   a. These youngsters, for instance, make 74% of their families' leisure decisions, according to a study by Stillman and his co-author, Lynne Lancaster.

   b. If they need to work extra hours, they want to know why.

   c. A surprising number of career books crossing my desk in recent months address the generation gap—or rather gaps.

   d. Respect is important to traditionalists.

> **WHY?** What leads you to give that answer? The word *surprising* makes Answer C an opinion, since not everyone would find this surprising. Answer A is a statistic, which can be verified. Answer B is suggested in this selection and can be verified in other sources, such as textbooks. Answer D is supported by paragraph 6.

Practice

____   10. Which of the following statements is a fact?

   a. Millennials have been taught to "put feelings on the table," Stillman says, and have had significant influence in how their families are run.

   b. Twentysomethings are more savvy at e-mail than traditionalists.

   c. Gen Xers are impatient because they are shaped by a culture of instant results.

   d. Baby boomers are workaholics because "they work to live."

WHY? What information in the selection leads you to give that answer? _____

_____

_____

_____

● Language in Use

The following words (or forms of them) were used in "Today's Generations Face New Communication Gaps." Now you can use them in different contexts. Put a word from the box into the blank lines in the following numbered sentences.

disparities	melding	savvy	collaborated
rapport	skeptical	leisure	attribute

1. It has been said that Clint Eastwood and Matt Damon have developed quite a _____ .

2. The _____ director is twice the age of the young but successful actor.

3. Despite the age difference, the two have _____ on at least two films so far.

4. When asked what has contributed to their friendship, they tend to joke, but it is obvious they respect each other and enjoy spending _____ time together.

5. To see them talk of their friendship on film and in magazines should be enough to convince even a _____ critic of Hollywood that they are sincere.

Previewing the Chapter

Flip through the pages of Chapter 2, and read all the headings that are printed like this:

Why Is Reading Important?

Write one piece of prior knowledge you have about one of the headings in Chapter 2.

_____

_____

Write down the heading of the section that you believe you will learn the most from.

_____

_____

Plan to come back and comment on your responses when you have finished working through the chapter to see if you were right.

_____

_____

 To access additional course materials for *Engage*, including quizzes, videos, and more, please visit www.cengagebrain.com. At the CengageBrain.com home page, search for the ISBN of *Engage* (from the back cover of your book) using the search box at the top of the page. This will take you to the product page where these resources can be found.

Videos Related to Readings

Vocab Words on Audio

Read and Talk on Demand

Read and Talk   ONLINE NEWSPAPER

In college, reading is just one aspect of how you will share new ideas with others in your class. So the first reading in each chapter of this book is meant to give you the chance to talk about reading. Read the article, and then use the four discussion questions to talk about your ideas with your classmates and your instructor.

Access the Reading CourseMate via **www.cengagebrain.com** to hear a reading of this selection and view a video about this topic.

CNN Reporter Sanjay Gupta Becomes Part of the Story in Haiti

Kathryn Blaze Carlson

1   Interchangeably dressed in a grey T-shirt or a black button-down, CNN's Dr. Sanjay Gupta has spent the past seven days and seven nights amid Haiti's ruins, at times abandoning the microphone and bright lights for gauze and a scalpel.

2   The 40-year-old medical correspondent and practicing neurosurgeon, who withdrew his name from consideration for the position of U.S. surgeon general, has stepped in to the fill the very **void** he was sent to Haiti to cover as a journalist.

void The next paragraph suggests the meaning of *void*. What is it?

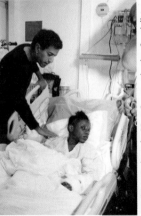

© U.S. Navy photo by Mass Communication Specialist 3rd Class Erin Oberholtzer/Released

perished Based on the general context of the earthquake, what do you think *perished* means?

USS *Carl Vinson* Given that this is anchored off the coast, what is it?

impromptu An earthquake has just occurred, and Gupta is running around lending a hand here and there. The scene is chaotic. What might *impromptu* mean?

3 "Many have asked: of course, if needed, I will help people with my neurosurgical skills," Dr. Gupta said on Twitter, the social networking site, the day after the 7.0 earthquake struck the Caribbean nation. "Yes, I am a reporter, but a doctor first."

4 Since he arrived in Haiti last Wednesday, Dr. Gupta has treated a 15-day-old Haitian girl whose mother **perished** in the earthquake, single-handedly staffed a field hospital after a Belgian medical team left the site over security concerns and, most recently, performed brain surgery on a 12-year-old Haitian girl aboard the USS *Carl Vinson*, which is anchored off the coast of Port-au-Prince.

5 "Honored to operate on a beautiful 12 yo girl, kimberly," he twittered on Monday morning, after he helped remove cement shrapnel from the girl's brain. "Suffered terrible brain inj was taken to uss carl vinson. she will do great!"

6 Between surgeries, **impromptu** consults, administering antibiotics and changing IV drips, Dr. Gupta—who was unavailable for an interview—has been filing regular field reports and interviewed U.S. Secretary of State Hillary Clinton over the weekend.

7 "You are a dad, I'm a mom," Ms. Clinton said in the Jan. 17 interview. "You know how you would feel if your child was injured . . . how desperate you would be and how you would go anywhere, to anybody, to try to help."

8 Dr. Gupta appears to have embraced this sense of duty, among chaos, looting and gunfire. "Pulling all nighter at haiti field hosp. lots of work, but all patients stable," he twittered at 3:45 a.m. on Jan. 16, referring to the field hospital that was left unstaffed after a Belgian medical team fled over fears of looters and riots. "Turned my crew into a crack med team tonight."

9 The day before, Dr. Gupta was filmed running down the street—sporting the grey T-shirt on this occasion, a backpack slung over his shoulder. "They're begging for a doctor," he said to the camera, out of breath. The cameras rolled as he was handed a tiny 15-day-old girl, who spanned the length of his forearm and was swaddled in a white blanket.

10 "Hi sweetie," Dr. Gupta whispered, as he lay her down on a wooden table, used a small light to check her eyes, and then confirmed she had not suffered a skull fracture.

11 With the help of a producer, he bandaged the child's head with gauze—a resource that, among many others, he has repeatedly said is in short supply.

12   Indeed, Dr. Gupta has emphasized the dire conditions in which he and other doctors are working, calling the situation "desperate" and "impossible."

13   "This is jungle medicine, this is primitive medicine," he said in a report outside a makeshift hospital. "There are IVs hanging from trees. That is what's happening here in Haiti."

14   "There are lots of patients waiting for care and hardly anyone to provide care," he said in another report, this time from Cité Soleil, a dense and lawless commune of Port-au-Prince.

15   Dr. Gupta, who in 2003 was named one of *People* magazine's "Sexiest Men Alive," has swapped his reporting hat for scrubs in the past, reporting live in 2003 from an Iraq operating room as he performed brain surgery, for example. He went on to perform four more life-saving brain surgeries as an embedded reporter with the U.S. Navy.

16   The Emmy-award winning University of Michigan graduate is not the only reporter-doctor deployed to Haiti—CBS's Jennifer Ashton wears scrubs and has reported from a clinic in an airport cargo building, and ABC's Richard Besser was filmed delivering a baby in a park.

17   Although this professional **duality** has raised some questions over journalistic ethics, the networks have defended their approach given the unimaginable devastation.

duality The previous paragraphs talk about people who are both doctors and reporters. What might *duality* mean?

18   Said CNN anchor Wolf Blitzer of Dr. Gupta: "He's going beyond amazing reporting and actually saving lives."

—Kathryn Blaze Carlson, "CNN Reporter Sanjay Gupta Becomes Part of the Story in Haiti." Material reprinted with the express permission of National Post Inc.

Talking About Reading

Respond in writing to the questions below and then discuss your answers with your classmates.

1. What are three things you have learned about Sanjay Gupta from reading this article?

_____

_____

_____

2. Based on television or other reports you have seen or read about earthquakes, what do you think were probably some of the most pressing needs in Haiti after this huge earthquake in 2010?

_____

_____

_____

3. Gupta is a journalist as well as a doctor. Most journalists are only observers of the events they report on, but Gupta is a participant as well. He also made his TV crew into a "crack med team," according to this article. What problems, if any, does his participation pose for Gupta as a reporter?

_____

_____

_____

4. Gupta was being considered for the position of surgeon general of the United States, but he decided he didn't want the job. Based on what you have learned about him from reading this article, make at least one guess about why he didn't take the job.

_____

_____

_____

Vocabulary Strategies

Three ways to develop your college vocabulary so that you can understand the many meanings of words are covered in Chapter 2:

- Defining words in context as you read.
- Learning the meaning of word parts to develop your vocabulary.
- Understanding the vocabulary of college.

Once you have learned a word, the next step is to use it in your daily life. You could *read* twenty new words a day and never *learn* one of them. The only way to truly learn a new word is to actively make it a part of your writing and speaking—that is, to use it in new contexts.

- **Use new words in writing.** As you write in your college courses, use the vocabulary you are learning. You can also use new words in a vocabulary notebook, a journal, letters, e-mails, blogs, texts, and IMs—anywhere you write.
- **Use new words in speaking.** You can transfer new words into your speaking vocabulary by learning how they are pronounced. For help, use the audio files that accompany the readings in each part of this book online at **www.cengagebrain.com**. Listen to the words, practice saying them, and then introduce them into your conversation.

Define Words As You Read Using Context Clues

As you work through this chapter, you will learn strategies to help you determine the meanings of words you do not know based on the **context** in which they are used. The context is the word's setting or environment. Words weave together to make meaning, and the meaning of a word changes—a lot or a little—depending on its context. Here is a pair of examples.

In the movie *Thank You for Smoking*, Nick Naylor (played by Aaron Eckhart) spends most of his time **spinning** the obviously false tale that smoking isn't linked to lung cancer. He does this by reporting the supposed research of The Academy of Tobacco Studies, a group funded by cigarette manufacturers.

©20thCentFox/Courtesy Everett Collection

During the economic slump of the seventeenth century, Europe's peasants and urban working poor, especially in the west, supplemented their incomes by making things at home. Many women **spun** wool into yarn and sold the surplus—the yarns they did not use themselves.

—From KIDNER. *Making Europe*, 1e (p. 512)
Copyright © 2009 Cengage Learning.

You can see from these two contexts that the word *spin* can mean two entirely different things. In the first example, you can figure out, at least roughly, the meaning of *spinning* by reading the excerpt. Naylor is lying (spinning a false tale) to get people to believe that smoking is healthy so that cigarette companies can make more money. In the second example, you probably know something about how yarn is made by spinning wool. The words surrounding *spinning* and *spun*—their context—help you determine their meanings.

Find Context Clues While Reading

Context clues are hints about the meaning of a word that are located in the surrounding words or sentences. When you are trying to figure out what a word means, look in the sentences surrounding the word. Clues to your word's meaning can be found anywhere within a paragraph, but they are often found in one or more of the following three places:

1. The sentence in which the unknown word appears.

2. The sentence before the one in which the word appears.

3. The sentence after the one in which the word appears.

Here is an example of a context clue for the word *dearth*.

There is a **dearth** of women who are self-made billionaires. Of the 1,011 billionaires in the world, only 14 are women who made their own fortunes. Among them is J. K. Rowling, the world's richest author.

—Information from Kroll, "The World's Richest Self-Made Women," Forbes.com, June 22, 2010

If you don't know what the word *dearth* means, you can figure it out from the second sentence. The clue is that only fourteen of 1,011 billionaires are women who made their own fortunes—not very many at all. *Dearth* means "lack" or "shortage." The numbers are a context clue that helps you understand the meaning.

The goal of using context clues is not always to find the exact definition of a word, although in your college classes, you will sometimes need to understand technical terms precisely. For much reading, however, you can use context clues for an approximate definition of a word—enough of an understanding so you can keep reading without having to stop to consult a dictionary.

Recognize Four Kinds of Context Clues

If you can remember the acronym EASY, you can remember the four common kinds of context clues: examples, antonyms, synonyms, and your own logic interacting with the words on the page:

Example
Antonym
Synonym
Your Logic

You won't necessarily use the context clues in this order, but the word EASY will help you remember four strategies to try when you don't know the meaning of a word.

Examples

Look for **examples** that might give you clues to a word's meaning. Examples may describe or explain an unknown word. At times, the author may use signal words like these to let you know an example is coming.

> **Words that signal examples:**
> *for example, for instance, such as, to illustrate*

Dental hygiene has changed considerably over the centuries. For instance, until recently, the daily practice of brushing, much less of flossing, was uncommon. Two hundred years ago, a 40-year-old might boast a nice set of implanted animal teeth or wooden dentures; poor people were often toothless. Today, dental hygiene, dentistry, and orthodontics allow people to enjoy a set of white, straight teeth for a lifetime, with bridges, crowns, and implants indistinguishable from the real thing.

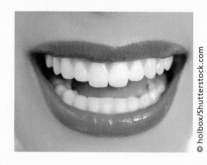

—From BRYM/LIE. *Sociology*, 3e (p. 352) Copyright © 2010 Cengage Learning.

As you can see, *dental hygiene* has to do with keeping the teeth and gums healthy. Since you already know that *dental* refers to teeth, you can figure out that *hygiene* relates to the actions a person needs to take in order to stay healthy.

INTERACTION 2–1 | **Identify Meaning Using Example Context Clues**

Each passage includes a **boldfaced** vocabulary word.

    A. Circle the signal word or words that point to an example.

    B. Underline the example.

    C. Guess the meaning of the vocabulary word and write it on the line.

1.

Beyoncé is a **gracious** person. To illustrate, at the 2009 MTV Video Music Awards, Kanye West had come onstage when Taylor Swift was starting her acceptance speech for winning Best Female Video, interrupting her to say that Beyoncé had filmed the best video. Later, when Beyoncé won her award, she invited Taylor back onstage to give her time to share her speech. She didn't have to do that.

• **Gracious:** _____

2.

> Gardeners experience **delayed gratification** several times a year, such as when they plant daffodil bulbs in October but don't see the flowers bloom until April and when they plant a pumpkin seed in May but don't get to eat pumpkin pie until September.

- Delayed gratification: _____

3.

> Because girls and boys form separate gender groups during middle childhood, socialization is specific to gender. A child doesn't get socialized to behave like an American—he gets socialized to behave like an American *boy,* or she gets socialized to behave like an American *girl.* The **norms** of behavior are different for both groups. Timidity and shyness, for instance, are acceptable in girls' groups but unacceptable in boys' groups.
>
> —Harris, *The Nurture Assumption,* p. 173

- Norms: _____

4.

> **Fidelity** to religious duties is important to worshippers. For example, in the Islamic faith, Muslims pray five times every day; this duty is known as *Salat.* Charity to others and fasting during Ramadan are also observed. Muslims who can afford it also make the *Hajj,* or sacred pilgrimage to Mecca, at least once.

- Fidelity: _____

5.

> When Oprah was a nationally known television host, it was very **advantageous** to be on her show. For example, writers whose books were shown on *The Oprah Winfrey Show* had a much better chance of becoming famous; in fact, *Publisher's Weekly* estimated that Oprah turned sixty-three books into bestsellers.

- Advantageous: _____

6.

> **Adherence** to certain healthy lifestyle choices can help many people prevent or control disease. To illustrate, maintaining healthy eating habits, exercising several times a week, and not smoking are three ways adults can maintain their health.

- Adherence: _____

Signal Words May Not Be Present

Signal words are not always used. However, if you think about the meaning of a sentence, you may find out that the author has given examples without making them obvious. Sometimes you can figure out if there are examples by trying some signal words in different places to see if they make sense. If they do, that's an example context clue. Notice how you can insert *for example* into the following sentence to help you determine the meaning of *stature*.

> Adaptations to cold climates have also resulted in changes to body **stature** over time. [For example] Being short and stocky and having short extremities is the ideal body type for conserving energy because it reduces surface area of the body for dissipation of heat.
>
> —From FERRARO. *Cultural Anthropology*, 6e (p. 152)
> Copyright © 2006 Cengage Learning.

© Bettmann/CORBIS

This won't always work, but it works often enough that you can use it to search for example context clues. However, use your common sense. Sometimes the way a sentence is put together doesn't allow you to insert *for example* or *such as,* but it can still include examples.

Punctuation Note: A Colon May Signal Examples

A colon (:) may introduce a series of examples:

> She loved the vivid **hues** of autumn: the brilliant <u>reds and oranges</u> of maple trees and the glowing <u>golds and yellows</u> of the other hardwoods.

INTERACTION 2–2	Identify Examples with No Signal Words

Each sentence includes a **boldfaced** vocabulary word.

    A. Underline the examples.

    B. Guess the meaning of the vocabulary word, and write it on the line.

1. Her father was a strict **disciplinarian,** punishing his children every time they broke a rule.

    • Disciplinarian: _____

2. A number of **factors** may contribute to heart disease: family history, lifestyle, diet, and stress are among them.

    • Factors: _____

3. The new laws were supposed to **stimulate** the economy by reducing taxes, increasing spending, and helping people find jobs and buy houses.

    • Stimulate: _____

Antonyms

Antonyms are words that have opposite meanings, such as *good* and *bad*. Sometimes you can figure out the meaning of a word by finding its antonym in a context that shows the author means to contrast (show the difference between) the two words.

> ### Words that signal contrast:
> *on the other hand, in contrast, however, but, yet, instead,*
> *even though, although, unlike, whether*

In the past, people often stayed in marriages even if they were dissatisfied with them. This traditional **constraint** no longer holds a man and woman together, however; people now have the freedom to end unhappy marriages.

—From BRYM/LIE. *Sociology*, 3e (p. 26)
Copyright © 2010 Cengage Learning.

© keith morris/Alamy

The word *however* signals a contrast between the two parts of the sentence that are divided by the semicolon (;). To figure out the meaning of *constraint,* you can use that signal word as a clue. The word with an opposing meaning is *freedom.* So *constraint* means (roughly) "not freedom." This is a **working definition** for the word *constraint.* Notice that we found the opposite word, and then put *not* in front of it. If the unknown word isn't a noun, you can use the word *doesn't* instead of *not* to help you form a working definition.

The words *traditional* and *now* offer another clue to the contrast in this sentence. Even when signal words for contrast aren't used, you can look for contrasts like these to more easily understand the author's meaning.

INTERACTION 2–3   **Identify Meaning Using Contrast Signal Clues**

Each passage includes a **boldfaced** vocabulary word.

   A. Circle the signal word or words that indicate a contrast.

   B. Underline the antonym.

   C. Guess the meaning of the vocabulary word and write it on the line.

Hint: Not all passages include signal words.

1.

   Even though these urban traffic solutions are **customary,** it's still worth thinking about adding more high-speed trains, encouraging bicycle use, and offering free public transportation. One more unusual idea that a *Slate* reader shared was to link cities to their suburbs with large roller coasters. That would be a fun commute!

• **Customary:** _____

2.

> In contrast to **bridewealth,** a dowry involves a transfer of goods or money in the opposite direction, from the bride's family to the groom or to the groom's family.
>
> —From FERRARO. *Cultural Anthropology*, 6e (p. 227)
> Copyright © 2006 Cengage Learning.

- Bridewealth: _____

_____

3.

> Unlike the bitter disputes that have broken out between TV networks and cable operators—Fox versus Time Warner Cable, ABC versus Cablevision—the latest round of fee negotiations between the Walt Disney Company and Time Warner have, so far, been quite **amicable.**
>
> —Barnes & Stetler, "In Cable Delivery, Rivals Are Pouncing,"
> *New York Times*, July 11, 2010

- Amicable: _____

4.

> Whether a person has normal mental function or mild **cognitive impairment,** regular physical exercise can lower the risk of developing Alzheimer's by up to 50 percent. A Japanese study found that among 265 people of both normal mental function and mild cognitive impairment, 70 percent of participants showed significant improvement in memory function after one year of moderate exercise.
>
> —Adapted from Weil, "Alzheimer's Disease," www.drweil.com

- Cognitive impairment: _____

5.

> Americans are so **chary** about cutting out of the office that career experts often chide them to take time away, refresh themselves, turn off the Blackberry, stop checking E-mail, and learn how to relax.
>
> —Wolgemuth, "7 Times You Shouldn't Take a Vacation,"
> *US News & World Report*, August 17, 2010

- Chary: _____

Synonyms

Synonyms are words that have similar meanings or the same meaning, such as *lovely* and *beautiful*. Sometimes you can figure out the meaning of a word by finding its synonym in a context that shows the author means to compare (show the similarities between) the two words. Other times the author actually defines the word, so be on the lookout for phrases that mean the same thing as the word.

> **Words that signal comparison:**
> *like, as, also, as well, or, in other words,*
> *similar to, that is, in the same way*

A well-designed roller coaster has enough **kinetic**, or moving, energy to complete its entire course.

© iStockphoto.com/
NicolasMcComber

The word *or* signals that the author is going to repeat the same idea using a different word. The word *kinetic* means the same thing as *moving.* These words are synonyms.

Punctuation Note: Dashes and Parentheses May Signal Synonyms or Definitions

1. A dash (—) or a pair of dashes may act as an equal sign.

Whether you solve a problem often hinges on <u>how you envision it</u>—your **representation** of the problem.

—From WEITEN. *Psychology,* 7e (p. 315) Copyright © 2008 Cengage Learning.

2. Parentheses may enclose definitions.

> To be creative requires **divergent** thinking (generating <u>many unique</u> ideas) and then **convergent** thinking (<u>combining</u> those ideas into the best result).
>
> —Bronson & Merryman, "The Creativity Crisis,"
> *Newsweek,* July 10, 2010

INTERACTION 2–4   **Identify Meaning Using Comparison Signal Clues**

Each passage includes a **boldfaced** vocabulary word.

  A. Circle the signal words or punctuation marks that indicate a similarity.

  B. Underline the synonym or definition.

  C. Guess the meaning of the vocabulary word and write it on the line.

Hint: Remember that signal words aren't always present; read carefully to find synonym clues.

1.
> Her **affinity** (feeling of attraction) to Mexican folk art could be seen throughout her living room, where there were several *retablos,* and in her kitchen, where hand-painted tile in warm colors and patterns predominated.

  • **Affinity:** _____

2.
> When Uggs came out, they quickly became **ubiquitous.** The same was true for Crocs; everyone had a pair.

  • **Ubiquitous:** _____

3.
> Proponents of a **core curriculum**—that is, a course of study every student would be required to take—argue that ever since the 1970s schools have focused on celebrating national diversity and pluralism but have failed to help students develop a shared national identity and common cultural framework.
>
> —From COOPER. *Those Who Can, Teach,* 12e (p. 155)
> Copyright © 2009 Cengage Learning.

- **Core curriculum:** _____

4.

> Another major advantage of participant-observation is that it enables the fieldworker to distinguish between **normative** and real behavior—that is, between what people should do and what people *actually do.*
>
> —From FERRARO. *Cultural Anthropology,* 6e (p. 102)
> Copyright © 2006 Cengage Learning.

- **Normative:** _____

5.

> Powerful interests opposed **suffrage** for women. Liquor interests feared that women voters would press for prohibition because many women had been active in the temperance (antiliquor) movement. Other businesses feared that women's voting would lead to reforms to improve working conditions for women and children. Southern whites feared that it would lead to voting by black women and then black men. Political bosses feared women would vote for political reform.
>
> —From WELCH. *Understanding American Government: The Essentials* (p. 174) Copyright © 2009 Cengage Learning.

- **Suffrage:** _____

Your Logic

You learned earlier that context clues for the meaning of a word are found in the surrounding words or sentences—that is, in the context of the reading selection. However, the reader's context plays a role, too, especially the context of how you think—your logic.

Your ability to understand logical connections as you interact with the words on the page will help you make meaning as you read. Starting with what you already understand, actively try to figure out what you don't yet know. This process of making **inferences** is one you should always use as you read. Here is an example.

Some people think that Americans are too **diverse** to share a common set of political values, and, in fact, some people argue that every country in the world is composed of "competing political cultures, not a single political culture."

—From WELCH. *Understanding American Government: The Essentials* (p. 11) Copyright © 2009 Cengage Learning.

© Andresr/Shutterstock.com

To discover what *diverse* means, read the sentence without it:

Some people think that Americans are too _____ to share a common set of political values.

You can see that the sentence would only make sense if the word *too* were followed by a word like *different*. And that is what *diverse* means: "different from one another."

In addition, you can look at other sentences nearby. In the second sentence of the example, the contrast between the words *competing* and *a single* offers another clue to the author's meaning.

INTERACTION 2–5	Determine Meanings Using Your Logic

Using your logic and your prior knowledge, figure out what the words in bold mean.

1.

> While he waited for the helicopter, he did what he could for Salander. He took a clean sheet from a linen cupboard and cut it up to make bandages. The blood had **coagulated** at the entry wound in her head, and he did not know whether he dared to put a bandage on it or not.
>
> —Larsson, *The Girl Who Kicked the Hornet's Nest*, p. 11

- Coagulated: _____

2.

> On July 15, 2010, Pink was performing a concert in Nuremberg, Germany, as part of her Funhouse Summer Carnival Tour, when the harness she was hooked into **malfunctioned,** sending her tumbling off stage right into a steel barricade.

- Malfunctioned: _____

3.

> The skies already are **saturated** with planes and passengers, but traffic is expected to double or even triple by 2050.
>
> —Dickey & McNicoll, "The Flying Prius," *Newsweek,* July 16, 2010

- Saturated: _____

4.

> **Deprived of** care and attention, the puppy started chewing shoes and barking constantly.

- Deprived of: _____

5.

> As was true throughout the western hemisphere, European guns and diseases rather quickly **decimated** the native American Indian population, making it easier to establish a new culture.
>
> —From WEEKS. *Population,* 10e (p. 48) Copyright © 2008 Cengage Learning.

- Decimated: _____

| INTERACTION 2–6 | Use Logic and Prior Knowledge to Determine Meanings |

Using your logic and prior knowledge, determine the meaning of each bold word.

1.

> President Barack Obama's **predecessor** was George W. Bush.

- Predecessor: _____

2.

> "Proximity" means *closeness*. (It comes from the same root as *approximate*.) Not surprisingly, we are most likely to become friends with people who live or work in proximity to us. One professor assigned students to seats randomly and followed up on them a year later. Students most often became friends with those who sat in **adjacent** seats.
>
> —From KALAT. *Introduction to Psychology*, 9e (p. 480)
> Copyright © 2011 Cengage Learning.

- **Adjacent:** _____

3.

> Cellphones, which in the last few years have become full-fledged computers with high-speed Internet connections, let people relieve the **tedium** of exercising, the grocery store line, stoplights or lulls in the dinner conversation.
>
> —Richtel, "Digital Devices Deprive Brain of Needed Downtime,"
> *New York Times*, August 24, 2010

- **Tedium:** _____

4.

> **Semiotics**—the science of signs—is an older theory of visual communication. The word is derived from the Greek words *sema*, meaning "sign," and *semelotikos* (observer of signs). From a semiotic point of view, a sign is anything that stands for something else.
>
> —From RYAN/CONOVER. *Graphic Communication Today*, 4e (p. 25)
> Copyright © 2004 Cengage Learning.

- **Semiotics:** _____

5.

> After exploding on the personal computer scene with the Macintosh, Apple continued to develop and market **innovative** technology options. Its iPod and iTunes products revolutionized the music industry.
>
> —From CILETTI. *Marketing Yourself*, 2e (p. 88)
> Copyright © 2004 Cengage Learning.

- **Innovative:** _____

Look for Signal Words

You have practiced working with signal words when you know which kind to expect. But of course, when you are reading you can't be sure what you will find. Here is an Interaction in which the kinds of context clues and signal words are varied.

INTERACTION 2–7	Use Signal Words to Determine Meanings

Determine what kind of context clue signals the meaning of the word in bold. Then write the definition.

1.

> Early music and dance have left no traces, but there is **abundant** evidence of painting and drawing.
>
> —From BULLIET. *The Earth and Its Peoples, Brief Edition, Complete,* 5e (p. 16)
> Copyright © 2012 Cengage Learning.

- Type of context clue: example   antonym   synonym   definition
- **Abundant:** _____

2.

> The human body must maintain its internal environment within narrow limits in order to remain healthy; this is known as **homeostasis.** Some examples of homeostasis are blood sugar levels, body temperature, and heart rate. This is the reason your doctor takes your temperature and blood pressure as part of a routine examination.
>
> —From RIZZO. *Fundamentals of Anatomy and Physiology,* 3e (pp. 13–14)
> Copyright © 2010 Cengage Learning.

- Two types of context clues: example   antonym   synonym   definition
- **Homeostasis:** _____

3.

> Although the financial **shenanigans** at Enron were complicated, once their basic outline is sketched, the wrongdoing is pretty easy to see: deception, dishonesty, fraud, disregarding one's professional responsibilities, and unfairly injuring others for one's own gain.
>
> —From SHAW. *Cengage Advantage Books: Business Ethics*, 7e (p. 6)
> Copyright © 2011 Cengage Learning.

- Type of context clue: example   antonym   synonym   definition
- **Shenanigans:** _____

4.

> Some common **phenotypes** that are associated with single pairs of genes include curly vs. straight hair, dark hair vs. blond hair, normal hearing vs. certain types of deafness, normal vision vs. nearsightedness, and type A vs. type O blood.
>
> —From KAIL/CAVANAUGH. *Cengage Advantage Books: Human Development*,
> 5e (p. 45) Copyright © 2010 Cengage Learning.

- Type of context clue: example   antonym   synonym   definition
- **Phenotypes:** _____

5.

> The hotter an object is, the more motion there is among its particles. The **agitated** particles, including electrons, collide with each other.

- Type of context clue: example   antonym   synonym   definition
- **Agitated:** _____

Create EASY Note Cards to Study Words

You need a way to keep your study of vocabulary organized, and it's a smart idea to keep reminding yourself of the meanings of new words so you can commit them to memory. Creating and then studying EASY note cards is a simple way to learn and remember enough about a new word so that you can start to use it comfortably.

The following kinds of information can go on an EASY note card.

The word

(the part of speech—
noun, verb, adjective, adverb)

Example—Write a sentence using the word that shows you know its meaning.

Antonym (if there are any)

Synonym (if there are any)

Your Logic—Use your logic to make up a definition in your own words.

Here is an example from the Read and Talk reading about Sanjay Gupta in Haiti.

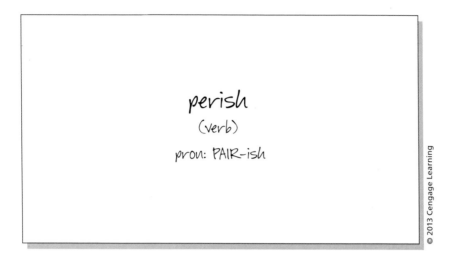

perish

(verb)

pron: PAIR-ish

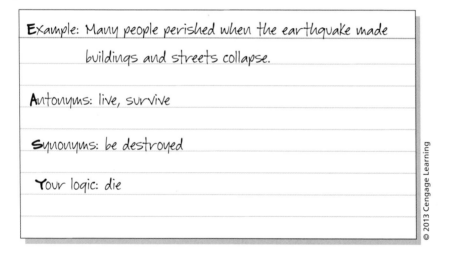

Example: Many people perished when the earthquake made

buildings and streets collapse.

Antonyms: live, survive

Synonyms: be destroyed

Your logic: die

As you learn about each word, you may find that other words are related to it. You can add this information to the front of the card as you learn it. You may also choose to draw a picture on the front of the card that reminds you of the meaning, or you can write how to pronounce the word. If you write the pronunciation, you can base it on the pronunciation key in a dictionary or you can use your own method, as shown on this card.

Section Review: Define Words as You Read Using Context Clues

A. Fill in the circles in the concept map to show what you have learned in this section of the chapter.

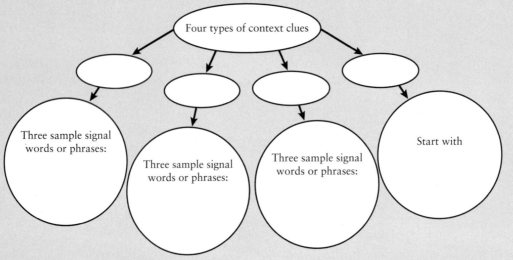

Four types of context clues

Three sample signal words or phrases:

Three sample signal words or phrases:

Three sample signal words or phrases:

Start with

B. Fill in an EASY note card for the word *amicable* from Interaction 2–3 on page 79.

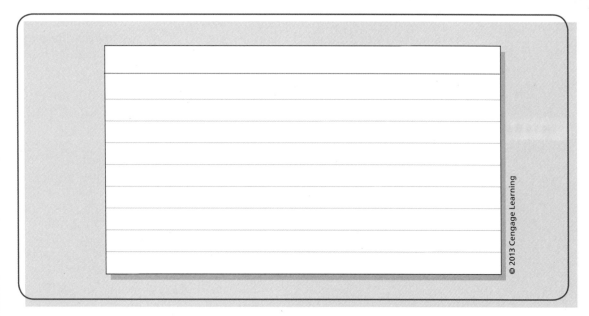

© 2013 Cengage Learning

Understand the Connotations of Some Words

Denotation is the most neutral meaning of a word. When you see *denotation,* think "d": denotation is the "dictionary definition." Every word has a denotative meaning. For instance, the denotative meaning of *home* is "the place where a person lives."

Connotation adds other associations to a word. When you see *connotation,* think "conn": connotation is the connection, or association, of a word to certain emotions or attitudes. Some words have positive connotations, and others have negative connotations. Connotations of the word *home* might include "warmth" and "love." In addition, certain words may have specific connotations for people based on their life experiences. For instance, if someone grew up in an abusive family, the connotations of *home* might include "danger" and "fear." (The context in which a word appears in a piece of writing adds much to its connotative meaning, and these connotations influence the tone of the writing. More on this topic will be discussed in Chapter 8.)

Child: a young person

      denotative meaning

Brat: a young person who misbehaves

   denotative meaning + negative connotative meaning

All words have a more neutral, denotative meaning, and some words also have a more emotional meaning as well. When you are reading, be sure to notice both levels of meaning. Authors use words deliberately in order to achieve their purpose, and you can tell a lot about their purpose and attitude from the words they select.

INTERACTION 2–8	Identify Neutral and Emotional Words

In each pair of words, write "D" next to the neutral, more denotative word and "C" next to the emotional, more connotative word. Then, for each connotative word, circle "positive" or "negative" for the type of connotation the word has.

1. facial expression _____   grin _____   positive   negative

2. angel _____   baby _____   positive   negative

3. overgrown _____   weedy _____   positive   negative

4. finished _____   washed-up _____   positive   negative

5. leave _____   abandon _____   positive   negative

6. candid _____   direct _____   positive   negative

7. enormous _____   mighty _____   positive   negative

8. top _____   pinnacle _____   positive   negative

9. compel _____   make _____   positive   negative

10. slow-moving _____   sluggish _____   positive   negative

Section Review: Understand the Connotations of Some Words

Fill in the rectangles in the concept map to show what you have learned in this section of the chapter.

Definition of a word

D = _____ meaning   Conn = _____ meaning

Study Vocabulary Systematically Using Word Parts

The single most powerful way to quickly expand your vocabulary is to learn word parts. Learning one word part can increase your understanding of hundreds of unfamiliar words. In this section you will learn some of the most productive word parts in the English language. If you learn all the word parts covered in this lesson, you will know the approximate meanings of thousands of words you have never seen before.

Definitions of Word Parts

- **Root:** The root carries the main meaning of a word. A word usually has at least one root. It can have more than one. The root can be found at the beginning, middle, or end of a word.

- **Prefix:** Placed before a root, the prefix changes the meaning of the word. Not all words have prefixes. Some words have one prefix; others have more than one.

- **Suffix:** Placed after a root, the suffix sometimes changes the part of speech (from verb to noun, for example) and thus changes the way the word acts in the sentence. Not all words have suffixes. Some words have one suffix; others have more than one.

Figure 2.1 Words Composed of Word Parts

A word has at least one root, but it may not have any prefixes or suffixes. Or it may have more than one of each. Read across each line to put the word parts together to form a whole word.

prefix	+ prefix	+ root	+ root	+ suffix	+ suffix
		mind			
		mercy		ful	
		beauty		ful	ly
	un	real		ist	ic
	re	mind		er	
re	con	struct		ed	
		demo	graph	y	

When you combine roots with other word parts, sometimes their spelling changes. For example, if you combine *mercy* and *-ful*, the resulting word is *merciful*. It has an *i* instead of a *y*. Word parts often have alternative spellings depending on what other word parts they are attached to.

A reference list of roots, prefixes, and suffixes that you can use while you read is provided on pages 103–105. In this section we'll look at a small number of roots and some of the other word parts they can be combined with. You'll learn how to analyze the word parts and then how to infer the meaning from the word parts and the reading context.

Roots Carry the Basic Meaning

Roots: Sight, Hearing, and Touch

Let's start with some roots that have to do with using your senses of sight, hearing, and touch. Study the three roots for seeing, hearing, and touching. (When roots are given with a slash between them, that means they can be spelled in the different ways shown.) As you read each root, picture using the sense listed under the heading "Basic meaning."

Root	Basic meaning	Example words
vid/vis	see	video, visible, visionary
aud	hear	audio, audible, audience
tact/tang/tig	touch	contact, tangible, contiguous

Combining Word Parts

Notice that each root can be combined with the suffix *-ible*. This suffix can also be spelled *-able*, and that's what the suffix means: "able to be."

- *Visible* means "able to be seen."

- *Audible* means "able to be heard."

- *Tangible* means "able to be touched."

You can tell from these examples that sometimes you have to put the meaning of the suffix in front of the meaning of the root so that the definition of the whole word will make sense.

Roots: Leading, Carrying, and Pulling

Study these three roots for different kinds of movement. Make a mental movie of each action to help you remember it.

Root	Basic meaning	Example words
duc/duce/duct	lead, bring, take	induction, produce, conduct
port	carry	comport, export, import
tract/trah	pull, drag, draw	contract, extract, protract, retraction

Combining Word Parts

Notice that each root can be combined with the prefix *com-*, which can also be spelled *con-*. This prefix means "together."

- *Conduct* means "lead together."

- *Comport* means "carry together."

- *Contract* means "draw together."

Notice that in the definition of these words, the root is before the prefix. When you are analyzing word parts, play with their order until you arrive at a phrase that makes sense as a definition.

More prefixes Other prefixes are used in the example words in the table above:

- *in- /im- /il- /ir-* means "not."

- *in-* means "in."

- *ex-* means "out."

- *pro-* means "forward" and "forth."

You can see from the first two items in this list that some prefixes, such as *in-*, have more than one meaning. If you see a word that begins with a prefix with two or more meanings, you need to test each possible meaning. Read the sentence and the surrounding sentences carefully to decide which meaning is more logical.

Prefixes Add Information to the Meaning

Roots carry the basic meaning of the word, but prefixes change that meaning. Look at the following table of prefixes. Memorize these five prefixes, and you will gain a partial understanding of more than 60 percent of all English words that have prefixes. Notice that half of them can mean "not."

As you read the example words, divide them into word parts to figure out what they mean. For even better practice, write them on a separate piece of paper and divide them into word parts with plus signs between each part.

Prefix	Basic meaning	Example words
un-	not	unkind, unproductive, unstoppable
re-	again; back	reduce, reproduce, retract
in-/il-/im-/ir-	not	inactive, illegal, impossible, irresistible
dis-	not; apart	disrespect, distrust, distract
en-/em-	cause to	enlarge, enrage, embolden

On pages 103–105, you'll find an alphabetical list of word parts you can refer to as you read.

INTERACTION 2–9 | **Identify Roots and Their Meanings**

A. In each word, underline the part that seems to be the root.

B. Check your answers using the Word Parts Glossary on pages 103–105 and change any that are incorrect.

C. Write the meaning of the correct root next to each word.

1. **dormitory**   Root meaning: _____

2. **factual**   Root meaning: _____

3. **graphic**   Root meaning: _____

4. **democracy**   Root meaning: _____

5. **satisfy**   Root meaning: _____

INTERACTION 2–10 | **Identify Roots and Prefixes**

A. In each word, underline the part that seems to be the root.

B. Check your answers using the Word Parts Glossary on pages 103–105 and change any that are incorrect.

C. Write the meaning of the correct root next to each word.

D. Write the prefix and its meaning.

1. project   Root meaning: _____

              Prefix _____

              Meaning: _____

2. conduct   Root meaning: _____

              Prefix _____

              Meaning: _____

3. import   Root meaning: _____

              Prefix _____

              Meaning: _____

4. advertise   Root meaning: _____

              Prefix _____

              Meaning: _____

5. circumvent   Root meaning: _____

              Prefix _____

              Meaning: _____

Suffixes Show How Words Act in Sentences

Suffixes follow roots, and they show the function of the word in the sentence.

Suffixes that can indicate actions—verbs:

- -*s* (-*s* on a verb indicates actions that happen again and again): *plays, ends, happens*

  *But note that -*s* on a noun means "more than one."

- *-ing* (*-ing* indicates action happening now): *laughing, remembering, choosing*
- *-ed* (*-ed* indicates action that happened in the past): *touched, lighted, described*

When you see a verb in a sentence, you can ask, "Who or what is doing this? When is this happening?" Figuring out who is doing what in a sentence will improve your reading comprehension.

Suffixes that can indicate conditions or processes—nouns:

- *-ance/-ence*: *guidance, dependence, tolerance*
- *-hood*: *neighborhood, manhood, statehood*
- *-ion/-sion/-tion*: *suspension, vacation, completion, partition*

When you see a noun in a sentence, you can ask, "What is this thing doing? What relationship is there between this noun and other nouns?" To understand sentences fully, you need to understand the relationships between words.

Suffixes that can indicate characteristics—adjectives:

- *-ly* (typical of): *fatherly, miserly, homely*
- *-less* (without): *motherless, waterless, loveless*
- *-ing, -ed* (also used as verb endings, these endings can indicate adjectives that are describing people, places, things, and ideas): *caring brother, expected visitor*

When you find an adjective, you can ask, "Who or what is this word describing?"

Suffixes that can indicate how, when, or where an action is done—adverbs:

- *-ly* (characteristic of): *nicely, instinctively, carefully*
- *-fully* (full of): *faithfully, joyfully, fearfully*
- *-wise* (in a certain direction or position; with respect to): *clockwise, moneywise*

When you see an adverb in a sentence, you can ask, "What verb or other word is this describing?"

See pages 103–105 for a list of suffixes that you can consult while you are reading.

INTERACTION 2–11 | **Identify Suffixes**

A. Underline the suffix in each bold word.

B. Write the suffix and its meaning, consulting the lists above or the Word Parts Glossary on pages 103–105 as needed.

1.

> Researchers have **conducted** numerous studies to determine what it is that police do and why people call on their **services**.

- **Conducted**   Suffix: _____   Meaning: _____
- **Services**   Suffix: _____   Meaning: _____

2.

> As far back as 1965, Elaine Cumming and her colleagues reported that the ordinary work routines of police officers included **relatively** little law enforcement and comprised a large variety of other activities that came to be known as peacekeeping and order **maintenance**.

- **Relatively**   Suffix: _____   Meaning: _____
- **Maintenance**   Suffix: _____   Meaning: _____

3.

> In a classic study of patrol activities in a city of 400,000, John Webster found that **providing** social service functions and performing **administrative** tasks accounted for 55 percent of police officers' time and 57 percent of their calls.

- **Providing**   Suffix: _____   Meaning: _____
- **Administrative**   Suffix: _____   Meaning: _____

4.

> Robert Lilly found that of 18,000 calls to a Kentucky police **department** made during a four-month period, 60 percent were for **information**, and 13 percent concerned traffic problems.

- **Department**   Suffix: _____   Meaning: _____
- **Information**   Suffix: _____   Meaning: _____

5.

> Carl B. Klockers, in *Idea of Police*, broadly **defines** the basic function of the police as dealing with all those problems that may require the use of coercive force.

- **Defines**   Suffix: _____   Meaning: _____

6.

> The police role is extremely diverse, **ambiguous**, and dynamic.
>
> —From DEMPSEY/FORST. *An Introduction to Policing*, 5e (p. 142)
> Copyright © 2010 Cengage Learning.

- **Ambiguous**   Suffix: _____   Meaning: _____

Using Your Knowledge of Word Parts to Make Meaning

To use word parts to figure out the meaning of a word, you first need to discover the meaning of each word part and then combine their meanings. Often, you then need to consider the word's context so you know how to interpret the meaning. Here is an example.

Although time is ticking away, I allow myself a few minutes to sit in the kitchen. It has an abandoned quality with no fire on the hearth, no cloth on the table. I mourn my old life here. We barely scraped by, but I knew where I fit in, I knew what my place was in the tightly **inter-woven** fabric that was our life. I wish I could go back to it because, in **retrospect**, it seems so secure compared with now, when I am so rich and so famous and so hated by the authorities in the Capitol.

—Collins, *Catching Fire*, p. 7

© Dieterlen/photocuisine/Corbis

The two words in bold each combine word parts:

interwoven

inter- + woven

_____ + woven

retrospect

retro- + spect

_____ + _____

Go to the Word Parts Glossary on pages 103–105 to see what the prefixes *inter-* and *retro-* and the root *spect* mean. Write the meanings in the blanks above.

A root carries the main meaning of the word, so it is smart to begin to construct the word's meaning with the root. Prefixes then change the basic meaning. *Interwoven* means "woven between." *Retrospect* means "looking back."

Reread the passage, and notice how the meaning of the whole paragraph is a clue to the meaning of *retrospect*. The narrator compares her old life with her new life, and she feels sad that she no longer has her old life. In order to make the comparison, she has to look back at the past. When she looks at her new life, she's rich and famous but also hated. In contrast, in her old life, she was very poor, but she seemed to have a place in the life of her community, a "tightly **interwoven** fabric." This description suggests that she was held in place by her relationships with others, which was a comfort to her.

INTERACTION 2–12	Use Word Parts and Context Clues to Define Words

A. Each bold word below is broken into word parts. Use the Word Parts Glossary on pages 103–105 to find the meaning of each word part.

B. Read the sentence that uses the word in context.

C. Using both word parts and context as clues, decide on the word's meaning.

D. Answer the comprehension question.

1.

> The website I was visiting, UrbanLegendsOnline.com, **dispelled** my fears about a scary story my friend had told me.

Dispel: *dis-* _____ + *pel* _____

Meaning: _____

Did the speaker still believe that the scary story had actually happened?

Yes   No

2.

> The chef became **disenchanted** with her suppliers when she started to receive stringy old beef and limp vegetables.

Disenchanted: *dis-* _____ + *enchant* (word) _____ + *-ed* _____

_____

Meaning: _____

Had the chef been angry at her suppliers previously?

      Yes   No

3.

> The pistons inside a car's engine are **unobservable** even though a mechanic can recognize when they are not working properly.

Unobservable: *un-* _____ + *observe* _____ + *-able* _____
Meaning: _____

Are the pistons on top of the motor or inside it?

       On top   Inside

4.

> The town council decided on a policy of **progressive** change rather than trying to accomplish all the goals at once.

Progressive: *pro-* _____ + *gress* _____ + *-ive* _____
Meaning: _____

Did the town budget provide money for the changes over a period of years?

      Yes   No

5.

> A **profusion** of flowers greeted the hotel guests.

Profusion: *pro-* _____ + *fus* _____ + *-sion* _____
Meaning: _____

Was the hotel well-maintained?

      Yes   No

Word Parts Glossary

The following 150 commonly used word parts are organized alphabetically so they will be easy to find while you read. Read down the column that describes the word part you are searching for. Remember that sometimes a word starts with a root, rather than a prefix.

Prefixes	Roots	Suffixes
ab-/abs-: away	annu: year	-able: able to
ad-: to, toward	anthrop: human	-age: condition or state of
ante-: before	aster/astro: star	-al: characteristic of
anti-: against	aud: hear	-ance: state, condition, action
auto-: self	bio: life	-ate: act upon
bi-: two	cap: take, seize	-ation: condition, process of
circum-: around	cede/ceed/cess: go, yield, surrender	-ative: adjective form of a noun
com-/con-: together, bring together	chron: time	-cracy: government
counter-: opposite	cog/gnosi: know	-ed: happened in the past (on a verb), or characteristic of (on an adjective)
de-: reverse, remove, reduce	corp: body	-en: made of
demi-: half	dem: people	-ence: condition or state of
dis-: not, apart	dict: say	-ent: causing or being in a certain condition
en-/em-: cause to	dorm: sleep	-eous: possessing the qualities of
ex-/e-/ec-/ef-: out, up	duc/duce/duct: lead, bring, take	-er: comparative (faster = more fast)
fore-: before	fact: make	-er: person who
hemi-: half	flu: flow	-es: noun plural (boxes)
hyper-: above, more	fund/fus: pour	-est: superlative (happiest = most happy)
hypo-: under, less	geo: earth	-ful: full of
in-/im-: in, into	graph: write	-hood: condition or process of (neighborhood)

Prefixes	Roots	Suffixes
in-/im-/ir-/il-: not	gress: walk	-ial: characteristic of
inter-: between, among	gyny: woman	-ible: able to
intra-: within	ject: throw	-ic: characteristic of
macro-: large, long	junct: join	-ical: characteristic of
mal-: bad, wrong	log/logue: word, thought, speech	-ing: present participle of verb (enjoying)
micro-: small	man/manu: by hand	-ion: condition, process of
mid-: middle	merc: money received for work, price	-ious: possessing the qualities of
mis-: wrongly	mit/mitt/miss: send	-ish: characteristic of
mis-/miso-: hatred	morph: form	-ism: state, quality, or condition
mono-: one	mors/mori/mort: dead	-ist: one who; characterized by
non-: not	nom: name, term	-ity: state of
over-: too much	path/pat: feeling, suffering	-ive: performing a specified action
pan-: all	ped/pedo: children	-ize: make
poly-: many	pel: drive	-less: without
post-: after	pend: hang	-ly: characteristic of
pre-: before	philo/phil: love	-ment: state of
pro-: forward	phobia: irrational fear	-ness: state of, condition of
pseudo-: false	phon: sound	-nym: name
re-: again, back	plic: fold	-ology: field of study
retro-: back	port: carry	-or: person who
semi-: half	sat/satis: enough	-ous: possessing the qualities of
sub-: under	scrib/script: write	-s: verb (swims); noun plural (trees)
super-: above	spect: see	-sion: condition, process of
sur-: more, above, over	sta: stand	-some: characteristic of
syn-/sym-: together, with, united	struct: build	-tion: condition, process of
trans-/tres-: across	tact/tang/tig: touch	-ty: state of

Prefixes	Roots	Suffixes
tri-: three	theo: God	-wise: in a specified direction, manner, or position
un-: not	tract/trah: pull, drag, draw	-worthy: worthy of, capable of
under-: too little	trib: pay, bestow	-yze: verb (analyze)
ultra-: beyond, exceeding	ven/veni/vent: come	
uni-: one	vert: turn	
	vis/vid: see	
	viv: life	

What if a word part is not in the Word Parts Glossary? Look in a college dictionary. The word parts are often given toward the beginning or end of an entry. Because word parts show which languages a word comes from, you will often see the word *Latin* or *Greek* (or an abbreviation such as *Lat., L., Gr., Gk.,* or *G.*) with the word parts. Here is an example from the *Concise Oxford English Dictionary* (11th edition):

abrupt adj. 1. sudden and unexpected. 2. brief to the point of rudeness; curt. 3. (of a slope) steep.
—DERIVATIVES **abruptly** adv. **abruptness** n.
—ORIGIN C16: from L. *abruptus*, 'broken off, steep,' from *abrumpere*, from *ab-* 'away, from,' + *rumpere*, 'break.'

In this dictionary, centuries are designated with "C," so "C16" means "sixteenth century."

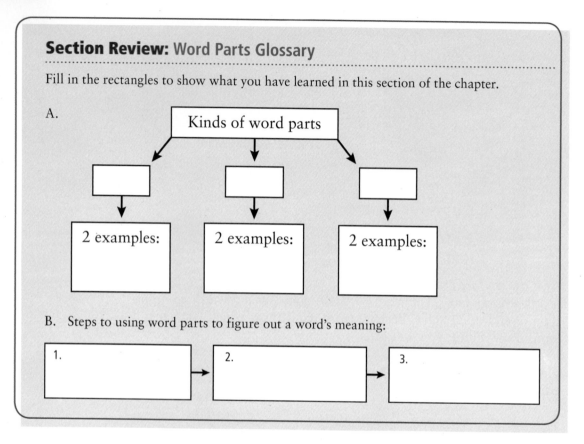

Section Review: Word Parts Glossary

Fill in the rectangles to show what you have learned in this section of the chapter.

A.

Kinds of word parts

2 examples:

2 examples:

2 examples:

B.   Steps to using word parts to figure out a word's meaning:

1.

2.

3.

Understand the Vocabulary of College

The fields you can study in college and career schools are called the *curriculum*. Many of these fields end with the suffix *-logy*, which means "the study of." The roots of some of these fields are shown in Figure 2.2. The names of many other important fields aren't formed using the *-logy* suffix: for example, composition, literature, mathematics, and chemistry.

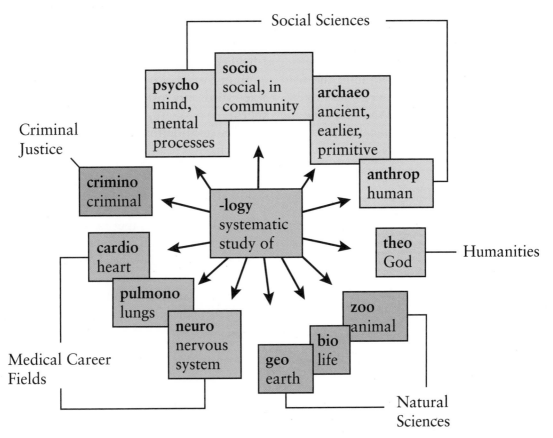

Figure 2.2 Some Fields in the College Curriculum and Careers That End in -logy

—From HESS/HESS ORTHMANN. *Criminal Investigation*, 9e (p. 685)
Copyright © 2010 Cengage Learning.

| INTERACTION 2–13 | Use the Vocabulary of College |

Using the root words in Figure 2.2, decide which one best fits in the blank.

1. When researchers study the remains of ancient civilizations, they look at the _____logical record.

2. Doctors who specialize in treating the heart are called _____logists.

3. _____logy includes the study of religious beliefs.

4. Different layers, or strata, of the earth interest _____logists.

5. How a person puts thoughts together affects the quality of his or her life, and thus _____logists can have a real impact.

Focus: How Textbooks Show Which Words Are Important

Each subject in college and field of work has its own vocabulary that helps people in the field communicate accurately with each other. In your college textbooks, these words are often printed in bold and defined the first time they appear.

A typical pattern you'll find is term-definition-example. Pay close attention when you see this pattern.

Example from an introduction to psychology text

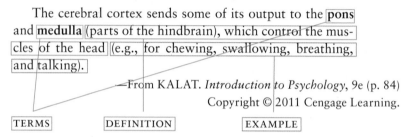

The cerebral cortex sends some of its output to the **pons** and **medulla** (parts of the hindbrain), which control the muscles of the head (e.g., for chewing, swallowing, breathing, and talking).

—From KALAT. *Introduction to Psychology*, 9e (p. 84)
Copyright © 2011 Cengage Learning.

TERMS   DEFINITION   EXAMPLE

Note that the abbreviation *e.g.* means "for example."

Example from a business marketing text

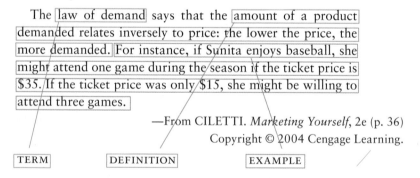

The **law of demand** says that the amount of a product demanded relates inversely to price: the lower the price, the more demanded. For instance, if Sunita enjoys baseball, she might attend one game during the season if the ticket price is $35. If the ticket price was only $15, she might be willing to attend three games.

—From CILETTI. *Marketing Yourself*, 2e (p. 36)
Copyright © 2004 Cengage Learning.

TERM   DEFINITION   EXAMPLE

You will also find a list of important terms in the glossary of your textbooks. Here is part of a page from a glossary that shows words being defined in specialized ways in the field of criminal justice.

Example from a criminology textbook glossary

Number in parentheses is the chapter in which the term is discussed.

A

accelerants substances that cause fires to burn faster and hotter. (16)

active voice in which the subject performs the action of the sentence; contrasts with passive voice. (3)

adipocere soapy appearance of a dead body left for weeks in a hot, moist location. (8)

administrative warrant official permission to inspect a given property to determine compliance with city regulations; for example, compliance with fire codes. (16)

admission statement containing some information concerning the elements of a crime, but falling short of a full confession. (6)

adoptive admission occurs when someone else makes a statement in a person's presence and under circumstances where it would be logical to expect the person to make a denial if the statement falsely implicated him or her, but the person does not deny the allegations. (6)

adversary system justice system used in the United States; establishes clearly defined roles for both the prosecution and the defense and sets the judge as the neutral party. (21)

adware type of spyware used by advertisers to gather consumer and marketing information. (17)

aggravated arson intentionally destroying or damaging a dwelling or other property, real or personal, by means of fire or explosives, creating an imminent danger to life or great bodily harm, which risk was known or reasonably foreseeable to the suspect. (16)

aggravated assault (felonious assault) unlawful attack by one person on another to inflict severe bodily injury. (9)

algor mortis postmortem cooling process of the body. (8)

alligatoring checking of charred wood giving the appearance of alligator skin. Large, rolling blisters indicate rapid, intense heat; small, flat blisters indicate slow, less intense heat. (16)

analogs drugs created by adding to or omitting something from an existing drug. (18)

Antichrist son of Satan. (19)

anticipatory warrant one based upon prior knowledge or an affidavit showing probable cause that at some future time (but not presently) certain evidence of crime will be located at a specified place. Such warrants are constitutional if a proper showing is made that contraband or evidence will likely be found at the target location at a given time, or when a specific triggering event occurs. (4)

arrest taking a person into custody in the manner authorized by law. (7)

arson malicious, willful burning of a building or property. *See also* **aggravated arson**. (16)

asphyxiation death or unconsciousness resulting from insufficient oxygen to support the red blood cells reaching the body tissues and the brain. (8)

assault unlawfully threatening to harm another person, actually harming another person or attempting to do so. Formerly referred to threats of or attempts to cause bodily harm, but now usually includes *battery*. (9)

associative evidence links a suspect with a crime. (5)

asymmetric warfare combat in which a weaker group attacks a superior group not head-on but by targeting areas where the adversary least expects to be hit, causing great psychological shock, along with loss of life among random victims. (20)

autoerotic asphyxiation accidental death from suffocation, strangulation or chemical asphyxia resulting from a combination of ritualistic behavior, oxygen deprivation, danger and fantasy for sexual gratification. (8)

automated fingerprint identification system (AFIS) computerized system of reviewing and mapping fingerprints. (5)

B

backing marking photographs on their back with a felt-tip pen or label to indicate the photographer's initials, date photo was taken, a brief description of what it depicts and the direction of north. Evidence can be circled on the back of the photo in the same way. (2)

bait money currency for which serial numbers are recorded and that is placed so it can be added to any robbery loot. (12)

ballistics the study of the dynamics of projectiles, from propulsion through flight to impact; a narrower definition is the study of the functioning of firearms. (5)

baseline (plotting) method establishes a straight line from one fixed point to another from which measurements are taken at right angles. (2)

battery actually hitting or striking someone. (9)

beachheading interrogation technique where an officer questions a custodial suspect without giving the *Miranda* warnings and obtains incriminating statements; the officer then gives the warning, gets a waiver and repeats the interrogation to obtain the same statement. (6)

Beelzebub powerful demon, subordinate only to Satan, according to Satanists. (19)

bench trial is before a judge without a jury. (21)

best evidence original object, or the highest available degree of proof that can be produced. (5)

685

—From HESS/HESS ORTHMANN. *Criminal Investigation*, 9e (p. 685)
Copyright © 2010 Cengage Learning.

Focus: Learning Vocabulary via Diagrams

As you read textbooks, keep in mind that they have images as well as words that can help you learn the vocabulary of the field. Diagrams—drawn figures with labels—can be particularly helpful because the labels often use important vocabulary in the field.

Some courses of study, such as health sciences, rely on diagrams more than others. There are many different fields of study and corresponding career fields in health sciences, but in all of them, students and health practitioners need to be able to discuss the human body with precision. The illustration that follows is from a health occupations textbook, and it shows the word parts used for various parts of the body.

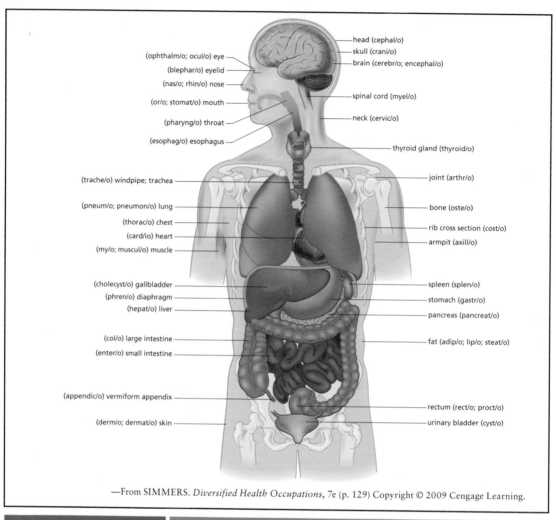

—From SIMMERS. *Diversified Health Occupations*, 7e (p. 129) Copyright © 2009 Cengage Learning.

INTERACTION 2–14 | **Use Key Terms from Health Science**

Fill in the correct root based on the diagram above.

1. The stomach is filled with _____ic juices.

2. The heart and lungs are in the _____ic cavity.

3. The vertebrae in the neck are the _____al vertebrae.

4. _____plasty is plastic surgery of the nose.

5. A disease in which the brain swells is _____itis.

6. Inflammation of the joints is known as _____itis.

7. Inflammation of the spinal column is called _____itis.

8. When teenagers get acne, they sometimes go to a _____atologist.

9. If older adults don't exercise enough, their bones may become porous and break more easily. This condition is called _____porosis.

10. At about age fifty, people ought to get a _____scopy since colon cancer detected in an early stage is curable, but colon cancer detected at a late stage is a certain killer.

When you begin to study a new subject in college, take time to learn its new vocabulary. Pay attention to how your instructor and the author of your textbook use each new word. Write down the exact definitions of words, and memorize the most important ones. You can prepare paper flashcards or use online flashcards to help you. Online flashcards are available on the website of some textbooks.

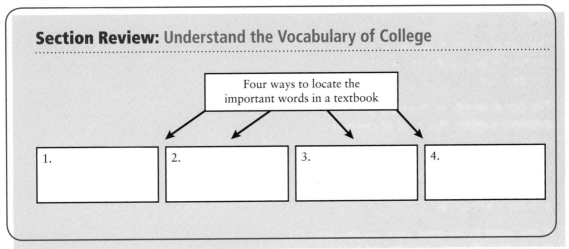

Section Review: Understand the Vocabulary of College

Four ways to locate the important words in a textbook

1.

2.

3.

4.

Chapter Summary Activity: Expanding Your Vocabulary

Chapter 2 has discussed how to expand your vocabulary by using context clues as you read and systematically developing your understanding of word parts. You've also learned about the vocabulary of college. Fill in the following Reading Guide by completing each idea on the left with information from Chapter 2 on the right. You can return to this guide throughout the course as a reminder of how to expand your vocabulary.

Reading Guide to Expanding Your Vocabulary

Complete this idea	with information from Chapter 2.
The only way to truly learn a new word is to	1. _____
The setting or environment of a word is called its	2. _____

Complete this idea	with information from Chapter 2.
Context clues are	3. _____ _____
Four kinds of context clues are	4. _____ 5. _____ 6. _____ 7. _____
The signal words *that is* and *in other words* may suggest this kind of context clue:	8. _____
The signal words *however* and *in contrast* may suggest this kind of context clue:	9. _____
The signal words *to illustrate* and *for example* suggest this kind of context clue:	10. _____
When you use your logic to figure out what a word probably means, the process is known as	11. _____
If you want to increase your vocabulary in a systematic way, you should learn the meanings of	12. _____
Three kinds of word parts that you can use to figure out the meaning of a word are:	13. _____ 14. _____ 15. _____
The main meaning of the word is carried by the	16. _____
The word part that changes the meaning of the root is the	17. _____
The word part that changes the way a word is used in the sentence is the	18. _____
To understand a word's meaning, you might need to use both	19. _____ 20. _____

Complete this idea	with information from Chapter 2.
If a particular word part is not in the Word Parts Glossary, you can	21. _____
The *college curriculum* is	22. _____ _____
The names of many fields of study end in this suffix:	23. _____
In college textbooks, a typical pattern you will find for important vocabulary is	24. _____

25. Think about what your vocabulary strategies were before you read Chapter 2. How did they differ from the suggestions here? Write your thoughts.

_____

_____

_____

ENGAGE YOUR SKILLS
Expanding Your Vocabulary

A. Read the following excerpts from a psychology textbook and determine the meanings of the boldfaced words by using context clues.

Achievement Motivation

Why do some people try harder than others to succeed?

1   This sentence was written at 6 A.M. on a beautiful Sunday in June. Why would someone get up that early to work on a weekend? Why do people take their work seriously and try to do the best that they can? People work hard partly due to **extrinsic** motivation, a desire for external rewards such as money. But work and other human activities also reflect **intrinsic motivation**, a desire for internal satisfaction.

1. extrinsic: _____

2. intrinsic: _____

3. motivation: _____

2   The next time you visit someone's home or office, notice the **mementos** displayed there. Perhaps there are framed diplomas and awards, trophies and ribbons, and photos of children and grandchildren. These badges of achievement **affirm** that a person has accomplished tasks that **merit** approval or establish worth. Much of human behavior is motivated by a desire for approval, admiration, and a sense of achievement—in short, for **esteem**—from others and from within.

4. mementos: _____

5. affirm: _____

6. esteem: _____

Need for Achievement

3   Many athletes who already hold world records still train **intensely;** many people who have built multimillion-dollar businesses still work fourteen-hour days. What motivates these people? One answer is achievement motivation (also called the need for achievement, abbreviated *n-Ach*). People with high achievement motivation seek to master tasks—such as sports, business **ventures,** occupational skills, intellectual puzzles, or artistic creation—and feel intense satisfaction from doing so. They work hard at **striving** for excellence, enjoy themselves in the process, and take great pride in achieving a high level.

7. intensely: _____

8. ventures: _____

9. striving: _____

4   *Individual Differences.* How do people with strong achievement motivation differ from others? To find out, researchers gave children a test to measure their need for achievement and then asked them to play a ring-toss game. Most of the children who scored low on the need-for-achievement test stood either so close to the ring-toss target that they couldn't fail or so far away that they could not succeed. In contrast, children scoring high on the need-for-achievement test stood at a **moderate** distance from the target, making the game challenging but not impossible.

—From BERNSTEIN. *Essentials of Psychology*, 5e (pp. 316–317) Copyright © 2011 Cengage Learning.

10. **moderate:** _____

B. Read the following sentences. For each word in bold:

- Write down a neutral word or phrase that has the same denotative meaning.

- Add some words to the denotation to show the word's emotional connotations.

> When I did finally **flop** into the dusty **gloom** and **clambered** to my feet, I was surprised to find a secret door.
>
> —Bryson, *At Home*, p. 1

11. **flop:** _____

12. **gloom:** _____

13. **clambered:** _____

> Our part of District 12, nicknamed the Seam, is usually **crawling** with coal miners heading out to the morning shift at this hour. Men and women with hunched shoulders, swollen knuckles, many who have long since stopped trying to rub the coal dust out of their broken nails, the lines of their **sunken** faces. But today the black cinder streets are empty.
>
> —Collins, *The Hunger Games*, p. 4

14. **crawling:** _____

15. **sunken:** _____

C. Use word parts to figure out the meaning of each word in bold, consulting the Word Parts Glossary on pages 103–105 as needed.

> 1   Cross-cultural studies further complicate our understanding of gender. In the United States, we generally envision only two genders, male and female, leaving no room for other gender alternatives such as **intersexed** or androgynous individuals. **Westerners,** uncomfortable with these ambiguous gender identities, tend to explain them away by categorizing them as pathological, **illegitimate,** and perhaps even criminal. However, some cultures not only accommodate the ambiguities of these gender alternatives but see them as legitimate and, in some cases, as powerful. One stunning example is the male/female Hijra role found in Hindu India.

2   The notion of a combined male/female role is a major theme in Hindu art, religion, and **mythology.** For example, androgynous people and **impersonators** of the opposite sex are found widely in Hindu mythology among both humans and their deities. These same themes are played out in parts of contemporary India.

—From FERRARO. *Cultural Anthropology*, 6e (p. 264) Copyright © 2006 Cengage Learning.

16. intersexed: _____

17. Westerners: _____

18. illegitimate: _____

19. mythology: _____

20. impersonators: _____

MASTER YOUR SKILLS
Expanding Your Vocabulary

Read each passage and answer the vocabulary questions that follow.

As is often reported in the popular press, the achievement gap between minority students and mainstream learners continues to increase. One indicator, in addition to low standardized test scores, is the overrepresentation of minority students and those labeled disabled in remedial and special education classes. Schools that serve predominantly minority populations also tend to have more vocational, remedial, and "resource" (special education) programming. Researchers have also found that low achievers are stigmatized by being continually placed in low-level tracks. Thus, these students are plagued by poor self-esteem and often remain unengaged and unmotivated by the curricula presented to them.

—From HUERTA. *Educational Foundations* (p. 180)
Copyright © 2008 Cengage Learning.

1. Are there more or fewer minority students in special education classes than is actually called for?

          more   fewer

What word from the paragraph suggests this situation? _____

2. Students who don't learn as quickly or as well as other students are regarded by others in what way?

approvingly   disapprovingly

What word from the paragraph includes this idea? _____

3. Students who are placed in classes for those of lower ability often think about themselves in what way?

"I'm not very smart."   "I'm very smart."

What phrase of four words from the paragraph suggests this idea? _____

_____

4. Some schools have more work-oriented programs of study than others do. What is another word for "work-oriented" from this paragraph? _____

5. Which kind of school has more work-oriented programs of study?

schools that mostly serve minority students schools that mostly serve majority students

What word from the paragraph means about the same thing as "mostly" in this context? _____

Two computer programmers at an oil company plant who were responsible for the company's purchasing files created a **fictitious** supply company. They altered the company's computer database so that the oil company bought its supplies twice: once from the real supplier and once from the fictitious supply company, resulting in an **embezzlement** of several million dollars over two years. The crime was discovered during a surprise **audit**, but the company declined to prosecute, not wanting to **publicize** how vulnerable its database was or how long it took to discover the embezzlement. **Ironically**, rather than being dismissed, the two embezzlers were promoted and placed in charge of computer security.

—From HESS/HESS ORTHMANN. Criminal Investigation, 9e (pp. 501–502)
Copyright © 2010 Cengage Learning.

_____ 6. **Fictitious** most nearly means
 a. Having to do with facts.
 b. Related to fractions.
 c. Characterized by fiction.
 d. Similar to opinion.

____ 7. The definition of **embezzlement** is
   a. Making something more beautiful through decoration.
   b. Violating trust by stealing.
   c. Dazzling to behold.
   d. Robbing from the rich in order to help the poor.

____ 8. In this context, **audit** means
   a. An examination of financial accounts.
   b. The decision to take a class pass/fail.
   c. A party for accountants.
   d. A deliberation by a team of lawyers.

____ 9. The word **publicize** means to make _____.
   a. Personable
   b. Perfect
   c. Public
   d. Particular

____ 10. The meaning of **ironically** as used here is
   a. Creating a contrast between the apparent and the intended meaning.
   b. In marked contrast to what a person might expect.
   c. Pretended ignorance.
   d. Weirdly.

Sociology at the Movies:
Sweet Home Alabama (2002)

1   *Sweet Home Alabama* is a Cinderella story with a twist: The successful heroine from humble beginnings gets the handsome prince but is not sure he is truly what she wants.

2   In the seven years since Melanie Carmichael (Reese Witherspoon) left her small-town Alabama home, she has achieved impressive upward social **mobility.** Beginning as a daughter of the working class, she has become a world-famous fashion designer in New York City. As the film begins, the mayor's son is courting Melanie. Andrew (Patrick Dempsey) proposes to her in Tiffany's, the upscale jewelry store that **epitomizes** upper-class consumption in the popular imagination. She says yes, but before she can marry him she has to clear up a not-so-minor detail: She needs a divorce from Jake (Josh Lucas), the childhood sweetheart she left behind.

3   Most of the story unfolds back in rural Alabama, in a town where friends climb the local water tower to drink beer and watch the folks pass by below, where major social events include Civil War **reenactments** and catfish festivals, and where special hospitality is shown by offering guests hot pickles "right out of the grease." Melanie finds herself caught between two classes and two **subcultures,** and the film follows her struggle to **reconcile** her conflicting identities. Her **dilemma** will require her to acknowledge and reconnect with her mother (Mary Kay Place), who lives in a trailer park, while standing up to her future mother-in-law, the mayor of New York City (Candice Bergen).

4   In the end, Melanie returns to Jake, while Andrew, briefly heartbroken, pleases his mother by marrying a woman of his own class. Melanie's homecoming does not, however, require that she return to life in a trailer park. She discovers that while she was in New York, Jake **transformed** himself. The working-class "loser" built a successful business as a glassblower. This change allows Melanie to imagine an upwardly mobile future by Jake's side.

5   *Sweet Home Alabama* sends the message that people are happiest when they marry within their own class and subculture. That message is comforting because it helps the audience **reconcile** itself to two realities. First, although many people want to "marry up," most Americans do not in fact succeed in doing so. We tend to marry within our own class. Second, marrying outside your class and subculture is likely to be unsettling insofar as it involves abandoning old norms, roles, and values and learning new ones. It is therefore in some sense a relief to learn you're better off marrying within your own class and subculture, especially since you will probably wind up doing just that.

6   There is an **ideological** problem with this message, however. Staying put in your own class and subculture denies the American Dream of upward mobility. *Sweet Home Alabama* resolves the problem by holding out the promise of upward mobility without having to leave home, as it were. Melanie and the transformed Jake can enjoy the best of both worlds, moving up the social **hierarchy** together without forsaking the community and the subculture they cherish. *Sweet Home Alabama* achieves a happy ending by denying the often difficult process of adapting to a new subculture as one experiences social mobility.

—From BRYM/LIE. *Sociology*, 3e (p. 220) Copyright © 2010 Cengage Learning.

_____ 11. **Epitomizes** means

    a. Suggests without saying.

    b. Represents with a typical example.

    c. Clearly connects to an imaginary world.

    d. Atomizes.

_____ 12. **Reconcile** is used twice in this selection. In paragraph 3, it means

    a. Reestablish a close relationship.

    b. Regain.

    c. Bring oneself to accept.

    d. Allow a difference.

_____ 13. In paragraph 5, **reconcile** means

    a. Reestablish a close relationship.

    b. Regain.

    c. Bring oneself to accept.

    d. Allow a difference.

_____ 14. Which of the following is the best example of a **reenactment**?

    a. A dream of a new land.

    b. A pretense.

    c. A Fourth of July parade.

    d. A Christmas nativity play.

_____ 15. The **hierarchy** discussed in this selection refers to

    a. Norms, roles, and values.

    b. Catfish festivals.

    c. Social class.

    d. The American Dream.

_____ 16. Which of the following does the word **transform** most closely suggest?

    a. A major change.

    b. Replacing something.

    c. A hardly noticeable difference.

    d. Varying a behavior.

_____ 17. What does the prefix in the word **subculture** suggest?

    a. There is more than one type of culture.

    b. One culture is less important than another culture.

    c. One culture is underground.

    d. A culture can also be a superculture.

_____ 18. **Ideology** most nearly means

    a. The study of the id in psychology.

    b. A system or network of ideas.

    c. Ideas about logic.

    d. Arguments about ideas.

_____ 19. A synonym for **dilemma** is

    a. Situation.

    b. Scenario.

    c. Problem.

    d. Belief.

_____ 20. What is the root of the word **mobility**?

    a. mob

    b. move

    c. nab

    d. noble

Focus on Health

College Health App

The following reading is linked to these fields of . . .

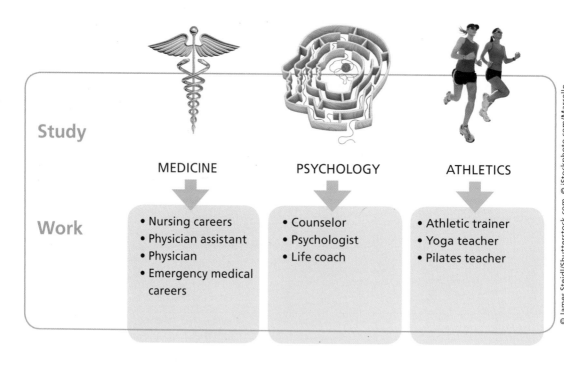

Study	MEDICINE	PSYCHOLOGY	ATHLETICS
Work	• Nursing careers • Physician assistant • Physician • Emergency medical careers	• Counselor • Psychologist • Life coach	• Athletic trainer • Yoga teacher • Pilates teacher

● Pre-Reading the Selection

The excerpt that begins on page 124 comes from the health textbook *An Invitation to Health*. The excerpt is titled "How Can I Change a Bad Health Habit?"

Surveying the Reading

Survey the textbook selection that follows. Then check the elements that are included in this reading.

_____ Title

_____ Headings

_____ First sentences of paragraphs

_____ Words in bold or italic type

_____ Images and captions

Guessing the Purpose

Based on the source and the title of the reading selection, do you think the authors' purpose is mostly to persuade, inform, or express? _____

Predicting the Content

Based on your survey, what are three things you expect the reading selection to discuss?

- _____

- _____

- _____

Activating Your Knowledge

Think about any bad habits you have effectively changed. What did you do? Or think about a bad habit you want to change. What are some thoughts on how you might do that based on your prior knowledge?

- _____

- _____

- _____

● Reading with Pen in Hand

Students who annotate as they read are more successful than students who do not annotate. That's why you will annotate each reading in *Engage* as you read. In the reading that follows, use the following symbols:

★ or (Point)   to indicate a main idea

① ② ③   to indicate major details

Access the Reading CourseMate via www.cengagebrain.com to hear vocabulary words from this selection and view a video about this topic.

Reading Journal

○ Think about what sort of risk change involves.

prospect The contrast of *prospect of reward* with *involves risk* gives a clue. What does *prospect* mean?

beneficial What word starts with the same root? And what kind of change is being discussed? What does *beneficial* mean?

○ Which of these approaches have you tried?

predisposition You know the prefix *pre-* means "before," and you have the clue *forces beyond your control*. What does *predisposition* mean?

How Can I Change a Bad Health Habit?

1   Change is never easy—even if it's done for the best possible reasons. When you decide to change a behavior, you have to give up something familiar and easy for something new and challenging. Change always involves risk—and the **prospect** of rewards.

© Danylchenko Iaroslav/Shutterstock.com

2   Researchers have identified approaches that people use to make **beneficial** changes. In the moral model, you take responsibility for a problem (such as smoking) and its solution; success depends on adequate motivation, while failure is seen as a sign of character weakness. In the enlightenment model, you submit to strict discipline to correct a problem; this is the approach used in Alcoholics Anonymous. The behavioral model involves rewarding yourself when you make positive changes. The medical model sees the behavior as caused by forces beyond your control (a genetic **predisposition** to being overweight, for example) and employs an expert to provide advice or treatment. For many people, the most effective approach is the compensatory model, which doesn't assign blame but puts

responsibility on individuals to acquire whatever skills or power they need to overcome their problems.

3   Before they reach the stage where they can and do take action to change, most people go through a process comparable to religious **conversion**. First, they reach a level of accumulated unhappiness that makes them ready for change. Then they have a moment of truth that makes them want to change. One pregnant woman, for instance, felt her unborn baby quiver when she drank a beer and swore never to drink again. As people change their behavior, they change their lifestyles and identities as well. Ex-smokers, for instance, may start an aggressive exercise program, make new friends at the track or gym, and participate in new types of activities, like racquetball games or fun runs.

4   Think about the behavior you want to change. Now think about which of the six stages of change you are in with regard to that behavior. Table 2.1 lists some appropriate change goals for each stage. Set your goal and go for it!

Table 2.1 Stages of Lifestyle Change

Stage of Change	Appropriate Change Goal
1. **Precontemplation:** You are not truly convinced about the importance of the lifestyle goal.	Get more information about the value of the lifestyle change goal.
2. **Contemplation:** You have no definite plan for when to begin but would like to change.	Set a date for making the change.
3. **Preparation:** You have set a date to begin the new behavior and are planning the best strategy to carry out the change.	Develop a plan and tell others about the change.
4. **Action:** You are engaged in making changes.	Adjust to new lifestyle and manage unexpected emotional and physical reactions.
5. **Maintenance:** You are working to integrate the lifestyle changes into normal day-to-day life.	Continue to pay attention to the behavior and work through any **relapse**. Help others achieve similar lifestyle goals.
6. **Termination/Moving On:** You have maintained the change for six months to a year and are ready to move on to other lifestyle interests.	Set new health-enhancing goals. Move on from support systems that are focused exclusively on the prior lifestyle goal.

—Reprinted by permission of the author Judd Allen, Ph.D. www.healthyculture.com

—From HALES. *An Invitation to Health*, 12e (pp. 37–38)
Copyright © 2007 Cengage Learning.

conversion What happens to someone who finds religion? What is *conversion*?

Do you know of anyone who has gone through this conversion experience?

What behavior do you want to change?

Which stage would you say you are at with the behavior you thought about in paragraph 4?

contemplation This stage comes after *precontemplation* but before a plan is made. What does *contemplation* mean?

relapse If you are working to make a lifestyle change, what might a *relapse* be?

exclusively You no longer need to focus *exclusively* on the change since you already made it. *Exclusively* means what?

● Comprehension Questions

Write the letter of the answer on the line. Then explain your thinking.

Main Idea

_____ 1. Which of the following best states the main idea of paragraph 3?

    a. Before they reach the stage where they can and do take action to change, most people go through a process comparable to religious conversion.

    b. First, they reach a level of accumulated unhappiness that makes them ready for change.

    c. One pregnant woman, for instance, felt her unborn baby quiver when she drank a beer and swore never to drink again.

    d. As people change their behavior, they change their lifestyles and identities as well.

WHY? What information in the selection leads you to give that answer? _____

_____

_____

_____

_____ 2. Which of the following statements is the best main idea of paragraph 2?

    a. Researchers have identified approaches that people use to make beneficial changes.

    b. In the enlightenment model, you submit to strict discipline to correct a problem; this is the approach used in Alcoholics Anonymous.

    c. The behavioral model involves rewarding yourself when you make positive changes.

    d. For many people, the most effective approach is the compensatory model, which doesn't assign blame but puts responsibility on individuals to acquire whatever skills or power they need to overcome their problems.

WHY? What information in the selection leads you to give that answer? _____

_____

_____

_____

Supporting Details

____ 3. Which of the following details is *least* relevant to the topic of Table 2.1?

    a. Contemplation.

    b. Moving on.

    c. Setting a date.

    d. Action.

WHY? What information in the selection leads you to give that answer? _____

_____

_____

_____

____ 4. Based on the details given in the reading selection, what is the best approach to use in order to make a behavioral change?

    a. Enlightenment.

    b. The compensatory model.

    c. Precontemplation.

    d. Religious conversion.

WHY? What information in the selection leads you to give that answer? _____

_____

_____

_____

Author's Purpose

____ 5. What is the purpose of the table at the end of the passage?

    a. To entertain readers with amusing thoughts of bad habits.

    b. To inform readers of the various stages and goals of successful changes in behavior.

    c. To persuade readers that no matter what their bad habits are, they can change if they try hard enough.

    d. To persuade readers that when following the stages of lifestyle change they must avoid relapse.

WHY? What information in the selection leads you to give that answer? _____

_____

_____

_____

_____ 6. Why does the author compare the incentive for changing a behavior to a religious conversion?

    a. To explain that religion is a bad habit.

    b. To suggest that people need to find religion.

    c. To illustrate the idea that change is hard, and it takes an emotional readiness and a moment of truth to help make the first step of change.

    d. To inform readers how to incorporate religious conversions into the stages of lifestyle change.

WHY? What information in the selection leads you to give that answer? _____

_____

_____

_____

Relationships

_____ 7. What is the main relationship shown in Table 2.1?

    a. Comparison or similarity

    b. Cause and effect

    c. Process

    d. Contrast or difference

WHY? What information in the selection leads you to give that answer? _____

_____

_____

_____

_____ 8. What relationship is stated in paragraph 2?

    a. Cause and effect

    b. Comparison or similarity

    c. Space order

    d. Classification

WHY? What information in the selection leads you to give that answer? _____

_____

_____

_____

Fact, Opinion, and Inference

____ 9. Which of the following statements is an opinion?

    a. The behavioral model involves rewarding yourself when you make positive changes.

    b. Change is never easy.

    c. First, they reach a level of accumulated unhappiness that makes them ready for change.

    d. Think about the behavior you want to change.

WHY? What leads you to give that answer? _____

_____

_____

_____

____ 10. Which of the following is a logical inference based on the information in Table 2.1?

    a. There are several changes that were not included in this table.

    b. Every six months you must make a new lifestyle change.

    c. An example of maintenance (stage 5) could be incorporating a consistent physical fitness routine into your daily life.

    d. A person can usually make a change without actually thinking about it.

WHY? What leads you to give that answer? _____

_____

_____

_____

● Language in Use

The following words (or forms of them) were used in "How Can I Change a Bad Health Habit?" Now you can use them in different contexts. Put a word from the box into the blank lines in the following numbered sentences.

> prospect beneficial predisposition conversion
>
> contemplation relapse exclusively

1. Certain individuals have a genetic _____ toward specific diseases, including mental illnesses.

2. One example of a mental illness is depression. Research has shown that depression does run in some families; however, depression is not _____ a genetic issue.

3. Many people face the _____ of becoming depressed because their environment isn't conducive to health. Any kind of abuse, certain medications, the death of a loved one, and serious conflict may all be environmental factors.

4. Although science is _____ in helping us understand more about why some people are depressed when others are not, it has not given us all the answers yet.

5. It will take more research and _____ before we will completely understand the cause of depression.

● EASY Note Cards

Make a note card for each of the vocabulary words from the reading that you did not know. On one side, write the word. On the other side, divide the card into quarters and label them E, A, S, and Y. Add a word or phrase in each area so that you wind up with an example sentence, an antonym, a synonym, and, finally, a definition that shows you understand the meaning of the word with your logic. Remember that a synonym or antonym may have appeared in the reading.

Career Health App   WEBSITE

● Pre-Reading the Selection

The excerpt that begins on page 132 comes from the website of UNICEF, a nonprofit organization working to help children around the world. The excerpt is titled "Join Our Fight Against AIDS."

Surveying the Reading

Survey the selection that follows. Then check the elements that are included in this reading.

_____ Title

_____ Headings

_____ First sentences of paragraphs

_____ Words in bold or italic type

_____ Images and captions

Guessing the Purpose

Based on the source and the title of the reading selection, do you think the author's purpose is mostly to persuade, inform, or express? _____

Predicting the Content

Based on your survey, what are three things you expect the reading selection to discuss?

- _____

- _____

- _____

Activating Your Knowledge

What do you already know about HIV or AIDS? Do you know anyone with personal experience with the virus?

- _____

- _____

- _____

Common Knowledge

AIDS *(paragraph 1)* Acquired immune deficiency syndrome, the last stage of infection of the HIV virus. AIDS attacks the immune system, leaving the person with no defenses against common bacteria, yeast, parasites, viruses, and cancers.

HIV-positive *(paragraph 1)* A condition caused by the human immunodeficiency virus, which gradually destroys the immune system. HIV is spread during unprotected sex or in other situations in which body fluids are exchanged.

UNICEF *(paragraph 2)* The United Nations Children's Fund, a nonprofit organization whose mission is to reduce to zero the number of children around the world who die from preventable causes.

sub-Saharan Africa *(paragraph 5)* *Sub-* means "below," so this term refers to the part of Africa that lies south of the Sahara Desert.

● Reading with Pen in Hand

Students who annotate as they read are more successful than students who do not annotate. That's why you will annotate each reading in *Engage* as you read. In the reading that follows, use the following symbols:

★ or (Point)   to indicate a main idea

① ② ③   to indicate major details

Access the Reading CourseMate via www.cengagebrain.com **to hear vocabulary words from this selection and view a video about this topic.**

Reading Journal

● Picture what would happen in your community if it were overwhelmed by this disease.

impeding Use your logic. Is *impeding* more like "helping" or "hindering"?

● What other diseases have been nearly wiped out by focusing on protecting children?

transmission Use the Word Parts Glossary to figure out the meaning.

Join Our Fight Against AIDS

Breaking the Cycle

1   The AIDS epidemic began over 25 years ago, and the disease continues to prey upon millions of children around the world. **Over 2.1 million children are HIV-positive,** with more than 400,000 children becoming newly infected with HIV/AIDS each year. This disease affects non-infected children as well—many are left orphaned or grow up in communities overwhelmed by the disease. These children are at increased risk of poverty, illiteracy, malnutrition, disease and early death without proper care and support. As HIV/AIDS continues to take its toll, **the disease is also** impeding **progress in health care, education and quality of life.**

© AP Photo/John Robinson

2   UNICEF has placed children center stage in the fight against AIDS with the "Unite for Children, Unite against AIDS" campaign. The global initiative uses the framework of the "4 P's" to identify the most urgent areas:

Prevention of mother-to-child transmission through testing and treatment of pregnant women;

Providing pediatric HIV/AIDS treatment;

Preventing infection among young people; and

Protecting and supporting children affected by HIV/AIDS.

3   UNICEF-supported programs provide care and education for millions of HIV-positive children, as well as those who are orphaned by the disease and those who are living with infected caregivers. UNICEF programs also teach adolescents and young adults about HIV prevention and educate communities about the harmful **stigmas** surrounding the disease. These stigmas, and the discrimination they produce, remain a considerable barrier to testing, treatment and prevention.

- What would it be like to live with infected caregivers?

stigmas Based on the context, are *stigmas* marks of disgrace or marks of approval?

Achieving an AIDS-Free Generation

4   Through these programs, **UNICEF and its partners have made significant strides in the fight against HIV/AIDS.** The latest Stocktaking Report shows trends that can result in a generation free of AIDS.

- Think carefully about the differences in numbers and percentages in each detail.

The number of people receiving **antiretroviral therapy** (ART) in low- and middle-income countries has increased dramatically, from 400,000 in 2003 to more than 4 million last year.

antiretroviral HIV is a retrovirus. Considering the word parts, what does *antiretroviral* mean?

The proportion of **HIV-positive pregnant women** receiving antiretroviral drugs in those countries has grown from 10% in 2004 to about 53% in 2009.

The number of children under age 15 benefiting from these **life-prolonging drugs** was more than 356,000 in 2009, meaning 28% of children estimated to be in need of ART are receiving it.

5   Despite these achievements, the majority of children with HIV and AIDS in need of treatment are still not getting it. Infants are particularly vulnerable to the effects of HIV, which has lent **urgency** to the global campaign for early infant diagnosis. **Every day, nearly 1,000 babies in sub-Saharan Africa are infected with HIV** through mother-to-child transmission. Without treatment, about half of the infants infected with HIV die before their second birthday.

- Think about how the details from the previous paragraph relate to the details in this paragraph.

urgency Think about what the root of this word means. What is *urgency*?

- Imagine someone saying the words in bold type. How would you describe that person's attitude?

6   UNICEF staff and partners are at the forefront of a global movement to care for the victims of this disease and to halt its **devastation**—and **we will not rest until every child has been reached.**

devastation AIDS destroys lives. What noun form of the verb "destroy" is a synonym for *devastation*?

A Terrible Inheritance

7   Nearly 30 years into the HIV/AIDS pandemic, the number of **children with HIV** continues to grow. Every day more than 1,000 babies are infected through transmission from their mother—during pregnancy, labor and delivery, and breastfeeding. Without treatment, an estimated 1/2 of HIV-positive infants die before their second birthday.

- How many babies in a year are infected through their mothers?

virtually Use your logic to decide what *virtually* means.

● Why is this one sentence set off in its own paragraph and put in bold type?

● Imagine being a mother and receiving these services. What would that be like?

● Imagine the actual activities being summarized here.

● Do you agree?

This doesn't have to happen. When a mother has access to antiretroviral therapy, the chance of HIV transmission is **virtually** zero.

8   **Prevention of mother-to-child-transmission (PMTCT) is the most effective way to create an HIV-free generation.**

9   UNICEF is working to provide the HIV testing, counseling, medication and support mothers need to protect their children. The success shows: in 2009, 53% of pregnant women living with HIV in low- and middle-income countries received antiretrovirals (ARVs) to prevent mother-to-child transmission, compared to 45% in 2008. One of the most significant increases occurred in Eastern and Southern Africa, where the proportion jumped 10 percentage points to 68% in 2009.

UNICEF at Work Worldwide

10   UNICEF's efforts in PMTCT also focus on training health care workers, expanding the reach of programs, and helping governments develop national strategies to respond to HIV in children.

11   But the real measure of UNICEF's success has been the healthy, HIV-negative babies born to mothers living with HIV.

—From www.unicef.org. Reproduced by permission.

● Comprehension Questions

Write the letter of the answer on the line. Then explain your thinking.

Main Idea

_____ 1. Which of the following is the best main idea of paragraph 1?

     a. The AIDS epidemic began over 25 years ago, and the disease continues to prey upon millions of children around the world.

     b. **Over 2.1 million children are HIV-positive,** with more than 400,000 children becoming newly infected with HIV/AIDS each year.

     c. This disease affects non-infected children as well—many are left orphaned or grow up in communities overwhelmed by the disease.

     d. As HIV/AIDS continues to take its toll, **the disease is also impeding progress in health care, education and quality of life.**

WHY? What information in the selection leads you to give that answer? _____

_____

_____

_____

____ 2. Which of the following statements is the topic sentence of paragraph 4?

    a. Through these programs, **UNICEF and its partners have made significant strides in the fight against HIV/AIDS.**

    b. The number of people receiving **antiretroviral therapy** (ART) in low- and middle-income countries has increased dramatically, from 400,000 in 2003 to more than 4 million last year.

    c. The proportion of **HIV-positive pregnant women** receiving antiretroviral drugs in those countries has grown from 10% in 2004 to about 53% in 2009.

    d. The number of children under age 15 benefiting from these **life-prolonging drugs** was more than 356,000 in 2009, meaning 28% of children estimated to be in need of ART are receiving it.

WHY? What information in the selection leads you to give that answer? _____

_____

_____

_____

Supporting Details

____ 3. Which sentence from paragraph 2 is *not* a supporting detail?

    a. The global initiative uses the framework of the "4 P's" to identify the most urgent areas.

    b. **Prevention** of mother-to-child transmission through testing and treatment of pregnant women.

    c. **Providing** pediatric HIV/AIDS treatment.

    d. **Preventing** infection among young people.

WHY? What information in the selection leads you to give that answer? _____

_____

_____

_____

____ 4. Which of the following sentences in paragraph 5 provides the supporting details?

    a. Sentences 1, 2, 3, and 4

    b. Sentences 2, 3, and 4

    c. Sentences 1, 3, and 4

    d. Sentences 2 and 4

> **WHY?** What information in the selection leads you to give that answer? _____

_____

_____

_____

Author's Purpose

_____ 5. What is the main purpose of the passage?

a. To express feelings of horror at what is happening to children living with HIV/AIDS.

b. To express a strong sense of optimism about UNICEF's mission.

c. To persuade readers to get involved in UNICEF's mission by informing them about the effects of HIV/AIDS on children.

d. To persuade readers that AIDS is a devastating disease.

> **WHY?** What information in the selection leads you to give that answer? _____

_____

_____

_____

_____

_____ 6. What is the purpose of the first paragraph?

a. To persuade readers that their local communities are threatened.

b. To suggest UNICEF's concern about a continuing problem.

c. To establish the widespread nature of the problem so that readers will understand how important it is.

d. To share with readers the heartbreaking story of AIDS.

> **WHY?** What information in the selection leads you to give that answer? _____

_____

_____

_____

Relationships

_____ 7. What is the relationship between paragraphs 4 and 5?

a. Cause and effect

b. Example

c. Contrast

d. Space order

WHY? What information in the selection leads you to give that answer? _____

_____

_____

_____

_____ 8. In paragraph 2, what pattern organizes the supporting details?

   a. Cause and effect

   b. Classification

   c. Time order

   d. Definition

WHY? What information in the selection leads you to give that answer? _____

_____

_____

_____

Fact, Opinion, and Inference

_____ 9. In the following sentence, which words indicate an opinion? _But the real measure of UNICEF's success has been the healthy, HIV-negative babies born to mothers living with HIV._

   a. But

   b. Real

   c. HIV-negative

   d. Mothers

WHY? What leads you to give that answer? _____

_____

_____

_____

_____ 10. What can you infer about UNICEF's assumptions about the people who visit their website?

   a. Our readers do not know much about HIV/AIDS.

   b. Our readers need to understand exactly how their money will be spent.

   c. Our readers have been directly affected by HIV/AIDS.

   d. Our readers will respond to us once they understand what is happening.

WHY? What leads you to give that answer? _____

_____

_____

_____

● Language in Use

The following words (or forms of them) were used in "Join Our Fight Against AIDS." Now you can use them in different contexts. Put a word from the box into the blank lines in the following numbered sentences.

> antiretroviral   devastation   impeded   stigma
>
> transmitted   urgency   virtually

1. Recent hurricanes, tornadoes, and earthquakes have left a path of _____ behind them.

2. In Japan on March 11, 2011, for instance, the largest earthquake ever to hit that island nation caused a tsunami, a huge wave of ocean water, to strike the northeastern coast of the country and wipe out many communities. However, one village, Fudai, remained intact because of a 51-foot concrete seawall that _____ the water's progress.

3. Many Internet sites _____ raw video footage of the tsunami flooding towns, lifting up warehouses, and causing massive destruction in a matter of minutes.

4. Another terrible effect of the tsunami was the breakdown of the Fukushima Daiichi nuclear power plant, which spewed large amounts of radioactive waste into the air, endangering Japanese citizens. For a country that always claimed its nuclear power plants were safe, it's a _____ that this nuclear disaster is the worst one seen since the Chernobyl nuclear accident of 1986.

5. This nuclear accident added a new sense of _____ to Japan's need to develop other sources of renewable energy.

● EASY Note Cards

Make a note card for each of the vocabulary words from the reading that you did not know. On one side, write the word. On the other side, divide the card into quarters and label them E, A, S, and Y. Add a word or phrase in each area so that you wind up with an example sentence, an antonym, a synonym, and, finally, a definition that shows you understand the meaning of the word with your logic. Remember that a synonym or antonym may have appeared in the reading.

Identifying Topics and Main Ideas

3

Previewing the Chapter

Flip through the pages of Chapter 3, and read all the major headings. Look at all the photos and figures, and read their captions.

Predict three topics this chapter will cover.

_____

_____

_____

Based on the figures in the chapter, write a statement about the topic of the chapter.

_____

_____

_____

Plan to come back and comment on your predictions and statement when you have finished working through the chapter.

_____

_____

To access additional course materials for *Engage,* including quizzes, videos, and more, please visit www.cengagebrain.com. At the CengageBrain.com home page, search for the ISBN of *Engage* (from the back cover of your book) using the search box at the top of the page. This will take you to the product page where these resources can be found.

Videos Related
to Readings

Vocab Words
on Audio

Read and Talk
on Demand

Read and Talk

MAGAZINE

In college, reading is just one aspect of how you will share new ideas with others in your class. So the first reading in each chapter of this book is meant to give you the chance to talk about reading. Read the article, and then use the four discussion questions to talk about your ideas with your classmates and your instructor.

Access the Reading CourseMate via www.cengagebrain.com to hear a reading of this selection and view a video about this topic.

Breaking Out: One School System's Success with Autistic Children

Lisa Fine

uncanny Does the use of the word *masters* in the next sentence suggest that Robert's knowledge is common or uncommon?

1   Robert Goodfellow, age six, has Asperger's syndrome, a mild form of autism that combines **uncanny** knowledge and awkward social skills. Students with Asperger's syndrome may be masters in mathematics, science, or computers, for example, but require daily drilling on such basics as how to make eye contact or maintaining appropriate distance from other children.

2   Before he joined a special program in the Seattle school system, Robert would sit alone in his yard, peeling bark off sticks he would find. He seemed fascinated by the process of removing the bark,

© Synchronista/Dreamstime.com

often singing songs over and over again as he worked on the sticks. He also refused to bathe, clip his nails, or comb his hair.

3   Robert has benefited greatly from a new program in the Seattle school district. With his teachers' encouragement, Robert has channeled his **obsessiveness** in more socially accepted ways. He has become an expert on the Seattle Mariners baseball team and has learned to juggle extremely well. His new knowledge about the batting averages and other **minutia** of the Mariners, plus his juggling, have enabled Robert to relate better socially with his peers. They now admire his new knowledge and skills.

obsessiveness Based on the example of the stick and your knowledge of word parts, what does this word probably mean?

minutia Does the context suggest that Robert has just broad knowledge or very detailed knowledge of the Mariners?

4   Students with Asperger's syndrome tend to excel in subjects that interest them, but other aspects of school may be difficult for them. For example, the hustle and bustle of recess or lunch can be extremely stressful. The Seattle program aims to help children like Robert function in their world without **alienating** others by their **eccentric** behavior. Robert and other Asperger's students attend mainstream classes as much as possible, sometimes with a school aide, and only go to small special education classes when they need to work on a particular skill. The special education teachers function as case managers for the children, monitoring their schedules, serving as their advocates, and teaching them lessons on behavior, social skills, and life skills. Students in grades 1–4 are given visual cue cards to remind them of appropriate classroom behavior, such as raising their hands before speaking and sitting still.

alienating This word can be divided into *alien* + *ate* + *ing*. What does it probably mean?

eccentric Based on how Robert has acted in the past, does *eccentric* more likely mean "ordinary" or "strange"?

5   There is no cure for autism disorders, but "high-functioning" people with autism can make useful—even outstanding—contributions to society. The Seattle school district began its program in 1997 with a single elementary-school **pilot** class for such high-functioning autistic children. Two years later the program was expanded districtwide, and twelve classes are now offered in elementary, middle, and high schools. There are plans to add even more classes in upcoming school years.

pilot Look up this word in the dictionary and select the most appropriate meaning for this context.

6   Because autism is one of the fastest-growing categories of disability in special education, it presents new challenges to school districts. The Seattle program has attracted considerable attention, and educators from around the United States (and even from Japan and Korea) have visited to learn more about how to help high-functioning children succeed in school.

—Lisa Fine, "Cracking the Shell," *Education Week*, November 21, 2001, pp. 22–29. Excerpted by permission of Editorial Projects in Education.

Talking About Reading

Respond in writing to the questions below, and then discuss your answers with your classmates.

1. What is Asperger's syndrome? Use your own words to define it.

   _____

   _____

   _____

2. The first sentence of paragraph 4 says students with Asperger's "tend to excel in subjects that interest them, but other aspects of school may be difficult for them." Can you relate to this idea regarding your own schooling? What has interested you? What have you found difficult?

   _____

   _____

   _____

3. Paragraph 4 also notes certain parts of school that are stressful for these students. What parts of your schooling have you found stressful? You might consider the school day, teacher-student relationships, student-student relationships, or specific subjects.

   _____

   _____

   _____

4. What are some of the kinds of knowledge you have had through the years that have caused others to appreciate you or look up to you?

   _____

   _____

   _____

MAPPS: A Reading Plan

Have you ever gotten into the car and started a long trip without any plans—with no idea of how to get where you were going? Probably not. Maybe you have thought about doing this, or you think it sounds adventurous or cool. It might be spontaneous, but it is not very practical. Even spontaneous people have maps or navigation systems in their car or use AAA, GoogleMaps, MapQuest, or some other source to help them figure out the best way to get to their destination.

Bloomberg via Getty Images

Just as it is important to have a road map while driving, it is also important to have a map for reading. Reading without a plan is about the same as driving without a clue about where you are going. You end up driving in circles, retracing your steps, wasting time, or worse, never arriving where you want to go. Similarly, if you read without a plan, you often end up "reading in circles"—rereading the same information again and again and becoming frustrated that you don't understand what you want to read. Or worse, maybe you just give up and never even complete the reading.

To successfully navigate when you are driving, there are always at least three things you need to know:

- Where you are.

- Where you are going.

and . . .

- How to get from point A to point B (a map)!

It's the same with reading. To successfully navigate a reading, you need to know:

- What you are reading.
- Your purpose for reading.
- A reading strategy: MAPPS.

MAPPS is a mnemonic device for a visual outline that can help you organize what you are reading and lead you to better comprehension. It is based on surveying a reading, asking "wh" questions (who, what, when, where, why, how, to what extent), and then marking the answers to your questions while you read, which encourages active reading. After you read, filling in the MAPPS outline will allow you to check your understanding as well as give you a convenient way to review important content for tests.

Mark = Mark the answers to your questions.

About = Topic: What is the reading about?

Point = Main idea: What is the point?

Proof = Supporting detail: What is the proof?

Summary = A combination of the topic, point, and proof.

In this chapter you'll learn how to figure out what a reading is about—the **topic**—and what the author's **point** is—the main idea. In Chapter 4, you'll learn about the **proof**—the supporting details and the patterns in which they are arranged.

Marking the Answers to Your Questions

Reading actively means asking questions as you read and searching for the answers in the reading.

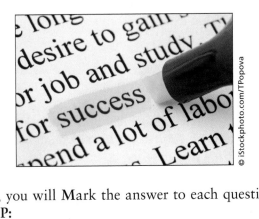

Using MAPPS, you will **Mark** the answer to each question associated with **A**, **P**, and **P**:

A: What is the reading about? (the topic)

P: What is the point? (the main idea)

P: What is the proof? (the supporting details)

The **A**, **P**, and **P** each represent a level of information in a reading. The topic (**A**) is the most general. The main idea (**P**) narrows the topic down to the point the author wants to discuss. The supporting details (**P**) are the most specific ideas; they explain the main idea.

To help you distinguish (tell apart) these three information levels, mark each level in some way. You'll see examples of how to do this throughout this chapter and Chapter 4.

What Is the Reading About? The Topic

Asking the simple question "What is the reading about?" will lead you to the **topic**. The topic is *who* or *what* a reading is about. Sometimes you will find the topic stated in the title, but even in single paragraphs, words related to the topic are often repeated throughout the paragraph in different ways. Topics are normally stated in a single word or a phrase. If your reading has a title, start by reading it to figure out what the topic is. If there is no title, look for people, places, things, or concepts that are repeated throughout the reading. Also, use your knowledge of words as you search for repetition—for example, if you see the word *equal*, you can also be on the lookout for the related word *equality*.

Look at the following example from a memoir:

Aaron is a year older than I. We should have been fratty, since we went to the same school, had the same teachers, read the same books. I should have had crushes on his friends, but his friends were severe science types, like him. His crowd hung out in Mr. Handwerker's homeroom, where there was a darkroom for printing black-and-white artistic images of garden slugs—pardon me, of *Arion distincti*—that might win a prize at the Fresno Fair! Aaron and his friends wore their T-shirts tucked into their pants, and wherever one met these boys, they smelled of chemical developer, stop bath, or formaldehyde.

—Janzen, *Mennonite in a Little Black Dress*, p. 138

There are two main threads in this paragraph. One has to do with Aaron, the narrator's brother. The paragraph starts by naming him and then refers to him several times with the pronouns *his* and *him*. The other thread has to do with Aaron's friends, who are also called "his crowd" and "these boys," and who are referred to with the words *they* and *their*. If you had to write a title for this paragraph that would reveal its topic, you could combine these two threads and call it "Aaron and His Friends."

Follow these steps when searching for the topic:

1. If there is a title, consider it first.

2. Look for repeated words, phrases, or concepts. Use your knowledge of words to find all the related words. Don't forget about pronouns like *he, she, him, her,* and *they*.

3. If you are reading a textbook, look for **bold** or *italicized* terms for clues to possible topics.

INTERACTION 3–1   **Identify the Topic of a Paragraph**

Read each paragraph and decide what the topic is.

A. Ask the question "What is this about?"

B. Look for repeated words, and mark them as you read.

C. Look for related words and pronouns.

D. When you are finished reading, create a title for the paragraph based on your findings.

1.

Angelina Jolie refuses to celebrate Thanksgiving because it is a celebration of one culture's crushing of another culture. She calls Thanksgiving a story of murder. To make sure that her family did not take part in Thanksgiving in 2010, Jolie took her family out of the country. Brad Pitt, however, said their family would cook a turkey somehow.

© Entertainment Press/Shutterstock.com

Title: _____

_____

2.

You can save money by shopping online if you know what you're doing. First, you can avoid driving anywhere to shop, which saves you gas money. Second, you can find the same exact item in many different online stores, and purchase it from the store that is selling it the cheapest. Third, many states don't charge a sales tax for goods you buy online.

Title: _____

_____

3.

Airport security methods are very invasive. Passengers at more than fifteen major airports may now have to submit to full-body scans, in which a person in a distant room can see their naked body, minus the head, to check for bombs and guns. If a traveler doesn't want to be scanned, he or she may need to submit to a pat-down, in which a security guard touches him or her in intimate places. Many people question whether these invasive security methods would keep air travel safe unless every single passenger went through these procedures.

Title: _____

_____

4.

> More than 50 million Indian people are suffering from diabetes, making India the country with the most diabetes patients in the world. Why? Sadly, it's because of the increasing number of Indians who are doing well in the world. The bodies of people who were born into poverty are geared to make the most of the scant amount of food they have to eat. When those people become more prosperous, their bodies can't handle the extra calories they can now afford and the decreased physical activity now that they don't have to do hard physical labor to survive. For many Indians, the result is diabetes.

Title: _____

_____

5.

> Jay-Z's book *Decoded* was published in the fall of 2010. The rapper's life story includes revealing details about his writing habits when he was first starting to put rhymes together. He carried a notebook everywhere he went, and each time he thought up a new rhyme, he would stop to write it down. Later, he practiced memorizing rhymes since it wasn't always easy to write them down while he was dealing crack. In *Decoded*, Jay-Z also talks about how he brings into his lyrics emotions that young men don't often share with each other, such as regret and longing.

Title: _____

_____

INTERACTION 3–2 | **Identify More Topics of a Paragraph**

Read each paragraph and decide what the topic is.

  A. Ask the question "What is this about?"

  B. Look for repeated words, and mark them as you read.

  C. Look for related words and pronouns.

  D. When you are finished reading, name the topic—what the reading is about.

1.

Even when product labels provide pertinent information, they are often difficult to understand or even misleading, and what they omit may be more important than what they say. For example, organic milk often comes from cows that are not on pasture, and products that bear the label "organic" or "USDA organic" are not necessarily 100 percent organic but may contain the same kind of synthetics that conventional food processors use.

USDA/National Organic Program

—From SHAW. *Cengage Advantage Books: Business Ethics*, 7e (p. 232) Copyright © 2011 Cengage Learning.

What is this paragraph about? _____

2.

What causes you to look like one or both of your parents or, perhaps, your grandparents? It is the genes you inherit from your parents and from your ancestors before them. **Genes** are long molecules of deoxyribonucleic acid (DNA) at various locations on chromosomes within the cell nucleus. Physical characteristics such as hair and eye color and, to a certain extent, height and weight are determined—or at least strongly influenced—by genetic endowment.

—From DURAND/BARLOW. *Essentials of Abnormal Psychology*, 5e (p. 35) Copyright © 2010 Cengage Learning.

What is this paragraph about? _____

3.

"Saga" stems from a Norse word for "say." It refers to spoken accounts of the Viking Age (roughly A.D. 800 to 1050) that were later written down by medieval clerks. Sagas tell of real people, real places, and real events, typically feuds. The prose is matter-of-fact. But sagas also inhabit a twilight zone where the normal and the paranormal intersect.

—Horwitz, *A Voyage Long and Strange*, p. 14

What is this paragraph about? _____

4.
> Action plans for intermediate and long-term goals are big-picture plans. Whether you follow your plans and achieve your goals will depend on managing your time well on a daily, weekly, and monthly basis. Otherwise, time can easily slip away. Procrastinating, not having enough time, wasting time, and misusing time can add up to a life spent without reaching your goals and your potential. If you want to be in control of your life and achieve your goals, you will have to take charge of your time.
>
> —From THROOP/CASTELLUCCI. *Reaching Your Potential*, 4e (p. 41)
> Copyright © 2011 Cengage Learning.

What is this paragraph about? _____

_____

5.
> The moderate drinker consumes no more than one or two drinks a day—one drink for a woman, two drinks for a man. Three drinks on a single occasion represent the *upper* limit of moderate alcohol consumption. It is important to remember that both the number of drinks and the distribution of drinks over time are important in defining moderate consumption. For example, people who do not drink all week so that they can have more than three drinks per episode during the weekend would *not* qualify as moderate drinkers.
>
> —From ROBINSON/MCCORMICK. *Concepts in Health and Wellness*, 1e
> (p. 324) Copyright © 2011 Cengage Learning.

What is the paragraph about? _____

_____

INTERACTION 3–3 | **Identify the Topic of a Paragraph in Longer Selections**

Read each paragraph and decide what the topic is.

A. Ask the question "What is this about?"

B. Look for repeated words within and across paragraphs, and mark them as you read.

C. Look for related words and pronouns within and across paragraphs.

D. When you are finished reading, name the topic of each paragraph.

From *Population: An Introduction to Concepts and Issues*

1   It has been said that "the past is a foreign country; they do things differently there." Population change and all that goes with it is an integral part of creating a present that seems foreign by comparison to the past, and it will create a future that will make today seem strange to those who look back on it several decades from now. Compare the United States in the year 1900 with the year 2000. Although the population of the United States grew considerably during that century, from 76 million to 281 million, it did not keep pace with overall world population growth and so accounted for a slightly smaller fraction of the world's population in 2000 than it had in 1900. Mortality levels dropped substantially over the century, leading to a truly amazing 30-year rise in life expectancy, from 47 in 1900 to 77 in 2000.

© Everett Collection Inc./Alamy

2   Fertility also declined, although by world standards fertility was already fairly low (3.5 children per woman) in 1900. Still, the drop from 3.5 to 2.1 clearly makes a huge difference in the composition of families. Americans rearranged themselves considerably within the country over that century, and the westward movement is exemplified by the change in the fraction of the population living in California. It went from only 2 percent in 1900 to 12 percent in 2000. Consider that in 1900 Los Angeles had about the same population as Buffalo, New York, but in 2000, Los Angeles was 35 times more populous than Buffalo.

3   In the latter part of the twentieth century, much of that growth in Los Angeles was fueled by immigrants from Mexico and Central America, but over the course of the century the composition of international immigrants had shifted substantially. In the decade following the 1900 census, there were about 50,000 Mexican immigrants to the U.S., compared to 2 million Italian immigrants in the same time period. By contrast, in the decade prior to Census 2000, the numbers were essentially reversed, with 63,000 Italian immigrants and at least 2.2 million Mexican immigrants. Yet, as strange as it might seem in an era when there is so much talk about immigrants, the data show that the foreign-born population actually represented a greater fraction of the nation in 1900 than it did a century later.

—From WEEKS. *Population*, 10e (pp. 3–4) Copyright © 2008 Cengage Learning.

1. What is the first paragraph about? _____

2. What is the second paragraph about? _____

   _____

3. What is the third paragraph about? _____

   _____

From *Thrive: Finding Happiness the Blue Zones Way*

1   It's ten o'clock on a Sunday morning in Hojancha, a small town in rural Costa Rica, and I'm on a mission. A few years ago, I met a woman here, the daughter of a Cuban revolutionary, who raised four children by herself on the edge of the jungle. Her name was Panchita, and when I first got to know her she had just celebrated her 99th birthday. Wearing a colorful dress, carnival beads, and hooped earrings, she would sit on a wooden plank on the patio of her tin-roofed house, dangle her legs above the dirt floor, and tell stories with friends and relatives who came to visit. She punctuated her conversations with a gentle touch and, depending on the topic, a sympathetic sigh or a whooping laugh. At sunset, once her guests had departed, she would make herself a simple meal of beans and handmade tortillas, say her prayers, and go to bed.

© Steve Cukrov/Shutterstock.com

2   Recently I heard that Panchita had a medical setback and moved out of her farmhouse into a one-room shack behind her son's place. I'm on my way to see her now.

3   A modest community of cinder-block houses, shops, and stables, Hojancha is populated mainly by farmers and *sabaneros,* the leathery-tough cowboys of Central America. Set apart from the rest of Costa Rica on the Nicoya Peninsula, people here have been left to themselves to follow the rhythms of their Mesoamerican ancestors. Something about their lifestyle—perhaps the lime-soaked corn tortillas called *nixtamale,* the wildly exotic fruits they grow in their gardens, the off-the-charts levels of calcium and magnesium in their tap water, their ability to shed stress with laughter and conversation, or even their penchant for extramarital

sex—has given people in this region the extraordinary gift of long life. In fact, the Nicoya Peninsula represents one of the most impressive pockets of longevity in the entire Western Hemisphere—a Blue Zone, as I've come to call such places. For the past eight years I've been studying the world's longevity Blue Zones. I've met more than 250 centenarians on five continents, some of whom still work as lawyers, stand on their heads, climb trees, or compete in karate matches.

4   Yet few have charmed me like Panchita.

—Buettner, *Thrive: Finding Happiness the Blue Zones Way*, pp. ix–x

4. What is the topic of the first and second paragraphs? _____

5. What is the topic of the third paragraph? _____

_____

Section Review: What Is the Reading About? The Topic

A. Fill in the APP rectangles with the appropriate question to ask to uncover their level of information.

Mark the answers to your questions.

About: _____

Point: _____

Proof: _____

Summary: A combination of the topic, main idea, and supporting details.

B. Name three steps you can follow to find the topic of a paragraph after you ask the question "What is this about?"

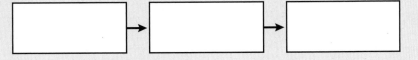

What Is the Point of the Reading? The Main Idea

Asking "What is the point?" as you read will lead you to the **main idea.** The main idea limits the topic to what the author wants to discuss. For example, suppose the topic is exercise. Exercise is a very broad topic. An author could explore any number of main ideas in regard to exercise. Here are a few examples.

<u>Many health benefits are associated with</u> [exercise].

[Exercise] <u>can be accomplished with or without the help of specialized equipment.</u>

[Exercise] <u>causes each muscle to shorten and contract.</u>

If you have a knee operation, you'll need to [exercise] <u>afterward to reach your previous level of fitness.</u>

© Syrota Vadym/Shutterstock.com

In these sentences, the topic is in brackets and the main idea is underlined. When the topic and the main idea appear in a single sentence, that sentence is called the *topic sentence.* Use this formula as a memory aid:

$$T \quad + \quad MI \quad = \quad TS$$
topic plus main idea equals topic sentence

Notice that in all of the examples, the topic is *exercise.* The main idea, however, is different in each topic sentence. Each main idea is about a different aspect of exercise. As a result, each topic sentence would lead to a paragraph with different supporting details. Here is an example using the APP of MAPPS.

About: Exercise

Point: can be accomplished with or without the help of specialized equipment.

Proof: 1. You can use an elliptical trainer to exercise your legs.
2. But you can also walk to the store, which requires no equipment.
3. You can use weights to strengthen your arms.
4. Or you can lift books or canned food using similar motions.

Notice that the first and third supporting details are examples of exercising with specialized equipment and the second and fourth supporting details are examples of exercising without specialized equipment.

Tips for Finding Topics and Main Ideas in the Topic Sentence

1. In the topic sentence, the topic may come before or after the main idea. To decide what is the topic and what is the main idea, look at the other sentences. Their details will explain the main idea.

> The most highly desirable gem in the world is [the diamond]. (The details are about the desirability of the diamond compared to the desirability of other gems.)

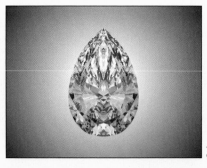

© Arsgera

continued

2. The topic can be more than a single word.

> [Eating well] is good for the body, mind, and spirit.
>
> [What I love the most about reading novels] is finding out how the characters change over time.

3. There may be words in the topic sentence that report the topic and main idea. Phrases like "Researchers Harriet King and Pedro Velasquez have found that..." and "Reporter Jennifer Steinhauser writes that..." indicate that the topic and main idea are later in the sentence.

INTERACTION 3–4   **Find the Topic Sentence of a Paragraph**

What is the topic sentence of each paragraph?

A. Look for repeated ideas to help you find the topic.

B. To figure out the main idea, think about how the author is limiting the topic to the point he or she wants to discuss.

C. Look for a sentence in which T + MI = TS.

D. In the topic sentence, put [brackets] around the topic and underline the main idea.

1.

My first direct contact with instruments and music came from my mother's Indian relatives. They all played something, and when the uncles and cousins visited, one guy played a mandolin and another played guitar, et cetera. They could all do something—it had a country, folk music kind of flavor. When I saw them, I wanted to be able to do it too. What's the trick, I thought.

© Carlos Caetano/Shutterstock.com

> —Interview with Robbie Robertson in Bonzai, *Faces of Music: 25 Years of Lunching with Legends*, p. 251

2.

> Participating in sports has many benefits for youth. In addition to improved physical fitness, sports can enhance participants' self-esteem and can help them learn initiative. Athletes also learn about teamwork and competitiveness by playing sports.
>
> —From KAIL/CAVANAUGH. *Cengage Advantage Books: Human Development*, 5e (p. 306) Copyright © 2010 Cengage Learning.

3.

> What's displayed on the computer screen is not a solid image. It's made up of small dots of colored light. Each dot is referred to as a pixel (picture element), which is the smallest unit that can be displayed on a computer monitor. Pixels are arranged in rows and columns. The number of pixels in each row and column defines the display device's resolution.
>
> —Adapted from ANDERSON/FERRO/HILTON. *Connecting with Computer Science*, 2e (p. 267) Copyright © 2011 Cengage Learning.

4.

> Over time, however, some human groups have adapted genetically to the challenges of living in specific environments in ways that make them a bit different from other groups of humans. That is, human groups living over time may evolve specialized adaptations to particular dietary environments. Lactose tolerance offers a classic example of this type of population-level difference. While most people in the world are unable to digest lactose—the principal sugar found in milk—after they reach adulthood, some people share a gene that allows them to produce large enough amounts of the enzyme lactase to continue consuming milk products throughout their lifetimes. The frequency with which this gene is found varies remarkably among populations. Almost the entire population of people living in Sweden, Czechoslovakia, Denmark, and Britain carry the gene for digesting lactose. In northern Italy, the gene frequency is about 49%. In most of Asia, Africa (except among a few groups such as the Tussi, Fulani, and Hilma), and South America it is well below 20%. Virtually no one from Taiwan or Singapore can digest lactose.
>
> —From BRYANT/COURTNEY/DEWALT/SCHWARTZ. *The Cultural Feast: An Introduction to Food and Society*, 2e (pp. 6–7) Copyright © 2004 Cengage Learning.

5.

> Special Agent Michael J. Bulzomi, a legal instructor at the FBI Academy, writes that drug detection dogs remain extremely important in drug detection. They represent a highly efficient and cost-effective way to establish quickly whether probable cause exists to execute a search for contraband. The use of drug detection dogs has met with few real legal challenges in the courts. The only notable area that has been challenged is a dog's reliability. Drug detection dog handlers should be prepared to establish a dog's reliability by providing prosecutors with a complete record of the dog's training, success rate, and certification in drug detection.
>
> —From DEMPSEY/FORST. *An Introduction to Policing*, 5e (p. 422)
> Copyright © 2010 Cengage Learning.

INTERACTION 3–5	Find More Topic Sentences of a Paragraph

What is the topic sentence of each paragraph?

A. Look for repeated ideas to help you find the topic.

B. To figure out the main idea, think about how the author is limiting the topic to the point he or she wants to discuss.

C. Look for a sentence in which T + MI = TS.

D. In the topic sentence, put [brackets] around the topic and underline the main idea.

1.

> Most writers don't need long to figure out that a detailed sentence is more memorable and convincing than an unproven generalization. "My father rarely laughs," one of my students wrote. After a quick revision, the same description read: "My father's laughter is a beautiful silver fish that leaps from a quiet stream." Another student told us that her father was "an asshole," a description she revised to read: "My mother doesn't appreciate my father's habit of showing our dinner guests photos of his mistresses."
>
> —From POLLACK. *Creative Nonfiction* (p. 11)
> Copyright © 2010 Cengage Learning.

2.

> The **free enterprise system** is a system in which most economic resources are privately owned and individuals are free to decide what they will produce with the resources. A free enterprise system makes entrepreneurship possible by allowing business interactions to be governed by the laws of supply and demand and not restrained by government interference, regulation, or subsidy. This freedom gives business owners the opportunity to reap the full rewards—and risks—of the ventures they choose to operate, in the way they choose to operate them.
>
> —Adapted from CILETTI. *Marketing Yourself*, 2e (pp. 316–317)
> Copyright © 2004 Cengage Learning.

3.

> The content of dreams varies culturally because people dream about things they experience in their daily lives. For instance, the Eskimo of two centuries ago had no basis for having dreams that included snowmobiles or jumbo jets. And the dreams of the traditional Zuni of the American Southwest might have included both desert vegetation and katchina rain gods, but not igloos. A contemporary Canadian's dreams might include religious figures, but probably not the ones that Eskimo or Zuni would recognize. Whereas Americans and Japanese both experience anxiety-filled dreams about taking tests, the Maasai herders of Kenya and dairy ranchers from Wyoming both have dreams about cattle. In simple terms, people dream about their own realities.
>
> —From PRICE/CRAPO. *Cross-Cultural Perspectives*, 4e (p. 30)
> Copyright © 2002 Cengage Learning.

4.

> What's it like to be single in the United States? It's tougher than you might think. DePaulo (2006) points out that there are numerous stereotypes and biases against single people. Her research found that young adults characterized married people as caring, kind, and giving about 50% of the time compared with only 2% for single people. And single people receive less compensation at work than married people do, even when age and experience are equivalent. DePaulo also found that rental agents preferred married couples 60% of the time.
>
> —Adapted from KAIL/CAVANAUGH. *Cengage Advantage Books: Human Development*, 5e (p. 406) Copyright © 2010 Cengage Learning.

5.

> Stress triggers complex changes in the body's endocrine, or hormone-secreting, system. When you confront a stressor, the adrenal glands, two triangle-shaped glands that sit atop the kidneys, respond by producing stress hormones, including catecholamines, cortisol (hydrocortisone), and epinephrine (adrenaline), that speed up heart rate and raise blood pressure and prepare the body to deal with the threat. This "fight-or-flight" response prepares you for quick action: Your heart works harder to pump more blood to your legs and arms. Your muscles tense, your breathing quickens, and your brain becomes extra alert. Because it's nonessential in a crisis, your digestive system practically shuts down.
>
> —From HALES. *An Invitation to Health*, 12e (p. 84)
> Copyright © 2007 Cengage Learning.

| INTERACTION 3–6 | Find More Topic Sentences of a Paragraph |

What is the topic sentence of each paragraph?

A. Look for repeated ideas to help you find the topic.

B. To figure out the main idea, think about how the author is limiting the topic to the point he or she wants to discuss.

C. Look for a sentence in which T + MI = TS.

D. In the topic sentence, put [brackets] around the topic and <u>underline</u> the main idea.

1.

> A few journalists achieve wealth, fame, and glamour. Most do not. They receive modest pay and recognition, and they report from unglitzy places such as courthouses, city halls, and state capitols. Amid recent turmoil in the media industry, they worry about making a secure living. And they sometimes face danger, especially when covering warfare or terrorism. During the Iraq war, columnist Michael Kelly died when the army vehicle in which he was traveling careened off the road while evading enemy fire. Bomb blasts severely injured ABC reporter Bob Woodruff and CBS reporter Kimberly Dozier. In Pakistan, terrorists kidnapped *Wall Street Journal* reporter Daniel Pearl, and when the American government did not give in to their demands, they beheaded him. Late in 2008, Taliban terrorists kidnapped *New York Times* reporter David Rohde in Afghanistan. Out of concern for his safety, the *Times* kept the abduction a secret until he escaped seven months later. As the Afghanistan war heated up in 2009, CBS reporter Cami McCormick suffered serious wounds in a roadside bombing.
>
> —From BESSETTE/PITNEY. *American Government and Politics* (p. 370)
> Copyright © 2012 Cengage Learning.

2.

> Most sensory illusions are not terribly important. Unless you are a vision scientist or an amputee or Captain John Ross, they have pretty much the status of parlor tricks. Occasionally, though, the quirks of our perceptual system leave us vulnerable to more serious errors. Take, for instance, a phenomenon known as inattentional blindness. There is a rather amazing experiment—which I'm about to ruin for you—in which subjects are shown a video of a group of people playing a fast-paced ball game and are asked to count how many times the ball is passed back and forth. At some point during the video, a gorilla (more precisely, a person dressed in a gorilla costume) wanders into the middle of the group of players, stands around for a bit, beats its chest a few times, and then wanders off again. Here's the amazing part: between 33 and 50 percent of subjects don't see this happen. Perhaps this bears repeating: one-third to one-half of people instructed to pay close attention to a video fail to see a gorilla beating its chest in the middle of it.
>
> —Schultz, *Being Wrong*, p. 62

3.

> Suppose you find this book on the floor and you pick it up and put it on your desktop. In doing this you have to use a certain amount of muscular force to move the book, and you have done work. In scientific terms, work is done when any object is moved a certain distance (work = force × distance). Also, whenever you touch a hot object such as a stove, heat flows from the stove to your finger. Both of these examples involve energy: the capacity to do work or to transfer heat.
>
> —From MILLER/SPOOLMAN. *Living in the Environment*, 17e (p. 44)
> Copyright © 2012 Cengage Learning.

4.

> **Milestones** are formal project review points used to assess progress and performance. For example, a company that has put itself on a 12-month schedule to complete a project must schedule milestones at the 3-month, 6-month, and 9-month points on the schedule. By making people regularly assess what they're doing, how well they're performing, and whether they need to take corrective action, milestones provide structure to the general chaos that follows technological discontinuities. Milestones also shorten the innovation process by creating a sense of urgency that keeps everyone on task.
>
> —From WILLIAMS. *Management*, 4e (p. 215)
> Copyright © 2004 Cengage Learning.

5.

> From a developmental perspective, the most important function that families serve in all societies is to care for and socialize their young. **Socialization** refers to the process by which children acquire the beliefs, motives, values, and behaviors deemed significant and appropriate by older members of their society. And the socialization of each successive generation serves society in at least three ways. First, it is a means of regulating children's behavior and controlling their undesirable impulses. Second, socialization promotes the personal growth of the individual. As children interact with and become like other members of their culture, they acquire the knowledge, skills, motives, and aspirations that should enable them to adapt to and function effectively within their communities. Finally, socialization perpetuates the social order. Appropriately socialized children become competent, adaptive, prosocial adults who will impart what they have learned to their own children.
>
> —From SHAFFER. *Social and Personality Development*, 6e (pp. 370–371)
> Copyright © 2009 Cengage Learning.

Section Review: What Is the Point? The Main Idea

A. Fill in three possible main ideas for the topic "my favorite movie."

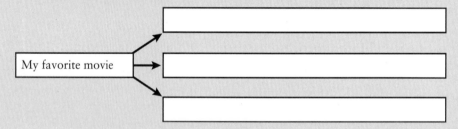

B. Select one of the topic sentences you created in A. Fill in the MAPP with the Point and three details that support it with Proof.

About: My favorite movie

Point:

Proof:

Proof:

Proof:

Location of the Topic Sentence: Anywhere

Topic sentences can appear anywhere in a paragraph. It is not the location of the topic sentence that is important; it is the relationships between the ideas in the paragraph that matter.

Think about this analogy. You may live in a city, a state, or even a country far away from the rest of your family. Let's say, for example, that you live in Miami, Florida, and your parents live in Bogota, Colombia. Are you still their child? Are they still your parents? Of course! It is the relationship between you and your parents that matters, not your respective locations.

In a paragraph, it is the same for the topic, main idea, and supporting details. It does not matter where they are located; their relationship is always the same.

- The topic is a broad, general idea.

- The main idea narrows the topic to the specific point the author wants to discuss.

- The major and minor details support the main idea with even narrower, more specific ideas.

In the following example, the topic sentence has been bracketed and underlined for you. Notice that it is in the middle of the paragraph.

Plain soaps do, at best, a middling job disinfecting. Their detergents remove loose dirt and grime, but fifteen seconds of washing reduces bacterial counts by only about an order of magnitude. Semmelweis recognized that ordinary soap was not enough and used a chlorine solution to achieve disinfection. Today's antibacterial soaps contain chemicals such as chlorhexidine to disrupt microbial membranes and proteins. <u>Even with the right soap, however, [proper handwashing] requires a strict procedure</u>. First, you must remove your watch, rings, and other jewelry (which are notorious for trapping bacteria). Next, you wet your hands in warm tap water. Dispense the soap and lather all surfaces, including the lower one-third of the arms, for the full duration recommended by the manufacturer (usually fifteen to thirty seconds). Rinse off for thirty full seconds. Dry completely with a clean disposable towel. Then use the towel to turn the tap off. Repeat after any new contact with a patient.

—Gawande, *Better: A Surgeon's Notes on Performance*, pp. 17–18

Let's put this paragraph into the diagram we've been using to visualize these relationships.

Figure 3.1 Three Levels of Information

broad   **A**bout: Proper handwashing

   narrower   **P**oint: requires a strict procedure.

     narrowest   **P**roof: 1. Remove watch and jewelry.
2. Wet hands with warm water.
3. Lather all surfaces, including lower arms, for full recommended duration.
4. Rinse for thirty seconds.
5. Dry completely with clean, disposable towel.
6. Turn off tap with the towel.
7. Repeat after any contact with a patient.

Did you notice that the first four sentences in the paragraph are not in Figure 3.1? That's because they relate to the phrase at the beginning of the topic sentence:

> Even with the right soap, however . . .

Notice how the sentences before the topic sentence support this phrase.

1. Plain soaps do, at best, a middling job of disinfecting.

2. Their detergents remove loose dirt and grime, but fifteen seconds of washing reduced bacterial counts by only about an order of magnitude.

3. Semmelweis recognized that ordinary soap was not enough and used a chlorine solution to achieve disinfection.

4. Today's antibacterial soaps contain chemicals such as chlorhexidine to disrupt microbial membranes and proteins.

You can see that the first sentences of the paragraph support and lead up to the first part of the topic sentence. Then, the majority of the paragraph explains the main part of the topic sentence.

Common Uses of the First Sentence of a Paragraph

Sometimes the first sentence of a paragraph is the topic sentence. But there are several other common uses of the first sentence:

1. The first sentence can be a **transition** from previously discussed ideas to the topic sentence of the paragraph. In the following example, the first part of the sentence refers to what the author has already talked about:

> **Given the wide-ranging causes of delinquency,** it would be naive to expect a single or simple cure.

The author has previously discussed many causes of delinquency. The second part of the sentence sets up readers for the topic sentence, which comes next:

> Instead, [delinquency] <u>must be attacked along several fronts simultaneously</u>.
>
> —From KAIL/CAVANAUGH. *Cengage Advantage Books: Human Development*, 5e (p. 350) Copyright © 2010 Cengage Learning.

2. The first sentence can offer specific **examples** of an idea the author will later explain in the topic sentence.

> St. Patrick's Cathedral, containing many monuments and plaques; Christ Church's vaulted crypt; Dublin Castle, part of which dates back to the Celts; Trinity College, with a collection of old book treasures; the National Museum, holding one of the world's great gold collections (with some Bronze Age pieces). [Dublin, the capital of Ireland], <u>offers a rich collection of medieval history and modern arts</u>.
>
> —From MANCINI. *Selling Destinations*, 4e (p. 253) Copyright © 2010 Cengage Learning.

continued

3. The first sentence of a paragraph may be a **question** that helps readers feel personally engaged in the main idea to come:

> Have you ever tried a new or "improved" product and been disappointed when it didn't work as expected? Everyone learns, sometimes the hard way, how useful it can be to cast a skeptical eye on advertising claims or get an unbiased evaluation of, say, a used car you are considering buying. This objective evaluation of information is called [*evidence-based* or **critical thinking**].
>
> —From STARR/MCMILLAN. *Human Biology*, 8e (p. 8)
> Copyright © 2010 Cengage Learning.

4. The first sentence may introduce a **general idea** that is then narrowed down by other sentences, leading to the specific main idea to be discussed:

> All self-help groups are formed by people who share a similar problem they want to solve. More specifically, twelve-step programs are for people who are addicted to alcohol, drugs, gambling, and other compulsive behaviors. Alcoholics Anonymous was the first twelve-step program. . . .

When you are searching for the topic sentence of a paragraph, look at the relationships among the ideas—which ideas are broadest, narrower, and narrowest—rather than looking in a particular location.

| INTERACTION 3–7 | Find the Topic Sentence |

Remember the formula T + MI = TS. Locate the topic sentence of each of the following paragraphs. Then mark the parts of the topic sentence: put [brackets] around the topic, and underline the main idea.

1.

East Asian economies have followed a flying-geese pattern of economic growth in which countries gradually move up in technological development by following in the pattern of countries ahead of them in the development process. For example, Taiwan and Malaysia take over leadership in apparel and textiles from Japan as Japan moves into the higher-technology sectors of automotive, electronic, and other capital goods. A decade or so later, Taiwan and Malaysia are able to upgrade to automotive and electronics products, while the apparel and textile industries move to Thailand, Vietnam, and Indonesia.

© Ginosphotos/Dreamstime

—From CARBAUGH. *International Economics*, 12e (p. 256)
Copyright © 2008 Cengage Learning.

2.

Three people with increased body temperature and nasal congestion may interpret the causes and treat the symptoms quite differently. A person who believes in a biomedical health model might describe it as a viral infection, caused by contact with an infectious person, and treat it by staying in bed, drinking plenty of fluids, and taking an analgesic. A proponent of complementary medicine might chalk it up to stress and use herbal remedies and visualization as the road to recovery. A person who explains it in spiritual terms might search for a violation of supernatural norms and perform a ritual dance to relieve the symptoms.

—From BRYANT/COURTNEY/DEWALT/SCHWARTZ. *The Cultural Feast: An Introduction to Food and Society*, 2e (p. 236)
Copyright © 2004 Cengage Learning.

3.

On February 28, 1953, two men walked into a pub in Cambridge, England, and offered drinks all around. "We have discovered the secret of life!" proclaimed one of the men. He was James Watson. With his colleague, Francis Crick, he had found the structure of deoxyribonucleic acid, or DNA, the chemical that makes up genes. During cell division, a single DNA molecule uncoils into two strands. New, identical molecules are formed from each strand. In this way, growth takes place and traits are passed from one generation to the next. It was one of the most important scientific discoveries ever.

—From BRYM/LIE. *Sociology*, 3e (p. 178) Copyright © 2010 Cengage Learning.

4.

It is difficult to believe, but our brains definitely play tricks on us. Our perception is limited, and the way we view our surroundings may not accurately reflect what is really there. Perception is faulty; it is not always accurate, and it does not always reflect reality. For example, our brains will fill in information that is not really there. If we are reading a sentence and a word is missing, we will often not notice the omission but instead predict the word that should be there and read the sentence as though it is complete.

—From BERTINO. *Forensic Science: Fundamentals and Investigations* (pp. 4–5) Copyright © 2010 Cengage Learning.

5.

All families go through times of chaos and upheaval. Your family life, like other aspects of your life, has ups and downs and good days and bad days. Some families, however, have many more relationship difficulties among their members than average. Sometimes you hear such a family referred to as a dysfunctional family. What does it mean to be a dysfunctional family? Experiencing occasional problems in family relationships, even if those problems are serious, doesn't make a family dysfunctional. A dysfunctional family is one in which family interactions continually negatively affect the physical, emotional, and social development of the individuals in the family. In a dysfunctional family, the sum total of all the relationship experiences in the family over time creates pain rather than pleasure.

—From ROBINSON/MCCORMICK. *Concepts in Health and Wellness*, 1e (p. 148) Copyright © 2011 Cengage Learning.

Section Review: Location of the Topic Sentence: Anywhere

A. Fill in the rest of each word:

T	+	M i	=	T s

B. Match the term on the left with the definition on the right.

Topic	Narrow, specific ideas
Main idea	A broad, general idea
Supporting details	The point the author wants to make

Thesis Statements in Textbook Sections

Single paragraphs have topic sentences that control which specific details will be included as support. Longer passages, such as sections of textbook chapters or groups of related paragraphs, may also have a sentence or two that summarizes the topic and main idea. This sentence might be called the thesis statement, the central point, or simply the main idea. (The idea may not always be stated, and Chapter 7 addresses that situation.)

Here is an example from the textbook *An Introduction to Policing*, 5th edition. As you read, highlight the topic sentence in each paragraph and underline any thesis statements that apply to a group of paragraphs:

- Paragraphs 1 and 2: topic sentence

- Paragraphs 3–6: thesis statement and three paragraph-level topic sentences

- Paragraph 7: topic sentence

Drug Undercover Investigations

1   Most law enforcement agencies have devoted resources to drug enforcement. Nine of 10 local law enforcement agencies perform drug enforcement functions. Although only 18 percent of all local departments operate a special unit for drug enforcement with one or more full-time officers assigned, most departments serving populations of greater than 50,000 have a full-time drug enforcement unit. Nationally, approximately 12,300 local police officers are

assigned full-time to drug enforcement, for an average of six officers per department. What do these officers do? What type of drug enforcement do they do?

2   Undercover drug operations can be very dangerous. Drug dealers are usually armed, the encounter may be a rip-off and not an actual deal, and the dealers may be in a paranoid state or under the influence of narcotics at the time of the deal. Caution also needs to be taken to make sure that the deal is not being done between two law enforcement agencies. That has happened in the past, and most agencies now have procedures in place to check that out before the deal goes down.

3   At least three general methods can be used in conducting drug undercover investigations. The first involves infiltrating criminal organizations that sell large amounts of drugs. The method is to buy larger and larger amounts of drugs so the buyer can reach as high as possible into the particular organizational hierarchy. Lower members of the criminal hierarchy have access only to a fixed quantity of drugs. To obtain larger amounts, they have to introduce the investigator to their source or connection, who is generally someone in the upper echelon of the organization or a member of a more sophisticated organization. These operations generally require sophisticated electronic surveillance measures and large sums of money. They can be very lengthy and dangerous to undercover investigators.

4   The next method that can be used to attack drug syndicates or drug locations is the process of staking out (a fixed surveillance) a particular location and making detailed observations of the conditions that indicate drug sales, such as the arrival and brief visit of numerous autos and people. These observations are best if recorded on video to establish probable cause for obtaining a search warrant. If a judge agrees with the probable cause, he or she can issue a search warrant, which can then be executed against a particular person, automobile, or premises. These investigations can be very lengthy and involve extensive sophisticated electronic surveillance.

5   The third method is the undercover "buy-bust," an operation in which an undercover police officer purchases a quantity of drugs from a subject, then leaves the scene, contacts the backup team, and identifies the seller. The backup team, in or out of uniform, responds to the

location of the sale and arrests the seller, based on the description given by the undercover officer. The legal basis of the arrest is probable cause to believe that a crime was committed and that the subject is the perpetrator of the crime. Based on the legal arrest, the backup team can search the subject and seize any illegal drugs. If the arrest occurs inside the premises, the backup team can seize any illegal substances that are in plain view. The undercover officer then goes to the police facility the subject was brought to and makes a positive identification of the subject from a hidden location, generally through a one-way mirror or window. By viewing the suspect through the one-way mirror or window, the undercover officer cannot be seen and can be used again in the same role. The buy-bust is generally used in low-level drug operations that receive numerous complaints from the community. The purpose is to take the person into custody as quickly as possible to relieve the quality-of-life problem in the neighborhood. A sufficient number of officers is extremely important in undercover buy-bust operations. This generally includes

- The undercover officer (U/C).
- The ghost officer. This officer closely shadows or follows the U/C as she or he travels within an area and approaches the dealer.
- The backup team. This should consist of at least five officers, if possible, who can watch from a discreet location to ensure the safety of the U/C and ghost and who can move in when ready to arrest the dealer.
- The supervisor. This critical member of the team plans and directs the operation and makes all key decisions.

6 Often, the undercover officer will make numerous purchases over time and then obtain an arrest warrant for the dealer, and a team will go in and make the arrest. This is good strategy because the dealer is less likely to make a connection to the buyer/officer, and it allows the officer to build probable cause and a stronger case.

7 Sometimes, law enforcement may then conduct a reverse-sting operation. This is where after the buy-bust, an officer poses as the drug dealer and arrests the buyers that come to purchase drugs. This is usually done in areas that readily attract buyers. As soon as an exchange is made, the backup team makes the bust. This type of operation can often lead to accusations of entrapment, so officers must be thoroughly versed in their state laws and court rulings regarding entrapment.

—From DEMPSEY/FORST. *An Introduction to Policing*, 5e (pp. 322–323)
Copyright © 2010 Cengage Learning.

Note the thesis statement in paragraph 3: "At least three general methods can be used in conducting drug undercover investigations." A thesis statement can cover an entire section in a textbook, or it can cover several paragraphs within a section, as in this reading. Notice that right after that first sentence in paragraph 3 is the topic sentence for paragraph 3: "The first involves infiltrating criminal organizations that sell large amounts of drugs."

Here are the thesis statement and the topic sentences of paragraphs 3 to 6 in the APP of MAPPS:

About: At least three general methods
       Point: can be used in conducting drug undercover investigations.
         Proof: 1. The first involves infiltrating criminal organizations that sell large amounts of drugs. (paragraph 3)
                   2. The next method that can be used to attack drug syndicates or drug locations is the process of staking out (a fixed surveillance) a particular location and making detailed observations of the conditions that indicate drug sales. (paragraph 4)
                   3. The third method is the undercover "buy-bust," an operation in which an undercover police officer purchases a quantity of drugs from a subject, then leaves the scene, contacts the backup team, and identifies the seller. (paragraphs 5–6)

You can see from this example that the same kinds of relationships that are found between a topic sentence and supporting details also exist between a thesis statement and topic sentences.

When you are reading textbooks, look for thesis statements. They are more commonly used than you might expect, and they can often help you understand the relationship among ideas.

| INTERACTION 3–8 | Identify Thesis Statements in a Textbook Section |

Read the following section from the textbook *Essentials of Ecology*. Highlight the topic sentence in each paragraph and underline any thesis statements that apply to a block of paragraphs. Then answer the questions following the reading.

Communities and Ecosystems Change Over Time: Ecological Succession

1   The types and numbers of species in biological communities and ecosystems change in response to changing environmental conditions such as fires, volcanic eruptions, climate change, and the clearing of forests to plant crops. The normally gradual change in species composition in a given area is called **ecological succession**.

2   Ecologists recognize two main types of ecological succession, depending on the conditions present at the beginning of the process. **Primary ecological succession**

involves the gradual establishment of biotic communities in lifeless areas where there is no soil in a terrestrial ecosystem or no bottom sediment in an aquatic ecosystem. Examples include bare rock exposed by a retreating glacier (Figure 3.2), newly cooled lava, an abandoned highway or parking lot, and a newly created shallow pond or reservoir. Primary succession usually takes hundreds to thousands of years because of the need to build up fertile soil or aquatic sediments to provide the nutrients needed to establish a plant community.

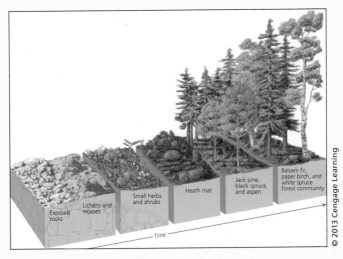

Exposed rocks

Lichens and mosses

Small herbs and shrubs

Heath mat

Jack pine, black spruce, and aspen

Balsam fir, paper birch, and white spruce forest community

Time

© 2013 Cengage Learning

Figure 3.2 Primary Ecological Succession

Over almost a thousand years, these plant communities developed, starting on bare rock exposed by a retreating glacier on Isle Royal, Michigan (USA) in northern Lake Superior. The details of this process vary from one site to another.

3   The other, more common type of ecological succession is called **secondary ecological succession,** in which a series of communities or ecosystems with different species develop in places containing soil or bottom sediment. This type of succession begins in an area where an ecosystem has been disturbed, removed, or destroyed, but some soil or bottom sediment remains. Candidates for secondary succession include abandoned farmland, burned or cut forests, heavily polluted streams, and land that has been flooded. Because some soil or sediment is present, new vegetation can begin to germinate, usually within a few weeks. It begins with seeds already in the soil and seeds imported by wind or in the droppings of birds and other animals.

4   Primary and secondary ecological succession are important natural services that tend to increase biodiversity, and thus the sustainability of communities and ecosystems, by increasing species richness and interactions among species. Such interactions in turn enhance sustainability by promoting population control and

by increasing the complexity of food webs. This then enhances the energy flow and nutrient cycling, which are functional components of biodiversity. As part of the earth's natural capital, both types of succession are examples of *natural ecological restoration*. Ecologists have been conducting research to find out more about the factors involved in ecological succession.

—From MILLER/SPOOLMAN. *Essentials of Ecology*, 6e (pp. 118–119)
Copyright © 2012 Cengage Learning.

1. What is the topic of this textbook section? _____

2. What is the main idea overall? _____

   _____

3. Where do you find a thesis statement?

   Paragraph _____   Sentence _____

4. Which paragraphs does the thesis statement control?

   Paragraphs _____

5. Which paragraph describes the benefits of ecological succession?

   Paragraph _____

6. What is the main difference between the two types of ecological succession? ___

   _____

   _____

   _____

7. Which type of ecological succession can get started more quickly?

   Primary   Secondary

8. Which type is more common?

   Primary   Secondary

9. Why would that type be more common? _____

   _____

10. What broader idea (besides ecological succession) are both types of succession examples of? _____

Section Review: Thesis Statements in Textbook Sections

Indicate on this MAPP where thesis statements would fit within a textbook section.

About:
        Point:
                Proof 1:
                Proof 2:

Explain your answer here. _____

_____

Chapter Summary Activity: Identifying Topics and Main Ideas

Chapter 3 has discussed how to identify the topic and main idea of a reading selection. Fill in the following Reading Guide by completing each idea on the left with information from Chapter 3 on the right. You can return to this guide throughout the course as a reminder of how to identify the topic and the main idea.

Reading Guide to Identifying Topics and Main Ideas

Complete this idea	with information from Chapter 3.
The reading strategy you have learned in this chapter is called	1. _____
State the meaning of each letter of MAPPS.	2. M: _____
	3. A: _____
	4. P: _____
	5. P: _____
	6. S: _____
When you ask "What is this reading about?" you are searching for the	7. _____
The first part of a reading selection you should examine to find the topic is the	8. _____

Complete this idea	with information from Chapter 3.
Next, you can look for	9. _____
Third, look for repeated	10. _____
As you look for repetitions, remember to consider both _____ and _____.	11. _____ 12. _____
When you ask the question "What's the point?", you are searching for the reading's	13. _____
The main idea of a reading selection limits the topic to	14. _____
When both the topic and the main idea appear in the same sentence, that sentence is called the	15. _____
The main idea can come either _____ or _____ the topic in the topic sentence.	16. _____ 17. _____
Do the supporting details of a paragraph explain the topic or the main idea?	18. _____
The topic sentence can appear _____ in a paragraph.	19. _____
It is the _____ between the topic, main idea, and supporting details that will help you find the topic sentence.	20. _____
Four common uses of the first sentence of a paragraph, stated briefly, are:	21. _____ 22. _____ 23. _____ 24. _____

25. Think about what your reading strategies were before you read Chapter 3. How did they differ from the suggestions here? Write your thoughts.

_____

_____

_____

ENGAGE YOUR SKILLS
Identifying Topics and Main Ideas

A. Find the topic of each paragraph from the textbook *Health Promotion in Nursing,* 2nd edition.

1.

> Frequently, when planning an exercise or fitness program, variables such as culture or lack of personal motivation are not taken into account. These variables are quite obvious and yet health promotion planners may not be aware of their impact on the decision to exercise. For example, people may be motivated to exercise to music if the type of music is relevant to their age group, lifestyle, or culture. An older American may adhere to an exercise plan using music referred to as "Golden Oldies" while younger adults may prefer rap music.
>
> —From MAVILLE/HUERTA. *Health Promotion in Nursing*, 2e (p. 328)
> Copyright © 2008 Cengage Learning.

What is this paragraph about? _____

2.

> Research has found that exercise programs that take into account culture create personal interest and increased adherence. One study conducted by researchers from the University of California—San Francisco School of Nursing found that 96 percent of the participants completed a 12-week Tai Chi exercise program for older Chinese women at risk for coronary heart disease. The researchers attributed the success of the program to the fact that it was culturally in tune with the exercise group. Incorporating culture into exercise routines may prove beneficial in other ethnic populations. For example, use of salsa music in an exercise regimen has been found to spark the interest of Cuban Americans as well as other Hispanic groups.
>
> —From MAVILLE/HUERTA. *Health Promotion in Nursing*, 2e (p. 328)
> Copyright © 2008 Cengage Learning.

What is this paragraph about? _____

B. Read the following selection from the textbook *Those Who Can, Teach*. For the topic sentence in each paragraph, bracket the [topic] and underline the <u>main idea</u>.

3.

Homelessness

For families in or close to poverty, the threat of homelessness is very real. Poor families often pay more than one-half of their annual incomes in rent. With such a large percentage of income consumed by rent payments, a single incident or emergency in the family can disrupt this tenuous equilibrium and jeopardize the family's ability to maintain a home. Imagine, for example, the domino effect that could occur from mechanical difficulties with the one family car. Even minor repairs costing $50 to $100 may be beyond the family's budget. Without a car, the family breadwinner may be unable to get to work and the children unable to get to day care. It does not take long in such a situation to lose a job or a long-awaited slot in a child care center. If the main earner cannot work, paying rent can soon become impossible. It is easy to see why housing, which consumes so much of annual income, is a particular source of vulnerability for families in poverty.

4.   Approximately 1.3 million children and youth in the United States are homeless at some point each year. Imagine the obstacles for homeless children trying to get an education. Uprooted from their homes, many live in shelters or other locations in distant parts of town. Attending school may require extensive transportation, which parents are not likely to be able to afford. Enrolling children in a school near a shelter may be a difficult and intimidating process for parents struggling with daily survival. Many parents, believing they will be homeless only for a short time, may not even try to transfer their child's enrollment. As days turn into weeks and months, the child may miss a great deal of school. If the child is fortunate enough to attend school, other difficulties may arise, such as the stigma of wearing dirty and ragged clothes, being unwelcome by other children or school officials, or being unable to stay awake in class.

5.   Some homeless children are on their own, having run away from home or been thrown out by their families. Many of these chronically homeless youth have been physically or sexually abused, and may suffer from drug or alcohol abuse, poor nutrition, inadequate sleep, exposure to the elements, and lack of health care. Schools can be a stabilizing force in the lives of these children, but it can also exacerbate their problems.

6.   In 1987, Congress passed the Stewart B. McKinney Homeless Assistance Act, which is intended to provide protection for the educational needs of homeless children and youth. This legislation provides grants to states to make available money for the educational needs of homeless children. It also requires states to ensure that these children are educated with the rest of the youth in their area and are not isolated and stigmatized.

7.   You may have homeless children in your classroom; if so, they are likely to require support and understanding from you. Some may be malnourished or physically dirty because they lack access to shower or tub facilities. They may show emotional needs. Other children may make fun of them. Your support and caring could provide these children with hope and be crucial in improving their chances for success.

8.

> More than anything else, homeless children need homes. As their teacher, you cannot be expected to provide the homes they need, but hundreds of local and federal programs serve runaway and homeless youth, and these agencies will help work with these youngsters. Through them, some may find shelter.
>
> —From COOPER. *Those Who Can, Teach*, 12e (pp. 104–106)
> Copyright © 2009 Cengage Learning.

Answer the following questions.

9. Think about the topic of this textbook section. Is the title of this section

        too general   just right   too specific

10. Respond to either a or b below, depending on your answer to question 9.

    a.   If you chose "too general" or "too specific," provide a revised title that is at the right level of generality: _____

        _____

        _____

        _____

    b.   If you chose "just right," explain why you think so. _____

        _____

        _____

        _____

MASTER YOUR SKILLS
Identifying Topics and Main Ideas

A. MAPP the topic and main idea of each of the following paragraphs.

1.

> The basic purpose of any investigation report is to record the facts. A fact is a statement that can be proven. (It may be proven false, but it is still classified as a factual statement.) Consider how to clearly distinguish between three basic types of statements.
>
> • Fact: A statement that can be proven.
>
> Example: The man has a bulge in his black leather jacket pocket.

- Inference: A conclusion based on reasoning.

  Example: The man is probably carrying a gun.

- Opinion: A personal belief.

  Example: Black leather jackets are cool.

  —From HESS/HESS ORTHMANN. *Criminal Investigation*, 9e (p. 78)
  Copyright © 2010 Cengage Learning.

About: _____

   Point: _____

2.

    Because of its great natural beauty and the warmth of its people, Brazil inevitably makes a powerful first impression. Those incredible sea- and landscapes, with their vivid hues of green, blue, and white! The beaches, the pulsing music, the year-round sunshine, the easygoing tropical vibe! Everything about Brazil seems designed to provoke wonderment at the presence of so much splendor and abundance. The fifth biggest country in the world, Brazil is larger than the continental United States, with some states that are bigger than any country in Europe, and it also ranks fifth in population, with nearly 200 million inhabitants. As a people, Brazilians blend European, African, Amerindian, and Asian backgrounds and values in a way found nowhere else on earth, and their vibrant culture also reflects that intermingling. Where is the largest concentration of people of Japanese descent outside Japan? In São Paulo, Brazil's most populous city and state. Where is the biggest concentration of people of Italian descent outside Italy? Also in São Paulo.

                —Rohter, *Brazil on the Rise*, p. 5

About: _____

   Point: _____

           _____

3.

    The economy is the institution that organizes the production, distribution, and exchange of goods and services. Conventionally, analysts divide the economy into three sectors. The primary sector includes farming, fishing, logging, and mining. In the secondary sector, raw materials are turned into finished goods; manufacturing takes place. Finally, in the tertiary sector, services are bought and sold. These services include the work of nurses, teachers, lawyers, hairdressers, computer programmers, and so forth. Often, the three sectors of the economy are called the "agricultural," "manufacturing," and "service" sectors.

—From BRYM/LIE. *Sociology*, 3e (p. 373) Copyright © 2010 Cengage Learning.

About: _____

Point: _____

4.

Each society has a set of emotional display rules that specify the circumstances under which various emotions should or should not be expressed. Children in many cultures, for example, learn that they are supposed to express happiness or gratitude when they receive a gift from grandma and, by all means, to suppress any disappointment they may feel should the gift turn out to be underwear. These emotional "codes of conduct" are rules that children must acquire and use in order to get along with other people and to maintain their approval.

—From SHAFFER. *Social and Personality Development*, 6e (p. 121)
Copyright © 2009 Cengage Learning.

About: _____

Point: _____

B. MAPP the topic and main idea of the following paragraphs from the textbook *Management*, 4th edition.

5.

Diversity in Organizations

Diversity means variety. Therefore, diversity exists in organizations when there is a variety of demographic, cultural, and personal differences among the people who work there and the customers who do business there. For example, step into Longo Toyota in El Monte, California, one of Toyota's top-selling dealerships, and you'll find diversity in the form of salespeople who speak Spanish, Korean, Arabic, Vietnamese, Hebrew, and Mandarin Chinese. In fact, the 60 salespeople at Longo Toyota speak 30 different languages. Surprisingly, this level of diversity was achieved without a formal diversity plan in place.

—From WILLIAMS. *Management*, 4e (pp. 384–385)
Copyright © 2004 Cengage Learning.

About: _____

Point: _____

_____

6.

> By contrast, some companies lack diversity, in their workforce, their customers, or both. For example, Denny's restaurants paid $54.4 million to settle a class-action lawsuit alleging discriminatory treatment of black customers at its restaurants. Edison International, a California-based utility company, paid more than $11 million for wrongly rejecting job applicants on the basis of race. And phone company Bell Atlantic paid a whopping $500 million to African American employees who were unfairly passed over for promotions. (Bell Atlantic and GTE have now merged and become Verizon Communications.)
>
> —From WILLIAMS. *Management*, 4e (p. 385) Copyright © 2004 Cengage Learning.

About: _____

Point: _____

7.

> Today, however, Denny's, Edison International, and Verizon have made great improvements in their level of diversity. At Denny's, all of the company's charitable contributions now go to organizations that benefit minorities. Furthermore, minorities now comprise 29.1 percent, 28.6 percent, and 24.6 percent of managers at Denny's, Edison International, and Verizon, respectively, and 47.4 percent, 44.9 percent, and 32 percent, respectively, of their workers. In fact, these companies have increased their diversity so much that they consistently make *Fortune* magazine's list of the 50 best companies for minorities.
>
> —From WILLIAMS. *Management*, 4e (p. 385) Copyright © 2004 Cengage Learning.

About: _____

Point: _____

C. Highlight the topic sentences in each paragraph in the following section from the textbook *Cultural Anthropology*, 6th edition.

8.

Mate Selection: Whom Should You Marry?

Every society defines a set of kin with whom a person is to avoid marriage and sexual intimacy. In no society is it permissible to mate with one's parents or siblings (that is, within the nuclear family), and in most cases the restricted group of kin is considerably wider. Beyond this notion of incest, people in all societies are faced with rules either restricting their choice of marriage partners or strongly encouraging the selection of certain people as desirable mates. These are known as rules of **exogamy** (marrying outside of a certain group) and **endogamy** (marrying within a certain group).

9.

Because of the universality of the incest taboo, all societies have rules for marrying outside a certain group of kin. These are known as the rules of exogamy. In societies such as the United States and Canada, the exogamous group extends only slightly beyond the nuclear family. It is considered either illegal or inadvisable to marry one's first cousin and, in some cases, one's second cousin, but beyond that one can marry other more distant relatives and encounter only mild disapproval. In societies that are based on unilineal descent groups, however, the exogamous group is usually the lineage, which can include hundreds of people, or even the clan, which can include thousands of people who are unmarriageable.

10.

In contrast to exogamy, which requires marriage outside one's own group, the rule of endogamy requires a person to select a mate from within one's own group. Hindu castes found in traditional India are strongly endogamous, believing that to marry below one's caste would result in serious ritual pollution. Caste endogamy is also found in a somewhat less rigid form among the Rwanda and Banyankole of eastern Central Africa. In addition to being applied to caste, endogamy can be applied to other social units, such as the village or local community, as was the case among the Inca of Peru, or to racial groups, as was practiced in the Republic of South Africa for much of the twentieth century.

—From FERRARO. *Cultural Anthropology*, 6e (pp. 213–214)
Copyright © 2006 Cengage Learning.

Focus on Education

College Education App

The following reading is linked to these fields of . . .

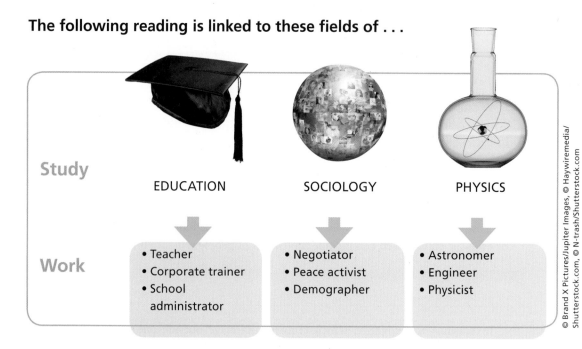

Study

EDUCATION   SOCIOLOGY   PHYSICS

Work

- Teacher
- Corporate trainer
- School administrator

- Negotiator
- Peace activist
- Demographer

- Astronomer
- Engineer
- Physicist

● Pre-Reading the Selection

The excerpt that begins on page 185 comes from the education textbook *So You Want to Be a Teacher?* The excerpt is titled "Technology and Learning."

Surveying the Reading

Survey the textbook selection that follows. Then check the elements that are included in this reading.

_____ Title

_____ Headings

_____ First sentences of paragraphs

_____ Words in bold or italic type

_____ Images and captions

Guessing the Purpose

Based on the source and the title of the reading selection, do you think the author's purpose is mostly to persuade, inform, or express? _____

Predicting the Content

Based on your survey, what are three things you expect the reading selection to discuss?

- _____
- _____
- _____

Activating Your Knowledge

Think about how you use technology while learning. What types of technology do you use and how do they help you learn? Does your school (or do your instructors) use technology to enhance learning? How?

- _____
- _____
- _____

● Reading with Pen in Hand

Students who annotate as they read are more successful than students who do not annotate. That's why you will annotate each reading in *Engage* as you read. In the reading that follows, use the following symbols:

 ★ or (Point)   to indicate a main idea

① ② ③   to indicate major details

Access the Reading CourseMate via **www.cengagebrain.com** to hear vocabulary words from this selection and view a video about this topic.

Technology and Learning

Reading Journal

1   Learning requires active engagement of the learner with the material to be learned. Many educators believe that technology encourages this process. In fact, in a national survey, more than half of the participating teachers said that technology helped them engage their students in learning, and 75% believed that technology use in schoolwork had increased students' achievement.

● Does technology help you become more engaged in learning?

2   But how exactly does technology help get students involved in learning? Entire books have been written on this subject, but here is

● Think of something in school you have learned better by doing rather than just hearing about.

one key point: because new technologies are interactive, it is easier to create environments in which students can learn by doing, receive feedback, and continually **refine** their understanding. Through this process, students take charge of their own learning. By integrating technology into the classroom, you promote students' passionate involvement in their own learning, allowing them to be adaptable and flexible and go beyond "education as usual."

refine If students are learning by doing and receiving immediate feedback, what will happen to their understanding? What does *refine* mean?

Three Ways Technology Supports Learning

3 The interactivity of computer-based technologies takes many forms, but from my perspective, there are three **paramount** ways it supports learning: by allowing students to deal with real-world problems as part of the curriculum; by expanding the possibilities for simulations and modeling; and by creating local and global communities of learners.

● Can you predict an example of each of the three ways based on your experience?

paramount The author says interactivity takes many forms, but narrows these down to three. Does she consider these three to be the most or least important? What does *paramount* mean?

Real-World Problems

4 Technology **fosters** the use of real-world, exciting problems in the classroom curriculum. Imagine you are working with middle school students on a unit about weather and global warming. Using the Internet, students can find real-time weather data about present conditions as well as archival data showing trends over time (see Figure 3.3). They can focus on a given part of the world or compare different areas.

● What technology do you use related to weather?

fosters Find the similar information in paragraph 3. The author goes a bit further here. What does the technology do?

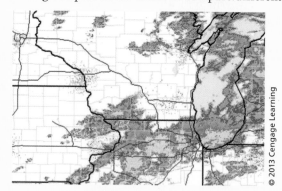

© 2013 Cengage Learning

Figure 3.3 An Interactive Weather Map

Online, interactive maps allow students to study weather developments in real time. This one from the National Weather Service shows a rainstorm in the Midwest.

5   Now imagine that a high school social studies class is exploring world population, comparing the number of births per day in China, India, and the United States. From the Internet, students gather the most current information related to population growth in these countries—data that have far-reaching **implications** for consumption of natural resources. This kind of real-world context makes the unit come alive for students. Yet the data retrieval requires only about as much time as it takes to read this paragraph!

● Do you know how many people live in each of these countries?

implications This word is composed of the verb *imply* + *-ation* + *-s*. What does *implications* mean?

Simulations and Modeling

6   Students can learn a great deal through simulations. (A simulation is a computer program or other procedure that imitates a real-world experience.) Often these imitate real-world activities that would be impossible to bring into the classroom. Say you want your students to understand the movements of planets in the solar system. Obviously you can't bring Mars and Venus to class, but you can use simulation software that shows the planets in motion and allows students to view the system from different positions. As another example, if you are teaching biology, your school system may not want to use dead animals, like frogs, for dissections, but you can turn to computer simulations of a frog dissection. In Net Frog (http://frog.edschool.virginia.edu), one of the most famous such tools, students can perform a simulated dissection online.

● Visualize the planets.

7   Another example is an online simulation of a **pendulum** that allows students to experiment with the way different factors influence the pendulum's speed. A similar experiment using a real pendulum would be difficult to set up in the classroom, and students' measurements of the speed would be tedious and inexact. With the simulation, they can change the weight, length, and maximum angle of the pendulum and instantly see the effect on the speed.

pendulum *Pendulum* is based on the root *pend*. What does pend mean?

8   Similarly, students often learn by creating models. For years, science students have created models of atoms and molecules, usually static ones made of plastic or Styrofoam pieces. With a computer, students can create atomic models in which the electrons move in cloud-like orbitals, and the software provides feedback about the correct number of protons and neutrons.

● Did you ever make a plastic or Styrofoam model in elementary or high school?

dilemmas If the students are looking for solutions to *dilemmas,* what do you think this word means?

● Have you ever worked with a social issue as described in this paragraph?

9   Do you suppose that simulations and models are useful mainly in the physical sciences? That's far from true. In social science, for example, simulations can model social **dilemmas** and engage students in finding their own creative solutions (see Figure 3.4). One software tool, Clover, was developed to provide middle school students with a way to look at important issues such as social justice, honesty, and conflict resolution. With Clover, students construct their own animated story and share it with their peers.

Figure 3.4 Simulating the Writing of the U.S. Constitution

This screenshot is from *The Constitution,* part of the Decisions, Decisions software series. In this simulation, students prepare a constitution for a fictional republic that resembles the United States in the 1780s.

10   Besides giving immediate feedback to users, many simulation and modeling technologies also provide opportunities for later reflection and discussion—and this point leads us to the third key benefit of technology.

Communities of Learners

11   Many classes have their own webpage, a site where teachers communicate with students and create an online extension of the classroom. The shared class webspace has many uses; announcements and schedules can be posted, and areas for more informal communication can be created.

● Do any of your classes use courseware or a blog?

12   On any given topic, teachers can promote focused discussions online through the use of discussion boards or forums. You may already have participated in such reflective discussions using Black-

board courseware or a similar tool in your college classes. Many teachers have added weblogs, or blogs, to their courses. Such technology-supported conversations can help students refine their thinking, and they help build a sense that everyone is working together in a learning community.

13   In fact, technology can easily extend the learning community beyond the immediate classroom. Students from around the world can collaborate to solve problems and share their cultures. Using technology, students from different places can work on the same projects with multiple solutions and collaborate with each other via shared classroom websites and e-mail. A deep sense of community is created as the groups work toward shared goals and communicate with one another about the strategies needed to solve a **mutual** problem.

—From KOCH. *So You Want to Be a Teacher?* (pp. 204–207)
Copyright © 2009 Cengage Learning.

● Have you had the opportunity to share your culture, or experience someone else's, through a class project?

mutual If several groups are working together, what does *mutual* mean?

● Comprehension Questions

Write the letter of the answer on the line. Then explain your thinking.

Main Idea

_____ 1. Which of the following best states the main idea of the passage?

     a. Technology is a requirement for successful learning in the classroom.

     b. Learning is supported by technology in several ways.

     c. Technology is interactive.

     d. Technology easily extends education beyond the physical classroom.

WHY? What information in the selection leads you to give that answer? _____

_____

_____

_____

_____ 2. Which of the following statements is the best main idea of the section entitled "Real-World Problems"?

a. Using the Internet, students can find real-time weather data about present conditions as well as archival data showing trends over time.

b. Now imagine that a high school social studies class is exploring world population, comparing the number of births per day in China, India, and the United States.

c. This kind of real-world context makes the unit come alive for students.

d. Technology fosters the use of real-world, exciting problems in the classroom curriculum.

WHY? What information in the selection leads you to give that answer? _____

_____

_____

_____

Supporting Details

_____ 3. Which of the following details is *least* relevant to the topic of this reading?

a. Technology allows students to deal with real-world problems as part of the curriculum.

b. Technology expands the possibilities for simulations and modeling.

c. Technology creates local and global communities of learners.

d. One software tool, Clover, was developed to provide middle school students with a way to look at important issues such as social justice, honesty, and conflict resolution.

WHY? What information in the selection leads you to give that answer? _____

_____

_____

_____

_____ 4. Which of the following is not supported by the details of the reading?

a. A learner must be actively involved in the learning process in order to learn.

b. Technology can create classroom frustrations when it does not work.

c. Technology can make learning about some things simpler.

d. Saving time is one advantage of using technology.

WHY? What information in the selection leads you to give that answer? _____

_____

_____

_____

Author's Purpose

_____ 5. What is the main purpose of the reading?

    a. To inform readers of the benefits of models and simulations.

    b. To inform readers of the various ways that technology supports learning.

    c. To persuade readers that they must use technology to improve their learning.

    d. To encourage readers with inspirational stories of successful employment of technology in education.

WHY? What information in the selection leads you to give that answer? _____

_____

_____

_____

_____

_____ 6. What is the purpose of the last sentence of paragraph 1?

    a. To explain the exact number of educators who use technology in their classrooms.

    b. To suggest that educators should use education more in their classrooms.

    c. To support the claim of the previous sentence.

    d. To show how knowledgeable the author is.

WHY? What information in the selection leads you to give that answer? _____

_____

_____

_____

_____

Relationships

_____ 7. What is the relationship between the major ideas of this reading?

    a. Comparison or similarity

    b. Cause and effect

    c. Process

    d. Contrast or difference

WHY? What information in the selection leads you to give that answer? _____

_____

_____

_____

_____ 8. What is the relationship between the first and second sentences of paragraph 6?

    a. Cause and effect

    b. Definition

    c. Space order

    d. Classification

WHY? What information in the selection leads you to give that answer? _____

_____

_____

_____

Fact, Opinion, and Inference

_____ 9. Which of the following statements is an opinion?

    a. As another example, if you are teaching biology, your school system may not want to use dead animals, like frogs, for dissections, but you can turn to computer simulations of a frog dissection.

    b. A similar experiment using a real pendulum would be difficult to set up in the classroom, and students' measurements of the speed would be tedious and inexact.

    c. Using the Internet, students can find real-time weather data about present conditions as well as archival data showing trends over time.

    d. Imagine you are working with middle school students on a unit about weather and global warming.

WHY? What leads you to give that answer? _____

_____

_____

_____

_____ 10. Which of the following is a logical inference based on the information in this reading?

    a. Overall, educators are resistant to technology due to the cost of new hardware and software.

    b. Traditional classrooms are more interactive than those utilizing technology.

    c. The author of this reading probably uses technology in his or her classroom.

    d. High schools are more likely to use new technologies than elementary or middle schools.

WHY? What leads you to give that answer? _____

_____

_____

_____

● Mapping the Reading

This reading includes headings and subheadings, which help give you a better understanding of how the reading is organized and how the ideas are related. Based on this information, fill out the following visual map.

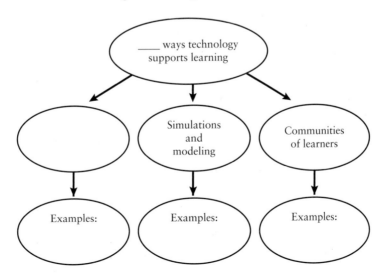

● Language in Use

The following words (or forms of them) were used in "Technology and Learning." Now you can use them in different contexts. Put a word from the box into the blank lines in the following numbered sentences.

> refine   paramount   foster   implicated
> pendulum   dilemma   mutual

1. The American Psychological Association released a study in February 2007 entitled *Sexualization of Girls.* The study showed that the number and frequency of sexualized images in the media is directly_____ in causing mental health issues in girls and women: eating disorders, self-image problems, and depression.

2. To _____ the meaning of *sexualization,* the psychologists said a sexualized person is someone who believes he or she has value only because of sexual appeal or behavior rather than other qualities, or someone who is "sexually objectified, e.g., made into a thing for another's sexual use."

3. The study also showed that parents may_____ sexualization in their daughters by linking self-worth to outer beauty, either through gender stereotyping or in more extreme ways, like giving a plastic surgery procedure as a high school graduation present.

4. This finding leaves many parents with the_____ of having to look at their own behaviors before laying blame on the "ever-evil" media.

5. The chair of the study, Dr. Eileen Zurbriggen, stated it was_____ that our society "replace all of these sexualized images with ones showing girls in positive settings—ones that show the uniqueness and competence of girls. The goal should be to deliver messages to all adolescents—boys and girls—that lead to healthy sexual development."

—APA Monitor, July/August 2011, "Protecting Girls"

● EASY Note Cards

Make a note card for each of the vocabulary words from the reading that you did not know. On one side, write the word. On the other side, divide the card into quarters and label them E, A, S, and Y. Add a word or phrase in each area so that you wind up with an example sentence, an antonym, a synonym, and, finally, a definition that shows you understand the meaning of the word with your logic. Remember that a synonym or antonym may have appeared in the reading.

Career Education App

● Pre-Reading the Selection

The excerpt that begins on page 196 comes from the *Bowling Green Daily News*. The excerpt is titled "School Texts :(: Educators Differ on How to Handle Cell Phones in Classrooms."

Surveying the Reading

Survey the selection that follows. Then check the elements that are included in this reading.

_____ Title

_____ Headings

_____ First sentences of paragraphs

_____ Words in bold or italic type

_____ Images and captions

Guessing the Purpose

Based on the source and the title of the reading selection, do you think the author's purpose is mostly to persuade, inform, or express? _____

Predicting the Content

Based on your survey, what are three things you expect the reading selection to discuss?

● _____

● _____

● _____

Activating Your Knowledge

Think about any experience you have had with your cell phone at school. What is your school's policy on cell phones? What different policies do you see among the instructors at your school?

● _____

● _____

● _____

● Reading with Pen in Hand

Students who annotate as they read are more successful than students who do not annotate. That's why you will annotate each reading in *Engage* as you read. In the reading that follows, use the following symbols:

★ or (Point)   to indicate a main idea

① ② ③   to indicate major details

Access the Reading CourseMate via www.cengagebrain.com to hear vocabulary words from this selection and view a video about this topic.

Reading Journal

School Texts :(: Educators Differ on How to Handle Cell Phones in Classrooms

Joanie Baker

© Robert Davies/Shutterstock.com

○ What does the image suggest about the reading?

morgue The quotation marks mean the word is not being used literally. What does *morgue* mean in this context?

confiscate What did the teacher *confiscate*? This should help you understand the meaning.

○ Is the situation described here similar to the one in your high school or college?

1   Fifteen-year-old Bethany Hill looked down into the "morgue" of cell phones at Warren East High School in Bowling Green, KY and saw her own with a sticky note attached that read "Bethany." The drawer sometimes holds as many as 12 phones a day after teachers confiscate the devices from students texting or pulling them out during class. Bethany, a sophomore at the school, said everyone who has a cell phone sends texts throughout the day, despite school regulations that say cell phones must be shut off and out of sight. School officials say the electronic note passing is becoming a problem as students use it for cheating, bullying and even starting "drama" in a whole other wing of the school. Some teachers note that excessive texting is having an impact on student writing and

communication skills, while some professors argue that it appears students can still **differentiate** between writing styles.

2   For Bethany, texting has become a form of addiction, she said. Averaging 13,000 texts a month, she said she has memorized the keypad to send messages **undetected** in class by pecking away from the safety of her bulky Carhartt jacket pocket. At least, she did until Friday. That's when a teacher noticed her looking at the screen and confiscated it for the first time, adding her device to the nearly 15 others housed at the front desk until the end of the day, when students are allowed to **retrieve** them. "When you have your phone, it's an urge to text and you have to control yourself not to get it out and text," Bethany said.

3   Some parents are taking advantage of parental controls on children's cell phones, allowing them to set time limits on what times the phones can send or receive texts. Some also can control to whom texts can be sent or from whom messages can be received during those times. But many parents are unaware of how the phones are being used in schools, Warren East Assistant Principal Edwin Moss said, until they are required to come to the school to pick them up. Each school has determined its own cell phone policy, which usually begins with a warning and confiscation, while repeat offenses eventually lead to in-school suspension. Jon Akers of the Kentucky Center for School Safety recently issued a newsletter to school officials giving reasons why cell phones should be **prohibited** in kindergarten through grade 12 schools. Akers lists 12 problems caused by students with phones, including bullying, cheating, secretly taking inappropriate photographs and even **facilitating** drug deals at school. Moss said texting has caused problems at the school such as students photographing a test and "texting" it to another student for answers.

4   School officials have looked at blocking cell phone signals in schools, Moss said, but found it cannot be legally done. In some states, cell phones are collected by school officials before class begins, then redistributed at the end of the day, Moss said. While officials look for solutions to solve the communication distraction in schools, others look to the long-term effects the thumb exercise is having on student writing. Bethany said she has caught herself slipping text **jargon** into her formal writing by occasionally using "C" rather than "see" or "U" for "you." While editing her personal narrative for class, she said she even noticed "mii" in the

differentiate The students are *differentiating* between writing styles. What does *differentiate* mean?

● How many texts do you send and/or receive each month?

undetected Use the prefix and the example context to determine the meaning of *undetected*.

retrieve The students do this at the end of each day. What does *retrieve* mean?

● What kinds of problems have you seen cell phones cause at school?

prohibited Based on the reasons in the next sentence, what does *prohibited* mean?

facilitating Use the context to determine the meaning of *facilitating*.

jargon Use the context to help determine the meaning of *jargon*.

● How has texting affected your formal writing?

deterioration Read Fife's opinion carefully. Use the context to determine the meaning of *deterioration.*

● What impression do you want to give in your writing on Facebook?

lines of her writing instead of "me." But the fact that she caught it leads some to believe that students can differentiate their text type from formal writing. And officials argue that the increased writing among students, especially if corralled by teaching opportunities, could enhance writing skills. Western Kentucky University professor Jane Fife, who teaches many levels of writing classes, said she hasn't noticed texting impacting student work, but rather sees it as a chance to teach reflection. "I hear those stories about their writing skills deteriorating, and I just don't see it," she said. "They really are aware of that and won't do it in a formal setting." Fife said one of her students wrote a reflection on his writing experiences, citing that he noticed some **deterioration** in his writing from texting, but then realized he was paying close attention to what he wrote on Facebook and MySpace.

5   "On Facebook, he would really read what he was writing because he didn't want to look like an idiot," she said. "He realized this was not a spur of the moment thing, like texting, it was going to be archived and a lot of people would see it." Fife said teaching the students to be reflective of what they are writing, whether a blog or Facebook entry, makes them better writers. "There's great potential for improving writing because any time you think about 'should I use this word' or 'how will this impact the reader,' you're being a more thoughtful writer," she said. "Just the fact that they are (texting or blogging) is not making them better writers, but if we can help them be aware of what they are doing in situations and how similar or different that is in formal writing, they can become better writers."

6   A study by the Pew Internet & American Life Project showed that while teens are writing more with e-mails, texts and social networks, they don't think of it as writing. "This disconnect matters because teens believe good writing is an essential skill for success and that more writing instruction at school would help them," the report stated. The survey of teens, ages 12 to 17, showed that while 85 percent use some form of electronic communication, 60 percent do not think of these "electronic texts" as writing. But 50 percent of the students surveyed admitted to using some informal writing styles or improper capitalization and punctuation in school assignments, such as using text shortcuts, like "LOL" for "laughing out loud." But the study reported more teens enjoy writing for school when it is similar to their form of communication. "In our

focus groups, teens said they are motivated to write when they can select topics that are relevant to their lives and interests, and report greater enjoyment of school writing when they have the opportunity to write creatively," the report read. "Teens also report writing for an audience motivates them to write and write well."

7   As Bethany tries to tackle her texting "addiction," her mother, April Witt, said she is investing in the $2 charge for parental controls and will be holding on to her daughter's phone during school. "It's become an **epidemic** for our children, it's sickening," she said. "But of course, I pay the bill and allow it."

—From Joanie Baker, "School Texts :(: Educators Differ on How to Handle Cell Phones in Classrooms." Bowling Green Daily News. Copyright © 2009 by MCCLATCHY-TRIBUNE REGIONAL NEWS. Reproduced with permission of MCCLATCHY-TRIBUNE REGIONAL NEWS.

○ What topics do you enjoy writing about?

epidemic What is Witt referring to? Use the context and your prior knowledge to determine the meaning of *epidemic*.

● Comprehension Questions

Write the letter of the answer on the line. Then explain your thinking.

Main Idea

_____ 1. Which of the following is the best topic sentence for paragraph 2?

a. For Bethany, texting has become a form of addiction, she said.

b. Averaging 13,000 texts a month, she said she has memorized the keypad to send messages undetected in class by pecking away from the safety of her bulky Carhartt jacket pocket.

c. At least, she did until Friday.

d. That's when a teacher noticed her looking at the screen and confiscated it for the first time, adding her device to the nearly 15 others housed at the front desk until the end of the day, when students are allowed to retrieve them.

WHY? What information in the selection leads you to give that answer? _____

_____

_____

_____

_____ 2. Which of the following statements is the best thesis statement of paragraphs 4 and 5?

    a. In some states, cell phones are collected by school officials before class begins, then redistributed at the end of the day, Moss said.

    b. While officials look for solutions to solve the communication distraction in schools, others look to the long-term effects the thumb exercise is having on student writing.

    c. Western Kentucky University professor Jane Fife, who teaches many levels of writing classes, said she hasn't noticed texting impacting student work, but rather sees it as a chance to teach reflection.

    d. Fife said teaching the students to be reflective of what they are writing, whether a blog or Facebook entry, makes them better writers.

WHY? What information in the selection leads you to give that answer? _____

_____

_____

_____

Supporting Details

_____ 3. Which of the following best supports the credibility of the author?

    a. The opinions of the school officials lend credibility to the author.

    b. The personal story of Bethany Hill makes the author more personable.

    c. The multiple examples of educators' views and the Pew study give the author credibility.

    d. The author's lack of statistical evidence weakens her credibility.

WHY? What information in the selection leads you to give that answer? _____

_____

_____

_____

_____ 4. Based on the details given in the reading selection, what is the best support for the claim that cell phones can be used for cheating?

    a. Akers lists 12 problems caused by students with phones, including bullying, cheating, secretly taking inappropriate photographs and even facilitating drug deals at school.

    b. Each school has determined its own cell phone policy, which usually begins with a warning and confiscation, while repeat offenses eventually lead to in-school suspension.

c. The drawer sometimes holds as many as 12 phones a day after teachers confiscate the devices from students texting or pulling them out during class.

d. Moss said texting has caused problems at the school such as students photographing a test and "texting" it to another student for answers.

WHY? What information in the selection leads you to give that answer? _____

_____

_____

_____

Author's Purpose

_____ 5. What is the overall purpose of the reading?

a. To horrify students with the possibility that their cell phones might be confiscated while they are at school.

b. To inform readers of the problems that cell phones are causing in the classroom and how educators are responding.

c. To persuade readers that cell phones are distracting and even dangerous for students.

d. To make readers aware of the technological capabilities of modern cell phones.

WHY? What information in the selection leads you to give that answer? _____

_____

_____

_____

_____ 6. What is the purpose of the text symbol :(: in the title?

a. It is cute and will be entertaining to the readers.

b. It will persuade the readers that the author is clever.

c. It illustrates both the positive and negative side to the issue of texting in school.

d. It was a typo; the author only intended to have a colon in the title.

WHY? What information in the selection leads you to give that answer? _____

_____

_____

_____

Relationships

_____ 7. What is the main relationship found in the following sentence? *But 50 percent of the students surveyed admitted to using some informal writing styles or improper capitalization and punctuation in school assignments, such as using text shortcuts, like "LOL" for "laughing out loud."*

   a. Comparison

   b. Cause and effect

   c. Example

   d. Contrast

WHY? What information in the selection leads you to give that answer? _____

_____

_____

_____

_____ 8. What is the relationship in paragraph 5?

   a. Cause and effect

   b. Comparison or similarity

   c. Space order

   d. Classification

WHY? What information in the selection leads you to give that answer?_____

_____

_____

_____

Fact, Opinion, and Inference

_____ 9. Which of the following statements contains an opinion?

   a. Some parents are taking advantage of parental controls on children's cell phones, allowing them to set time limits on what times the phones can send or receive texts.

   b. School officials have looked at blocking cell phone signals in schools, Moss said, but found it cannot be legally done.

   c. Only contemptuous students have memorized their phone keypads in order to send text messages undetected in class.

   d. "On Facebook, he would really read what he was writing because he didn't want to look like an idiot," she said.

WHY? What leads you to give that answer? _____

_____

_____

_____

_____ 10. Which of the following best states the author's point of view concerning cell phones?

a. She is against cell phone use in the classroom.

b. She is for cell phone use in the classroom.

c. There is not enough information to say whether the author is for or against cell phone use in the classroom.

d. The author would prefer cell phones not be used in her classroom, but she is flexible about some use.

WHY? What leads you to give that answer? _____

_____

_____

_____

● Mapping the Reading

Fill in the following APP from MAPP based on the details of the text and what you marked while reading.

About: _____

Point: _____

Proof: _____

_____

_____

Proof: _____

_____

_____

• Language in Use

The following words (or forms of them) were used in "School Texts :(: Educators Differ on How to Handle Cell Phones in Classrooms." Now you can use them in different contexts. Put a word from the box into the blank lines in the following numbered sentences.

> morgue   confiscate   differentiate   undetected   retrieve
> prohibits   facilitate   jargon   deterioration   epidemic

1. An estimated 285 million people worldwide deal with diabetes, which makes this disease an _____.

2. It is predicted that by 2020 half of the U.S. population could be affected by diabetes. Today about one in ten have diabetes, with many thousands more having _____ symptoms.

3. Diabetes _____ the body from regulating insulin and controlling blood sugar levels.

4. Diabetes comes in two types: type 1 and type 2. It is often difficult or confusing to _____ between the two.

5. In general, type 1 is a true disease and not preventable. Only about 15 percent of those with diabetes have type 1 and must take insulin in order to live. Type 2 is characterized by a _____ of the body's ability to produce insulin (usually caused by an unhealthy lifestyle) and is preventable.

• EASY Note Cards

Make a note card for each of the vocabulary words from the reading that you did not know. On one side, write the word. On the other side, divide the card into quarters and label them E, A, S, and Y. Add a word or phrase in each area so that you wind up with an example sentence, an antonym, a synonym, and, finally, a definition that shows you understand the meaning of the word with your logic. Remember that a synonym or antonym may have appeared in the reading.

Noticing Patterns of Supporting Details 4

Previewing the Chapter

Flip through the pages of Chapter 4, and read all the headings that are printed like this:

Why Is Reading Important?

What are the main ideas you want to understand from this chapter? Change each heading into a question that you can answer as you read.

- _____

- _____

- _____

- _____

Plan to come back and comment on what you've learned about each main idea when you have finished working through the chapter.

_____

_____

 To access additional course materials for *Engage,* including quizzes, videos, and more, please visit www.cengagebrain.com. At the CengageBrain.com home page, search for the ISBN of *Engage* (from the back cover of your book) using the search box at the top of the page. This will take you to the product page where these resources can be found.

 Videos Related to Readings

 Vocab Words on Audio

 Read and Talk on Demand

Read and Talk CRIMINAL JUSTICE TEXTBOOK

In college, reading is just one aspect of how you will share new ideas with others in your class. So the first reading in each chapter of this book is meant to give you the chance to talk about reading. Read the article, and then use the four discussion questions to talk about your ideas with your classmates and your instructor.

Access the Reading CourseMate via www.cengagebrain.com to hear a reading of this selection and view a video about this topic.

Gunfire on Campus: Lesson Learned

1   Just after 3 pm on February 14, 2008, Stephen Kazmierczak kicked in an exit door that led into a lecture hall on the campus of Northern Illinois University (NIU) in DeKalb, Illinois. The twenty-seven-year-old, armed with a 12-gauge shotgun and three handguns, proceeded to fire more than fifty rounds of buckshot and bullets into the terrified crowd of students before turning one of the weapons on himself. Including the shooter, six people died and sixteen were wounded as a result of Kazmierczak's violent outburst.

2   **Silver linings** were notably absent on that dark day, as the DeKalb community struggled to come to grips with the **carnage.** NIU's response to Kazmierczak's actions did, however, merit praise. Only ten months earlier, another university had become the

silver linings This is part of an expression: "Every cloud has a silver lining." What kind of attitude does this saying express? Is that the attitude expressed in the article?

carnage If you speak Spanish, you know that *carne* is meat. What do people do to animals to turn them into meat?

Scott Olson/Getty Images

scene of the deadliest shooting **rampage** in American history when Cho Seung Hui killed thirty-two people at Virginia Tech in Blacksburg, Virginia. Officials from that school came under widespread criticism for failing to notify the campus community about the first two deaths, providing Cho with several hours of preparation time before continuing his murderous assault in a separate building.

rampage When a person shoots in a crowded place, killing and injuring many others, what words would describe their actions? A *rampage* is an act of _____.

3   Putting into operation a plan designed in the wake of the Virginia Tech killings, NIU officials placed the campus on alert at 3:07 pm, with all students and personnel **confined** to dorms, classrooms, and administrative offices. Within twenty minutes, the university posted a warning on its Web site and through e-mail: "There has been a report of a possible gunman on campus. Get to a safe area and take precautions until given the all clear." By 4:14 pm, the school issued another message, announcing that the threat has passed. "Their response time was amazing," said one appreciative NIU student. "They had this whole campus on lockdown in seven minutes."

confined Based on the context in this sentence and the e-mailed words, what does *confined* probably mean?

—From GAINES/MILLER. *Criminal Justice in Action*, 5e (p. 4)
Copyright © 2011 Cengage Learning.

Talking About Reading

Respond in writing to the questions below, and then discuss your answers with your classmates.

1. Had you ever heard before of the situations described in the reading selection or any other similar situations? What did you hear?

_____

_____

_____

2. Has anyone on your campus ever shared information about what to do in case of a shooter? If so, what have they said to do? If not, what do you think you should do?

_____

_____

_____

3. Some states allow students to carry concealed weapons on campus so they can defend themselves against such shootings. Is this a good idea? Why or why not?

_____

_____

_____

4. What role would you expect instructors to play in these kinds of dangerous situations? Would you expect them to know better than you what to do? Why or why not?

_____

_____

_____

What Is the Proof? The Supporting Details

You have learned to ask questions that will lead you to the topic and the main idea of a reading selection. When the topic and main idea appear together in the same sentence, that sentence is called the **topic sentence.**

Asking "What is the proof?" leads you to the author's **supporting details.** The details are called "supporting" because they give support—evidence or proof—for the author's point. The support might consist of examples, statistics, facts, anecdotes (little stories), or expert opinions. To find the supporting details in a paragraph, turn the topic sentence into a question and look for the answers. Each one should be a supporting detail. Let's look at an example from a criminal investigation textbook. The topic sentence is underlined.

The behavior of an armed robber is unpredictable. In some cases when the victim resists, the robber may flee without completing the robbery. In one case, a man armed with a shotgun demanded and obtained $10,000 from a bank teller. Instead of leaving, he talked to the teller for 15 minutes, telling her that he was drunk and considering suicide. Then he handed the money back to the teller and walked out of the bank. In another case, a robber handed a bank teller a note that said, "Please put the money in this bag and no one will get hurt. Thank you very much." The teller called a bank guard and handed him the note. The guard read the note and told the robber, "Get out, you bum, or I'll blow your brains out." The robber quickly left the bank. In other instances, however, resisting victims have been injured or killed.

—From HESS/HESS ORTHMANN. *Criminal Investigation*, 9e (p. 379)
Copyright © 2010 Cengage Learning.

If you were to fill in the APP in MAPPS, it would look like this:

About: The behavior of an armed robber

   Point: is unpredictable.

   To find the proof, form a question from the topic sentence: How is the behavior of an armed robber unpredictable? Look for each answer the author gives.

   Proof: 1. In one case, a man armed with a shotgun demanded and obtained $10,000 from a bank teller. Instead of leaving, he talked to the teller for 15 minutes, telling her that he was drunk and considering suicide. Then he handed the money back to the teller and walked out of the bank.

   2. In another case, a robber handed a bank teller a note that said, "Please put the money in this bag and no one will get hurt. Thank you very much." The teller called a bank guard and handed him the note. The guard read the note and told the robber, "Get out, you bum, or I'll blow your brains out." The robber quickly left the bank.

   3. In other instances, however, resisting victims have been injured or killed.

   Thinking about the supporting details will help you understand an author's point and decide whether you agree with it.

INTERACTION 4–1 | Map the Details

Reread paragraphs 2, 3, and 5 from Interaction 3–4 in Chapter 3. **Mark** the topic and the main idea in each paragraph if you haven't already done so. Then form a question from each of the topic sentences, and complete the following outlines with the supporting details.

1. Paragraph 2 on page 157 (Interaction 3–4)

   About: _____

   Point: _____

   Form a question from the topic sentence: _____

   _____

   Proof: 1. _____

   2. _____

   3. _____

   4. _____

2. Paragraph 3 on page 157 (Interaction 3–4)

   About: _____

   Point: _____

   Form a question from the topic sentence: _____

   _____

   Proof: 1. _____

   _____

   2. _____

   _____

   3. _____

   _____

   4. _____

   _____

3. Paragraph 5 on page 158 (Interaction 3–4)

About: _____

Point: _____

Form a question from the topic sentence: _____

_____

Proof: 1. _____

_____

2. _____

_____

3. _____

_____

4. _____

_____

_____

Section Review: What Is the Proof? The Supporting Details

A. What kinds of information might you find as supporting details?

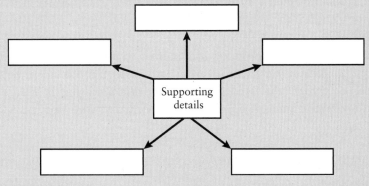

B. What two steps can you take to find the supporting details?

Step 1:

Step 2:

Major versus Minor Details

There are two types of supporting details: major and minor. Major details directly support the main idea. Minor details support the major details. Imagine a cheerleading squad or a gymnastics team making a human pyramid. The star of the show is on the very top. The star is supported by two other people holding him or her up. In turn, those two people are supported by three people holding them up. There can be as many levels of supporters as the athletes can form.

© Trinity Mirror/Mirrorpix/Alamy

In a reading, the star is the main idea. The ideas holding up the main idea are the major details, and the ideas holding up the major details are the minor details. There can be just a few layers of information in a reading, or there can be many. The number of levels depends on how long and how complex a reading is.

Let's look at the difference between major and minor details by examining the following passage.

1   Currently there are two approaches to schooling that influence student assessment strategies. The traditional approach, which is associated with B.F. Skinner and Edward L. Thorndike, is based on the idea that students need to be reinforced for their learning. Schools that follow this model tend to teach academic fields separately (e.g., math, English, science, history), breaking down the content into small chunks of information that are taught in sequence. This particular model focuses on tests, quizzes, and homework that measure declarative knowledge and skills and uses traditional grades as measures of student achievement.

2   In the progressive approach to learning, however, they learn by doing. Students are encouraged to ask questions, work cooperatively, and learn in mentor-apprenticeship relationships. Students in this learning situation are more likely to be assessed via performance assessments and authentic assessments. **Performance assessments** measure how well a particular skill is completed, be it rebuilding a car engine or writing a formal letter. **Authentic assessments** imitate real-world experiences.

—From HUERTA. *Educational Foundations* (p. 201) Copyright © 2008 Cengage Learning.

Here is a MAPP of these two paragraphs:

About: Currently there are two approaches to schooling

Point: that influence student assessment strategies.

Form a question from the topic sentence: What two approaches to schooling influence student assessment strategies?

The supporting details that directly answer the question are the major supporting details.

Proof: 1. The traditional approach (major supporting detail).

Proof: 2. The progressive approach (major supporting detail).

You can form a question by combining the first major detail with the main idea: How does the traditional approach influence student assessment strategies?

The details that answer the question are the minor supporting details.

a. Schools that follow this model tend to teach academic fields separately (e.g., math, English, science, history), breaking down the content into small chunks of information that are taught in sequence.

b. This particular model focuses on tests, quizzes, and homework that measure declarative knowledge and skills and uses traditional grades as measures of student achievement.

Form a question by combining the second major detail with the main idea: How does the progressive approach influence student assessment strategies?

The details that answer the question are minor supporting details.

a. Students are encouraged to ask questions, work cooperatively, and learn in mentor-apprenticeship relationships.

b. Students in this learning situation are more likely to be assessed via performance assessments and authentic assessments.

This minor supporting detail is then supported by two other points.

i. **Performance assessments** measure how well a particular skill is completed, be it rebuilding a car engine or writing a formal letter.

ii. **Authentic assessments** imitate real-world experiences.

In general, **proof** refers to both major and minor supporting details. However, only the major details provide direct proof for the main idea and give organizational structure to the paragraph. The minor details give extra information about the major details.

| INTERACTION 4–2 | Map the Minor Details |

A. Read the following selection from a business ethics textbook. Mark the APP within each paragraph.

Place brackets around the [topic].
Underline the <u>main idea</u>.
Use circled numbers to indicate the major supporting details ①②③.

B. Fill in the MAPP.

1　　One way that business assumes responsibilities to consumers for product quality and reliability is through *warranties,* which are obligations to purchasers that sellers assume. There are two types of warranties. **Express warranties** are the claims that sellers explicitly state—for example, that a product is "shrinkproof" or will require no maintenance for two years. Express warranties include assertions about the product's character, assurances of product durability, and other statements on warranty cards, labels, wrappers, and packages or in the advertising of the product. Many companies offer detailed warranties that are very specific about what defects they cover. Few go as far as L. L. Bean does with its "100% guarantee," which allows customers to return any purchase at any time for a full refund if it proves unsatisfactory.

2　　**Implied warranties** include the claim, implicit in any sale, that a product is fit for its ordinary, intended use. The law calls this the implied warranty of merchantability. It's not a promise that the product will be perfect; rather, it's a guarantee that it will be of passable quality or suitable for the ordinary purpose for which it is used. Implied warranties can also be more specific. For example, it's an implied warranty when the seller knows that a buyer has a particular purpose in mind and is relying on the seller's superior skill or judgment to furnish goods adequate for that purpose.

—From SHAW. *Cengage Advantage Books: Business Ethics,* 7e (p. 226)
Copyright © 2011 Cengage Learning.

About: _____

Point: _____

Form a question from the topic sentence: _____

_____

Proof: 1. _____

Form a question from the major supporting detail: _____

_____

    a. _____

    _____

    _____

    b. _____

    _____

    _____

    c. _____

    _____

    _____

    d. _____

    _____

    _____

Proof: 2. _____

Form a question from the major supporting detail: _____

_____

    a. _____

    _____

        i. _____

    _____

    _____

ii. _____

_____

_____

b. _____

_____

_____

i. _____

_____

_____

| INTERACTION 4–3 | Identify the Proof in an Article |

A. Mark the APP in this selection about Zumba.

Place brackets around the [topic].
Underline the <u>main idea</u>.
Use circled numbers to indicate the major supporting details ①②③.

B. Fill in the MAPP. Put only the major supporting details under "Proof."

Hint: Find the APP of paragraph 1 separately, and then find the APP of paragraphs 2–6 together.

Zumba Secrets: How to Get a Workout at Da Club This Weekend

Jenny Everett

1   It's hard not to be intrigued by Zumba—the popular Latin dance-inspired fitness craze that more than seven-and-half million people have tried worldwide. The name alone is interesting and, lately, it seems like everyone is talking about it. On top of new versions of the class, including Aqua Zumba and Zumba Toning (more strength-focused), one of the reasons for the buzz is that Zumba Fitness has started offering classes in nightclubs—starting with SOB's in downtown New York City. You literally show up in the evening post-work (generally, around 7 p.m.), a Zumba instructor leads you through a dance party, then you stay, have a drink (doesn't have to be alcohol) and mingle. Count us in!

2   We talked to Edmee Cherdieu d'Alexis, a Zumba instructor and Group Fitness Manager at Equinox in New York City, to find out how you can tweak your dance party routine (whether it's in your living room or at a local hot spot) to add some bonus fat burning to your weekend fun.

Copyright © 2011 Zumba Fitness, LLC | Zumba®, Zumba Fitness® and the Zumba Fitness logos are registered trademarks of Zumba Fitness, LLC | 800 Silks Run, Suite 2310, Hallandale, FL 33009

3   **Treat it like an interval workout:** A Zumba class can burn 500 to 1000 calories an hour—and so can your average night of dancing. "What makes Zumba such a great workout is that you're constantly moving," says Cherdieu d'Alexis. "It's a cardio work-out, but on top of endurance it also improves agility and strengthens your lower body, legs, hips, butt, and thighs, which women love." If you're out dancing with your friends, take breaks as you need to—rest, socialize, flirt, whatever—then jump back in. This pat-tern of raising your heart rate and recovering is a great way to boost your metabolism.

4   **Go big:** "Zumba is all about the music and the dancing and having fun," says Cherdieu d'Alexis. "Try to make your dance movements a little bigger than you usu-ally would and focus on making them crisper. This will make it more intense." A little bit goes a long way, so don't feel like you need to flail to the point of freaking out the people around you!

5   **Work on your posture:** According to Cherdieu d'Alexis, it's key to brace your core and be conscious about doing so as you dance. This will not only help you get an abs workout (as you bend forward and back, and rotate side to side), but also make you more agile and light on your feet.

6   **Jump, jump!** Every time you jump, it amps up your heart rate. Generally, people wear sneakers to Zumba classes, however, Cherdieu d'Alexis says that a pair of cute supportive heels (might want to leave the 5-inch stilettos at home) are totally manageable on the dance floor.

        —Jenny Everett, "Zumba Secrets: How to Get a Workout at Da Club This Weekend."
Reprinted by permission of Condé Nast Publications.

*The facts in this article were accurate as of August 2010.

About (paragraph 1): _____

    Point: _____

    Form a question from the topic sentence: _____

_____

Proof: 1. _____

2. _____

3. _____

About (paragraphs 2–6): _____

Point: _____

Form a question from the topic sentence: _____

_____

Proof: 1. _____

2. _____

3. _____

4. _____

Section Review: Major versus Minor Details

A. Show the relationship between the topic, main idea, major supporting details, and minor supporting details in the following outline.

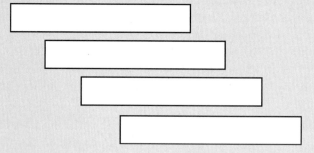

B. As you move from topic to main idea to major supporting details to minor supporting details, the ideas become:

More general   More specific

Patterns that Organize Supporting Details

Identifying patterns is a significant help in making sense of what you read. It can help you forecast what kinds of information you will be reading about, which will help you sort through all the ideas the author writes about to find the ones that are most important. This ability to sort more important ideas from less important ones is the most crucial skill you can develop to improve your reading comprehension.

The major details of a paragraph or longer passage are often organized in a certain pattern. For example, if you buy a new TV, it comes with directions about how to set it up. The directions are written in the order in which you should complete the steps. This step-by-step order is called **process order.** The arrangement of the information is directly related to what you need to do with it. Think how difficult it would be to set up the TV if you had to guess which steps should come first, in the middle, and last.

At times, you will find that a topic sentence (of a paragraph) or a thesis statement (of a longer piece of writing) forecasts not only the content of the major supporting details but also the pattern in which they are organized. Here is an example of such a sentence:

> Most anthropologists distinguish three types of societies based on levels of social inequality.
>
> —From FERRARO. *Cultural Anthropology*, 6e (p. 322) Copyright © 2006 Cengage Learning.

This is the thesis statement for a section of an anthropology textbook chapter. First, you can form a question from it:

What three types of societies based on levels of social inequality do most anthropologists distinguish?

Second, you can mentally prepare a structure for the answers to this question, which you would learn by reading the piece. Your mental structure for the thesis statement above would look like this:

First type: ?

Second type: ?

Third type: ?

or like this:

| Type 1: ? | Type 2: ? | Type 3: ? |

As you read the section, you see that it is divided into three smaller subsections. The first is called "Egalitarian Societies," the second is titled "Rank Societies," and the third is called "Stratified Societies." If we put these into our MAPP format, it looks like this:

About: Societies based on levels of social inequality

    Point: Most anthropologists distinguish three types of these.

        Proof: 1. Egalitarian societies

                    2. Rank societies

                    3. Stratified societies

However, you could also arrange the proof more visually to help you remember that these are three individual types that do not overlap:

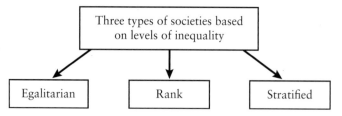

You could then add the minor supporting details of each type directly under each heading, which would later allow for easier comparisons among the three. For example, you could add the definition of each one:

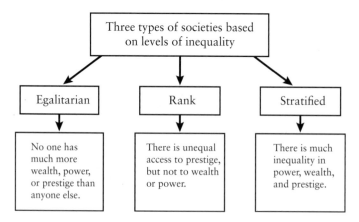

Notice how this format allows you to easily review the three types and remember how they differ.

| INTERACTION 4–4 | Form Mental Structures from Main Ideas |

A. Turn each topic sentence or thesis statement into a question.

B. Make a list or diagram to show what kinds of ideas you would be looking for in order to answer the question. Use question marks to indicate the missing answers.

1. There are three main causes of the Civil War.

   Question: _____

   Kinds of answers you would look for: _____

2. Management teams are composed of five kinds of leaders.

   Question: _____

   Kinds of answers you would look for: _____

3. Setting up your new DVR requires just a few steps.

   Question: _____

   Kinds of answers you would look for: _____

Types of Organizational Patterns

Each organizational pattern reflects a different kind of thought process that people have based on their natural curiosity. Each one answers a certain kind of general question—the kinds of questions people ask each other every day.

- What **kinds** of cameras are there? (classification pattern)
- How is the Toyota Matrix **similar to** the Corolla? (comparison pattern)
- How is Jennifer Aniston's acting **different from** her father John's acting? (contrast pattern)
- **What is** a tax credit? (definition pattern)
- What are some **examples** of songs that Taylor Swift has recorded this year? (example pattern)
- **Why** did Denzel Washington get a Golden Globe award for his role in *American Gangster*? (cause pattern)
- How does your daughter feel **when** you treat her that way? (effect pattern)
- OMG, what happened **after** that? (time pattern)
- **Where** in the world is Carmen Sandiego? (space pattern)

As you can see in some of these examples, certain words and phrases are signals that a certain pattern is being called for. For instance, in the second example, the words *similar to* signal that a comparison is being asked for. These are called **signal words,** or **transitions.** Not all paragraphs include signal words, but when they do, these words can help you figure out what relationship between the ideas the author is establishing.

Classification: What Kinds Are There?

Classification answers the question "What kinds are there?" Suppose someone asks you, "What kinds of TV programs do you like?" You might answer, "I like sitcoms, reality shows, and cartoons." These are categories, or types, of TV shows. They are not specific examples of such shows.

Reading Strategy for Classification

As you read, mentally slot the details into the following categories:

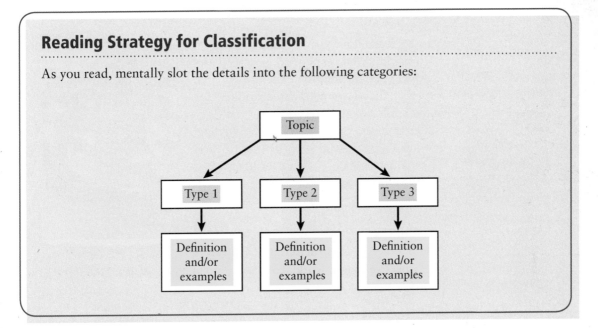

Signal Words (Transitions) for Classification

When you are reading, look for phrases that signal classification into types.

- several kinds
- certain forms
- three patterns
- four types
- different groups
- separate categories
- divided into
- classified by
- split up

Classification Paragraph

Study this paragraph about learning theories. Notice that the color of the highlights matches the colors used in the diagram above. The topic, signal words, and names of the four kinds of learning theories are highlighted.

Learning theories are formal ideas about how learning may happen. Over the past hundred years or so, psychologists and others have used the developmental theories of their time to describe conditions that they have considered optimal for learning. These fall into four main categories. **Behaviorism** is an approach in which students learn the correct responses through rewards and punishments handed out by the teacher. **Cognitive learning theories** center on students' active role in learning. Students form symbolic mental constructions to help them process information. **Social learning theories** are somewhat learner-centered. In this theory, learners' internal mental processes are important, but learning also occurs through experiences shared with others. **Constructivism** is entirely learner-centered. Learners construct individual perspectives of the world, based on individual experiences and internal knowledge structures.

© Tim Pannell/CORBIS

—From KOCH. *So You Want to Be a Teacher?* (pp. 94, 102)
Copyright © 2009 Cengage Learning.

Comparison and Contrast: How Are These the Same? How Do They Differ?

Comparisons show how two things are similar. Contrasts show how they are different. Sometimes the word *comparison* is used more generally to indicate both of these organizational patterns.

Reading Strategy for Comparison and Contrast

Mentally or on paper, form two lists, one for each item being compared or contrasted in the reading selection under "Comparison Paragraphs." As the author gives each piece of information for an item, place it in the appropriate list.

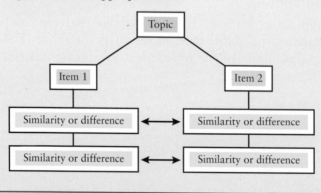

Signal Words (Transitions) for Comparisons

As you read, check for words that signal comparison.

- the same, identical
- similar, similarly, similarity
- alike, like, likewise
- both
- not only . . . but also

Comparison Paragraphs

Study the following paragraphs on Google and Yahoo! The topic, the items being compared, and the signal words are highlighted.

Photo by Eric Sander

Michael Grecco/Hulton Archive/Getty Images

1 Two incredibly successful Web search engines—Google and Yahoo!—both had their beginnings in academia. In fact, they were both invented by students at Stanford University.

2 The future founders of Google met at Stanford. Larry Brin was a second-year student in computer science, and Sergey Page was an engineering major who would attend Stanford to get his Ph.D. Page decided to work on the idea of ranking Web sites according to how many other sites link to them, as well as on how important each of those sites is based on the number of sites linking to *them*. This idea posed a difficult mathematical challenge, but Brin's incredible math skills were up to the task. He and Page soon realized that they had created a search engine that often gave better results than existing search engines. Not only that, but they realized that the larger the Web grew, the better their search engine would become because of the way it was structured. So they called their search engine "Google," which is the number 1 followed by 100 zeroes, to express this thought.

3 Similarly to the Google founders, the two creators of Yahoo! also attended Stanford University. David Filo and Jerry Wang were both Ph.D. students in electrical

engineering. They started lists of the Web sites they particularly liked visiting, and as their lists grew longer and longer, they had to divide them into categories. As the categories filled up, they had to divide those into subcategories. Other people, first those at Stanford and later many others, started using Filo's and Wang's subject directories. These creative students had developed bookmarks, which then became the basis of Yahoo!'s later subject lists, a hugely popular way to search the Web. The word "Yahoo" means "Yet Another Hierarchical Officious Oracle," so just like Google's name, it describes very well Yahoo!'s basic method of organization.

4   Although their products are organized differently, both Google and Yahoo! help people search the Web effectively and efficiently. And both search engines are the products of students who later became billionaires for their famous ideas.

Signal Words (Transitions) for Contrasts

As you read, check for words that signal contrast.

- differs from, differs by, a difference
- contrasts with, in contrast, to the contrary
- on the one hand . . . on the other hand
- however, although, but, while
- instead, rather
- distinguishes, distinguish between

Contrast Paragraph

Study this paragraph. The two aspects of art (form and content) are being contrasted, and the signal words are highlighted.

Discussions of art often distinguish between two aspects, form and content. Form is the purely visual aspect, the manipulation of the various elements and principles of design. Content implies the subject matter, story, or information that the artwork seeks to communicate to the viewer. Content is what artists want to say; form is how they say it. The poster reprinted here can be appreciated for a successful relationship between form and content.

—From LAUER/PENTAK. *Design Basics*, 8e (p. 5)
Copyright © 2012 Cengage Learning.

Definition: What Is This? What Does It Mean?

Definition tells what a word or idea means—what it is. Definitions include the term being taught and a description of its meaning. Often, examples are given to illustrate the meaning of the term. Sometimes, illustrations of what the term does *not* mean are also provided.

Reading Strategy for Definition

As you read a definition, mentally slot the various parts of the definition into these categories:

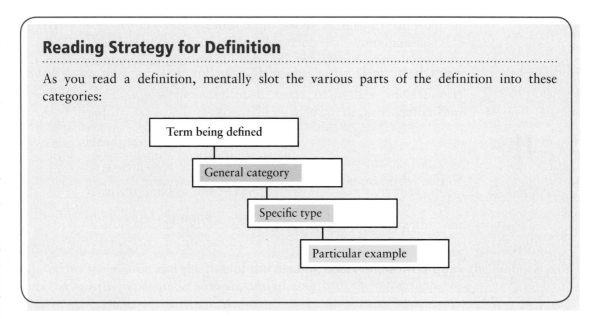

Signal Words (Transitions) for Definitions

As you read, look for words that suggest definitions are being used.

- is, that is
- is called, can be understood as, refers to
- means, has come to mean
- defined as
- consists of
- is not; rejected the idea (used to show what a term does not mean)

Definition Paragraph

Study this paragraph about Gestalt psychology. The parts of the definition are highlighted. Notice that the colors of the highlights are the same as the colors in the diagram above.

Your ability to perceive something in more than one way is the basis of **Gestalt psychology,** a field of psychology that focuses on our ability to perceive overall patterns. *Gestalt* (geh-SHTALT) is a German word meaning pattern or configuration. The founders of Gestalt psychology rejected the idea that a perception can be broken down into its component parts. A melody broken up into individual notes is no longer a melody. Their slogan was, "The whole is different from the sum of its parts."

—From KALAT. *Introduction to Psychology*, 9e (p. 128) Copyright © 2011 Cengage Learning.

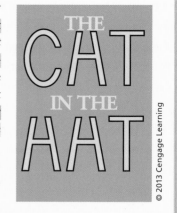

Examples: What Are Examples of This General Idea?

Examples give the specific, down-to-earth details that help readers understand the general statements a writer is making. Examples help make general statements come alive. Examples are often provided for definitions as well.

Reading Strategy for Examples

As you read, create a mental list of the examples the author is providing.

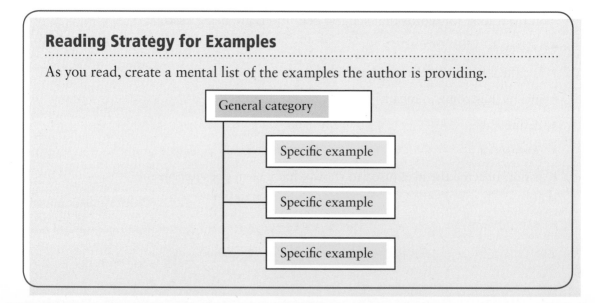

Signal Words (Transitions) for Examples

As you read, check for words that signal examples are being used.

- for instance,
- to illustrate,
- namely,
- for example,

Note that example phrases are often followed by a comma.

Example Paragraph

Study this paragraph. The topic sentence is highlighted, and so are the signal words for examples.

Students in elementary and high schools do better when their parents are involved in their education. For example, students excel more, regardless of socioeconomic status, cultural background, or the parents' own educational opportunities or achievements. As another example, students display more positive attitudes toward school when their parents are involved.

—From HUERTA. *Educational Foundations* (p. 193)
Copyright © 2008 Cengage Learning.

© Rob Marmion/Shutterstock.com

An Important Note About the Listing Pattern and Reading Tests

Some reading exit tests include a pattern called *enumeration* or *listing*. Here is an example:

Fruit includes apples, oranges, and grapes.

The three fruits are listed in a series, with commas between the words and an *and* before the last word. You can see why this pattern would be called *listing* or *enumeration* (which means "numbering of"). Apples are one fruit, oranges are a second, and grapes are a third.

When you think about the sentence, though, you will see that two other patterns also indicate the relationship between fruit on the one hand and apples, oranges, and grapes on the other:

- Classification, because apples, oranges, and grapes are kinds of fruit.

- Example, because apples, oranges, and grapes are all examples of fruit.

The listing pattern overlaps with the patterns of classification and example. If you are taking a reading test that includes "enumeration" or "listing" as an answer choice, see if "classification" or "example" is also a choice that makes sense. If one of these more precise words makes sense, choose it. If they aren't listed or don't make sense, select "enumeration" or "listing."

Cause and Effect: What Made This Happen? What Does This Lead To?

Cause-and-effect paragraphs may focus on the causes of an event, in which case they answer a question such as "What made this happen?" or "What's the reason this occurred?" When it focuses on the effects that could come about because of something else, a cause-and-effect paragraph answers a question like "What does this lead to?" or "What is the result of this action?"

A cause-and-effect paragraph may describe how a single cause leads to multiple effects, or how multiple causes create a single effect. A piece of writing may even describe how one cause leads to an effect, which then becomes the cause of a second effect, which then becomes the cause of a third effect, and so on. Think of dominoes falling. This type of organization is called a causal chain.

© oksana2010/Shutterstock.com

A causal chain

Reading Strategy for Cause and Effect

As you read, visualize that causes and effects are linked by arrows:

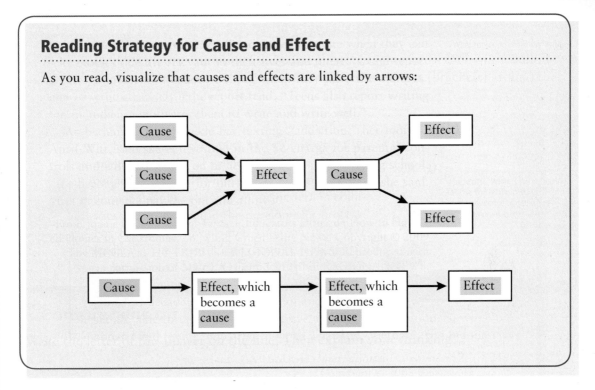

Signal Words (Transitions) for Cause and Effect

As you read, look for the words that signal cause and effect. The lines in the columns below tell you whether the cause or effect precedes or follows the signal word.

Signal Words for Causes

_____ causes

_____ creates

_____ allows for

_____ leads to

_____ makes

_____ produces

are due to _____

because _____

reason is _____

Signal Words for Effects

causes _____

leads to _____

makes (or made) _____

consequences are _____

produces _____

_____ depends on

_____ were the effects

_____ is the result

thus _____

Cause-and-Effect Paragraph

Study this paragraph. The causes and effects are highlighted, and so are the signal words for causes and effects. Which effects become causes?

Methamphetamine is an addictive stimulant that is less expensive and possibly more addictive than cocaine or heroin. It has become America's leading drug problem. Methamphetamine causes the release of large amounts of dopamine, which creates a sensation of euphoria, increased self-esteem, and alertness. Users also report a marked increase in sexual appetite, which often leads to risky sexual behaviors while under the drug's influence. Even small amounts of methamphetamine can increase wakefulness and physical activity, depress appetite, and raise body temperature. Other effects on the central nervous system include irritability, insomnia, confusion, tremors, convulsions, anxiety, paranoia, and aggressiveness.

—From HALES. *An Invitation to Health*, 12e (p. 323)
Copyright © 2007 Cengage Learning.

Photo by Jonathan Torgovnik/Getty Images

Time Order: When Did That Happen? What Steps Does It Take?

Time order tells readers when things happen (yesterday, this morning) and in what order (first, second, third). Two kinds of writing often use time order: narrative writing (also called narration) and process writing.

Reading Narrative Writing: When Did That Happen?

One kind of time order is called **narration,** or story. In narrative writing, the author uses time order to show what events a person, character, or group experiences. Often, time-order paragraphs do not have a topic sentence. This is especially true in fiction. However, the author deliberately presents details in a certain order to create a certain impression.

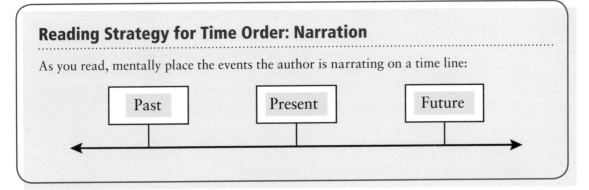

Reading Strategy for Time Order: Narration

As you read, mentally place the events the author is narrating on a time line:

Past	Present	Future

Signal Words (Transitions) for Time Order

As you read, look for phrases that will help you figure out when things have occurred.

- before, during, after
- first, second, third
- next, then, later
- preceding, following, afterward
- as soon as, when, while, until, since
- days, dates, and times, such as Monday through Friday; on March 17, 2010; since 2009; during the week

Time Order: Narrative Paragraph

Study this paragraph. The signal words for time order are highlighted.

Shadows dance upon walls, and people look at images that tell of their lives and imagined tales and dreams. At the dawn of humanity, people crawled, torches in hand, into deep caves to paint and then see images of hunters and their prey. Since then, we have returned time and again to darkened spaces to watch stories illuminated upon walls. Now, you can sit in plush seats and look up at the light and shadows playing as the sounds that accompany them resound in a man-made cavern.

—From CASHINGHINO. *Moving Images: Making Movies, Understanding Media* (p. 121) Copyright © 2010 Cengage Learning.

© Fox Searchlight Pictures

Reading Process Writing: What Steps Does It Take?

A second kind of time order is called **process**. In process writing, the author tells readers what steps need to occur to achieve a goal and in what order. Sometimes, words like *first step, second phase, next stage,* and *finally* are used to show the main steps. Numbers may also mark the steps or stages of the process.

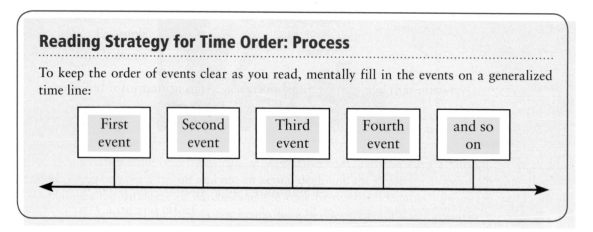

Reading Strategy for Time Order: Process

To keep the order of events clear as you read, mentally fill in the events on a generalized time line:

| First event | Second event | Third event | Fourth event | and so on |

Signal Words (Transitions) for Process Writing

As you read, look for phrases that will help you figure out in what order steps have to occur in order to achieve the desired result.

- first step, second step, third step; first stage, second stage; first phase, second phase
- first, next, then, eventually, last
- start, continue, end
- any of the words from the narration list on page 233

Time Order: Process Paragraph

Study this paragraph. Signal words for process writing are highlighted.

If you have been sedentary, it's best to launch a walking program **before** attempting to jog or run. **Start** by walking for 15 to 20 minutes three times a week at a comfortable pace. **Continue** at this same level **until** you no longer feel sore or unduly fatigued the day after exercising. **Then** increase your walking time to 20 to 25 minutes, speeding up your pace as well.

—From HALES. *An Invitation to Health*, 12e (p. 120)
Copyright © 2007 Cengage Learning.

© iStockphoto.com/Sportstock

Space Order: Where Are Things Located?

Space order, also called spatial order, shows readers where things are located in space. Some signal words for space order are *above, below, behind, in front of,* and *near.* Space order is often used in **descriptions.** In a description, the author asks the reader to use sight, hearing, and touch to imagine experiencing events or items.

Reading Strategy for Space Order

As you read, mentally use your senses, especially your sense of sight, to re-create the scene the author is describing.

Signal Words (Transitions) for Space Order

As you read, look for words that signal how the author wants you to picture the scene and how the elements of the scene are arranged.

- on the left, in the middle, on the right
- in front of, in back of
- above, below, underneath, behind, forward
- off in the distance, beyond, up close, near, far
- at, in, on (as in at the store, in the wilderness, on the table)
- inside, outside, inward, outward
- ten feet away, a mile in the distance, 2½ inches from the top

Space Order Paragraph

Study this paragraph. The signal words for space order are highlighted.

In all societies, people communicate by manipulating the space that separates them from others. Sociologists commonly distinguish four zones that surround us. The size of these zones varies from one society to the next. In North America, an intimate zone extends about 18 inches from the body. It is restricted to people with whom we want sustained, intimate physical contact. A personal zone extends from about 18 inches to 4 feet away. It is reserved for friends and acquaintances. We tolerate only a little physical intimacy from such people. The social zone is situated in the area roughly 4 feet to 12 feet away from us. Apart from a handshake, no physical contact is permitted from people we restrict to this zone. The public zone starts around 12 feet from our bodies. It is used to distinguish a performer or a speaker from an audience.

—From BRYM/LIE. *Sociology*, 3e (p. 143) Copyright © 2010 Cengage Learning.

Notice in this example that another pattern is at work: classification. In many reading selections, you will find a mix of patterns. Remember that knowing a pattern is a tool, not a rule. The tool can help you dig up the major supporting details or even the main idea. But there's no rule that authors have to follow only one pattern at a time.

Each Pattern Answers a Question

Each pattern of organization answers a general question, as shown in the review chart that follows. Notice that the question and the signal words go naturally together.

Pattern of organization	General question	Sample signal words
Classification	What kinds are there?	types, kinds, forms
Comparison and contrast	How are these the same? How do they differ?	similar, alike; in contrast, however
Cause and effect	What made this happen? What does this lead to?	reasons, because, consequences
Definition	What is this? What does it mean?	means, is, namely

Pattern of organization	General question	Sample signal words
Example	What are examples of this general idea?	for example, to illustrate
Time order (narration)	When did that happen?	yesterday, today, then, now
Time order (process)	What steps are needed, and in what order?	first, second, steps, stages
Space (or spatial) order	Where are things located?	above, below, to the right

INTERACTION 4–5　Apply Your Knowledge of Patterns to Paragraphs

A. In each paragraph, circle any signal words. Note that some paragraphs do not include any.

B. Think about what general question the paragraph's details answer. Write the question.

C. Name the pattern that organizes the major details.

1.

> If you drink at a party or at a bar, take responsibility for how much and how often you drink by taking the following steps. First, if you are at a party or bar, start with a soft drink. You will drink much faster if you are thirsty, so have a nonalcoholic drink to quench your thirst before you start drinking alcohol. Second, pace yourself. Every second or third drink, have a soft drink instead of an alcoholic one. Third, stay busy. You will drink less if you play pool or dance rather than just sitting and drinking. Throughout the evening, drink slowly. Take sips and not gulps. Put your glass down between sips. Finally, be assertive. Don't be pressured into drinking more than you want or intend to. Say "Thanks, but no thanks."
>
> —From HALES. *An Invitation to Health*, 12e (pp. 348–349)
> Copyright © 2007 Cengage Learning.

General question that the details answer: _____

Organizational pattern: _____

2.

> Southeast Asia was an important early center of pig domestication. Studies tell us that the eating of pork became highly ritualized in this area and that it was sometimes allowed only on ceremonial occasions. On the other side of the Indian Ocean, wild swine were common in the Nile swamps of ancient Egypt. There, too, pigs took on a sacred role, being associated with the evil god Set, and eating them was prohibited.
>
> —From BULLIET. *The Earth and Its Peoples, Brief Edition, Complete, 5e* (p. 224) Copyright © 2012 Cengage Learning.

General question that the details answer: _____

Organizational pattern: _____

3.

> Plenty of art thefts are spectacular, the stuff of movies. In the Boston heist, the Gardner thieves tricked the night watchman with a ruse and bound them eyes to ankles with silver duct tape. In Italy, a young man dropped a fishing line down a museum skylight, hooked a $4 million Klimt painting, and reeled it up and away. In Venezuela, thieves slipped into a museum at night and replaced three Matisse works with forgeries so fine they were not discovered for sixty days.
>
> —Wittman, *Priceless,* p. 15

General question that the details answer: _____

Organizational pattern: _____

4.

> According to Professor Warren Bennis, the primary difference between leaders and managers is that leaders are concerned with doing the right thing, while managers are concerned with doing things right. In other words, leaders begin with the question, "What should we be doing?" while managers start with "How can we do what we're already doing better?" Leaders focus on vision, mission, goals, and objectives, while managers focus on productivity and efficiency. Managers see themselves as preservers of the status quo, while leaders see themselves as promoters of change and challengers of the status quo in that they encourage creativity and risk taking.
>
> —From WILLIAMS. *Management,* 4e (p. 451) Copyright © 2004 Cengage Learning.

General question that the details answer: _____

Organizational pattern: _____

5.

> **Depth of field** is the range of the image that is in focus for a specific shot. Imagine that you are photographing an actor. Your camera is on a tripod and you measure the distance between the film plane and the exact spot of the actor, which is five feet. You adjust the lens so that everything that is five feet from the camera is in exact focus. This is the **plane of focus.** The depth of field is the space in front of and behind that plane that is also in focus.
>
> —From CASHINGHINO. *Moving Images: Making Movies, Understanding Media* (pp. 135–136) Copyright © 2010 Cengage Learning.

General question that the details answer: _____

Organizational pattern: _____

INTERACTION 4–6   Apply Your Knowledge of Patterns to a Passage

Read this selection from *Management,* a business textbook. On the line next to each paragraph, write the pattern used to organize the paragraph.

How Do You Make Ethical Decisions?

_____ 1   On a cold morning in the midst of a winter storm, schools were closed, and most people had decided to stay home from work. Nevertheless, Richard Addessi had already showered, shaved, and dressed for the office. Addessi was just four months short of his 30-year anniversary with the company. Addessi kissed his wife Joan goodbye, but before he could get to his car, he fell dead on the garage floor of a sudden heart attack. Having begun work at IBM at the age of 18, he was just 48 years old.

_____ 2   You're the vice president in charge of benefits at IBM. Given that he was four months short of full retirement, do you award full retirement benefits to Mr. Addessi's wife and daughters? If the answer is yes, they will receive his full retirement benefits of $1,800 a month and free lifetime medical coverage. If you say no, Mrs. Addessi and her daughters will receive only $340 a month. They will also have to pay $473 a month just to continue their current medical coverage. As the VP in charge of benefits at IBM, what would be the ethical thing to do?

Influences on Ethical Decision Making

3   So, what did IBM decide to do? Since Richard Addessi was four months short of 30 years with the company, IBM officials felt they had no choice but to give Joan Addessi and her two daughters the smaller, partial retirement benefits. Do you think IBM's decision was ethical? Probably many of you don't. You wonder how the company could be so heartless as to deny Richard Addessi's family the full benefits to which you believe they were entitled. Yet others might argue that IBM did the ethical thing by strictly following the rules laid out in its pension benefit plan. After all, being fair means applying the same rules to everyone. Although some ethical issues are easily solved, many do not have clearly right or wrong answers.

Ethical Intensity of the Decision

4   Managers don't treat all ethical decisions the same. The manager who has to decide whether to deny or extend full benefits to Joan Addessi and her family is going to treat that decision much more seriously than the decision of how to deal with an assistant who has been taking computer paper home for personal use. These decisions differ in their ethical intensity, or the degree of concern people have about an ethical issue. When addressing an issue of high ethical intensity, managers are more aware of the impact their decision will have on others. They are more likely to view the decision as an ethical or moral decision rather than as an economic decision. They are also more likely to worry about doing the "right thing."

5   Ethical intensity depends on six factors:

- magnitude of consequences
- social consensus
- probability of effect
- temporal immediacy
- proximity of effect
- concentration of effect.

6   **Magnitude of consequences** is the total harm or benefit derived from an ethical decision. The more people who are harmed or the greater the harm to those people, the larger the consequences. **Social consensus** is agreement on whether behavior is bad or good. **Probability of effect** is the chance that something will happen and then result in harm to others. If we combine these factors, we can see the effect they can have on ethical intensity. For example, if there is a clear agreement (social consensus) that a managerial decision or action is certain (probability of effect) to have large negative consequences (magnitude of effect) in some way, then people will be highly concerned about that managerial decision or action, and ethical intensity will be high.

7   **Temporal immediacy** is the time between an act and the consequences the act produces. Temporal immediacy is stronger if a manager has to lay off workers next week as opposed to three months from now. **Proximity of effect** is the social, psychological, cultural, or physical distance of a decision maker from those affected by his or her decisions. Thus, proximity of effect is greater for the manager who works with employees who are to be laid off than it is for a manager who works where no layoffs will occur. Finally, whereas the magnitude of consequences is the total effect across all people, **concentration of effect** is how much an action affects the average person. Temporarily laying off 100 employees for 10 months without pay is a greater concentration of effect than temporarily laying off 1,000 employees for 1 month.

8   Which of these six factors has the most impact? Studies indicate that managers are much more likely to view decisions as ethical decisions when the magnitude of consequences (total harm) is high and there is a social consensus (agreement) that a behavior or action is bad.

9   Many people will likely feel IBM was wrong to deny full benefits to Joan Addessi. Why? In this situation, IBM's decision met five of the six characteristics of ethical intensity. The difference in benefits (more than $23,000 per year) was likely to have serious consequences for the family. The decision was certain to affect them and would do so immediately. We can closely identify with Joan Addessi and her daughters (as opposed to IBM's faceless, nameless, corporate identity). And the decision would have a concentrated effect on the family in

terms of their monthly benefits ($1,800 and free medical coverage if full benefits were awarded versus $340 a month and medical care that costs $473 per month if they weren't).

10   The exception is social consensus. Not everyone will agree that IBM's decision was unethical. The judgment also depends on your level of moral development and which ethical principles you use to decide.

—From WILLIAMS. *Management*, 4e (pp. 108–109)
Copyright © 2004 Cengage Learning.

Section Review: Types of Organizational Patterns

For each pattern shown here, fill in the kinds of information you would find in each rectangle. Then name each pattern.

A. Name: _____

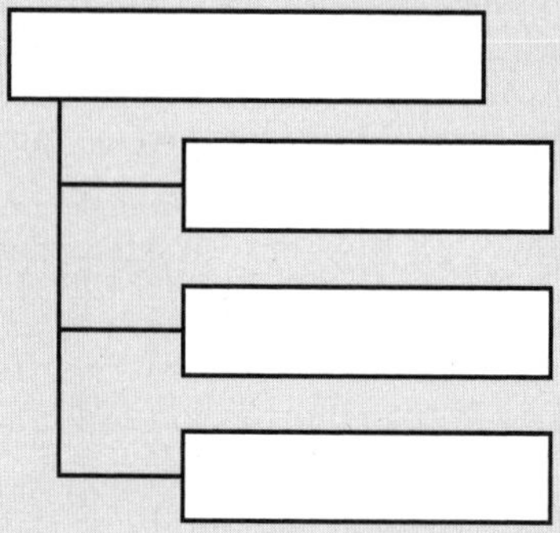

B. Name: _____

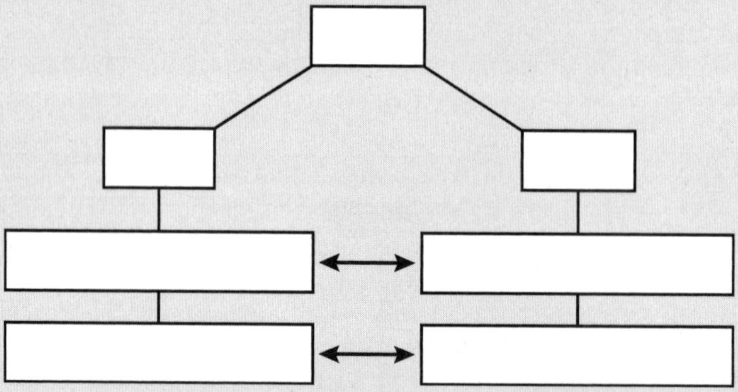

C. Name: _____

D. Name: _____

E. Name: _____

F. Name: _____

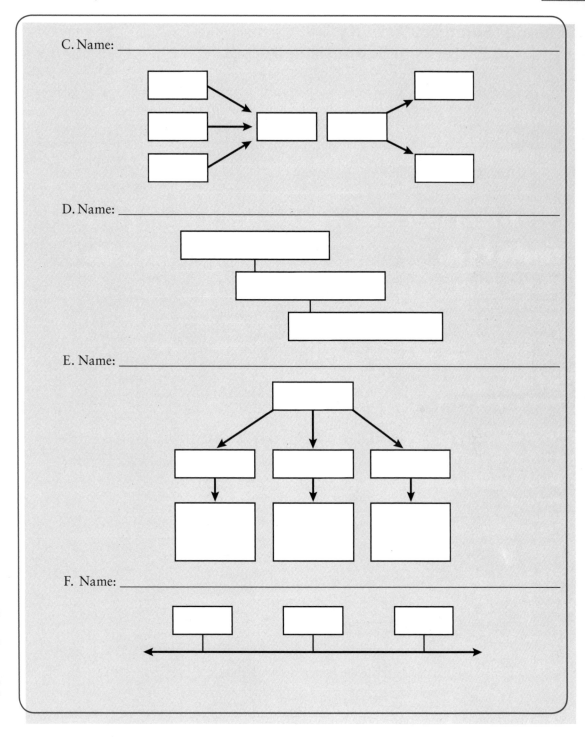

Chapter Summary Activity:
Noticing Patterns of Supporting Details

Chapter 4 has discussed how to identify the details that support the main idea of a paragraph or passage, how to distinguish major from minor supporting details, and how to identify the patterns that authors use to arrange the details. Fill in the following Reading Guide by completing each idea on the left with information from Chapter 4 on the right. You can return to this guide throughout the course as a reminder of how to identify the levels of information in a paragraph.

Reading Guide to Noticing Patterns of Supporting Details

Complete this idea	with information from Chapter 4.
The most important reading comprehension skill is the ability to	1. _____ _____
To identify the supporting details in a paragraph or longer passage, you can ask:	2. _____
To find the supporting details, turn the topic sentence into a ____ and then ____.	3. _____ 4. _____
Major supporting details provide direct evidence for the author's	5. _____
Minor supporting details provide direct evidence for the	6. _____
The kind of details that give organizational structure to the paragraph are the	7. _____
The major supporting details of a paragraph are often organized in a certain	8. _____
At times, you can forecast the pattern of organization when you read the	9. _____
After you make a question out of the topic sentence, you can mentally	10. _____ _____
Each pattern of organization answers a certain _____ question.	11. _____

Complete this idea	with information from Chapter 4.
The classification pattern answers the question:	12. _____
The comparison and contrast pattern answers the questions:	13. _____
The definition pattern answers the questions:	14. _____
The example pattern answers the question:	15. _____
The cause-and-effect pattern answers the questions:	16. _____
The time order pattern of narration answers the question:	17. _____
The time order pattern of process answers the question:	18. _____
The space order pattern answers the question:	19. _____
The word *because* signals the pattern of	20. _____
The word *afterward* suggests	21. _____
The phrase *to illustrate* suggests	22. _____
Process organization is signaled by words such as	23. _____
Contrast is signaled by words such as	24. _____

25. Think about what your reading strategies were before you read Chapter 4. How did they differ from the suggestions here? Write your thoughts.

_____

_____

_____

ENGAGE YOUR SKILLS
Noticing Patterns of Supporting Details

Read this passage from a psychology textbook and answer the questions that follow.

Overestimating the Improbable

1   Various causes of death are paired up below. In each pairing, which is the more likely cause of death?

Asthma or tornadoes?

Accidental falls or shooting accidents?

Tuberculosis or floods?

Suicide or murder?

2   Table 4.1 shows the actual mortality rates for each of the causes of death just listed. As you can see, the first choice in each pair is the more common cause of death. If you guessed wrong for several pairings, don't feel bad. Like many other people, you may be a victim of the tendency to overestimate the improbable. People tend to greatly overestimate the likelihood of dramatic, vivid—but infrequent—events that receive heavy media coverage. Thus, the number of fatalities due to tornadoes, floods, food poisonings, and murders is usually overestimated. Fatalities due to asthma and other common diseases, which receive less media coverage, tend to be underestimated. For instance, a majority of subjects estimate that tornadoes kill more people than asthma, even though asthma fatalities outnumber tornado fatalities by a ratio of 80 to 1. The tendency to exaggerate the improbable has generally been attributed to operation of the *availability heuristic*. Instances of floods, tornadoes, and such are readily available in memory because people are exposed to a great deal of media coverage of such events.

Table 4.1 Actual Mortality Rates for Selected Causes of Death

Cause of death	Rate	Cause of death	Rate
Asthma	2,000	Tornadoes	25
Accidental falls	6,021	Firearms accidents	320
Tuberculosis	400	Floods	44
Suicide	11,300	Homicide	6,800

Note: Mortality rates are per 100 million people and are based on the *Statistical Abstract of the United States, 2001.*

3 As a general rule, people's beliefs about what they should fear tend to be surprisingly inconsistent with actual probabilities. This propensity has been especially prominent in the aftermath of 9/11, which left countless people extremely worried about the possibility of being harmed in a terrorist attack (as the terrorists intended). To date, one's chances of being hurt in a terrorist attack are utterly microscopic in comparison to one's chances of perishing in an automobile accident, yet people worry about the former and not the latter. People tend to overestimate the likelihood of rare events when their estimates are based on descriptive information (such as media coverage) as opposed to when their estimates are based on personal experiences.

—From WEITEN. *Psychology*, 7e (pp. 327–328) Copyright © 2008 Cengage Learning.

1. What is the topic sentence of paragraph 2?

    a. If you guessed wrong for several pairings, don't feel bad.

    b. Like many other people, you may be a victim of the tendency to overestimate the improbable.

    c. People tend to greatly overestimate the likelihood of dramatic, vivid—but infrequent—events that receive heavy media coverage.

    d. Thus, the number of fatalities due to tornadoes, floods, food poisonings, and murders is usually overestimated.

2. Write the two major supporting details of the topic sentence of paragraph 2.

    • _____

      _____

    • _____

      _____

3. What relationship exists between the topic sentence and the two major details?

    a. Comparison

    b. Cause and effect

    c. Time order

    d. Classification

4. What transition is a clue to the relationship in question 3? _____

5. In the topic sentence, a cause-and-effect relationship is implied (suggested rather than directly stated). Fill in the map of this relationship.

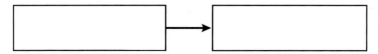

____ 6. What is the relationship of paragraph 1 to paragraph 2?

    a. Definition

    b. Cause

    c. Narrative

    d. Example

____ 7. The sentence in paragraph 2 that starts "For instance" is what kind of detail?

    a. Major

    b. Minor

8. What pattern does that sentence demonstrate? _____

____ 9. Which sentence of paragraph 3 is the topic sentence?

    a. First sentence

    b. Second sentence

    c. Third sentence

    d. Fourth sentence

10. In the following sentence, what is the organizational pattern? _____

> To date, one's chances of being hurt in a terrorist attack are utterly microscopic in comparison to one's chances of perishing in an automobile accident, yet people worry about the former and not the latter.

MASTER YOUR SKILLS
Noticing Patterns of Supporting Details

Read each textbook selection and answer the questions that follow.

A.

> 1   An **economic system** is a social institution through which goods and services are produced, distributed, and consumed to satisfy people's needs and wants, ideally in the most efficient way possible.
>
> 2   Three types of capital, or resources, are used to produce goods and services. **Natural capital** includes resources and services produced by the earth's natural processes, which support all economies and all life. **Human capital,** or human resources, includes people's physical and mental talents that provide labor, organizational and management skills, and innovation. **Manufactured capital,** or manufactured resources, refers to items such as machinery, equipment, and factories made from natural resources with the help of human resources.
>
> —From MILLER/SPOOLMAN. *Living in the Environment*, 17e (p. 614)
> Copyright © 2012 Cengage Learning.

_____ 1. What pattern characterizes this passage overall?

  a. Example

  b. Classification

  c. Cause and effect

  d. Contrast

_____ 2. What other organizational pattern is used extensively?

  a. Cause and effect

  b. Definition

  c. Spatial order

  d. Comparison

  3. Innovation is a (or an) _____ of human capital.

_____ 4. The word *or,* used after **human capital** and after **manufactured capital,** indicates which of the following?

  a. A contrast

  b. A comparison

  c. An antonym (word with the opposite meaning)

  d. A synonym (word with the same or similar meaning)

B.

1   "Like many identical twins reared apart, Jim Lewis and Jim Springer found they had been leading eerily similar lives. Separated four weeks after birth in 1940, the Jim twins grew up 45 miles apart in Ohio and were reunited in 1979. Eventually, they discovered that both drove the same model blue Chevrolet, chain-smoked Salems, chewed their fingernails, and owned dogs named Toy. Each had spent a good deal of time vacationing at the same three-block strip of beach in Florida. More important, when tested for such personality traits as flexibility, self-control, and sociability, the twins responded almost exactly the same."

2   So began a *Time* magazine summary of a major twin study conducted at the University of Minnesota Center for Twin and Adoption Research. Since 1979 the investigators at this center have been studying the personality resemblances of identical twins reared apart. Not all the twin pairs have been as similar as Jim Lewis and Jim Springer, but many of the parallels have been uncanny. Identical twins Oskar Stohr and Jack Yufe were separated soon after birth. Oskar was sent to a Nazi-run school in Czechoslovakia while Jack was raised in a Jewish home on a Caribbean island. When they were reunited for the first time during middle age, they showed up wearing similar mustaches, haircuts, shirts, and wire-rimmed glasses! A pair of previously separated female twins both arrived at the Minneapolis airport wearing seven rings on their fingers. One had a son named Richard Andrew and the other had a son named Andrew Richard!

3   Could personality be largely inherited? These reports of striking resemblances between identical twins reared apart certainly raise this possibility.

—From WEITEN. *Psychology*, 7e (p. 491) Copyright © 2008 Cengage Learning.

_____ 5. Which pattern is most evident in paragraph 1?

a. Definition

b. Cause

c. Effect

d. Comparison

6. List six signal words that point to that pattern.

- _____
- _____
- _____
- _____
- _____
- _____

_____ 7. In paragraph 1, the second and third sentences use which pattern of organization?

    a. Classification

    b. Definition

    c. Time order (narrative)

    d. Contrast

8. List four signal words or phrases that point to that pattern.

- _____

- _____

- _____

- _____

_____ 9. What is the topic sentence of paragraph 1?

    a. The sentence that begins "Like many identical twins . . ."

    b. The sentence that begins "Separated four weeks . . ."

    c. The sentence that begins "Eventually . . ."

    d. The sentence that begins "Each had spent . . ."

_____ 10. What is the main pattern of organization in paragraph 2?

    a. Cause and effect

    b. Time order

    c. Contrast

    d. Definition

C.

> What do the terms _child maltreatment_ and _child abuse_ mean to you? When asked what constitutes child maltreatment, many people first think of cases that involve severe physical injuries or sexual abuse. However, neglect is the most frequent form of child maltreatment. Child neglect occurs when children's basic needs—including emotional warmth and security, adequate shelter, food, health care, education, clothing, and protection—are not met, regardless of cause. Neglect often involves acts of omission (where parents or caregivers fail to provide adequate physical or emotional care for children) rather than acts of commission (such as physical or sexual abuse). Of course, what constitutes child maltreatment differs from society to society.
>
>   —From KENDALL. _Sociology in Our Times_, 6e (p. 112)
>   Copyright © 2008 Cengage Learning.

_____ 11. What is the relationship between the second and third sentences?

    a. Contrast

    b. Comparison

    c. Spatial order

    d. Classification

_____ 12. The words inside the dashes in the fourth sentence are part of what pattern?

    a. Cause

    b. Effect

    c. Comparison

    d. Enumeration

_____ 13. What other patterns could be the answers to question 12?

    a. Cause and effect

    b. Comparison and contrast

    c. Classification and example

    d. Definition and spatial order

_____ 14. In the last sentence, what is the relationship between the word _omission_ and the words that follow it in parentheses?

    a. Definition

    b. Time order

    c. Spatial order

    d. Classification

_____ 15. What is the relationship of the word _commission_ and the words that follow it in parentheses?

    a. Definition

    b. Example

    c. Effect

    d. Comparison

16. List three transitions from the paragraph that signal contrast.

    • _____

    • _____

    • _____

D.

1   When you stretch a muscle, you are primarily stretching the connective tissue. The stretch must be intense enough to increase the length of the connective tissue without tearing it.

2   **Static stretching** involves a gradual stretch held for a short time (10 to 30 seconds). A shorter stretch provides little benefit; a longer stretch does not provide additional benefits. Since a slow stretch provokes less of a reaction from the stretch receptors, the muscles can safely stretch farther than usual. Fitness experts most often recommend static stretching because it is both safe and effective. An example of such a stretch is letting your hands slowly slide down the front of your legs (keeping your knees in a soft, unlocked position) until you reach your toes and holding this final position for several seconds before slowly straightening up. You should feel a pull, but not pain, during this stretch.

3   In **passive stretching,** your own body, a partner, gravity, or a weight serves as an external force or resistance to help your joints move through their range of motion. You can achieve a more intense stretch and a greater range of motion with passive stretching. There is a greater risk of injury, however, because the muscles themselves are not controlling the stretch. In working with a partner, it's very important that you communicate clearly so as not to force a joint outside its normal functional range of motion.

4   Research on stretching demonstrates a 5 to 20 percent increase in static flexibility within four to six weeks of stretching. Much of this long-term increase in range of motion is due to an increased level of "stretch tolerance," or ability to tolerate the discomfort of a stretched position.

5   **Active stretching** involves stretching a muscle by contracting the opposing muscle (the muscle on the opposite side of the limb). In an active seated hamstring stretch, for example, the stretch occurs by actively contracting the muscles on the top of the shin, which produces a reflex that relaxes the hamstring. This method allows the muscle to be stretched farther with a low risk of injury.

6   The disadvantage of active stretching is that a person may not be able to produce enough of a stretch to increase flexibility only by means of contracting opposing muscle groups. Although active stretching is the safest and most convenient approach, an occasional passive assist can be helpful.

—From HALES. *An Invitation to Health,* 12e (p. 129)
Copyright © 2007 Cengage Learning.

_____ 17. The overall pattern of organization in this passage is

    a. Cause

    b. Time order (process)

    c. Contrast

    d. Classification

____ 18. The example of static stretching is given using what organizational pattern?

    a. Time order (process)

    b. Comparison

    c. Spatial order

    d. Effect

____ 19. The advantages and disadvantages of different kinds of stretching are

    a. Causes

    b. Effects

    c. Time order (narrative)

    d. Definitions

____ 20. In the last sentence of paragraph 4, what is the relationship between *stretch tolerance* and the words that come after it?

    a. Definition

    b. Comparison

    c. Contrast

    d. Time order (process)

Focus on Criminal Justice

College Criminal Justice App   CRIMINAL JUSTICE TEXTBOOK

The following reading is linked to these fields of . . .

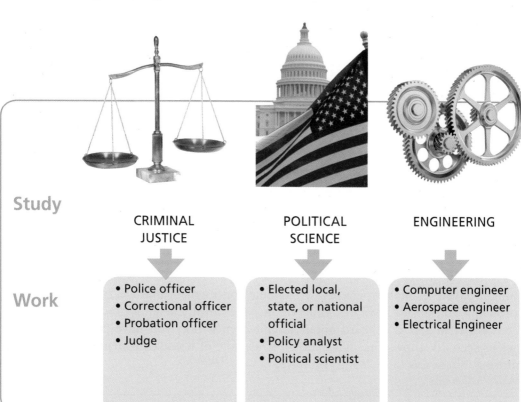

Study

CRIMINAL
JUSTICE

POLITICAL
SCIENCE

ENGINEERING

Work

- Police officer
- Correctional officer
- Probation officer
- Judge

- Elected local, state, or national official
- Policy analyst
- Political scientist

- Computer engineer
- Aerospace engineer
- Electrical Engineer

● Pre-Reading the Selection

The excerpt that begins on page 257 comes from the criminal justice textbook *Criminal Justice in Action*. The excerpt is titled "Home Confinement and Electronic Monitoring."

Surveying the Reading

Survey the textbook selection that follows. Then check the elements that are included in this reading.

_____ Title

_____ Headings

_____ First sentences of paragraphs

_____ Words in bold or italic type

_____ Images and captions

Guessing the Purpose

Based on the source and the title of the reading selection, do you think the authors' purpose is mostly to persuade, inform, or express? _____

Predicting the Content

Based on your survey, what are three things you expect the reading selection to discuss?

- _____

- _____

- _____

Activating Your Knowledge

You might have personal experience with home confinement and electronic monitoring, but probably you do not. Maybe someone in your family, neighborhood, or school has direct experience and you heard about it. But even if not, you have probably watched movies or seen TV shows that have shown some sort of home confinement or electronic monitoring. Share any knowledge you have.

- _____

- _____

- _____

● Reading with Pen in Hand

Students who annotate as they read are more successful than students who do not annotate. That's why you will annotate each reading in *Engage* as you read. In the reading that follows, use the following symbols:

★ or (Point)   to indicate a main idea

① ② ③   to indicate major details

Access the Reading CourseMate via **www.cengagebrain.com** to hear vocabulary words from this selection and view a video about this topic.

Home Confinement and Electronic Monitoring

Reading Journal

1   Various forms of **home confinement**—in which offenders serve their sentences not in a government institution but at home—have existed for centuries. It has often served, and continues to do so, as a method of political control. For example, the military government of Myanmar (Burma) has **confined** Nobel Peace Prize winner Aung San Suu Kyi to her home for years at a time since she won an election for leadership of that country in 1990.

confined Use context clues to decide what *confined* means.

◉ Have you heard of Aung San Suu Kyi? Can you locate Myanmar (Burma) on a map?

AP Photo/Itsuo Inouye

2   For purposes of general law enforcement, home confinement was **impractical** until relatively recently. After all, one could not expect offenders to "promise" to stay at home, and the personnel costs of guarding them were too high. In the 1980s, however, with the

◉ Why was home confinement impractical?

impractical Look at the reasons in the next sentence. What does *impractical* mean?

advent Contrast this sentence with the one before it to decide what *advent* means.

advent of electronic monitoring, or using technology to "guard" the prisoner, home confinement became more practical. Today, all fifty states and the federal government have home monitoring programs with about 120,000 offenders participating at any one time.

The Levels of Home Monitoring and Their Benefits

• Can you identify with these levels, having been a teenager?

restriction Look at the examples that follow to determine the meaning of *restriction*.

3   Home monitoring has three general levels of **restriction**:

1. *Curfew,* which requires offenders to be in their homes at specific hours each day, usually at night.

2. *Home detention,* which requires that offenders remain home at all times, with exceptions being made for education, employment, counseling, or other specified activities such as the purchase of food or, in some instances, attendance at religious ceremonies.

incarceration As the highest level of restriction, what does *incarceration* mean?

3. *Home incarceration*, which requires the offender to remain home at all times, save for medical emergencies.

• What are the goals of intermediate sanctions?

4   Under ideal circumstances, home confinement serves many of the goals of intermediate sanctions. [Discussed previously in this criminal justice textbook, **intermediate sanctions** are sentencing options that are more restrictive than probation and less restrictive than imprisonment.] It protects the community. It saves public funds and space in correctional facilities by keeping convicts out of **institutional** incarceration. It meets public expectations of punishment for criminals. Uniquely, home confinement also recognizes that convicts, despite their crimes, play important roles in the community, and it allows them to continue in those roles. An offender, for example, may be given permission to leave confinement to care for elderly parents.

institutional A kind of institution is mentioned earlier. What does *institutional* mean here?

Types of Electronic Monitoring

• Does it surprise you that a comic book inspired electronic monitors?

5   According to some reports, the inspiration for electronic monitoring was a *Spiderman* comic book in which the hero was trailed by the use of an electronic device on his arm. In 1979, a New Mexico judge named Jack Love, having read the comic, convinced an executive at Honeywell, Inc., to begin developing similar technology to supervise convicts.

• Visualize the two major types of electronic monitoring.

6   Two major types of electronic monitoring have grown out of Love's initial concept. The first is a "programmed contact" program, in which the offender is contacted periodically by telephone or beeper to **verify** his or her whereabouts. Verification is obtained via a computer that uses voice or visual recognition techniques

verify Think of how the electronic monitoring system helps authorities keep tabs on criminals. What might *verify* mean?

or by requiring the offender to enter a code in an electronic box when called. The second is a "continuously signaling" device, worn around the convict's wrist, ankle, or neck. A transmitter in the device sends out a continuous signal to a "receiver-dialer" device located in the offender's **dwelling**. If the receiver device does not detect a signal from the transmitter, it informs a central computer, and the police are notified.

dwelling Think about where the offender is being kept. What is a *dwelling*?

Technological Advances in Electronic Monitoring

7   As electronic monitoring technology has evolved, the ability of community corrections officials to target specific forms of risky behavior has greatly increased. A Michigan court, for example, has begun placing black boxes in the automobiles of repeat traffic law violators. Not only do these boxes record information about the offenders' driving habits for review by probation officers, but they also **emit** a loud beep when the car goes too fast or stops too quickly. Another device—an ankle bracelet—is able to test a person's sweat for alcohol levels and transmit the results over the Internet.

emit *Emit* is a verb. Use *loud beep* to help you decide the meaning of *emit*.

8   The advance with perhaps the greatest potential for transforming electronic monitoring is the **global positioning system** (GPS). GPS technology is a form of tracking technology that relies on twenty-four military satellites orbiting 12,000 miles above the earth. The satellites transmit signals to each other and to a receiver on the ground, allowing a monitoring station to determine the location of the receiving device to within a few feet.

9   GPS provides a much more precise level of electronic monitoring. The offender wears a transmitter, similar to a traditional electronic monitor, around his or her ankle or wrist. The transmitter communicates with a small box called a portable tracking device (PTD), which uses the military satellites to determine the offender's movements. GPS technology can be used either "actively," to constantly monitor the offender's whereabouts, or "passively," to ensure that the offender is within the confines of his or her limited space. Inclusion and exclusion zones are also very important to GPS supervision. Inclusion zones are areas such as a home or workplace where the offender is expected to be at certain times. Exclusion zones are areas such as parks, playgrounds, and schools where the offender is not permitted to go. GPS-linked computers can alert officials immediately when a zone has been **breached** and create a record of all the offender's movements to review at a later time.

How would you explain the three technological advances to someone else?

breached Use the word *zone* and refer to the previous two sentences. What does *breached* mean?

—From GAINES/MILLER. *Criminal Justice in Action*, 5e (pp. 300–302)
Copyright © 2011 Cengage Learning.

● Comprehension Questions

Write the letter of the answer on the line. Then explain your thinking.

Main Idea

_____ 1. Which of the following sentences is the best main idea for paragraph 4?

   a. Under ideal circumstances, home confinement serves many of the goals of intermediate sanctions.

   b. It protects the community.

   c. It saves public funds and space in correctional facilities by keeping convicts out of institutional incarceration.

   d. Uniquely, home confinement also recognizes that convicts, despite their crimes, play important roles in the community, and it allows them to continue in those roles.

WHY? What information in the selection leads you to give that answer? _____

_____

_____

_____

_____ 2. Which of the following statements is the best main idea of the section titled "Types of Electronic Monitoring"?

   a. According to some reports, the inspiration for electronic monitoring was a *Spiderman* comic book in which the hero was trailed by the use of an electronic device on his arm.

   b. In 1979, a New Mexico judge named Jack Love, having read the comic, convinced an executive at Honeywell, Inc., to begin developing similar technology to supervise convicts.

   c. Two major types of electronic monitoring have grown out of Love's initial concept.

   d. The second is a "continuously signaling" device, worn around the convict's wrist, ankle, or neck.

WHY? What information in the selection leads you to give that answer? _____

_____

_____

_____

Supporting Details

_____ 3. Which of the following is a major detail in the section "Technological Advances in Electronic Monitoring"?

   a. As electronic monitoring technology has evolved, the ability of community corrections officials to target specific forms of risky behavior has greatly increased.

   b. A Michigan court, for example, has begun placing black boxes in the automobiles of repeat traffic law violators.

   c. Not only do these boxes record information about the offenders' driving habits for review by probation officers, but they also emit a loud beep when the car goes too fast or stops too quickly.

   d. GPS technology is a form of tracking technology that relies on twenty-four military satellites orbiting 12,000 miles above the earth.

WHY? What information in the selection leads you to give that answer? _____

_____

_____

_____

_____ 4. Which of the following is not supported by the details of the passage?

   a. Technology has helped usher in more effective home monitoring.

   b. The global positioning system is a fourth level of home monitoring.

   c. Home detention is less extreme of a restriction than home incarceration.

   d. Exclusion zones are areas that are prohibited to the offender being monitored.

WHY? What information in the selection leads you to give that answer? _____

_____

_____

_____

Author's Purpose

_____ 5. What is the overall purpose of this reading selection?

   a. To persuade readers that without technology, home monitoring would not exist.

   b. To inform readers of the types of home monitoring.

   c. To persuade readers that home monitoring reduces crime.

   d. To inform readers of the relationship between home confinement, electronic monitoring, and technology.

WHY? What information in the selection leads you to give that answer? _____

_____

_____

_____

____ 6. What is the purpose of paragraph 2?

    a. To convince the reader of the overdependence of home confinement practices by law enforcement.

    b. To criticize law enforcement for their underutilization of home confinement prior to the 1980s.

    c. To suggest that technology is ensuring that home monitoring is here to stay.

    d. To inform the readers of how many criminals are being monitored in an electronic format.

WHY? What information in the selection leads you to give that answer? _____

_____

_____

_____

Relationships

____ 7. What is the relationship of paragraph 9 to paragraph 8?

    a. Paragraph 9 provides support and paragraph 8 states the main idea.

    b. Paragraph 9 restates the ideas in paragraph 8.

    c. Paragraph 9 gives a solution and paragraph 8 gives the problem.

    d. Paragraph 9 gives the cause and paragraph 8 provides the effects.

WHY? What information in the selection leads you to give that answer? _____

_____

_____

_____

____ 8. The heading "Types of Electronic Monitoring" suggests what relationship?

    a. Cause and effect

    b. Time order

    c. Space order

    d. Classification

WHY? What information in the selection leads you to give that answer? _____

_____

_____

_____

Fact, Opinion, and Inference

____ 9. Which of the following statements is an opinion?

    a. GPS provides a much more precise level of electronic monitoring.

    b. Today, all fifty states and the federal government have home monitoring programs with about 120,000 offenders participating at any one time.

    c. Home confinement is an unreasonable punishment for intermediate sanctions.

    d. As electronic monitoring technology has evolved, the ability of community corrections officials to target specific forms of risky behavior has greatly increased.

WHY? What leads you to give that answer? _____

_____

_____

_____

____ 10. Which of the following statements would the author probably agree with?

    a. Electronic monitoring is too costly an expense for society to be burdened by.

    b. There should be a fourth level of home confinement.

    c. Law enforcement will increase its use of electronic monitoring devices as technological advances continue to be refined.

    d. The author does not believe that a *Spiderman* comic inspired electronic monitoring.

WHY? What leads you to give that answer? _____

_____

_____

_____

● Mapping the Reading

This textbook reading centers on classification: the levels of home confinement and the benefits and types of electronic monitoring. Fill in the following visual maps.

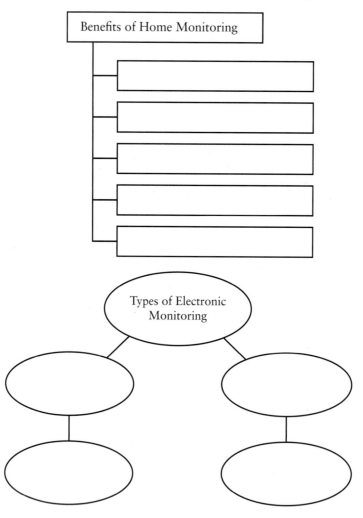

● Language in Use

The following words (or forms of them) were used in "Home Confinement and Electronic Monitoring." Now you can use them in different contexts. Put a word from the box into the blank lines in the following numbered sentences.

confined   impractical   advent   restriction   incarceration

institutional   verify   dwellings   emit   breached

1. Many a river has _____ its banks and caused serious flooding.

2. It wouldn't take long to _____ hundreds or even thousands of examples of flooding around the world.

3. Every year, flooding causes thousands of _____ to be destroyed, with many lives lost as well.

4. The lucky ones may only be _____ for a few days in an unlikely place, like a rooftop or tree.

5. If someone lives in an area prone to flooding, it is _____ to think that they may not be affected one day and so they should prepare by having an evacuation plan and an updated emergency kit.

● EASY Note Cards

Make a note card for each of the vocabulary words from the reading that you did not know. On one side, write the word. On the other side, divide the card into quarters and label them E, A, S, and Y. Add a word or phrase in each area so that you wind up with an example sentence, an antonym, a synonym, and, finally, a definition that shows you understand the meaning of the word with your logic. Remember that a synonym or antonym may have appeared in the reading.

Career Criminal Justice App   WEBSITE

● Pre-Reading the Selection

The excerpt that begins on page 266 comes from a law firm's blog. The excerpt is titled "Dogs Trained to Smell Cell Phones Will Fight Prison Drug Crimes."

Surveying the Reading

Survey the selection that follows. Then check the elements that are included in this reading.

_____ Title

_____ Headings

_____ First sentences of paragraphs

_____ Words in bold or italic type

_____ Images and captions

Guessing the Purpose

Based on the source and the title of the reading selection, do you think the author's purpose is mostly to persuade, inform, or express? _____

Predicting the Content

Based on your survey, what are three things you expect the reading selection to discuss?

- _____
- _____
- _____

Activating Your Knowledge

Think about other ways dogs are used in law enforcement. What other ways can you think of? Do you know anything about how cell phones are used to do drug deals?

- _____
- _____
- _____

● Reading with Pen in Hand

Students who annotate as they read are more successful than students who do not annotate. That's why you will annotate each reading in *Engage* as you read. In the reading that follows, use the following symbols:

★ or (Point)   to indicate a main idea

① ② ③   to indicate major details

Access the Reading CourseMate via www.cengagebrain.com to hear vocabulary words from this selection and view a video about this topic.

Reading Journal

○ Why is there a battle against cell phones in prisons?

illicit Are inmates allowed to have cell phones or are they banned? What might *illicit* mean?

Dogs Trained to Smell Cell Phones Will Fight Prison Drug Crimes

1   The Tennessee Department of Correction has introduced a new strategy in its effort to reduce drug crimes in prison. The Department plans to train three dogs, which are already trained to discover drug possession, to sniff out **illicit** cell phones. The Department argues that prison inmates are increasingly running criminal drug enterprises from their cells. Prisons and jails nationwide struggle to

stop inmates from continuing their criminal enterprises via smuggled cell phones.

AP Photo/Southern Illinoisan, Joe Jines

2   "We probably will find one at least once a week here, sometimes more often," warden Ricky Bell of Riverbend Maximum Security Institution told the *Tennessean*. "We get reports from people in the community that they're getting threatening phone calls. That happens pretty often."

3   Corrections officers have confiscated 1,684 illicit cell phones at 12 Tennessee prisons in the last year alone, and other states report similar problems. Despite regular searches and a ban on corrections officers carrying cell phones while on duty, the phones still find their way to inmates. "People have used some creative ways to get them in, by hiding them, how do I say this, in certain parts of their bodies," said Department of Correction spokeswoman Dorinda Carter. Friends and family members also toss phones over prison fences and use other methods.

confiscated Use the context of the battle against cell phones in prison, as well as who is doing the *confiscating*, to determine the meaning.

◉ Can you imagine having the job of searching for cell phones?

Department Trying Various Strategies to Stop Cell Phones and Prison Drug Crimes

4   In the ongoing effort to reduce illegal drug possession and trafficking within prisons, the Department views jamming cell phone signals within prisons as the most promising strategy. Currently, FCC rules prohibit cell phone jamming, but a bill exempting prisons from that rule has been passed by the U.S. Senate and is currently up for a House committee vote. John Shaffer, a consultant with ITT Defense, a producer of cell phone tracking technology for prisons,

◉ Do you think prisons should jam cell phone signals? Why?

prohibit Is cell phone jamming allowed? What does *prohibit* mean?

admits that the jamming technology has its limits. Since jamming cell phone signals is illegal, it has never been tested in prisons. It also might affect legitimate cell phone service near prison properties. Jamming could also have another downside. Currently, officers may be able to get information from inmates who are illegally using cell phones. Jamming the signal will stop the calls, but it would also stop that information gathering.

○ What might be the reason the dogs are limited in how often they can search?

5   The cell phone-sniffing dogs are a backup plan. The dogs are already being used effectively in Rhode Island. The dogs "are very effective at sniffing out the odor of cell phones," Shaffer said. "Most handlers believe it has to do with the battery in the cell phone." However, the dogs are expensive, both in training and maintenance. Each dog's training could cost up to $7,000. They are also limited in how often they can search.

6   The problem of illegal cell phone use may be worth that cost. It goes beyond drug trafficking and other illegal business activities. Inmates have also used cell phones in prison breaks, some of which have resulted in officers being shot.

albeit Think about the contrast. What does *albeit* mean?

7   On the other hand, shutting down cell phone use in prisons could have a real impact on prisoners who are merely trying (albeit illegally) to save a little money for their families. The only legal means they have of communication are written letters and collect phone calls. "I have to admit, the calls are a little pricey," said Warden Bell.

○ Do you think the cost of collect calls justifies the use of cell phones? Why?

—Reprinted by permission of Gasaway Long & Associates, PLLC.

● Comprehension Questions

Write the letter of the answer on the line. Then explain your thinking.

Main Idea

_____   1. Which of the following sentences is the best main idea for paragraph 1?

   a. The Tennessee Department of Correction has introduced a new strategy in its effort to reduce drug crimes in prison.

   b. The Department plans to train three dogs, which are already trained to discover drug possession, to sniff out illicit cell phones.

   c. The Department argues that prison inmates are increasingly running criminal drug enterprises from their cells.

   d. Prisons and jails nationwide struggle to stop inmates from continuing their criminal enterprises via smuggled cell phones.

WHY? What information in the selection leads you to give that answer? _____

_____

_____

_____

_____ 2. Which of the following statements is the best main idea of paragraph 3?

    a. Corrections officers have confiscated 1,684 illicit cell phones at 12 Tennessee prisons in the last year alone, and other states report similar problems.

    b. Despite regular searches and a ban on corrections officers carrying cell phones while on duty, the phones still find their way to inmates.

    c. "People have used some creative ways to get them in, by hiding them, how do I say this, in certain parts of their bodies," said Department of Correction spokeswoman Dorinda Carter.

    d. Friends and family members also toss phones over prison fences and use other methods.

WHY? What information in the selection leads you to give that answer? _____

_____

_____

_____

Supporting Details

_____ 3. Which of the following details is *most* relevant to the main idea of the section entitled "Department Trying Various Strategies to Stop Cell Phones and Prison Drug Crimes"?

    a. In the ongoing effort to reduce illegal drug possession and trafficking within prisons, the Department views jamming cell phone signals within prisons as the most promising strategy.

    b. The cell phone-sniffing dogs are a backup plan.

    c. The problem of illegal cell phone use may be worth that cost.

    d. Both a and b are major details that support the main idea.

WHY? What information in the selection leads you to give that answer? _____

_____

_____

_____

_____ 4. Which of the following is *not* supported by the details of the passage?

a. The use of cell phones in prisons helps perpetuate crime.

b. Cell phone-sniffing dogs are probably the best weapon in the battle against illicit cell phone use in American prisons.

c. Corrections officers are unable to keep up with the influx of cell phones into prisons.

d. Not all prisoners use their illicit cell phones for criminal purposes.

WHY? What information in the selection leads you to give that answer? _____

_____

_____

_____

Author's Purpose

_____ 5. What is the overall purpose of this reading?

a. To inform readers of a struggle in the Tennessee Department of Correction, and what is being done to fight it.

b. To persuade readers of the importance of not committing crimes because of the violence present in prisons.

c. To encourage readers that fighting crime sometimes brings rewards.

d. To entertain readers with the ongoing drama between the correction officers and the inmates in the Tennessee prisons.

WHY? What information in the selection leads you to give that answer? _____

_____

_____

_____

_____ 6. What is the purpose of the section entitled "Department Trying Various Strategies to Stop Cell Phones and Prison Drug Crimes"?

a. To inform the readers of how dogs are trained to find cell phones.

b. To inform the readers of two main plans the Department of Correction will use to battle the proliferation of illicit cell phone use.

c. To ensure the readers that they have nothing to fear concerning criminals because the Department of Correction is winning the war on illicit cell phone abuse within the prison system.

d. To inform readers of why cell phone use in prisons has become such a problem.

WHY? What information in the selection leads you to give that answer? _____

_____

_____

_____

Relationships

_____ 7. What relationship is found in the following sentence? *Currently, FCC rules prohibit cell phone jamming, but a bill exempting prisons from that rule has been passed by the U.S. Senate and is currently up for a House committee vote.*

   a. Comparison

   b. Cause and effect

   c. Time order

   d. Contrast

WHY? What information in the selection leads you to give that answer? _____

_____

_____

_____

_____ 8. What is the overall pattern that drives this reading?

   a. Cause and effect

   b. Time order

   c. Space order

   d. Classification

WHY? What information in the selection leads you to give that answer? _____

_____

_____

_____

Fact, Opinion, and Inference

____ 9. Which of the following statements is an opinion?

    a. Since jamming cell phone signals is illegal, it has never been tested in prisons.

    b. In the ongoing effort to reduce illegal drug possession and trafficking within prisons, the Department views jamming cell phone signals within prisons as the most promising strategy.

    c. The Department argues that prison inmates are increasingly running criminal drug enterprises from their cells.

    d. "We probably will find one at least once a week here, sometimes more often," warden Ricky Bell of Riverbend Maximum Security Institution told the *Tennessean*.

WHY? What leads you to give that answer? _____

_____

_____

_____

____ 10. Which of the following best lends credibility to the author(s) of this reading selection?

    a. The author's presentation of a balanced view, as well as factual details, gives the reader confidence in the author's credibility.

    b. The author's credibility is called into question because he or she takes the inmates' point of view in paragraph 7.

    c. The most important statement that gives the author credibility is, "The problem of illegal cell phone use may be worth that cost."

    d. The lengthy quotes and personal opinions presented in the text raise doubt as to the credibility of the author.

WHY? What leads you to give that answer? _____

_____

_____

_____

● Mapping the Reading

Summarize the issue of cell phone use in prison as presented in this reading.

_____

_____

_____

_____

_____

_____

● Language in Use

The following words (or forms of them) were used in "Dogs Trained to Smell Cell Phones Will Fight Prison Drug Crimes." Now you can use them in different contexts. Put a word from the box into the blank lines in the following numbered sentences.

> illicit   enterprises   confiscated   prohibited   albeit

1. Mandated by the Eighteenth Amendment, Prohibition in the United States was a period from 1919 to 1933 when the production, selling, transportation, and consumption of alcohol were _____.

2. And for a while, the Eighteenth Amendment did have what supporters saw as a positive effect: The consumption of alcohol decreased, and millions of gallons of alcohol were _____.

3. However, Prohibition also had an unwanted side effect. Competing _____ to smuggle liquor were created by Mafia bosses, like the legendary Al Capone, that caused an increase in crime, much of it violent.

4. In response to increased crime, as well as loss of jobs and revenue, public sentiment toward Prohibition changed, and the wheels began to move in the direction of a repeal, _____ slowly.

5. In 1933, President Franklin Roosevelt signed the Twenty-first Amendment into law. This law made production and consumption of alcoholic beverages (such as beer and wine) legal, but the making of distilled spirits at home, like moonshine, remained _____ (and still is to this day).

● EASY Note Cards

Make a note card for each of the vocabulary words from the reading that you did not know. On one side, write the word. On the other side, divide the card into quarters and label them E, A, S, and Y. Add a word or phrase in each area so that you wind up with an example sentence, an antonym, a synonym, and, finally, a definition that shows you understand the meaning of the word with your logic. Remember that a synonym or antonym may have appeared in the reading.

Applying Reading Comprehension Skills through Note Taking

5

Previewing the Chapter

Flip through the pages of Chapter 5, and read all the major headings. Look at all the photos and figures, and read their captions.

Predict four topics this chapter will cover.

- _____

- _____

- _____

- _____

Based on the figures in the chapter, write a statement about the topic of the chapter.

_____

Plan to come back and comment on how accurate your predictions were when you have finished working through the chapter.

_____

_____

To access additional course materials for *Engage*, including quizzes, videos, and more, please visit www.cengagebrain.com. At the CengageBrain.com home page, search for the ISBN of *Engage* (from the back cover of your book) using the search box at the top of the page. This will take you to the product page where these resources can be found.

Videos Related to Readings   **Vocab Words on Audio**   **Read and Talk on Demand**

Ask Questions and Mark the Answers

When you genuinely want to know something, you ask a lot of questions about it until you learn the information you want or need to know. So when you need to learn from a reading selection, ask questions about it. This simple strategy offers three advantages.

1. Searching for the answers to your questions gives you a well-defined purpose for reading.

2. Stating your purpose for reading will motivate you to read actively and clarify what information you are looking for. When you find this information, you should highlight, annotate, or mark it in some way.

3. When studying for a test, the key information is clearly marked for you to review, saving you time and effort.

Wow! That's a lot of potential return from the simple investment of asking a few questions!

Turn Titles, Headings, and Subtitles into Questions

Start with the title, heading, or subtitle; turn it into a question, and then look for the answer as you read. This establishes a purpose for reading. Your mission, should you choose to accept it, is to find the answer to your question.

Table 5.1 gives some titles of nonfiction trade books (non-textbooks) and some headings from college textbooks, along with questions that you might form from them.

Table 5.1 Questions Formed from Titles and Headings

Title or heading	Question
Major Categories of Child Abuse (sociology textbook heading)	What are the major categories of child abuse?
Starting Your Own Business (book title)	What are the steps to starting your own business?
Why People Keep Smoking (health textbook heading)	Why do people keep smoking?
Importing and Preparing Audio Files (media textbook heading)	How do you import and prepare audio files?
Piaget's Theory (psychology textbook heading)	Who is Piaget and what is his theory?
Events Leading to the American Revolution (history textbook heading)	How did these events cause the American Revolution?
MTV to Build a Wider Audience: Looking Beyond *Jersey Shore* (newspaper heading)	How is MTV looking beyond *Jersey Shore* to build a wider audience?

The first thing to notice is that the main words of each title or heading were used to form the question. These are the words that carry much of the meaning. For example, in the last heading, the subtitle, "Looking Beyond *Jersey Shore*," is connected somehow to the title, "MTV to Build a Wider Audience," but how? That is the information to look for while you read. The simple act of turning a title into a question can improve your focus while reading by giving you a clearly defined purpose.

Another important strategy is to try to predict what kind of information might be coming or how it might be organized. For example, the heading "Events Leading to the American Revolution" seems to indicate a cause-and-effect relationship, so using the word *cause* in the question helps you understand how the author organized the important information in the reading. In addition, more than one question might be necessary, especially when there is a title and a subtitle.

| INTERACTION 5–1 | Form Your Question, Set Your Reading Purpose, and Activate Your Prior Knowledge |

Create a question based on each of the following headings or titles. Then write what your reading purpose related to each heading or title might be. Describe any prior knowledge you have about that topic.

1. *The 7 Habits of Highly Effective People* (self-help book title)

Question: _____

_____

Purpose: To find and understand _____

_____

Prior Knowledge: _____

_____

2. "The New Jewish Immigration" (history textbook heading)

Question: _____

_____

Purpose: To understand _____

_____

Prior Knowledge: _____

_____

3. "MySpace for Musicians" (marketing textbook heading)

Question: _____

_____

Purpose: To understand _____

_____

Prior Knowledge: _____

_____

4. *Eat That Frog!: 21 Great Ways to Stop Procrastinating and Get More Done in Less Time* (self-help book title)

Question: _____

_____

Purpose: To find and understand _____

_____

Prior Knowledge: _____

_____

5. "Decimals: A Better Way to Work with Rational Numbers" (math textbook heading)

   Question: _____

   _____

   Purpose: To find and understand _____

   _____

   Prior Knowledge: _____

   _____

Read to Answer the Question, Then Mark the Answer, and Repeat

When you have formed a question from the heading, stated a purpose for reading, and thought about any prior knowledge you may have, you are ready to read for the answer.

The answer to your question is the main idea of the section. When you reach an idea or fact that helps to answer the question you formed from the heading, mark it in some way. Highlight it, underline it, or otherwise mark it as a main idea. Be careful to mark only the ideas that directly answer the question you asked. Let's look at an example from a health and wellness textbook.

Defense Mechanisms

Defense mechanisms are mental strategies and behaviors used to avoid painful feelings caused by difficult situations. They provide a distraction or escape from having to directly confront and deal with events or circumstances we find upsetting. They also serve as protection when we are faced with unpleasant thoughts, emotions, or situations that threaten our self-esteem or contradict our perceptions of reality. The occasional use of defense mechanisms is common.

—From ROBINSON/MCCORMICK. *Concepts in Health and Wellness*, 1e (pp. 89–90) Copyright © 2011 Cengage Learning.

Question: What are defense mechanisms?

As you can see, the answer to your question is in the first sentence. Although this does not always happen, you will often find the answer to your question soon after the title, especially in textbooks.

Once you find the main idea, you also need to understand the major details of the paragraph. You do this by repeating the questioning process with the main idea. The main idea is "mental strategies and behaviors used to avoid painful feelings caused by difficult situations." You can turn that into a question such as "How are defense mechanisms used to avoid painful feelings caused by difficult situations?" Now continue reading to find and mark the details that answer this question. Here is the same paragraph with the main idea highlighted in yellow and the major details highlighted in green:

Defense Mechanisms

Defense mechanisms are mental strategies and behaviors used to avoid painful feelings caused by difficult situations. They provide a distraction or escape from having to directly confront and deal with events or circumstances we find upsetting. They also serve as protection when we are faced with unpleasant thoughts, emotions, or situations that threaten our self-esteem or contradict our perceptions of reality. The occasional use of defense mechanisms is common.

—From ROBINSON/MCCORMICK. *Concepts in Health and Wellness*, 1e (pp. 89–90)
Copyright © 2011 Cengage Learning.

Repeating the questioning strategy allows you to drill down from the main idea to the major details. If you consistently mark the main idea one way and the major details in another, then when you review, you will automatically see the relationship between the ideas you are studying. In addition, as you read through entire sections, you can repeat this process, and later you can combine all the information in notes or an outline to effectively study (more about this later).

INTERACTION 5–2	**Turn Headings into Questions, and Read to Find the Answer**

Review the headings in the following reading from a criminal justice text. Create questions based on the title and headings, and then read to find the answers. When you do, highlight the answer. Then repeat the questioning process with the main idea. Finally, use your highlights to answer the questions that follow the reading.

The Purposes of Criminal Law

© zimmytws/Shutterstock.com

Question: _____

Why do societies need laws? Many criminologists believe that criminal law has two basic functions: one relates to the legal requirements of a society, and the other pertains to its need to maintain and promote social values.

Notice that the next two headings are the main idea that you should have annotated.

Protect and Punish: The Legal Function of the Law

Question: _____

_____

The primary legal function of the law is to maintain social order by protecting citizens from criminal harm. This term refers to a variety of harms that can be generalized to fit into two categories:

Question based on the main idea: _____

1. Harms to individual citizens' physical safety and property, such as the harm caused by murder, theft, or arson.
2. Harms to society's interests collectively, such as the harm caused by unsafe foods or consumer products, a polluted environment, or poorly constructed buildings.

The first category is self-evident, although even murder has different degrees, or grades, of offense to which different punishments are assigned. The second, however, has proved more problematic, for it is difficult to measure society's "collective" interests. Often, laws passed to reduce such harms seem overly intrusive and only marginally necessary. An extreme example would seem to be the Flammable Fabrics Act, which makes it a crime for a retailer to willfully remove a precautionary instruction label from a mattress that is protected with a chemical fire retardant. Yet even in this example, a criminal harm is conceivable. Suppose a retailer removes the tags before selling a large number of mattresses to a hotel chain. Employees of the chain then unknowingly wash the mattresses with an agent that lessens their flame-resistant qualities. After the mattresses have been installed in the rooms, a guest falls asleep while smoking a cigarette, starting a fire that burns down the entire hotel and causes several deaths.

Maintain and Teach: The Social Function of the Law

Question: _____

If criminal laws against acts that cause harm or injury to others are almost universally accepted, the same cannot be said for laws that criminalize "morally" wrongful activities that may do no obvious, physical harm outside the families of those involved. Why criminalize gambling or prostitution if the participants are consenting?

The answer lies in the social function of criminal law. Many observers believe that the main purpose of criminal law is to reflect the values and norms of society, or at least of those segments of society that hold power. Legal scholar Henry Hart has stated that the only justification for criminal law and punishment is "the judgment of community condemnation."

Question based on the main idea: _____

Take, for example, the misdemeanor of bigamy, which occurs when someone knowingly marries a second person without terminating her or his marriage to an original husband or wife. Apart from moral considerations, there would appear to be no victims in a bigamous relationship, and indeed many societies have allowed and continue to allow bigamy to exist. In the American social tradition, however, as John L. Diamond of the University of California's Hastings College of the Law points out:

> Marriage is an institution encouraged and supported by society. The structural importance of the integrity of the family and a monogamous marriage requires unflinching enforcement of the criminal laws against bigamy. The immorality is not in choosing to do wrong, but in transgressing, even innocently, a fundamental social boundary that lies at the core of social order.

When discussing the social function of criminal law, it is important to remember that a society's views of morality change over time. Puritan New England society not only had strict laws against adultery, but also considered lying and idleness to be criminal acts. Today, such acts may carry social stigmas, but only in certain extreme circumstances do they elicit legal sanctions. Furthermore, criminal laws aimed at minority groups, which were once widely accepted in the legal community as well as society at large, have increasingly come under question.

Some scholars believe that criminal laws not only express the expectations of society, but "teach" them as well. Professor Lawrence M. Friedman of Stanford University thinks that just as parents teach children behavioral norms through punishment, criminal justice "'teaches a lesson' to the people it punishes, and to society at large."

Question based on the main idea: _____

Burglary is one example. Making burglary a crime, arresting burglars, placing them in jail—each step in the criminal justice process reinforces the idea that burglary is unacceptable and is deserving of punishment. This teaching function can also be seen in traffic laws. There is nothing "natural" about most traffic laws; Americans drive on the right side of the street, the British on the left side, with no obvious difference in the results. These laws, such as stopping at intersections, using headlights at night, and following speed limits, do lead to a more orderly flow of traffic and fewer accidents—certainly socially desirable goals. Various forms of punishment for breaking traffic laws teach drivers the social order of the road.

—From GAINES/MILLER. *Criminal Justice in Action*, 5e (pp. 80–81)
Copyright © 2011 Cengage Learning.

1. What are the purposes of criminal law? _____

_____

2. What is the legal function of law? _____

_____

3. Give one example of the legal function of law. _____

_____

4. What is the social function of law? _____

_____

5. Give one example of the social function of law. _____

_____

Mark Only the Most Important Ideas

Questioning should become an internal habit that you use for every passage, article, section, chapter, or book you read. Good questions lead not only to better thinking but also to more effective study habits.

Notice that answering the questions about the headings or the main idea from the Interaction reading did not require rewriting the whole reading selection. You simply had to look back at the text you had highlighted based on your questions. That's because most of the words a writer uses are details and examples that help readers understand the main idea. It's the main ideas and major details that you are searching for now. Only highlight the answers to the questions you asked about the headings and the main ideas.

Should You Highlight or Annotate?

Both highlighting and annotating can be effective. It really depends on which method you prefer or which is better suited to the material you are reading. You might find using both together is most effective for your retention of information.

To clarify, highlighting is marking important text with a highlighter, pen, or pencil. Annotating is when you write notes in the margin and/

def ⟶ or use abbreviations and symbols.

The purpose of highlighting and annotating while you read is to leave a record for yourself of what you understand to be important.

Later, when you are studying or preparing to take a test, you won't have to reread everything. Instead, you should be able to go back to your highlights or annotations for focused review and studying.

Highlighting

Your highlighting should be complete enough to include the topic, main idea, and major details. It is easy to mark too much, but then when you are studying, you will have to reread more than you need to. It is also easy to mark too little, but then you might have to reread the entire passage to remember the relationship of ideas. Both too much and too little highlighting can bog you down and are to be avoided! Although each reading is different, your general goal should be to mark about 20 percent of a selection. Look at the following example to see the right amount of highlighting.

Food Security or Insecurity?

Food security includes "(1) the ready availability of nutritionally adequate and safe foods, and (2) an ensured ability to acquire acceptable foods in socially acceptable ways (that is, without resorting to emergency food supplies, scavenging, stealing, or other coping strategies)" (Economic Research Service 2001). To assess food security, the U. S. Census Bureau conducts an 18-question survey of a nationally representative sample of about 50,000 households covering topics from worry about running out of food to the number of entire days children go without eating (Nord 2001).

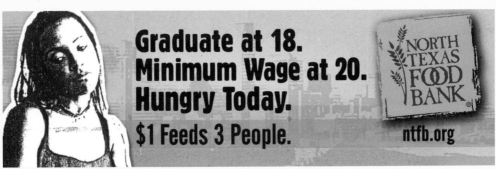

Graduate at 18.
Minimum Wage at 20.
Hungry Today.
$1 Feeds 3 People.

NORTH TEXAS FOOD BANK®

ntfb.org

North Texas Food Bank

Using these data, households are classified as food secure—they had ensured access at all times to enough food for an active, healthy life; food insecure—they were uncertain of having or unable to acquire adequate food to meet basic needs because there was not enough money for food; and food insecure with hunger—one or more household members were hungry at some time during the year because they could not afford enough food. In 1999 approximately 10% of households were classified as food insecure, including 3%, or 3.1 million households, in which people were hungry at times during the year because they could not afford enough food. (For a more complete description of how food security is measured, visit the Economic Research Service Web site at http://www.ers.usda.gov/briefing/foodsecurity/.)

—From BRYANT/COURTNEY/DEWALT/SCHWARTZ. *The Cultural Feast:*
An Introduction to Food and Society, 2e (p. 363)
Copyright © 2004 Cengage Learning.

As you can see in this example, only the important information is highlighted: the topic, the main idea, and the major details. The highlighting is intentional and follows how the key information is related.

To effectively highlight, you can follow the "APP" of the MAPP reading plan—something you have been practicing. You have marked answers to the questions you formed from headings, which are the "Points" the author wants to make, and you have turned the main ideas into questions and then marked those answers, which are the major details or "Proof" the author uses to support the main points.

Annotating: Symbols, Abbreviations, and Marginal Notes

If you use only one color of highlighting, everything you marked looks the same, and this can slow down your reviewing, because you have to rediscover the relationships of the ideas you have read. Fortunately, there is another strategy.

Abbreviations and symbols can help you be more precise about the information you are marking. They allow you to clearly label each idea for quick reference. Table 5.2 provides some basic suggestions if you choose to annotate.

Table 5.2 Use Symbols and Abbreviations to Point Out Important Ideas

Use this symbol or abbreviation	to indicate . . .
[ ]	The topic
main or MI or key or * or _____	The main idea or important point
① ② ③	List of details or steps in a sequence
def	Definition of a key term
imp EX	An important example
! or ?	Personal reactions to the material
Exam	Possible exam questions

As you can see from Table 5.2, annotation can help you clarify exactly how an idea relates to the ideas around it. And there is great flexibility using symbols. For example, if you want to underline definitions instead of main ideas, that's perfectly fine! As long as *you* know what you mean, then it will be helpful. The following paragraphs, which were used earlier to illustrate highlighting, show how you can use annotation.

Food Security or Insecurity?

Food security includes "(1) the ready availability of nutritionally adequate and safe foods, and (2) an ensured ability to acquire acceptable foods in socially acceptable ways (that is, without resorting to emergency food supplies, scavenging, stealing, or other coping strategies)" (Economic Research Service 2001). To assess food security, the U.S. Census Bureau conducts an 18-question survey of a nationally representative sample of about 50,000 households covering topics from worry about running out of food to the number of entire days children go without eating (Nord 2001).

3 def

Summary
finding

Using these data, households are classified as (food secure)—they had ensured access at all times to enough food for an active, healthy life; (food insecure)—they were uncertain of having or unable to acquire adequate (food) to meet basic needs because there was not enough money for food; and (food insecure with hunger)—one or more household members were hungry at some time during the year because they could not afford enough food. In 1999 approximately 10% of households were classified as food insecure, including 3%, or 3.1 million households, in which people were hungry at times during the year because they could not afford enough food. (For a more complete description of how food security is measured, visit the Economic Research Service Web site at http://www.ers.usda.gov/briefing/foodsecurity/.)

—From BRYANT/COURTNEY/DEWALT/SCHWARTZ. *The Cultural Feast: An Introduction to Food and Society*, 2e (p. 363)
Copyright © 2004 Cengage Learning.

As you can see in this example, only the important information is annotated, and the annotation is intentional and clarifies how the key information is related.

Ultimately, it may be easiest to understand your markings later if you combine the methods we have been discussing. For example, drawing a big star and writing the word *Point* in the margin next to the highlighted main idea will help you focus on that main idea first when you go back to review the book. If you make additional notes in the margin about the topic and pattern of organization, the notes will help jog your memory later about the major details. Whatever markings you decide to use, make sure that they make sense to you so you can use them effectively.

Turning Highlights and Annotations into an Outline

Students who highlight and annotate can then convert their markings to an outline or summary to study from. This is a powerful tool to help you move information from short-term memory into long-term memory. Here is an outline applying the APP from MAPP to the example reading.

Food Security or Insecurity?

About: Food security and insecurity

    Point: are defined in the following ways.

        Proof: 1. Food security means having easy access to nutritionally adequate and safe foods and being able to buy it.

              2. Households are then labeled in one of the following ways:

- Food secure—enough food for an active, healthy life.

- Food insecure—uncertain of having or being able to purchase food.

- Food insecure with hunger—some household members were hungry at some time during the year because they could not afford enough food.

              3. In 1999 approximately 10% of households were classified as food insecure.

Now you are prepared to study the notes that you have made based on your highlights or annotations from a textbook reading. This strategy might take a little extra time until you master it, but in the long run it saves time and is guaranteed to help you improve your academic skills, your knowledge, and your test grades.

INTERACTION 5–3 | **Highlight Only the Important Ideas**

A. Highlight each of the following paragraphs. Pay attention to whether the amount of highlighting you do is too little, too much, or just right. Let three questions guide you:

- Have you highlighted the answers to your questions?

- Are the key words of the topic, main idea, and major details highlighted?

- Is about 20 percent of the reading highlighted?

Also, turn each heading into a question.

Types of Public Speaking

Question: _____

1   Whether you have decided, been asked, or are required to participate in the public dialogue, your first step is to select the type of speech you will give. There are four different types of speeches: informative, invitational, persuasive, and speeches for special occasions. Each type has its own distinctive goal and character. Understanding what's expected of these different speech types is an important part of helping you understand and manage speech anxiety more effectively.

Informative Speeches

Question: _____

2   When the goal of a speech is to share information with others, the speech is informative. An informative speech communicates knowledge about a process, an event, a person, a place, an object, or a concept and it does so by describing, explaining, clarifying, or demonstrating information about its subject. Informative speeches are given in a wide range of situations, from informal to formal, and can vary in length depending on the situation and the audience's need.

3   In an informative speech, your ethical responsibilities are to focus on accuracy and respect. The information you provide your audience must be factually correct and clearly presented. Your audience must also understand why that information is important to them and, if appropriate, how they can use it.

Invitational Speeches

Question: _____

4   In an invitational speech, your goal is to establish a dialogue with an audience to clarify positions, explore issues and ideas, or share beliefs and values. With these speeches, you seek a reciprocal exchange of ideas and information, an exchange in which your audience participates along with you in exploring the many sides of a complex issue. As a result of your invitational speech, both you and your audience leave the interaction with a better understanding of the issue, its complexity, and why people hold the positions on it they do. Thus, invitational speaking most closely resembles an actual dialogue in which your speech initiates the conversation, setting the stage for an exchange of ideas and facilitating that exchange during or after the speech.

5   Invitational speeches are usually given in two contexts. In the first context, we want to present an issue that has many sides to it, and an invitational speech helps us explore the issue thoroughly with an audience before we decide what to do about it. In the second context, we want to speak about an issue that has polarized an audience and we know we can't persuade them to change. In this context, an invitational speech allows us and our audience to continue communicating with one another, even when we disagree profoundly. Rather than try to change other people, we speak invitationally to try to understand them. In this context, we try to see the world as our audience does and understand its views so that we can be more respectful of its positions and perspectives.

6   The primary ethical consideration in invitational speaking is your relationship to an audience. As an invitational speaker, you want to share your own views, but you also want to hear the views of your audience, especially if they are very different from your own. Because of this relationship, people who speak invitationally are ethically bound to create an environment in which all the participants are able to articulate their differences, similarities, and perspectives without judgment or attempts to change them. The goal is to create an atmosphere in which people can listen to one another with respect and openness.

Persuasive Speeches

Question: _____

7   A persuasive speech is one whose message attempts to change or reinforce an audience's thoughts, feelings, or actions. When we speak to persuade, we act as advocates, encouraging or discouraging certain thoughts and actions. We urge our audience to accept our views or solutions, take a particular action, buy certain products, or adopt specific proposals. When we persuade others, we defend an idea and ask our audience to agree with us rather than someone else. We seek to change or reinforce our audience's attitudes (positive or negative feelings about something), beliefs (ideas about what is real or true), or values (ideas of what is good or worthy).

8   Because persuasive speakers act as advocates for positions concerning complicated, often polarizing issues, their words and actions carry unique ethical responsibilities. Persuasive speakers must advocate their position without threatening, intimidating, or belittling their audience. They also must present their position without distorting or omitting important details or facts that make their case more persuasive. Finally, they must recognize the audience's right to make its own decision concerning the issue.

Speaking on Special Occasions

Question: _____

9   The type of speech you give at special occasions such as award ceremonies, banquets, weddings, and retirement parties is very different from informative, invitational, and persuasive speeches. Your goal with a special occasion speech is to mark an event as distinct and to help your audience reflect on the special nature of the gathering. With special occasion speeches, you introduce (yourself, someone else, or an event), commemorate (another person for his or her accomplishments), or accept (an award or special recognition).

10   When you present information with the intention of introducing yourself, another person, or an event to an audience, you are giving an introductory speech. In an introductory speech, your goal is to give the audience a compelling perspective on yourself or another person or to welcome the audience to an event and familiarize them with it. Introductory speeches often take place in formal settings (ceremonial events, job interviews, professional gatherings) and usually are quite short.

11   When you introduce yourself, you share with an audience what is interesting about you and relevant to the occasion. You may describe your skills, talents, and the events in your life that have shaped who you are and what you value, but whatever you say about yourself, you want your audience to be glad they've had the opportunity to meet you. When you introduce another person, you describe his or her contributions, qualifications, or talents with the aim of stimulating the audience's recognition and interest. When you introduce an event, you set the stage for a particular program or activity. You explain the importance of the event, what's to come, and, if appropriate, offer information about how the audience can or should participate in the event. Remember that a person's or an event's reputation and credibility rest at the heart of an introductory speech. Thus, you are ethically bound to tell the truth and to create an environment that fosters awareness, appreciation, respect, and understanding.

12   When you give a commemorative speech, sometimes called a speech of tribute, you praise, honor, recognize, or pay tribute to a person, an event, an idea, or an institution. Commemorative speeches often take place in formal settings such as retirement parties, weddings, anniversaries, birthday parties, and memorial services. Your goal in a commemorative speech is to share what is unique and special about someone or something and to express appreciation for special qualities and contributions. A commemorative speaking environment emphasizes values and celebrates accomplishments and contributions that have positively affected others. Your ethical responsibility as a speaker is to tell the truth about who or what you are commemorating. You should also only share information that is appropriate and relevant to fostering recognition and appreciation in the audience for the person, event, idea, or institution.

13   When you give an acceptance speech, your goal is to communicate your gratitude, appreciation, and pleasure at receiving an honor or a gift in recognition of your accomplishments. Acceptance speeches are often given at formal gatherings, such as awards ceremonies or banquets, but they may also be given in more informal or casual situations, such as after a competition. When you give an acceptance speech, your ethical responsibilities are to express sincere appreciation for the recognition you are receiving. You can do this by conveying your understanding of the meaning and importance of the award. You also can do so by acknowledging those who have helped you reach your goals.

AP Photo/Mark J. Terrill

14   As you learn to give these various types of speeches, you will discover that each is appropriate to particular situations and requires a particular kind of environment or tone. You may find you are more comfortable with some types of speeches than you are with others. However, note that each type of speech has its place in the public dialogue, and learning to give each will help you be more successful in that dialogue once you complete your public speaking class.

—From GRIFFIN. *Invitation to Public Speaking*, 3e (pp. 23–28)
Copyright © 2009 Cengage Learning.

B. You have already "Marked" this passage. Now fill in the APP outline below using your highlighting.

About: _____

  Point: _____

    Proof: 1. _____

                _____

          2. _____

                _____

a. _____

b. _____

3. _____

_____

4. _____

_____

a. _____

_____

_____

b. _____

_____

c. _____

_____

_____

INTERACTION 5–4   **Annotate Only the Important Ideas**

A. Read through the following passage. Use symbols, marginal abbreviations, and annotations to mark the important information you will need: topic, main idea, and major details. Also, turn each heading into a question.

Defining Culture

Question: _____

1   Culture is the complex system of meaning and behavior that defines the way of life for a given group or society. It includes beliefs, values, knowledge, art, morals, laws, customs, habits, language, and dress, among other things. Culture includes ways of thinking as well as patterns of behavior. Observing culture involves studying what people think, how they interact, and the objects they use.

2   In any society, culture defines what is perceived as beautiful and ugly, right and wrong, good and bad. Culture helps hold society together, giving people a sense of belonging, instructing them on how to behave, and telling them what to think in particular situations. Culture gives meaning to society.

Culture Is Both Material and Nonmaterial

Question: _____

3   Material culture consists of the objects created in a given society—its buildings, art, tools, toys, print and broadcast media, and other tangible objects. In the popular mind, material artifacts constitute culture because they can be collected in museums or archives and analyzed for what they represent. These objects are significant because of the meaning they are given. A temple, for example, is not merely a building, nor is it only a place of worship. Its form and presentation signify the religious meaning system of the faithful.

4   Nonmaterial culture includes the norms, laws, customs, ideas, and beliefs of a group of people. Nonmaterial culture is less tangible than material culture, but it has a strong presence in social behavior. Examples of nonmaterial culture are numerous and found in the patterns of everyday life. In some cultures, people eat with silverware; in others, with chopsticks; and in some, with their fingers. Such are the practices of nonmaterial culture, but note that the eating utensils are part of material culture.

5   There is a link between nonmaterial and material culture: Material culture can be the manifestation of nonmaterial culture; at the same time, nonmaterial culture can be shaped by material culture (such as when widespread marketing fosters a culture of consumerism).

Characteristics of Culture

Question based on the title/topic: _____

6   Across societies, certain features of culture are noted by sociologists. These different characteristics of culture are examined here.

7   Culture is shared. Culture would have no significance if people did not hold it in common. Culture is not idiosyncratic; rather, it is collectively experienced and collectively agreed upon. The shared nature of culture makes human society possible. The shared basis of culture may be difficult to see in complex societies where groups have different traditions, perspectives, and ways of thinking and behaving. In the United States, for example, different racial and ethnic groups have unique histories, languages, and beliefs—that is, different cultures. Even within these groups, there are diverse cultural traditions. Latinos, for example, comprise many groups with distinct origins and cultures. Still, there are features of Latino culture, such as the Spanish language and some values and traditions, that are shared. The different groups constituting Latino culture also share a culture that is shaped by their common experiences as minorities in the United States. Similarly, African Americans have created a rich and distinct culture

that is the result of their unique experience within the United States. What identifies African American culture are the practices and traditions that have evolved from both the U.S. experience and African and Caribbean traditions. Placed in another country, such as an African nation, African Americans would likely recognize elements of their culture, but they would also feel culturally distinct as Americans.

8   Within the United States, culture varies by age, race, region, gender, ethnicity, religion, class, and other social factors. A person growing up in the South is likely to develop different tastes, modes of speech, and cultural interests than a person raised in the West. Despite these differences, there is a common cultural basis to life in the United States. Certain symbols, language patterns, belief systems, and ways of thinking are distinctively American and form a common culture even though great cultural diversity exists.

9   Culture is learned. Cultural beliefs and practices are usually so well learned that they seem perfectly natural, but they are learned nonetheless. How do people come to prefer some foods to others? How is musical taste acquired? Culture may be taught through direct instruction, such as a parent teaching a child how to use silverware or teachers instructing children in songs, myths, and other traditions in school.

10   Culture is also learned indirectly through observation and imitation. Think of how a person learns what it means to be a man or a woman. Although the "proper" roles for men and women may never be explicitly taught, one learns what is expected from observing others. A person becomes a member of a culture through both formal and informal transmission of culture. Until the culture is learned, the person will feel like an outsider. The process of learning culture is referred to by sociologists as socialization.

11   Culture is taken for granted. Because culture is learned, members of a given society seldom question the culture of which they are a part, unless for some reason they become outsiders or establish some critical distance from the usual cultural expectations. People engage unthinkingly in hundreds of specifically cultural practices every day; culture makes these practices seem "normal." If you suddenly stopped participating in your culture and questioned each belief and every behavior, you would soon find yourself feeling detached and perhaps a little disoriented; you would also become increasingly ineffective at functioning within your group. Little wonder that tourists stand out so much in a

foreign culture. They rarely have much knowledge of the culture they are visiting and, even when they are well informed, typically approach the society from their own cultural orientation.

12   Think, for example, of how you might feel if you were a Native American student in a predominantly White classroom. Many, though not all, Native American people are raised to be quiet and not outspoken. If students in a classroom are expected to assert themselves and state what is on their minds, a Native American student may feel awkward, as will others for whom these expectations are contrary to their cultural upbringing. If the professor is not aware of these cultural differences, he or she may penalize students who are quiet, resulting perhaps in a lower grade for the student from a different cultural background. Culture binds us together, but lack of communication across cultures can have negative consequences, as this example shows.

13   Culture is symbolic. The significance of culture lies in the meaning it holds for people. Symbols are things or behaviors to which people give meaning; the meaning is not inherent in a symbol but is bestowed by the meaning people give it. The U.S. flag, for example, is literally a decorated piece of cloth. Its cultural significance derives not from the cloth of which it is made, but from its meaning as a symbol of freedom and democracy, as was witnessed by the widespread flying of the flag after the terrorist attacks on the United States on September 11, 2001.

14   That something has symbolic meaning does not make it any less important or influential than objective facts. In fact, symbols are powerful expressions of human life. Protests over the flying of the Confederate flag provide a good example. Those who object to the flag being displayed on public buildings see the Confederate flag as a symbol of racism and the legacy of slavery. Those who defend the flying of the flag see it as representing Southern heritage, a symbol of group pride and regional loyalty. Similarly, the use of Native American mascots to name and represent sports teams is symbolic of the exploitation of Native Americans. (Think of the Washington Redskins, the Cleveland Indians, the Atlanta Braves' "tomahawk chop," and various college mascots.) Native American activists and their supporters see these mascots as derogatory and extremely insulting, representing gross caricatures of Native American traditions. The protests that have developed over controversial symbols are indicative of the enormous influence of cultural symbols.

15   Symbols mean different things in different contexts. The U.S. flag, for example, is to Shiite extremists in Iraq and Iran a despised symbol of U.S. imperialism. A flag tattooed on someone's arm has a meaning different from a flag insignia stitched on a military uniform. Similarly, a cross on a church altar has a meaning different from a cross burning in someone's front yard.

16   One interesting thing about culture is the extent to which symbolic attachments guide human behavior. For example, people stand when the national anthem is sung and may feel emotional from displays of the cross or the Star of David. Under some conditions, people organize mass movements to protest what they see as the defamation of important symbols, such as the burning of a flag or the burning of a cross. The significance of the symbolic value of culture can hardly be overestimated. Learning a culture means not just engaging in particular behaviors but also learning their symbolic meanings within the culture.

17   Culture varies across time and place. Culture develops as humans adapt to the physical and social environment around them. Since this environment varies from one society to another, and since human beings use their creative imagination to develop cultural solutions to the challenges they face, culture is not fixed from one place to another. In the United States, for example, there is a strong cultural belief in scientific solutions to human problems; consequently, many think that problems of food supply and environmental deterioration can be addressed by scientific breakthroughs, such as genetic engineering to create high-yield tomatoes or bacteria that eat oil spills. In another cultural setting, other solutions may seem preferable. Indeed, a religious culture might think that genetic engineering trespasses on divine territory, and in many cultures science may be seen as creating more problems than it solves (Harding 1998).

18   Because culture varies from one setting to another, the meanings that develop within a culture must be seen in their cultural context. Cultural relativism is the idea that something can be understood and judged only in relationship to the cultural context in which it appears. This does not make every cultural practice morally acceptable, but it suggests that without knowing the cultural context, it is impossible to understand why people behave as they do. For example, in the United States, burying or cremating the dead is the cultural practice. It may be difficult for someone from this culture to understand that in Tibet, with a ruggedly cold climate and the inability to dig the soil, the dead are cut into pieces and left for vultures to eat.

Although this would be repulsive (and illegal) in the United States, within Tibetan culture, this practice is understandable.

19   Not only does culture vary from place to place, it also varies over time. As people encounter new situations, the culture that emerges is a mix of the past and present. Second-generation immigrants to the United States are raised in the traditions of their culture of origin, and children of immigrants typically grow up with both the traditional cultural expectations of their parents' homeland and the cultural expectations of a new society. Adapting to the new society can create conflict between generations, especially if the older generation is intent on passing along their cultural traditions. The children may be more influenced by their peers and may choose to dress, speak, and behave in ways that are characteristic of their new society but unacceptable to their parents (Portes and Rumbaut 2001).

20   To sum up: Culture is concrete because we can observe the cultural objects and practices that define human experience. Culture is abstract because it is a way of thinking, feeling, believing, and behaving. Culture links the past and the present because it is the knowledge that makes us part of human groups. Culture gives shape to human experience.

—From ANDERSEN/TAYLOR. *Sociology*: *The Essentials*, 4e
(pp. 36–40) Copyright © 2007 Cengage Learning.

B. Use the title and headings from the reading to summarize the key terms and concepts.

1. What is culture? _____

_____

2. What is material culture? _____

_____

3. What is nonmaterial culture? _____

_____

4. What are the characteristics of culture? Give an example of each.

a. _____

_____

b. _____

_____

c. _____

_____

d. _____

_____

e. _____

_____

Section Review: Ask Questions and Mark the Answers

Fill in the following visual outlines based on the information from this section.

> Forming questions from headings has three benefits for the reader:

1.
2.
3.

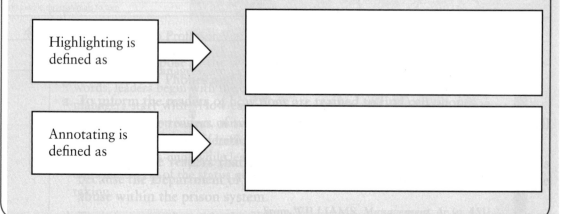

Highlighting is defined as ⟹ [ ]

Annotating is defined as ⟹ [ ]

Use Cornell Notes to Record Ideas

Once you have asked the questions and marked the answers in a reading, you can use a notebook to take notes on the main points and key details you want to remember. A classic and helpful system is the Cornell note-taking system; it is named for the university at which Walter Pauk, the creator of the system, taught. This system is highly effective for both notes on reading assignments and notes from lectures in class. To use this system, make two columns in your notebook. Here is what it looks like:

Cornell Notes	
Main points, big ideas, key terms, and questions:	**Notes: Key details, examples, explanations**
↓	1. During reading/lecture
	Take notes in this space
	← 6 inches →
2. Soon after reading/ lecture	To study, cover this section with your hand and attempt to recall the details of the main points, big ideas, key terms, or questions written on the left.
Read through your notes soon after taking them and pull out the main ideas in the form of key terms, phrases, or questions to create clues to help yourself recall the details. ↓	
← 2.5 inches →	
Summary:	
3. Recall your notes on the lecture/reading when studying for a test. Summarize your notes into a few sentences. This can be done at the bottom of each page of notes, after a section, or after a chapter.	

↑ 2 inches ↓

There are several advantages of the Cornell note-taking system:

- It helps you get an overview of key ideas in longer readings or lectures.
- It allows you to organize your ideas from big to small.
- It gives you a chance to summarize concepts you might be tested on.
- It gives you a structure for effective studying.

Look at the following example of a Cornell note-taking entry. It is based upon the article "Defining Culture" from pages 295–301.

Culture	A complex system of meaning, thinking, and behavior that defines the way of life for a given group or society.
Material culture	The objects created in a given society. • Buildings, art, tools, toys, ads, etc.
Nonmaterial culture	The norms, laws, customs, ideas, and beliefs of a group of people.
Characteristics of culture	(1) Shared (2) Learned (3) Taken for granted (4) Symbolic (5) Varies across time and place

Summary:

Culture is a complicated system of meaning, thinking, and behavior that a group or society follows. There are two kinds of culture: material, which includes things like buildings, art, and toys, and nonmaterial, which includes things like laws, customs, and beliefs. Culture has several characteristics: It is shared, learned, taken for granted, symbolic, and varies over time and location.

In the right column, you can see the detailed notes. In the left column, headings or key words summarize a main idea or identify key terms.

You can use the MAPP strategy, short outlines, or lists to write down the major supporting details while you are taking notes. Here are some hints:

- Use words or images that will help you remember the pattern of relationship between the ideas. Ideas are easier to remember when you understand their relationship.

- Use numbered lists. After you have reviewed your notes several times, you will remember how many points there are in a particular answer. You can use that knowledge as a check to see whether you are remembering all of the points.

- Abbreviate as you like. Develop a system of abbreviations you can use in all your classes to make note taking more efficient.

INTERACTION 5–5 | **Create Cornell Notes**

Ask questions, read, and highlight or annotate the main ideas and supporting details in the following short passages. Fill in the Cornell notes at the end of the reading based on your markings, with the main idea on the left side and the key details on the right.

1.

Strategies for Problem Solving

1   When you are trying to get from one place to another, the best path may not necessarily be a straight line. In fact, obstacles may require going in the opposite direction to get around them. So it is with problem solving. Sometimes the best strategy does not involve mental steps aimed straight at your goal. For example, when a problem is especially difficult, it can sometimes be helpful to allow it to "incubate" by setting it aside for a while. A solution that once seemed out of reach may suddenly appear after you have been thinking about other things. The benefits of incubation probably arise from forgetting incorrect ideas that may have been blocking the path to a correct solution (Anderson, 2000). Other effective problem-solving strategies are more direct.

2   One of these strategies is called means-end analysis. It involves continuously asking where you are in relation to your final goal and then deciding on the means by which you can get one step closer to that goal (Newell & Simon, 1972). In other words, rather than trying to solve the problem all at once, you identify a subgoal that will take you toward a solution (this process is also referred to as decomposition). After reaching that subgoal, you identify another one that will get you even closer to the solution, and you continue this step-by-step process until the problem is solved. Some students apply this approach to the problem of writing a major term paper. The task might seem overwhelming at first, but their first subgoal is simply to write an outline of what they think the paper should cover. When the outline is complete, they decide whether a paper based on it will satisfy the assignment. If it will, the next subgoal might be to search the library and the Internet for information about each section. If they decide that this information is adequate, the next subgoal would be to write a rough draft of the introduction, and so on.

3   A second strategy in problem solving is to work backward. Many problems are like a tree. The trunk is the information you are given; the solution is a twig on one of the branches. If you work forward by taking the "givens" of the problem and trying to find the solution, it's easy to branch off in the wrong direction. Sometimes the more efficient approach is to start at the twig end and work backward. Consider the problem of planning a climb to the summit of Mount Everest. The best strategy is to figure out, first, what equipment and supplies are needed at the highest camp on the night before the attempt to reach the summit, then how many people are needed to stock that camp the day before, then how many people are needed to supply those who must stock the camp, and so on until a plan for the entire expedition is established. People often overlook the working-backward strategy because it runs counter to the way they have learned to think. It is hard to imagine that the first step in solving a problem could be to assume that you have already solved it. Sadly, it was partly because of failure to apply this strategy that six climbers died on Everest in 1996 (Krakauer, 1997).

4   A third problem-solving strategy is trying to find analogies, or similarities, between today's problem and others you have encountered before. A supervisor may discover that a seemingly hopeless problem between co-workers can be resolved by the same compromise that worked during a recent family squabble. Of course, to take advantage of analogies, you must first recognize the similarities between current and previous problems. Then you will be in a position to recall the solution that worked before. Unfortunately, most people are surprisingly poor at seeing the similarities between new and old problems (Anderson, 2000). They tend to concentrate on the surface features that make problems appear different.

—From BERNSTEIN. *Essentials of Psychology*, 5e (pp. 258–259)
Copyright © 2011 Cengage Learning.

Andres Peiro Palmer/istockphoto.com

2.

Parenting Styles

European American parents tend to employ one of four distinct parenting styles (Baumrind, 1991; Maccoby & Martin, 1983). Authoritarian parents tend to be strict, punishing, and unsympathetic. They value obedience from children and try to curb children's wills and shape their children's behavior to meet a set standard. They do not encourage independence. They are detached and seldom praise their youngsters. In contrast, permissive parents give their children complete freedom and provide little discipline. Authoritative parents fall between these two extremes. They reason with their children, encouraging give and take. They allow children increasing responsibility as they get older and better at making decisions. They are firm but understanding. They set limits but also encourage independence. Their demands are reasonable, rational, and consistent. Uninvolved parents are indifferent to their children. They invest as little time, money, and effort in their children as possible, focusing on their needs before their children's. These parents often fail to monitor their children's activities, particularly when the children are old enough to be out of the house alone.

—From BERNSTEIN. *Essentials of Psychology*, 5e (p. 369)
Copyright © 2011 Cengage Learning.

_____

3.

The Structure of Personality

1   Freud believed that people are born with basic needs or instincts—not only for food and water but also for sex and aggression (Schultz & Schultz, 2009). He believed that needs for love, knowledge, security, and the like arise from these more fundamental desires. He said that each of us has to find ways of meeting our needs in a world that often frustrates our efforts. Our personalities develop, said Freud, as we struggle with this task and are reflected in the way we satisfy a wide range of urges.

2   Freud described the personality as having three major components: the id, the ego, and the superego (Allen, 2006; see Figure 11.1). The id represents the inborn, unconscious portion of the personality where life and death instincts reside. The life instincts promote positive, constructive behavior; the death instincts are responsible for human aggression and destructiveness (Carver & Scheier, 2004). The id operates on the pleasure principle, seeking immediate satisfaction of both kinds of instincts, regardless of society's rules or the rights and feelings of others. The hungry person who pushes to the front of the line at Burger King would be satisfying an id-driven impulse.

3   As parents, teachers, and others place ever greater restrictions on the expression of id impulses, a second part of the personality, called the ego (or "self"), emerges from the id. The ego is responsible for organizing ways to get what a person wants in the real world, as opposed to the fantasy world of the id. Operating on the reality principle, the ego makes compromises as the id's demands for immediate satisfaction run into the practical realities of the social world. The ego would influence that hungry person at Burger King to wait in line and think about what to order rather than risk punishment by pushing ahead.

4   As children gain experience with the rules and values of society, they tend to adopt them. This process of internalizing parental and cultural values creates the third component of personality. It is called the superego, and it tells us what we should and should not do. The superego becomes our moral guide, and it is just as relentless and unreasonable as the id in its demands to be obeyed. The superego would make the person at Burger King feel guilty for even thinking about violating culturally approved rules about waiting in line.

—From BERNSTEIN. *Essentials of Psychology*, 5e (p. 427)
Copyright © 2011 Cengage Learning.

4.

Stages of Personality Development

1   Freud proposed that during childhood, personality evolves through several stages of psychosexual development. Failure to resolve the conflicts that appear at any of these stages can leave a person fixated—that is, unconsciously preoccupied with the area of pleasure associated with that stage. Freud believed that the stage at which a person became fixated in childhood can be seen in the person's adult personality characteristics.

2   In Freud's theory, a child's first year or so is called the oral stage because the mouth—which infants use to eat and to explore everything from toys to their own hands and feet—is the center of pleasure during this period. Personality problems arise, said Freud, when oral needs are either neglected or overindulged. For example, early or late weaning from breastfeeding or bottle feeding may leave a child fixated at the oral stage. The resulting adult characteristics may range from overeating or childlike dependence (late weaning) to the use of "biting" sarcasm (early weaning).

Andres Peiro Palmer/istockphoto.com

3   The anal stage occurs during the second year, when the child's ego develops to cope with parental demands for socially appropriate behavior. For example, in most Western cultures, toilet training clashes with the child's freedom to have bowel movements at will. Freud said that if toilet training is too harsh or begins too early, it can produce an anal fixation that leads, in adulthood, to stinginess or excessive neatness (symbolically withholding feces). If toilet training is too late or too lax, however, the result could be a kind of anal fixation that is reflected in adults who are disorganized or impulsive (symbolically expelling feces).

4   According to Freud, between the ages of three and five the focus of pleasure shifts to the genital area. Because he emphasized the psychosexual development of boys, Freud called this period the phallic stage (phallus is another word for penis). It is during this stage, he claimed, that the boy experiences sexual feelings for his mother and a desire to eliminate, or even kill, his father, with whom the boy competes for the mother's affection. Freud called this set of impulses the Oedipal complex because it reminded him of the plot of the classical Greek play Oedipus Rex. (In the play, Oedipus unknowingly kills his father and marries his mother.) The boy's fantasies create so much fear, however, that the ego represses his incestuous desires and leads him to "identify" with his father and try to be like him. In the process, the child's superego begins to develop.

5   According to Freud, a girl begins the phallic stage with a strong attachment to her mother. However, when she realizes that boys have penises and girls don't, she supposedly develops penis envy and transfers her love to the father. (This sequence has been called the Electra complex because it echoes the plot of Electra, another classical Greek play, but Freud never used this term.) To avoid her mother's disapproval, the girl identifies with and imitates her, thus forming the basis for her own superego.

6   Freud believed that unresolved conflicts during the phallic stage create a fixation that is reflected in many kinds of adult problems. These problems can include difficulties with authority figures and an inability to maintain a stable love relationship.

7   As the phallic stage draws to a close and its conflicts are coped with by the ego, there is an interval of psychological peace. During this latency period, which lasts through childhood, sexual impulses stay in the background as the youngster focuses on education, same-sex peer play, and the development of social skills.

8   During adolescence, when sexual impulses reappear at the conscious level, the genitals again become the focus of pleasure. Thus begins what Freud called the genital stage, which lasts for the rest of the person's life. The quality of relationships and the degree of fulfillment experienced during this final stage, he claimed, are influenced by how intrapsychic conflicts were resolved during the earlier stages.

—From BERNSTEIN. *Essentials of Psychology*, 5e (pp. 428–430)
Copyright © 2011 Cengage Learning.

Summary:

Andres Peiro Palmer/istockphoto.com

Section Review: Use Cornell Notes to Record Ideas

Complete the Cornell notes.

Four advantages of Cornell note taking:	1.
	2.
	3.
	4.

Paraphrase to Recall Ideas

A paraphrase is a restatement of someone else's ideas using your own words. Paraphrasing an author's thoughts is a good way to improve your comprehension of text.

Because paraphrasing takes a little time, you should use it particularly for short sections of text you don't understand but believe are important to know in detail. It is also often applicable when you need to write a paper and want to avoid plagiarizing.

Two methods of paraphrasing will be covered here:

1. Switch it, flip it, tweak it: Use synonyms for key words and change the order of phrases when applicable.

2. Flesh it out: Reduce the text to an outline, map, double-column notes, or a list, and then rewrite the details into paragraph form. (To flesh out an idea means to give it substance with specific details.)

Switch It, Flip It, Tweak It

This technique works very well when you need to paraphrase a sentence. It can also make short work of quotes. You focus on the key words, and you switch in similar words. Then you look at clauses or phrases to see if the order can be flipped. This technique is flexible because you can switch then flip, or flip then switch, or only do one, or play with any variation until you get a nice-sounding sentence. Here is an example:

There is nothing so rewarding as to make [making] people realize that they are worthwhile in this world.

—Bob Anderson

Flip it: Making people realize that they are worthwhile in this world, there is nothing so rewarding.

Switch it: Helping people appreciate that they have value is the most enriching thing one can do.

The switch holds the meaning of the quote but uses different words. And you can always tweak your sentence if that will make it sound better. Say, for example, you decide to change the word *enriching* to *fulfilling* and *thing* to *action* and *do* to *accomplish*. Now, your paraphrased saying is this:

Helping people appreciate that they have value is the most fulfilling action one can accomplish.

You can use the same strategies on different words to make the paraphrase sound as natural as possible. You have now flipped, switched, and tweaked it. But more importantly, you have made it your own!

INTERACTION 5–6 | **Switch It, Flip It, Tweak It (As Needed)**

Read the following quotes and practice the switch-it-and-flip-it strategy. Tweak your versions as needed until you get the one you like best.

1. "Behold the turtle, he makes progress only when he sticks his neck out." —James Bryant Conant

   Switch it: _____

   Flip it: _____

   Tweak it: _____

2. "Buy land, they're not making it anymore." —Mark Twain

   Switch it: _____

   Flip it: _____

   Tweak it: _____

3. "The weak can never forgive. Forgiveness is the attribute of the strong." —Mahatma Gandhi

Switch it: _____

Flip it: _____

Tweak it: _____

4. "Always look at what you have left. Never look at what you have lost." —Robert Schuller

Switch it: _____

Flip it: _____

Tweak it: _____

5. "Our greatest weakness lies in giving up. The most certain way to succeed is always to try one more time." —Thomas Edison

Switch it: _____

Flip it: _____

Tweak it: _____

The switch it, flip it, tweak it approach can also work with definitions. This is especially helpful in life science or social science classes, which often have many new concepts, processes, and terms.

INTERACTION 5–7 | **Switch It, Flip It, Tweak It Applied to Definitions**

Read the following terms and their definitions, taken from *Introduction to Business*, 4th edition, by Jeff Madura.

1. **auditing:** an assessment of the records that were used to prepare a firm's financial statements.

Switch it: _____

Flip it: _____

Tweak it: _____

_____

2. **business plan:** a detailed description of the proposed business, including a description of the product or service, the types of customers it would attract, the competition, and the facilities needed for production.

Switch it: _____

Flip it: _____

Tweak it: _____

_____

3. **consumerism:** the collective demand by consumers that businesses satisfy their needs.

Switch it: _____

Flip it: _____

Tweak it: the idea that _____

_____

4. **expectancy theory:** holds that an employee's efforts are influenced by the expected outcome (reward) for those efforts.

Switch it: _____

Flip it: _____

Tweak it: _____

_____

5. **participative management:** employees are allowed to participate in various decisions made by their supervisors or others.

Switch it: _____

Flip it: _____

Tweak it: _____

_____

You have practiced this technique on simple sentences and definitions; however, this technique can also work on multiple sentences or paragraphs. You simply work through one sentence at a time until you finish the paragraph.

Flesh It Out

This technique works best when you need to paraphrase the content of paragraphs or longer passages that you must understand in entirety. Simply read the passage normally, highlighting and annotating as you read. You may also use a dictionary to look up any words you do not know, or a thesaurus to find an easier synonym for a complicated word. Then reduce the text to an outline, map, Cornell notes, or a list, and rewrite the details into paragraph form. For example, this might be necessary in a government class. Many times students need to learn the Bill of Rights (the first ten amendments to the U.S. Constitution) or maybe even all twenty-seven amendments. The flesh-it-out paraphrasing method would work well with learning the amendments. Here is an example using the First Amendment:

Amendment I

Congress shall make no law respecting an establishment of religion, or prohibiting the free exercise thereof; or abridging the freedom of speech, or of the press; or the right of the people peaceably to assemble, and to petition the Government for a redress of grievances.

© 2013 Cengage Learning

Outline or Key Words from Annotation

Congress cannot make laws

Denying freedom of religion

Freedom of speech, the press, or demonstrations

Can appeal wrongdoing and expect a remedy

Flesh It Out

Congress cannot make any laws that favor one religion over another; they cannot stop freedom of religion, speech, the news, or the right to demonstrate. In addition, the people can appeal any wrongdoing and expect a solution.

INTERACTION 5–8 | **Flesh Out a Paragraph**

Read the following amendments to the U.S. Constitution, marking key words as you go. Paraphrase each amendment when you are done, using key words or concepts from your annotations or highlights. You may use a dictionary or thesaurus if needed. Then flesh out your notes into a new paragraph.

> # Amendment IV
>
> The right of the people to be secure in their persons, houses, papers, and effects, against unreasonable searches and seizures, shall not be violated, and no Warrants shall issue, but upon probable cause, supported by Oath or affirmation, and particularly describing the place to be searched, and the persons or things to be seized.

Outline or key words from annotation:

_____

_____

_____

Flesh it out:

_____

_____

_____

Amendment V

No person shall be held to answer for a capital, or otherwise infamous crime, unless on a presentment or indictment of a Grand Jury, except in cases arising in the land or naval forces, or in the Militia, when in actual service in time of War or public danger; nor shall any person be subject for the same offence to be twice put in jeopardy of life or limb; nor shall be compelled in any criminal case to be a witness against himself, nor be deprived of life, liberty, or property, without due process of law; nor shall private property be taken for public use, without just compensation.

Outline or key words from annotation:

_____

_____

_____

_____

Flesh it out:

_____

_____

_____

Amendment VI

In all criminal prosecutions, the accused shall enjoy the right to a speedy and public trial, by an impartial jury of the State and district wherein the crime shall have been committed, which district shall have been previously ascertained by law, and to be informed of the nature and cause of the accusation; to be confronted with the witnesses against him; to have compulsory process for obtaining witnesses in his favor, and to have the Assistance of Counsel for his defense.

Outline or key words from annotation:

_____

_____

_____

_____

Flesh it out:

_____

_____

_____

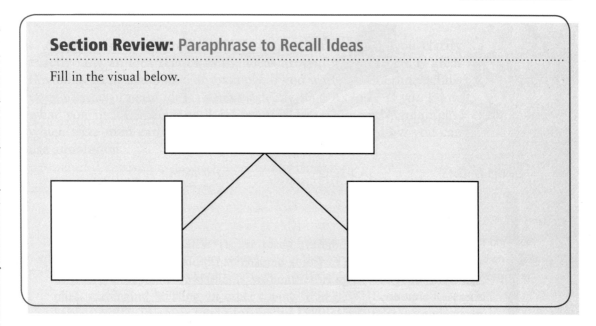

Section Review: Paraphrase to Recall Ideas

Fill in the visual below.

Chapter Summary Activity:
Applying Reading Comprehension Skills through Note Taking

Chapter 5 has discussed how to ask questions and mark the answers, highlighting, annotating, using the "APP" outline, Cornell note taking, and paraphrasing. Fill in the following Reading Guide by completing each idea on the left with information from Chapter 5 on the right. You can return to this guide throughout the course as a reminder of how to take notes on important information.

Reading Guide to Applying Reading Comprehension Skills through Note Taking

Complete this idea	with information from Chapter 5.
Asking questions offers the following three advantages:	1. _____ 2. _____ 3. _____
To use the questioning strategy, turn the _____, _____, or _____ into a question.	4. _____ 5. _____ 6. _____
Read until you find the answer to your question and then _____ it.	7. _____
When you are highlighting, you should only mark about _____ of the text.	8. _____
Two easy errors to make when highlighting is to mark too _____ or too _____.	9. _____ 10. _____
Annotating uses marginal notes, _____, and _____.	11. _____ 12. _____
The symbol recommended to use for a topic is a	13. _____
The symbol recommended to use for a main idea is a	14. _____
The symbol recommended for major details is	15. _____
Cornell note taking can help you in four ways by providing	16. _____ 17. _____ 18. _____ 19. _____
A paraphrase can be defined as:	20. _____ _____

Complete this idea	with information from Chapter 5.
Changing the key words and order of phrases or clauses is one way to paraphrase. What three parts does this method have?	21. _____ 22. _____ 23. _____
Condensing a paragraph or longer reading into Cornell notes and then rewriting it in your own words is called _____.	24. _____

25. Think about what your reading strategies were before you read Chapter 5. How did they differ from the suggestions here? Write your thoughts.

_____

_____

_____

PART 2

"I have had dreams and I have had nightmares, but I have conquered my nightmares because of my dreams."

—Jonas Salk, the scientist who discovered the polio vaccine

Critical Reading Strategies

The theme of the movie *Inception* (2010) is that an idea can be planted into a person's subconscious (a dream within a dream). In order to achieve this, the main character, Dom Cobb (Leonardo DiCaprio), creates several layers of a dream within the target's mind and then endures hair-raising adventures to accomplish the "inception." Things never quite work out as planned, and the characters have to scramble as well as think critically in order to solve problems and survive. However, each is driven by a goal or dream. Cobb's goal is to be reunited with his children.

Life is like that! We have a dream, set a plan, but it never quite works out as easily as it looked in our mind's eye. However, as *Inception* illustrates, there are two strategies that can bring us closer to our dreams. (1) Take action. Set a goal. Make a plan. Move toward it. (2) Think critically. When a problem arises, think about how you can solve it. Be creative and flexible. If one attempt doesn't work, try again. It's okay to change strategies based on what you learn. The more critical thinking strategies you have to draw on, the better you will become at solving problems.

. . . .

Share Your Prior Knowledge

Brainstorm with a classmate about movies or TV shows you have enjoyed where the main character had to use his or her brains to overcome or survive.

1. _____

2. _____

3. _____

Now share a time where you have had to think critically in order to overcome a problem. List three strategies you used.

1. _____

2. _____

3. _____

6 Asking Critical Thinking Questions

Previewing the Chapter

Flip through the pages of Chapter 6, and read all the major headings. Look at all the images, both photos and figures, and read their captions.

Predict four topics this chapter will cover.

- _____
- _____
- _____
- _____

Based on the figures in the chapter, write a statement about the topic of the chapter.

_____

_____

Plan to come back and comment on the accuracy of your statement when you have finished working through the chapter.

_____

_____

To access additional course materials for *Engage,* including quizzes, videos, and more, please visit www.cengagebrain.com. At the CengageBrain.com home page, search for the ISBN of *Engage* (from the back cover of your book) using the search box at the top of the page. This will take you to the product page where these resources can be found.

Videos Related to Readings

Vocab Words on Audio

Read and Talk on Demand

Read and Talk

MEMOIR

In college, reading is just one aspect of how you will share new ideas with others in your class. So the first reading in each chapter of this book is meant to give you the chance to talk about reading. Read the article, and then use the four discussion questions to talk about your ideas with your classmates and your instructor.

Access the Reading CourseMate via www.cengagebrain.com to hear a reading of this selection and view a video about this topic.

Lone Survivor

Marcus Luttrell and Patrick Robinson

© U.S. Navy photo

Navy SEALs (Sea, Air, Land) operating in Afghanistan in support of Operation Enduring Freedom. From left to right: Sonar Technician–Surface 2nd Class (SEAL) Matthew G. Axelson, 29, of Cupertino, Calif.; Information Systems Technician Senior Chief (SEAL) Daniel R. Healy, 36, of Exeter, N.H.; Quartermaster 2nd Class (SEAL) James Suh, 28, of Deerfield Beach, Fla.; Hospital Corpsman 2nd Class (SEAL) Marcus Luttrell; Machinist Mate 2nd Class (SEAL) Eric S. Patton, 22, of Boulder City, Nev.; Lt. (SEAL) Michael P. Murphy, 29, of Patchogue, N.Y. With the exception of the lone survivor, Luttrell, all were killed June 28, 2005, by enemy forces while supporting Operation Redwing.

1   Would this ever become easier? House to house, freeway to freeway, state to state? Not so far. And here I was again, behind the wheel of a hired SUV, driving along another Main Street, past the shops and the gas station, this time in a windswept little town on Long Island, New York, South Shore, down by the long Atlantic

beaches. Winter was coming. The skies were platinum. The white-caps rolled in beneath dark, lowering clouds. So utterly appropriate, because this time was going to be worse than the others. A whole lot worse.

2   I found my landmark, the local post office, pulled in behind the building, and parked. We all stepped out of the vehicle, into a chill November day, the remains of the fall leaves swirling around our feet. No one wanted to lead the way, none of the five guys who accompanied me, and for a few moments we just stood there, like a group of mailmen on their break.

3   I knew where to go. The house was just a few yards down the street. And in a sense, I'd been there before—in Southern California, northern California, and Nevada. In the next few days, I still had to visit Washington and Virginia Beach. And so many things would always be precisely the same.

devastated You saw this word in Chapter 5 referring to boll weevils. Here it describes sadness. What does *devastated* mean in this context?

4   There would be the familiar devastated sadness, the kind of pain that wells up when young men are cut down in their prime. The same hollow feeling in each of the homes. The same uncontrollable tears. The same feeling of desolation, of brave people trying to be brave, lives which had uniformly been shot to pieces. Inconsolable. Sorrowful.

inconsolable If tears are "uncontrollable," what do you think *inconsolable* means? Also notice the prefix *in-* and the suffix *-able*.

5   As before, I was the bearer of the terrible news, as if no one knew the truth until I arrived, so many weeks and months after so many funerals. And for me, this small gathering in Patchogue, Long Island, was going to be the worst.

6   I tried to get a hold of myself. But again in my mind I heard that terrible, terrible scream, the same one that awakens me, bullying its way into my solitary dreams, night after night, the confirmation of guilt. The endless guilt of the survivor.

7   "Help me, Marcus! Please help me!"

8   It was a desperate appeal in the mountains of a foreign land. It was a scream cried out in the echoing high canyons of one of the loneliest places on earth. It was the nearly unrecognizable cry of a mortally wounded creature. And it was a plea I could not answer. I can't forget it. Because it was made by one of the finest people I ever met, a man who happened to be my best friend.

plea A synonym is used in the first sentence of paragraph 8 and an example is in paragraph 7. What is a *plea*?

—Luttrell & Robinson, *Lone Survivor: The Eyewitness Account of Operation Redwing and the Lost Heroes of SEAL Team 10*, pp. 3–4

Talking About Reading

Respond in writing to the questions below and then discuss your answers with your classmates.

1. What task does the narrator of this reading have?

_____

_____

_____

2. Imagine what it would be like to have the task the author describes in this reading. Discuss what would make it so difficult to carry out.

_____

_____

_____

3. Do you have a family member or friend who has sacrificed his or her life as a soldier? If so, share a memory of this person with a classmate. If you do not, listen to someone who does.

_____

_____

_____

4. Describe your best friend to a classmate. Discuss what makes him or her the "best," and then make a list of the top five qualities you feel are essential to being a good friend.

_____

_____

_____

Critical Thinking Is a Learning Process

It's a habit for many people to read an article quickly, make a snap judgment about it, and then act on that judgment as though it is truth. In college, however, one of the most important things you can learn is to slow down and not come to such quick conclusions. If you take the time to examine an author's ideas closely and then form a conclusion based on the evidence you find, you will be thinking critically.

You could say that one goal of education is to teach people to think critically. In all fields of study, instructors want to help their students learn to go beyond impulsive reactions in order to reach a more thoughtful response.

Reading is not an activity you can do on autopilot. You need to:

• Actively question the author's words.

• Think about the ideas behind the words.

• Add your own thoughts into the mix.

• Make decisions or solve problems based on the understanding you have formed.

To help you form the habit of using a critical thinking process, you are going to explore a series of six critical thinking levels. The levels are arranged according to a format of increasing complexity that Benjamin Bloom, a professor at the University of Chicago, devised. His critical thinking levels are often referred to as Bloom's Taxonomy. (Lorin W. Anderson and David R. Krathwohl revised the system. Their labels for each level are used here.) Figure 6.1 shows the six levels.

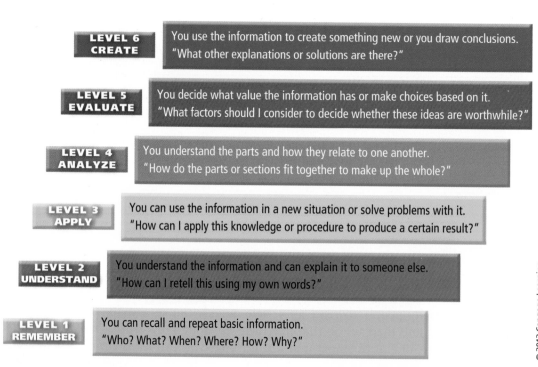

LEVEL 6 CREATE — You use the information to create something new or you draw conclusions. "What other explanations or solutions are there?"

LEVEL 5 EVALUATE — You decide what value the information has or make choices based on it. "What factors should I consider to decide whether these ideas are worthwhile?"

LEVEL 4 ANALYZE — You understand the parts and how they relate to one another. "How do the parts or sections fit together to make up the whole?"

LEVEL 3 APPLY — You can use the information in a new situation or solve problems with it. "How can I apply this knowledge or procedure to produce a certain result?"

LEVEL 2 UNDERSTAND — You understand the information and can explain it to someone else. "How can I retell this using my own words?"

LEVEL 1 REMEMBER — You can recall and repeat basic information. "Who? What? When? Where? How? Why?"

Figure 6.1 Bloom's Taxonomy with Questions

Level 1: Remembering

When you remember, you can recall and repeat basic information that answers the questions "who," "what," "where," "when," "why," and "how." You actually began practicing this level of critical thinking in Chapter 1 when you learned about the process of reading interactively: survey, mark, review. Level 1 is remembering the basic information about the subject—important dates and places, key terms, and other important details that stand out in what you read.

Level 2: Understanding

When you understand, you can explain the ideas in a reading selection using your own words. You have been practicing this level when you answer the "Why?" questions in the College and Career App readings found at the end of each chapter. Level 2 is about demonstrating that you comprehend ideas. Your ability to create a MAPP, summarize, use Cornell notes, or explain the information to someone else verbally is proof that you understand. Understanding is built upon remembering.

Level 3: Applying

When you apply information, you can use it in a new situation or solve problems with it. Think of Chapters 3 and 4, in which you practiced finding the main idea and identifying patterns of organization. You practiced these skills in class, and then you were expected to find the main idea or organizational pattern in a new paragraph on your own. Applying what you have learned helps you solve problems you haven't seen before. Applying builds upon remembering and understanding.

Level 4: Analyzing

When you analyze a reading selection (or anything else), you learn about its parts and how they relate to one another. For example, Chapter 3 asked you to analyze the parts of a word and then decide what they mean when they are combined. You also learned how a word sometimes needs to be analyzed for both its connotative and denotative meanings in order to fully understand the word as well as the author's intended meaning. Analyzing is about breaking a whole into pieces and examining the pieces to understand how they work together, and then putting them back together to see what you have learned about the whole.

Throughout this book, you have learned to analyze various aspects of reading selections. Here are just some of the things you can examine when you are analyzing a paragraph or longer selection:

- The topic, main idea, and supporting details.

- What the author did to connect one sentence to the next or one paragraph to the next.

- Signal words that indicate relationships between ideas.

- The author's word choices—synonyms, antonyms, and connotative words.

After you have examined these specifics, ask yourself what the overall effect is, and then generalize from the details.

Level 5: Evaluating

When you evaluate a reading selection, you decide what value the information has, or you make choices based on it. Evaluating a selection involves answering questions such as "Does this make sense?" and "Does this author support his main ideas well?" and "What bias does this author have?" **Bias** is an author's support for or opposition to a certain idea, belief, or action. Depending on your evaluation, you may choose to agree with the author or not. Level 5 is about value that is either inherent in a piece of writing or that a reader or observer assigns to it.

Level 6: Creating

When you create, you use information to draw a conclusion or come up with your own ideas. You might make a prediction or think of a question that the reading did not answer. You may also read several sources about the same topic and combine the ideas, or synthesize them, into a new form or new idea. Level 6 is about the type of work you do when you are writing a paper. Another application of Level 6 is using information you have read to create a plan for improving yourself or some part of your life, such as exercise or time management.

Thinking Critically About Munch's *The Scream*

Create. You can **design** or **draw** your own version of an expressionist work that evokes strong emotional responses from viewers. Or you can write a paper **synthesizing** a variety of sources or **make** an original presentation about Munch and *The Scream* based on what you have learned.

Evaluate. You can **assess** the **quality** of *The Scream* as an expressionist piece as well as decide whether it is **appealing**. You can evaluate the emotions that this painting makes you feel.

Analyze. You can **examine** *The Scream*; you can **explain** what medium Munch used and how he used color, line, and distortion to create this expressionist work.

Apply. You can **demonstrate** how this painting represents expressionist work and **show** that it is consistent with Munch's tendency to create art that illustrates human pain and suffering. You can **apply** this knowledge to identify works by other expressionist artists.

Understand. You can **explain** what the painting *The Scream* looks like, and what you know of the artist, style, and period of the painting.

Remember. You can **recognize** the work of art entitled *The Scream*. You can recall that it is an expressionist work created by the Norwegian artist Edvard Munch and that it was painted in 1893 and is housed in the National Gallery of Norway.

INTERACTION 6–1 — Reasons Why You Decided to Attend School

Pair up with another student. Write your answers to the Level 1 question and then discuss your answers with each other. Then move to Level 2 and beyond, and discuss each level's question until you reach Level 6. When you are finished, be prepared to discuss with the class how your answers became more involved as you moved from Level 1 to Level 6.

Level 1—Remember: You can recall and repeat basic information.

"What are your reasons for attending school?"

_____

_____

_____

Level 2—Understand: You understand the information and can explain it to someone else.

"How would you explain your reasons for attending school to someone who doesn't think school is important?"

_____

_____

_____

Level 3—Apply: You can use the information in a new situation or solve problems with it.

"How can your reasons for attending school apply in this class?"

_____

_____

_____

Level 4—Analyze: You understand the parts and how they relate to one another.

"What are the steps you have to take in order to reach your educational goal?"

_____

_____

_____

Level 5—Evaluate: You decide what value the information has or make choices based on it.

"What factors should you consider when deciding whether school is worthwhile?"

_____

_____

_____

Level 6—Create: You use information to create something new or draw conclusions.

"What are solutions to obstacles you will face while attending school?" (such as getting sick, not having enough time, getting distracted, and lacking motivation)

_____

_____

_____

Bloom's Taxonomy Summary

Critical thinking is a systematic process of thinking and learning that includes the following kinds of activities:

Create: Form new ideas or create something new based on this thinking process.
Skills: write a paper, make a plan, create an experiment
Verbs: *develop, design, adapt, imagine, plan*

Evaluate: Judge the usefulness or worth of the subject based on relevant criteria.
Skills: identify bias, logic, strength of ideas
Verbs: *assess, rank, critique, justify, judge*

Analyze: Study the parts of the subject to find out how they are related.
Skills: Investigate point of view, tone, purpose, fact or opinion, inference
Verbs: *compare, examine, explain, investigate, imply*

Apply: Think about how ideas can be applied in different situations.
Skills: Discern main idea, details, pattern of organization
Verbs: *diagram, demonstrate, solve, illustrate, organize*

Understand: Gain clarity about what the subject means or how it acts.
Skills: Develop outlines, MAPPs, or summaries
Verbs: *summarize, explain, discuss, exemplify, restate*

Remember: Gather information about a subject and remember it accurately.
Skills: Name who, what, when, where, why, and how, basic details, topic
Verbs: *identify, list, reproduce, define, locate*

Section Review: Critical Thinking Is a Learning Process

Write in the basic task corresponding to each critical thinking level. Use your understanding of these tasks when you are thinking about readings and lectures.

Critical
thinking level

Tasks that can help you think
about any reading or lecture

Level 6:

Level 5:

Level 4:

Level 3:

Level 2:

Level 1:

Using Critical Thinking to Determine Hierarchy

Hierarchy is the arrangement or classification of ideas or things, usually in a vertical structure. Hierarchy can also be arranged from general to specific, as is often found in written works:

Articles	Paragraph
Title	Topic
Heading	Main idea
Subheading	Major details
Bullet	Minor details

Hierarchy can also be arranged top-to-bottom or by level of importance, as in businesses or governments:

Corporation	American government
Board	President
CEO	Vice president
Vice president	Speaker of the House of Representatives
General manager	President pro tempore of the Senate
Manager	Secretary of State
Supervisor	Secretary of the Treasury

You should be familiar with the hierarchy of ideas in readings at this point and understand that it is the use of the first four levels of critical thinking, especially analyzing, that enables you to recognize and understand the author's hierarchy.

For example, given the following list of items about the Free Application for Federal Student Aid (FAFSA), you should be able to identify the topic, the details, and the pattern, as well as organize it in a visual diagram.

Gather all documents needed to fill out the FAFSA.

Fill out the FAFSA.

Submit the FAFSA online or by mail.

Completely fill out each section of the FAFSA.

"Fill out the FAFSA" would be the broad topic, and the rest of the items are **steps** that make up the **process** of filling out the FAFSA (which is the pattern). A visual organization of this material could look like this:

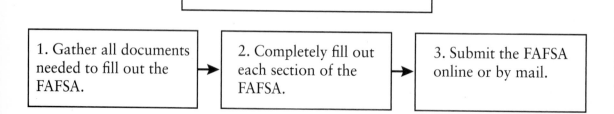

| INTERACTION 6–2 | Think Critically to Recognize General to Specific Ideas |

Analyze each list of ideas. Circle the most general idea, which would be the topic (or heading) of the other three. Then describe the relationship of the details to the topic.

1. a. Complete detoxification of the body

   b. Yoga promotes physical benefits.

   c. Massaging internal organs of the body

   d. Increased mobility of joints

   _____

2. a. Install antivirus software and update daily.

   b. Uninstall programs no longer in use.

   c. Keeping PCs running smoothly

   d. Defrag the hard drive frequently.

   _____

3. a. Rock, or *ishi*

   b. Ornaments, or *tenkebutsu*

   c. Water, or *mizu*

   d. Japanese garden, or *nihon teien*

   _____

4. a. Engrossing, entertaining, and outrageous characters

   b. A provocative musical score

   c. *Anna Nicole: The Opera*

   d. Shameless yet poignant scenes

   _____

5. a. Encouraging nonconformist behavior

   b. Limiting time spent watching television

   c. Encouraging creativity in children

   d. Buying toys that involve building something

| INTERACTION 6–3 | Think Critically to Recognize Hierarchy |

Each of the following hierarchical lists was taken from a college textbook table of contents. Each has a hierarchical order that has been scrambled. Put the ideas in order by numbering each one. Number the highest level 1, the next highest 2, and so on.

1. American Government

   ____ Religious Freedom

   ____ Civil Liberties

   ____ Free Exercise of Religion

   ____ Liberties and Rights

2. Mathematics

   ____ What's Math Anyway? Unifying Ideas

   ____ Different Kinds of Numbers

   ____ What Are Numbers?

   ____ Rational Numbers

3. Business Communications

   ____ Communication Climate

   ____ Oral and Nonverbal Communication

   ____ The Elements of Interpersonal Communication

   ____ Interpersonal Communication and Teamwork

4. Psychology

   ____ Sensing and Perceiving the World

   ____ Sensation and Perception

   ____ Sensory Systems

   ____ Colorblindness

   ____ Seeing

5. Political Science

____ Measuring Opinion

____ Types of Polls

____ Democratic Politics and Public Deliberation

____ Exit Polls

____ Public Opinion and Political Participation

Working through a list of ideas is simpler than working through a reading; however, the process is the same. You, as the reader, have to understand, apply, and analyze the relationships of ideas you find. Without doing this, you will be confused, frustrated, or even lost. Thinking critically about hierarchy can help you avoid these traps.

Section Review: Using Critical Thinking to Determine Hierarchy

Pick one of the items from Interaction 6–2 and create an example of the hierarchy using a visual diagram that reflects the relationships or pattern of organization.

Using Critical Thinking to Analyze Test Questions

Tests are a fact of life when you are a student. They are how your understanding is evaluated. Let's take a look at test question examples that might apply to each level of Bloom's Taxonomy.

1. Remember: These questions include specific details, such as dates, names, and important terms.

   • Who is the "father of behaviorism"?

   • What is the name of the person who invented Coca-Cola; when and where was it invented?

   • What is a cell?

   Note that these types of questions are not often asked on college tests. Rather, it is presumed you will have already transferred this type of basic information into long-term memory when you were studying.

2. Understand: These questions focus on the relationships between ideas. Do you understand processes, steps, requirements, the timeline of events, and so on?

   • Why did John Watson reject the "law of effect?"

   • Explain the events surrounding the invention of Coca-Cola.

   • Explain the cell theory.

   Test questions usually begin at this level. However, many instructors skip this level of question, presuming your ability to remember and understand the material will be better evaluated with questions that ask you to apply this knowledge.

3. Apply: These questions focus on your ability to understand a process and apply it to a familiar or a new situation.

   • How did Watson apply the theory of classical conditioning in the "Little Albert" experiment?

   • Coke's formula remains a heavily guarded secret. At least that's how the story goes. Actually, this was marketing hype to make the beverage seem special. What other products have applied a similar marketing strategy?

   • Identify the parts of a prokaryotic cell on the following diagram.

4. Analyze: These questions break events, materials, or processes into parts to figure out how the parts relate to one another and to the overall topic.

- Many modern psychology students have criticized Watson's experiments. Analyze his experiments from the perspective of the day when they were carried out. Explain how they would have been perceived in Watson's day.

- Coca-Cola is one of the most recognized brands in the world today. Analyze the strategies that have led to its extraordinary success.

- Compare and contrast prokaryotic and eukaryotic cells.

5. Evaluate: These questions ask you to decide on the criteria that should be used to assess the value of something and then judge it based on these criteria.

- Critique Watson's behavioral theory based on what modern psychology understands about human behavior.

- Evaluate the social impact that Coca-Cola has had in America.

- View the provided cell under a microscope. Determine whether it is whole or defective. If irregularities are noted, diagnose the genetic disorder.

6. Create: These questions ask you to produce something—usually a paper, project, or presentation—synthesizing a variety of information from multiple sources.

- Write a paper explaining John Watson's view on the nature-versus-nurture debate.

- Create a visual presentation of Coca-Cola advertisements from its early days to its latest commercials.

- Write a paper arguing for or against the use of stem cells. Be sure to include the different types of stem cells that can be used. A minimum of five sources is required, and only one can be from the Internet.

When you read a question, attempt to identify the critical thinking verb and decide what level of thinking is called for. For example, suppose you see this writing prompt on an American government test:

Identify all of the causes for impeaching a president.

Seeing the verb *identify,* you know that this question is about the lowest level of critical thinking. You simply need to list the causes to prove that you remember them.

In contrast, suppose you get this prompt:

> Only two presidents have been impeached: Andrew Johnson and Bill Clinton. However, both were acquitted after a trial and completed their presidential terms. Choose either Johnson or Clinton. Assess the facts for the case brought against the president you chose; do you agree he should have been acquitted or do you think he should have been formally charged and forced out of office? State your opinion and explain your thinking.

Reading the verbs *assess, agree,* and *think,* you know that this question is much more complex. You need to understand impeachment, but you also need to know the facts of each case and decide whether the judgment was correct, plus support your evaluation of the case with convincing details. The question calls for you to form an opinion based on all the facts. The verb *explain* is a clue that you will need to analyze each factor before you make a decision.

The first question, at critical thinking Level 1, is more likely to appear on a test as a question requiring a short answer than as an essay question. The second question, at Level 5, is more likely an essay question. It's too complicated to be answered in just a few sentences; you might need five or six paragraphs to explain your evaluation. The following table gives a few examples of typical verbs used in each level of question.

Level 6: Create	develop	design	adapt	imagine
Level 5: Evaluate	assess	rank	critique	justify
Level 4: Analyze	compare	examine	explain	investigate
Level 3: Apply	diagram	demonstrate	solve	illustrate
Level 2: Understand	paraphrase	conclude	match	exemplify
Level 1: Remember	identify	list	reproduce	define

Tests in your college classes, such as literature, history, and even math, may include several varieties of questions: short answer, essay, and multiple choice. Multiple-choice test questions can range from Level 2 to Level 5 in Bloom's Taxonomy. In addition, the question might not always include a key critical thinking verb. This means that you must use critical thinking Levels 1–5 when you are answering a multiple-choice question, no matter what the level of the question is. Here is an example from a biology test:

> Which of the following statements about metabolic pathways is not correct?

Notice that even though there is no key critical thinking verb, the question is on the Level 5 evaluating level because it is asking you to choose which answer is not correct. In order to answer this question correctly, you need to involve *all* of the following levels:

Level 1: Remember what metabolic pathways are.

Level 2: Understand how metabolic pathways work.

Level 3: Apply your knowledge to this question.

Level 4: Analyze each answer to see what each one means.

Level 5: Evaluate and then choose the best answer.

INTERACTION 6–4	Use Critical Thinking to Analyze Test Questions

Read the following test questions. Then determine which critical thinking level each one might require and circle the number of the level. Remember to look for key verbs.

1 = Remember
2 = Understand
3 = Apply
4 = Analyze
5 = Evaluate
6 = Create

1. Neoclassical style is which of the following?

1   2   3   4   5   6

2. Seth learned the state capitals in fifth grade. He had forgotten them by college, but he was delighted to find they were much easier to learn the second time. Faster relearning is an example of which of the following?

1   2   3   4   5   6

3. *Dances with Wolves* illustrates which of the following categories of film?

1   2   3   4   5   6

4. What are the four things all plants need?

1   2   3   4   5   6

5. Which of the following images shows an example of stimulus response?

1 2 3 4 5 6

6. Explain Lincoln's argument against the South's secession.

1 2 3 4 5 6

7. Which of the following statements is the most accurate description of a hypokinetic disease?

1 2 3 4 5 6

8. Develop a personal mission statement.

1 2 3 4 5 6

9. Summarize Williams's definition of "social responsibility" as found in Chapter 2.

1 2 3 4 5 6

10. What are some comparisons between Martin Luther King, Jr. and Mahatma Gandhi?

1 2 3 4 5 6

Section Review: Using Critical Thinking to Analyze Test Questions

A. Create some example test questions that fit into the following critical thinking levels.

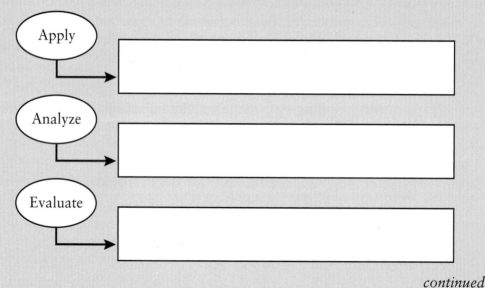

continued

B. Fill in appropriate critical thinking verbs for each level.

Create			
Evaluate			
Analyze			
Apply			
Understand			
Remember			

Applying Critical Thinking to Reading Passages

The true test of critical thinking comes in your ability to apply it to what you are reading. Each level is critical for overall comprehension of the chapter, the book, and the class. The best way to think critically about what you read is to apply the reading strategies you have already been practicing since Chapter 1. Make sure you apply all the strategies of being an active reader as you work through your college reading (and beyond).

INTERACTION 6–5	Use Critical Thinking to Analyze Reading Passages

Read the following passage. Turn the title into a question, read to find the answers, and mark them when you find them. Continue to ask questions as you read. When you are done, answer the questions relating to the six levels of critical thinking that follow the reading.

Types of Social Movements

1   There are three broad types of social movements: personal transformation movements, social change movements, and reactionary movements. **Personal transformation movements** aim to change the individual. Instead of pursuing social change, they focus on the development of new meaning within individual lives (Klapp 1972). The New Age movement is a personal transformation movement that defines mainstream life as stressful and overly rational and promotes relaxation and spiritualism as an emotional release and route to expanded perceptions. New Age music, crystals, massage therapy, and meditation are intended to restore the New Age person to a state of unstressed wholeness. Like many other social movements, New Ageism is supported by an array of dues-charging organizations and commercial products, from tapes and crystals to sessions with the spirits of the dead, retreats in yoga ashrams, and guided tours of Native American holy sites.

2   Religious and cult movements are also personal transformation movements. The rise in evangelical religious movements can be explained in part by the need people have to give clear meaning to their lives in a complex and sometimes perplexing society. In personal transformation movements, participants adopt a new identity—one they use to redefine their lives, both current and former states.

3   **Social change movements** aim to change some aspect of society. Examples are the environmental movement, the gay and lesbian movement, the civil rights movement, the animal rights movement, the religious right movement, and the Green Party. All seek social change, although in distinct and sometimes oppositional ways. Some movements want radical change in existing social institutions; others want a retreat to a former way of life or even a move to an imagined past (or future). Social movements use a variety of tactics, strategies, and organizational forms to achieve their goals. The civil rights movement in the early 1950s used collective action in sit-ins, mass demonstrations, and organizational activities to overturn statutes that supported the "separate but equal" principle of segregation. These efforts culminated in the Supreme Court decision *Brown v. Board of Education,* which declared the "separate but equal" doctrine unconstitutional (Morris 1999).

4   Movements also form alliances with other movements, and many social change movements involve a vast network of diverse groups organized around broadly

similar, but also unique, goals. The Asian American movement, for example, includes Asian American women's organizations such as Pan Asia and the National Network of Asian and Pacific Women, Asian workers' groups such as the Six Companies and the Chinese Consolidated Benevolent Association, and other groups of Asian activists (Wei 1993; Espiritu 1992).

5   Social change movements may be *norm focused* (trying to change the prescribed way of doing things) or they may be *value focused* (trying to change a fundamental idea or something everyone holds dear; Turner and Killian 1988). Often, they are both. The civil rights movement tried to change the law of the land and the attitudes of its people at the same time. The broad charter of the civil rights movement spawned offspring movements devoted to the special interests of such groups as Chicanos, feminists, and lesbians and gays, among many others.

6   Social change movements may be either reformist or radical. **Reform movements** seek change through legal or other mainstream political means, typically working within existing institutions. **Radical movements** seek fundamental change in the structure of society. Although most movements are primarily one or the other, within a given movement there may be both reformist and radical factions. In the environmental movement, for example, the Sierra Club is a classic reform movement that lobbies within the existing political system to promote legislation protecting the environment. Greenpeace is a more radical group that sometimes uses tactics that disrupt the activities the group finds objectionable, such as the killing of whales. The distinction between reform and radical movements is not absolute. Social movements can contain elements of both and may change their orientation in midstride upon meeting success or failure. Moreover, whether a group is defined as radical or reformist is to a great degree a matter of public perception. Just as one person's rebel is another's freedom fighter on the world stage, the definition of a social movement often depends on its social legitimacy and its ability to control how it is defined in the media and other public forums (Killian 1975).

7   **Reactionary movements** organize to resist change or to reinstate an earlier social order that participants perceive to be better and are reacting against contemporary changes in society. The New Right provides a case in point. It has emerged in opposition to changes such as the legalization of abortion, the high divorce rate, women's liberation, and greater freedom for gays and lesbians. To the New Right, these changes symbolize a decline in moral values and traditions (Esterberg 2003). Thus, the New Right is organized to resist the social changes that participants in this conservative movement find deeply objectionable.

—From ANDERSEN/TAYLOR. *Sociology: The Essentials*, 4e (pp. 601–603)
Copyright © 2007 Cengage Learning.

CRITICAL THINKING LEVEL 1: REMEMBER

What are the three types of social movements? Name and define each one based on the information in the reading.

_____

_____

_____

CRITICAL THINKING LEVEL 2: UNDERSTAND

Create an APP for this reading based on your markings.

About: _____

    Point: _____

       Proof: 1. _____

                    _____

                   a. _____

                   b. _____

             2. _____

                    _____

                   a. _____

                      _____

                   b. _____

                      _____

                   c. _____

                      _____

                   d. _____

                      _____

                   e. _____

                      _____

3. _____

_____

a. _____

CRITICAL THINKING LEVEL 3: APPLY

Label each organization or movement with the category of social movement it belongs to. (Some may belong in more than one movement.) Use the following letters to represent each movement.

A. Personal transformation movement

B. Social change movement (reform)

C. Social change movement (radical)

D. Reactionary movement

1. _____ PETA (People for the Ethical Treatment of Animals)

2. _____ NRA (National Rifle Association)

3. _____ The Tea Party (a conservative political movement)

4. _____ Feminism (women's liberation movement)

5. _____ The AFL-CIO (a federation of unions, in which workers band together)

6. _____ Society for the Environment (promotes sustainability and environmental matters)

7. _____ Habitat For Humanity International (builds housing for the poor)

8. _____ Focus on the Family (promotes conservative family values)

9. _____ Art of Living Satsang (an Indian philosophy)

10. _____ Militia movement (a political movement advocating the right to bear arms against a tyrannical government)

CRITICAL THINKING LEVEL 4: ANALYZE

Analyze the following mission statements (taken from the organizations' websites) and write a sentence explaining what type of social movement the organization represents.

Sierra Club Mission Statement

To explore, enjoy, and protect the wild places of the earth;

To practice and promote the responsible use of the earth's ecosystems and resources;

To educate and enlist humanity to protect and restore the quality of the natural and human environment; and to use all lawful means to carry out these objectives.

—Reproduced from sierraclub.org with permission of the Sierra Club

---

_____

_____

About Greenpeace

Our core values are reflected in our environmental campaign work: We "bear witness" to environmental destruction in a peaceful, non-violent manner. We use non-violent confrontation to raise the level and quality of public debate. In exposing threats to the environment and finding solutions we have no permanent allies or adversaries. We ensure our financial independence from political or commercial interests. We seek solutions to environmental dilemmas and promote open, informed debate about society's environmental choices.

Mission Statement

Greenpeace is the leading independent campaigning organization that uses peaceful protest and creative communication to expose global environmental problems and to promote solutions that are essential to a green and peaceful future.

—Reprinted by permission of Greenpeace

_____

_____

_____

CRITICAL THINKING LEVEL 5: EVALUATE

Look at the following visual entitled "The Influence of Social Movements: What the Public Perceives." Read the questions and see if you agree with the public perception. If possible, do this with a classmate or two, so you can discuss your assessment of the information.

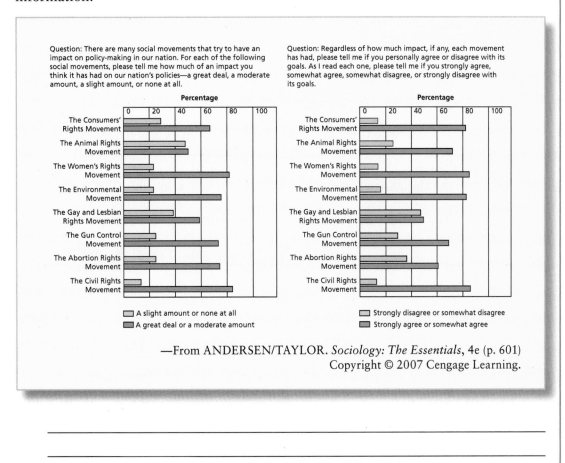

—From ANDERSEN/TAYLOR. *Sociology: The Essentials*, 4e (p. 601)
Copyright © 2007 Cengage Learning.

_____

_____

_____

CRITICAL THINKING LEVEL 6: CREATE

Come up with an idea for either a reactionary or a reform movement and describe an organization that would support the movement. Base it on something you are dissatisfied with, whether it is on the world, the national, or the local level, or within a particular organization. If you cannot think of an issue that bothers you, then choose one that someone else is concerned about or use your prior knowledge or imagination.

_____

_____

_____

_____

_____

Chapter Summary Activity:
Asking Critical Thinking Questions

Chapter 6 has discussed how to think and read critically as well as how to ask critical thinking questions based on Bloom's Taxonomy. Fill in the following Reading Guide by completing each idea on the left with information from Chapter 6 on the right. You can return to this guide throughout the course as a reminder of how to think critically about ideas.

Reading Guide to Asking Critical Thinking Questions

Complete this idea	with information from Chapter 6.
List the six levels of Bloom's Taxonomy:	1. _____ 2. _____ 3. _____ 4. _____ 5. _____ 6. _____
A Level 1 activity is to	7. _____
A Level 2 activity is to	8. _____
A Level 3 activity is to	9. _____ _____
A Level 4 activity is to	10. _____
A Level 5 activity is to	11. _____ _____ _____
A Level 6 activity is to	12. _____ _____

Complete this idea	with information from Chapter 6.
Hierarchy refers to	13. _____ _____ _____
List two critical thinking verbs for Level 1.	14. _____ 15. _____
List two critical thinking verbs for Level 2.	16. _____ 17. _____
List two critical thinking verbs for Level 3.	18. _____ 19. _____
List two critical thinking verbs for Level 4.	20. _____ 21. _____
List two critical thinking verbs for Level 5.	22. _____ 23. _____
List two critical thinking verbs for Level 6.	24. _____ 25. _____
If you were discussing the aspects of the plot of a short story in a literature class, which level of critical thinking would you be illustrating?	26. _____
If you wrote a job résumé based on the guidelines given in your marketing class, which level of critical thinking would you be illustrating?	27. _____
If you solved a math problem using a theorem you had learned in class, which level of critical thinking would you be illustrating?	28. _____
If you recited the Gettysburg Address in government class, which level of critical thinking would you be illustrating?	29. _____

30. Think about what your reading strategies were before you read Chapter 6. How did they differ from the suggestions here? Write your thoughts.

_____

_____

_____

ENGAGE YOUR SKILLS
Asking Critical Thinking Questions

A. Read the following cartoon and then answer the questions that follow.

1. What critical thinking level is Calvin (the boy) expressing in the first frame of this cartoon? _____

2. What critical thinking level is Calvin expressing in the second frame of this cartoon? _____

3. What critical thinking level is Calvin expressing in the third frame of this cartoon? _____

4. What critical thinking level is Hobbes (the tiger) expressing in the fourth frame of this cartoon? _____

5. What critical thinking level is Calvin expressing in the fourth frame of this cartoon? _____

B. Read the following passage and answer the questions that follow.

Vegetarians

There is a wide range in the diets of those who call themselves vegetarians. The list below describes general categories of vegetarians.

- **Lacto-ovo vegetarians** eat dairy products (lacto) and eggs (ovo), but no meat. This is the most common type of vegetarian.
- **Vegans** (pronounced vee-gans) eat no dairy products, eggs, or meat, and generally avoid honey and leather products too.
- **Natural hygienists** eat plant foods combined in particular ways and fast periodically.
- **Fruitarians** eat fruit, nuts, seeds, and some vegetables.
- **Raw foodists** eat only uncooked nonmeat products.
- **Semivegetarians** include small amounts of meat in their diets, but predominantly eat foods from plants.

Some people come up with creative ways of describing their diets. For example, one man called himself a "pancake-o-vegan" because he ate pancakes with eggs and milk every weekend, but did not eat eggs or milk during the week.

—From BRYANT/COURTNEY/DEWALT/SCHWARTZ. *The Cultural Feast: An Introduction to Food and Society*, 2e (p. 80) Copyright © 2004 Cengage Learning.

1. Based on the definition above of lacto-ovo vegetarians, define the term *lacto vegetarian:*

_____

2. Based on the definition above of lacto-ovo vegetarians, define the term *ovo vegetarian:*

_____

3. What is the highest critical thinking level you used to answer questions 1 and 2 above?

_____

4. How would you describe your eating habits?

_____

5. What critical thinking level did you use to answer question 4?

_____

6. Which type of vegetarianism would be the hardest for you?

_____

7. What critical thinking level did you use to answer question 6?

_____

8. Come up with a creative way to describe your diet.

_____

9. What critical thinking level did you use to answer question 8?

_____

10. What type of hierarchy is represented in this reading?

_____

MASTER YOUR SKILLS
Asking Critical Thinking Questions

Read the following excerpt from a college textbook and then answer the critical thinking questions that follow.

A Brief History of Vegetarianism

1   The most significant examples of religious basis for vegetarian diets are found in religions of the Asian culture. Hinduism, though not requiring a strictly vegetarian diet, promoted a strong tradition of vegetarianism for more than two millennia. Vegetarianism is more widespread in Buddhism and Jainism, which promote nonviolent treatment of all beings and so prohibit the killing of animals for food (Whorton 2000).

2   Religion has been a component of the history of vegetarianism in the West, but philosophical and scientific influences have been stronger contributors. Vegetarian doctrine in the West can be traced to Pythagoras, the Greek natural philosopher of the sixth century B.C. (known for the geometric theorem). He believed that human spirits were reborn in other creatures and so animals were as worthy of moral treatment as humans were. Killing an animal was seen as murder, eating it was seen as cannibalism (Whorton 2000). In the fourth century B.C., Plato wrote in *The Republic* that a vegetarian diet was best suited for the ideal society because plant foods were better for health and required less land to produce than animal foods.

3   In later antiquity, during the first two centuries of the Christian era, Ovid and Plutarch both described slaughtering animals for food as cruel treatment of innocent animals. Plutarch's essay "Of Eating of Flesh" added health arguments, stating that flesh foods caused "grievous oppressions and qualmy indigestions" and brought "sickness and heaviness on the body" (Plutarch 1998:14). Porphyry, of the third century, promoted a flesh-free diet for spiritual purification (Porphyry 1965).

4   With the Fall of Rome and the spread of Christianity across Europe, vegetarian ideas became less pronounced. Christian thinkers such as Saint Augustine of Hippo (354–430) and Saint Thomas Aquinas (1225–1274) proposed that only people had free will, rationality, and immortal souls and that animals were placed on the earth for the use of humans. Using Genesis 1:28 as a guide, they saw meat eating as the right of humans: "God blessed them and said to them 'Be fruitful and increase, fill the earth and subdue it, have dominion over the fish in the sea, the birds of the air and every living thing that moves on the earth.'" Vegetarianism was practiced during these times in some Christian abbeys, however.

5   Both medical and moral arguments were central to vegetarian philosophies throughout the 1700s. Thomas Tryon wrote the most broad-based argument to date for a vegetable diet in *The Way to Health, Long Life and Happiness* (1683). He quoted Genesis 1:29 to support vegetarian diets: "I give you every seed-bearing plant of the whole earth and every tree that has fruit with seed in it. They will be yours for food." Tryon also raised the issue of health to a new level, noting "Nothing so soon turns to putrification as meat" (Tryon 1683:376).

6   A vegetarian "renaissance" unfolded in the nineteenth century. This new view was woven into the American humanitarian reform movements. It was not uncommon for vegetarians to be involved in other issues of social change such as antislavery, women's rights, and utopian socialism. Sylvester Graham (as in the cracker) was a Presbyterian minister, turned temperance lecturer, who promoted an all-inclusive program of physical and moral reform that included vegetarian practices (Whorton 2000). Later the term *vegetarian* was coined, originating from the Latin word *vegetus,* which means "vigorous" or "active." The term has led many to believe that vegetarians eat only vegetables, an inaccurate notion.

7   The formation of the Bible Christian Church, founded by William Cowherd in 1809 in England, is said to be the start of the organized modern vegetarian movement. Followers believed that a vegetarian diet kept one in better health so as to be better able to serve God. They formed the Vegetarian Society in 1847. Cowherd gave lectures and distributed pamphlets that taught that eating plant-based diets would lead to universal brotherhood, increased happiness and a more civilized society. This group still exists and is now called the Vegetarian Society of Great Britain.

8   In some people's minds, Darwin's theory narrowed the distance between humans and animals and so disrupted the religious and philosophical defense for humans to eat meat. The vegetarian movement continued to build in the twentieth century with proponents such as Seventh-Day Adventists, George Bernard Shaw, and Mohandas Gandhi. John Harvey Kellogg (the man we have to thank for cornflakes) headed the Seventh-Day Adventist Battle Creek Sanitarium where he invented nuttose, the first meat analog made from peanuts and flour. Visitors to his sanitarium included Admiral Richard Byrd, John D. Rockefeller, J. C.

Penney, Mrs. Knox of gelatin fame, Alfred duPont, Montgomery Ward, and Thomas Edison (Carson 1957). Upton Sinclair wrote *The Jungle* in 1905, featuring graphic descriptions of the unsanitary conditions in slaughterhouses, which brought more people into the vegetarian movement. A popular restaurant in New York City at the turn of the century was the Physical Culture and Strength Restaurant, which featured vegetarian food (Messina 1996).

9   By the mid-twentieth century, with the discovery of vitamins and government-sponsored food guides, meat-based diets were promoted as the most healthful. All food guides developed at the time encouraged generous helpings of both meat and dairy products. Nonetheless, in 1942 the Gallup Poll showed that 2% of the U.S. population, or 2.5 million Americans, were vegetarian. In 1944 the term *vegan* was coined for people who ate no meat, dairy products, or eggs, and the Vegan Society was formed in Great Britain the same year (Messina 1994).

10   During the social upheavals of the 1960s and 1970s, a variety of influences converged that had major effects on the course of vegetarianism. These included an increased understanding of the relationship between diet and health, an interest in Eastern philosophy and religion, anti-war sentiment, and the environmental and animal rights movements. Out of this stew of social change, the modern era of vegetarianism grew.

11   There were two books published during this era that had major impact on increasing the popularity of the practice of vegetarianism. The 1971 publication of Frances Moore Lappe's book, *Diet for a Small Planet,* linked diets to global concerns and focused attention on the negative effects of meat production on the planet. The discovery of the meat, dairy, and egg industries' harsh treatment of animals described in Australian philosopher Pete Singer's 1975 book, *Animal Liberation,* galvanized the animal ethics movement.

12   The number of vegetarians in the United States doubled between 1985 and 1992. A 1992 Gallup Poll showed that 12 million Americans identified themselves as vegetarian. Nearly half had been eating this way for 10 years, and a quarter had been vegetarian for more than 20 years (Messina and Messina 1996). As throughout history, vegetarianism in this age is often part of an overall worldview.

—From BRYANT/COURTNEY/DEWALT/SCHWARTZ. *The Cultural Feast: An Introduction to Food and Society,* 2e (pp. 74–76) Copyright © 2004 Cengage Learning.

CRITICAL THINKING LEVEL 1: REMEMBER

List at least four reasons for vegetarianism throughout history, based on the above reading.

_____

_____

_____

_____

_____

CRITICAL THINKING LEVEL 2: UNDERSTAND

In your own words, explain the views of the following people mentioned in the reading.

1. Pythagoras: _____

_____

2. Plato: _____

_____

3. Thomas Tryon: _____

_____

4. William Cowherd: _____

_____

5. Peter Singer: _____

_____

CRITICAL THINKING LEVEL 3: APPLY

Vegetarian diets have the potential to be very healthy. However, there can be some disadvantages. Think about some reasons why most Americans might have difficulty with a healthy vegetarian diet.

_____

_____

_____

_____

_____

CRITICAL THINKING LEVEL 4: ANALYZE

The following meal plan is from EatingWell.com. Compare and contrast this meal plan with what you eat on a typical day.

EatingWell's 28-Day Vegetarian Meal Plan
(1800 calorie menu—Day 1)

Breakfast

German Apple Pancake
Grapefruit (1/2)
Skim Milk

Lunch

Leek, Asparagus & Herb Soup
Mushroom Risotto or Rice & Corn Cakes with Spicy Black Beans
Skim Milk

Snack

Apple
Spiced Almonds

Dinner

Curried Cashew Burgers or Spinach & Cheese Stuffed Shells
Cool Zucchini Slaw
Double Raspberry Soufflés

—"EatingWell's 28-Day Vegetarian Meal Plan," EatingWell.com

_____

_____

_____

_____

CRITICAL THINKING LEVEL 5: EVALUATE

Analyze the following quotations. Then decide whether you agree with each one and explain your evaluation.

1. "I am not a vegetarian, but I eat animals that are." —Groucho Marx

_____

_____

2. "The hardest part about being vegan is shoes. I mean, really, that's the only difficult part, finding shoes that don't have leather on them." —Lisa Edelstein

_____

_____

3. "Nothing will benefit human health and increase the chances for survival of life on Earth as much as the evolution to a vegetarian diet." —Albert Einstein

_____

_____

4. "If slaughterhouses had glass walls, everyone would be a vegetarian." —Paul McCartney

_____

_____

5. "For as long as men massacre animals, they will kill each other. Indeed, he who sows the seed of murder and pain cannot reap joy and love." —Pythagoras

_____

_____

6. "If a group of beings from another planet were to land on Earth—beings who considered themselves as superior to you as you feel yourself to be to other animals—would you concede them the rights over you that you assume over other animals?" —George Bernard Shaw

_____

_____

CRITICAL THINKING LEVEL 6: CREATE

On a separate piece of paper, create a timeline that represents "A Brief History of Vegetarianism."

Focus on Visual Arts

College Visual Arts App

The following reading is linked to these fields of . . .

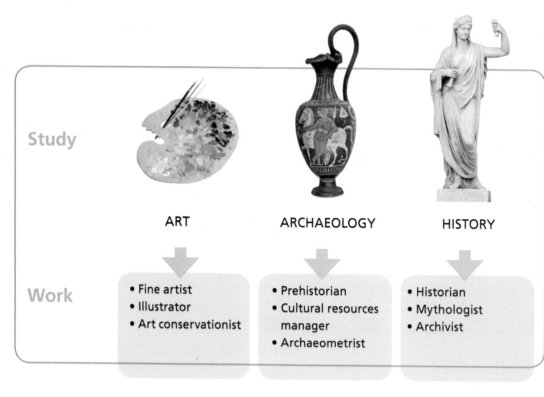

Study

ART   ARCHAEOLOGY   HISTORY

Work

- Fine artist
- Illustrator
- Art conservationist

- Prehistorian
- Cultural resources manager
- Archaeometrist

- Historian
- Mythologist
- Archivist

● Pre-Reading the Selection

The excerpt that begins on page 364 comes from the art history textbook *Gardner's Art Through the Ages*. The excerpt is titled "Paleolithic Cave Painting."

Surveying the Reading

Survey the textbook selection that follows. Then check the elements that are included in this reading.

_____ Title

_____ Headings

_____ First sentences of paragraphs

_____ Words in bold or italic type

_____ Images and captions

Guessing the Purpose

Based on the source and the title of the reading selection, do you think the author's purpose is mostly to persuade, inform, or express? _____

Predicting the Content

Based on your survey, what are three things you expect the reading selection to discuss?

- _____

- _____

- _____

Activating Your Knowledge

Think about what you know about cave art. Where are some places in the world that have cave art? Have you ever seen any cave art? What types of images are found in cave art? Who created cave art? Write your thoughts below.

- _____

- _____

- _____

● Reading with Pen in Hand

Students who annotate as they read are more successful than students who do not annotate. That's why you will annotate each reading in *Engage* as you read. In the reading that follows, use the following symbols:

★ or (Point)   to indicate a main idea

① ② ③   to indicate major details

Access the Reading CourseMate via www.cengagebrain.com to hear vocabulary words from this selection and view a video about this topic.

Reading Journal

● Imagine how it would feel to walk through a prehistoric cave like Altamira, Pech-Merle, or Lascaux.

choked You are familiar with this word from a different context. Use that to determine the meaning of *choked*.

Paleolithic Cave Painting

1   The caves of Altamira (Fig. 6.2), Pech-Merle (Fig. 6.3), Lascaux (Figs. 6.4 and 6.6), and other sites in prehistoric Europe are a few hundred to several thousand feet long. They are often choked, sometimes almost impassably, by deposits, such as stalactites and stalagmites. Far inside these caverns, well removed from the cave mouths early humans often chose for habitation, painters sometimes made pictures on the walls. Examples of Paleolithic painting now have been found at more than 200 sites, but prehistorians still regard painted caves as rare occurrences, because the images in them, even if they number in the hundreds, were created over a period of some 10,000 to 20,000 years.

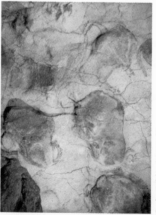

© akg/Bildarchiv Steffens

Figure 6.2. Bison, detail of a painted ceiling in the cave at Altamira, Spain, ca. 12,000–11,000 BCE. Each bison 5′ long.

As in other Paleolithic caves, the painted ceiling at Altamira has no ground line or indication of setting. The artist's sole concern was representing the animals, not locating them in a specific place.

2   To illuminate the surfaces while working, the Paleolithic painters used stone lamps filled with marrow or fat, with a wick, perhaps, of moss. For drawing, they used chunks of red and yellow ocher. For painting, they ground these same ochers into powders they mixed with water before applying. Recent analyses of the pigments used show that Paleolithic painters employed many different minerals, attesting to a technical sophistication surprising at so early a date.

3   Large flat stones served as palettes. The painters made brushes from reeds, bristles, or twigs, and may have used a blowpipe of reeds or hollow bones to spray pigments on out-of-reach surfaces. Some caves have natural ledges on the rock walls upon which the painters could have stood in order to reach the upper surfaces of the naturally formed chambers and corridors. One Lascaux gallery has holes in one of the walls that once probably anchored a scaffold made of saplings lashed together. Despite the difficulty of making the tools and pigments, modern attempts at replicating the techniques of Paleolithic painting have demonstrated that skilled workers could cover large surfaces with images in less than a day.

○ Imagine what these caves looked like when lighted with torches and bustling with artists.

pigments This paragraph explains what the Paleolithic painters used. Paragraph 3 also uses *pigments* twice. Using this context, what are *pigments*?

palettes The next sentence explains brushes. What do you think the artists used the flat stones or *palettes* for?

○ What instruments do you think artists used to create the art shown in Figure 6.3 (the spotted horses)?

bpk, Berlin/Wolfgang Ruppert/Art Resource, NY

Figure 6.3. Spotted horses and negative hand imprints, wall painting in the cave at Pech-Merle, France, ca. 22,000 BCE. 11′ 2″ long.
The purpose and meaning of Paleolithic art are unknown. Some researchers think the painted hands near the Pech-Merle horses are "signatures" of community members or of individual painters.

Art in the Old Stone Age

4   From the moment in 1879 that cave paintings were discovered at Altamira (Fig. 6.2), scholars have wondered why the hunters of the Old Stone Age decided to cover the walls of dark caverns

○ What theories of the meaning of the cave paintings are presented in paragraphs 4 and 5?

with animal images like those found at Altamira, Pech-Merle (Fig. 6.3), Lascaux (Figs. 6.4 and 6.6), and Vallon-Pont-d'Arc (Fig. 6.5). Scholars have proposed various theories including that the painted and engraved animals were mere decoration, but this explanation cannot account for the narrow range of subjects or the inaccessibility of many of the representations. In fact, the remoteness and difficulty of access of many of the images, and indications that the caves were used for centuries, are precisely why many researchers have suggested that the prehistoric hunters attributed magical properties to the images they painted and sculpted. According to this argument, by confining animals to the surfaces of their cave walls, the Paleolithic hunters believed they were bringing the beasts under their control. Some prehistorians have even hypothesized that rituals or dances were performed in front of the images and that these rites served to improve the hunters' luck. Still others have stated that the animal representations may have served as teaching tools to instruct new hunters about the character of the various species they would encounter or even to serve as targets for spears.

5   In contrast, some scholars have argued that the magical purpose of the paintings and reliefs was not to facilitate the destruction of bison and other species. Instead, they believe prehistoric painters and sculptors created animal images to assure the survival of the herds on which Paleolithic peoples depended for their food supply and for their clothing. A central problem for both the hunting-magic and food-creation theories is that the animals that seem to have been diet staples of Old Stone Age peoples are not those most frequently portrayed. For example, faunal remains show that the Altamirans ate red deer, not bison.

6   Other scholars have sought to reconstruct an elaborate mythology based on the cave paintings and sculptures, suggesting that Paleolithic humans believed they had animal ancestors. Still others have equated certain species with men and others with women and postulated various meanings for the abstract signs that sometimes accompany the images. Almost all of these theories have been discredited over time, and most prehistorians admit that no one knows the intent of these representations. In fact, a single explanation for all Paleolithic animal images, even ones similar in subject, style, and composition (how the motifs are arranged on the surface), is unlikely to apply universally. The works remain an enigma—and always will, because before the invention of writing, no contemporaneous explanations could be recorded.

---

remoteness This word has the suffix *-ness,* which makes it a noun. Use the word parts and the general context to determine what *remoteness* means.

faunal Use the phrase that follows *faunal* to determine its meaning.

○ What two theories of the meaning of the cave paintings are presented in paragraph 6?

enigma Use the context to determine the meaning of *enigma.* As a hint, paragraphs 4, 5, and 6 all talk of discredited theories of why Stone Age hunters painted these animal images.

PIERRE ANDRIEU/AFP/Getty Images

Figure 6.4. Hall of the Bulls (left wall) in the cave at Lascaux, France, ca. 15,000– 13,000 BCE Largest bull 11' 6" long.

Several species of animals appear together in the Hall of the Bulls. Many are colored silhouettes, but others were created by outline alone—the two basic approaches to painting in the history of art.

The World's Oldest Paintings?

7 One of the most spectacular archaeological finds of the past century came to light in December 1994 at Vallon-Pont-d'Arc, France, and was announced at a press conference in Paris on January 18, 1995. Unlike some other recent "finds" of prehistoric art that proved to be forgeries, the paintings in the Chauvet Cave (named after the leader of the exploration team, Jean-Marie Chauvet) seemed to be **authentic.** But no one, including Chauvet and his colleagues, guessed at the time of their discovery that radiocarbon dating (a measure of the rate of degeneration of carbon 14 in organic materials) of the paintings might establish that the murals in the cave were more than 15,000 years older than those at Altamira (Fig. 6.2). When the scientific tests were completed, the French archaeologists announced that the Chauvet Cave paintings were the oldest yet found anywhere, datable around 30,000–28,000 BCE.

8 This new early date immediately caused scholars to reevaluate the scheme of "stylistic development" from simple to more complex forms that had been nearly universally accepted for decades. In the Chauvet Cave, in contrast to Lascaux (Fig. 6.4), the horns of the aurochs (extinct long-horned wild oxen) are shown naturalistically,

authentic The sentence gives an antonym of *authentic*. What does *authentic* mean?

● Take a moment to absorb how long ago 30,000 BCE really is.

● Can you explain why "stylistic development" does not seem like a valid idea now?

one behind the other, not in the twisted perspective thought to be universally characteristic of Paleolithic art. Moreover, the two rhinoceroses at the lower right of Fig. 6.5 appear to confront each other, suggesting to some observers that the artist intended a narrative, another "first" in either painting or sculpture. If the paintings are twice as old as those of Lascaux, Altamira (Fig. 6.2), and Pech-Merle (Fig. 6.3), the assumption that Paleolithic art "evolved" from simple to more sophisticated representations is wrong.

sophisticated *Sophisticated* has an antonym clue within the sentence where it is found. Based on this clue, what does *sophisticated* mean?

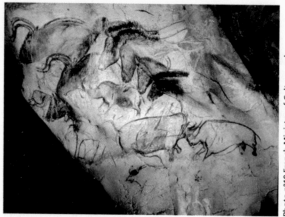

Figure 6.5. Aurochs, horses, and rhinoceroses, wall painting in the Chauvet Cave, Vallon-Pont-d'Arc, France, ca. 30,000–28,000 or ca. 15,000–13,000 BCE.
The date of the Chauvet Cave paintings is the subject of much controversy. If the murals are the oldest paintings known, they exhibit surprisingly advanced features, such as overlapping animal horns.

contested You probably know the meaning of this word when it is used as a noun. Here it is a verb. What does *contested* mean?

◉ How do you think finding and studying the world's oldest art would feel?

9   Much research remains to be conducted in the Chauvet Cave, but already the paintings have become the subject of intense controversy. Recently, some archaeologists have contested the early dating of the Chauvet paintings on the grounds that the tested samples were contaminated. If the Chauvet animals were painted later than those at Lascaux, their advanced stylistic features can be more easily explained. The dispute exemplifies the frustration—and the excitement—of studying the art of an age so remote that almost nothing remains and almost every new find causes art historians to reevaluate what had previously been taken for granted.

bpk, Berlin/Wolfgang Ruppert/Art Resource, NY

Figure 6.6. Rhinoceros, wounded man, and disemboweled bison, painting in the well of the cave at Lascaux, France, ca. 15,000–13,000 BCE. Bison 3'8" long.
If these paintings of two animals and a bird-faced (masked?) man deep in a Lascaux well shaft depict a hunting scene, they constitute the earliest example of narrative art ever discovered.

—From KLEINER. *Gardner's Art Through the Ages*, 13e (pp. 20–23)

Copyright © 2011 Cengage Learning.

● Comprehension Questions

Write the letter of the answer on the line. Then explain your thinking.

Main Idea

_____ 1. Which of the following best states the main idea of the section entitled "Art in the Old Stone Age"?

a. From the moment in 1879 that cave paintings were discovered at Altamira, scholars have wondered why the hunters of the Old Stone Age decided to cover the walls of dark caverns with animal images like those found at Altamira, Pech-Merle, Lascaux, and Vallon-Pont-d'Arc.

b. Scholars have proposed various theories including that the painted and engraved animals were mere decoration, but this explanation cannot account for the narrow range of subjects or the inaccessibility of many of the representations.

c. In contrast, some scholars have argued that the magical purpose of the paintings and reliefs was not to facilitate the destruction of bison and other species.

d. Other scholars have sought to reconstruct an elaborate mythology based on the cave paintings and sculptures, suggesting that Paleolithic humans believed they had animal ancestors.

WHY? What information in the selection leads you to give that answer? _____

_____

_____

_____

____ 2. What is the best main idea of paragraph 8?

a. This new early date immediately caused scholars to reevaluate the scheme of "stylistic development" from simple to more complex forms that had been nearly universally accepted for decades.

b. In the Chauvet Cave, in contrast to Lascaux (Fig. 6.4), the horns of the aurochs (extinct long-horned wild oxen) are shown naturalistically, one behind the other, not in the twisted perspective thought to be universally characteristic of Paleolithic art.

c. Moreover, the two rhinoceroses at the lower right of Fig. 6.5 appear to confront each other, suggesting to some observers that the artist intended a narrative, another "first" in either painting or sculpture.

d. If the paintings are twice as old as those of Lascaux, Altamira (Fig. 6.2), and Pech-Merle (Fig. 6.3), the assumption that Paleolithic art "evolved" from simple to more sophisticated representations is wrong.

WHY? What information in the selection leads you to give that answer? _____

_____

_____

_____

Supporting Details

____ 3. Which of the following would be an "ocher" as discussed in paragraph 2?

a. Stone lamp

b. Marrow

c. Water

d. Pigment

WHY? What information in the selection leads you to give that answer? _____

_____

_____

_____

___ 4. Which of the following is not a theory presented to explain the meaning of prehistoric cave art?

    a. The art is simply decorative.

    b. The art represents the hierarchy of status within the tribal structure of the Old Stone Age peoples.

    c. The art is representative of animal ancestors.

    d. The art was meant to ensure the survival of the Paleolithic people's food sources.

WHY? What information in the selection leads you to give that answer? _____

_____

_____

_____

Author's Purpose

___ 5. What is the overall purpose of the passage?

    a. To persuade readers of the important need to discover why Paleolithic peoples painted caves.

    b. To inform readers of the tribal structure of the Old Stone Age peoples.

    c. To inform readers what is known, debated, and unknown about Paleolithic peoples.

    d. To entertain readers with stories of discovering Paleolithic cave paintings.

WHY? What information in the selection leads you to give that answer? _____

_____

_____

_____

___ 6. What is the purpose of the section entitled "Art in the Old Stone Age"?

    a. To explain the process of how art in the Old Stone Age was created.

    b. To suggest that Old Stone Age hunters painted to bring luck to their hunts.

    c. To categorize all of the different types of art that represent the era of the Old Stone Age peoples.

    d. To inform the reader that despite the numerous theories proposed, no one really knows the purpose of cave painting.

WHY? What information in the selection leads you to give that answer? _____

_____

_____

_____

Relationships

_____ 7. Which of the following is an accurate statement about the relationship between the figures and the paragraphs in this reading?

a. The figures show the main ideas; the paragraphs give support.

b. Both the paragraphs and figures have the same role in the reading.

c. There is no relationship between the paragraphs and the figures.

d. The figures illustrate the ideas found within the paragraphs.

WHY? What information in the selection leads you to give that answer? _____

_____

_____

_____

_____ 8. What two patterns of organization are found in the first two sentences of paragraph 7?

a. Cause and effect; time order

b. Definition; contrast

c. Time order; contrast

d. Classification; comparison

WHY? What information in the selection leads you to give that answer? _____

_____

_____

_____

Fact, Opinion, and Inference

____ 9. Which of the following statements is an opinion?

a. The dispute exemplifies the frustration—and the excitement—of studying the art of an age so remote that almost nothing remains and almost every new find causes art historians to reevaluate what had previously been taken for granted.

b. This new early date immediately caused scholars to reevaluate the scheme of "stylistic development" from simple to more complex forms that had been nearly universally accepted for decades.

c. A central problem for both the hunting-magic and food-creation theories is that the animals that seem to have been diet staples of Old Stone Age peoples are not those most frequently portrayed.

d. Examples of Paleolithic painting now have been found at more than 200 sites, but prehistorians still regard painted caves as rare occurrences, because the images in them, even if they number in the hundreds, were created over a period of some 10,000 to 20,000 years.

WHY? What leads you to give that answer? _____

_____

_____

_____

____ 10. Which of the following statements would the author of this selection most likely agree with?

a. The discovery of cave art is probably the most important within the art world.

b. The next discovery of caves containing art from the Paleolithic era will cause historians to reconsider what they thought they knew about cave art.

c. The cave at Lascaux, France, is the most visually impressive example of cave art that we have.

d. Discoveries like the Chauvet Cave in 1994 probably cause many art historians to want to change professions.

WHY? What leads you to give that answer? _____

_____

_____

_____

● Mapping the Reading

Create a timeline of each of the caves mentioned in the above reading.

● Critical Thinking Questions

CRITICAL THINKING LEVEL 3: APPLY

This chapter has talked about Bloom's Taxonomy and levels of critical thinking. These concepts do not simply exist in the classroom. Explain how the archaeologist researchers at the Chauvet Caves (or other sites of prehistoric art) use critical thinking in their jobs.

_____

_____

_____

_____

CRITICAL THINKING LEVEL 4: ANALYZE

Explain the effect that a discovery of caves containing paintings from 45,000–35,000 BCE could have on the art world.

_____

_____

_____

_____

CRITICAL THINKING LEVEL 5: EVALUATE

Which of the five images from this reading do you find the most impressive, mysterious, or awe-inspiring? Explain your thoughts.

_____

_____

_____

_____

● Language in Use

The following words (or forms of them) were used in "Paleolithic Cave Painting." Now you can use them in different contexts. Put a word from the box into the blank lines in the following numbered sentences.

> choked   pigments   palettes   remoteness   faunal
>
> enigma   authentic   sophisticated   contested

1. Kate Middleton is one _____ young lady, having made the best-dressed list in *People, Vanity Fair,* and Style.com.

2. If you find her name to be an _____, well, she is Prince William of Wales's wife.

3. The dreams of many a young English woman were _____ in November 2010, when the official announcement came of the engagement between William and Kate.

4. And even though Kate's family heritage includes working-class laborers and miners, no one has _____ the wedding between a royal and a commoner.

5. But don't worry. Kate didn't stay a commoner for long; she became _____ royalty when she married Prince William in Westminster Abbey on April 29, 2011.

● EASY Note Cards

Make a note card for each of the vocabulary words from the reading that you did not know. On one side, write the word. On the other side, divide the card into quarters and label them E, A, S, and Y. Add a word or phrase in each area so that you wind up with an example sentence, an antonym, a synonym, and, finally, a definition that shows you understand the meaning of the word with your logic. Remember that a synonym or antonym may have appeared in the reading.

Career Visual Arts App ONLINE EDUCATION JOURNAL

● Pre-Reading the Selection

The excerpt that begins on page 377 comes from the website of *New Horizons for Learning,* an educational journal associated with Johns Hopkins University School of Education. The excerpt is titled "Every Child Needs the Arts."

Surveying the Reading

Survey the selection that follows. Then check the elements that are included in this reading.

_____ Title

_____ Headings

_____ First sentences of paragraphs

_____ Words in bold or italic type

_____ Images and captions

Guessing the Purpose

Based on the source and the title of the reading selection, do you think the author's purpose is mostly to persuade, inform, or express? _____

Predicting the Content

Based on your survey, what are three things you expect the reading selection to discuss?

- _____

- _____

- _____

Activating Your Knowledge

What does the author mean by "the arts" in the title? How many of "the arts" can you name?

- _____

- _____

- _____

● Reading with Pen in Hand

Students who annotate as they read are more successful than students who do not anno-tate. That's why you will annotate each reading in *Engage* as you read. In the reading that follows, use the following symbols:

★ or (Point)   to indicate a main idea

① ② ③   to indicate major details

  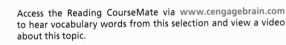

Access the Reading CourseMate via www.cengagebrain.com to hear vocabulary words from this selection and view a video about this topic.

Every Child Needs the Arts

Charles Fowler, D.M.A.

Reading Journal

1   The arts are windows on the world in the same way that sci-ence helps us see the world around us. Literature, music, theater, the visual arts, the media (film, photography, and television), archi-tecture, and dance reveal **aspects** about ourselves, the world around us, and the relationship between the two. In 1937, German planes flying for Franco in the Spanish civil war bombed a defenseless vil-lage as a laboratory experiment, killing many of the inhabitants. In *Guernica,* Pablo Picasso painted his outrage in the form of a vicious bull smugly surveying a scene of human beings screaming, suffer-ing, and dying. These powerful images etch in our minds the horror of a senseless act of war.

○ Think of a movie that expresses something important or interesting about the relationship between people and the world.

aspects Look at the list of items in this sentence as well as the example that follows. What does *aspects* mean?

2   Similar themes have been represented in other art forms. Ben-jamin Britten's *War Requiem* gives poignant musical and poetic expression to the unpredictable misfortunes of war's **carnage.** Brit-ten juxtaposes the verses of Wilfred Owen, a poet killed during World War I, with the ancient scriptures of the Mass for the Dead. In Euripides' play *The Trojan Women,* the ancient art of theater expresses the grievous sacrifices that war forces human beings to endure. The film *Platoon,* written and directed by Oliver Stone, is a more recent exposition of the meaning of war, a theme that has been treated again and again with telling effect in literature throughout the ages. The theme of human beings inflicting suffering upon other human beings has also been expressed through dance. One example is *Dreams,* a modern dance choreographed by Anna Sokolow, in which the dreams become nightmares of Nazi concentration camps.

carnage What happens in war? The next sentence gives a clue. What does *carnage* mean?

○ Visualize one of the examples (if you are familiar with any of them), or think of an antiwar story, movie, play, or song you are familiar with.

3

This theme and many others are investigated, expressed, and communicated through the arts. Through such artistic representations, we share a common humanity. What would life be without such shared expressions? How would such understandings be conveyed? Science is not the sole conveyor of truth. While science can explain a sunrise, the arts convey its emotive impact and meaning. Both are important. If human beings are to survive, we need all the symbolic forms at our command because they permit us not only to preserve and pass along our accumulated wisdom but also to give voice to the invention of new visions. We need all these ways of viewing the world because no one way can say it all.

4

The arts are *acts of intelligence* no less than other subjects. They are forms of thought every bit as potent as mathematical and scientific symbols in what they convey. The Egyptian pyramids can be "described" in mathematical measurements, and science and history can hypothesize about how, why, and when they were built, but a photograph or painting of them can show us other equally important aspects of their reality. The arts are symbol systems that permit us to give representation to our ideas, concepts, and feelings in a variety of forms that can be "read" by other people. The arts were invented to enable us to react to the world, to analyze it, and to record our impressions so that they can be shared. Like other symbol systems, the arts require study before they can be fully understood.

© c./Shutterstock.com

5

Is there a better way to gain an understanding of ancient Greek civilization than through their magnificent temples, statues, pot-

○ What would life be like without art?

conveyor A form of this word is used three times in this paragraph. Read the context of each to determine what *conveyor* means.

○ How is art an act of intelligence?

potent Art is compared to science and math as being just as *potent*. What does *potent* mean?

○ Can you think of some art piece or style that represents a culture or a time period?

tery, and poetry? The Gothic cathedrals inform us about the Middle Ages just as surely as the skyscraper reveals the Modern Age. The arts may well be the most telling imprints of any civilization. In this sense they are living histories of eras and peoples, and records and revelations of the human spirit. One might well ask how history could possibly be taught without their **inclusion.**

6   Today's schools are concerned, as they rightly should be, with teaching literacy. But literacy should not—must not—be limited to the written word. It should also encompass the symbol systems of the arts. If our concept of literacy is defined too narrowly as referring to just the symbol systems of language, mathematics, and science, children will not be equipped with the breadth of symbolic tools they need to fully represent, express, and communicate the full **spectrum** of human life.

7   What constitutes a good education anyway? Today, one major goal has become very practical: employability. Children should know how to read, write, and compute so that they can assume a place in the work force. Few would argue with that. Considering the demands that young people will face tomorrow in this technological society, the need for literacy in English language, mathematics, science, and history is critical. But this objective should not allow us to overlook the importance of the arts and what they can do for the mind and spirit of every child and the **vitality** of American schooling.

8   Educational administrators and school boards need to be reminded that schools have a fundamental obligation to provide the fuel that will ignite the mind, spark the aspirations, and illuminate the total being. The arts can often serve as that fuel. They are the ways we apply our imagination, thought, and feeling through a range of "languages" to illuminate life in all its mystery, misery, delight, pity, and wonder. They are fundamental enablers that can help us engage more significantly with our inner selves and the world around us. As we first engage one capacity, we enable others, too, to emerge. Given the current dropout rate, whether the entry vehicle to learning for a particular human being happens to be the arts, the sciences, or the humanities is less important than the assured existence of a variety of such vehicles.

9   The first wave of the education reform movement in America focused on improving the quality of public education simply by

inclusion Look at the word parts: *inclu* + *-sion*. Use your logic and the word parts to give the meaning of *inclusion.*

● Think about how art encourages literacy.

spectrum The author wants to expand literacy and open up children's options for communication. What is a *spectrum*?

● How would you answer the question "What constitutes a good education?"

vitality The root *vital* means "having life." This paragraph answers the question of what makes for good education. What would art add to an education? What does *vitality* mean?

● Does art fuel your imagination, thoughts, or emotions?

● What are the three waves of educational reform?

induce *Induce* is a verb. Look at it in reference to *self-discipline*. What does *induce* mean?

● What is the purpose of art, according to this paragraph? Do you agree?

conjuring up Connect *conjuring up* with the previous phrase *play make-believe* to determine the meaning.

raising standards and introducing more challenging course requirements at the high school level. The second wave has focused on improving the quality of the nation's teachers. The third wave should concentrate on the students—how to activate and inspire them, how to induce self-discipline, and how to help them to discover the joys of learning, the uniqueness of their beings, the wonders and possibilities of life, the satisfaction of achievement, and the revelations that literacy, broadly defined, provides. The arts are a central and fundamental means to attain these objectives.

10   We do not need more and better arts education simply to develop more and better artists. There are far more important reasons for schools to provide children with an education in the arts. Quite simply, the arts are the ways we human beings "talk" to ourselves and to each other. They are the language of civilization through which we express our fears, our anxieties, our curiosities, our hungers, our discoveries, and our hopes. They are the universal ways by which we humans still play make-believe, conjuring up worlds that explain the ceremonies of our lives. The arts are not just important; they are a central force in human existence. Every child should have sufficient opportunity to acquire familiarity with these languages that so assist us in our fumbling, bumbling, and all-too-rarely brilliant navigation through this world. Because of this, the arts should be granted major status in every child's schooling. That is a cause worthy of our energies.

—Charles Fowler, D.M.A. "Every Child Needs the Arts" in *Creating the Future: Perspectives on Educational Change.* Copyright © 1991, 1996, 1998, 2002 New Horizons for Learning, all rights reserved. Reprinted by permission.

● Comprehension Questions

Write the letter of the answer on the line. Then explain your thinking.

Main Idea

_____ 1. Which of the following sentences is the best main idea for paragraph 1?

    a. The arts are windows on the world in the same way that science helps us see the world around us.

    b. Literature, music, theater, the visual arts, the media (film, photography, and television), architecture, and dance reveal aspects about ourselves, the world around us, and the relationship between the two.

    c. In 1937, German planes flying for Franco in the Spanish civil war bombed a defenseless village as a laboratory experiment, killing many of the inhabitants.

    d. In *Guernica,* Pablo Picasso painted his outrage in the form of a vicious bull smugly surveying a scene of human beings screaming, suffering, and dying.

WHY? What information in the selection leads you to give that answer? _____

_____

_____

_____

_____ 2. Which of the following sentences is the best topic sentence of paragraph 6?

    a. Today's schools are concerned, as they rightly should be, with teaching literacy.

    b. But literacy should not—must not—be limited to the written word.

    c. It should also encompass the symbol systems of the arts.

    d. If our concept of literacy is defined too narrowly as referring to just the symbol systems of language, mathematics, and science, children will not be equipped with the breadth of symbolic tools they need to fully represent, express, and communicate the full spectrum of human life.

WHY? What information in the selection leads you to give that answer? _____

_____

_____

_____

Supporting Details

____ 3. Which of the following answers is *most* relevant to the main idea of this reading: *Children should be taught the arts?*

   a. The first wave of the education reform movement in America focused on improving the quality of public education simply by raising standards and introducing more challenging course requirements at the high school level.

   b. Today, one major goal has become very practical: employability.

   c. The arts are not just important; they are a central force in human existence.

   d. Science is not the sole conveyor of truth.

WHY? What information in the selection leads you to give that answer? _____

_____

_____

_____

____ 4. What type of evidence does the author give in paragraphs 1 and 2 to support the idea that "the arts are windows on the world"?

   a. Causes

   b. Examples

   c. Anecdotes

   d. Reasons

WHY? What information in the selection leads you to give that answer? _____

_____

_____

_____

Author's Purpose

____ 5. Which of the following most accurately describes the purpose of this reading?

   a. To persuade readers that children being educated in the arts is more important than their being educated in math and science.

   b. To persuade readers that teaching the arts in schools should have been the first wave of educational reform.

   c. To persuade readers of the importance of teaching the arts so that children can become better artists.

   d. To persuade readers that children need to learn the language of art because it is essential to being human.

WHY? What information in the selection leads you to give that answer? _____

_____

_____

_____

_____ 6. What is the author's purpose in mentioning the Egyptian pyramids, ancient Greek civilization, and Gothic cathedrals?

    a. To show how art is the best strategy for explaining ancient cultures.

    b. To give examples of how ancient cultures were more artistic than modern-day cultures.

    c. To illustrate that art is essential in fully understanding these structures and civilizations.

    d. To help the student fully understand what art is.

WHY? What information in the selection leads you to give that answer? _____

_____

_____

_____

Relationships

_____ 7. What is the relationship of the second sentence to the first? *Educational administrators and school boards need to be reminded that schools have a fundamental obligation to provide the fuel that will ignite the mind, spark the aspirations, and illuminate the total being. The arts can often serve as that fuel.*

    a. Comparison or similarity

    b. Cause and effect

    c. Process

    d. Contrast or difference

WHY? What information in the selection leads you to give that answer? _____

_____

_____

_____

____ 8. What is the relationship between paragraphs 1 and 2?

   a. Paragraph 1 sets up a cause; paragraph 2 explains an effect.

   b. Paragraph 1 gives a timeline; paragraph 2 gives a location.

   c. Paragraph 1 gives a comparison; paragraph 2 gives a contrast.

   d. Paragraph 1 introduces an idea; paragraph 2 gives more examples.

WHY? What information in the selection leads you to give that answer? _____

_____

_____

_____

Fact, Opinion, and Inference

____ 9. Which of the following statements is a fact?

   a. These powerful images etch in our minds the horror of a senseless act of war.

   b. Like other symbol systems, the arts require study before they can be fully understood.

   c. The arts may well be the most telling imprints of any civilization.

   d. The arts should be granted major status in every child's schooling.

WHY? What leads you to give that answer? _____

_____

_____

_____

____ 10. Which of the following quotes would the author most likely agree with?

   a. "A guilty conscience needs to confess. A work of art is a confession." —Albert Camus

   b. "An artist is somebody who produces things that people don't need to have." —Andy Warhol

   c. "Abstract art: a product of the untalented sold by the unprincipled to the utterly bewildered." —Al Capp

   d. "Art disturbs, science reassures." —Georges Braque

WHY? What leads you to give that answer? _____

_____

_____

_____

● Mapping the Reading

Create a visual map showing the author's reasoning for why children need art.

● Critical Thinking Questions

CRITICAL THINKING LEVEL 3: APPLY

The excerpt mentioned that the movie *Platoon* has the theme of expressing the meaning of war. We live in a culture full of movies. Can you think of one or more movies that have the following themes?

- Parent-child issues: _____
- Redemption: _____
- Freedom: _____
- Loss (grief, death, etc.): _____
- Being wrongly accused: _____
- Perseverance: _____

CRITICAL THINKING LEVEL 4: ANALYZE

The title of this excerpt is "Every Child Needs the Arts." List five major details the author uses to support this claim.

1. _____

2. _____

3. _____

4. _____

5. _____

CRITICAL THINKING LEVEL 5: EVALUATE

Do you think the arts are part of what constitutes a good education? Should the arts be taught in school? Why or why not? Support your answer.

_____

_____

_____

_____

● Language in Use

The following words (or forms of them) were used in "Every Child Needs the Arts." Now you can use them in different contexts. Put a word from the box into the blank lines in the following numbered sentences.

> aspect carnage convey potent inclusion
>
> spectrum vitality induce conjure up

1. There is a wide _____ of views about what constitutes ethical treatment of animals.

2. On one extreme is PETA (People for the Ethical Treatment of Animals), which believes strongly in a vegetarian world. Its members are against eating, wearing, testing, or abusing animals in any way. They show graphic videos of the _____ of animals on their website to get their point across.

3. On the other extreme are cultures that view some animals as pests and kill them indiscriminately (Tasmanian tiger, Javan tiger). Still other cultures believe that particular parts of some animals are _____ (turtle blood for longevity and bear gallbladder for increased sexual power) and have consequently hunted certain species of those animals to extinction.

4. In fact, the current demand for restricted animal products, such as tiger penis, rhinoceros horn, and bear foot, has created a black market of such great _____ that it is estimated to be worth $10 to $20 billion per year.

5. Although most people fall somewhere between these extremes—they eat meat but don't abuse animals and certainly don't want to cause any more species to become extinct—it is not hard to _____ reasons for a code of ethics for the treatment of the animals that share our planet.

● EASY Note Cards

Make a note card for each of the vocabulary words from the reading that you did not know. On one side, write the word. On the other side, divide the card into quarters and label them E, A, S, and Y. Add a word or phrase in each area so that you wind up with an example sentence, an antonym, a synonym, and, finally, a definition that shows you understand the meaning of the word with your logic. Remember that a synonym or antonym may have appeared in the reading.

7 Inferring Meaning from Details

Previewing the Chapter

Preview Chapter 7. Name four things you intend to learn from this chapter.

- _____

- _____

- _____

- _____

Plan to come back to your list when you have finished working through the chapter to make sure you have learned all that you meant to. Write your notes here.

_____

_____

_____

_____

 To access additional course materials for *Engage,* including quizzes, videos, and more, please visit www.cengagebrain.com. At the CengageBrain.com home page, search for the ISBN of *Engage* (from the back cover of your book) using the search box at the top of the page. This will take you to the product page where these resources can be found.

Videos Related   **Vocab Words**   **Read and Talk**
to Readings   **on Audio**   **on Demand**

Read and Talk   MAGAZINE

In college, reading is just one aspect of how you will share new ideas with others in your class. So the first reading in each chapter of this book is meant to give you the chance to talk about reading. Read the article, and then use the four discussion questions to talk about your ideas with your classmates and your instructor.

Access the Reading CourseMate via www.cengagebrain.com to hear a reading of this selection and view a video about this topic.

Illegal Fireworks Likely Cause of Massive Arkansas Blackbird Deaths

Alisa Opar

© R. Gino Santa Maria/Shutterstock.com

1   Professional-grade fireworks probably caused the deaths of thousands of red-winged blackbirds in Beebe, Arkansas, on New Year's Eve, 2011. The loud noises, combined with birds' poor night vision and large winter gathering, likely led 4,000 to 5,000 birds to crash to their deaths. That's the Arkansas Game and Fish Commission's "strong working hypothesis," according to Karen Rowe, a Commission **ornithologist**.

2   Here's what officials have pieced together:

3   At 10 p.m., residents heard several extremely loud, "window-shaking" noises that are believed to have come from professional-grade fireworks, which no one had permission to set off. The blasts came from an area near the birds' winter roost.

ornithologist Based on the subject Rowe is discussing, what is the meaning of this word?

disorientation Considering the word parts, what does this word mean?

necropsy *Necros* means "corpse." What is the meaning of the whole word?

hemorrhaging Guess the meaning based on context and your knowledge.

prolific Use your logic. What does *prolific* mean?

4 About 15 minutes later several folks went outside when they heard the whooshing wings of a blackbird flock flying at its normal fast speed. "But when they looked up, instead of the birds being above treetop level, like they usually are, they were at rooftop level," says Rowe. "They crashed into houses, cars, trees, mailboxes, shrubbery. Everything around."

5 Blackbirds don't usually fly at night. The big booms apparently flushed the birds from their roost, and then poor eyesight and disorientation stymied them from making it back safely.

6 "Necropsy report shows trauma primarily to the chest," says Rowe. "Hemorrhaging in the body cavity, bruised skulls, blood clots in brain. It's consistent with crashing into something rather than falling." Toxins don't appear to be a factor, says Rowe, adding that the death toll is difficult to estimate because feral cats, raccoons, and other scavengers likely made a meal out of the fallen creatures.

7 The loss of any animals is regrettable, says Rowe. "I don't want to see it again, but I especially hope we don't see it with any declining species like cerulean warblers."

8 Beebe residents aren't likely to see a repeat of the freak event on the Fourth of July, the only other day the city allows fireworks. Blackbirds will be spread out on their individual nests then, instead of congregating in their winter roost.

9 It appears that similarly mysterious bird deaths in Louisiana around the same time are unrelated. "Initial findings indicate that these are isolated incidents that were probably caused by disturbance and disorientation," says Greg Butcher, Audubon's director of bird conservation.

10 The birds—red-winged blackbirds, common grackles, brownheaded cowbirds and European starlings—are abundant species that flock together in large nighttime roosts during the winter months. Roosts can contain from tens of thousands to 20 million individuals or more.

11 Blackbirds are so prolific that during the Christmas Bird Count this year, Rowe says she and another biologist commented that they spent so much time counting blackbirds that they didn't get to search out more rare species. "This will teach us," she says wryly.

—Alisa Opar, "Illegal Fireworks Likely Cause of Massive Arkansas Blackbird Deaths." Copyright © 2011 Audubon Magazine. Reprinted by permission.

Talking About Reading

Respond in writing to the questions below and then discuss your answers with your classmates.

1. Should the people who set off the illegal fireworks be found and punished? Why or why not?

_____

_____

_____

_____

2. Does your response to the first question depend at all on how many red-winged blackbirds there are? Why or why not?

_____

_____

_____

_____

3. What factors did residents of Beebe and ornithologists take into account as they tried to figure out why so many blackbirds died at once?

_____

_____

_____

_____

4. Does this story of the interaction between people and birds seem similar to or different from other stories you've heard of people's interactions with animals, birds, and fish? What aspects are similar or different?

_____

_____

_____

_____

The Process of Making Inferences

When the people of Beebe, Arkansas, went outside on New Year's Day in 2011 and saw dead blackbirds littering their streets and yards, they wanted to know what had happened. What caused the death of all these birds? They started gathering all the evidence they could find—the sequence of events on New Year's Eve, their knowledge of black-birds, and the information they gained from examining the birds' bodies—to see what it added up to. They created a theory that would explain all the details.

They also discarded explanations that didn't fit the facts. For instance, the birds were probably not killed from falling to the ground or by toxins. When the scientists looked at the birds' dead bodies, they didn't find any details to support those hypotheses (interpretations of a situation). Discarding ideas that don't fit the facts is a crucial step in forming inferences. No matter how attractive or commonsensical, if an idea doesn't fit the facts, it must be left behind.

Using inference, an investigator begins with a set of facts, and then tries to figure out what they mean. In this particular case, the facts are effects, and the cause of the events is unknown. The causes need to be inferred. In other cases, the relationship between the known and the unknown may be different.

The Process of Making an Inference About Causes

Notice that making inferences is a critical thinking process.

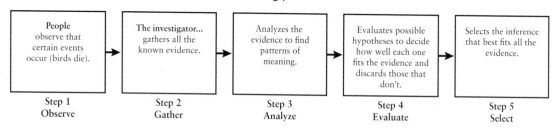

People observe that certain events occur (birds die).	The investigator... gathers all the known evidence.	Analyzes the evidence to find patterns of meaning.	Evaluates possible hypotheses to decide how well each one fits the evidence and discards those that don't.	Selects the inference that best fits all the evidence.
Step 1 Observe	Step 2 Gather	Step 3 Analyze	Step 4 Evaluate	Step 5 Select

When scientists use inferences to try to understand the world, they are as logical at each step as possible. They carefully consider what they know and what they don't know. They have other scientists check their work to see if they get the same results. In contrast, when we read, we make lots of inferences that don't go through any kind of sci-entific process. Mostly, the inferences we make are quite unconscious. One of the goals of this chapter is for you to become consciously aware of the inferences you are making so you can decide whether they really are warranted by the words on the page.

INTERACTION 7–1 | **Make Inferences about Causes**

With a group of classmates, discuss all the different possible causes you can think of for each of the following situations.

1. You're watching a YouTube video of a new band on your computer (full screen), and the computer screen goes black. _____

_____

2. You and a friend are at a restaurant, and suddenly she springs to her feet and screams. _____

_____

3. The husband in a married couple does all the cooking and shopping. _____

_____

4. A girl has pronounced dark circles under her eyes. _____

_____

5. A seventeen-year-old boy comes home from a party much earlier than expected.

_____

_____

Section Review: The Process of Making Inferences

For the first four steps in the process of making inferences about causes, write a question that an investigator could ask.

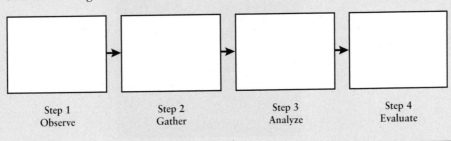

| Step 1 Observe | Step 2 Gather | Step 3 Analyze | Step 4 Evaluate | Step 5 Select |

Inferences that Fit All the Details

The task in Interaction 7–1 was simple, because each sentence included only one or two facts that you had to think of explanations for. But you didn't have enough information to tell which explanation was most likely.

The more details that a sentence includes, the fewer hypotheses or inferences will fit all the facts. For example, what if we added one new fact to sentence 2 in Interaction 7–1?

> You and a friend are at a restaurant **in Hollywood,** and suddenly she springs to her feet and screams.

Maybe you already had as one of your hypotheses that your friend saw a movie star. Now, it seems even more likely. Of course, you still don't know if it's true. If the writer had provided one more detail, you might feel even more convinced:

> You and a friend are at a restaurant in Hollywood, and suddenly she springs to her feet and screams, **"Oh, my God, there he is!"**

With these additional details, it's easy to discard some of your earlier hypotheses. If you hypothesized that she got stung by a bee, for example, you now know that isn't true—unless she got stung by a bee at the same moment that she saw Brad Pitt.

Stephen Lovekin/Getty Images

INTERACTION 7–2   **Make Inferences that Fit All the Details**

For each item, make inferences that fit *all* the facts. If you think an inference might be true but you're not 100 percent sure, use words like *might* and *may* in your explanation.

1. Every pass the quarterback for the Green Bay Packers made was caught by a receiver. The average distance the quarterback ran in each play was twenty-five yards. The other team had lost nine of their last ten games. _____

   _____

   _____

2. The subway train ran slower and slower. Eventually, it stopped, even though it was between stations. No announcement was made about the cause of the unexpected stop. _____

   _____

   _____

3. A dog was trotting down the road. It was panting and drooling. It had a broken leash trailing behind it. Its head was moving from side to side twenty or thirty times a minute. _____

   _____

   _____

4. The girl tried to scratch her head, but she couldn't move her arm. She tried to look around because she couldn't remember where she was, or why. But she felt dizzy and sick. Another wave of blackness overcame her. _____

   _____

   _____

5. A young man is in a video store, and he's looking around a lot. He goes to the back of the store and lingers there for a few minutes. All the other customers leave. Then he takes a video case off the shelf and goes to the counter. _____

   _____

   _____

INTERACTION 7–3 | **Play with Inference Riddles**

Each of the following numbered items is a riddle to solve. There is a list of clues for each item. See how many clues you have to read to figure out what is being implied. To do this, put a sheet of paper over all but the first clue. Make an inference when you read that clue. Then move the sheet of paper down, read the second clue, and see if it confirms your original inference or suggests something new. Work your way through the clues until you are assured of your inferences, then write what you think the clues are describing on the blank line.

1. Inference: _____

- People depend on me.
- I hurt people, and I help people.
- I may have a specialty.
- I wear white.
- I took the Nightingale Pledge.

2. Inference: _____

- They tell stories.
- Many young people like to look at them.
- Those who sell them may work behind a counter.
- They can be funny.
- Often, they are filled with color.

3. Inference: _____

- They can be ninety feet high.
- They have a somewhat irregular but still rhythmic motion.
- Distant winds affect them.
- They may foam.
- They may bring unwanted gifts with them.

4. Inference: _____

- It takes over an otherwise vacant spot when allowed to.
- It can be destroyed by chemicals or by cutting.
- Women only like them on others.
- Tom Selleck (from *Magnum P.I.*) wears his with a smile.
- Recently, caring for it has been referred to as "manscaping."

5. Inference: _____

- It gets you what you want, but it also may take a lot in return.
- It might even reward you.
- Twenty-nine percent of Americans don't have one.
- The name of one popular kind suggests that it will get you into another country.
- It can be placed horizontally into a slot.

Section Review: Inferences that Fit All the Details

Think about a recent situation in which you weren't sure why something happened. In the boxes on the right, write the facts (the effects of the unknown cause) that you knew. If you need to, add more boxes or write between the boxes. On the left, write down your inference about the cause or causes. Is your inference supported by all the facts? If not, try to think of an inference that is.

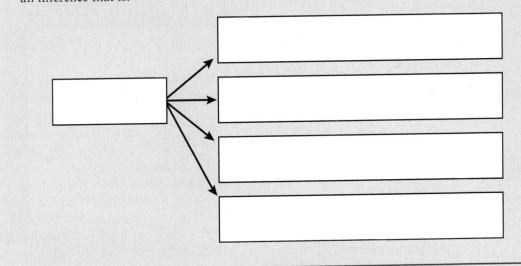

The Role of Prior Knowledge in Making Inferences

If you had no knowledge of the world, you would not be able to make inferences from what you read and the events you experience. For example, suppose you were an alien visiting from Mars who had never seen water before. You see a river. You would be unlikely to make the inferences an earthling would, such as "I can drink this water" or "I can go swimming here" or "I'm going to get wet if I cross the river."

Furthermore, if you have enough knowledge of water to think "I can drink this water," you can make the further inference "If I set up camp near this river, I won't go thirsty." Once you think "I can go swimming here," you can also infer "If the day gets hot, I'll jump in and cool off." And when you think "I'm going to get wet if I cross the river," you can also infer "If I don't want to get my sneakers wet, I should take them off before I go wading."

When you read, the words on a page are like the river. They activate all kinds of prior knowledge about how the physical world works, how different kinds of people act and why, and the many other pieces of knowledge you have acquired through the years. Because reading requires you to activate this knowledge, books have been called an act of creation shared by the writer and the reader.

As a reader, you have a responsibility to the author. If you hold a belief that isn't shared by the author, you can't let it derail the author's meaning. If the author's words contradict your prior knowledge, you have an obligation to suspend your own ideas, at least for a while, in order to understand the author's ideas. Inferences that you build must be based on the solid ground of the text in front of you.

INTERACTION 7–4 | **Make Meaning from Words on the Page**

Work with a partner or in a small group to complete this Interaction.

A. The items that follow are chunks of sentences from pages 3 and 4 of the novel *Naked,* by David Sedaris. Use a piece of paper to cover all the items except the first one. Read it, and then make as many inferences as you can about the situation. Uncover the next item, refine your inferences, and repeat the process for all eleven items.

1. When my sisters were taken,

_____

_____

2. my father crumpled the ransom note and tossed it

_____

_____

3. into the eternal flame that burns beside the mummified Pilgrim we keep in the dining hall

_____

_____

4. of our summer home in Olfactory.

_____

_____

5. We don't negotiate with criminals, because it's not in our character.

_____

_____

6. Every now and then we think about my sisters and hope they're doing well,

_____

_____

7. but we don't dwell upon the matter, as that only allows the kidnappers to win.

_____

_____

8. My sisters are gone for the time being but, who knows, maybe they'll return someday, perhaps when they're older and have families of their own.

   _____

   _____

9. In the meantime, I am left as the only child and heir to my parents' substantial fortune.

   _____

   _____

10. Is it lonely? Sometimes. I've still got my mother and father and, of course, the servants, several of whom are extraordinarily clever despite their crooked teeth and lack of breeding. Why, just the other day I was in the stable with Duncan when . . .

    _____

    _____

11. "Oh, for God's sake," my mother said, tossing her wooden spoon into a cauldron of chipped-beef gravy.

    _____

    _____   _____

B. Answer the following questions based on the inferences you made.

12. In items 1 through 10, what inference were you making?

    _____ The family is rich.

    _____ The family is poor.

13. What does the author say to lead you to this conclusion? Quote statements by the author in the left column. In the right column, describe your prior knowledge about the statements in the left column that led you to your inference. The first one is done as an example.

Evidence:	Prior knowledge that connects evidence to inference:
"my sisters were taken"	Only children of rich families are kidnapped because only rich people can pay a ransom.

14. In items 1 through 10, what inference were you making?

_____ The narrator loves his family very much.

_____ The narrator doesn't care about his family.

15. What does the author say to lead you to this conclusion? What pieces of your prior knowledge led you to that inference?

Evidence:	Prior knowledge that connects evidence to inference:

16. In items 1 through 10, what inference were you making?

_____ The narrator is a child.

_____ The narrator is an adult.

17. What does the author say to lead you to this conclusion? What pieces of your prior knowledge led you to that inference?

Evidence:	Prior knowledge that connects evidence to inference:

18. In item 11, what inference did you make?

_____ The mother is upper-class.

_____ The mother is middle-class or lower-class.

19. What does the author say to lead you to this conclusion? What pieces of your prior knowledge led you to that inference?

Evidence:	Prior knowledge that connects evidence to inference:

20. After you read item 11, what inference did you make?

    _____ The narrator has been daydreaming.

    _____ The narrator has been asleep and dreaming.

21. What evidence supports your answer to question 20? Think about the contrasts between items 1 through 10, on the one hand, and item 11, on the other hand. Also, consider all of the inferences you have made so far. Fill in the table.

Evidence from items 1 through 11 and from the inferences you drew about them:	Prior knowledge that connects evidence to inference:

Section Review: The Role of Prior Knowledge in Making Inferences

A. Fill in the prior knowledge boxes with information that connects the evidence to the inference.

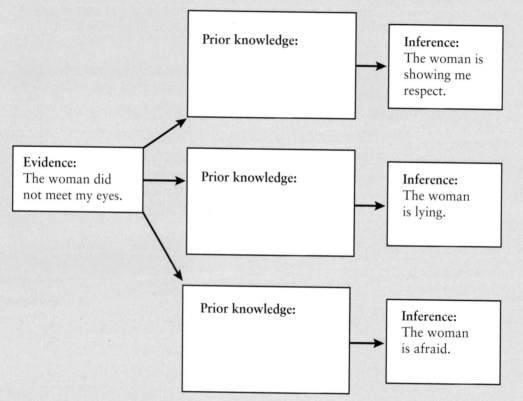

B. If you were reading a passage with the sentence "The woman did not meet my eyes," how would you figure out what inference was the most likely? _____

_____

_____

Generalizing by Identifying Patterns among Ideas

All kinds of relationships among ideas can be implied by the author and then inferred by the reader. For instance, the story of the Arkansas blackbirds was about a cause-and-effect relationship, when the effects were known but the cause was unknown. The example about the alien from Mars encountering a river was about the opposite kind of relationship: knowing the cause and inferring the effects.

Another kind of inference readers need to make are generalizations. The author gives a number of specific examples, types, or other kinds of details, and the reader must determine what generalization best encompasses them all. You practiced identifying generalizations when you learned how to locate the topic sentence of a paragraph. Now you can practice creating generalizations. Consider these sentences:

- Cohabitation, that is, living together, is often a practice run at marriage for young Americans.

- Cohabitation is a common and accepted alternative to marriage in Sweden, where nearly one in four cohabiting Swedes are not legally married and tend to marry only to legalize the relationship for their children's sake.

- In China, cohabitation occurs mostly in rural villages where couples are below the legal age for marriage.

To arrive at an accurate generalization, first you need to decide what larger categories link the ideas in each sentence. Here is one link between specific examples and a more general category:

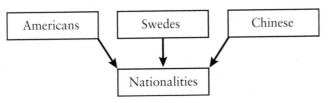

Americans, Swedes, and Chinese people are different nationalities. But the idea of "nationalities" is only one link between the sentences.

Another kind of information given across sentences is reasons (causes) for cohabiting:

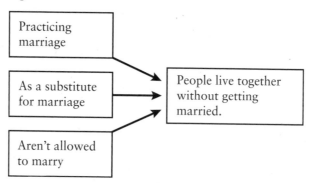

When you put together these two links, you get this generalization, which is also an inference:

People in different countries cohabit for different reasons.

Typically, when you are generalizing from details, you won't actually take the time to diagram the relationships between the details and the missing element, such as the general categories the ideas fit into. But if you get stuck and aren't sure what the author is getting at, run through the organizational patterns in your mind to get ideas about what the relationships could be. (See pages 236–237 for a review of patterns.)

INTERACTION 7–5   Use Visuals to Practice Generalizing

Practice using visuals to determine what generalization will fit the details.

- Read each set of supporting details to figure out the topic.
- Fill in the information about the patterns that go across sentences.
- Create an inference from the details, and add the main idea into the APP.
- Write a topic sentence that covers the topic and main idea.

1. About: _____

   Point: _____

          _____

      Proof: 1. When the United States went to war in World War II, we did not view ourselves as going off to commit violence.

             2. When citizens of ancient Sparta threw "unfit" babies off of cliffs, they did not see themselves as committing violence.

3. When a Yanomamo man pounds the chest of another man or hits his wife, he does not deem himself to be committing violence.

4. When eighteenth-century slavers captured and sold Africans as slaves, they did not regard themselves as committing violence.

—From ELLER. *Violence and Culture* (p. 1)
Copyright © 2006 Cengage Learning.

Patterns across sentences:

a. What groups of people are mentioned? What do these groups all have in common, according to the sentences?

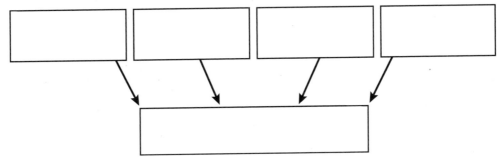

b. What actions are represented? *Make an inference* by figuring out what effect all these actions have in common (besides the stated one of each group not viewing its own acts as violent).

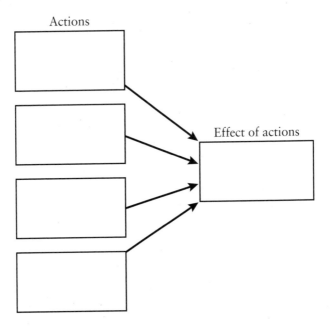

c. Write the topic sentence: _____

_____

2. About: _____

    Point: _____

        Proof: 1. First, when a pregnant woman experiences stress, her body secretes hormones that reduce the flow of oxygen to the fetus while increasing its heart rate and activity level.

               2. Second, stress can weaken a pregnant woman's immune system, making her more susceptible to illness, which can, in turn, damage fetal development.

               3. Third, pregnant women under stress are more likely to smoke or drink alcohol and are less likely to rest, exercise, and eat properly.

—From KAIL/CAVANAUGH. *Cengage Advantage Books: Human Development,* 4e (p. 64)
Copyright © 2010 Cengage Learning.

Patterns across sentences:

a. What cause-and-effect chains (like falling dominoes) are represented in these sentences? Fill in the boxes in the diagram.

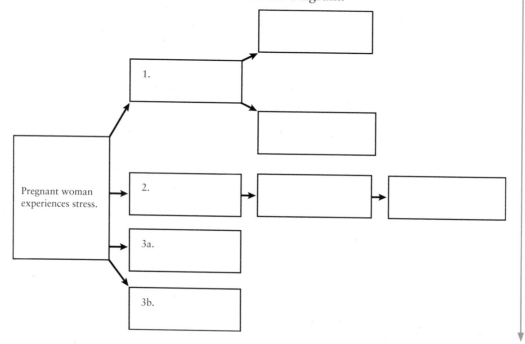

b. *Make an inference* by extending each causal chain that starts with 1, 3a, and 3b out to its final effect. What effect will that be? _____

_____

Note that causal chain 2 already ends with the final outcome of that chain.

c. Write the topic sentence: _____

_____

3. About: _____

    Point: _____

        Proof: 1. The police motorcycle's maneuverability and acceleration make it ideal for traffic enforcement, escort details, and crowd control.

               2. Bicycles are quiet and efficient and provide a bridge between motorized vehicles and foot patrol. They provide efficient transportation to areas that are normally available only by walking, such as parks, public housing developments with limited street access, tourist areas, college campuses, business plazas, and sports arenas.

               3. Electric bikes provide all of the advantages of the pedal bike but require less physical effort by the rider.

               4. Scooters are more maneuverable than cars, yet offer many of the features of a car in a compact space. They also may provide shelter from the weather and enable officers to carry more equipment than bicycles do.

           —From DEMPSEY/FORST. *An Introduction to Policing*, 5e (p. 286)

           Copyright © 2010 Cengage Learning.

Patterns across sentences:

a. What kinds of things are being discussed? What do these things all have in common?

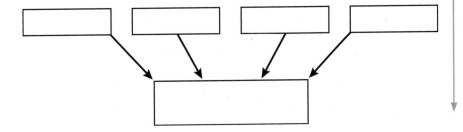

b. What does each sentence say about these things? On the left, list the attributes (characteristics) of the things, and on the right, list the effects of these attributes. The first one is provided as an example.

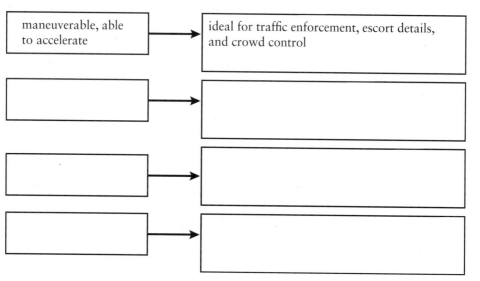

| maneuverable, able to accelerate | → | ideal for traffic enforcement, escort details, and crowd control |

c. *Make an inference* by generalizing first about the qualities on the left. What general word accounts for all of these? _____

What general phrase takes into account all of the information on the right side? _____

d. Write the topic sentence. _____

_____

| INTERACTION 7–6 | Make Generalizations |

Make a generalization about each set of details by noticing patterns that go across sentences.

1. Generalization: _____

_____

- In less-developed countries, the indoor burning of wood, charcoal, dung, crop residues, coal, and other fuels in open fires or in unvented or poorly vented stoves exposes people to dangerous levels of particulate air pollution.

- Workers, including children, are also exposed to high levels of indoor air pollution in countries where there are few if any air pollution laws or regulations.

- According to the WHO and the World Bank, indoor air pollution is the most serious air pollution problem, especially for poor people.

> —From MILLER/SPOOLMAN. *Living in the Environment*, 17e (p. 481)
> Copyright © 2012 Cengage Learning.

2. Generalization: _____

_____

- In recent years, violent aggressive driving—which some dub *road rage*—has exploded.
- Sideline rage at amateur and professional sporting events has become so widespread that a Pennsylvania midget football game ended in a brawl involving more than 100 coaches, players, parents, and fans.
- Women fly off the handle just as often as men, although they are less likely to get physical.
- The young and the infamous, including several rappers and musicians sentenced to anger management classes for violent outbursts, may seem more volatile.
- However, ordinary senior citizens have erupted into "line rage" and pushed ahead of others simply because they feel they've "waited long enough" in their lives.
- Sybil Evans, a conflict resolution expert, singles out three primary culprits: time, technology, and tension.

> —From HALES. *An Invitation to Health*, 12e (p. 89)
> Copyright © 2007 Cengage Learning.

3. Generalization: _____

_____

- *Palatability.* The better food tastes, the more of it people consume.
- *Quantity available.* A powerful determinant of the amount eaten is the amount available. People tend to consume what is put in front of them.
- *Variety.* Humans and animals increase their consumption when a greater variety of foods is available.

> • *Presence of others.* On average, individuals eat 44% more when they eat with other people than when they eat alone.
>
> —From WEITEN. *Psychology*, 7e (pp. 380–381)
> Copyright © 2008 Cengage Learning.

4. Generalization: _____

_____

> • The great importance of the church in the lives of older African American women is supported by results from four national surveys of African American adults.
> • The women participants report that they are more active in church groups and attend services more frequently than African American men or either European American men or women.
> • In addition, spirituality influences many African American women's daily lives in some less obvious ways.
> • For example, many women came to the conclusion that domestic violence was not part of God's plan for their lives.
>
> —From KAIL/CAVANAUGH.
> *Cengage Advantage Books: Human Development*, 4e (p. 587)
> Copyright © 2007 Cengage Learning.

5. Generalization: _____

_____

> • In many areas of America in the early 1800s, school lasted only about 75 to 80 days a year because the entire family was needed to work the farm.
> • By the 1830s, only about half of all children attended school and then only for this short period of time.
> • But as the industrial revolution drew people to the cities for work and common schools flourished, more children began attending school, and by the end of the 1890s, over 70 percent of children were receiving schooling.
> • There was such a great need for schools between 1890 and 1914 that a new high school was added every day.
>
> —From KOCH. *So You Want to Be a Teacher?* 1e (p. 67)
> Copyright © 2009 Cengage Learning.

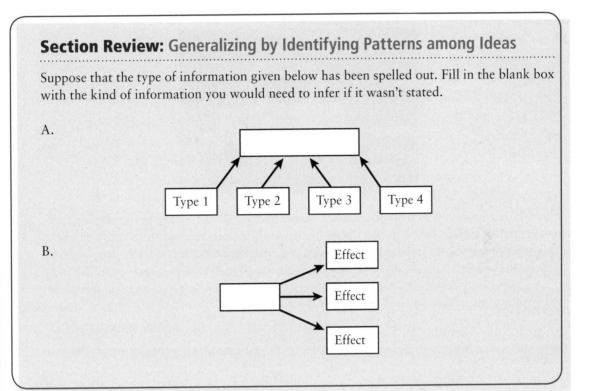

Inferring Implied Main Ideas

Authors carefully select every detail in order to make an overall point—that is, to support the main idea. When the author doesn't state the main idea directly but instead lets readers infer it, or make an educated guess about it, the main idea is called an **implied main idea**. As a reader, you have to generalize from the details of the passage in order to draw a conclusion about the author's meaning.

Inferring the Topic Sentence of a Paragraph

You can use a MAPP to figure out the implied main idea, even if you just use it in your mind instead of on paper. Mark (or just note) the topic, list the details, and then infer what the main idea must be. Let's look at an example.

The coffee served in the coffeehouses wasn't necessarily very good coffee. Because of the way coffee was taxed in Britain (by the gallon), the practice was to brew it in large batches, store it cold in barrels, and reheat it a little at a time for serving. People went to coffeehouses to meet people of shared interests, gossip, read the latest journals and newspapers—a brand-new word and concept in the 1660s—and exchange information of value to their lives and businesses.

—Bryson, *At Home*, p. 180

What is the paragraph **about**? The first two sentences are about coffee. The third sentence is about why people went to coffeehouses.

About: Coffee and why people went to British coffeehouses in the 1660s

Point: ?

What **proof** is given for the implied point? Here are the two main supporting details.

Proof: 1. The coffee wasn't very good.

2. People went to coffeehouses to talk to others, read the news, and exchange information.

Now it's time to make an inference. What **point** can you think of that would include both supporting details? Here is one way to say it:

Point: In Britain in the 1660s, people didn't go to coffeehouses for the great coffee; instead, they went to get the latest news and gossip.

Notice a few particulars about this point:

- It limits the time and place to the ones the author is discussing. It would be wrong to leave out "In Britain in the 1660s," because people worldwide have had many reasons for going to coffeehouses, one of which is clearly to drink fine coffee. (Think Starbucks.)

- You might expect that people in Britain in the 1660s might, like so many others, go to a coffeehouse to drink great coffee. But the first two sentences of the paragraph clearly state the opposite. The point has to include this idea, so we used *didn't* and *instead* to express that idea.

- The point includes a generalization from the details in the third sentence but still conveys the idea that people liked going for information about the world (the news) and information about their neighbors (the gossip).

Compare your own topic sentence to the one Bill Bryson actually used in this paragraph:

> So coffee's appeal in Britain had less to do with being a quality beverage than with being a social lubricant.

Bryson put it more elegantly than we did, but the point remains the same.

INTERACTION 7–7 State the Implied Topic Sentence of Paragraphs

Create a topic sentence for each paragraph.

1. Topic sentence: _____

_____

> People care about creating the right impression online through the timeliness of their responses, the use of chat room nicknames, and their use of vocabulary, grammar, and manners (sometimes called netiquette). Initial interaction online often begins with the question A/S/L?, which asks for someone's age, sex, and location. This is a get-to-know-you question, which allows someone to reduce uncertainty about the other person. Creating personal home pages also relates to self-identity and first impressions. Creating a personal home page is an opportunity for people to reflect upon themselves and to think about how they want to represent themselves to the world. It is an attempt to influence others' first impressions of you.
>
> —From VERDERBER/VERDERBER/SELLNOW. *COMM*, 1e (p. 25)
> Copyright © 2009 Cengage Learning.

2. Topic sentence: _____

_____

> The mentor helps a young worker avoid trouble ("Be careful what you say around Harry."). He or she also provides invaluable information about the unwritten rules that govern day-to-day activities in the workplace (not working too fast on the assembly line, wearing the right clothes, and so on), with mentors being sensitive to the employment situation (such as guarding against playing favorites). As part of the relationship, a mentor makes sure that his or her protégé is noticed and receives credit for good work from supervisors. Thus, occupational success often depends on the quality of the mentor-protégé relationship and the protégé's perception of its importance.
>
> —From KAIL/CAVANAUGH.
> *Cengage Advantage Books: Human Development*, 4e (pp. 456–457)
> Copyright © 2007 Cengage Learning.

3. Topic sentence: _____

_____

> Being a professional cheapskate, I'm frequently asked if I buy bottled water. "Heck, no," I say in all truthfulness, "I don't even buy bottled wine." Prepare for shock and awe: 1.5 million barrels of oil are used every year to manufacture disposable plastic water bottles for the U.S. market. That's enough to fuel 100,000 cars for a year. The bottling process itself uses two gallons of water for every gallon of water it bottles. But regardless of whether or not the cheapskates next door are environmentalists, here's why they ain't buyin' it: Bottled water is 240 to 10,000 times more expensive than water from the tap, usually costing more than $10 a gallon … Think about that the next time you complain about gas prices. And bottled water is actually subjected to less rigorous testing and purity standards than tap water here in the United States.
>
> —Yeager, *The Cheapskate Next Door*, p. 108

4. Topic sentence: _____

_____

> Tropical forests play a particularly important role in cleansing the atmosphere of carbon dioxide and replenishing it with oxygen. High prices and sustained demand for tropical hardwoods from Central Africa and Indonesia, however, have led lumber companies to fell vast areas of forest, sometimes bribing politicians to evade environmental regulations. In Brazil, rising grain prices give farmers an incentive to clear the forest for agriculture, especially when they can grow more sugar cane for ethanol. In 2008 the minister for the environment, Marina Silva, resigned when she lost a battle to stop government transportation projects that would hasten the extension of the country's agricultural frontier into the rainforest.
>
> —Hansen & Curtis, *Voyages in World History,* p. 961

5. Topic sentence: _____

_____

> Did you ever wonder how lobster could be so wondrously cheap at those chain restaurants next to the mall? Despite the old-fashioned lobster traps hanging on the wall, what you're eating isn't actually Maine lobster; it's spiny or rock lobster from the waters off Central America. Close to 100 percent of the divers who harvest those lobsters off the sea bottom show signs of neurological damage, according to a 1999 World Bank report, because they use ancient scuba equipment, without depth gauges or even an indicator to tell them how much air they have left, and because, as the lobsters have gotten scarcer thanks to the endless all-you-can-eat lobster buffets back home, the divers have fished out the 40-foot depths. They're down at 120 feet, 130 feet.
>
> —Bryon, *Deep Economy*, p. 59

INTERACTION 7–8	State the Implied Topic Sentence of a Paragraph

Create a topic sentence for each paragraph.

1. Topic sentence: _____

_____

> If you see someone selling neckties from a table set up on the street corner, you have less confidence in that "firm" than you would have in the Nordstrom store across the street, so you might be willing to pay more for the same tie at Nordstrom than at the street vendor. The reason is at least partly that Nordstrom has devoted huge resources to that large building. You see many types of firms trying to assure customers of their reliability by locating in large buildings or beautiful offices or by spending lavishly on advertisements. For some products, a guarantee or warranty is an important signal that the product is of high quality.
>
> —From BOYES/MELVIN. *Economics*, 8e (p. 550)
> Copyright © 2011 Cengage Learning.

2. Topic sentence: _____

_____

> According to Gary W. Cordner and Robert Sheehan, police departments seem to discourage applicants from applying. Sheehan and Cordner also point to the low esteem in which police are held in some communities and the fictitious television image of the police as other factors that discourage qualified applicants from applying for police jobs. Some potential candidates may have negative images of police, whereas others may perceive the physical attributes as being beyond their reach. Since September 11, 2001, the law enforcement occupation has been more favorably viewed and, as the media focused on the heroes who served on 9/11, many realized they were everyday people with a desire to help and contribute to society. With dedication and hard work, these individuals had attained their goals.
>
> —From DEMPSEY/FORST. *An Introduction to Policing*, 5e (p. 118)
> Copyright © 2010 Cengage Learning.

3. Topic sentence: _____

_____

The goal of user testing is to determine whether your website is easy to navigate and provides easy access to content. Following are some considerations to take into account when planning for user testing of your site. First, vary your subjects. Draw your test subjects from a variety of backgrounds, if possible. Gather test subjects who are representative of your target audience. Find users with varying computing skills and familiarity with the information. Second, formalize your testing by creating replicable methods of testing your website. Prepare a series of questions that users have to answer after viewing the website. Compare the results from different users to find any problem areas in navigation. Third, develop a feedback form that users can fill out after they have tested the website.

—From SKLAR. *Principles of Web Design*, 4e (pp. 83–84)
Copyright © 2009 Cengage Learning.

4. Topic sentence: _____

_____

One of our most basic human needs is to establish meaningful connections with other humans. Dating helps you decide whether you want to be more intimately connected and perhaps marry that person or to have a more casual relationship. The process of dating also allows you to discover more about yourself as you relate to others. Through dating, you can experiment with different roles and different types of relationships to discover the ones that are most satisfying to you. No relationship is perfect. Self-discovery can give you insights that help you develop empathy, tolerance, acceptance, and readiness for change.

—From ROBINSON/MCCORMICK. *Concepts in Health and Wellness*, 1e (p. 162)
Copyright © 2011 Cengage Learning.

5. Topic sentence: _____

_____

In 1971, university students were invited by Stanford Psychology Professor Philip Zimbardo to participate in an experiment. All the students were in good mental and physical condition, all were well-adjusted (for example, none had a record of criminal or disorderly conduct), and all were male. Professor Zimbardo was interested in exploring the interactions between individuals in situations wherein some had authority over others; to accomplish this objective, he set up a mock prison in the basement of the Psychology Department and he randomly assigned some of the student participants to be "guards" and others to be "inmates." He intended for the experiment to last two weeks. However, by the end of the second day, guards were acting aggressively toward inmates. By the fifth day, guards were forcing inmates to surrender their clothing, to wear head coverings, to endure sleep deprivation, and to submit to sexual humiliation. Upon the urging of a former graduate student, Professor Zimbardo called an end to the experiment after six days rather than allow the physical, sexual, and verbal taunts to continue.

—From GRIGSBY. *Analyzing Politics*, 4e (p. 11)
Copyright © 2009 Cengage Learning.

Inferring the Thesis Statement of a Longer Selection

The process used to infer the thesis statement of a longer selection is the same as the one used to infer the topic sentence of a paragraph.

- Search for the topic.

- Find the major supporting details (which may be the topic sentences of paragraphs).

- Look for patterns among them.

- Generalize from the details.

- Combine the generalization with the topic to arrive at the implied thesis statement.

As you read this passage, highlight repeated words or phrases that might be the topic. Underline sentences that seem to be the topic sentences of paragraphs or major supporting details.

What Is Reality?

Stephen Hawking and Leonard Mlodinow

1   A few years ago the city council of Monza, Italy, barred pet owners from keeping goldfish in curved goldfish bowls. The measure's sponsor explained the measure in part by saying that it is cruel to keep a fish in a bowl with curved sides because, gazing out, the fish would have a distorted view of reality. But how do we know we have the true, undistorted picture of reality? Might not we ourselves be inside some big goldfish bowl and have our vision distorted by an enormous lens? The goldfish's picture of reality is different from ours, but can we be sure it is less real?

2   The goldfish view is not the same as our own, but goldfish could still formulate scientific laws governing the motion of the objects they observe outside their bowl. For example, due to the distortion, a freely moving object that we would observe to move in a straight line would be observed by the goldfish to move along a curved path. Nevertheless, the goldfish could formulate scientific laws from their distorted frame of reference that would always hold true and that would enable them to make predictions about the future motion of objects outside the bowl. Their laws would be more complicated than the laws in our frame, but simplicity is a matter of taste. If a goldfish formulated such a theory, we would have to admit the goldfish's view as a valid picture of reality.

3   A famous example of different pictures of reality is the model introduced around AD 150 by Ptolemy (ca. 85–ca. 165) to describe the motion of the celestial bodies. Ptolemy published his work in a thirteen-book treatise usually known under its Arabic title, *Almagest*. The *Almagest* begins by explaining reasons for thinking that the earth is spherical, motionless, positioned at the center of the universe, and negligibly small in comparison to the distance of the heavens. Despite Aristarchus's heliocentric model, these beliefs had been held by most

educated Greeks at least since the time of Aristotle, who believed for mystical reasons that the earth should be at the center of the universe. In Ptolemy's model the earth stood still at the center and the planets and the stars moved around it in complicated orbits involving epicycles, like wheels on wheels.

4   This model seemed natural because we don't feel the earth under our feet moving (except in earthquakes or moments of passion). Later European learning was based on the Greek sources that had been passed down, so that the ideas of Aristotle and Ptolemy became the basis for much of Western thought. Ptolemy's model of the cosmos was adopted by the Catholic Church and held as official doctrine for fourteen hundred years. It was not until 1543 that an alternative model was put forward by Copernicus in his book *De revolutionibus orbium coelestium* (*On the Revolutions of the Celestial Spheres*), published only in the year of his death (though he had worked on his theory for several decades).

5   Copernicus, like Aristarchus some seventeen centuries earlier, described a world in which the sun was at rest and the planets revolved around it in circular orbits. Though the idea wasn't new, its revival was met with passionate resistance. The Copernican model was held to contradict the Bible, which was interpreted as saying that the planets moved around the earth, even though the Bible never clearly stated that. In fact, at the time the Bible was written people believed the earth was flat. The Copernican model led to a furious debate as to whether the earth was at rest, culminating in Galileo's trial for heresy in 1633 for advocating the Copernican model and for thinking "that one may hold and defend as probable an opinion after it has been declared and defined contrary to the Holy Scripture." He was found guilty, confined to house arrest for the rest of his life, and forced to recant. He is said to have muttered under his breath *"Eppur si muove,"* "But still it moves." In 1992 the Roman Catholic Church finally acknowledged that it had been wrong to condemn Galileo.

6   So which is real, the Ptolemic or Copernican system? Although it is not uncommon for people to say that Copernicus proved Ptolemy wrong, that is not true. As in the case of our normal view versus that of the goldfish, one can use either picture as a model of the universe, for our observations of the heavens can be explained by assuming either the earth or the sun to be at rest. Despite its role in philosophical debates over the nature of our universe, the real advantage of the Copernican system is simply that the equations of motion are much simpler in the frame of reference in which the sun is at rest.

7   A different kind of alternative reality occurs in the science fiction film *The Matrix*, in which the human race is unknowingly living in a simulated virtual reality created by intelligent computers to keep them pacified and content while the computers suck their bioelectrical energy (whatever that is). Maybe this is not so far-fetched, because many people prefer to spend their time in the simulated reality of websites such as Second Life. How do we know we are not just characters in a computer-generated soap opera? If we lived in a synthetic imaginary world, events would not necessarily have any logic or consistency or obey any laws. The aliens in control might find it more interesting or amusing to see our reactions, for example, if the full moon split in half, or everyone in the world on a diet developed an uncontrollable

craving for banana cream pie. But if the aliens did enforce consistent laws, there is no way we could tell there was another reality behind the simulated one. It would be easy to call the world the aliens live in the "real" one and the synthetic world a "false" one. But if—like us—the beings in the simulated world could not gaze into their universe from the outside, there would be no reason for them to doubt their own pictures of reality. This is a modern version of the idea that we are all figments of someone else's dream.

—From THE GRAND DESIGN by Stephen W. Hawking and Leonard Mlodinow, copyright © 2010 by Stephen W. Hawking and Leonard Mlodinow. Used by permission of Bantam Books, a division of Random House, Inc.

The topic of this passage is "pictures of reality." The authors discuss four examples of pictures of reality: the goldfish in the bowl, the Ptolemic model of the universe, the Copernican model of the universe, and a hypothetical model in which our world is controlled by aliens. Let's look at the topic sentences of the individual paragraphs, which are also the major supporting details of the implied main idea.

- The measure's sponsor explained the measure in part by saying that it is cruel to keep a fish in a bowl with curved sides because, gazing out, the fish would have a distorted view of reality.

- A famous example of different pictures of reality is the model introduced around AD 150 by Ptolemy (ca. 85–ca. 165) to describe the motion of the celestial bodies.

- Ptolemy's model of the cosmos was adopted by the Catholic Church and held as official doctrine for fourteen hundred years.

- Although it is not uncommon for people to say that Copernicus proved Ptolemy wrong, that is not true.

- But if—like us—the beings in the simulated world could not gaze into their universe from the outside, there would be no reason for them to doubt their own pictures of reality.

The major details discuss how someone else's view of reality (the fish's) may seem distorted when seen from the outside, by someone with a different view. A particular view may hold sway for thousands of years (Ptolemy's model) until replaced by a new view (Copernicus's model). But that doesn't necessarily make the new view better or more true than the old one. In fact, it's impossible for anyone to understand distortions in his or her view of reality when viewing it from inside the system (aliens and humans).

Taken together with the topic, we could boil down these ideas to state the implied main idea something like this:

> People believe that their own picture of reality is true and that others' views are distorted, but it's only possible to see the distortions in the picture when outside it.

INTERACTION 7–9   Infer the Thesis Statement of a Longer Selection

Infer the implied thesis statement of the following passage by taking these steps:

- Search for the topic.

- Find the major supporting details (which may be the topic sentences of paragraphs).

- Look for patterns among them.

- Generalize from the details.

- Combine the generalization with the topic to arrive at the implied thesis statement.

Implied thesis statement: _____

_____

Computer Operators. This field declined by 31% from 2004 to 2009 and lost 42,000 workers, and the Bureau of Labor Statistics expects continued deterioration. With most professionals using personal computers with ever more sophisticated data processing, jobs based solely on entering commands and monitoring computer terminals are outdated or increasingly specialized.

Stage Performers. The five-year decline for this career path, which includes magicians, jugglers, clowns and dancers, was a startling 61%—one of the steepest on this list. According to jobs researcher Laurence Shatkin, Ph.D., live performances have fallen out of fashion and have been almost entirely replaced with movies and home entertainment technologies.

Postal Service Mail Sorters. After losing almost 57,000 jobs between 2004 and 2009, the BLS expects a further 30% decline in this occupation by 2018. With more automated processes for mail sorting and increasing correspondence via e-mail and fax, this job is quickly becoming unnecessary.

Holistic Healers. Alternative medicine specialists like acupuncturists, homeopathic doctors and hypnotherapists may be an endangered species. The field declined 44% between 2004 and 2009, losing about 26,000 jobs. Because health insurance companies typically do not cover these specialties, alternative medicine may be becoming a more niche, luxury service.

Office and Administrative Support Workers. About 300,000 administrative jobs disappeared between 2004 and 2009, and the BLS projects continued contraction throughout the next decade. Secretaries and file clerks are no longer in demand as companies cut costs. Moreover, technologies like voicemail and easy-to-use word processors have enabled professionals to do their own clerical work.

—Jenna Goudreau, "Job Outlook: Careers Headed for the Trash Pile."
Copyright © 2011. Reprinted by Permission of Forbes Media LLC.

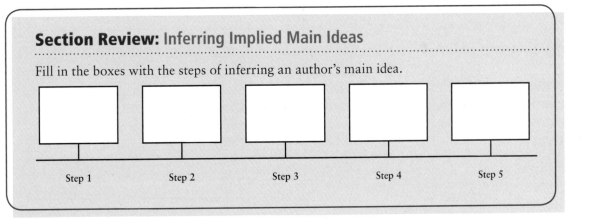

Section Review: Inferring Implied Main Ideas

Fill in the boxes with the steps of inferring an author's main idea.

| Step 1 | Step 2 | Step 3 | Step 4 | Step 5 |

Chapter Summary Activity:
Inferring Meaning from Details

Chapter 7 has discussed the process of creating inferences about causes and effects, and how to generalize from details—for example, how to infer an implied main idea. Fill in the following Reading Guide by completing each idea on the left with information from Chapter 7 on the right. You can return to this guide throughout the course as a reminder of how to infer meaning from supporting details.

Reading Guide to Inferring Meaning from Details

Complete this idea	with information from Chapter 7.
All inferences must start with paying close attention to the	1. _____
When you are reading, this comes from	2. _____ _____
The next step in inferring unstated meaning is to	3. _____ _____
As you continue reading, you almost automatically do the next step:	4. _____ _____
As you read more and more details, you probably will make fewer and fewer	5. _____
Why is that?	6. _____ _____
As a reader, you use your _____ to evaluate the possible inferences.	7. _____
When you are inferring meaning, what carries more weight, the author's words or your knowledge?	8. _____
Why is that?	9. _____ _____ _____ _____ _____
Two common patterns of organization that call for inferences are:	10. _____ 11. _____
If a paragraph's topic sentence or main idea is implied, your two most important pieces of evidence for inferring it are:	12. _____ 13. _____
Once you have found these two important pieces of evidence, what are your next steps?	14. _____ 15. _____ _____ 16. _____ _____

17. Think about what your reading strategies were before you read Chapter 7. How did they differ from the suggestions here? Write your thoughts.

_____

_____

_____

ENGAGE YOUR SKILLS
Inferring Meaning from Details

A. Select the best inference for each item.

_____ 1.

> Today, 95 of every 100 senior management positions at the level of vice president and above are held by white men, even though white men constitute only about 29 percent of the overall work force.
>
> —From KENDALL. *Sociology in Our Times*, 6e (p. 429)
> Copyright © 2008 Cengage Learning.

a. White men are smarter than everyone else.
b. White men start working younger than others, so they have longer to climb to the top.
c. White men have an unfair advantage in the workplace.

_____ 2.

> The Boca Raton, Florida, police officer noticed twenty black people walking up from the beach together. They were all soaking wet. Most of them didn't speak English. They seemed hungry, cold, and tired.

a. They were on the French swim team.
b. They had just swum from San Francisco out to Alcatraz Island.
c. They were drug smugglers from Morocco.
d. They were shipwrecked immigrants from Haiti.

_____ 3.

> In 1938, Edith Hahn was a 24-year-old studying law in Austria. In the same year, Nazi Germany incorporated Austria into its political domain. Forced to leave school, Edith worked at home as a seamstress. In 1939, she was assigned the middle name Sarah, was transferred into a ghetto, and was required to carry an identity card. In 1941, she was assigned to a Nazi labor camp.
>
> —From GRIGSBY. *Analyzing Politics*, 4e (p. 128)
> Copyright © 2009 Cengage Learning.

a. Edith Hahn was Jewish.

b. Edith Hahn was married.

c. Edith Hahn died in 1942.

d. Edith Hahn could never work again.

_____ 4.

> In many societies, shops close and activities are curtailed in the afternoon to permit people to enjoy a 1- to 2-hour midday nap. These "siesta cultures" are found mostly in tropical regions of the world. There, this practice is adaptive in that it allows people to avoid working during the hottest part of the day. The siesta is not a fixture in all tropical societies, however. It is infrequent among nomads and those that depend on irregular food supplies. As a rule, the siesta tradition is not found in industrialized societies, where it conflicts with the emphasis on productivity and the philosophy that "time is money." Moreover, when industrialization comes to a siesta culture, it undermines the practice. For instance, modernization in Spain has led to a decline in midday napping there.
>
> —From WEITEN. *Psychology*, 7e (p. 183) Copyright © 2008 Cengage Learning.

a. Most cultures in the world encourage some form of napping.

b. Adaptive behaviors are those that serve a purpose.

c. Napping in the middle of the day causes cultures to remain backward.

d. "Time is money" represents well the attitudes of those nomads who do not nap.

_____ 5.

> She said that although she had recently traveled to Ontario, to Colorado, and to Connecticut with her husband, she would not have been able to do this by herself, as she had only a few years before. She felt that she remained quite capable of looking after herself at home when Claude was away. Still, she said, "When I am alone, it's lousy. I'm not complaining—I'm describing."
>
> —Sacks, *The Mind's Eye*, p. 26

a. She is mute.

b. She is blind and deaf.

c. She has a degenerative illness.

d. She has a mental illness.

B. Infer and write down the implied main idea of the following paragraph.

6. Implied main idea: _____

_____

The average American eats more than 200 pounds of meat per year. Producing a pound of beef can use more than 13,000 gallons of water. By comparison, it takes about 21 gallons of water to produce a pound of tomatoes. Adding insult to injury, livestock waste has polluted more than 27,000 miles of rivers. And talk about gassy: Between the methane emitted from cow farts and manure and the CO_2 emitted in transporting feed to farms and meat to consumers, producing one hamburger patty gives off as much greenhouse gas as a 6-mile car ride. It takes as much land to provide one person with a meat-based diet as it does to feed six people on a plant-based diet.

—Matheson, *Green Chic*, p. 84

C. Read the passage below and answer the questions that follow.

1　　Mathematicians of the Southern Song Empire introduced the use of fractions, first employing them to describe the phases of the moon. From lunar observations, Song astronomers constructed a very precise calendar and, alone among the world's astronomers, noted the explosion of the Crab Nebula in 1054. Song inventors drew on their knowledge of celestial coordinates, particularly the Pole Star, to refine compass design. The magnetic compass, an earlier Chinese invention, shrank in size in Song times and gained a fixed pivot point for the needle. With a protective glass cover, the compass now became suitable for seafaring, a use first attested in 1090.

2　　Development of the seaworthy compass coincided with new techniques in building China's main oceangoing ship, the junk. A stern-mounted rudder improved the steering of the large ship in uneasy seas, and watertight bulkheads helped keep it afloat in emergencies. The shipwrights of the Persian Gulf soon copied these features in their ship designs.

mandylina/BigStockPhoto.com

3   Because they needed iron and steel to make weapons for their army of 1.25 million men, the Song rulers fought their northern rivals for control of mines in north China. Production of coal and iron soared. By the end of the eleventh century cast iron production reached about 125,000 tons (113,700 metric tons) annually, putting it on a par with the output of eighteenth-century Britain. Engineers became skilled at high-temperature metallurgy using enormous bellows, often driven by water wheels, to superheat the molten ore. Military engineers used iron to buttress defensive works because it was impervious to fire or concussion. Armorers mass-produced body armor. Iron construction also appeared in bridges and small buildings. Mass-production techniques for bronze and ceramics in use in China for nearly two thousand years were adapted to iron casting and assembly.

4   To counter cavalry assaults, the Song experimented with gunpowder, which they initially used to propel clusters of flaming arrows. During the wars against the Jurchens in the 1100s the Song introduced a new and terrifying weapon. Shells launched from Song fortifications exploded in the midst of the enemy, blowing out iron shrapnel and dismembering men and horses. The short range of these shells limited them to defensive uses.

—From BULLIET. *The Earth and Its Peoples, Brief Edition, Complete*, 5e (p. 263)
Copyright © 2012 Cengage Learning.

7. What is the implied main idea of paragraph 1? _____

_____

8. Which is larger, a ton or a metric ton?   ton   metric ton

Explain your answer.

_____

_____

9. Infer from the context in paragraph 3 what *impervious* means.

_____

10. What is the implied thesis statement of the passage?

_____

_____

MASTER YOUR SKILLS
Inferring Meaning from Details

For each selection, write a statement of the main idea.

1. Main idea: _____

_____

Table 7.1 The Development of the Mass Media

1906	First radio voice transmission
1920	First regularly scheduled radio broadcast, Pittsburgh
1925	78 rpm records chosen as a standard
1928	First commercial TV broadcast
1949	Network TV begins in the United States
1952	VCR invented
1961	First cable television, San Diego
1969	First four nodes of the United States Defense Department's ARPANET (precursor of the Internet) set up at Stanford University, UCLA, UC Santa Barbara, and the University of Utah
1975	First microcomputer marketed
1983	Cell phone invented
1989	World Wide Web conceived by Tim Berners-Lee at the European Laboratory for Particle Physics in Switzerland

—From BRYM/LIE. *Sociology*, 3e (p. 533) Copyright © 2010 Cengage Learning.

2. Main idea: _____

_____

- *Art.* Robert Mapplethorpe is one of several artists whose work has elicited debate between conservatives and liberals. Mapplethorpe's portfolio includes photographs of gay men. Critics have often described these works as pornographic, whereas many supporters have countered that they are representations of gay erotica. Should public dollars be used to subsidize and promote such art? Politics involves making such decisions.

- *Love.* Two people in love may not believe that politics has anything to do with their relationship. However, politics greatly influences the ways in which love may be expressed. At what age may couples get married, for instance? Why can some couples (heterosexual) get married, whereas others (gay) cannot? Governments answer such political questions.
- *Emotion.* What could be more personal than emotion? How can your emotions have anything to do with politics? Your emotions are very political if, for instance, you are accused of committing what the government defines as a crime. A person's "state of mind" may be one of the variables considered when the state brings charges and makes recommendations for sentencing in criminal cases.

—From GRIGSBY. *Analyzing Politics*, 4e (p. 8) Copyright © 2009 Cengage Learning.

3. Main idea: _____

_____

Religion deals with the major issues of human existence, such as the meaning of life, death, and one's spiritual relationship with deities. In contrast, magic is directed toward specific, immediate problems, such as curing an illness, bringing rain, or ensuring safety on a long journey. Religion uses prayer and sacrifices to appeal to or petition supernatural powers for assistance. Magicians, on the other hand, believe they can control or manipulate nature or other people by their own efforts. Religion by and large tends to be a group activity whereas magic is more individually oriented. Whereas religion is usually practiced at a specified time, magic is practiced irregularly in response to specific and immediate problems. Religion usually involves officially recognized functionaries such as priests, whereas magic may be performed by a wide variety of practitioners who may or may not be recognized within the community as having supernatural powers.

—From FERRARO. *Cultural Anthropology*, 6e (p. 352)
Copyright © 2006 Cengage Learning.

4. Main idea: _____

_____

1   Near the city of Eliat, Israel, at the northern tip of the Red Sea, is a magnificent coral reef, which is a major tourist attraction. To help protect the reef from excessive development and destructive tourism, Israel set aside part of the reef as a nature reserve.

2   But tourism, industrial pollution, and inadequate sewage treatment have destroyed most of the remaining reef. Enter Reuven Yosef, a pioneer in reconciliation ecology, who has developed an underwater restaurant called the Red Sea Star Restaurant. Patrons take an elevator down two floors below street level and walk into a restaurant surrounded with windows looking out into a beautiful coral reef.

© Jeffrey Rotman/Corbis

3   This part of the reef was created from pieces of broken coral. Typically, when coral breaks, the pieces become infected and die. But researchers have learned how to treat the coral fragments with antibiotics and to store them while they are healing in large tanks of fresh seawater. Yosef has such a facility, and when divers find broken pieces of coral in the reserve near Yosef's restaurant, they bring them to his coral hospital. After several months of healing, the fragments are taken to the underwater area outside the Red Sea Star Restaurant's windows where they are wired to panels of iron mesh cloth. The corals grow and cover the iron matrix. Then fish and other creatures begin to appear in and around the new reef.

—From MILLER/SPOOLMAN. *Living in the Environment*, 17e (p. 264)
Copyright © 2012 Cengage Learning.

5. Main idea: _____

_____

_____

1   When people are getting to know others, they begin by sharing information that they perceive to be low risk. This is information usually shared freely among people with that type of relationship in that culture and might include information about hobbies, sports, school, and views of current events. One way to determine what information is appropriate to disclose is to ask yourself whether you would feel comfortable having the person disclose that kind of information to you.

2   There is always some risk that disclosure will distress or alarm your partner and damage your relationship, but the better you know your partner, the more likely it is that a difficult disclosure will be well received. Incidentally, this guideline explains why people sometimes engage in inappropriate intimate self-disclosure with bartenders or with people they meet in travel. They perceive the disclosures as safe (representing reasonable risk) because the person either does not know them or is in no position to use the information against them.

3   Research suggests that people expect a kind of equity in self-disclosure. When it is apparent that self-disclosure is not being returned, you should consider limiting the amount of disclosure you make. Someone's choice not to reciprocate indicates that the person does not yet feel comfortable with this level of self-disclosure. If the response you receive to your self-disclosure implies that it was inappropriate, try to find out why so that you may avoid this problem in the future.

4   Because receiving self-disclosure can be as threatening as giving it, most people who receive it become uncomfortable when the level of disclosure exceeds their expectations. As a relationship develops, the depth of disclosure should gradually increase. So we disclose biographical and demographic information early in a relationship and more closely held, personal information later, in a more developed relationship.

5   Disclosures about intimate matters are appropriate in close, well-established relationships. When people disclose very personal information to acquaintances or business associates, they are not only taking a risk of being exposed; the disclosure may also threaten their partner. Making intimate disclosures before a bond of trust is established risks alienating the other person. Moreover, people are often embarrassed by and hostile toward others who try to saddle them with intimate information in an effort to establish a personal relationship where none exists.

—From VERDERBER/VERDERBER/SELLNOW. *COMM*, 1e (p. 92)
Copyright © 2009 Cengage Learning.

Focus on Environmental Science

College Environmental Science App ECOLOGY TEXTBOOK

. . . .

The following reading is linked to these fields of . . .

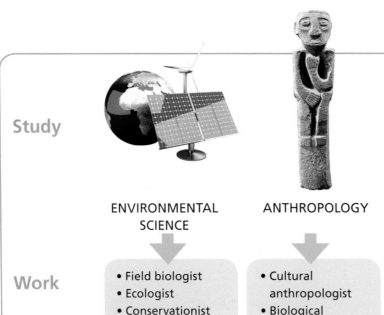

Study	ENVIRONMENTAL SCIENCE	ANTHROPOLOGY	ART
Work	• Field biologist • Ecologist • Conservationist	• Cultural anthropologist • Biological anthropologist • Linguist	• Art historian • Sculptor • Photographer

● Pre-Reading the Selection

The excerpt that begins on page 437 comes from the ecology textbook *Essentials of Ecology*. The excerpt is titled "Easter Island: Some Revisions in a Popular Environmental Story."

Surveying the Reading

Survey the textbook selection that follows. Then check the elements that are included in this reading.

_____ Title

_____ Headings

_____ First sentences of paragraphs

_____ Words in bold or italic type

_____ Images and captions

Guessing the Purpose

Based on the source and the title of the reading selection, do you think the authors' purpose is mostly to persuade, inform, or express? _____

Predicting the Content

Based on your survey, what are three things you expect the reading selection to discuss?

- _____

- _____

- _____

Activating Your Knowledge

Think about what you know about Easter Island, the earth's life-support systems, or the Polynesians. Do you have any ideas about where Easter Island's huge statues came from, for example? Write any thoughts you have below.

- _____

- _____

- _____

● **Reading with Pen in Hand**

Students who annotate as they read are more successful than students who do not annotate. That's why you will annotate each reading in *Engage* as you read. In the reading that follows, use the following symbols:

★ or (Point)   to indicate a main idea

① ② ③   to indicate major details

Access the Reading CourseMate via **www.cengagebrain.com** to hear vocabulary words from this selection and view a video about this topic.

Easter Island: Some Revisions in a Popular Environmental Story

Reading Journal

1   For years, the story of Easter Island has been used in textbooks as an example of how humans can seriously **degrade** their own life-support system. It concerns a civilization that once **thrived** and then largely disappeared from a small, isolated island located about 3,600 kilometers (2,200 miles) off the coast of Chile in the great expanse of the South Pacific.

2   Scientists used **anthropological** evidence and scientific measurements to estimate the ages of some of the more than 300 large statues (Figure 7.1) found on Easter Island. They hypothesized that about 2,900 years ago, Polynesians used double-hulled, seagoing canoes to colonize the island. The settlers probably found a paradise with fertile soil that supported dense and diverse forests and lush grasses. According to this hypothesis, the islanders thrived, and their population increased to as many as 15,000 people.

● Do you have any prior knowledge of Easter Island?

degrade You are familiar with a form of this word with the prefix *up-*. What does *degrade* mean?

thrived Reread the previous sentence. Under these conditions, what does *thrived* mean?

anthropological This word has three parts: *anthrop-, ology, -ical.* Use these word parts to decode the meaning of *anthropological*.

● Imagine the journey the Polynesians took to reach Easter Island.

© gary yim/Shutterstock.com

Figure 7.1 These and many other massive stone figures once lined the coasts of Easter Island and are the remains of technology created on the island by an ancient civilization of Polynesians. Some of these statues are taller than an average five-story building and can weigh as much as 89 metric tons (98 tons).

● If this sounds familiar, why?

unsustainably Use what follows this word in the sentence to determine its meaning.

plummeted What would happen to the Polynesians' food supplies under the stated conditions?

● Can you predict an alternative hypothesis?

artifacts Use the example of an *artifact* mentioned earlier in this sentence to determine the meaning.

● Summarize Hunt's conclusions.

regenerated What do seeds do? Also look at the word parts to determine what *regenerated* means.

3   Measurements made by scientists seemed to indicate that over time, the Polynesians began living **unsustainably** by using the island's forest and soil resources faster than they could be renewed. They cut down trees and used them for firewood, for building seagoing canoes, and for moving and erecting the gigantic statues. Once they had used up the large trees, the islanders could no longer build their traditional seagoing canoes for fishing in deeper offshore waters, and no one could escape the island by boat.

4   It was hypothesized that without the once-great forests to absorb and slowly release water, springs and streams dried up, exposed soils were eroded, crop yields **plummeted**, and famine struck. There was no firewood for cooking or keeping warm. According to the original hypothesis, the population and the civilization collapsed as rival clans fought one another for dwindling food supplies, and the island's population dropped sharply. By the late 1870s, only about 100 native islanders were left.

5   In 2006, anthropologist Terry L. Hunt, Director of the University of Hawaii Rapa Nui (Easter Island) Archeological Field School at the University of Hawaii, evaluated the accuracy of past measurements and other evidence and carried out new measurements to estimate the ages of various statues and other **artifacts**. He used these data to formulate an alternative hypothesis describing the human tragedy on Easter Island.

6   Hunt used the data he gathered to come to several new conclusions. First, the Polynesians arrived on the island about 800 years ago, not 2,900 years ago. Second, their population size probably never exceeded 3,000, contrary to the earlier estimate of up to 15,000. Third, the Polynesians did use the island's trees and other vegetation in an unsustainable manner, and by 1722, visitors reported that most of the island's trees were gone.

7   But one question not answered by the earlier hypothesis was, why did the trees never grow back? Recent evidence and Hunt's new hypothesis suggest that rats (which either came along with the original settlers as stowaways or were brought along as a source of protein for the long voyage) played a key role in the island's permanent deforestation. Over the years, the rats multiplied rapidly into the millions and devoured the seeds that would have **regenerated** the forests.

8   Another of Hunt's conclusions was that after 1722, the population of Polynesians on the island dropped to about 100, mostly from contact with European visitors and invaders. Hunt hypothesized that these newcomers introduced fatal diseases, killed off

some of the islanders, and took larger numbers of them away to be sold as slaves.

9   This story is an excellent example of how science works. The gathering of new scientific data and the reevaluation of older data led to a revised hypothesis that challenges earlier thinking about the decline of civilization on Easter Island. As a result, the tragedy may not be as clear an example of human-caused ecological collapse as was once thought.

○ Can you think of any other scientific hypotheses that have been revised?

10   **Critical Thinking.** Does the new doubt about the original Easter Island hypothesis mean that we should not be concerned about using resources unsustainably on the island in space that we call earth? Explain.

○ How would you answer the question posed in this paragraph?

—From MILLER/SPOOLMAN. *Essentials of Ecology*, 6e (p. 35)
Copyright © 2012 Cengage Learning.

● Comprehension Questions

Write the letter of the answer on the line. Then explain your thinking.

Main Idea

_____ 1. Which of the following best states the main idea of this reading?

a. Easter Island is a textbook example of how humans can seriously degrade their own life-support system.

b. Scientists used anthropological evidence and scientific measurements to estimate the ages of some of the more than 300 large statues found on Easter Island.

c. Some new conclusions have been drawn about the fate of Easter Island and its inhabitants.

d. One question not answered by the earlier hypothesis was, why did the trees never grow back?

WHY? What information in the selection leads you to give that answer? _____

_____

_____

_____

_____ 2. What is the best main idea of paragraph 9?

    a. This story is an excellent example of how science works.

    b. The gathering of new scientific data and the reevaluation of older data led to a revised hypothesis that challenges earlier thinking about the decline of civilization on Easter Island.

    c. As a result, the tragedy may not be as clear an example of human-caused ecological collapse as was once thought.

    d. Paragraph 9 has no main idea. Instead, it continues to support the ideas in paragraph 8.

WHY? What information in the selection leads you to give that answer? _____

_____

_____

_____

Supporting Details

_____ 3. Which of the following details is never explained in the reading?

    a. Why the trees did not repopulate.

    b. When Easter Island became inhabited.

    c. The fate of the Easter Islanders.

    d. The purpose of the giant statues.

WHY? What information in the selection leads you to give that answer? _____

_____

_____

_____

_____ 4. How many major details about Hunt's hypothesis does this reading include?

    a. Three

    b. Five

    c. Four

    d. Seven

WHY? What information in the selection leads you to give that answer? _____

_____

_____

_____

Author's Purpose

_____ 5. What is the overall purpose of the passage?

    a. To persuade modern readers of the important need to conserve resources.

    b. To inform readers of the Easter Island day-to-day cultural practices.

    c. To inform readers of a new hypothesis concerning Easter Island.

    d. To horrify the readers with the destruction caused by the Polynesian inhabitants of Easter Island as well as the European settlers who came in the 1700s.

WHY? What information in the selection leads you to give that answer? _____

_____

_____

_____

_____ 6. What is the purpose of paragraph 10?

    a. To use reverse psychology on the reader so that they will not worry about the overuse of natural resources.

    b. To suggest that the Easter Island tragedy is our fault.

    c. To cause the reader to think critically about the meaning of the example of Easter Island.

    d. To inform the reader that despite the new theories proposed, no one really knows what happened on Easter Island.

WHY? What information in the selection leads you to give that answer? _____

_____

_____

_____

Relationships

_____ 7. Which of the following is the main pattern of organization of paragraphs 1–4?

    a. Time order

    b. Cause and effect

    c. Compare and contrast

    d. Space order

WHY? What information in the selection leads you to give that answer? _____

_____

_____

_____

____ 8. What is the relationship of paragraphs 5–8 to paragraphs 1–4?

 a. Cause and effect

 b. Definition

 c. Time order

 d. Contrast

WHY? What information in the selection leads you to give that answer? _____

_____

_____

_____

_____

Fact, Opinion, and Inference

____ 9. Which of the following statements is an accurate fact based on the information presented within this reading?

 a. 2,900 years ago, Polynesians used double-hulled, seagoing canoes to colonize the island.

 b. Rats were central in causing Easter Island's deforestation.

 c. The main reason for the population loss was internal strife.

 d. The giant statues represented ancient chiefs worshipped by the Polynesian peoples of Easter Island.

WHY? What leads you to give that answer? _____

_____

_____

_____

____ 10. Which of the following statements is a valid conclusion to draw from this reading?

 a. Easter Island's fate could have been prevented.

 b. The Polynesians of Easter Island were cannibals.

 c. Even though it was not mentioned in the passage, rats were kept as pets by the Polynesian children. The aversion to eating pets could be why the rat population exploded.

 d. Hunt took more accurate measurements of age than the scientists who originally hypothesized what happened in the ill-fated history of Easter Island.

WHY? What leads you to give that answer? _____

_____

_____

_____

● Mapping the Reading

Create a chart contrasting the traditional hypothesis about the cause of the fate of Easter Island with Hunt's 2006 hypothesis.

Original hypothesis	Hunt's hypothesis

● Critical Thinking Questions

CRITICAL THINKING LEVEL 3: APPLY

Considering any prior knowledge you may have about how the stones of Stonehenge (in England) or the pyramids (in Egypt) were moved to their permanent locations, form a hypothesis to explain how the stones for the huge statues of Easter Island could have been moved.

_____

_____

_____

_____

CRITICAL THINKING LEVEL 4: ANALYZE

Analyze the situation that scientists find themselves in when they attempt to explain something like the abandonment of Easter Island. What are some of the factors that make it difficult to reach a clear understanding of why this happened?

_____

_____

_____

_____

CRITICAL THINKING LEVEL 5: EVALUATE

Answer the critical thinking question posed in paragraph 10 of the reading excerpt: *Does the new doubt about the original Easter Island hypothesis mean that we should not be concerned about using resources unsustainably on the island in space that we call earth?*

_____

_____

_____

_____

● Language in Use

The following words (or forms of them) were used in "Easter Island: Some Revisions in a Popular Environmental Story." Now you can use them in different contexts. Put a word from the box into the blank lines in the following numbered sentences.

> degraded thriving anthropological unsustainable
>
> plummeted artifacts regenerate

1. The reproduction of one of our most beloved fruits is _____ without a helping hand from humans. You see, the banana has a dark secret: it's impotent.

2. Bananas are able to _____ only because farmers cultivate them from sucker cuttings taken from the underground stem of the main banana tree "trunk."

3. The most common variety of banana is the Cavendish, and it is _____ in smoothies, ice cream treats, and on grocery store shelves the world over.

4. However, because of the genetic constancy of this fruit, it is especially vulnerable to pests and plague. In fact, about 100 years ago, the most popular banana variety, the Gros Michel (Big Mike), was devastated by a fungus. Crops around the world _____ in numbers so dramatic that growers started growing the Cavendish instead.

5. Cavendish has been the banana hero for years, but a villain disease has reemerged that is threatening our beloved yellow fruit. The answer may be genetic modification. However, most consumers view genetically modified foods as _____ in quality. Let's hope a favorable solution is found, or our favorite yellow fruit may disappear.

● EASY Note Cards

Make a note card for each of the vocabulary words from the reading that you did not know. On one side, write the word. On the other side, divide the card into quarters and label them E, A, S, and Y. Add a word or phrase in each area so that you wind up with an example sentence, an antonym, a synonym, and, finally, a definition that shows you understand the meaning of the word with your logic. Remember that a synonym or antonym may have appeared in the reading.

Career Environmental Science App   NONFICTION BOOK

● Pre-Reading the Selection

The excerpt that begins on page 446 comes from the book *Eaarth: Making a Life on a Tough New Planet,* by environmentalist Bill McKibben. The excerpt is titled "A New World."

Surveying the Reading

Survey the selection that follows. Then check the elements that are included in this reading.

_____ Title

_____ Headings

_____ First sentences of paragraphs

_____ Words in bold or italic type

_____ Images and captions

Guessing the Purpose

Based on the source and the title of the reading selection, do you think the author's purpose is mostly to persuade, inform, or express? _____

Predicting the Content

Based on your survey, what are three things you expect the reading selection to discuss?

- • _____
- • _____
- • _____

Activating Your Knowledge

What do you know about global warming or changes that have occurred in our environment over the last few decades?

- • _____
- • _____
- • _____

● Reading with Pen in Hand

Students who annotate as they read are more successful than students who do not annotate. That's why you will annotate each reading in *Engage* as you read. In the reading that follows, use the following symbols:

★ or (Point)   to indicate a main idea

① ② ③   to indicate major details

Access the Reading CourseMate via www.cengagebrain.com to hear vocabulary words from this selection and view a video about this topic.

Reading Journal

● Can you see the planet you are asked to imagine?

inhospitable Look at the description of the planet. Also look at the word parts. What does *in-hospit-able* mean?

A New World

Bill McKibben

1   Imagine we live on a planet. Not our cozy, taken-for-granted earth, but a planet, a real one, with melting poles and dying forests and a heaving, corrosive sea, raked by winds, strafed by storms, scorched by heat. An inhospitable place.

2 It's hard. For the ten thousand years that constitute human civilization, we've existed in the sweetest of sweet spots. The temperature has barely **budged**; globally averaged, it's swung in the narrowest of ranges, between fifty-eight and sixty degrees Fahrenheit. That's warm enough that the ice sheets retreated from the centers of our continents so we could grow grain, but cold enough that mountain glaciers provided drinking and irrigation water to those plains and valleys year-round; it was the "correct" temperature for the marvelously diverse planet that seems right to us. And every aspect of our civilization reflects that particular world. We built our great cities next to seas that have remained tame and level, or at altitudes high enough that disease-bearing mosquitoes could not overwinter. We refined the farming that has swelled our numbers to take full advantage of that predictable heat and rainfall; our rice and corn and wheat can't imagine another earth either. Occasionally, in one place or another, there's an abrupt departure from the norm—a hurricane, a drought, a freeze. But our very language reflects their rarity: freak storms, disturbances.

- Did you realize our planet was so ideal?

budged Look at the temperature example given later in this sentence to establish a meaning for *budged*.

3 In December 1968 we got the first real view of that stable, secure place. *Apollo 8* was orbiting the moon, the astronauts busy photographing possible landing zones for the missions that would follow. On the fourth orbit, Commander Frank Borman decided to roll the craft away from the moon and tilt its windows toward the horizon—he needed a navigational fix. What he got, instead, was a sudden view of the earth, rising. "Oh my God," he said, "Here's the earth coming up." Crew member Bill Anders grabbed a camera and took the photograph that became the **iconic** image of perhaps all time. "Earthrise," as it was eventually known, that picture of a blue-and-white marble floating amid the vast backdrop of space, set against the barren edge of the lifeless moon. Borman said later that it was "the most beautiful, heart-catching sight of my life, one that sent a torrent of nostalgia, of sheer homesickness, surging through me. It was the only thing in space that had any color to it. Everything else was simply black or white. But not the earth." The third member of the crew, Jim Lovell, put it more simply: the earth, he said, suddenly appeared as a "grand oasis."

- Imagine what it would feel like to see the earth from space as described here.

iconic This is the first image ever taken of the earth from space. What status do you think it might gain? What might *iconic* mean?

4 *But we no longer live on that planet.* In the four decades since, that earth has changed in profound ways, ways that have already taken us out of the sweet spot where humans so long thrived. We're every day less the oasis and more the desert. The world hasn't ended,

oasis *Oasis* is contrasted with *desert*. What does *oasis* mean?

but the world as we know it has—even if we don't quite know it yet. We imagine we still live back on that old planet, that the disturbances we see around us are the old random and freakish kind. But they're not. It's a different place. A different planet. It needs a new name. Eaarth. Or Monnde, or Tierrre, Errde, оккучивать. It still looks familiar enough—we're still the third rock out from the sun, still three-quarters water. Gravity still pertains; we're still earth*like*. But it's odd enough to constantly remind us how profoundly we've altered the only place we've ever known. I am aware, of course, that the earth changes constantly, and that occasionally it changes wildly, as when an asteroid strikes or an ice age relaxes its grip. This is one of those rare moments, the start of a change far larger and more thoroughgoing than anything we can read in the records of man, on a **par** with the biggest dangers we can read in the records of rock and ice.

5   Consider the veins of cloud that streak and **mottle** the earth in that glorious snapshot from space. So far humans, by burning fossil fuel, have raised the temperature of the planet nearly a degree Celsius (more than a degree and a half Fahrenheit). A NASA study in December 2008 found that warming on that scale was enough to trigger a 45 percent increase in thunderheads above the ocean, breeding the spectacular anvil-headed clouds that can rise five miles above the sea, generating "supercells" with torrents of rain and hail. In fact, total global rainfall is now increasing 1.5 percent a decade. Larger storms over land now create more lightning; every degree Celsius brings about 6 percent more lightning, according to the climate scientist Amanda Staudt. In just one day in June 2008, lightning sparked 1,700 different fires across California, burning a million acres and setting a new state record. These blazes burned on

---

○ How did reading paragraph 4 make you feel?

par *On a par with* is used to compare "the start of a change . . ." with "the biggest dangers . . . ." What does *par* mean?

mottle *Mottle* is an adjective describing how the clouds make the earth look. Look at the picture to get a visual suggestion of the meaning.

○ Did you see images of the California fires mentioned here? If not, picture them in your mind's eye.

the new earth, not the old one. "We are in the mega-fire era," said Ken Frederick, a spokesman for the federal government. And that smoke and flame, of course, were visible from space—indeed anyone with an Internet connection could watch the video feed from the space shuttle *Endeavour* as it circled above the towering **plumes** in the Santa Barbara hills.

plumes What is it that can be seen from the air above the hills? What are *plumes*?

6   Or consider the white and frozen top of the planet. Arctic ice has been melting slowly for two decades as temperatures have climbed, but in the summer of 2007 that gradual thaw suddenly accelerated. By the time the long Arctic night finally descended in October, there was 22 percent less sea ice than had ever been observed before, and more than 40 percent less than the year that the Apollo capsule took its picture. The Arctic ice cap was 1.1 million square miles smaller than ever in recorded history, reduced by an area twelve times the size of Great Britain. The summers of 2008 and 2009 saw a virtual repeat of the **epic** melt; in 2008 both the Northwest and Northeast passages opened for the first time in human history. The first commercial ship to make the voyage through the newly opened straits, the *MV Camilla Desgagnés,* had an icebreaker on standby in case it ran into trouble, but the captain reported, "I didn't see one cube of ice."

◎ Imagine the size of the ice that melted: twelve times the size of Great Britain.

epic Connect *epic* to the kind of melt that is being described. What is *epic*?

7   This is not some **mere** passing change; this is the earth shifting. In December 2008, scientists from the National Sea Ice Data Center said the increased melting of Arctic ice was accumulating heat in the oceans, and that this so-called Arctic amplification now penetrated 1,500 kilometers inland. In August 2009, scientists reported that lightning strikes in the Arctic had increased twentyfold, igniting some of the first tundra fires ever observed. According to the center's Mark Serreze, the new data are "reinforcing the **notion** that the Arctic ice is in its death spiral." That is, within a decade or two, a summertime spacecraft pointing its camera at the North Pole would see nothing but open ocean. There'd be ice left on Greenland—but much less ice. Between 2003 and 2008, more than a trillion tons of the island's ice melted, an area ten times the size of Manhattan. "We now know that the climate doesn't have to warm any more for Greenland to continue losing ice," explained Jason Box, a geography professor at Ohio State University. "It has probably passed the point where it could maintain the mass of ice that we remember." And if the spacecraft pointed its camera at the South Pole? On the last day of 2008, the *Economist* reported that temperatures on the Antarctic Peninsula were rising faster than anywhere else on earth, and that the West Antarctic was losing ice 75 percent faster than just a decade before.

mere There is a contrast in this sentence between *change* and *shifting*. Think of this relationship and how *mere* is used. What does *mere* mean?

notion If the data is reinforcing the *notion*, what does *notion* mean?

◎ How heavy is a trillion tons? What else might weigh that much?

● Do you agree about what reaction you should be experiencing?

barrages Compare *barrages* with *blows* and *thuds*. What does *barrages* mean?

8   Don't let your eyes glaze over at this parade of statistics (and so many more to follow). These should come as body blows, as mortar **barrages**, as sickening thuds. The Holocene is staggered, the only world that humans have known is suddenly reeling. I am not describing what will happen if we don't take action, or warning of some future threat. This is the current inventory: more thunder, more lightning, less ice. Name a major feature of the earth's surface and you'll find massive change.

9   For instance: a U.S. government team studying the tropics recently concluded that by the standard meteorological definition, they have expanded more than two degrees of latitude north and south since 1980—"a further 8.5 million square miles of the Earth are now experiencing a tropical climate." As the tropics expand, they push out the dry subtropics ahead of them, north and south, "with grave implications for many millions of people" in these newly arid regions. In Australia, for instance, "westerly winds bringing much needed rain" are "likely to be pushed further south, dumping their water over open ocean rather than on land." Indeed, by early 2008 half of Australia was in drought, and forecasters were calling it the new normal. "The inflows of the past will never return," the executive director of the Water Services Association of Australia told reporters. "We are trying to avoid the term 'drought' and are saying this is the new reality." They are trying to avoid the term *drought* because it implies the condition may someday *end*. The government warned in 2007 that "exceptionally hot years," which used to happen once a quarter century, would now "occur every one or two years." The brushfires ignited by drought on this scale claimed hundreds of Australian lives in early 2009; four-story-high walls of flame "raced across the land like speeding trains," according to news reports. The country's prime minister visited the scene of the worst blazes. "Hell and its fury have visited the good people of Victoria," he said.

● Can you imagine a forty-foot wall of flames traveling like a train across your town?

AP Photo/FILE

10   And such hell is not confined to the **antipodes**. By the end of 2008 hydrologists in the United States were predicting that drought across the American Southwest has become a "permanent condition." There was a 50 percent chance that Lake Mead, which backs up on the Colorado River behind the Hoover Dam, could run dry by 2121. (When that happens, as the head of the Southern Nevada Water Authority put it, "you cut off supply to the fifth largest economy in the world," spread across the American West.) But the damage is already happening: researchers calculate that the new **aridity** and heat have led to reductions in wheat, corn, and barley yields of about 40 million tons a year. The dryness keeps spreading. In early 2009 drought wracked northern China, the country's main wheat belt. Rain didn't fall for more than a hundred days, a modern record. The news was much the same in India, in southern Brazil, and in Argentina, where wheat production in 2009 was the lowest in twenty years. Across the planet, rivers are drying up. A massive 2009 study looked at streamflows on 925 of the world's largest rivers from 1948 to 2004 and found that twice as many were falling as rising. "During the life span of the study, fresh water discharge into the Pacific Ocean fell by about six percent—or roughly the annual volume of the Mississippi," it reported.

11   From the flatlands to the highest peaks. The great glaciologist Lonnie Thompson, drilling cores on a huge Tibetan glacier in 2008, found something odd. Or rather, didn't find: one of the usual marker layers in any ice core, the radioactive particles that fell out from the atomic tests of the 1960s, were missing. The glacier had melted back through that history, wiped it away. A new Nepalese study found temperatures rising a tenth of a degree Fahrenheit annually in the Himalayas. That would be a degree every *decade* in a world where the mercury barely budged for ten millennia. A longstanding claim that Himalayan glaciers might disappear by 2035 has been discredited, but across the region the great ice sheets are already shrinking fast: photos from the base of Mount Everest show that three hundred vertical feet of ice—a mass as tall as the Statue of Liberty—have melted since the Mallory expedition took the first photographs of the region in 1921. But already, while there's still some glacier left, the new heat is flustering people. The rhododendrons that dominate Himalayan hillsides are in some places blooming forty-five days ahead of schedule, wrecking the annual spring flower festival and "creating confusion among folk artists." The same kind of confusion is gripping mountaineers; one experienced high-altitude guide recently reported abandoning some mountains

antipodes The previous paragraphs have discussed changes in the Arctic and changes in Australia and south of Australia. Think of a globe. What does *antipodes* mean?

aridity Look at the sentences before this one. What is *aridity*?

● Do you know of any fresh water sources near where you live that have shrunk or dried up? Does your city control the use of water for lawns? Do you think there is a connection here?

● Of all the changes mentioned, which ones would you find the most confusing if they happened in your area?

he'd climbed for years because "of the melting of the ice that acts as a glue, literally holding the mountains together."

12 It's not just the Himalayas. In the spring of 2009, researchers arriving in Bolivia found that the eighteen-thousand-year-old Chacaltaya Glacier is "gone, completely melted away as of some sad, undetermined moment early this year." Once the highest ski run in the world, it is now nothing but rocks and mud. But it's not the loss of a ski run that really matters. These glaciers are the reservoirs for entire continents, watering the billions of people who have settled downstream precisely because they guaranteed a fresh supply. "When the glaciers are gone, they are gone. What does a place like Lima do?" asked Tim Barnett, a climate scientist at Scripps Oceanographic Institute. "In northwest China there are 300 million people relying on snowmelt for water supply. There's no way to replace it until the next Ice Age."

● What do you predict will happen in Lima, Peru, and northwest China?

● Why is the author telling this story?

13 When I read these accounts, I flash back to a tiny village, remote even by Tibetan standards, where I visited a few years ago. A gangly young man guided me a mile up a riverbank for a view of the enormous glacier whose snout towered over the valley. A black rock the size of an apartment tower stuck out from the middle of the wall of ice. My guide said it had appeared only the year before and now grew larger daily as its dark surface absorbed the sun's heat. We were a hundred miles from a school, far from TV; no one in the village was literate. So out of curiosity I asked the young man: "Why is it melting?" I don't know what I expected—some story about angry gods? He looked at me as if I was visiting from the planet Moron.

● Why does the author share this information?

14 "Global warming," he said. "Too many factories."

—"A New World" from the book *Eaarth: Making a Life on a Tough New Planet* by Bill McKibben. Copyright © 2010 by Bill McKibben. Reprinted by permission of Henry Holt and Company, LLC.

● Comprehension Questions

Write the letter of the answer on the line. Then explain your thinking.

Main Idea

_____ 1. Which of the following sentences best represents the main idea for this entire passage?

    a. Name a major feature of the earth's surface and you'll find massive change.

    b. Arctic ice has been melting slowly for two decades as temperatures have climbed, and lightning has increased twentyfold in the past four decades.

    c. "Earthrise," as it was eventually known, showed a picture of a blue-and-white marble floating amid the vast backdrop of space, set against the barren edge of the lifeless moon.

    d. The earth is not experiencing some small passing changes; the earth is shifting.

WHY? What information in the selection leads you to give that answer? _____

_____

_____

_____

_____ 2. Which of the following sentences is the best topic sentence of paragraph 2?

    a. We refined the farming that has swelled our numbers to take full advantage of that predictable heat and rainfall; our rice and corn and wheat can't imagine another earth either.

    b. For the ten thousand years that constitute human civilization, we've existed in the sweetest of sweet spots.

    c. Every aspect of our civilization reflects that particular world.

    d. The temperature has barely budged; globally averaged, it's swung in the narrowest of ranges, between fifty-eight and sixty degrees Fahrenheit.

WHY? What information in the selection leads you to give that answer? _____

_____

_____

_____

Supporting Details

____ 3. Which paragraphs contain most of the examples of how the earth has changed?

    a. Paragraphs 5, 6, 7, 9, and 10

    b. Paragraphs 1, 2, 4, and 6

    c. Paragraphs 4, 8, and 10

    d. Paragraphs 3, 5, 7, and 9

WHY? What information in the selection leads you to give that answer? _____

_____

_____

_____

____ 4. Which of the following details contradicts the information presented in the reading?

    a. More than 200 Australians were burned to death in 2009.

    b. Lightning strikes in the Arctic have increased approximately 2,000 percent over the past forty years.

    c. Due to "supercells," in 2009, China experienced its wettest year in modern history, causing floods and destroying crops.

    d. In fifty-six years, the amount of fresh water flowing into the Pacific decreased by about 6 percent.

WHY? What information in the selection leads you to give that answer? _____

_____

_____

_____

Author's Purpose

____ 5. Which of the following purposes most accurately describes this reading?

    a. To persuade readers that the earth as we know it is no more and that we need to change our disregard of earth before it is too late.

    b. To inform readers that the main cause for the degradation of the earth is linked to the space exploration of the late 1960s.

    c. To inform readers that the earth has changed and give some of the current scientific data to show proof of this reality.

    d. To shock readers with gloom-and-doom statistics about the end of the earth.

WHY? What information in the selection leads you to give that answer? _____

_____

_____

_____

____ 6. What is the purpose of paragraph 8?

    a. To remind the reader of the many statistics that will be given in this reading.

    b. To emphasize the importance of the statistics the author is giving about the current status of earth.

    c. To compare our treatment of the earth to the Holocaust.

    d. To warn the reader of some future effect that might happen on earth based on current behavioral patterns.

WHY? What information in the selection leads you to give that answer? _____

_____

_____

_____

Relationships

____ 7. What is the relationship of paragraphs 9–12 to paragraph 8?

    a. Paragraph 8 is an example; paragraphs 9–12 give the point.

    b. Paragraph 8 gives the point; paragraphs 9–12 give support.

    c. All of these paragraphs offer major supporting details.

    d. Paragraphs 8 and 9–12 are being compared to each other.

WHY? What information in the selection leads you to give that answer? _____

_____

_____

_____

____ 8. What is the main pattern of organization for this passage?

    a. Contrast

    b. Narration

    c. Cause and effect

    d. Process

WHY? What information in the selection leads you to give that answer? _____

_____

_____

_____

Fact, Opinion, and Inference

_____ 9. Which of the following answers contains an opinion?

a. What he got, instead, was a sudden view of the earth, rising. "Oh my God," he said, "Here's the earth coming up."

b. So far humans, by burning fossil fuel, have raised the temperature of the planet nearly a degree Celsius (more than a degree and a half Fahrenheit).

c. We imagine we still live back on that old planet, that the disturbances we see around us are the old random and freakish kind. But they're not. It's a different place. A different planet. It needs a new name.

d. On the last day of 2008, the *Economist* reported that temperatures on the Antarctic Peninsula were rising faster than anywhere else on earth, and that the West Antarctic was losing ice 75 percent faster than just a decade before.

WHY? What leads you to give that answer? _____

_____

_____

_____

_____ 10. Which of the following can be inferred based on the information from the passage?

a. It should be obvious by now that earth has been seriously affected by global warming.

b. All of the ice in the Arctic will be gone within the next five years if immediate changes are not made.

c. If humans change their reckless behavior, then we can return the earth to its former "sweet spot."

d. The shift in the earth's status has been so severe in some places that gravity has been affected.

WHY? What leads you to give that answer? _____

_____

_____

_____

● Mapping the Reading

Create a visual map showing the author's support for how the earth has changed since 1968 when the iconic photo "Earthrise" was taken.

● Critical Thinking Questions

CRITICAL THINKING LEVEL 3: APPLY

Suppose the author is correct about what is happening to the planet. What would Eaarth look like from space?

_____

_____

_____

_____

CRITICAL THINKING LEVEL 4: ANALYZE

How does the author's use of language in paragraph 1 support his main idea? Discuss at least four individual words in your answer.

_____

_____

_____

_____

CRITICAL THINKING LEVEL 5: EVALUATE

How effective do you find the author's use of the image of earth from space? Rate its effectiveness on a scale from 1 to 10, with 10 being the most effective. Explain your answer by discussing what function the image performs in the reading excerpt.

_____

_____

_____

_____

● Language in Use

The following words (or forms of them) were used in "A New World." Now you can use them in different contexts. Put a word from the box into the blank lines in the following numbered sentences.

> inhospitable budged iconic oasis par mottle plumes
>
> epic mere notion barraged antipodes aridity

1. Gene Simmons, also known as "The Demon," cofounded and plays bass for the _____ band KISS.

2. KISS was formed in New York in 1973 and by 1977 was considered the most popular band in America. They were not only on _____ with other rock legends, but surpassed the biggest band of them all—the Beatles—by breaking their record of sold-out back-to-back concerts with their Japanese debut concert series.

3. By 1979 KISS's popularity had peaked. They had four platinum albums, estimated worldwide sales of more than $100 million, and their largest attendance to date for their _____ live concerts.

4. To see KISS was to have your senses _____. Each KISS member sported outlandish makeup and costumes. They played hard to heavy metal music, and their concerts included pyrotechnics, smoking guitars, levitating drums, fire breathing, and more.

5. The _____ that their popularity would decline within a few short years was not even considered. However, by the early 1980s, KISS had lost two band members, experienced a marked decline in record sales and concert attendance, and fired their manager.

6. But don't worry about KISS. Despite a few years of life being _____, the band has done extremely well. As of 2010, KISS had a total of twenty-four gold records with sales of more than 100 million albums worldwide.

● EASY Note Cards

Make a note card for each of the vocabulary words from the reading that you did not know. On one side, write the word. On the other side, divide the card into quarters and label them E, A, S, and Y. Add a word or phrase in each area so that you wind up with an example sentence, an antonym, a synonym, and, finally, a definition that shows you understand the meaning of the word with your logic. Remember that a synonym or antonym may have appeared in the reading.

8 Evaluating the Author's Purpose and Tone

Previewing the Chapter

Flip through the pages of Chapter 8, and read all the major headings. Look at all the photos and figures, and read their captions.

Predict three topics this chapter will cover.

_____

_____

_____

Based on the figures in the chapter, write a statement about the topic of the chapter.

_____

_____

Plan to come back and comment on your predictions and statement when you have finished working through the chapter.

_____

_____

 To access additional course materials for *Engage,* including quizzes, videos, and more, please visit www.cengagebrain.com. At the CengageBrain.com home page, search for the ISBN of *Engage* (from the back cover of your book) using the search box at the top of the page. This will take you to the product page where these resources can be found.

**Videos Related
to Readings**

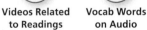
**Vocab Words
on Audio**

**Read and Talk
on Demand**

Read and Talk   TEXTBOOK

In college, reading is just one aspect of how you will share new ideas with others in your class. So the first reading in each chapter of this book is meant to give you the chance to talk about reading. Read the article, and then use the four discussion questions to talk about your ideas with your classmates and your instructor.

Access the Reading CourseMate via www.cengagebrain.com to hear a reading of this selection and view a video about this topic.

Now What Was My Password? . . .

Spencer

1   Have you ever noticed that the only "cool" computer people in movies are computer hackers? It's not often you see a scene with dramatic music playing in the background while Larry from down the hall sits in his cubicle and **configures** his router.

2   Sometimes I wish that I were a computer hacker. I don't want to break into government files or the university **database**. (Not even a hacker could make my grades look good.) I just want to be able to get into my computer the day after I change my password.

3   We've all heard that changing your password frequently is important to make your computer more secure.

4   The only problem with this advice is that my brain seems to contain only "**virtual** memory" these days. As soon as I "shut down" at night, the password information disappears from my brain.

5   Trying to guess your password is almost like a game. "Okay, so I was thinking about my aunt when I created this password. She has a dog named Fluffy. She got Fluffy in May. My password must be "fluffymay!" BUZZ! "mayfluffy?" BUZZ! "05fluffy?" BUZZ! "fluffy05?" BUZZ! "$%*&!" BUZZ! "Where's Chloe from 24 when I need her?!"

6   I've finally **resorted** to writing my usernames and passwords on yellow sticky notes that I paste all over my monitor. So now I'm completely secure—as long as someone isn't sitting at my computer. (Professional hackers would have a hard time getting into my computer from around the globe, but a kindergartner sitting at my desk shouldn't have any problem.)

configures Using word parts, guess what the word *configures* means.

database Consider your prior knowledge and the example in this sentence of *data*. What is a *database*?

virtual The idea plays on two meanings of the word *virtual*. Use your dictionary to find the meaning that is unrelated to computer memory.

resorted Based on the general ideas here, what phrase could replace *resorted*?

7   Yellow sticky notes are an essential tool for any computer person. My computer often resembles a big yellow piñata. Besides holding my username and password information, the yellow sticky notes on my monitor also contain appointments, to-do lists, important phone numbers and dates, dates' phone numbers, reminders to pay bills, and the names of the Jonas Brothers (just in case).

8   One thing I could do to improve my personal security is to clean my desk. I'm currently on the annual cleaning schedule. At this very moment, I face the risk of paper avalanche in my office. I'm considering buying one of those cannons that ski resorts use to prevent avalanches. I'd better check to see if one's available on eBay. Now, what was my password . . . ?

Dorling Kindersley/Getty Images

—From ANDERSON/FERRO/HILTON. *Connecting With Computer Science*, 2e (p. 48) Copyright © 2011 Cengage Learning.

Talking About Reading

Respond in writing to the questions below, and then discuss your answers with your classmates.

1. What image comes to mind when you hear the term *hacker*?

_____

_____

_____

2. Have any of your accounts (or those of anyone you know) ever been hacked?

_____

_____

_____

3. Discuss how you approach online passwords. For example, how often do you change them; how many do you have; how do you structure your passwords?

_____

_____

_____

4. What would you say the tone of this reading is and why?

_____

_____

_____

Three Main Purposes (PIE Review)

As you learned in Chapter 1, an author usually has one of three broad purposes, which are organized into the mnemonic "PIE."

> **Persuasive purpose:** Attempts to change the reader's or viewer's thoughts, attitudes, or behaviors.
>
> **Informative purpose:** Attempts to teach the reader or viewer about key information, usually factual.
>
> **Expressive purpose:** Attempts to express an emotion or to cause readers or viewers to feel emotions, such as amusement, sadness, horror, and so on, often by using stories.

You also learned two basic ways to predict an author's purpose.

1. Read the title and headings.

2. Consider the source and the genre.

Use Interaction 8–1 to review your purpose-finding skills.

INTERACTION 8–1	Determine the Purpose of a Passage

Read the following passages and determine their purpose. Consider the title, the heading, and the source, if you can tell what it is.

1.

Not All Lotto Winners Win

1   Many people think that winning the lottery would be a dream come true, the "cat's meow," or just plain awesome. However, not all who win the lottery ride off into the sunset and live happily ever after.

2   Several winners have been murdered. One 20 million dollar winner, Jeffrey Dampier, was kidnapped and murdered by his sister-in-law and her boyfriend. Another winner of $30 million, Abraham Shakespeare, was approached by a poser, Dee Dee Moore, who claimed she wanted to write a book about him, but ended up not only stealing his money, but his life as well.

3   Many lottery winners can't handle the pressures of their newfound financial freedom, and quickly end up broke. One winner won more than $5 million but quickly gambled it away and is now living in a trailer park. Others lose their winnings on bad investments, pesky friends and family, or lavish lifestyles. They think the money will last forever, but it is gone within a few years, and they are worse off than before they won.

What is the purpose of this reading?

Persuasive   Informative   Expressive

2.

A Letter

My Little One,

1   My precious unknown child . . . I should have written this long ago, but never knew quite what to say. Though it is a casual comment often said without truth, I think I really have thought about you every day since we lost you . . . I lost something over the days we lost you, but I have never been sure what it really was. I grieved but was strong for your mother who was devastated; she has such a tender heart and had already given it all to you. We both lost part of our heart that weekend, of all times, our anniversary weekend, which is supposed to be full of joy and romance. But your mom and I married "for better or for worse," and this was definitely a worse part. I think the worst part . . . but don't feel bad; we have had many wonderful times and will have many, many more . . . and you will always be a part of them. You are our history.

2   I have spent some months trying to figure out what hurt the most. Was it the death before a life really began (life is so precious even though it is an uncherished commodity by many in our amoral culture—your mom and I were in awe of your life barely begun)? Was it that I had to deal with my grief and that of my wife (infinitely harder because I want to protect her from all hurt, but I can't)? Was it the fact that I do not even know whether you were a sweet little boy (which we wanted ever so much) or if you were a precious little girl (which we would have loved more than words can even begin to claim because that is how I love you still . . .)? I think it is all those things . . . and so much more.

3   But I have finally boiled it down. What hurt the most (and still does) is the time that was lost. I will never be able to spend time with you, except in my mind and heart. I will never hear your first cry for air, never know your soft touch or sweet baby smell, as you lay on my chest skin to skin, my heart will never be warmed by your smiles or laughter, I will never thrill at your first word (which would have been "Da, Da", of course). . . . There are so many memories that I will never have with you, and that is what hurts the most . . . and sometimes it leaves me feeling so empty . . .

4   But here is what I promise: The emptiness will always remind me to take the time I have forever lost with you and transfer it. I promise that I will always cherish the two beautiful sisters you have and do my best to never take them for granted. I will love your mother for the queen she is and honor her so that I make her blessed among women. This is my love promise to you, the precious child I lost but will always love. I will try to make you proud, while you are looking down from heaven, to call me . . .

                                                                                          Your Daddy

What is the purpose of this reading?

Persuasive   Informative   Expressive

3.

Sources of Motivation

Human motivation stems from four main sources. First, we can be motivated by *physiological factors*, such as the need for food and water. Second, *emotional factors* can motivate behavior. Panic, fear, anger, love, and hatred can influence behavior ranging from selfless giving to brutal murder. *Cognitive factors* provide a third source of motivation. Your perceptions of the world, your beliefs about what you can do, and your expectations of how others will respond generate certain behaviors. For example, even the least musical contestants who try out for *American Idol* and other talent shows seem utterly confident in their ability to sing. Fourth, motivation can stem from *social factors*, including the influence of parents, teachers, siblings, friends, television, and other sociocultural forces. Have you ever bought a jacket or tried a particular hairstyle not because you liked it but because it was in fashion? This is just one example of how social factors can affect almost all human behavior.

—From BERNSTEIN. *Essentials of Psychology*, 5e (p. 299)
Copyright © 2011 Cengage Learning.

What is the purpose of this reading?

Persuasive   Informative   Expressive

4.

Excerpt from *The Girl Who Kicked the Hornet's Nest*

Stieg Larsson

Friday, April 8

1   Dr. Jonasson was woken by a nurse five minutes before the helicopter was expected to land. It was just before 1:30 in the morning.

2   "What?" he said, confused.

3   "Rescue Service helicopter coming in. Two patients. An injured man and a younger woman. The woman has gunshot wounds."

4   "All right," Jonasson said wearily.

5   Although he had slept for only half an hour, he felt groggy. He was on the night shift in the ER at Sahlgrenska hospital in Göteborg. It had been a strenuous evening.

6   By 12:30 the steady flow of emergency cases had eased off. He had made a round to check on the state of his patients and then gone back to the staff bedroom to try to rest for a while. He was on duty until 6:00, and seldom got the chance to sleep even if no emergency patients came in. But this time he had fallen asleep almost as soon as he turned out the light.

7   Jonasson saw lightning out over the sea. He knew that the helicopter was coming in the nick of time. All of a sudden a heavy downpour lashed at the window. The storm had moved in over Göteborg.

8   He heard the sound of the chopper and watched as it banked through the storm squalls down towards the helipad. For a second he held his breath when the pilot seemed to have difficulty controlling the aircraft. Then it vanished from his field of vision and he heard the engine slowing to land. He took a hasty swallow of his tea and set down the cup.

—Larsson, *The Girl Who Kicked the Hornet's Nest*, p. 1

What is the purpose of this reading?

Persuasive   Informative   Expressive

5.

Got Milk? For Many People, There Are Reasons To Get Rid Of It

Milton Mills

1   In mid-March, People for the Ethical Treatment of Animals sparked controversy with its campaign promoting beer's advantages over cow's milk to college students. Certainly, few health professionals would advocate beer as a health tonic, yet many mistakenly regard milk as a necessarily wholesome choice. Indeed, saying "don't drink your milk" may initially sound as un-American as "don't eat apple pie." But PETA's anti-milk points are well-taken.

2   For generations, most parents and physicians have kept urging children to drink their glasses of milk. To be sure, they generally had good intentions—but they also had been flooded with endless promotions and ads from the financially well-set dairy industry. More recently, it's hard to miss those here, there and everywhere milk-mustache and "Got Milk?" billboards, bus ads, print ads, TV spots, and classroom promotions. The milk industry even hit the road with its "Better Bones Tour," visiting 100 U.S. cities with trucks carrying displays claiming a beneficial relationship between dairy and osteoporosis.

3   Science, however, has been raining on dairy's parade. Observations in South African black townships, with virtually no dairy consumption, showed residents there experience almost no osteoporosis, while the chronic bone disease afflicts millions in dairy-devouring places such as Scandinavia, Canada, and the United States. In a finding published in the *American Journal of Public Health* in June 1997, the 12-year Harvard Nurses' Study of almost 78,000 people found those regularly consuming dairy products had no protection at all against hip and forearm fractures. Indeed, women drinking three glasses of milk daily had more fractures than women who rarely or never touched milk.

4   Other studies are investigating dairy's links with breast cancer, ovarian cancer, iron deficiency, insulin-dependent diabetes, cataracts, food allergies, heart disease, asthma and colic. Common toxic contaminants in dairy include pesticides, drugs and antibiotic traces.

5   In attacking cow's milk, PETA actually echoes the growing number of nutritionists and doctors—the late pediatrician Benjamin Spock among them—wiping off their milk mustaches.

6   From my perspective as an African-American physician, there is another troubling side to dairy promotions, and especially to government recommendations that it be part of every school lunch meal and similar nutrition programs.

7   While only about 15 percent to 20 percent of U.S. whites are intolerant of the milk sugar lactose, some 95 percent of Asian Americans, about 70 percent of African Americans and Native Americans, and more than 50 percent of Mexican-Americans cannot digest it. Many get quite sick from it. Nature starts to remove the enzymes that digest milk sugar once we have passed the age of weaning.

8   Indeed, one can call lactose intolerance nature's normal warning signal not to "do dairy," akin to the protective pain signals prompting you to snatch your hand away from a hot stove. Of course, some advocate taking lactose-tolerance pills or adding small amounts of dairy at intervals throughout the day to "trick" the body into accepting milk, ice cream, and so on. But, if you wouldn't want to trick your hand into not feeling a searingly painful stove, why would you want to temporarily mask the unhealthy downside of dairy? Being lactose-intolerant really constitutes genetic good luck.

9   It's bad enough that current federal dietary guidelines encourage meat consumption, though they do list nutritionally sound alternatives, such as legumes (beans and peas). However, the 1992-issued federal Food Guide Pyramid's "dairy section" doesn't even bother to list substitutes, though the 2000 Dietary Guidelines for Americans draft does finally mention soymilk. Indeed, healthy dairy-free alternatives such as fortified soymilk and calcium-set tofu have become increasingly available in supermarkets, as well as in health food stores and food co-ops.

10   Calcium, dairy's big "health" selling point, does indeed strengthen teeth and bones. But it's readily absorbable from broccoli, kale, mustard greens, turnip greens, Brussels sprouts, pinto beans, navy beans, black-eyed peas, calcium-set tofu, and, of course, the new fortified orange juice and apple juice products. And none of those haul the health-damaging freight that dairy does.

11   So, for your health's sake, why not replace cow's milk with soymilk and other alternatives?

—Mills, "Got Milk? For Many People, There Are Reasons To Get Rid Of It,"
San Jose Mercury News, March 27, 2000. Copyright © 2000
San Jose Mercury News. Reprinted by permission.

What is the purpose of this reading?

Persuasive   Informative   Expressive

In each of the passages from Interaction 8–1, you predicted the author's purpose based on the title or the source, but you used more than that. You also looked at the tone of the reading, even if you were not really aware of doing that. For instance, in the letter from the father to the never-to-be-born child, the author's tenderness and grief shine through and mark the general purpose as being emotionally expressive. Contrast that passage with the article about lactose intolerance, in which the author uses phrases such as "Why would you want to . . ." and "It's bad enough . . .". These phrases show that the author wants to persuade readers to his point of view.

The rest of this chapter will discuss the nuances of tone and then circle back around to connect author's purpose and tone.

Section Review: Three Main Purposes (PIE Review)

A. Fill in the following visual about authors' purposes.

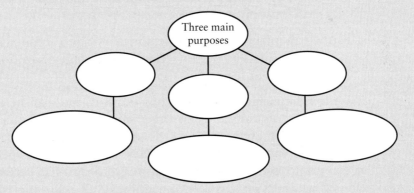

B. Fill in the following visual with strategies for determining an author's purpose.

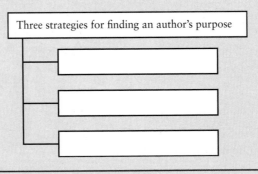

Distinguishing Between Denotation and Connotation

How can you tell if someone is happy, sad, or mad? The short answer is that you can use **inference**. Based on what people say and how they say it, you can infer how they are feeling. Here's the long answer.

- You can listen closely to the speaker's tone of voice and, using your prior knowledge about different tones of voice in different circumstances, you can understand what that tone implies (that is, what it suggests without saying).

- You can listen to the words a person says and, based on your memories of your experiences (again, your prior knowledge), you can understand what shade of meaning he or she is using. For example, "I'm glad to meet you" means something different than "I'm so delighted to meet you!" The first sentence usually means the person is just being polite. The second suggests that the person has been waiting to meet you for some time or has a special reason for wanting to meet you.

- You can imagine what the person is trying to accomplish with her or his words. The person's emotions probably have something to do with her or his purpose for speaking.

Written language also has a tone—and it, too, can be happy, sad, mad, or any of thousands of other emotions. The difference is, of course, that you are reading words, not listening to and seeing a person. But the basic idea is the same. The author chooses specific words to get you to understand and even to get you to feel certain feelings. One way authors do this is by imagining what associations, or connotations, readers will have for certain words. What memories, emotions, or experiences will a word call up for readers?

Denotation is the literal meaning of a word. It is straightforward. When you see *denotation*, think "d": denotation is the dictionary definition. When you look up a word in the dictionary, the definition is the denotation of that word.

ab•scond (ab-'skänd) *v.* 1. to depart secretly and hide oneself

—*Merriam-Webster* Online, www.merriam-webster.com/dictionary/abscond

Connotation, as you learned in Chapter 2, is a word's associations. When you see *connotation,* think "conn": connotation is the **conn**ection or association of a word to certain emotions or attitudes. Some words have positive connotations, and others have negative connotations. Connotations are related to the context in which a word appears.

Let's contrast denotation and connotation. Here are three words and their denotations, or dictionary definitions.

© Marquis/Shutterstock.com

smile   to form a facial expression where one's mouth slightly turns up at the corners

grin   to smile widely (from ear to ear)

beam   to smile joyfully

Now read each sentence below. Based on the different verbs that are used, what does each sentence connote? Pay attention to what is being implied about the girl's emotions.

A. The girl **smiled** at her boyfriend.
B. The girl **grinned** at her boyfriend.
C. The girl **beamed** at her boyfriend.

Minimal emotion is suggested by the verb *smiled* in sentence A. The word has a simple, positive connotation in this situation. In sentence B, the verb *grinned* suggests that the girl may be joking or being silly with her boyfriend, and it is more intense than the word *smiled*. In sentence C, *beaming* is even more intense and suggests that the girl feels extremely happy, as if her boyfriend did something really special—maybe even proposed. As you can see, the emotional connotation of each word becomes stronger with each sentence, even though denotatively these words are similar; each would be considered synonyms of the other.

You use **inference** to determine what a word connotes. You base your reading of connotations on your experiences. Your memories of smiling, grinning, or beaming, and how these are connected to certain emotional states, all come into play. The other important part of understanding connotation is knowing what words mean. Use the strategies you learned in Chapter 2 to figure out the meaning of words.

| INTERACTION 8–2 | Note the Connotations of Words |

Think of a situation that shows the connotation of each of the following words. You can do this independently or collaboratively. Circle whether the context you come up with shows a positive (**+**) or negative (**−**) connotation. Some might be both.

1. Disobedient: _____

_____

+   **−**

Rebellious: _____

_____

+   **−**

Mischievous: _____

_____

+   **−**

2. Aggressive: _____

_____

+   **−**

Argumentative: _____

_____

+   **−**

Violent: _____

_____

+   −

3. Burglar: _____

_____

+   −

Shoplifter: _____

_____

+   −

Embezzler: _____

_____

+   −

4. Woo: _____

_____

+   −

Chase: _____

_____

+   −

Date: _____

_____

+   −

5. Strong: _____

_____

+   −

Muscular: _____

_____

+   −

Stalwart: _____

_____

+   −

Connotations Suggest a Subjective Tone

When an author uses words that have connotations, you can assume that the tone is subjective. **Subjective** means that the author is putting himself or herself into the writing as one of the subjects. It's like someone in a conversation giving his or her opinion. The opinion becomes part of what you then respond to. Of course, sometimes authors give opinions directly—for example, with phrases such as "I believe," "I think," "people should," and "in my opinion." But whether directly or by connotation, the tone is subjective. Once you determine the tone is subjective, you can then consider whether it is positive or negative.

Example of Subjective Tone

Grandparents should lavish attention on their grandchildren.

AUTHOR'S   POSITIVE

OPINION   CONNOTATION

The police abuse their power too frequently.

NEGATIVE   AUTHOR'S

CONNOTATION   OPINION

Lack of Connotations Suggests an Objective Tone

Some words are simply denotative. They possess meaning but not connotation. You might call these words the neutral version of all the choices the author could have made. A lack of connotations suggests that the tone is objective, or factual. **Objective** means the author is ignoring his or her own opinions and is focusing on the object of the writing—the facts or ideas he or she is reporting.

Example of Objective Tone

Many grandparents pay attention to their grandchildren.

NEUTRAL WORDS

Police can misuse their power.

NEUTRAL WORDS

INTERACTION 8–3 | Understand Tone Based on Connotation

A. In the readings below, underline or circle any words that have some kind of connotation or suggest the author's opinion.

B. Choose the tone of the reading (objective or subjective). If you find connotation, the tone is subjective. Decide if the connotation is positive (**+**) or negative (**−**). If there is no connotation, then the tone would be denotative, objective, or neutral (**N**).

1.

> Immediately Tyrone raised his hand. The teacher called on him to come to the front of the class to tell what he and his family did over summer vacation. He excitedly told of his trip to the beach, his sister getting sunburned, and catching a shark on a fishing trip.

Tone: objective   N

subjective   **+**   **−**

2.

> 1   She took one hand from his and stroked his head where the hair hung long and ragged and said, "If I do not do this thing, then it may go on and on. 'Nothing of the greater good comes without struggle and sacrifice in equal measure, be you man or woman, and in this way we are freed from tyranny.' Those are your words."
>
> 2   He made an impatient gesture and said, "They are not my words but words of those who gained from them by being murdered and put to rot in unmarked graves."
>
> —Kent, *The Heretic's Daughter*, pp. 175–176

Tone: objective   N

       subjective   +   −

3.

> 1   *Demography* is the scientific study of human populations. The term itself was coined in 1855 by Achille Guillard, who used it in the title of his book *Éléments de Statistique Humaine ou Demographie Comparée*. The word he invented is a combination of two Greek words: *demos,* which means people, and *graphien,* which means to write about a particular subject (in this instance, population).
>
> 2   Guillard defined demography as "the mathematical knowledge of populations, their general movements, and their physical, civil, intellectual and moral state" (Guillard 1855; xxvii). This is generally in tune with how we use the term today in that modern demography is the study of the determinants and consequences of population change. . . .
>
> —From WEEKS. *Population*, 10e (pp. 2–3)
> Copyright © 2008 Cengage Learning.

Tone: objective   N

       subjective   +   −

4.

> 1   Scientists say they have discovered the first fossil of a dinosaur in Angola, and that it's a new creature, heralding a research renaissance in a country slowly emerging from decades of war.

2   A paper published Wednesday in the *Annals of the Brazilian Academy of Sciences* describes a long-necked, plant-eating sauropod, among the largest creatures ever to have walked the earth. The international team that found and identified the fossilized forelimb bone say it is from a previously unknown dinosaur, citing unique skeletal characteristics.

3   The fossil was found along with fish and shark teeth in what would have been a sea bed 90 million years ago, leading its discoverers to believe the dinosaur might have been washed into the sea and torn apart by ancient sharks.

4   The new dinosaur has been dubbed Angolatitan adamastor—Angolatitan means "Angolan giant" and the adamastor is a sea giant from Portuguese sailing myths.

—Donna Bryson, "1st Dinosaur Fossil Discovered in Angola."
Copyright © 2011 by The Associated Press. Reprinted by permission.

Tone: objective   N

subjective   +   −

5.

HERE IS A SMALL FACT

You are going to die.

I am in all truthfulness attempting to be cheerful about this whole topic, though most people find themselves hindered in believing me, no matter my protestations. Please, trust me. I most definitely can be cheerful. I can be amiable. Agreeable. Affable. And that's only the A's. Just don't ask me to be nice. Nice has nothing to do with me.

—Zusak, *The Book Thief*, p. 1

Tone: objective   N

subjective   +   −

Section Review: Distinguishing Between Denotation and Connotation

Fill in the following visual.

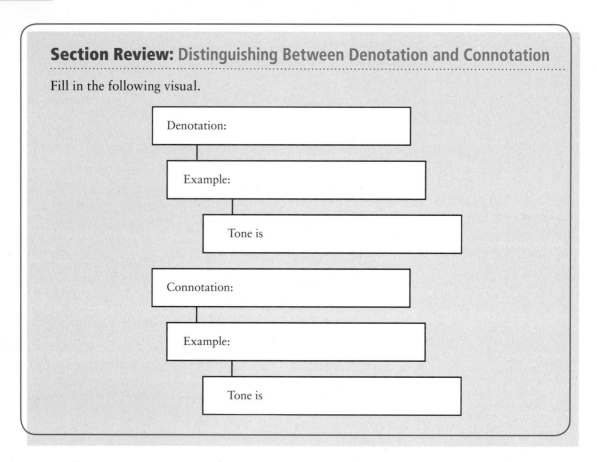

Considering a Word's Degree of Intensity

Several kinds of words can have connotations. For example, one noun that has connotations is *home* ("home is where the heart is"), and one verb with connotations is *scurry* (rats scurry). However, another kind of word, the adjective, has the job of stating outright what the characteristics of a person, place, thing, or idea are. Examples of adjectives are *gorgeous, manipulative,* and *ecstatic.*

When you are trying to understand an author's tone, look for adjectives that will show you the degree of intensity with which the author describes ideas and events. Many words can have the same basic meaning, but they express different degrees of intensity. Look at these words, which all share the definition of "not cold":

cool lukewarm warm hot boiling

LOW INTENSITY ⟶ HIGH INTENSITY

The words are arranged from least hot to most hot. Knowing what degree of intensity an author is using can help you understand the tone. Here's an example:

> Victor was lukewarm about the delay.

> Victor was boiling about the delay.

The words *lukewarm* and *boiling* here suggest different emotional states. In the first sentence, Victor isn't terribly bothered by the delay, but he's not happy about it either. In the second sentence, he is very angry. The first sentence suggests low intensity, the second sentence high intensity.

INTERACTION 8–4 | **Identify Degrees of Intensity**

Each numbered item shown here starts with a definition that begins with the word *not*. The group of words following that all share this common definition. (Look up the words whose meanings you don't know in a dictionary.) Number the words so that the lowest-intensity word is 1, the medium-intensity word is 2, and the highest-intensity word is 3.

1. "not dark"   _____ gleaming   _____ glowing   _____ glaring

2. "not brand new" _____ shabby   _____ threadbare   _____ old-fashioned

3. "not mature"   _____ immature   _____ inexperienced   _____ naïve

4. "not polluted"   _____ clear   _____ pristine   _____ uncontaminated

5. "not big"   _____ minuscule   _____ petite   _____ small

Section Review: Considering a Word's Degree of Intensity

Put the following words in order based on intensity from lowest to highest.

rich   wealthy   affluent   millionaire   comfortable

lowest intensity ←————————————————————→ highest intensity

Learning to Use More Specific Tone Words

The words *subjective* and *objective* are very general. It is helpful to become familiar with a range of more specific words you can use to describe an author's tone, especially a subjective tone. If you want to be able to talk in class about an author's ideas or write about them for a college assignment, you will need to use words that describe the author's tone more specifically.

You have been looking at connotation and denotation in the sense of positive, neutral, and negative, and you can also use that spectrum to think about the specific description of the tone of a piece of writing.

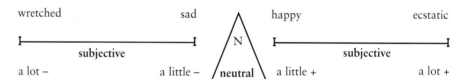

| wretched | sad | happy | ecstatic |

As you read and are trying to determine tone, you can ask yourself if the author is using words that are positive (a lot or a little), negative (a lot or a little), or neutral, and then choose a term to describe the tone used. Here are some examples:

− Negative −	Neutral	+ Positive +
alarmed	balanced	amused
angry	denotative	appreciative
annoyed	factual	blessed
apathetic	impartial	celebratory
bitter	informative	cheerful
cynical	just	elated
desperate	matter-of-fact	excited
disbelieving	objective	humorous
frustrated	unbiased	inspirational
hyperbolic	unprejudiced	intrepid
indignant		loving
ironic		nostalgic
irreverent		optimistic
mocking		relieved
outraged		respectful
panicked		righteous

— Negative —	Neutral	+ Positive +
pessimistic		sensational
reticent		sincere
sarcastic		supportive
shocked		suspenseful
skeptical		thoughtful
urgent		wry

Here is an example of how you can apply this strategy when you are reading.

1. Circle the connotative words and indicate with a + or − whether they are positive or negative.

> Bonnie and Clyde's image as skilled gangsters was a (farce.) The reality is that they were (blundering) criminals whose two-year crime spree was a (reign of error.)

2. Determine from your markings whether the tone is objective and neutral, or subjective in either the positive or negative direction.

   Tone: objective   N

        (subjective)   +   (−)

3. If the tone is subjective, think about the intensity and meanings of the connotations and decide on a specific word that best describes the tone. If the tone is objective, you could write "factual" (or some other neutral word).

   Specific tone word based on the intensity and meanings of the connotation:

   Mocking _____

INTERACTION 8–5   **Find the Specific Tone Word**

Read the following passages. Pay attention to the tone as you are reading. Circle any connotative tone words. Determine if the tone is objective and neutral, or subjective in either the positive or negative direction. Then choose the best specific tone word for that passage.

1.

> Zainab Salbi is Founder and CEO of Women for Women International, a grassroots humanitarian and development organization helping women survivors of wars rebuild their lives. Since 1993, the organization has helped 299,000 women survivors of wars access social and economic opportunities through a program of rights awareness training, vocational skills education, and access to income generating opportunities, thereby ultimately contributing to the political and economic health of their communities. In its 17-year history, the organization has distributed more than $95 million in direct aid and micro credit loans and has impacted more than 1.6 million family members. For its work "alleviating human suffering," Women for Women International was awarded the 2006 Conrad Hilton Humanitarian Award, becoming the first women's organization to receive this honor.
>
> —Copyright © Women for Women International. www.womenforwomen.org.
> Reprinted by permission.

Tone: objective   N

   subjective   +   −

Specific tone word based on the intensity of the connotation:

_____

2.

> He had lied to her, I realized, and lied to me. He had taken advantage of my own cross-country trip to slip away—a week ago, she was saying, by bus, right after I had set out myself—and had gone off for some reason unknown to either of us. It had taken the Zdrevkov clinic staff three whole days to track my grandma down after he died, to tell her and my mother that he was dead, arrange to send his body. It had arrived at the City morgue that morning, but by then, I was already four hundred miles from home, standing in the public bathroom at the last service station before the border, the pay phone against my ear, my pant legs rolled up, sandals in hand, bare feet slipping on the green tiles under the broken sink.
>
> —Obreht, *The Tiger's Wife*, pp. 8–9

Tone: objective   N

   subjective   +   −

Specific tone word based on the intensity of the connotation:

_____

3.

> 1 The silence was deafening. Laura Frye sat in the corner of a leather sofa in the den, hugged her knees and listened to it, minute after minute after minute. The wheeze of the heat through the vents couldn't pierce it. Nor could the slap of the rain on the windows, or the rhythmic tic of the ship's clock on the shelf behind the desk.
>
> 2 It was five in the morning and her husband still wasn't home. He hadn't called. He hadn't sent a message. His toothbrush was in the bathroom along with his razor, his after shave, and the sterling comb and brush set Laura had given him for their twentieth anniversary the summer before. The contents of his closet were intact, right down to the small duffel he took with him to the sports club every Monday, Wednesday, and Friday. If he had slept somewhere else, he was totally ill equipped, which wasn't like Jeffrey at all, Laura knew. He was a precise man, a creature of habit. He never traveled, not for so much as a single night, without fresh underwear, a clean shirt, and a bar of deodorant soap.
>
> 3 More than that, he never went anywhere without telling Laura, and that was what frightened her the most. She had no idea where he was or what had happened.
>
> —Delinsky, *A Betrayed Woman*, p. 1

Tone: objective   N

subjective   +   −

Specific tone word based on the intensity of the connotation:

_____

4.

> We've known each other since we were boys; we went to school together. He was one of my closest friends, with thick glasses, reddish hair that he hated, and a voice that cracked when he was emotional. I didn't know he was still alive and then one day I was walking down East Broadway and I heard his voice. I turned around. His back was to me, he was standing in front of the grocer's asking for the price of some fruit. I thought: You're hearing things, you're such a dreamer, what is the likelihood—your boyhood friend? I stood frozen on the sidewalk. He's in the ground, I told myself. Here you are in the United States of America, there's McDonald's, get a grip. I waited just to make sure. I wouldn't have recognized his face. But. The way he walked

was unmistakable. He was about to pass me, I put my arm out. I didn't know what I was doing, maybe I was seeing things, I grabbed his sleeve. *Bruno,* I said. He stopped and turned. At first he seemed scared and then confused. *Bruno.* He looked at me, his eyes began to fill with tears. I grabbed his other hand, I had one sleeve and one hand. *Bruno.* He started to shake. He touched his hand to my cheek. We were in the middle of the sidewalk, people were hurrying past, it was a warm day in June. His hair was thin and white. He dropped the fruit. *Bruno.*

—Krauss, *The History of Love,* pp. 5–6

Tone: objective   N

subjective   +   –

Specific tone word based on the intensity of the connotation:

_____

5.

1   The thousand injuries of Fortunato I had borne as I best could, but when he ventured upon insult, I vowed revenge. You, who so well know the nature of my soul, will not suppose, however, that I gave utterance to a threat. At length I would be avenged; this was a point definitively settled—but the very definitiveness with which it was resolved precluded the idea of risk. I must not only punish, but punish with impunity. A wrong is unredressed when retribution overtakes its redresser. It is equally unredressed when the avenger fails to make himself felt as such to him who has done the wrong.

2   It must be understood that neither by word nor deed had I given Fortunato cause to doubt my good will. I continued as was my wont, to smile in his face, and he did not perceive that my smile NOW was at the thought of his immolation.

—Poe, "The Cask of Amontillado"

Tone: objective   N

subjective   +   –

Specific tone word based on the intensity of the connotation:

_____

Section Review: Learning to Use More Specific Tone Words

Place the following words into the correct columns of the table.

anxious	embittered	impartial	lighthearted
balanced	fair	incensed	respectful
charming	fortunate	informative	uncaring
denotative	grateful	irritated	

– Negative –	Neutral	+ Positive +

Understanding the Different Tones of Literal and Figurative Language

- "It's raining cats and dogs." This statement is a figure of speech (more specifically, it is hyperbole—an intentional exaggeration).

- "It is raining very hard." This statement is literal.

Figurative language, like connotation, has a subjective tone: it reveals the author's emotions about whatever he or she is describing. Literal language, on the other hand, is linked to denotation. Literal language often appears in the form of facts, and it has a matter-of-fact or objective tone.

We will discuss four common figures of speech—simile, metaphor, personification, and hyperbole.

A Simile Is Like a Metaphor, but a Metaphor Is Not a Simile

Simile: An indirect comparison of two things using the words "like" or "as" (A is like B).

Metaphor: A direct comparison of two things without using the words "like" or "as" (A is B).

Here are two examples for you to compare:

Simile: During the campaign for the presidency, many saw Barack Obama as a rock star. (Notice the indirect comparison of Obama and a rock star.)

Metaphor: Barack Obama is hope and change. (Notice the direct comparison of Obama to hope and change. In other words, he is a direct representation of hope and change.)

INTERACTION 8–6 | **Identify Metaphors and Similes**

Can you determine whether the following statements from popular songs (from a variety of eras and genres) are metaphors or similes? Circle the correct choice.

1. "It seems to me you lived your life like a candle in the wind." —Elton John, "Candle in the Wind," 1973 and 1997

   metaphor   simile

2. "I am a rock. I am an island." —Simon and Garfunkel, "I Am a Rock," 1966

   metaphor   simile

3. "Now pump it up and back it up like a Tonka truck." —Jennifer Lopez, "On the Floor," 2011

   metaphor   simile

4. "You are the sunshine of my life." —Stevie Wonder, "You Are the Sunshine of My Life," 1973

metaphor   simile

5. "We all fall down like toy soldiers." —Eminem, "Like Toy Soldiers," 2004

metaphor   simile

Personification

Personification is the act of giving an inanimate object (something that isn't alive or can't move) characteristics of an animate being (something that is alive or can move):

The tears [inanimate] ran [animate] down her face.

Fuse/Jupiter Images

Think of cartoons. These are inanimate objects that are animated. Get it? Animation!

Look for examples of personification in this classic poem by Carl Sandburg:

Fog

Carl Sandburg (1878–1967)

The fog comes
on little cat feet.

It sits looking
over harbor and city
on silent haunches
and then moves on.

—Carl Sandburg, "The Fog" from CHICAGO POEMS. Copyright 1916 by Holt, Rinehart and Winston, renewed 1944 by Carl Sandburg. Reprinted by permission of Houghton Mifflin Harcourt Publishing Company.

This short poem personifies fog. The fog "comes on little cat feet" and "sits looking" and "moves on"—all actions of a living being.

INTERACTION 8-7 **Find Personification in Poetry**

Read the following poem and mark the personifications you find. Then explain how personification is present in the poem.

Two Sunflowers Move in the Yellow Room

William Blake (1757–1827)

"Ah, William, we're weary of weather,"
said the sunflowers, shining with dew.
"Our traveling habits have tired us.
Can you give us a room with a view?"

They arranged themselves at the window
and counted the steps of the sun,
and they both took root in the carpet
where the topaz tortoises run.

Explain the personification: _____

_____

Hyperbole

"If I've told you once, I've told you a thousand times!" If your parent or significant other ever hurled these words at you, their point was to make you realize you haven't been paying close enough attention to their wishes. Hyperbole is intentional exaggeration to make or empha-size a point. Hyperbole is meant to be taken figuratively.

Some examples of hyperbole include:

- Someone rich might "have more money than God."

- Someone waiting a long time might say, "That took forever!"

- Someone hungry might say, "I am so hungry I could eat a horse."

INTERACTION 8–8 | **Think About Hyperbole**

By yourself or collaboratively, remember or create one hyperbolic statement for the following topics.

1. Poverty or wealth

_____

2. Time

_____

3. Food

_____

INTÉRACTION 8–9 | **Metaphor, Simile, Personification, or Hyperbole?**

Read the following passage and identify (by highlighting, circling, underlining, or bracketing) the metaphor, simile, personification, or [hyperbole] used within it.

> How does one tell the angel he has just met that he is smitten by her? Might she think it's a line—a dishonorable come-on? Or maybe think that he is a shaky boat riding on shallow emotions tossed around like the waves of the beach where he met her? Or maybe he is the devil. But that's a bit too strong . . . She'll just be flattered and humor him because, after all, she is as sweet as the Mediterranean breeze, and she knows that he is leaving soon, after all. You know it's funny how one's mind gets captured by the fear of the unknown, frozen with the possibility

of rejection, and barraged by "what ifs" when all it really takes is the timing of mutual truth, a common interest, and the guiding hand of Providence. I wonder if the breeze carries my thoughts to the girl on my left, or if I'll be brave enough to take a deep breath and say what I'm sure my actions reveal. I know my eyes do because they are the ever-honest windows to the timidity of my soul. If the rest of me was as courageously revealing as my eyes ... But words must be spoken to carry the confirmation of "smittenness;" otherwise, the moment fades and no stances are ever taken and time wanders into anonymity ...

Understanding Irony

A famous pair of lines from the poem "The Rime of the Ancient Mariner," written in 1798 by Samuel Coleridge, illustrates irony:

Alperium/BigStockPhoto.com

Water, water, everywhere,
Nor any drop to drink.

This is ironic because men are on a ship surrounded by water but dying of thirst because it is salt water, so they cannot drink it.

In general, irony is the use of words or images to express the opposite of what is said. To understand irony, you need to understand (infer) what the expected response or action would have been in the situation.

There are three common types of irony.

1. **Verbal irony:** The words used have an unexpected meaning. For example, we often say "Oh, great!" or "That's fantastic!" when something bad happens. We do not mean those words literally; we actually mean the opposite.

2. **Situational irony:** What happens is unexpected or is the opposite of our expectations. For example, you save for six months to buy yourself an iPad and then you get one as a gift a week later.

3. **Dramatic irony:** The audience or reader knows more about what is going on than the character does. The ending of the iconic play *Romeo and Juliet* is a great example. The audience knows Juliet is simply sleeping, but Romeo thinks she is dead and so takes his own life.

INTERACTION 8–10   **Identify Irony**

A. What kind of irony is represented in the images below? Circle the type of irony and explain your answer.

1.

Jim West Photography

Verbal   Situational   Dramatic

Explanation: _____

_____

2.

Janet Fekete/Workbook Stock/Getty Images

Verbal   Situational   Dramatic

Explanation: _____

_____

3.

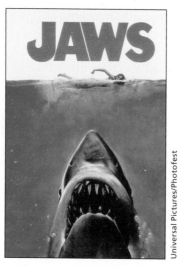

Universal Pictures/Photofest

Verbal   Situational   Dramatic

Explanation: _____

_____

4.

© Bob Hosea/Shutterstock.com

Verbal   Situational   Dramatic

Explanation: _____

_____

B. Find and explain the irony in the following poem.

5.

> # We Real Cool
>
> ### Gwendolyn Brooks (1917–2000)
>
> THE POOL PLAYERS.
> SEVEN AT THE GOLDEN SHOVEL.
>
> We real cool. We
> Left school. We
>
> Lurk late. We
> Strike straight. We
>
> Sing sin. We
> Thin gin. We
>
> Jazz June. We
> Die soon.
>
> —Gwendolyn Brooks, from BLACKS. Copyright © 1991 by Gwendolyn Brooks
> Blakely. Reprinted by consent of Brooks Permissions.

What kind of irony is found in this poem?

Verbal   Situational   Dramatic

Explanation: _____

_____

C. Find and explain the irony in the following quotes.

6. "The deeper that sorrow carves into your being, the more joy you can contain. Is not the cup that holds your wine the very cup that was burned in the potter's oven?" —Kahlil Gibran

Explanation: _____

_____

7. "I was seldom able to see an opportunity until it had ceased to be one."
   —Mark Twain

   Explanation: _____

   _____

8. "In order to save the relationship / We will never see each other again." —Bob Hulman

   Explanation: _____

   _____

9. "We spend the first 12 months of our children's lives teaching them to walk and talk and the next 12 [years] teaching them to sit down and shut up."
   —Phyllis Diller

   Explanation: _____

   _____

10. "I am free of all prejudices. I hate everyone equally." —W.C. Fields

    Explanation: _____

    _____

Section Review: Understanding the Different Tones of Literal and Figurative Language

Define and give an example of each of the following terms.

Term	Definition	Example
Simile		
Metaphor		
Personification		
Hyperbole		
Verbal irony		
Situational irony		
Dramatic irony		

Understanding How Tone Supports the Author's Purpose

As you reviewed in the beginning of this chapter, an author's general purpose might be to persuade readers, to inform readers, or to express and evoke emotions. The author's tone supports the purpose. (See Table 8.1.)

Table 8.1 Tone Supports Purpose

General purpose	General tone
To inform (teach) readers	Objective: Focusing on facts and not on the author's feelings about the facts, matter-of-fact, impersonal
To express the feelings or thoughts of the writer (or, in fiction, those of the characters being developed) to the reader, or to evoke the reader's emotions	Subjective: Emotional (sad, happy, funny, exciting, and every other emotion), personal
To persuade readers to believe or do something	Subjective: Personal

Subjective writing uses words with connotations and different degrees of intensity. The author's goal is to create emotional states—either persuading readers to feel certain emotions or being expressive by revealing the writer's emotions to the reader. However, the writing may still include facts and information.

Objective writing uses words without many connotations and with fewer degrees of intensity. The author's goal is to help readers understand with their minds rather than to feel emotions. Because connotations suggest the author's emotional stance, the lack of words with such meanings suggests an attempt to be objective rather than subjective.

Here are some examples of the connection between purpose and tone.

Informative Purpose and Objective Tone

Greg Mortenson and David Oliver Relin wrote *Three Cups of Tea: One Man's Mission to Promote Peace . . . One School at a Time.* This is the story of Greg Mortenson's attempt to overcome issues of poverty and cross-cultural divides through educating girls in rural villages in Pakistan and Afghanistan.

BOOKS-AUTHORS/MORTENSON REUTERS/ Central Asia Institute/Handout

These sentences inform readers about the book's title, the authors' names, and the book's subject. It doesn't give the writer's thoughts or feelings about the author or the book. It just reports the facts. So it has an objective tone.

Expressive Purpose and Subjective Tone

1   Arriving in Korphe with Dr. Greg, Bhangoo and I were welcomed with open arms, the head of a freshly killed ibex, and endless cups of tea. And as we listened to the Shia children of Korphe, one of the world's most impoverished communities, talk about how their hopes and dreams for the future had grown exponentially since a big American arrived a decade ago to build them the first school their village had ever known, the general and I were done for.

2   "You know," Bhangoo said, as we were enveloped in a scrum of 120 students tugging us by the hands on a tour of their school, "flying with President Musharraf, I've become acquainted with many world leaders, many outstanding gentlemen and ladies. But I think Greg Mortenson is the most remarkable person I've ever met."

—Relin, Introduction to *Three Cups of Tea: One Man's Mission to Promote Peace . . . One School at a Time*, pp. 2–3

This is an excerpt from the introduction to *Three Cups of Tea*. In it, the co-author, David Oliver Relin, expresses feelings from his own experiences. The tone is subjective.

Persuasive Purpose and Subjective Tone

Three Cups of Tea is a nicely written as well as engaging book. It gives a genuine portrait of spirited people. It is a fantastic and stirring story of an incredible man and his journey of failures and successes. It is a must read!

These sentences tell readers what a reviewer thinks about the book and tells you that you "must" read it. Others might not agree. The purpose is persuasive, and the tone is subjective.

INTERACTION 8–11 | **Understand How Tone Supports the Author's Purpose**

Read the following excerpts and answer the questions that follow.

> She watched his hands, but what pulled on her was the dark green glint of his eyes. He observed her acutely, seeming to evaluate her hill-inflected vowels for the secrets behind her "yep" and "nope." His grin turned down on the corners instead of up, asking a curved parenthetical question above his right-angled chin. She could not remember a more compelling combination of features on any man she'd ever seen.
>
> —Kingsolver, *Prodigal Summer*, p. 4

1. What is the general purpose of this reading?

    a. To persuade the reader that the man is good-looking.

    b. To inform the reader about what the man looks like.

    c. To express to the readers the main character's first meeting with a man she finds attractive.

2. Circle the general tone of this reading.

    objective   N

    subjective   +   −

3. What is the specific tone of this passage? _____

> And then our mom got sick, sicker than a person should ever be allowed to get. I was twelve when she got her diagnosis and I was furious. There is no justice and no logic, the cancer doctors cooed around me; I don't remember the exact words they used, but I could not decode a note of hope. One of the nurses brought me chocolate duds from the vending machine that stuck in my throat. These doctors were always stooping to talk to us, or so it seemed to me, like every doctor on her ward was a giant, seven or eight feet tall. Mom fell through the last stages of her cancer at a frightening speed. She no longer resembled our mother. Her head got soft and bald like a baby's head. We had to watch her sink into her own face. One night she dove and she didn't come back. Air cloaked the hole that she left and it didn't once tremble, no bubbles, it seemed she really wasn't going to surface. Hilola Jane Bigtree, world-class alligator wrestler, terrible cook, mother of three, died in a dryland hospital bed in West Davey on an overcast Wednesday, March 10, at 3:12 p.m.
>
> —Russell, *Swamplandia!*, p. 7

4. What is the general purpose of this reading?

    a. To persuade the reader that cancer is a horrible way to die.

    b. To inform the reader of how cancer can take any one of us, from children to mothers.

    c. To express to the readers an emotional description of the loss of a mother.

5. Circle the general tone of this reading.

    objective   N

    subjective   +   −

6. What is the specific tone of this passage? _____

---

1   "I can get married anytime I want to," Lucy said stubbornly. "I won't have to ask your permission. I'll be a grown-up woman."

2   "That's the spirit, Lucy," I applauded. "Don't listen to a thing your parents say. That's the only rule of life I want you to be sure and follow."

3   "You don't mean that. You're just talking, Daddy," Chandler said, leaning her head back under my chin. "I mean Dad," she corrected herself.

4   "Remember what I told you. Nobody told me this kind of stuff when I was a kid," I said seriously, "but parents were put on earth for the sole purpose of making their children miserable. It's one of God's most important laws. Now listen to me. Your job is to make me and Mama believe that you're doing and thinking everything we want you to. But you're really not. You're thinking your own thoughts and going out on secret missions. Because Mama and I are screwing you up."

5   "How are you screwing us up?" Jennifer asked.

6   "He embarrasses us in front of our friends," Lucy suggested.

7   "I do not. But I know we're screwing you up a little bit every day. If we knew how we were doing it, we'd stop. We wouldn't do it ever again, because we adore you. But we're parents and we can't help it. It's our job to screw you up. Do you understand?"

8   "No," they agreed in a simultaneous chorus.

9   "Good," I said, taking a sip of my drink. "You're not supposed to understand us. We're your enemies. You're supposed to wage guerrilla warfare against us."

10   "We're not gorillas," Lucy said primly. "We're little girls."

—Conroy, *Prince of Tides*, p. 12

7. What is the general purpose of this reading?

   a. To persuade the reader that parents and children are indeed enemies even though they love each other.

   b. To inform the reader of how one father's wit and humor makes family life enjoyable for his family.

   c. To express to the readers a witty and innocent exchange between a father and his young daughters.

8. Circle the general tone of this reading.

   objective   N

   subjective   +   −

9. What is the specific tone of this passage? _____

Can You Go to College Without Debt?

1   Harvard fees and tuition can run more than $50,000 per year. But do you need to go to Harvard? Probably not. While state schools cost money too, their yearly tuition averages only around $7,000–8,000. The question is, can you go to college without accumulating a bunch of debt? The answer is yes. Here are a few ideas to mull over.

2   Apply for scholarships. Don't just apply for one or two, but apply for many. Ben Kaplan, who wrote *How to Go to College Almost for Free*, says that most people only apply for one or two and then quit. He says that by this time you have done 60 percent of the work and should apply for 10. He should know. He applied and received over $90,000 in scholarships and graduated with a Harvard degree almost free! Keep in mind, the worst that can happen is you are told no, but what if you are told yes?

3   Work. Your family or roommates might think you are crazy, but if you work two or three jobs while going to school, you can pay as you go. Now, you have to be dedicated and motivated, but can you just imagine how it would feel to graduate without any school loans? Not to mention, being busy would keep you out of trouble! One specific benefit that this can give you is that you will have some nice work experience when you graduate. This will give you a competitive edge in a tough job market.

4   Consider two-year schools. While most people seem to want the prestigious four-year school experience, the reality is that those schools are expensive and many freshmen fail out. A better (and cheaper) plan might be to attend a community college (while living at home). You can earn your

two-year degree and then transfer to a four-year school. This will save you tons of money, plus many universities give scholarships to students in clubs like Phi Theta Kappa, an honors society. However, be sure to stay in-state, which will save you even more money.

5   While a degree is essential in this day and age, debt isn't. Be smart about your schooling. Plan ahead, work hard, and be creative. You might just find yourself graduating debt-free, which means no stress. The sky's the limit!

10. What is the general purpose of this reading?

   a. To persuade the reader that they can graduate with a college degree and be debt-free.

   b. To inform the reader of how much it costs to go to an Ivy League school like Harvard versus a state school.

   c. To express to the readers stories of students who have graduated debt-free.

11. Circle the general tone of this reading.

   objective   N

   subjective   +   −

12. What is the specific tone of this passage? _____

1   Take a look at the following list of numbers: 4, 8, 5, 3, 9, 7, 6. Read them out loud to yourself. Now look away, and spend twenty seconds memorizing that sequence before saying them out loud again.

2   If you speak English, you have about a 50 percent chance of remembering that sequence perfectly. If you're Chinese, though, you're almost certain to get it right every time. Why is that? Because as human beings we store digits in a memory loop that runs for about two seconds. We most easily memorize whatever we can say or read within that two second span. And Chinese speakers get that list of numbers—4, 8, 5, 3, 9, 7, 6—right every time because—unlike English speakers—their language allows them to fit all those seven numbers into two seconds.

3   That example comes from Stanislas Dehaene's book "The Number Sense," and as Dehaene explains:

   Chinese number words are remarkably brief. Most of them can be uttered in less than one-quarter of a second (for instance, 4 is 'si' and 7 'qi'). Their English equivalents—"four," "seven"—are longer: pronouncing them takes about one-third of a second. The

> memory gap between English and Chinese apparently is entirely due to this difference in length. In languages as diverse as Welsh, Arabic, Chinese, English and Hebrew, there is a reproducible correlation between the time required to pronounce numbers in a given language and the memory span of its speakers. In this domain, the prize for efficacy goes to the Cantonese dialect of Chinese, whose brevity grants residents of Hong Kong a rocketing memory span of about 10 digits.
>
> —Gladwell, *Outliers*, pp. 227–228

13. What is the general purpose of this reading?

   a. To persuade the reader that the Chinese are smarter at math than the rest of the world.

   b. To inform the reader how the shorter amount of time taken to pronounce numbers in Chinese leads to Chinese speakers' ability to remember numbers.

   c. To express to readers an interesting story of why Chinese are better at math than the rest of the world.

14. Circle the general tone of this reading.

   objective   N

   subjective   +   −

15. What is the specific tone of this passage? _____

Section Review: Understanding How Tone Supports the Author's Purpose

Fill in the following box.

General purpose	General tone
Persuasive	
Informative	
Expressive	

Chapter Summary Activity:
Evaluating the Author's Purpose and Tone

Chapter 8 has discussed how to think about an author's purpose and how to read and recognize an author's tone based on the words he or she uses. Fill in the following Reading Guide by completing each idea on the left with information from Chapter 8 on the right. You can return to this guide throughout the course as a reminder of how to recognize an author's purpose and tone.

Reading Guide to Evaluating the Author's Purpose and Tone

Complete this idea	with information from Chapter 8.
List the three general purposes of writing:	1. _____ 2. _____ 3. _____
Name three strategies to predict purpose:	4. _____ 5. _____ 6. _____
Denotation is defined as	7. _____ _____
Connotation is defined as	8. _____ _____
Pick a word that describes the tone of denotation:	9. _____
Pick three broad words that describe the tone of connotation:	10. _____ 11. _____ 12. _____
The part of speech that explicitly states connotation is the	13. _____
Many words can have the same basic meaning, but they express different	14. _____
A simile is defined as	15. _____
Two words that indicate a simile are:	16. _____ 17. _____
A metaphor is defined as	18. _____
A personification is defined as	19. _____ _____
Hyperbole can be defined as	20. _____
The three types of irony are:	21. _____ 22. _____ 23. _____

Complete this idea	with information from Chapter 8.
The following is an example of what type of irony? A headline that reads "Olympic Swimmer, Gold Medalist Drowns"	24. _____
25. Think about what your reading strategies were before you read Chapter 8. How did they differ from the suggestions here? Write your thoughts. _____ _____ _____	

ENGAGE YOUR SKILLS
Evaluating the Author's Purpose and Tone

A. Purpose and Tone

Determine the purpose and tone of the following excerpts.

> One person's picture postcard is someone else's normal. This was the landscape whose every face we knew: giant saguaro cacti, coyotes, mountains, the wicked sun reflecting off bare gravel. We were leaving it now in one of its uglier moments which made good-bye easier but also seemed like a cheap shot—like ending a romance right when your partner has really bad bed hair. The desert that day looked like a nasty case of prickly heat caught in a long naked wince.
>
> —Kingsolver, *Animal Vegetable Miracle: A Year of Food Life*, p. 1

1. What is the general purpose of this reading?

   a. To persuade the reader that the desert is an ugly place.

   b. To inform the reader of what deserts look like.

   c. To express to readers a vivid description of moving from a place one loves.

2. Circle the general tone of this reading.

   objective   N

   subjective   +   –

3. What is the specific tone of this passage? _____

Myth: Shark Attacks Are Common

1   Despite the media hype, the fact is that sharks do not target humans as the source of a good meal. Occasionally, sharks do mistake humans for their usual food or feel threatened and react to protect themselves, but such incidents are extremely rare.

2   According to the International Shark Attack File (ISAF), in 2006, there were 62 confirmed cases of unprovoked shark attacks on humans worldwide. Of these attacks, 4 proved to be fatal. In that same year, there were 39 attacks and no fatalities in the United States.

3   You have a better chance of dying by a lightning strike, or a dog bite. More children are killed while playing in a beach sand hole that collapses or while being inadvertently left in a closed car on a hot day, than there are people killed by a shark attack. A recent *New York Times* article sums it up pretty well by saying you have double the chance of dying from a coconut falling on your head.

—"Myth: Shark Attacks Are Common" from www.sharksavers.org.
Copyright © 2011 Shark Savers Inc. All rights reserved. Reprinted by permission.

---

4. What is the general purpose of this reading?

   a. To persuade the reader not to swim in the ocean due to potential shark attacks.

   b. To inform the reader of the slim statistical chance of being attacked by a shark.

   c. To express to readers the funny contrast between being killed by a falling coconut or a shark attack.

5. Circle the general tone of this reading.

   objective   N

   subjective   +   −

6. What is the specific tone of this passage? _____

Napoleon Hill says in his book *Think and Grow Rich,* "More than 500 of the most successful individuals this country has ever known told me that their greatest success came just one step beyond the point at which defeat had overtaken them. Failure is a trickster with a keen sense of irony and cunning. It takes great delight in tripping one when success is almost within reach." (p. 23)

7. What is the general purpose of this reading?

   a. To persuade the reader to read *Think and Grow Rich.*

   b. To inform the reader of what Napoleon Hill says about how success found more than 500 successful individuals.

   c. To express to the reader an interesting quote about how failure is a trickster.

8. Circle the general tone of this reading.

   objective   N

   subjective   +   −

9. What is the specific tone of this passage? _____

B. Figurative Language

   Read the following poems and decide if they contain metaphor, simile, personification, or hyperbole. Mark the example within each poem and then circle the type of figurative language used. (More than one type may be used in a single poem.) Also, describe each poem's tone.

   My life unraveled
   Like a tattered dress
   And fell to the gravel
   In a cluttered mess

10. Metaphor   Simile   Personification   Hyperbole

11. What is the specific tone of this poem? _____

   Time is so impatient . . .
   Is decorum too much to offer?
   Time waits for none
   Come to think of it . . .
   I'm not one for waiting either.

12. Metaphor   Simile   Personification   Hyperbole

13. What is the specific tone of this poem? _____

I keep trying to find some kryptonite
To lower your defense
But try as I might
My efforts are futile
You're not Superman
You're Wonder Woman

14. Metaphor   Simile   Personification   Hyperbole

15. What is the specific tone of this poem? _____

Homework! Oh, homework!

Jack Prelutsky

Homework! Oh, homework!
I hate you! You stink!
I wish I could wash you
away in the sink.
If only a bomb
would explode you to bits.
Homework! Oh, homework!
You're giving me fits
I'd rather take baths
with a man-eating shark,
or wrestle a lion
alone in the dark,
eat spinach and liver,
pet ten porcupines,
than tackle the homework
my teacher assigns.
Homework! Oh, homework!
You're last on my list.
I simply can't see
why you even exist.
If you just disappeared
it would tickle me pink.
Homework! Oh, homework!
I hate you! You stink!

—Copyright © 2003 by Jack Prelutsky. Reprinted by permission of School Survival,
www.school-survival.net

16. Metaphor   Simile   Personification   Hyperbole

17. What is the specific tone of this poem? _____

C. Irony

Read each of the following quotes and then explain how each is ironic.

18. "I dream for a living." —Steven Spielberg

    Explanation: _____

    _____

19. "A man is never more truthful than when he acknowledges himself a liar." —Mark Twain

    Explanation: _____

    _____

20. "Health consists of having the same diseases as one's neighbors." —Quentin Crisp

    Explanation: _____

    _____

MASTER YOUR SKILLS
Evaluating the Author's Purpose and Tone

A. Purpose and Tone

Read the following passages and answer the questions that follow.

Intensive Agriculturalists

1   In North America, and in most other parts of the industrialized world, resources such as land are allocated according to the principle of private individual ownership. Most English-speaking people have no difficulty understanding the concept of private ownership. When we say we "own" a piece of land, the term means that we have absolute and exclusive rights to it. We are able to sell it, give it away, rent it, or trade it for another piece of property, if we so choose. In other words, we have 100 percent rights to that piece of land. This association between private individual land ownership and intensive agriculture is at least partially due to the possibility of using the land year after year, thereby giving the land a permanent and continual value.

2   This concept of individual property rights is so entrenched in our thinking and our culture that we sometimes fail to realize that many other cultures do not share that principle with us. This cultural myopia led some early anthropologists to ask the wrong types of questions when they first encountered certain nonwestern peoples. To illustrate, when studying a small group of East African horticulturalists who also kept cattle, some early anthropologists, using their own set of linguistic categories, asked what to them seemed like a perfectly logical question: "Who owns that brown cow over there?" In actual fact, no one "owned" the cow in our sense of the term because no single individual had 100 percent rights to the beast. Instead, a number of people may have had limited rights and obligations to the brown cow. The man we see with the cow at the moment may have rights to milk the cow on Tuesdays and Thursdays, but someone else has rights to milk it on Mondays and Wednesdays. The cows are actually controlled by the larger kinship group (the lineage or extended family); the individual merely has limited rights to use the cow. This fundamental difference in property allocation is reflected in the local East African language of Swahili, which contains no word that would be comparable to the English word *own*. The closest Swahili speakers can come linguistically to conveying the notion of ownership is to use the word *nina*, which means literally "I am with."

—From FERRARO. *Cultural Anthropology*, 6e (pp. 184–185) Copyright © 2006 Cengage Learning.

1. What is the general purpose of this reading?

   a. To persuade the reader of the dangers of cultural myopia.

   b. To inform the reader of differing views of property ownership.

   c. To express to the reader an anecdotal story about East African horticulturalists.

2. Circle the general tone of this reading.

   objective   N

   subjective   +   −

3. What is the specific tone of this passage? _____

Camelot

1   "Camelot—Camelot," said I to myself. "I don't seem to remember hearing of it before. Name of the asylum, likely."

2   It was a soft, reposeful summer landscape, as lovely as a dream, and as lonesome as Sunday. The air was full of the smell of flowers, and the buzzing of insects, and the twittering of birds, and there were no people, no wagons, there was no stir of life, nothing going on. The road was mainly a winding path with hoof-prints in it, and now and then a faint trace of wheels on either side in the grass—wheels that apparently had a tire as broad as one's hand.

3   Presently a fair slip of a girl, about ten years old, with a cataract of golden hair streaming down over her shoulders, came along. Around her head she wore a hoop of flame-red poppies. It was as sweet an outfit as ever I saw, what there was of it. She walked indolently along, with a mind at rest, its peace reflected in her innocent face. The circus man paid no attention to her; didn't even seem to see her. And she—she was no more startled at his fantastic make-up than if she was used to his like every day of her life. She was going by as indifferently as she might have gone by a couple of cows; but when she happened to notice me, THEN there was a change! Up went her hands, and she was turned to stone; her mouth dropped open, her eyes stared wide and timorously, she was the picture of astonished curiosity touched with fear. And there she stood gazing, in a sort of stupefied fascination, till we turned a corner of the wood and were lost to her view. That she should be startled at me instead of at the other man, was too many for me; I couldn't make head or tail of it. And that she should seem to consider me a spectacle, and totally overlook her own merits in that respect, was another puzzling thing, and a display of magnanimity, too, that was surprising in one so young. There was food for thought here. I moved along as one in a dream.

4   As we approached the town, signs of life began to appear. At intervals we passed a wretched cabin, with a thatched roof, and about it small fields and garden patches in an indifferent state of cultivation. There were people, too; brawny men, with long, coarse, uncombed hair that hung down over their faces and made them look like animals. They and the women, as a rule, wore a coarse tow-linen robe that came well below the knee, and a rude sort of sandal, and many wore an iron collar. The small boys and girls were always naked; but nobody seemed to know it. All of these people stared at me, talked about me, ran into the huts and fetched out their families to gape at me; but nobody ever noticed that other fellow, except to make him humble salutation and get no response for their pains.

—Twain, *A Connecticut Yankee in King Arthur's Court,* pp. 27–28

4. What is the general purpose of this reading?

   a. To persuade the reader that the narrator is strange and worthy of the attention he is getting.

   b. To inform the reader of what Camelot was, where it was, and what it looked like.

   c. To express to the reader a story full of vivid detail.

5. Circle the general tone of this reading.

   objective   N

   subjective   +   −

6. What is the specific tone of this passage? _____

Review of *Water for Elephants*

Bob Hoose

1   This adaptation of Sara Gruen's Depression-era romantic-adventure has a strong appeal. The film's big top production design, dodgy carny characters and colorful costumes come off as eye-catching and entertaining. And its depiction of the rough-and-tumble, poverty-ridden world of traveling circus shows rings true.

2   And the romance? Well, that side of this rail-riding yarn is involving, if not quite as compelling. *Twilight* heartthrob Robert Pattinson is still a bit glaze-eyed and bloodless, even though he's in a decidedly non-vampire role this time around. But his Jacob is handsome, kindhearted and easy to root for. And we can see why he falls for the fragile, golden-haired Marlena. We certainly understand why he wants to rescue her from the clutches of her hateful husband and take her away to a better life.

3   That romantic but forbidden affair, though, is the movie's biggest deceit. Let's face it: Animal cruelty, heavy drinking and coarse language are all easy things to spot. But the siren's song of seemingly justified infidelity is a much more subtle thing.

4   *Water* makes its moral lapses appear perfectly righteous by portraying husband August as a megalomaniacal killer. And so, from this pic's perspective it would almost be a crime if the heroic Jacob didn't steal the man's wife away so they could have babies together and a happily ever after of their own.

—Bob Hoose, "Water for Elephants," *Focus on the Family's Plugged In Online.*
Copyright © 2011 Focus on the Family. Reprinted by permission.

7. What is the general purpose of this reading?

    a. To persuade the reader that *Water for Elephants* is a decent film with some misplaced morality.

    b. To inform the reader of the plot of *Water for Elephants*.

    c. To express to the reader a reviewer's personal opinion of *Water for Elephants*.

8. Circle the general tone of this reading.

    objective   N

    subjective   +   –

9. What is the specific tone of this passage? _____

B. Figurative Language

10–17. The following poem contains more than one type of figurative language. Mark each that is relevant and identify it in the margin.

Poetry

Nikki Giovanni (1943–present)

poetry is motion graceful
as a fawn
gentle as a teardrop
strong like the eye
finding peace in a crowded room
we poets tend to think
our words are golden
though emotion speaks too
loudly to be defined
by silence

sometimes after midnight or just before
the dawn
we sit typewriter in hand
pulling loneliness around us
forgetting our lovers or children
who are sleeping
ignoring the weary wariness
of our own logic
to compose a poem
no one understands it
it never says "love me" for poets are
beyond love

it never says "accept me" for poems seek not
acceptance but controversy
it only says "i am" and therefore
i concede that you are too
a poem is pure energy
horizontally contained
between the mind
of the poet and the ear of the reader
if it does not sing discard the ear
for poetry is song
if it does not delight discard
the heart for poetry is joy

if it does not inform then close
off the brain for it is dead
if it cannot heed the insistent message
that life is precious

which is all we poets
wrapped in our loneliness
are trying to say

—Nikki Giovanni, "Poetry" from THE WOMEN AND THE MEN. Copyright © 1970, 1974, 1975 by Nikki Giovanni. Reprinted by permission of HarperCollins Publishers.

C. Irony

Read each of the following quotes and then explain how each is ironic.

18. "Illiterate? Write today for free help." —Unknown

Explanation: _____

_____

19. "You'd be surprised how much it costs to look this cheap." —Dolly Parton

Explanation: _____

_____

20. "He has Van Gogh's ear for music." —Billy Wilder

Explanation: _____

_____

Focus on Computer and Information Sciences

College Computer and Information Sciences App

COMPUTER SCIENCE TEXTBOOK

The following reading is linked to these fields of . . .

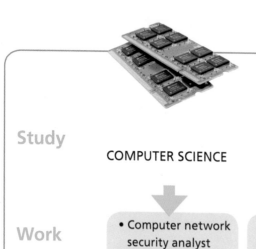  

Study

COMPUTER SCIENCE | INFORMATION SCIENCE | GRAPHIC ARTS

Work

- Computer network security analyst
- Computer programmer
- Website developer

- Database manager
- Information specialist
- Reference librarian

- Website designer
- User interface designer
- Media artist
- Animator

● Pre-Reading the Selection

The excerpt that begins on page 516 comes from the computer science textbook *Connecting with Computer Science*. The excerpt is titled "The Hacker."

Surveying the Reading

Survey the textbook selection that follows. Then check the elements that are included in this reading.

_____ Title

_____ Headings

_____ First sentences of paragraphs

_____ Words in bold or italic type

_____ Images and captions

Guessing the Purpose

Based on the source and the title of the reading selection, do you think the authors' purpose is mostly to persuade, inform, or express? _____

Predicting the Content

Based on your survey, what are three things you expect the reading selection to discuss?

- _____

- _____

- _____

Activating Your Knowledge

Think about what you know about hackers based on movies or personal experience. How would you describe a hacker? Write your thoughts below.

- _____

- _____

- _____

● Reading with Pen in Hand

Students who annotate as they read are more successful than students who do not annotate. That's why you will annotate each reading in *Engage* as you read. In the reading that follows, use the following symbols:

★ or ⟨Point⟩   to indicate a main idea

① ② ③   to indicate major details

Access the Reading CourseMate via www.cengagebrain.com to hear vocabulary words from this selection and view a video about this topic.

Reading Journal

● Can you explain the difference between a *hacker* and a *cracker*?

esoteric A synonym is given in a phrase following the word *art*. What is the meaning of *esoteric*?

subvert How did phreaks *subvert* the phone system? Determine the meaning of *subvert*.

● Can you explain what a *phreak* did?

beneficiaries Look at the example of John Draper and also consider the word parts to understand the meaning of *beneficiaries*.

The Hacker

1   The term *hacker* (or *cracker*) is often used to refer to an intruder who breaks into a computer system with malicious intent. The term originated in the 1960s, and it meant an insider who was able to manipulate a system for the good of the system. At that time, programming was a difficult and esoteric art practiced by very few people. The best programmers were called hackers as a sign of respect, and a good program that took advantage of the system as best it could was called a "hack." Over time, however, the connotation of "hacker" in the eyes of the general public has become more negative and synonymous with "cracker," although the computer security industry still differentiates between a hacker (technically proficient person) and a cracker (unwelcome system intruder).

© Pedro Miguel Sousa/Shutterstock.com

2   Around the same time, some people began illegally manipulating the AT&T phone system, mimicking certain tones to get free long-distance calls. A fellow who called himself Cap'n Crunch discovered that a whistle that came in boxes of this cereal could be used to subvert the phone system. The practice was called **phreaking,** and those who did it became known as phreaks.

3   Some phreaks were becoming more interested in computers as the microcomputer revolution took hold. In fact, some of these characters went legit and became beneficiaries of the revolution. Cap'n Crunch, whose real name is John Draper, helped write some of the most important applications for Microsoft. Unfortunately, a number of characters applied their technical proficiency to computers in a negative way. By breaking into mainframes and creating viruses,

they changed the word "hacker" from meaning a technically savvy insider helping to make the system better to a potentially dangerous outsider. The labels "cracker" or just plain "criminal" are also used.

○ Why did the term *hacker* change from having a positive to a negative meaning?

4   These hackers are now the semi-romantic figures from movies, books, and magazines who wear the "black hat" and threaten the world or the "white hat" and promise to save the world. Remember the movie *War Games*? Matthew Broderick was a computer "geek" immersed in computer games and dialed random numbers in the hope he could break into a company's system to play games. He ended up breaking into the Pentagon's defense system and almost started World War III. But who are these hackers in reality? Many intruders are fairly innocent computer users who stumble into a security hole and cause problems. Intentional intruders are generally divided into two classes: those motivated primarily by the challenge of breaking into a system, called **undirected** (or **untargeted**) hackers, and those motivated by greed or **malicious** intent, called **directed** (or **targeted**) hackers. In this book, "cracker," "malicious hacker," "directed hacker," and "undirected hacker" are used to indicate an unwanted system intruder.

○ What is the difference between a "white hat" and "black hat" hacker?

malicious Look at what the directed hackers do to determine what *malicious* means.

5   Generally, the cracker profile is a male between 16 and 35 years old considered by many to be a loner. The person also tends to be intelligent as well as technically savvy. **Novice** crackers who know how to use only existing tools earn the moniker **script kiddie.** Crackers intent on remaining anonymous while they steal or damage (directed hackers) are usually the most proficient.

○ What is the difference between a "cracker" and "script kiddie"?

novice Use your logic to determine the meaning of *novice.*

6   For undirected hackers, one of the biggest motivators for cracking is bragging rights. Often these undirected hackers comb the Internet looking for **vulnerable** systems that haven't yet been cracked. After they've cracked a system, they boast about it on Internet Relay Chat (IRC), on message boards, or in magazines such as *2600: The Hacker Quarterly*. Many crackers close the security hole that they've taken advantage of after they've gained entry so that no other cracker can follow. Their justification might be to have sole control of the system. Another justification is **hacktivism.** Many crackers believe they're doing society a favor by discovering these security holes before "real criminals" do. A document on the Internet called the **Hacker's Manifesto** justifies cracker activity for this very reason.

○ What two motivators are mentioned for undirected hackers?

vulnerable What do undirected hackers do with *vulnerable* systems? What does the word mean?

7   Greed tends to motivate directed hackers, who unfortunately are usually more proficient and do not advertise their **exploits.** This

exploits What are directed hackers doing that they do not want to advertise? What are *exploits*?

○ What motivates directed hackers?

type of hacker looks for information that can be sold or used to blackmail the organization that owns it. Hackers of this type tend to target corporations that have assets of monetary value. Smart young Russian hackers, for instance, are becoming a global threat by extorting money from banks and betting firms. The Russian police have said this particular racket is just the tip of the iceberg, and no one is safe from these attacks.

○ How are malicious hackers both directed and undirected?

8   Malicious hackers—interested in vandalizing or terrorism—can be both directed and undirected. Undirected hackers tend to write viruses and worms, without knowing where they will end up. They're content with the random violence of the act. These intrusions can damage systems at many levels. Some attacks are fairly

benign Use the contrast clue of the sentence to determine what *benign* means.

benign, but others can cause billions of dollars of damage. Directed hackers usually direct their efforts at organizations or individuals where there's some perceived wrong. For example, a directed hacker might vandalize a company's Web site because he or she was fired or was dissatisfied with the company's product. Directed hackers might also be interested in making political statements. Usually, directed hackers intend to damage, not gain quiet access.

9   Whether directed or undirected, malicious, greedy, or benign, hired by a competing corporation or the Mob, or part of a terrorist organization, hackers are an increasingly expensive and dangerous aspect of computing. In monetary terms, illegal hacking becomes more expensive each year, and there seems to be no end in sight. So how do unwanted visitors hack into systems?

monetary Look at the clue that follows the comma. What does *monetary* mean?

How Do They Get In?

○ How do hackers get in?

10   The sad truth is that most intrusions could have been avoided with good system configuration, proper programming techniques, and adherence to security policies: Directed hackers can quickly take advantage of these failures to follow sound security practices. Even more quick to take advantage of systems are malicious software programs, commonly known as viruses. It takes milliseconds for a virus (or worm) to invade an unprotected system over a network. Finally, crackers take advantage of the innocent human tendency to be helpful. By starting a friendly dialogue and then asking for help, often they can get answers that help them guess passwords, for example, and use them to break into a system. This nontechnical approach—called social engineering—is often one of the most effective tools for intruders.

—From ANDERSON/FERRO/HILTON. *Connecting with Computer Science,* 2e (pp. 50–52) Copyright © 2011 Cengage Learning.

• Comprehension Questions

Write the letter of the answer on the line. Then explain your thinking.

Main Idea

_____ 1. Which of the following best states the main idea of paragraphs 1–9?

    a. Hackers are technological intruders with malicious intent.

    b. The term _hacker_ has evolved in meaning since the 1960s and has come to be negatively associated with criminal computer activity that is increasingly expensive and dangerous.

    c. Technology experts feel stymied because hackers (or crackers) cost businesses around the world billions of dollars each year and have come to be considered a digital scourge with no end in sight.

    d. Hackers have become more sophisticated since the 1960s.

WHY? What information in the selection leads you to give that answer? _____

_____

_____

_____

_____ 2. Which of the following four sentences is the broadest?

    a. For undirected hackers, one of the biggest motivators for cracking is bragging rights.

    b. After they've cracked a system, they boast about it on Internet Relay Chat (IRC), on message boards, or in magazines such as _2600: The Hacker Quarterly._

    c. Many crackers close the security hole that they've taken advantage of after they've gained entry so that no other cracker can follow.

    d. Their justification might be to have sole control of the system.

WHY? What information in the selection leads you to give that answer? _____

_____

_____

_____

Supporting Details

_____ 3. Which of the following does *not* describe a directed hacker?

a. Motivated by greed

b. Vengeful

c. Wanting bragging rights

d. Making political statements

WHY? What information in the selection leads you to give that answer? _____

_____

_____

_____

_____ 4. Which of the following statements is accurate based on the information in this reading?

a. Crackers are equally male and female.

b. A directed, malicious hacker can be motivated by revenge or perceived injustice.

c. Directed hackers are motivated by bragging rights.

d. The term *hacker* has come to have a more positive connotation since the 1960s, when it was first coined.

WHY? What information in the selection leads you to give that answer? _____

_____

_____

_____

Author's Purpose

_____ 5. What is the overall purpose of the passage?

a. To persuade readers of the detrimental impact that hackers have on computer technology.

b. To inform readers of how the meaning of the term *hacker* has evolved since it was invented in the 1960s.

c. To inform readers of what is known about who become hackers and why they decide to enter this cyberworld.

d. To entertain readers with the history of hackers, crackers, phreaks, and script kiddies.

WHY? What information in the selection leads you to give that answer? _____

_____

_____

_____

_____ 6. What is the purpose of the section "How Do They Get In?"

    a. To categorize all the different types of hackers.

    b. To suggest that the issue is the lack of effective Internet security.

    c. To explain how hackers get into computer systems.

    d. To inform the reader that despite its frequency, hacking can be prevented with proper training and security patches.

WHY? What information in the selection leads you to give that answer? _____

_____

_____

_____

Relationships

_____ 7. What relationship is shown in the following sentence? _A fellow who called himself Cap'n Crunch discovered that a whistle that came in boxes of this cereal could be used to subvert the phone system._

    a. Cause and effect

    b. Definition

    c. Space order

    d. Contrast

WHY? What information in the selection leads you to give that answer? _____

_____

_____

_____

_____ 8. Which of the following best describes the overall pattern of this reading?

    a. Definition and example

    b. Cause and effect

    c. Compare and contrast

    d. Time order

WHY? What information in the selection leads you to give that answer? _____

_____

_____

_____

Fact, Opinion, and Inference

_____ 9. Which of the following statements is an opinion?

    a. By starting a friendly dialogue and then asking for help, often hackers can get answers that help them guess passwords, for example, and use them to break into a system.

    b. The Russian police have said this particular racket is just the tip of the iceberg, and no one is safe from these attacks.

    c. Whether directed or undirected, malicious, greedy, or benign, hired by a competing corporation or the Mob, or part of a terrorist organization, hackers are an increasingly expensive and dangerous aspect of computing.

    d. Undirected hackers tend to be more intelligent than directed hackers.

WHY? What leads you to give that answer? _____

_____

_____

_____

_____ 10. Which of the following statements would the author of this passage most likely agree with?

    a. Hackers are not to blame; rather, the faulty security of the Internet and the gullibility of some employees are responsible for the mounting cost of hacking.

    b. The open nature of the Internet makes it likely that hacking will continue.

    c. All successful hackers are lonely males who could be considered "geeks."

    d. Hackers or crackers are an essential part of the Internet and make it a safer place.

WHY? What leads you to give that answer? _____

_____

_____

_____

● Mapping the Reading

Create a visual map of each of the hacker terms given in the reading above. Define each term and give an example.

● Critical Thinking Questions

CRITICAL THINKING LEVEL 3: APPLY

Francis Bacon wrote, "Opportunity makes a thief." How does this idea relate to the ideas in "The Hacker"?

_____

_____

_____

_____

CRITICAL THINKING LEVEL 4: ANALYZE

What two words are combined to form the word *hacktivism*? Based on the definition of each word, define *hacktivism*.

_____

_____

_____

_____

CRITICAL THINKING LEVEL 5: EVALUATE

Are malicious hackers examples of *hacktivism*? Why or why not?

_____

_____

_____

_____

● Language in Use

The following words (or forms of them) were used in "The Hacker." Now you can use them in different contexts. Put a word from the box into the blank lines in the following numbered sentences.

> esoteric   subvert   beneficiaries   maliciously   novice
>
> vulnerable   exploits   benign   monetary

1. The names of the outlaws Bonnie and Clyde are still fairly well known today, even though their _____ took place in the 1930s. But do you know the true story?

2. Clyde started his criminal career as a petty thief. He soon went to prison after a series of arrests for burglary. He entered prison as a _____ delinquent from the wrong side of the tracks and not as a hardened criminal.

3. However, this changed dramatically in prison. An aggressive prisoner repeatedly raped Clyde. Before his release in 1932, an embittered Clyde _____ attacked the man with a lead pipe, committing his first murder.

4. The beginning of what became a criminal spree was simply an attempt to raise funds to _____ the system that allowed his abuse in prison.

5. Bonnie's initial crime was that she was _____ to love. She loved a man who was bent on self-destruction. What followed has become legend, fueled by hearsay and exaggeration. A recommended read to find out the true story of this infamous duo is *Go Down Together: The True, Untold Story of Bonnie and Clyde* by Jeff Guinn.

● EASY Note Cards

Make a note card for each of the vocabulary words from the reading that you did not know. On one side, write the word. On the other side, divide the card into quarters and label them E, A, S, and Y. Add a word or phrase in each area so that you wind up with an example sentence, an antonym, a synonym, and, finally, a definition that shows you understand the meaning of the word with your logic. Remember that a synonym or antonym may have appeared in the reading.

Career Computer and Information Sciences App   SOCIAL TECHNOLOGY BLOG

● Pre-Reading the Selection

The excerpt that begins on page 527 comes from loose wire blog, a social technology blog. The excerpt is titled "Social Media and Politics: Truthiness and Astroturfing."

Surveying the Reading

Survey the selection that follows. Then check the elements that are included in this reading.

_____ Title

_____ Headings

_____ First sentences of paragraphs

_____ Words in bold or italic type

_____ Images and captions

Guessing the Purpose

Based on the source and the title of the reading selection, do you think the author's purpose is mostly to persuade, inform, or express? _____

Predicting the Content

Based on your survey, what are three things you expect the reading selection to discuss?

- _____

- _____

- _____

Activating Your Knowledge

What do you know of how social media has been used in politics around the world? If you do not know anything particular, think about how social media sites, like Twitter or Facebook, could be used in this arena. Write your thoughts below.

- _____

- _____

- _____

● Reading with Pen in Hand

Students who annotate as they read are more successful than students who do not annotate. That's why you will annotate each reading in *Engage* as you read. In the reading that follows, use the following symbols:

★ or (Point)   to indicate a main idea

① ② ③   to indicate major details

Access the Reading CourseMate via www.cengagebrain.com to hear vocabulary words from this selection and view a video about this topic.

Social Media and Politics: Truthiness and Astroturfing

Jeremy Wagstaff

Reading Journal

1   Just how social is social media? By which I mean: Can we trust it as a measure of what people think, what they may buy, how they may vote? Or is it as easy a place to manipulate as the real world?

    ● Can we trust social media to reveal these things?

AP Photo/Maya Alleruzzo

2   The answers to these questions aren't of academic interest only. They go right to the heart of what may be our future. More and more of our world is online. And more and more of our online world is social media: A quarter of web pages viewed in the U.S. are on Facebook. So it's not been lost on those who care about such things that (a) what we say online may add up to be a useful predictor of what we may do at the shops, the movies, at the polling booth. And (b) that social media is a worthwhile place to try to manipulate what we think, and what we do at the shops, the movies—and at the ballot box.

    ● Of all the time you spend online, what percentage of the time are you on Facebook?

3   There is plenty of evidence supporting the former. Counting the number of followers a candidate has on Facebook, for example, is apparently a pretty good indicator of whether they'll do well at the ballot box. The Daily Beast set up something called the Oracle which scanned 40,000 websites—including Twitter—to measure whether comments on candidates in the recent U.S. elections were positive, negative, neutral or mixed. It predicted 36 out of 37 Senate races and 29 out of 30 Governors' races and nearly 98% of the House races. That's pretty good.

● What is your reaction to Oracle's success in predicting political winners?

● Do you think social media has caused more interest or involvement in voting?

4   Dan Zarrella, a self-styled social media scientist, counted the followers of the Twitter feeds of 30 Senate, House and Governor races and found that in 71% of the races, the candidate with the most Twitter followers was ahead in the polls. And Facebook found that candidates with more Facebook fans than their opponents won 74% of House races, and 81% of Senate races. More than 12 million people used the "I Voted" button this year, more than double that in 2008.

5   Why is this interesting? Well, social media, it turns out, is quite a different beast to even recent phenomena such as blogs. Social media, it turns out, really is social, in that more than previous Internet methods of communication, it reflects the views of the people using it. It is, one might say, democratic.

phenomena Both blogs and social media are described as *phenomena*. You probably also know another form of this word. Use this to determine the meaning of *phenomena*.

● How is social media democratic?

6   A study by researchers from the Technical University of Munich of the 2009 federal parliamentary elections in Germany, for example, revealed that, in contrast to the bulletin boards and blogs of the past, Twitter was reflective of the way Germans voted. Unlike bulletin boards and blogs, they wrote, "heavy users were unable to impose their political sentiment on the discussion." The large number of participants, they found, "make the information stream as a whole more representative of the electorate."

impose What was it that was not *imposed*? Using this context, what does *impose* mean?

7   In other words, social media is as much a battleground for hearts and minds as the rest of the world. Even more so, perhaps, because it's easier to reach people. Forget knocking on doors or holding rallies: Just build a Facebook page or tweet. And, maybe, hire some political operators to build a fake movement, aka astroturfing?

● What is *astroturfing*?

8   Astroturfing, for those not familiar with the term, is the opposite of grassroots. If you lack the support of ordinary people, or don't have time to get it, you can still fake it. Just make it look like you've got grassroots support. Since the term was coined in the mid 1980s it's become a popular activity by marketers, political operators and governments. Astroturfing, in short, allows a politician to seem a

grassroots *Grassroots* is contrasted with "astroturfing," which is defined. What does *grassroots* mean?

lot more popular than he really is by paying folk to say how great he is.

9 Whether social media is ripe for astroturfing isn't clear. On one hand, we know that the Internet is full of fakery and **flummery**: Just because your inbox is no longer full of spam doesn't mean the Internet isn't full of it—87%, according to the latest figures from MessageLabs. You don't see it because the filters are getting better at keeping it away from you. Twitter, by contrast, is much less spammy: the latest figures from Twitter suggest that after some tweaks earlier this year the percentage of unwanted messages on the service is about 1%.

10 So Twitter isn't spammy, and it broadly reflects the electorate. But can it be gamed? We already know that Twitter can spread an idea, or meme, rapidly—only four hops are needed before more or less everyone on Twitter sees it. In late 2009 Google unveiled a new product: Real time search. This meant that, atop the usual results to a search, Google would throw in the latest matches from the real time web—in other words, Twitter and its ilk. So getting your tweets up there would be valuable if, say, you were a political operator and you wanted people to hear good things about your candidate, or bad things about your rival. But were people doing this? Two researchers from Wellesley College in Massachusetts wondered.

11 Panagiotis Takis Metaxas and Eni Mustafaraj studied the local senate race and found that they were. They looked at 185,000 Twitter messages which mentioned the two competing candidates and found that there was plenty of astroturfing going on—where political supporters were creating fake accounts and repeating each other's messages, and sending them to likely sympathizers, in the hope of their messages hitting the mainstream.

12 The researchers found one group, apparently linked to an Iowa Republican group, was sending out one tweet a second linking to websites "exposing" their rival's missteps and misstatements. Overall, the message they sent reached more than 60,000 users. The researchers concluded that "the fact that a few minutes of work, using automated scripts and exploiting the open architecture of social networks such as Twitter, makes possible reaching a large audience for free ... raises concerns about the deliberate exploitation of the medium."

13 The point here is not merely that you're **propagating** a point of view. That's just spam. But by setting up fake Twitter accounts and

---

flummery Use the synonym clue to determine what *flummery* means.

• Do you still get a lot of spam in your inbox?

• What do you think the author means when he asks if Twitter can be "gamed"?

meme You are told that *meme* is an idea, but it is a specific type of idea. Look at how this idea is spread to determine the meaning.

ilk How would Twitter be classified? What is it grouped with? What is its *ilk*?

• How does the idea of being manipulated through Twitter make you feel?

exploiting Two forms of this word are given within the sentence. What action is taking place? What does *exploiting* mean?

propagating What is being *propagated*? What is the meaning of *propagating*?

tweeting and then repeating these messages, you're creating the illusion that these views are widespread. We may ignore the first Twitter message we see exposing these views and linking to a website, but will we ignore the second or the third?

○ What is *truthiness*?

14   This discovery of Twitter astroturfing in one race has prompted researchers at Indiana University to set up a tool they call Truthy—after comedian Stephen Colbert's term to describe something that someone knows intuitively from the gut—irrespective of evidence, logic or the facts. Their tool has exposed other similar attacks which, while not explosive in terms of growth, are, they wrote in an accompanying paper, "nevertheless clear examples of coordinated attempts to deceive Twitter users." And, they point out, the danger with these Twitter messages is that unless they're caught early, "once one of these attempts is successful at gaining the attention of the community, it will quickly become indistinguishable from an organic meme."

irrespective Use the word parts *ir-* + *spect.* Also look at the description in the sentence. What does *irrespective* mean?

15   This is all interesting, for several reasons. First off, it's only in the past few months that we've woken up to what political operators seem to be doing on Twitter. Secondly, while none of these cases achieves viral levels, the relative ease with which these campaigns can be launched suggests that a lot more people will try them out. Thirdly, what does this tell us about the future of political manipulation in social media?

16   I don't know, but it's naïve to think that this is just an American thing. Or a "what do you expect in a thriving democracy?" thing. Less democratically minded organizations and governments are becoming increasingly sophisticated about the way they use the Internet to control and influence public opinion. Evgeny Morozov points to Lebanon's Hezbollah, "whose suave manipulation of cyberspace was on display during the 2006 war with Israel." My journalist friends in Afghanistan say the Taliban are more sophisticated about using the Internet than the Karzai government or NATO.

○ How can Hezbollah or the Taliban effectively use social media?

○ How does social media increase the opportunity for manipulation?

17   The good news is that researchers are pushing Twitter to improve their spam catching tools to stop this kind of thing from getting out of hand. But I guess the bigger lesson is this: While social media is an unprecedented window on, and reflection of, the populace, it is also an unprecedented opportunity for shysters, snake oil salesmen and political operators to manipulate what we think we know.

shysters Look at who *shysters* share the sentence with and what they are doing. Who is a *shyster*?

18   It may be a great channel for the truth, but truthiness may also be one step behind.

—Copyright © 2011 by Jeremy Wagstaff. Reprinted by permission.

● Comprehension Questions

Write the letter of the answer on the line. Then explain your thinking.

Main Idea

_____ 1. Which of the following best states the main idea of paragraph 9?

　　a. Whether social media is ripe for astroturfing isn't clear.

　　b. On one hand, we know that the Internet is full of fakery and flummery.

　　c. Just because your inbox is no longer full of spam doesn't mean the Internet isn't full of it—87%, according to the latest figures from MessageLabs.

　　d. Twitter, by contrast, is much less spammy: the latest figures from Twitter suggest that after some tweaks earlier this year the percentage of unwanted messages on the service is about 1%.

WHY? What information in the selection leads you to give that answer? _____

_____

_____

_____

_____ 2. What is the best main idea of this reading?

　　a. More and more of our world is online.

　　b. Social media is a worthwhile place to try to manipulate what we think, and what we do at the shops, the movies—and at the ballot box.

　　c. Although social media is an unprecedented window on, and reflection of, the populace, it is also an unprecedented opportunity for shysters, snake oil salesmen and political operators to manipulate what we think we know.

　　d. We may ignore the first Twitter message we see exposing these views and linking to a website, but will we ignore the second or the third?

WHY? What information in the selection leads you to give that answer? _____

_____

_____

_____

Supporting Details

_____ 3. Which of the following would *not* be an example of truthiness as defined by this reading?

a. The use of astroturfing

b. Hezbollah's manipulation of cyberspace

c. The Taliban's sophisticated use of the Internet

d. Oracle's predictions

WHY? What information in the selection leads you to give that answer? _____

_____

_____

_____

_____ 4. Which of the following makes the author most credible?

a. The large amount of factual data coupled with asking questions and giving thoughtful answers.

b. The author's abundant knowledge of pop culture, as evidenced by his extensive use of technical terminology.

c. The overview given of the rise of Twitter use within the political arena.

d. The easy, friendly tone that the author takes allows the reader to feel the truthiness of the author.

WHY? What information in the selection leads you to give that answer? _____

_____

_____

_____

Author's Purpose

_____ 5. What is the overall purpose of the passage?

a. To persuade readers of the important need for Twitter to monitor their sites for truthiness and astroturfing.

b. To inform readers of how astroturfing works within the realm of social media.

c. To discuss how social media is a good indicator of public interest and thought and that it is a place to manipulate what our interests are and how we think.

d. To regale readers with statistics of how Oracle is a spot-on predictor of successful political candidates.

WHY? What information in the selection leads you to give that answer? _____

_____

_____

_____

_____ 6. What is the purpose of paragraph 18?

    a. To leave the reader with a reference to an inside joke from a comedian that the author finds riotously funny.

    b. To suggest that we need to watch how social media, like Twitter, is used so that it is not abused.

    c. To show that truthiness is more important than truth when it comes to social media.

    d. To persuade the reader of the inherent corruption of humanity.

WHY? What information in the selection leads you to give that answer? _____

_____

_____

_____

Relationships

_____ 7. Which of the following is an accurate statement of the relationship between paragraphs 5 and 6?

    a. Paragraph 6 is an example of what paragraph 5 states.

    b. Both the paragraphs have the same role in the reading.

    c. There is no relationship between the paragraphs.

    d. Paragraphs 5 and 6 compare social media's impact on elections in the U.S. and Germany.

WHY? What information in the selection leads you to give that answer? _____

_____

_____

_____

_____ 8. What pattern of organization is found in paragraph 15?

  a. Cause and effect

  b. Definition

  c. Time order

  d. Classification

WHY? What information in the selection leads you to give that answer? _____

_____

_____

_____

Fact, Opinion, and Inference

_____ 9. Which of the following statements is a fact?

  a. It is interesting that social media, it turns out, really is social.

  b. Social media is an easy venue for mass manipulation.

  c. Less democratically minded organizations and governments are becoming increasingly sophisticated about the way they use the Internet to control and influence public opinion.

  d. All politicians who use Twitter employ astroturfing techniques to get the votes they need to win.

WHY? What leads you to give that answer? _____

_____

_____

_____

_____ 10. Which of the following reflects an assumption the author holds?

  a. Blogs are more effective than social media for getting a pulse of what the populace is thinking.

  b. Astroturfing is the latest craze on social media sites, with politicians and retailers alike flocking to the practice in order to gain a following.

  c. Statistically, Twitter has more spam than the average e-mail inbox.

  d. Twitter has a responsibility to monitor its site to ensure that it is not used for manipulation.

WHY? What leads you to give that answer? _____

_____

_____

_____

● Mapping the Reading

Fill in the following outline of the reading selection, including the topic, main idea, and major and minor details.

Topic + main idea: _____

    Major detail 1: _____

                                _____

           Example: _____

                                  _____

    Major detail 2: _____

                                _____

           Example: _____

                                  _____

● Critical Thinking Questions

CRITICAL THINKING LEVEL 3: APPLY

How do politicians and their followers "astroturf" offline? That is, what other kinds of activities might they engage in to make voters believe they are popular?

_____

_____

_____

_____

CRITICAL THINKING LEVEL 4: ANALYZE

Do you tend to believe a piece of gossip or an idea more if you hear it from more than one person? If more than one person says something, does that automatically mean it's more likely to be true?

_____

_____

_____

CRITICAL THINKING LEVEL 5: EVALUATE

Which of the following situations would be an example of the word _truthiness_ (as made popular by Stephen Colbert)? Explain your choice.

1. Elderly workers are unable to adapt to new technology.

2. Social media has changed the way consumers and brands interact.

3. Kopi Luwak, the most expensive coffee in the world, is harvested from civet (a cat-like mammal) poop.

_____

_____

_____

_____

● Language in Use

The following words (or forms of them) were used in "Social Media and Politics: Truthiness and Astroturfing." Now you can use them in different contexts. Put a word from the box into the blank lines in the following numbered sentences.

> phenomenon impose grassroots flummery meme ilk
>
> exploiting propagating irrespective shysters

1. Most scientists are amused by the idea of a "Bigfoot" creature. The scientific community views the whole Sasquatch legend as _____.

2. Yet _____ of any hard scientific evidence, such as remains, clear photos, or video, belief persists. In fact, there are even societies established to study Bigfoot sightings, analyze photos and videos, and give tips on how to gather good Bigfoot evidence.

3. The oldest and largest organization, the Bigfoot Field Researchers Organization (BFRO), has made its mission to solve the mystery surrounding the Bigfoot _____.

4. Although they do not _____ their beliefs on nonbelievers, they do have plenty of arguments for Bigfoot's possible existence, as well as yearly expeditions and a website dedicated to their search (you can even post your own sighting, and they will contact you to investigate the legitimacy of your claim).

5. Whether unfounded legend or undiscovered scientific fact, Bigfoot remains a mystery. Only one thing is certain: Bigfoot and his (or her) _____ are a part of our cultural consciousness.

• EASY Note Cards

Make a note card for each of the vocabulary words from the reading that you did not know. On one side, write the word. On the other side, divide the card into quarters and label them E, A, S, and Y. Add a word or phrase in each area so that you wind up with an example sentence, an antonym, a synonym, and, finally, a definition that shows you understand the meaning of the word with your logic. Remember that a synonym or antonym may have appeared in the reading.

9 Evaluating Points of View

Previewing the Chapter

Preview the headings in Chapter 9. Consider what you already know about these topics. Give an example of each topic here.

- _____

- _____

- _____

- _____

Plan to come back to your list when you have finished working through the chapter to double-check your examples. Revise any that need to be changed to be better examples.

_____

_____

 To access additional course materials for *Engage,* including quizzes, videos, and more, please visit www.cengagebrain.com. At the CengageBrain.com home page, search for the ISBN of *Engage* (from the back cover of your book) using the search box at the top of the page. This will take you to the product page where these resources can be found.

 Videos Related to Readings

 Vocab Words on Audio

 Read and Talk on Demand

Read and Talk   ONLINE MAGAZINE

In college, reading is just one aspect of how you will share new ideas with others in your class. So the first reading in each chapter of this book is meant to give you the chance to talk about reading. Read the article, and then use the four discussion questions to talk about your ideas with your classmates and your instructor.

Access the Reading CourseMate via www.cengagebrain.com to hear a reading of this selection and view a video about this topic.

The Potential Lover:
Is This Person Attracted to Me?

Carlin Flora

1   "I was sitting with a male friend at a lecture," says Helen Fisher, a biological anthropologist at Rutgers University and a renowned love researcher. "It was a humid summer day. The woman in front of us shook her hair out and gathered it up into a pony tail. My friend said, 'Did you see that? She's hot for me.' I laughed—I'm pretty certain she was just plain hot and wanted to get her hair off her neck!"

2   The body language of flirting is elemental, hardwired into us, and yet sometimes it's difficult to know if someone wants you right now, might possibly want you, wants to be your friend, or is just a nice person who could transmit polite interest to a statue. As an expert in mating rituals, Fisher recognized in her friend the male tendency to overestimate overtures: "Men have everything to gain from a sexual encounter and very little to lose," she says. "So they might as well try." Women, on the other hand, have evolved to read potential suitors with a suspicious eye, since the consequences of sex—pregnancy and childbirth—are costly for them indeed.

3   That feminine skepticism, however, is sometimes obscured by a friendly facade that could be misread by anyone. Indiana University researchers had American subjects watch videos of speed-dating events in Germany, focusing on posture, tone of voice, and eye contact as they guessed whether or not the daters were sexually attracted

renowned The prefix *re-* here means "repeatedly," and *nown* means "named." What does *renowned* mean?

overtures Use the context to decide what this word means.

skepticism The sentence before this has a rough synonym for this word, except that you'll need to change it from an adjective to a noun. What is *skepticism*?

to each other. Male and female viewers were equally good at measuring men's interest but equally bad at judging women's interest. In five of the videos, in fact, 80 percent of the subjects thought the German women pictured were interested when they were just being sociable.

4   Men and women seeking to improve their hook-up hit rate can start by keeping an eye out for some of the behaviors that people automatically display when they are into each other. Amazingly, humans tend to throw out 70 such signals per hour while chatting up romantic prospects, Fisher says.

© vgstudio/Shutterstock.com

repertoire The examples that follow are a clue to this word's meaning.

5   Here's a sampling of that extensive repertoire: Men might draw attention to themselves with a loud laugh or by spreading their arms wide. Both men and women might flash a broad grin, showing all their teeth. Once a conversation begins, besotted women slip into sing-songy voices, while men drop theirs an octave. As interest accelerates, flirters tend to mimic each other's stance and movements. And finally, they make physical contact.

6   It's best to hang back until you witness a cluster of gestures, says Marsha Lucas, a neuropsychologist. "A good one to watch for: After making eye contact, she looks down a bit, gathers or otherwise preens her hair, and then looks up at you while her chin is tipped."

7   If you consistently miss amorous advances, get in tune with your own emotions, says Lucas, who recommends mindfulness exercises. "In as little as two weeks, you can change how well your brain integrates emotional information."

8   If, after a skillful sizing up of the situation, you still make the wrong call—the woman you thought was falling for you turns red and stumbles away after you invite her to dinner, "be brave and own the error," says Lucas. "If you offer a simple apology instead of getting pissed off at her for 'misleading' you, you might impress her enough to get a connection going after all."

—"Who Are You And What Do You Think Of Me (Excerpt: Is This Person Attracted To Me?)" by Carlin Flora. *Psychology Today* (Jan/Feb 2011). Copyright © 2011 by Psychology Today. www.psychologytoday.com. Reprinted by permission.

Talking About Reading

Respond in writing to the questions below, and then discuss your answers with your classmates.

1. Have you ever been in a situation in which you weren't sure whether or not someone was flirting with you? What caused the confusion?

_____

_____

_____

2. How can you tell "if someone wants you right now, might possibly want you, wants to be your friend, or is just a nice person who could transmit polite interest to a statue"?

_____

_____

_____

3. Paragraph 3 reports on a study that indicates people can easily tell whether men are flirting, but not whether women are. In a practical sense, what does this mean for men and for women when they are interacting with an interesting new person?

_____

_____

_____

4. Is flirting only appropriate if neither person is in a committed relationship? Why or why not?

_____

_____

_____

Fact, Opinion, and Bias

"The Potential Lover" demonstrates three kinds of ideas that this chapter will discuss: fact, opinion, and bias. A fact is an idea that can be verified as being true. The findings of the Indiana University research study described in paragraph 3 consist of facts: A certain number of Americans were able to tell which German men were flirting, and a certain number were not able to tell which German women were flirting. Even though this article doesn't mention the actual numbers, you could look them up if you were interested in knowing more.

An opinion is what the male friend of love researcher Helen Fisher declared when he saw a woman shaking out her hair: "She's hot for me." He interpreted a fact. Notice that Helen Fisher disagreed with his interpretation. This is a good way to tell fact from opinion: People can and often do disagree with others' opinions.

Finally, bias is a preference for a particular viewpoint. As you can see from Fisher's expert opinion of her friend's statement, sometimes bias is based in biology. In this case, men have a tendency to interpret women's gestures in a certain way because they have little to lose from the act of sex (if that should occur). Women have a different bias toward men's flirting because, for them, sex may result in pregnancy and motherhood. Bias can also be based in a person's social status or psychology and in the historical realities of a particular group of people. In fact, bias pervades every context. The trick is to notice its often invisible presence and to take it into account.

When you are reading, you need to be able to separate facts from opinions from the underlying biases of the author. As a critical thinker, you'll want to be able to form your own opinions based on the facts, not just accept someone else's. And when you are able to notice other people's biases, you can more easily notice your own.

Section Review: Fact, Opinion, and Bias

Provide the definition for each term by filling in the general category and specific type.

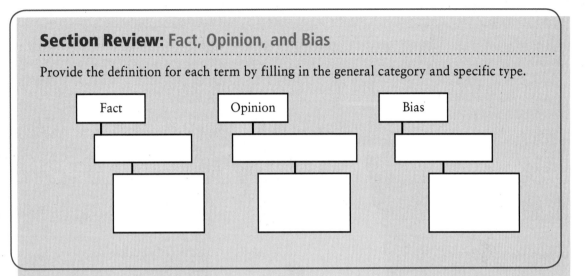

Facts Can Be Verified

You can think of a fact as an object, as in *objective*. **Objective** means not influenced by personal judgments or feelings. Facts exist externally. They are physical, observable things (like any object in the physical world). They exist separately from you and outside of you. They are independent of you. They can be verified—you can check to see if they are true. No matter what you do, believe, or feel, facts will still be facts. Facts are objective reality.

Sentence Stems that Introduce Facts

The following phrases typically introduce facts that should be verifiable—that is, they can be shown to be true or false. If they prove to be false, of course, they are not facts!

- According to **a study** by . . .
- The research **demonstrated** . . .
- The results of the test **showed** . . .
- Scientists **confirmed** . . .
- The poll **discovered** . . .

Here are some facts about the British Prince William's marriage to Kate Middleton.

An engagement photo.

- Kate Middleton and Prince William announced their plan to wed on November 16, 2010. They had become engaged while on a trip to Kenya.
- The two originally met when they were both attending St. Andrew's University in Scotland.
- Their wedding date was April 29, 2011, the day of the Feast of Saint Catherine.
- 1,900 guests were invited to the ceremony, but only 600 guests were invited to a lunchtime reception at Buckingham Palace, and 300 to the evening dinner hosted by Prince Charles.

This information about the royal wedding is factual. Each item can be proven true (or false). You can verify this information from many different sources, such as newspapers, magazines, and the official website of the British monarchy. Or the list—or items on it—could be proven false. Say, for example, that the number of guests was incorrect. That error would not make the information an opinion; it would just make it wrong. Once corrected, the information would be factual. Information that is proven correct is fact. Information that is proven wrong is fiction, a falsehood, make believe, an assumption, or even a lie. A fact must be verifiable.

INTERACTION 9–1	Identify Information that Can Be Verified

Put a check mark beside each sentence that contains information that could be verified by research, such as reading encyclopedias, other reference works, or websites.

_____ 1. As of February 27, 2011, the day before the Academy Awards, 32 percent of Yahoo! visitors who voted said that *Inception* should win Best Picture.

_____ 2. Emma Watson looks stunning with her short haircut.

_____ 3. According to the College Savings Plan Network, 529 plans contained about $135 billion by the end of June 2010.

_____ 4. Newborn mice's hearts can heal themselves, according to researchers at the University of Texas Southwestern Medical Center.

_____ 5. Everyone should live in tiny houses made of scavenged materials.

Section Review: Facts Can Be Verified

Check any kinds of information that would allow a statement to be verified.

_____ Specific names, dates, and times
_____ Generalizations about groups of people
_____ The writer's creative thoughts
_____ Particular ideas attributed to specific people

Opinions Are Subjective

Consider opinion as having to do with a subject, as in *subjective*. **Subjective** means based on or influenced by personal beliefs, feelings, or tastes. Opinions are internal. They exist inside you (or me or someone else). They depend upon the person who holds the opinion. So where does "subject" come in? Think of yourself as the subject of your life. Just as the subject of a sentence controls the action of a sentence, you control your opinions. Think of the ways you express your beliefs, feelings, preferences, and desires: Those are all opinions. Without you, they do not exist. Opinions are subjective reality. There is a difference between reality and "your reality." Reality is fact. "Your reality" is opinion.

Sentence Stems that Introduce Opinions

The following words introduce opinions that may be held by one person or one group of people.

- The defendant **claims** . . .
- The author **argues** that . . .
- My **point of view** is . . .
- Police **suspect** . . .
- Many **believe** . . .

What words in these sentences from David Kirkpatrick's book about Facebook tell you that he is giving you his opinion?

Excerpt from *The Facebook Effect*

The encounter of Van Natta [for Facebook] and Ballmer [for Microsoft] must have been a sight to see. Van Natta may be fearless, a belligerent and uncompromising negotiator, but Ballmer is big, loud, and consummately forceful himself. You don't screw around with him. Not to mention he's CEO of the most powerful technology company in the world. Ballmer didn't lose his cool. He reiterated that Microsoft had no interest in reopening the U.S. ad deal. What he was really interested in, he said, was buying Facebook.

© 1000 Words/Shutterstock.com

—Kirkpatrick, *The Facebook Effect*, p. 241

Here are the first four opinion words and phrases: *a sight to see, fearless, belligerent, uncompromising.* Underline the opinion words in the rest of the paragraph.

Unlike facts, opinions can't be verified by looking in dictionaries, encyclopedias, or newspapers. Because opinions are personal, they may be held by only one person, several people, or many people. A person can give reasons for holding a certain opinion, or facts to support it, and another person might still disagree.

| INTERACTION 9–2 | Compare Facts and Opinions |

For each pair of sentences, decide which one is the opinion. Circle the opinion word or words, and write **O** on the line.

_____ 1. Michelle Obama's "Let's Move!" campaign to end childhood obesity in the United States is a serious step in the right direction.

_____ The "Let's Move!" campaign helped pass a bill that gives the USDA the authority to set nutritional standards for all food regularly sold in schools.

_____ 2. Twenty-year-old Trevor Bayne is the youngest NASCAR driver to win the Daytona 500.

_____ Bayne is ridiculously inexperienced and is part of the tired old Ford team.

_____ 3. Kilim rugs are woven on looms in Iran, the Balkans, parts of Turkey, and elsewhere.

_____ Kilim rugs might have had their beginnings as early as 4000 BC.

_____ 4. The YouTube video "Perfect Red Lips" suggests several methods for selecting a red color that will complement your skin tone.

_____ You should watch "Perfect Red Lips" to find your perfect lip color.

_____ 5. Chris Medina suffered a heartbreaking loss when his fiancée got into a terrible accident.

_____ In his _American Idol_ audition, Chris Medina sang The Script's "Breakeven."

| INTERACTION 9–3 | Create Fact and Opinion Sentences |

Think about a movie (or television show) that you've seen and remember well. For each aspect of the movie, create one factual sentence and one opinion sentence. Then exchange sentences with a classmate and circle all the opinion words you find. Do you agree on which sentences state facts and opinions?

1. Actors

   a. Fact:

   _____

   _____

   b. Opinion:

   _____

   _____

2. Storyline

   a. Fact:

   _____

   _____

   b. Opinion:

   _____

   _____

3. Soundtrack

   a. Fact:

   _____

   _____

   b. Opinion:

   _____

   _____

4. Set or locations

   a. Fact:

   _____

   _____

   b. Opinion:

   _____

   _____

5. Camera work

a. Fact:

_____

_____

b. Opinion:

_____

_____

_____

Section Review: Opinions Are Subjective

Circle the careers that are based more on subjectivity than objectivity.

fine artist   mathematician   poet   journalist   police officer

house painter   child care worker   advertising copywriter

Words That Can Express Opinions

Facts and opinions are not always easy to distinguish. In this section you'll read about some kinds of words to pay close attention to. When you come to them in your reading, think carefully about whether you would be able to verify the information with other sources of information. If you can verify the information, you are reading facts. If you cannot, you are reading opinions.

Adjectives

Many words that tell you when an opinion is being expressed are adjectives. Adjectives describe nouns. In the following sentence, the adjective reveals the writer's opinion.

© epa/Corbis

Whitney Houston is the most talented female vocalist today.

The word *talented* is an adjective. (It is modified by the adverb *most*.) It describes the proper noun *Whitney Houston*. Since you could not look in a reference book to find out whether Whitney Houston is, indeed, the most talented female vocalist today, this is the opinion of the writer. One person might think Celine Dion is the best, and another might prefer Jennifer Lopez's voice. Other people might think that it depends on which songs are being discussed. Since people may disagree, it's an opinion.

Here are some adjectives:

abnormal	alive	bad	considerable
abstract	alternative	beautiful	consistent
academic	ambiguous	big	constant
accurate	antique	blunt	contrary
adequate	appropriate	capable	cooperative
adjacent	arbitrary	classical	definite
afraid	attached	compatible	different
aggressive	attractive	conservative	dramatic

dynamic	infinite	objective	reluctant
empirical	inherent	passive	restricted
enhanced	irrational	persistent	short
enormous	isolated	precise	stable
expert	liberal	primary	subjective
explicit	modern	prime	sufficient
finite	mature	professional	sustainable
hierarchical	maximum	radical	symbolic
identical	minimum	random	unique
immature	marginal	rational	visible
implicit	modified	reinforced	voluntary
incompatible	normal	relevant	widespread

Not all adjectives point to opinions, however. Sometimes they merely summarize facts. For example, read this sentence.

> As the earth's average temperature gets hotter, there is increased demand to reduce carbon emissions.

There are three adjectives here: *average, hotter,* and *increased.* But they all refer to facts that can be verified by checking an encyclopedia or other reference book. For instance, you could look in the *State of the Climate Report* (published jointly by the National Oceanic and Atmospheric Administration [NOAA] and its British counterpart) to find out what the average temperature of the earth has been through the years, whether it is getting hotter, by how much, and how quickly. You could also look in newspapers, magazines, and reference books to find out whether during that time, there were more calls for reducing carbon emissions than there were before the earth started getting hotter. So these adjectives do not point to opinions. They point to facts.

When you see adjectives, think carefully about whether they point to facts or opinions.

| INTERACTION 9–4 | Identify Adjectives and What They Point To |

A. Circle all of the adjectives in the following sentences.

1. With over 800,000 species, insects are the largest group of animals on earth. There are more individual insects on earth than any other animal as well.

2. Many groups of people capitalize on this fact and make insects a nutritious part of their diets. In parts of India, for example, insects are eaten with rice, in Myanmar they are used in stews, and in Egypt grasshoppers are skewered on sticks, roasted over fires, and then dipped in butter for a tasty snack. Some Peruvians use beetles as flavoring, and in Thailand over 50 insect species are consumed; they are roasted, boiled, sautéed, or pounded and added to pastes.

3. As a food source, insects offer many benefits. They are rich in calories and protein, carbohydrate, water, vitamins, and minerals. In terms of fat content, insects are a lot like fish and poultry, with between 10% and 30% of their weight made up of fat. Most edible species are cholesterol free and have a high ratio of polyunsaturated to saturated fats.

4. Because entomophagy (insect eating) has so many advantages, the almost total lack of insects from Euro-American diets is being challenged. Some colleges and universities now offer courses designed to increase the acceptance of insects as animal and human food.

5. Perhaps Euro-Americans don't eat insects because they find the thought disgusting.

> —Items 1–4 adapted from BRYANT/COURTNEY/DEWALT/SCHWARTZ.
> *The Cultural Feast: An Introduction to Food and Society*, 2e (p. 85)
> Copyright © 2004 Cengage Learning.

B. Write down the adjectives in each numbered passage that point to opinions rather than facts. Write "none" if there aren't any.

1. _____

2. _____

3. _____

4. _____

5. _____

INTERACTION 9–5   **Write About an Image**

- Select one of the photos below. On a separate sheet of paper, write two short paragraphs about it.

- Write one paragraph that uses adjectives that all point to opinions.

- Write a second paragraph in which some adjectives point to facts.

- Exchange your two paragraphs with a classmate without revealing which has factual adjectives and which has only opinion adjectives.

- Circle the adjectives in your partner's paragraphs that you think point to facts. Do you and your partner agree?

© Jeremy Richards/Dreamstime.com

© George Blonsky

Qualifiers

Some statements are qualified. That is, the writer describes how often something happens or how many members of a group are being discussed. **Qualifiers** may be used to express an opinion or fact. Often, they are used to limit the extent of whatever the writer is describing:

They *rarely* eat beef. [The sentence qualifies how often they eat beef.]

Some Americans go to worship services each week. [The number isn't definite, but it's fewer than all Americans.]

You got *all* the courses you wanted! I didn't get *any* of my top choices. [These qualifiers indicate how many.]

Here are some qualifiers that tell how often or how many:

a few	frequently	normally
all	often	rarely
always	nearly	some
any	never	sometimes
every	none	usually

Another group of qualifiers modify, or change, the meanings of the verbs that follow them:

can	must	should
could	have to	would
may	shall	
might	will	

These qualifiers indicate degrees of certainty, permission, and necessity. Notice how none of the following statements could really be called a fact:

I might do my hair. [It's not too certain that I will.]

I must do my hair. [I really have to do it.]

I will do my hair. [I'm going to do it.]

These statements are all opinions. The last one is considered an opinion because the event has not yet occurred. Future events can't be considered facts—not yet:

Our vacation will be over by the end of the month.

You are going to be my wife!

Some qualifiers, such as *all, always, never, none, must,* and *have to,* are absolute. In conversation, people often use absolute qualifiers when they are exaggerating:

She is *always* angry. [Has she never felt happy, even once?]

He *never* washes his hands. [Has he ever washed his hands, even one time?]

You *must* do it my way! [Can it be done even one other way?]

Because hardly anything is ever absolute, statements that use absolute qualifiers are usually not true. So if you see a statement with an absolute qualifier on a test, the statement is almost always false. The more extreme the qualifier (*all* or *none*), the more likely the statement is to be an opinion or simply incorrect.

Finally, it's worth mentioning that the absolute qualifier *all* is sometimes hidden; it is not in the sentence at all, even though its meaning is:

> If you read, "Homeless people are mentally disturbed," the author is really saying, "All homeless people are mentally disturbed."

> If you read, "Condos on Biscayne Bay are overpriced," the author is really saying, "All condos on Biscayne Bay are overpriced."

The unstated *all* is present when the author uses the word *are* to define the subject without using other qualifiers to limit the statement. Be on the lookout for this unstated *all*, and remember that things are rarely "all or nothing."

INTERACTION 9–6	**Think about Qualifiers**

The qualifiers in the sentences below are in bold type. If the sentence is true, write **T** on the line. If it is false, write **F**. If a statement is false, rewrite it using a different qualifier to make it true. Don't forget that the absolute qualifier *all* may not be stated in the sentence even though it is implied.

Example: <u> F </u> Soldiers **always** have troubled dreams.

<u>Soldiers **sometimes** have troubled dreams.</u>

_____ 1. **Every** person in the world needs to eat in order to survive.

_____

_____ 2. When you enter a dark theater on a sunny day, your eyes **always** need at least a moment or two to adjust.

_____

_____ 3. Rich people are **always** hated.

_____

_____ 4. One-month-old babies **never** speak in complete sentences.

_____

_____ 5. Tourists to Italy **must** travel by boat.

_____

_____ 6. Texans fear snakes.

_____

_____ 7. American drivers **normally** wear seat belts to avoid getting hurt in an accident.

_____

_____ 8. People who don't get high grades in high school **never** become successful.

_____

_____ 9. Stereotypes are **always** positive.

_____

_____ 10. Thin people have excellent self-control.

_____

Comparatives and Superlatives

Comparatives and superlatives are words you should think about carefully as you decide what is fact and what is opinion. A **superlative** compares one thing to all the other things of the same kind. Superlatives usually end with -est or have *most* before a word, as in *most intelligent*. Some examples of superlatives are *best, greatest, strongest, most intelligent, most clearly,* and *most often*. The **comparative** is typically used to compare two items: *better, greater, stronger, more intelligent, more clearly,* and *more often*. (As you may have noticed, comparatives and superlatives can be adjectives or adverbs.)

The question is whether we can find proof for a comparison so that we can consider it a fact. If someone notes that "the Japanese earthquake in 2011 was stronger than the Haitian earthquake of 2010," we can verify whether this is a true statement by finding out how strong each one was on the Richter scale, which is the accepted scientific scale for measuring earthquakes. (The Japanese earthquake measured 8.9, and the Haitian one measured 7.0.) The comparison is very specific. But what about a statement like "Chinese food is better than French food"? Can we prove this? No. The word *better* is so general and so based in personal opinion that it would be impossible to find proof for the statement. So sometimes, superlatives and comparatives are opinions, and other times they are verifiable as fact (or just plain wrong). Keep coming back to the question: Can I verify this statement?

| INTERACTION 9–7 | **Think About Comparisons** |

Write **Y** in the blank if the sentence can be proven. Write **N** if it cannot be proven. Explain your answer. If you aren't sure, discuss the sentence with classmates to see if you can agree on an answer.

_____ 1. The **largest** fire that ever burned in the recorded history of California took place around San Jose in 2008.

_____

_____

_____ 2. Sigmund Freud was a **better** psychologist than Dr. Ruth is.

_____

_____

_____ 3. The iPad 2 is **more significant** than the iPad 1.

_____

_____

_____ 4. Geoffrey Mutai is the **fastest** marathon runner in the world.

_____

_____

_____ 5. The whales in the St. Lawrence Estuary are **more interesting** than the river dolphins that live in the Amazon.

_____

_____

| INTERACTION 9–8 | **Identify Fact and Opinion in a Movie Review** |

Following is a review of the movie _Inception_. Read the review with careful attention to which parts are facts about the movie and which are the reviewer's opinions. As you read, circle any words (adjectives, qualifiers, comparatives, and superlatives) that point to the reviewer's opinion.

Inception: Christopher Nolan's Dazzling Sci-Fi Thriller Has Heart As Well As Brains

Jason Best

1   Christopher Nolan pulled off the year's most daring cinematic coup with his mind-boggling thriller *Inception.*

2   In a summer when the big studios mostly played safe with remakes, rip-offs and sequels, Nolan somehow managed to make a dazzlingly smart, deeply personal art-house movie on a blockbuster budget.

Photofest/Warner Bros. Pictures

3   Combining the conceptual daring of his thrifty debut film *Following* with the multi-million-dollar spectacle of his *Batman* blockbusters, *Inception* put its brain-dead rivals to shame with its dizzying intelligence and eye-popping visuals.

4   Imagine, for a moment, that Freud and Jung had decided to remake *The Sting* and hired MC Escher to do the production design and you'll begin to have a grasp of what Nolan has done.

5   *Inception* is a brain-twister, to be sure. But the fact that the plot demands attention only adds to the exhilaration. This is a story about dreams that requires the audience to stay awake.

6   Here, though, is a brief summary of what's in store. The setting is a near future in which Leonardo DiCaprio's corporate spy, Dom Cobb, steals industrial secrets by infiltrating his victims' dreams. Can this master 'Extractor,'

however, pull off the seemingly impossible feat of 'Inception' and implant a thought in the mind of the heir to a multi-billion-dollar energy company?

7   If that's challenging enough to get your head around, it gets even trickier. To accomplish the task, Cobb and his team have to penetrate a labyrinth of dreams within dreams, encountering ever more perilous hazards on every level—many of them springing from Cobb's guilty sub-conscious memories of his dead wife, Marion Cotillard's Mal.

8   As this suggests, *Inception* keeps its viewers on their toes. Stripped down to its essence, however, Nolan's film is basically a 'guys on a mission' tale, with DiCaprio's leader the conflicted hero who must carry out 'one last job.' In Cobb's case, the motivation is his desire to end his exile from his children, which complicates things no end for the team of specialists he assembles for the enterprise.

9   As in *The Sting*, Cobb's companions all have apt role-names. Joseph Gordon-Levitt's Arthur, Cobb's right-hand, is The Point Man. Ellen Page's Ariadne (named after the heroine of Greek myth who helped hero Theseus find his way through the Cretan labyrinth) is The Architect whose job is to design the maze-like structures of the dreams.

10   Tom Hardy's wily, charming Eames is The Forger. Dileep Rao's Yusuf is The Chemist. Ken Watanabe's Saito, the mission's paymaster, is The Tourist. And Cillian Murphy's billion-heir, Robert Fisher Jr, is The Mark.

11   Cotillard's Mal, meanwhile, is the treacherous femme fatale whose presence threatens to sabotage the whole endeavor.

12   That should give you an idea of the genre pleasures that *Inception* fulfills. The film isn't just a cerebral puzzle; it's also an exciting thrill-ride. Indeed, all those different dreamscapes give Nolan the chance to reprise what I can well imagine are some of his favorite episodes of cinematic derring-do and adventure—from James Bond's alpine escapades in *On Her Majesty's Secret Service* to the scorching gun battles of *Heat*.

13   But *Inception* has another level, and it's one that prevents the film from being just a clever intellectual game. As my sometime Movie Talk colleague Heidi has observed elsewhere, there's also "a haunting tale of love and loss lurking inside all the mind-blowing FX and plot contortions." At every twist and turn in the narrative, we're grounded by the burden Cobb carries with him everywhere—his crushing grief over the death of his wife and his separation from his children. A movie with heart, then, as well as brains.

—Copyright © Jason Best/What's on TV/IPC+ Syndication. Reprinted by permission.

1. Which paragraphs include more factual summary of the movie's plot than the reviewer's opinions? _____

2. Who directed *Inception*? _____

3. What other movies by the same director does this reviewer compare *Inception* to? _____

4. What comparison does the author make between *Inception* and other movies that came out around the same time? _____

_____

5. Name one adjective, qualifier, comparative, or superlative the author uses that points to a fact, not an opinion, in each of the following paragraphs.

- Paragraph 6: _____
- Paragraph 7: _____
- Paragraph 9: _____

Section Review: Words That Can Express Opinions

Circle the word or phrase in each pair that is more likely to express an opinion.

should	worst	always
does	lightest	at times
reveals	longer	cooking
might reveal	better	enjoyable

Sources of Information

Suppose someone says, "That's not what I heard. I heard that *she* left *him*!" Although the speaker might have heard that "she left him," if you want to decide whether you believe the statement is true, you first have to determine if the speaker is trustworthy. Does this person usually speak honestly, often exaggerate, or have a reason to lie? Even if you trust the speaker, ultimately you would need to go to the people involved to determine what was true.

There are many sources for information. Generally they fall into two categories: trustworthy and not trustworthy. But there are shades of trust in between. Also keep in mind that mistakes and errors are always possible. Regardless, it is the speaker's or author's ethos, or credibility, that makes him or her believable. In order to decide whether to trust someone's facts or consider their opinion carefully, you should think about how credible the source is likely to be.

Let's look at three categories of sources: experts, people with informed opinions, and people on the street.

Expert Opinion

An **expert** is someone who earns our trust because he or she has gained extensive education and/or experience in a particular field of study. Or the expert may hold a position of authority or respect in the field. It is important to note that people are experts only in their own fields. Just because Kym Rock is an expert in karate does not mean we should follow her advice about rock climbing or parasailing.

Examples of experts

- Bill Phillips, author of *Body for Life*, is an expert on exercise and nutrition for body building.
- Deborah L. Smith, member of the international executive board of Amnesty International, is an expert on human rights.
- Natalie Goldberg, novelist, poet, and writing instructor, is an expert on teaching fiction writing.
- Basil Davidson, a historian who has written extensively about Africa, is an expert on African history.
- Dale Earnhardt, Jr., NASCAR racer, is an expert on stock car racing.

Experts get their information from other experts and from direct study or experience with the facts of their field. Experts usually build their opinions upon facts that they have studied or experienced. However, experts are not infallible: At times, they can be wrong. Also, sometimes experts build opposing opinions or interpretations from the same factual information.

Informed Opinion

People who are **informed** have researched or experienced something we have not and are sharing what they have learned. Included in this category are news journalists, TV news anchors, and other media people who gather and relay the news to the public. We expect them to know more than we do, but we don't necessarily accept their opinions.

Examples of informed people

- A student who researches a local environmental issue online and at local meetings

- A person who shares firsthand travel tips for a place she has been recently

- A newspaper reporter who interviews people in order to write a story

- A person who is concerned about an issue and who has read several books and articles on the topic

- A journalist or news anchor who has discussed a topic with several experts

People who are informed get their information directly from experts, from the media, and/or from personal experience. Informed opinions are often based on fact mixed with emotional experience. In terms of credibility, people who are informed are often credible, but they don't have the extensive knowledge of experts. More of their knowledge comes from other people's descriptions and interpretations of events.

People on the Street

People on the street are just ordinary people whose expertise is unknown. If you have ever seen interviews with sports fans after a big game, you know that every person has an opinion, but you may or may not care what it is. Is it based on the most important and relevant facts? It's often impossible to know.

Examples of people on the street

- Regular people who are interviewed about any recent event as they walk down the street

- People who write blogs to give their opinions on a wide variety of topics

- "Reporters" for "newspapers" that publish stories about alien babies and virgin pregnancies
- An expert in one field talking about an issue outside that field

People on the street are not necessarily uninformed; it's just difficult to know whether they are or not sometimes. (The alien babies aren't real!)

INTERACTION 9–9 | Identify the Credibility of Sources

Decide the level of credibility for the people listed below. Write **E** for expert sources, **I** for informed sources, and **S** for people on the street. If you don't recognize someone's name, use Google to search for information.

_____ 1. LeBron James on playing basketball

_____ 2. LeBron James on caring for new tattoos

_____ 3. Mia Hamm on international relations

_____ 4. Mia Hamm on soccer

_____ 5. Eric Clapton talking about guitars

_____ 6. Eric Clapton on the politics of immigration

_____ 7. Former President George W. Bush's book *Decision Points* on making presidential decisions

_____ 8. A college student's research paper on George W. Bush's presidential decisions

_____ 9. The *Autobiography of Mark Twain*

_____ 10. FloBots on writing alternative hip-hop lyrics

_____ 11. Best Friends Animal Society on caring for abused dogs

_____ 12. A circus trick horseback rider on caring for abused dogs

---

INTERACTION 9–10 | Evaluate Statements for Credibility

For each numbered item, give points for facts and points for sources of information. Add the two point values together to evaluate how credible the source is.

Facts (choose one):

Includes one fact: 1 point

Includes two facts: 2 points

Includes three facts: 3 points

Sources of information (choose one):

Expert: 5 points
Informed: 3 points
Person on the street: 0 points

1. Katy Perry says she wrote her album *Teenage Dream* because she wanted peo-
    ple to dance more while she is on tour.

    Fact points: _____

    Sources of information points: _____

    Total credibility points: _____

2. According to the Environmental Protection Agency, New York City needs to
    speed up its plan to replace light fixtures that are leaking toxic substances in area
    schools. The light fixtures are a source of PCBs, which are believed to be cancer-
    causing agents. High levels of PCBs have been found in the air students breathe.

    Fact points: _____

    Sources of information points: _____

    Total credibility points: _____

3. Researchers C. B. Zhong and S. E. Devoe of the University of Toronto con-
    ducted three experiments to find out whether exposure to fast food can cause
    impatient behavior in non-eating contexts. They found that exposure to fast
    food symbols increased people's reading speeds; this exposure also reduces
    people's willingness to save money. Their research was reported in *Psychologi-
    cal Science* in May of 2010.

    Fact points: _____

    Sources of information points: _____

    Total credibility points: _____

4. Ginny Baker, my stepson's friend, says that some state governments, such as
    Wisconsin, Ohio, Michigan, Tennessee, and Idaho, want to limit the right of
    public employees like teachers to collectively bargain for better salaries and
    benefits because they think unions lead to communism.

    Fact points: _____

    Sources of information points: _____

    Total credibility points: _____

5. The Detroit Bureau, which is run by journalists who provide news and commentary on the automotive world, states that the two most likely places your car will be stolen are, first, the West Commerce Street area of Dallas, where one out of every four cars is stolen, and, second, the Lubertha Johnson Park neighborhood of Las Vegas, where nearly one of every six cars is stolen.

Fact points: _____

Sources of information points: _____

Total credibility points: _____

6. Cancer survivor Frank Trepino noted that there are more cancer survivors alive in 2007 than there were in 2001.

Fact points: _____

Sources of information points: _____

Total credibility points: _____

7. Gail Collins, a regular columnist for the *New York Times*, reminded readers recently that Newt Gingrich started the process of divorcing his first two wives while each one was ill—the first, Jackie, recovering from cancer surgery and the second, Marianne, diagnosed with multiple sclerosis. Gingrich is now married for the third time.

Fact points: _____

Sources of information points: _____

Total credibility points: _____

8. In *American Psychologist*, Peng and Nisbett (1999) reported their finding that many more proverbs in Chinese than in English include seeming paradoxes, such as "Beware of your friends, not your enemies" and "Too humble is half proud."

Fact points: _____

Sources of information points: _____

Total credibility points: _____

9. Even when people consider themselves environmentalists, they may still oppose environmental projects that change their own neighborhoods, a common issue known as "Nimbyism." (*Nimby* is an abbreviation for "not in my backyard.") One example mentioned in a *New York Times* article is Park Slope, Brooklyn, residents who want to have a bike path removed because it makes driving a car there more difficult.

Fact points: _____

Sources of information points: _____

Total credibility points: _____

10. Many people find it creepy that data mining companies know so much about them from the websites they visit and the purchases they make online.

Fact points: _____

Sources of information points: _____

Total credibility points: _____

Section Review: Sources of Information

A. For the following topic, give a specific example of each type of source.

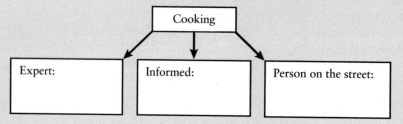

B. Rate each combination of fact/opinion and sources of information by giving the most credible combination a 10, the second a 5, and the third a 1.

Score: _

The writer, who is a person on the street, provides no facts but lots of opinions.

Score: _

The writer, who is informed, provides lots of opinions but no facts.

Score: __

The writer, who is an expert, provides many opinions, and then gives several facts to support each one.

Bias for a Viewpoint

A **bias** is a preference for a particular viewpoint—usually your own! When someone expresses an opinion, he or she also is expressing a bias. Both opinions and biases include words that express your values: what is right and wrong, beautiful and ugly, useful and useless, and so on.

Think about the opinions you have about the following subjects:

- What makes a person look good?

- What kind of music is the best?

- Is it important to go to college?

Suppose you answered the first question by saying:

> A person looks good when he or she is wearing stylish clothing.

This opinion reveals your bias, and to find out what that bias is, you can ask this question:

> *What does a person need to believe in order to believe that?*

Here is one possible answer:

> People ought to pay attention to changing fashion.

Notice that the question was another way to ask: What does this person value?

Once again, ask the question: What does a person need to believe in order to believe that?

One answer might be this:

> If you don't pay attention to changing fashion, you are stuck in the past.

If you want to dig even deeper into a person's beliefs, another revealing question to ask is this one:

> *And what's important about that?*

One answer that might come up is:

> People who live in the past don't understand that living in the moment is exciting.

Here is the original opinion with additional wording that now expresses more fully the bias behind it:

> I believe that people look good when they wear stylish clothing, because to me, such clothing indicates a person who understands that the present moment is exciting.

On the other hand, what is the bias of a person who holds this opinion?

> People look good when they are centered and happy.

Ask: What does a person need to believe in order to believe that? A possible answer:

> A person's emotions affect his or her appearance.

Ask: What does a person need to believe in order to believe that? A possible answer:

> The inner state of being affects the body.

Ask: And what's important about that? A possible answer:

> It allows you to understand that if you want to change your appearance, you can change your mind.

Here is the original opinion with additional wording that now expresses more fully the bias behind it:

> People look good when they are centered and happy, so if you want to change your appearance, change your inner state of being.

INTERACTION 9–11   Investigate Your Own Biases

State your opinion to answer each numbered question. Then investigate your own biases by answering the questions that follow.

1. What kind of music is the best?

   What is your opinion? _____

   _____

   What do you need to believe in order to believe that? _____

   _____

   What do you need to believe in order to believe that? _____

   _____

   And what's important about that? _____

   _____

2. Is it important to go to college?

   What is your opinion? _____

   _____

   What do you need to believe in order to believe that? _____

   _____

   What do you need to believe in order to believe that? _____

   _____

   And what's important about that? _____

   _____

3. Should college students be allowed to carry concealed weapons to class?

   What is your opinion? _____

   _____

   What do you need to believe in order to believe that? _____

   _____

   What do you need to believe in order to believe that? _____

   _____

   And what's important about that? _____

   _____

4. Should people read the newspaper every day?

What is your opinion? _____

_____

What do you need to believe in order to believe that? _____

_____

What do you need to believe in order to believe that? _____

_____

And what's important about that? _____

_____

INTERACTION 9–12 Investigate Authors' Biases

Based on the opinions expressed by the following authors, investigate their biases by using at least one of the following questions:

• What does the author need to believe in order to believe that?

• What's important about that?

1.

> If I donated all of my organs today, I could clear nearly 1 percent of my state's organ waiting list. I am 37 years old and healthy; throwing my organs away after I am executed is nothing but a waste.
>
> —Longo, "Giving Life after Death Row," *New York Times,* March 5, 2011

What opinion is stated?

_____

_____

What bias is behind the opinion?

_____

_____

_____

2.

> If a man aspires towards a righteous life, his first act of abstinence is from injury to animals.
>
> —Tolstoy, "The First Step"

What opinion is stated?

_____

_____

_____

What bias is behind the opinion?

_____

_____

_____

3.

> Society in every state is a blessing, but Government, even in its best state, is but a necessary evil; in its worst state an intolerable one: for when we suffer, or are exposed to the same miseries by a government, which we might expect in a country without government, our calamity is heightened by reflecting that we furnish the means by which we suffer. Government, like dress, is the badge of lost innocence; the palaces of kings are built on the ruins of the bowers of paradise. For were the impulses of conscience clear, uniform and irresistibly obeyed, man would need no other lawgiver; but that not being the case, he finds it necessary to surrender up a part of his property to furnish means for the protection of the rest; and this he is induced to do by the same prudence which in every other case advises him, out of two evils to choose the least. Wherefore, security being the true design and end of government, it unanswerably follows that whatever form thereof appears most likely to ensure it to us, with the least expense and greatest benefit, is preferable to all others.
>
> —Paine, _Common Sense_

What opinion is stated?

_____

_____

_____

What bias is behind the opinion?

_____

_____

_____

4.

> Abuse of power really can go both ways. If you're a boss, a parent, or a child, it's best to wield whatever power you have over your employees, children, or parents wisely. If you can't be gracious, don't spend time together. There's no gun being held to your head that says you have to associate with people who make you crazy. My family may be a little eccentric, but I would never talk cruelly to them—and certainly not in front of other people.
>
> —Gunn, *Gunn's Golden Rules*, p. 71

What opinion is stated?

_____

_____

_____

What bias is behind the opinion?

_____

_____

_____

5.

> When psychologists studied phobias, they went out and found hundreds of people with phobias. They went after the only people who did not know how to get over the problem! I took another approach. I went out and found two people who had a phobia and who got over it. Then I found out what they did.
>
> —Bandler, *Time for a Change*, p. 7

What opinion is stated?

_____

_____

_____

What bias is behind the opinion?

_____

_____

_____

INTERACTION 9–13 | **Identify Fact, Opinion, and Bias**

Read the selection and answer the questions that follow.

Bruce Sabath

Scott Barry Kaufman

1   "I'm sick of you . . . moaning about not being able to get up in the morning and go to work. If you could do anything you wanted with your time, what would you do?" Bruce Sabath's wife, Karen, asked him. For the first time out loud, he said, "Well, I would act." Pause. "But of course I can't do that." Puzzled, his wife asked, "Why not?" Despite a string of excuses, including money and potential rejection, his wife responded, "Well, if that's what you really want to do, why wouldn't you do that?"

2   Sabath soon quit his position in strategic planning at American Express and enrolled full-time in an acting program. Nine years later, he stars on Broadway in the revival of the musical _Company_.

3   "It never occurred to me to pursue acting as a career," says Sabath, who grew up surrounded by people who acted for fun but got 'real' jobs in medicine or law. After majoring in applied mathematics and computer science at Harvard, Sabath became a Wall Street whiz kid, taking acting classes "just for fun." "This isn't really it," he felt. He switched to finance. Not it, either. He went to Wharton Business School to do "real business." He still felt something was missing.

4   One day at American Express, a "superstar" consultant at the company walked into his office and told him she was quitting her job to pursue her love of painting. "It kind of blew the lid off my whole concept of who can do what," Sabath says.

5   He attributes his success to his later start. In the acting business, "the weeding out process is fast and unrelenting." By the time he started, at age 35, much of his competition—90 percent of it, he estimates—was gone. The pool of actors with whom he now competes for roles is indeed much smaller—if much better known.

6   Sabath no longer has any trouble getting up in the morning. And he confides that the major roadblock all along had been his own beliefs about what was possible.

—"Better Late Than Never," by Scott Barry Kaufman, _Psychology Today_
(November/December 2008). Copyright © 2008 by Psychology Today.
www.psychologytoday.com. Reprinted by permission.

1. What bias did Sabath have about being a professional actor?

_____

_____

2. What are two reasons for this bias?

_____

_____

3. Which two events led Sabath to decide to try an acting career?

_____

_____

4. What does Sabath say caused his success as an actor?

_____

_____

5. Reading between the lines, what are at least three other reasons for his success as an actor? Support each reason with facts.

_____

_____

_____

_____

Make connections to your life:

6. What biases do you have about who you cannot be?

_____

_____

7. Give one reason to support that idea that you could, in fact, be that.

_____

_____

8. What biases do you have about what you cannot do?

_____

_____

9. Give one reason to support that idea that you could, in fact, do that.

_____

_____

10. Suppose that, like Bruce Sabath, you worked at something you love for the next nine years with the purpose of becoming the best at it that you can be. What result would you expect?

_____

_____

Section Review: Bias for a Viewpoint

Fill in the boxes.

Questions to uncover an author's bias

Chapter Summary Activity:
Evaluating Points of View

Chapter 9 has discussed fact, opinion, and bias, and how to evaluate an author's point of view as you read by determining which is which. Fill in the following Reading Guide by completing each idea on the left with information from Chapter 9 on the right. You can return to this guide throughout the course as a reminder of how to distinguish fact from opinion and bias.

Reading Guide to Evaluating Points of View

Complete this idea	with information from Chapter 9.
Facts are different from opinions. For one thing, facts exist _____ the self.	1. _____
In contrast, opinions exist _____ the self.	2. _____
Objective reality is represented by	3. _____
Subjective reality is represented by	4. _____
Opinions are neither true nor false, but facts can be	5. _____
You can find out whether facts are true or not by	6. _____
For example, you could check these two sources of information:	7. _____ 8. _____
Several different kinds of words can be used to express opinions, although they may also express facts. They are:	9. _____ 10. _____ 11. _____ 12. _____
The words that describe nouns are called	13. _____
Three examples of words that show how often or how much something happens are:	14. _____ 15. _____ 16. _____
Two examples of absolute qualifiers are:	17. _____ 18. _____
Two examples of words that qualify the meaning of the verb that follows them are:	19. _____ 20. _____
To decide whether comparatives and superlatives are expressing facts or opinions, determine if	21. _____
To decide how much to trust someone's opinion, you can consider what kind of source the person is. Three types of sources and brief descriptions of them are:	22. _____ 23. _____ 24. _____
An opinion that an author expresses represents his or her	25. _____

Complete this idea	with information from Chapter 9.
The definition of *bias* is	26. _____ _____
The kinds of words that express a writer's bias are	27. _____
A person's biases, as well as opinions, help him or her distinguish	28. _____ _____
Two questions you can ask to uncover an author's bias are:	29. _____ _____ 30. _____

31. Think about what your reading strategies were before you read Chapter 9. How did they differ from the suggestions here? Write your thoughts.

_____

_____

_____

ENGAGE YOUR SKILLS
Evaluating Points of View

Read the following newspaper editorial.

A. For each highlighted adjective, determine whether it points to a fact or an opinion. Circle **F** or **O** in the margin next to the word.

The G.O.P.'s Abandoned Babies

Charles M. Blow

Republicans need to figure out where they stand on children's welfare. They can't be "pro-life" when the "child" is in the womb but indifferent when it's in the world. Allow me to illustrate just how schizophrenic their position has become through the prism of premature babies.

1. schizophrenic

   F O

Of the 33 countries that the International Monetary Fund describes as "advanced economies," the United States now has the highest infant mortality rate according to data from the World Bank. It took us decades to arrive at this dubious distinction. In 1960, we were 15th. In 1980, we were 13th. And, in 2000, we were 2nd.

2. advanced

   F O

3. highest

   F O

4. poor

F O

5. preterm

F O

6. bad

F O

7. special:

F O

8. immoral

F O

9. unborn

F O

10. economic

F O

Part of the reason for our poor ranking is that declines in our rates stalled after premature births—a leading cause of infant mortality as well as long-term developmental disabilities—began to rise in the 1990s.

The good news is that last year the National Center for Health Statistics reported that the rate of premature births fell in 2008, representing the first two-year decline in the last 30 years.

Dr. Jennifer L. Howse, the president of the March of Dimes, which in 2003 started a multimillion-dollar premature birth campaign focusing on awareness and education, has said of the decline: "The policy changes and programs to prevent preterm birth that our volunteers and staff have worked so hard to bring about are starting to pay off."

The bad news is that, according to the March of Dimes, the Republican budget passed in the House this month could do great damage to this progress. The budget proposes:

- $50 million in cuts to the Maternal and Child Health Block Grant that "supports state-based prenatal care programs and services for children with special needs."
- $1 billion in cuts to programs at the National Institutes of Health that support "lifesaving biomedical research aimed at finding the causes and developing strategies for preventing preterm birth."
- Nearly $1 billion in cuts to the Centers for Disease Control and Prevention for its preventive health programs, including to its preterm birth studies.

This is the same budget in which House Republicans voted to strip all federal financing for Planned Parenthood.

It is savagely immoral and profoundly inconsistent to insist that women endure unwanted—and in some cases dangerous—pregnancies for the sake of "unborn children," then eliminate financing designed to prevent those children from being delivered prematurely, rendering them the most fragile and vulnerable of newborns. How is this humane?

And it doesn't even make economic sense. A 2006 study by the Institute of Medicine of the National Academies estimated that premature births cost the country at least $26 billion a year. At that rate, reducing the number of premature births by just 10 percent would save thousands of babies and $2.6 billion—more than the proposed cuts to the programs listed, programs that also provide a wide variety of other services.

This type of budgetary policy is penny-wise and pound-foolish—and ultimately deadly. Think about that the next time you hear Republican representatives tout their "pro-life" bona fides. Think about that the next time someone uses the heinous term "baby killer."

—From *The New York Times*, February 25th, 2011. Copyright © 2011 *The New York Times*. All rights reserved. Used by permission and protected by the Copyright Laws of the United States. The printing, copying, redistributing, or transmission of this Content without express written permission is prohibited.

B. Answer the following questions.

11. What expert sources of information—people and organizations—does the author cite to support his case?

    • _____

    • _____

    • _____

    • _____

12. Would you say the author has a bias in favor of or against Republican ideas?

    in favor of   against

13. What information in the editorial leads you to say that? _____

    _____

    _____

14. Does the author believe in a woman's right to choose to have an abortion?

    yes   no

15. What information in the editorial leads you to say that? _____

    _____

    _____

16. Reread the title. (Note that G.O.P. stands for Grand Old Party, a nickname for the Republican Party.) What is the other adjective in the title, and what does it reveal about the author's bias? _____

    _____

    _____

C. This editorial garnered 268 comments from *New York Times* readers. Read responses 32 and 75, reprinted here, and answer the questions that follow.

Response 32

The allegations of poor infant mortality results in the USA are as groundless as they are commonplace. As reported in http://health.usnews.com . . .

The United States counts all births as live if they show any sign of life, regardless of prematurity or size. This includes what many other countries report as stillbirths. In Austria and Germany, fetal weight must be at least 500 grams (1 pound) to count as a live birth; in other parts of Europe, such as Switzerland, the fetus must be at least 30 centimeters (12 inches) long. In Belgium and France, births at less than 26 weeks of pregnancy are registered as lifeless. And some countries don't reliably register babies who die within the first 24 hours of birth. Thus, the United States is sure to report higher infant mortality rates. For this very reason, the Organization for Economic Cooperation and Development, which collects the European numbers, warns of head-to-head comparisons by country.

Infant mortality in developed countries is not about healthy babies dying of treatable conditions as in the past. Most of the infants we lose today are born critically ill, and 40 percent die within the first day of life. The major causes are low birth weight and prematurity, and congenital malformations. As Nicholas Eberstadt, a scholar at the American Enterprise Institute, points out, Norway, which has one of the lowest infant mortality rates, shows no better infant survival than the United States when you factor in weight at birth.

—Bernadine Healy, M.D., "Behind the Baby Count," *US News and World Report*, 9/24/06. Copyright © 2011 *US News and World Report* LP. All rights reserved. Reprinted by permission.

In other words, the allegedly superior health care systems of Europe get their superior results by just not counting all the dead babies. It makes you wonder what else they don't bother to report.

—RRD, *New York Times*, February 26, 2011

17. Which statement of Charles M. Blow's does this reader's comment respond to?

_____

_____

18. When you read Blow's editorial, did you consider this statement to be fact or opinion?

fact   opinion

19. Summarize in one sentence, using general terms, the problem with this statement.

_____

_____

Response 75

Despite all these comments on abortion, I have never seen a Democrat talk about accepting responsibility for one's actions.

I agree there needs to be support for the child before and after birth, but does everything have to be a Federal Program? There are routine collections in our Catholic Church for Birthrite and other organizations which support mothers before and after they give birth to their children.

—Mark, *New York Times*, February 26, 2011

---

20. Analyze the use of qualifiers in this response. Which ones are absolute?

_____

MASTER YOUR SKILLS
Evaluating Points of View

Read the following articles, and then decide which point of view is more credible by answering the questions that follow.

In-Car Breathalyzers

Mothers Against Drunk Driving

1   The average drunk driver has driven drunk 87 times before a first arrest. And on any given day, your family shares the roadways with more than 2 million drunk drivers who have had three or more prior convictions. While suspending the license of these individuals makes sense, in reality, three out of four of those with a suspended license still drive, threatening the safety of you and your loved ones. That is why MADD now supports the usage of ignition interlock devices, or in-car breathalyzers, which require all convicted drunk drivers to prove they are sober before the car will start.

Blow Before They Go

2   An ignition interlock is a device about the size of a cell phone. It is wired into the ignition system of a vehicle. A convicted drunk driver must blow in to the device in order to start their vehicle. If they have a measurable amount of alcohol in their system, the vehicle will not start. It is a simple and economical way to make sure that offenders can drive to and from work, but that they can't drive drunk.

—Copyright © 2011 by MADD. www.madd.org.
Reprinted by permission.

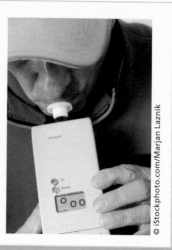

1. Consider the facts stated in these two paragraphs.

   • Which facts seem the easiest to verify? How could they be verified?

   _____

   _____

   • Which facts seem difficult to verify? Why?

   _____

   _____

2. Consider the rest of the Web page text. Is there any information here that would be difficult to verify?

                   yes   no

3. What overall opinion is stated or implied?

   _____

   _____

4. Consider the source of information. Is the Mothers Against Drunk Driving organization an expert, informed, or person-on-the-street source? Why do you say so?

   _____

   _____

5. What bias does this organization have?

   _____

   _____

6. What is the purpose of this Web page?

_____

_____

7. What is the tone of the Web page overall?

          objective   subjective

MADD Chalks Up Victory On In-Car Breathalyzers

Joseph Weisenthal

For some time, the organization Mothers Against Drunk Driving (MADD) has been promoting the use of in-car technology that will detect the presence of a drunk driver and prevent the car from starting. Heretofore, the technology has been pretty flaky and some studies even suggest that it's dangerous, but the organization claimed victory when Nissan recently announced that it had incorporated the technology into one of its concept cars. There's nothing wrong with car buyers (parents of teenagers most likely) wanting to get this feature, but MADD isn't content to see this as simply an option. The organization is clear that it would like to see this technology become mandatory, like seat belts. Of course, if you accept the logic that we could reduce crime by simply monitoring everyone's activities, there's a whole host of invasive technology we could conceivably employ for the betterment of society. What's particularly absurd about the Nissan technology is that it will work (well, supposedly work) by detecting alcohol in the air, which means that a drunk passenger could prevent the car from starting. So much for the campaign to get more designated drivers. Ultimately, some of the flaws with the existing technology could get worked out, so that it's effective. Unfortunately, once people feel that these devices work as advertised, politicians will have little reluctance to mandate them.

—Courtesy of www.techdirt.com

8. Does the first sentence include a verifiable fact?

                     yes   no

9. How can it be verified?

_____

_____

10. What opinion words does the second sentence include?

_____

_____

11. Are these opinions supported by facts in this article?

yes   no

12. Does the fourth sentence include a verifiable fact?

yes   no

13. Based on what you know, is the fact true? Explain.

_____

_____

14. The writer uses the opinion word *absurd*. What support is offered for this opinion?

_____

_____

15. Based on all you've read, does the opinion word *absurd* make sense? Why?

_____

_____

16. The MADD website information is from 2011. The TechDirt blog entry is from 2007. What is one possible explanation for the difference in information about the technology given in the two sources?

_____

_____

17. Should we consider the writer to be an expert, an informed source, or a person on the street? Why?

_____

_____

18. What bias does this writer have?

_____

_____

19. What is the writer's purpose?

_____

_____

20. What is the overall tone of this blog entry?

objective   subjective

Focus on Psychology

College Psychology App

PSYCHOLOGY TEXTBOOK

The following reading is linked to these fields of . . .

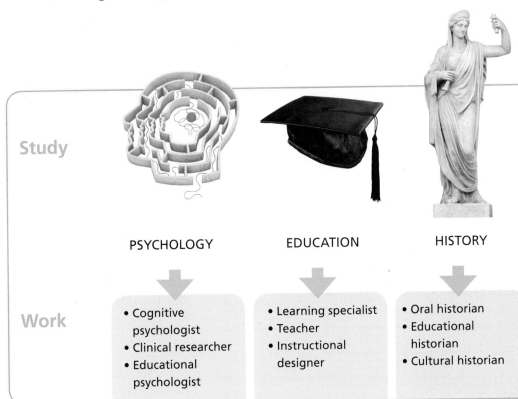

PSYCHOLOGY	EDUCATION	HISTORY
• Cognitive psychologist • Clinical researcher • Educational psychologist	• Learning specialist • Teacher • Instructional designer	• Oral historian • Educational historian • Cultural historian

Study

Work

● Pre-Reading the Selection

The excerpt that begins on page 587 comes from the textbook *Psychology*. The excerpt is titled "Improving Everyday Memory."

Surveying the Reading

Survey the textbook selection that follows. Then check the elements that are included in this reading.

_____ Title

_____ Headings

_____ First sentences of paragraphs

_____ Words in bold or italic type

_____ Images and captions

Guessing the Purpose

Based on the source and the title of the reading selection, do you think the author's purpose is mostly to persuade, inform, or express? _____

Predicting the Content

Based on your survey, what are three things you expect the reading selection to discuss?

- _____

- _____

- _____

Activating Your Knowledge

Explain your study strategies. How do you study for a test? How do you remember material you need to know? Are your strategies effective? Write your thoughts below.

- _____

- _____

- _____

● Reading with Pen in Hand

Students who annotate as they read are more successful than students who do not annotate. That's why you will annotate each reading in *Engage* as you read. In the reading that follows, use the following symbols:

★ or (Point)   to indicate a main idea

① ② ③   to indicate major details

Access the Reading CourseMate via **www.cengagebrain.com** to hear vocabulary words from this selection and view a video about this topic.

Improving Everyday Memory

Reading Journal

Answer the following "true" or "false."

_____ 1. Memory strategies were recently invented by psychologists.
_____ 2. Overlearning of information leads to poor retention.
_____ 3. Outlining what you read is not likely to affect retention.
_____ 4. Massing practice in one long study session is better than distributing practice across several shorter sessions.

1   ***Mnemonic devices* are strategies for enhancing memory.** They have a long and honorable history. In fact, one mnemonic device was described in Greece as early as 86–82 B.C. Actually, mnemonic devices were even more **crucial** in ancient times than they are today. In ancient Greece and Rome, for instance, writing instruments were not readily available for people to write down things they needed to remember, so they had to depend heavily on mnemonic devices.

● When were mnemonics first used?

crucial Look at the example that follows in the next sentence to determine the meaning of *crucial*.

My	Very	Excellent	Mother	Just	Sent	Us	Nine	Pizzas

| Mercury | Venus | Earth | Mars | Jupiter | Saturn | Uranus | Neptune | Pluto |

This mnemonic device (an acronym) helps people learn the order of the planets starting closest from the sun. Now that Pluto has been demoted to "dwarf planet," the mnemonic (and the meal) can change to "My Very Excellent Mother Just Served Us Nachos." If you aren't in the mood for nachos, you can use noodles, nectarines, nuts, naan, or nilla wafers!

(first seven images) NASA; *(Neptune)* NASA, L. Sromovsky, and P. Fry (University of Wisconsin–Madison); *(Pluto)* NASA, ESA, and M. Buie (Southwest Research Institute)

○ What is an example of a mnemonic?

2 Are mnemonic devices the key to improving one's everyday memory? No. Mnemonic devices can clearly be helpful in some situations, but they are not a cure-all. They can be hard to use and hard to apply to many everyday situations. Most books and training programs designed to improve memory probably overemphasize mnemonic techniques. Less exotic strategies such as increasing rehearsal, engaging in deeper processing, and organizing material are more crucial to everyday memory, and we will discuss these as we proceed through this Application. Along the way, you'll learn that all of our opening true-false statements are false.

3 In this Application, we will focus primarily (although not exclusively) on how to use memory principles to *enhance performance in academic pursuits*. Obviously, this is only one aspect of everyday memory. You may also want to improve your memory of phone numbers, passwords, addresses, others' names and faces, errands that you need to run, where you filed things, what you said to certain people, and so forth. For more advice on these diverse everyday memory tasks you may want to consult a couple of very practical books: *Memory Fitness* by Einstein and McDaniel (2004) and *Improving Memory and Study Skills* by Hermann, Raybeck, and Gruneberg (2002) (which has much broader coverage than its title suggests).

○ What is something you would like to remember better?

Engage in Adequate Rehearsal

○ How important do you think practice is when studying for a test?

4 Practice makes perfect, or so you've heard. In reality, practice is not likely to guarantee perfection, but it usually leads to improved retention. Studies show that retention improves with increased rehearsal. This improvement **presumably** occurs because rehearsal helps to transfer information into long-term memory. Although the benefits of practice are well-known, people have a curious tendency to overestimate their knowledge of a topic and how well they will perform on a **subsequent** memory test of this knowledge. That's why it is a good idea to informally test yourself on information that you think you have mastered before confronting a real test.

presumably *Presumably* is an adverb describing *occurs*. Focus on the words "improvement" and "because" as well to determine the meaning of *presumably*.

subsequent When do the memory tests occur? *Subsequent* means what?

remedy You are being given a strategy for what purpose? What does *remedy* mean?

○ "Overlearning" sounds harder than what you probably do! Do you think it is worth it?

5 Another possible remedy for overconfidence is trying to overlearn material. *Overlearning* refers to continued rehearsal of material after you first appear to have mastered it. In one study, after subjects had mastered a list of nouns (they recited the list without error), Krueger (1929) required them to continue rehearsing for 50% or 100% more trials. Measuring retention at intervals up to 28 days, Krueger found that greater overlearning was related to better recall of the list. Modern studies have also shown that overlearning can enhance perfor-

mance on an exam that occurs within a week, although the evidence on its long-term benefits (months later) is inconsistent.

6 One other point related to rehearsal is also worth mentioning. If you are memorizing some type of list, be aware of the serial-position effect, which is often observed when subjects are tested on their memory of lists. *The serial-position effect* **occurs when subjects show better recall for items at the beginning and end of a list than for items in the middle.** The reasons for the serial-position effect are complex and need not concern us, but its pragmatic implications are clear: If you need to memorize a list of, say, cranial nerves or past presidents, allocate extra practice trials to items in the middle of the list and check your memorization of those items very carefully.

● What is the serial-position effect?

pragmatic Read what follows the colon to get an idea of what *pragmatic* means.

allocate What are you doing if you are *allocating*?

Schedule Distributed Practice and Minimize Interference

7 Let's assume that you need to study 9 hours for an exam. Should you "cram" all your studying into one 9-hour period (massed practice)? Or would it better to distribute your study among, say, three 3-hour periods on successive days (distributed practice)? The evidence indicates that retention tends to be greater after distributed practice than after massed practice. This advantage is especially apparent if the intervals between practice periods are fairly long, such as 24 hours. For instance, Underwood (1970) studied children (ages 9 to 14) who practiced a list of words four times, either in one long session or in four separate sessions. He found that distributed practice led to better recall than a similar amount of massed practice. The superiority of distributed practice suggests that cramming is an ill-advised approach to studying for exams.

● Do you cram or use distributed practice?

retention Look at the cause-and-effect relationship given. *Retention* is the effect of what? What does *retention* mean?

8 Because interference is a major cause of forgetting, you'll probably want to think about how you can minimize it. This issue is especially important for students, because memorizing information for one course can interfere with the retention of information for another course. Thus, the day before an exam in a course, you should study for that course only—if possible. If demands in other courses make that plan impossible, you should study the test material last.

interference Consider word parts to determine what *interference* means.

● Have you ever experienced interference? What happened?

Engage in Deep Processing and Organize Information

9 Research on levels of processing suggests that how *often* you go over material is less critical than the *depth* of processing that you engage in. If you expect to remember what you read, you have to fully comprehend its meaning. Many students could probably benefit if they spent less time on rote repetition and devoted more effort

rote *Rote* repetition is contrasted with paying attention and analyzing. What does *rote* mean?

○ What is one way you can make material personal when you study?

hierarchical How are outlines organized? What does *hierarchical* mean?

○ What outlining technique have you learned in this book that could help you?

empirical Look at the word that follows *empirical*. What does *empirical* mean?

to actually paying attention to and analyzing the meaning of their reading assignments. In particular, it is useful to make material *personally* meaningful. When you read your textbooks, try to relate information to your own life and experience. For example, when you read about classical conditioning, try to think of your own responses that are attributable to classical conditioning.

10   It is also important to understand that retention tends to be greater when information is well organized. Gordon Bower (1970) has shown that hierarchical organization is particularly helpful when it is applicable. Thus, it may be a good idea to *outline* reading assignments for school, since outlining forces you to organize material hierarchically. Consistent with this reasoning, there is some empirical evidence that outlining material from textbooks can enhance retention of the material.

—From WEITEN. *Psychology*, 7e (pp. 291–292)
Copyright © 2008 Cengage Learning.

● Comprehension Questions

Write the letter of the answer on the line. Then explain your thinking.

Main Idea

_____ 1. Which of the following gives a simple thesis statement of this reading based on its pattern of organization?

a. There are several strategies for improving everyday memory.

b. There are four basic types of learning.

c. Improving everyday memory is important for success in school.

d. Mnemonic devices are strategies for enhancing memory.

WHY? What information in the selection leads you to give that answer? _____

_____

_____

_____

_____ 2. Which of the following four sentences is the broadest?

a. Overlearning refers to continued rehearsal of material after you first appear to have mastered it.

b. Another possible remedy for overconfidence is trying to overlearn material.

c. In one study, after subjects had mastered a list of nouns (they recited the list without error), Krueger (1929) required them to continue rehearsing for 50% or 100% more trials.

d. Modern studies have also shown that overlearning can enhance performance on an exam that occurs within a week, although the evidence on its long-term benefits (months later) is inconsistent.

WHY? What information in the selection leads you to give that answer? _____

_____

_____

_____

Supporting Details

____ 3. Which of the following would be considered a mnemonic device?

a. Studying for a seven-hour block of time the night before a test

b. Making the material meaningful to you

c. Creating a word using the first letters of the list of items that you need to memorize

d. Memorizing material using rote repetition

WHY? What information in the selection leads you to give that answer? _____

_____

_____

_____

____ 4. Which of the following statements is accurate based on the information in this reading?

a. Mass practice increases retention.

b. Mnemonics are the most important strategy for improving memory.

c. Practicing memorization techniques makes for a perfect memory.

d. Memory is increased by personalizing and systematizing information.

WHY? What information in the selection leads you to give that answer? _____

_____

_____

_____

Author's Purpose

_____ 5. What is the overall purpose of the passage?

    a. To persuade readers of the need to improve their poor memory strategies.

    b. To test readers on their reading and study strategies.

    c. To inform readers of effective strategies they can use to improve their memory.

    d. To entertain readers with the history of Greek memory techniques.

WHY? What information in the selection leads you to give that answer? _____

_____

_____

_____

_____ 6. What is the purpose of the four true-false questions?

    a. To cause readers to feel foolish if they do not know the answers to the quiz.

    b. To make readers feel confident of their study skills if they get the quiz questions right.

    c. To confirm for readers whether their knowledge about memorization techniques is correct, inaccurate, or some of both.

    d. To inform the reader of effective strategies for taking true-false quizzes in college, especially in psychology classes.

WHY? What information in the selection leads you to give that answer? _____

_____

_____

_____

Relationships

_____ 7. What main relationship pattern could this reading be said to have?

    a. Cause and effect

    b. Definition

    c. Time order

    d. Comparison

WHY? What information in the selection leads you to give that answer? _____

_____

_____

_____

_____ 8. Which two patterns are found in paragraph 1 of this reading?

    a. Definition and example

    b. Time order and cause and effect

    c. Time order and compare and contrast

    d. Process and time order

WHY? What information in the selection leads you to give that answer? _____

_____

_____

Fact, Opinion, and Inference

_____ 9. Which of the following statements is a fact?

    a. Books and training programs designed to improve memory overemphasize mnemonic techniques.

    b. The day before an exam in a course, you should study for that course only.

    c. It is always a good idea to outline all reading assignments for school.

    d. Studies show that retention improves with increased rehearsal.

WHY? What leads you to give that answer? _____

_____

_____

_____ 10. Which of the following statements would the author of this passage most likely agree with?

    a. By the time they reach college, students should know these memory improvement strategies.

    b. Success with memory is about studying smarter and not necessarily harder.

    c. When it comes to improving your memory, frequency of review is more important than depth of review.

    d. Improving memory is no easy task and there are no shortcuts.

WHY? What leads you to give that answer? _____

_____

_____

● Mapping the Reading

Create a visual map of each of the strategies for improving memory given in the reading.

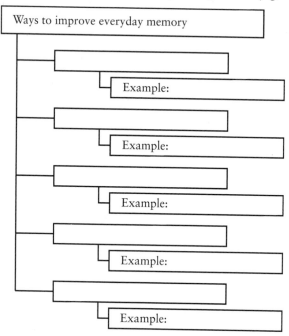

● Critical Thinking Questions

CRITICAL THINKING LEVEL 3: APPLY

The mnemonic device (acronym) for learning the order of the planets was given in paragraph 1 of this reading. Can you come up with other acronyms that you have learned for an academic subject, music, or any other area?

_____

_____

_____

_____

CRITICAL THINKING LEVEL 4: ANALYZE

Based on this reading, what are some problems associated with memorizing?

- _____

- _____

- _____

- _____
- _____
- _____

CRITICAL THINKING LEVEL 5: EVALUATE

This reading discusses several strategies for improving your memory. Evaluate which one would be most helpful to incorporate into your study habits. Explain your reasoning and how you will make this strategy part of your study techniques.

_____

_____

_____

_____

● Language in Use

The following words (or forms of them) were used in "Improving Everyday Memory." Now you can use them in different contexts. Put a word from the box into the blank lines in the following numbered sentences.

> crucial   presumably   subsequent   remedy   pragmatic   allocate
>
> retention   interference   rote   hierarchical   empirical

1. Teacher _____ is a critical issue on the national level: 50–60 percent of new teachers quit within five years.

2. In order to _____ this high attrition rate, an understanding of the reasons why teachers are leaving in droves must be developed.

3. _____ data from one study shows that workload is the biggest reason for teacher turnover. The teacher's workload involves not only the act of teaching but also lesson-plan creation, paperwork, club sponsorships, and a strong emphasis on meeting state testing standards.

4. Another big reason teachers leave is the _____ structure of schools. If teachers do not feel supported by the administration or mentored by veteran teachers, they become frustrated or disillusioned and leave.

5. It is _____ that solutions be found to increase teacher retention. It should be fairly straightforward to restructure workload requirements or implement programs, such as peer evaluations or mentoring, to make a new instructor feel integrated, appreciated, and effective.

● EASY Note Cards

Make a note card for each of the vocabulary words from the reading that you did not know. On one side, write the word. On the other side, divide the card into quarters and label them E, A, S, and Y. Add a word or phrase in each area so that you wind up with an example sentence, an antonym, a synonym, and, finally, a definition that shows you understand the meaning of the word with your logic. Remember that a synonym or antonym may have appeared in the reading.

Career Psychology App

● Pre-Reading the Selection

The excerpt that begins on page 597 comes from the website PsychologyToday.com. The excerpt is titled "Domestic Drama: On-Again, Off-Again."

Surveying the Reading

Survey the selection that follows. Then check the elements that are included in this reading.

_____ Title

_____ Headings

_____ First sentences of paragraphs

_____ Words in bold or italic type

_____ Images and captions

Guessing the Purpose

Based on the source and the title of the reading selection, do you think the author's purpose is mostly to persuade, inform, or express? _____

Predicting the Content

Based on your survey, what are three things you expect the reading selection to discuss?

- _____
- _____
- _____

Activating Your Knowledge

Do you know anyone who has been in an on-again, off-again relationship? Or have you ever been in one? Why do you think these types of relationships happen? Write your thoughts below.

- _____
- _____
- _____

● Reading with Pen in Hand

Students who annotate as they read are more successful than students who do not annotate. That's why you will annotate each reading in *Engage* as you read. In the reading that follows, use the following symbols:

★ or (Point)   to indicate a main idea

① ② ③   to indicate major details

Access the Reading CourseMate via www.cengagebrain.com to hear vocabulary words from this selection and view a video about this topic.

Domestic Drama: On-Again, Off-Again

Elizabeth Svoboda

Reading Journal

1   For Laura, a 35-year-old corporate recruiter from New York City, dating had always felt like a Ferris wheel ride. When a relationship started to feel wrong, she'd leave to get a new **vantage** point on things, but as the pain of singleness set in, she retreated to her former partner for comfort, ending up back where she started. She'd repeat the cycle several times before breaking things off permanently. "It became this crazy pattern," she says. "They weren't good guys at all, but whenever something in my life was difficult, I would go back."

vantage Use your prior knowledge to think of what a *vantage* point might be when you leave a relationship.

● Why did Laura go back?

• Are you among the 60 percent?

embarking What are they *embarking* on? What is the meaning of the word?

2   Laura's longtime boomeranging habit puts her in good company. The dynamic is quite common. University of Texas communications professor Rene Dailey found that 60 percent of adults have had a romantic relationship end and then gotten back together, and that three-quarters of those respondents had been through the breakup, makeup cycle at least twice. But **embarking** on this bumpy relational road takes an emotional toll: On-off couples have more relational stress than non-cyclical couples, she found.

© Dan Reynolds. Reproduction rights obtainable from www.CartoonStock.com.

fervent When you make a proclamation of love, what does it feel like? What might *fervent* mean?

• Can you think of a friend whose relationship fits this description?

fleeting In a rocky relationship, are the high moments common or few and far between? What does *fleeting* mean?

3   Given the obvious costs, why do couples keep dancing the on-and-off tango? Many who seesaw from freeze-outs to **fervent** proclamations of love know deep down that the relationship probably isn't right, says psychologist Steven Stosny. But when couples are faced with the loneliness and low self-esteem that accompany a breakup, they continually fall back on the temporary relief of reconciliation.

4   It's often the **fleeting** high points of a fundamentally rocky relationship that convince embattled partners to keep coming back for more, spurring a tortuous dynamic with no end in sight. "Often there is something that works very well for you about this person," says Gail Saltz, a Manhattan-based psychiatrist and author of *Becoming Real*. But when your mate's dreamy qualities are accompanied by deal-breaker ones like dishonesty or irresponsibility, it can be difficult to make a clear-headed assessment of whether to stay or leave.

• What is a deal-breaker quality for you?

hiatus "On-again, off-again" suggests that *hiatus* means what?

5   While problem behaviors may prompt a periodic **hiatus**, on-again, off-again couples continue to reunite out of a persistent hope that the moments of happiness and fulfillment they've known will someday constitute the entire relationship. "People say, 'I can fix

this other part of my partner,'" Saltz says, even though efforts at "remodeling" a mate are typically useless. The self-deprecating internal monologues serial on-off artists conduct after a breakup— "What was I thinking? I'll never meet someone as funny, smart, and attractive ever again!"—can also lead to repeated reconciliations.

● Have you ever tried to "fix" someone or vice versa?

6   While periodic **estrangement** is painful, some couples see a silver lining. By experiencing life without their significant others for a while, they come away with a deeper understanding of the value of their bond, even if the romance doesn't always have storybook qualities.

estrangement Use word parts to decide what *estrangement* means.

● Do you know a couple who stayed together permanently after a period of estrangement?

7   But this kind of "pruning" is no **panacea**. Virginia psychotherapist Toni Coleman warns couples to steer clear of the false epiphanies making up and breaking up can encourage. After an emotion-filled reunion, it's tempting to assume your partner has permanently changed for the better. But underlying conflicts that simmered before the breakup will resurface—just ask consummate on-off artists Pamela Anderson and Tommy Lee, who married and divorced twice before breaking up for good. "Things will change only if both people commit to working on the big issues," says Coleman.

panacea Read the entire paragraph to see how the author explains what *panacea* means.

● Can you name other stars who have been on-again, off-again?

8   Saltz recommends veterans of the breakup, makeup carousel take time to think about why they've been there so long in the first place. "The key is in recognizing that there is a pattern," she says. "You need to **elucidate** what the draw of this relationship really is for you." Some on-off cyclists, she explains, repeatedly return to partnerships with flaws that mirror those in their own parents' marriage, which they've unconsciously internalized as fundamental to any relationship. If your mother took her cheating partner back over and over again, you may be inclined to do the same. "Just the awareness of that can help you step out: 'Oh, my gosh, this is really me being my mother, and I don't want to recapitulate her love story,'" says Saltz.

elucidate Use the phrase "what the draw of this relationship really is for you" to determine what *elucidate* means.

● Are your parents good or bad relationship role models?

9   Another way to decide whether to fish or cut bait for good, Coleman says, is to take as long a view as possible. By forcing partners to consider the implications of "forever," so-called fast-forwarding scenarios may make them less likely to **acquiesce** to the temporary high of being "on" again with a problematic mate.

● Is this hard for you to do? Why or why not?

acquiesce Look at the cause-and-effect relationship. Less likely to *acquiesce* suggests what?

10   Since casting aside her most recent drama-ridden relationship, Laura has decided to steer clear of the dating world for a while. She sees her new freedom as a chance to step back and contemplate how to avoid the trap in the future. "The whole love industry makes you

● Do you think it is healthy to focus on yourself before you focus on a relationship?

feel like you have to be in a relationship all the time, but right now I'm just taking some time to figure things out," she says. "I truly am happy on my own."

Breaking the Breakup Cycle

11   On-again, off-again couples often find themselves caught between their desire for freedom and their fear of regret. Here's how to decide whether to sign on for the long haul or get out for good.

● What advice sounds best to you?

- Adopt a worst-case-scenario mindset. Many perpetual boomer-angers keep returning because they assume they can change their partner's worst habits. But that's wishful thinking, psychotherapist Toni Coleman says. "You have to assume that the behaviors you see will get more entrenched and worse over time. Ask yourself, 'If that turns out to be the case, would I still want to be in this relationship?'"

- Seek advice from a trusted third party. Therapists fill the bill nicely, but family and friends can be just as helpful. Because they don't have as much invested in your partner as you do, they can provide unbiased opinions as to whether smooth sailing is in your relationship's future.

- Take a time-out. In an on-again, off-again pairing, hiatuses are par for the course. But resolve to make this one different. Use the emotional distance to think clearly about what you want from a long-term relationship. Make a list if it helps you organize your thoughts. If your partner doesn't measure up, make the hiatus permanent.

—"Domestic Drama: On-Again, Off-Again," by Elizabeth Svoboda. *Psychology Today* (Mar/Apr 2008). Copyright © 2008 by Psychology Today. www.psychologytoday.com. Reprinted by permission.

● Comprehension Questions

Write the letter of the answer on the line. Then explain your thinking.

Main Idea

_____ 1. Which of the following best states the main idea of the section titled "Breaking the Breakup Cycle?"

a. Here's how to decide whether to sign on for the long haul or get out for good.

b. Adopt a worst-case-scenario mindset.

c. Seek advice from a trusted third party.

d. Take a time-out.

WHY? What information in the selection leads you to give that answer? _____

_____

_____

_____

_____ 2. Which of the following sentences from paragraph 8 is the broadest?

    a. Saltz recommends veterans of the breakup, makeup carousel take time to think about why they've been there so long in the first place.

    b. "The key is in recognizing that there is a pattern," she says. "You need to elucidate what the draw of this relationship really is for you."

    c. Some on-off cyclists, she explains, repeatedly return to partnerships with flaws that mirror those in their own parents' marriage, which they've unconsciously internalized as fundamental to any relationship.

    d. If your mother took her cheating partner back over and over again, you may be inclined to do the same.

WHY? What information in the selection leads you to give that answer? _____

_____

_____

_____

Supporting Details

_____ 3. Which of the following is *not* a reason why couples get back together?

    a. Low self-esteem

    b. False epiphanies

    c. Loneliness

    d. Elucidation

WHY? What information in the selection leads you to give that answer? _____

_____

_____

_____

_____ 4. Which of the following statements is accurate based on the information in this reading?

    a. On-again, off-again relationships are no more stressful than non-cyclical relationships.

    b. People who are involved in on-again, off-again relationships are probably emotionally immature.

c. Pamela Anderson and Tommy Lee are held up as a couple who successfully overcame the Ferris wheel of on-again, off-again relationships.

d. Thinking "short term" is a good strategy for breaking the cycle of on-again, off-again relationships.

WHY? What information in the selection leads you to give that answer? _____

_____

_____

_____

Author's Purpose

_____ 5. What is the overall purpose of the passage?

a. To persuade readers of the detrimental effects of being involved in an on-again, off-again relationship.

b. To inform readers of the types of relational stress that having an on-again, off-again relationship can cause and how to stop the cycle.

c. To inform readers of why 60 percent of American adults are in an on-again, off-again relationship.

d. To entertain readers with the sordid details of individuals and couples who are in on-again, off-again relationships.

WHY? What information in the selection leads you to give that answer? _____

_____

_____

_____

_____ 6. What is the purpose of the section titled "Breaking the Breakup Cycle?"

a. To categorize the different types of on-again, off-again relationships.

b. To suggest that only emotionally immature people become involved in on-again, off-again relationships.

c. To give some suggestions for breaking the cycle of on-again, off-again relationships.

d. To define for the reader the consequences of continuing in on-again, off-again relationships.

WHY? What information in the selection leads you to give that answer? _____

_____

_____

_____

Relationships

_____ 7. What two patterns are shown in the following sentences? *Many who seesaw from freeze-outs to fervent proclamations of love know deep down that the relationship probably isn't right, says psychologist Steven Stosny. But when couples are faced with the loneliness and low self-esteem that accompany a breakup, they continually fall back on the temporary relief of reconciliation.*

   a. Contrast and cause and effect

   b. Definition and time order

   c. Process and cause and effect

   d. Compare and contrast and description

WHY? What information in the selection leads you to give that answer? _____

_____

_____

_____

_____ 8. Which of the following is the most accurate statement of the overall pattern for paragraphs 1–10?

   a. Definition and example

   b. Cause and effect

   c. Compare and contrast

   d. Time order

WHY? What information in the selection leads you to give that answer? _____

_____

_____

_____

Fact, Opinion, and Inference

_____ 9. Which of the following statements is an opinion?

   a. University of Texas communications professor Rene Dailey found that 60 percent of adults have had a romantic relationship end and then gotten back together, and that three-quarters of those respondents had been through the breakup, makeup cycle at least twice.

   b. But when your mate's dreamy qualities are accompanied by deal-breaker ones like dishonesty or irresponsibility, it can be difficult to make a clear-headed assessment of whether to stay or leave.

    c. Virginia psychotherapist Toni Coleman warns couples to steer clear of the false epiphanies making up and breaking up can encourage.

    d. For Laura and many other thirty-something women, dating always feels like a Ferris wheel ride.

WHY? What leads you to give that answer? _____

_____

_____

_____

____ 10. Which of the following inferences can be made about the author, Elizabeth Svoboda?

    a. Elizabeth Svoboda wrote this article because she has been involved in numerous on-again, off-again relationships.

    b. Elizabeth Svoboda is biased against people who are involved in on-again, off-again relationships.

    c. Elizabeth Svoboda attempts to give a neutral presentation of some causes of and solutions for ending on-again, off-again relationships.

    d. Elizabeth Svoboda is a psychology student who has an interest in becoming a marriage and family counselor.

WHY? What leads you to give that answer? _____

_____

_____

_____

● Mapping the Reading

Start with this question: "Why do couples keep dancing the on-and-off tango?" Create a visual map of each of the reasons given in the reading.

● Critical Thinking Questions

CRITICAL THINKING LEVEL 3: APPLY

The reading mentioned Pamela Anderson and Tommy Lee as an example of an on-again, off-again couple. Can you think of any other examples of famous couples who are also examples? If not, do you know any couples in your circle of friends who would make a good example? Describe their situation.

_____

_____

_____

_____

CRITICAL THINKING LEVEL 4: ANALYZE

According to the reading, what are three causes that keep people in an on-again, off-again relationship?

● _____

● _____

● _____

CRITICAL THINKING LEVEL 5: EVALUATE

The last paragraph of this reading gives a three-bullet list of advice on whether to stay in an on-again, off-again relationship, or end it. Read this additional item of advice and evaluate if it fits with the reading.

● Think about the issue or issues that caused the initial breakup. If these issues have not changed, then maybe the relationship should be ended.

_____

_____

_____

_____

● Language in Use

The following words (or forms of them) were used in "Domestic Drama: On-Again, Off-Again." Now you can use them in different contexts. Put a word from the box into the blank lines in the following numbered sentences.

vantage	embarking	fervent	fleeting	hiatus

estrangement	panacea	elucidate	acquiesced

1. Life is _____, but sometimes we get a second chance. Such was the case for Maurice Hamonneau, a soldier in the French Foreign Legion during World War I.

2. He was wounded, which forced him to take a _____ from consciousness for several hours. When he awoke, he realized that the book he had in his breast pocket had saved his life.

3. The book was *Kim* by Rudyard Kipling; it had stopped a bullet. As you can imagine, he became a more _____ fan of Kipling than ever before.

4. When he heard that Kipling was mourning the loss of his own son, Maurice wrote a letter offering him not a _____, but the book that had saved his life (bullet still embedded), as well as a medal he had been given.

5. The gesture moved Kipling greatly. He _____ on the condition that the book and medal be returned if Maurice had a son. When Maurice did indeed have a son, Kipling returned the book and medal with a letter to the son, containing the advice that he should always carry a book of at least 350 pages in his left breast pocket for protection!

● EASY Note Cards

Make a note card for each of the vocabulary words from the reading that you did not know. On one side, write the word. On the other side, divide the card into quarters and label them E, A, S, and Y. Add a word or phrase in each area so that you wind up with an example sentence, an antonym, a synonym, and, finally, a definition that shows you understand the meaning of the word with your logic. Remember that a synonym or antonym may have appeared in the reading.

Applying Critical Thinking Skills to Visuals 10

Previewing the Chapter

Flip through the pages of Chapter 10, and read all the major headings. Look at all the photos and figures, and read their captions.

Based on the figures in the chapter, write a statement about the topic of the chapter.

_____

_____

Write down any strategies you use to interpret the meaning of visuals.

_____

_____

Plan to come back and write down any new strategies you learned about interpreting the meaning of visuals when you have finished working through the chapter.

_____

_____

 To access additional course materials for *Engage,* including quizzes, videos, and more, please visit www.cengagebrain.com. At the CengageBrain.com home page, search for the ISBN of *Engage* (from the back cover of your book) using the search box at the top of the page. This will take you to the product page where these resources can be found.

Videos Related   Vocab Words   Read and Talk
to Readings   on Audio   on Demand

Textbook Visuals

Visuals in textbooks may provide:

- Examples of the ideas being talked about.
- Specific numerical data to support the general statements in the text.
- A comparison of large amounts of information.

In college textbooks, some visuals include information that you must understand in order to comprehend the chapter completely. Other visuals are less important for comprehension but still interesting to look at. For example, the photo and caption from the College Psychology App in Chapter 9 (page 587) provide a mnemonic device that helps you understand the idea of the passage better. In contrast, the movie still from the 2010 version of *The Karate Kid* at the beginning of Part 1 (page 2) gives you the visual of the action that the text under the image refers to, but you could understand the idea without the photograph.

In the rest of this chapter we will discuss several major types of visual material, such as tables, pie charts, line graphs, bar graphs, flowcharts, and photographs. The following points, with some adaptations, apply to reading most of these different kinds of visuals.

Interpreting Visuals

1. **Read the title of the table or graphic carefully.** The title often provides information you need in order to understand the graphic. The title may function as the topic. Captions that appear under photographs are similarly important. Often, the caption functions as the main idea or the topic sentence of the graphic. Captions can also indicate the purpose of the visual.

2. **Read the headings of rows and columns or the labels on *x*- and *y*-axes carefully.** In a table, you should read the column headings so that you will know which groups are being compared. The information in the rows often consists of the points of comparison between the groups listed in the columns.

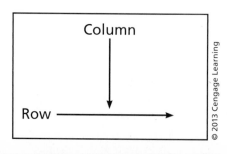

When you are reading graphs, the *y*-axis is the vertical line, and the *x*-axis is the horizontal line along the bottom of the figure. Read the labels carefully to make sure you understand how the information is set up.

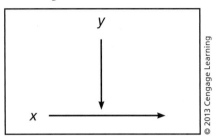

3. **If different colors are used, notice their meaning.** The parts of some graphs and charts may be printed in different colors that have specific meanings. Look for a key to tell you what the colors mean.

4. **Think critically about the implications of the headings, the numbers, and the way the information is presented.** Remember that graphics and tables summarize large amounts of data. In the process of reading so much information, sometimes it's easy to lose track of potential problems or questions that should be asked. Throughout the Interactions, we'll draw your attention to questions you might want to ask about specific graphics.

Interpret Tables

A table is an arrangement of information in rows and columns. Tables condense a lot of information into a small space, and they make pieces of information easy to compare. Tables may be comprised of information reported in words or in numbers.

INTERACTION 10–1 | **Analyze a Table from a Health Textbook**

Read the following passage, which includes a table, and answer the questions that follow. Remember to follow these four steps:

1. Read the title of the table carefully.

2. Read the headings of rows and columns carefully.

3. If different colors are used, notice their meaning.

4. Think critically about the implications of the headings, the numbers, and the way the information is presented.

Vitamins

1   **Vitamins,** which help put proteins, fats, and carbohydrates to use, are essential to regulating growth, maintaining tissue, and releasing energy from foods. Together with the enzymes in the body, they help produce the right chemical reactions at the right times. They're also involved in the manufacture of blood cells, hormones, and other compounds.

2   The body produces some vitamins, such as vitamin D, which is manufactured in the skin after exposure to sunlight. Other vitamins must be ingested.

3   Vitamins A, D, E, and K are fat-soluble; they are absorbed through the intestinal membranes and stored in the body.

4   The B vitamins and vitamin C are water-soluble; they are absorbed directly into the blood and then used up or washed out of the body in urine and sweat. They must be replaced daily. Table 10.1 summarizes key information about vitamins.

Table 10.1 Key Information about Vitamins

Vitamin/ Recommended Intake per Day	Significant Sources	Chief Functions	Signs of Severe, Prolonged Deficiency	Signs of Extreme Excess
FAT-SOLUBLE VITAMINS				
Vitamin A Males 19–50: 900 μg Females 19–50: 700 μg	Fortified milk, cheese, cream, butter, fortified margarine, eggs, liver; spinach and other dark, leafy greens, broccoli, deep orange fruits (apricots, cantaloupes) and vegetables (carrots, sweet potatoes, pumpkins)	Antioxidant; needed for vision, health of cornea, epithelial cells, mucous membranes, skin health, bone and tooth growth, reproduction, immunity	Anemia, painful joints, cracks in teeth, tendency toward tooth decay, diarrhea, depression, frequent infections, night blindness, keratinization, corneal degeneration, rashes, kidney stones	Nosebleeds, bone pain, growth retardation, headaches, abdominal cramps and pain, vomiting, diarrhea, weight loss, overreactive immune system, blurred vision, fatigue, irritability, hair loss, dry skin

Vitamin/ Recommended Intake per Day	Significant Sources	Chief Functions	Signs of Severe, Prolonged Deficiency	Signs of Extreme Excess
Vitamin D Males 19–50: 5 µg Females 19–50: 5 µg	Fortified milk or margarine, eggs, liver, sardines; exposure to sunlight	Mineralization of bones (promotes calcium and phosphorus absorption)	Abnormal growth, misshapen bones (bowing of legs), soft bones, joint pain, malformed teeth	Raised blood calcium, excessive thirst, headaches, irritability, loss of appetite, weakness, nausea, kidney stones, deposits in arteries
Vitamin E Males 19–50: 15 mg Females 19–50: 15 mg	Polyunsaturated plant oils (margarine, salad dressings, shortenings), green and leafy vegetables, wheat germ, whole-grain products, nuts, seeds	Antioxidant; needed for stabilization of cell membranes, regulation of oxidation reactions	Red blood cell breakage, anemia, muscle degeneration, difficulty walking, leg cramps	Augments the effects of anticlotting medication; general discomfort; blurred vision
Vitamin K Males 19–50: 120 µg Females 19–50: 90 µg	Green leafy vegetables, cabbage-type vegetables, soybeans, vegetable oils	Synthesis of blood-clotting proteins and proteins important in bone mineralization	Hemorrhage	Interference with anticlotting medication; jaundice

WATER-SOLUBLE VITAMINS

Vitamin/ Recommended Intake per Day	Significant Sources	Chief Functions	Signs of Severe, Prolonged Deficiency	Signs of Extreme Excess
Vitamin B$_6$ Males 19–50: 1.3 mg Females 19–50: 1.3 mg	Meats, fish, poultry, liver, legumes, fruits, whole grains, potatoes, soy products	Part of a coenzyme used in amino acid and fatty acid metabolism, helps make red blood cells	Anemia, depression, abnormal brain wave pattern, convulsions, skin rashes	Impaired memory, irritability, headaches, numbness, damage to nerves, difficulty walking, loss of reflexes

Vitamin/ Recommended Intake per Day	Significant Sources	Chief Functions	Signs of Severe, Prolonged Deficiency	Signs of Extreme Excess
Vitamin B$_{12}$ Males 19–50: 2.4 µg Females 19–50: 2.4 µg	Animal products (meat, fish, poultry, milk, cheese, eggs)	Part of a coenzyme used in new cell synthesis, helps maintain nerve cells	Anemia, nervous system degeneration progressing to paralysis, hypersensitivity	None known
Vitamin C Males 19–50: 90 mg Females 19–50: 75 mg	Citrus fruits, cabbage-type vegetables, dark green vegetables, cantaloupe, strawberries, peppers, lettuce, tomatoes, potatoes, papayas, mangoes	Antioxidant, collagen synthesis (strengthens blood vessel walls, forms scar tissue, matrix for bone growth), amino acid metabolism, strengthens resistance to infection, aids iron absorption	Anemia, pinpoint hemorrhages, frequent infections, bleeding gums, loosened teeth, muscle degeneration and pain, joint pain, blotchy bruises, failure of wounds to heal	Nausea, abdominal cramps, diarrhea, excessive urination, headache, fatigue, insomnia, rashes; deficiency symptoms may appear at first on withdrawal of high doses
Thiamin Males 19–50: 90 mg Females 19–50: 1.1 mg	Pork, ham, bacon, liver, whole grains, legumes, nuts; occurs in all nutritious foods in moderate amounts	Part of a coenzyme used in energy metabolism, supports normal appetite and nervous system function	Edema, enlarged heart, nervous/ muscular system degeneration, difficulty walking, loss of reflexes, mental confusion	None reported
Riboflavin Males 19–50: 1.3 mg Females 19–50: 1.1 mg	Milk, yogurt, cottage cheese, meat, leafy green vegetables, whole-grain or enriched breads and cereals	Part of a coenzyme used in energy metabolism, supports normal vision and skin health	Cracks at corner of mouth, magenta tongue, hypersensitivity to light, reddening of cornea, skin rash	None reported
Niacin Males 19–50: 16 mg Females 19–50: 14 mg	Milk, eggs, meat, poultry, fish, whole-grain and enriched breads and cereals, nuts, and all protein-containing foods	Part of a coenzyme used in energy metabolism	Diarrhea, black smooth tongue, irritability, loss of appetite, weakness, dizziness, mental confusion, flaky skin rash on areas exposed to sun	Nausea, vomiting, painful flush and rash, sweating, liver damage

Vitamin/ Recommended Intake per Day	Significant Sources	Chief Functions	Signs of Severe, Prolonged Deficiency	Signs of Extreme Excess
Folate Males 19–50: 400 µg Females 19–50: 400 µg	Leafy green vegetables, legumes, seeds, liver, enriched breads, cereal, pasta, and grains	Part of a coenzyme needed for new cell synthesis	Anemia, heartburn, frequent infections, smooth red tongue, depression, mental confusion	Masks vitamin B_{12} deficiency
Pantothenic acid Males 19–50: 5 mg Females 19–50: 5 mg	Widespread in foods	Part of a coenzyme used in energy metabolism	Vomiting, intestinal distress, insomnia, fatigue	Water retention (rare)
Biotin Males 19–50: 30 µg Females 19–50: 30 µg	Widespread in foods	Used in energy metabolism, fat synthesis, amino acid metabolism, and glycogen synthesis	Abnormal heart action, loss of appetite, nausea, depression, muscle pain, drying of facial skin	None reported

Source: Adapted from Sizer, Frances, and Ellie Whitney. *Nutrition: Concepts and Controversies,* 10th ed. Belmont, CA: Wadsworth, 2006.

—From HALES. *An Invitation to Health,* 12e (pp. 152–153)
Copyright © 2007 Cengage Learning.

1. What is the purpose of this table? _____

_____

2–3. What are two differences between fat-soluble and water-soluble vitamins?

   a. _____

   _____

   b. _____

   _____

4–8. What five categories are reported by this table?

- _____
- _____
- _____
- _____
- _____

9. If you needed to thin your blood, what vitamin and foods would you most likely need to limit or decrease? _____

_____

10. To strengthen your bones, you should ingest more of what? _____

_____

Interpret Pie Charts

A pie chart shows how a whole pie—100 percent of something—is divided up. Pie charts help readers compare the percentages or proportions of different components of a whole.

| INTERACTION 10–2 | Analyze a Financial Pie Chart |

Read the following passage, which includes a pie chart, and answer the questions that follow. Remember to follow these four steps:

1. Read the title of the graphic carefully.

2. Read the names of categories carefully.

3. If different colors are used, notice their meaning.

4. Think critically about the implications of the headings, the numbers, and the way the information is presented.

Budgeting Your Money

How We Spend Our Income

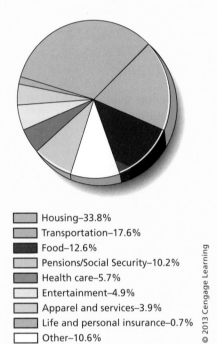

Housing–33.8%
Transportation–17.6%
Food–12.6%
Pensions/Social Security–10.2%
Health care–5.7%
Entertainment–4.9%
Apparel and services–3.9%
Life and personal insurance–0.7%
Other–10.6%

© 2013 Cengage Learning

Source: "Consumer Expenditures in 2006,"
Washington, DC: U.S. Department of Labor,
Bureau of Labor Statistics, Report 1010,
October 2008, p. 4.

1   The pie chart above tells you what the average American consumer spends income on. Three of those categories account for almost two-thirds of what we spend: food, housing, and transportation.

2   It's one thing to know where others spend their money, but it can be difficult to know where your money goes. While there are many financial experts and a variety of budgeting plans and software, and no budget is the same, the basic categories and expenditure percentages should be similar.

- Pay yourself first—save 10 percent

- Housing—no more than 35 percent of your income

- Transportation—10 to 20 percent

- Debt repayment—no more than 10 percent (the less you have the better)
- Food—5 to 15 percent
- Utilities—5 to 10 percent
- Medical—5 to 10 percent
- Entertainment/recreation—5 to 10 percent
- Personal/miscellaneous—5 to 10 percent

3   Even though each person's budget will be different, it is important to have a budget. You need to know where your money is going; otherwise, it is very easy to overspend and go into debt.

4   You can begin by tracking what you spend in each of the above categories. Once you know what you are spending, you can see if you are above or below the recommended percentages. Then you can start cutting back in areas that are not essential or in areas where you are spending more than you realized. Once you get a handle on your spending by following a budget, you can begin either paying down your debt or building up your savings. Whatever your financial state, a budget is essential in finding financial stability and success.

1. What is the purpose of the pie chart? _____

_____

2. What pattern of organization is shown in the pie chart? _____

3. What is the significance of each color? _____

4. What category do you think eating out would fit into? _____

_____

5. What category is your largest monthly expense? _____

6. Do you make a monthly budget? Why or why not? _____

_____

7. Visit the following website to see an interactive pie chart where you can enter your monthly take-home pay and see how much your pie-chart percentages should be: **www.cnbc.com/id/26641187**.

Interpret Line Graphs

Line graphs are used to show how a condition or behavior changes over time. The number of people engaging in a behavior is often plotted on the *y*-axis (the vertical line). The units of time, such as years, are plotted on the *x*-axis, or horizontal line. Line graphs help make it easy to see trends in data.

INTERACTION 10–3	Analyze a Line Graph from a Gallup Poll

Read the following passage, which includes a line graph, and answer the questions that follow. Remember to follow these four steps:

1. Read the title of the graphic carefully.

2. Read the labels on *x*- and *y*-axes carefully.

3. If different colors are used, notice their meaning.

4. Think critically about the implications of the headings, the numbers, and the way the information is presented.

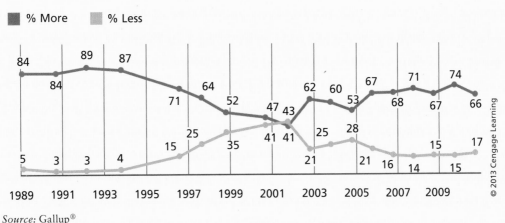

Americans Still Perceive Crime as on the Rise

Two-thirds say crime increasing in U.S., 49% in their local area

Jeffrey M. Jones

1 Two-thirds of Americans say there is more crime in the United States than there was a year ago, reflecting Americans' general tendency to perceive crime as increasing. Still, the percentage perceiving an increase in crime is below what Gallup measured in the late 1980s and early 1990s, but is higher than the levels from the late 1990s and early 2000s.

1989–2010 trend: Is there more crime in the U.S. than there was a year ago, or less?

■ % More   ■ % Less

Source: Gallup®

2   Americans are somewhat more positive about the trend in crime in their local area, but still are more likely to see it going up than going down.

1973–2010 trend: Is there more crime in your area than there was a year ago, or less?

■ % More   ▨ % Less

Source: Gallup®

3   These trends, based on Gallup's annual Crime survey, come at a time when both the FBI and the Bureau of Justice Statistics recently reported drops in property and violent crime from 2008 to 2009 in separate studies, as well as documenting longer-term declines in both types of crime. Though the latest Gallup estimates, from an Oct. 7–10, 2010, survey, would reflect a more up-to-date assessment of the crime situation than those reports do, Americans were also likely to perceive crime as increasing both locally and nationally in the 2009 Gallup Crime survey.

4   The apparent contradiction in assessments of the crime situation stems from Americans' general tendency to view crime as increasing. That said, the percentage holding this view appears to be higher when crime actually is increasing, as in the late 1980s and early 1990s, than when it is not.

5   Americans' perceptions of crime may also be influenced by their general assessments of how things are going in the country. Americans generally believe the crime situation to be better when their satisfaction with national conditions is high, as in the late 1990s, when the economy was strong, and in the wake of the 9/11 terror attacks, when patriotism and support for political leaders surged. Thus, the current estimates of increasing crime may to some degree be inflated due to widespread dissatisfaction with the state of the U.S. today.

6   Apart from whether the crime rate is increasing, 60% of Americans believe the crime problem in the U.S. is "extremely" or "very serious," up from 55% in 2009

and tied for the highest Gallup has measured since 2000. A majority of Americans have typically rated the U.S. crime problem as extremely or very serious in the 11-year history of this question.

7   As is usually the case, Americans are much less concerned about the crime problem in their local area, as 13% say the crime problem is extremely or very serious where they live.

2000–2010 trend: Overall, how would you describe the problem of crime in the United States/in the area where you live?

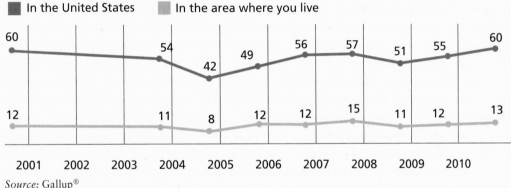

% Extremely/Very serious

■ In the United States   ■ In the area where you live

Source: Gallup®

8   Americans who have been victimized by crime in the past 12 months are about twice as likely as those who have not been victimized to describe the crime problem in their local area as very serious (18% to 10%). Crime victims are also substantially more likely to perceive crime as increasing in their local area (62% to 43%). However, being a victim of crime bears little relationship to the way one perceives the crime situation in the U.S.

—Jeffrey M. Jones, "Americans Still Perceive Crime as on the Rise." Copyright © 2011 by the Gallup Organization. Reprinted by permission.

1. What do these graphs measure? _____

   _____

2. What does the *y*-axis measure? _____

   _____

3. What does the *x*-axis measure? _____

_____

4. What does the dark green line represent in the first two line graphs? _____

_____

5. What does the light green line represent in the last line graph? _____

_____

6. What is the purpose of these graphs? _____

_____

7. What patterns of organization do the graphs represent? _____

8. Which year on the second graph shows the greatest difference in perceptions of

the amount of local crime? _____

9. Name two factors that affect Americans' view of crime. _____

_____

_____

_____

10. What conclusion can one draw from these graphs? _____

_____

_____

_____

Interpret Bar Graphs

Bar graphs help readers compare differences between groups. A bar graph can show the relationship between two sets of numbers, such as the number of people doing two different things over a certain number of years.

INTERACTION 10–4 | Analyze a Bar Graph from a Sociology Textbook

Read the following passage, which includes a bar graph, and answer the questions that follow. Remember to follow these four steps:

1. Read the title of the graphic carefully.

2. Read the labels on *x*- and *y*-axes carefully.

3. If different colors are used, notice their meaning.

4. Think critically about the implications of the headings, the numbers, and the way the information is presented.

Self-Report Surveys

1   First a word about crime statistics. Much crime is not reported to the police. For example, many common assaults go unreported because the assailant is a friend or a relative of the victim. Similarly, many rape victims are reluctant to report the crime because they are afraid they will be humiliated and stigmatized by making it public. Moreover, authorities and the wider public decide which criminal acts to report and which to ignore. For instance, if the authorities decide to crack down on drugs, more drug-related crimes will be counted, not because more drug-related crimes occur but because more drug criminals are apprehended. Third, many crimes are not incorporated in major crime indexes by the FBI. Excluded are many so-called **victimless crimes,** such as prostitution and illegal drug use, which involve violations of the law in which no victim steps forward and is identified. Also excluded from the indexes are most white-collar crimes.

2   Recognizing these difficulties, students of crime often supplement official crime statistics with other sources of information. **Self-report surveys** are especially useful. In such surveys respondents are asked to report their involvement in criminal activities, either as perpetrators or victims. In the United States, the main source of data on victimization is the National Crime Victimization Survey, conducted by the U.S. Department of Justice twice annually since 1973 and involving a nationwide sample of about 80,000 people in 43,000 households (Rennison, 2002). Among other things, such surveys show about the same rate of serious crime (e.g., murder and non-negligent manslaughter) as official statistics but two to three times the rate of less serious crime, such as assault. Figure 10.1 shows some of the results of an international self-report survey conducted in 1996. Among the 11 Western countries studied, the United States is at the high end with respect to violent offenses and household burglary and below average with respect to theft of personal property. Survey data, however, are influenced by peoples' willingness and ability to discuss criminal

experiences frankly. Therefore, indirect measures of crime are sometimes used as well. For instance, sales of syringes are a good index of the use of illegal intravenous drugs. Indirect measures are unavailable for many types of crime, however.

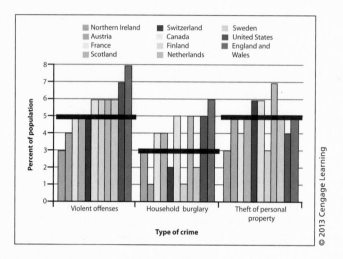

Figure 10.1 Percent of population victimized once or more in preceding 12 months, by type of crime

Note: Horizontal lines indicate international average for each type of crime. Data are for 1996.

Source: "Criminal Victimization," Sandra Besserer, *Juristat,* Vol. 18, No. 6, 1998.

—From BRYM/LIE. *Sociology: Your Compass for a New World,* Brief Edition (p. 149)

Copyright © 2010 Cengage Learning.

1. What is the purpose of this bar graph? _____

_____

2. What is the main pattern of organization of this bar graph? _____

3. What is the *y*-axis measuring? _____

4. What is the *x*-axis measuring? _____

5. What do the colors represent? _____

6. What does the horizontal black line represent? _____

7. What country has the lowest percentage of household burglaries? _____

_____

8. What category of crime ranks highest across countries? _____

What ranks the lowest? _____

Interpret Flowcharts

Flowcharts, also called process charts, show how different stages in a process are connected. You should read flowcharts from left to right and from top to bottom. Flowcharts can be simple or quite technical, with different box colors representing different aspects of the process.

INTERACTION 10–5 | **Analyze a Flowchart from a Population Textbook**

Read the text that accompanies the flowchart in Figure 10.2, and answer the questions that follow. Follow these four steps:

1. Read the title of the graphic carefully.

2. Read the headings or box content carefully.

3. Notice the flow of the boxes.

4. Think critically about the implications of the headings, the flow of the boxes, and the way the information is presented.

Reproductive Rights, Reproductive Health, and the Fertility Transition

1 As the life expectancy of the urban woman increased and as her childbearing activity declined, the lack of alternative activities was bound to create pressures for change, and over time the urban opportunities for women have multiplied. In the figure accompanying this essay (Figure 10.2), I have diagrammed the major paths by which mortality, fertility, and urbanization influence the status of women and lead to more egalitarian gender roles and improved reproductive health. Increased

longevity eventually lessens the pressure for high fertility and lessens the pressure to marry early. These changes permit a woman greater freedom for alternative activities before marrying and having children as well as providing more years beyond child-bearing. Women are left to search for alternatives, which are importantly wrapped up in higher levels of education. Society is then offered a "new" resource—nondomestic female labor. This creates new opportunities for a woman's economic independence, which is key to controlling her life, including her reproduction.

2   Having greater control over her own life, enhanced by lower fertility, also improves a woman's health in the process, even without government programs designed to increase reproductive health. Keep in mind, however, that public policy supporting gender equity, reproductive rights, and reproductive health can go a long way toward accelerating these changes in society. For its part, the fertility transition can be viewed as a key element in the broader pattern of changes involved in the demographic transition associated with women being able to take control of their lives and their bodies.

The Demographic Linkage Between the Fertility Transition and Reproductive Health

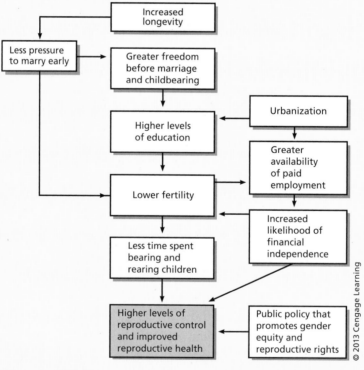

© 2013 Cengage Learning

Figure 10.2

—From WEEKS. *Population*, 10e (pp. 213, 215)
Copyright © 2008 Cengage Learning.

1. What pattern of organization is represented in this flowchart? _____

2. Explain what the box with the darker shading represents in this flowchart. ___

_____

3. Define *fertility transition*. _____

_____

4. List the three main influences in this flowchart:

   a. _____

   b. _____

   c. _____

5. Based on this flowchart, what two things does lower fertility lead to?

   a. _____

   b. _____

Interpret Photographs

Photographs are used in textbooks to illustrate the ideas being discussed. Photograph captions connect the photo to the idea being illustrated and should be read just as carefully as the title of a chart, a graph, or a table.

| INTERACTION 10–6 | Analyze a Photograph from an Anthropology Textbook |

Read the following passage, which includes a photo, and answer the questions that follow. Remember to follow these four steps:

1. Read the heading carefully.

2. Read the photo caption carefully.

3. Notice the relationships within the image as well as between the image and the text.

4. Think critically about the implications of the headings and the way the information is presented.

Malnutrition

1   In general, we are concerned with two types of nutrients when we talk of malnutrition. A shortfall in the intake of energy (calories) and protein is referred to as **protein-energy malnutrition (PEM)**. We group energy and protein together because it has been recognized since the 1970s that shortfalls in energy and protein go together. Individuals who don't have enough energy usually don't have enough protein and vice versa. The second form of malnutrition is **micronutrient malnutrition**, sometimes called "hidden hunger." This is caused by a shortfall in the amount of vitamins and minerals that a person consumes. The most easily recognized forms of PEM are kwashiorkor and marasmus, both of which are found predominantly in children under 6 years of age.

2   Initially recognized by Dr. Cicely Williams in West Africa in the early twentieth century, **kwashiorkor** is the indigenous name used to describe the disease that occurs when another baby displaces a child from the breast. And indeed, the condition clinically recognized as kwashiorkor most frequently develops several months after switching a child from breast milk to a starchy diet providing adequate caloric intake but insufficient protein. In its more extreme forms, kwashiorkor includes moderate to severe growth failure and muscles that are poorly developed and lack tone. Edema is usually severe, resulting in a large potbelly and swollen legs and face and masking the muscle loss that has occurred. The child has prolonged apathy and general misery, he or she whimpers, but does not generally cry or scream because to do so would take too much energy.

3   **Marasmus** results from a diet lacking in calories, while intakes of protein and other nutrients may be well balanced. Severe growth failure and emaciation are the most striking characteristics of the marasmic infant. The wasting of the muscles and lack of subcutaneous fat are extreme. Marasmus differs from kwashiorkor in several ways. The onset is earlier, usually in the first year of life; growth failure is more extreme; there is not edema; and the liver is not infiltrated with fat. The period of recovery is much longer. In both marasmus and kwashiorkor, height and weight-for-height are markedly retarded.

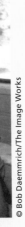

left Children suffering from a severe form of protein deficiency called kwashiorkor experience swelling in the arms, legs, and stomach area. The swelling hides the devastating wasting that is taking place within their bodies. This child has the characteristic "moon face" (edema), swollen belly, and patchy dermatitis (from zinc deficiency) often seen with kwashiorkor.
right Individuals with marasmus look starved. People with this condition lack both protein and calories. This child is suffering from the extreme emaciation of marasmus.

—From BRYANT/COURTNEY/DEWALT/SCHWARTZ. *The Cultural Feast: An Introduction to Food and Culture*, 2e (pp. 282–284) Copyright © 2004 Cengage Learning.

1. What is the purpose of the two photos in the reading selection? _____

_____

_____

2. What patterns of organization do the photos illustrate? _____

3. What is edema? _____

4. What causes kwashiorkor? _____

5. What causes marasmus? _____

6. Which PEM is more severe? Support your answer with details. _____

_____

7. How does seeing these photos affect you? _____

_____

Chapter Summary Activity: Applying Critical Thinking Skills to Visuals

Chapter 10 has discussed how to interpret the meaning of visuals, such as tables, pie charts, line graphs, bar graphs, flowcharts, and photographs. Fill in the following Reading Guide by completing each idea on the left with information from Chapter 10 on the right. You can return to this guide throughout the course as a reminder of how to interpret visuals.

Reading Guide to Applying Critical Thinking Skills to Visuals

Complete this idea	with information from Chapter 10.
The four steps to interpreting visuals are:	1. _____ _____ 2. _____ _____ 3. _____ _____ 4. _____ _____
A table arranges information in	5. _____ _____
Pie charts help readers understand	6. _____ _____
Line graphs are used to	7. _____ _____
Bar graphs help readers	8. _____ _____
Flowcharts, also called process charts, show	9. _____ _____

Complete this idea	with information from Chapter 10.
Photographs are used in textbooks to	10. _____ _____

11. Think about what your reading strategies were before you read Chapter 10. How did they differ from the suggestions here? Write your thoughts.

_____

_____

_____

PART 3

"If you're trying to build for the future, you must build its foundation strong."

—Russell Crowe as Robin Hood in the film *Robin Hood*

Reading Across the Disciplines

The story of Robin Hood revolves around miscommunication and the inability to compromise. For example, in one scene from the most recent movie version, Eleanor of Aquitaine (the queen) says to her son, Prince John (the bad guy), "Milking a dried udder gets you nothing but kicked off the milking stool!" Prince John responds, "Mother, spare me your farmyard memories; you have none and I don't understand them."

The mother was trying to warn her son that taxing people who had no money would cause trouble, but he did not even try to understand.

Sometimes it's hard to hear (and understand) what people mean. The keys to comprehension—in conversation and in reading—are paying careful attention, using prior knowledge, and understanding context clues. As you work through the readings in Part 3, see if you can find any common ground with the content by applying the skills covered in Chapters 1–10. Attend to what the author is saying; connect the information to what you already know; ask questions to resolve any conflict you might be having with the text. Use the foundation you have built for a strong reading future.

. . . .

Focus on Your Prior Knowledge

In Chapter 1 (on page 3) you were asked to share three things that help you focus. Go back and review those. Then write three more strategies that you have learned or improved upon in regard to your focus while working through Chapters 1 through 9.

1. _____

2. _____

3. _____

What advice would you give to someone who is struggling with his or her focus?

_____

_____

_____

Reading A

● Pre-Reading the Selection

The excerpt that begins on page 633 comes from the health textbook *An Invitation to Health*. The excerpt is titled "Stress on Campus."

Surveying the Reading

1. Survey the textbook selection that follows. Then check the elements that are included in this reading.

_____ Title

_____ Headings

_____ First sentences of paragraphs

_____ Words in bold or italic type

_____ Images and captions

Guessing the Purpose

2. Based on the source and the title of the reading selection, do you think the author's purpose is mostly to persuade, inform, or express? _____

Predicting the Content

3. Based on your survey, what are three things you expect the reading selection to discuss?

- _____

- _____

- _____

Activating Your Knowledge

4. What types of stress have you felt as a student? What causes you the most stress as a student?

- _____

- _____

- _____

● Reading with Pen in Hand

Students who annotate as they read are more successful than students who do not annotate. That's why you will annotate each reading in *Engage* as you read. In the reading that follows, use the following symbols:

★ or ⟨Point⟩   to indicate a main idea

①②③   to indicate major details

Access the Reading CourseMate via **www.cengagebrain.com** to hear vocabulary words from this selection and view a video about this topic.

Stress on Campus

1   You've probably heard that these are the best years of your life, but being a student—full-time or part-time, in your late teens, early twenties, or later in life—can be extremely stressful. You may feel pressure to perform well to qualify for a good job or graduate school. To meet steep tuition payments, you may have to juggle part-time work and coursework. You may feel stressed about choosing a major, getting along with a difficult roommate, passing a particularly hard course, or living up to your parents' and teachers' expectations. If you're an older student, you may have children, housework, and homework to balance. Your days may seem so busy and your life so full that you worry about coming apart at the seams. One thing is for certain: You're not alone.

2   After a steady surge upward in the 1990s, the percentage of students who say they are "frequently overwhelmed by all they have to do" has declined from the peak of 30.7 percent in 1999 to 27.4 percent in 2004. However, women are more than twice as likely to report stress as men. According to surveys of students at colleges and universities around the country and the world, stressors are remarkably similar. Among the most common are:

- **Test pressures.**
- **Financial problems.**
- **Frustrations,** such as delays in reaching goals.
- **Problems in friendships** and dating relationships.
- **Daily hassles.**

- **Academic failure.**
- **Pressures** as a result of competition, deadlines, and the like.
- **Changes,** which may be unpleasant, disruptive, or too frequent.
- **Losses,** whether caused by the breakup of a relationship or death of a loved one.

3 Many students bring complex psychological problems with them to campus, including learning disabilities and mood disorders like depression and anxiety. "Students arrive with the underpinnings of problems that are brought out by the stress of campus life," says one counselor. Some have grown up in broken homes and bear the scars of family troubles. Others fall into the same patterns of alcohol abuse that they observed for years in their families or suffer lingering emotional scars from childhood physical or sexual abuse.

4 Students aren't the only ones complaining about stress on campus. Professors working toward tenure also report high stress levels—particularly women. The reason for this gender difference may be that women take on more responsibility for mentoring female students and for teaching independent study courses with individual students.

Students Under Stress

5 More than a quarter of freshmen feel overwhelmed by all they have to do at the beginning of the academic year; by the year's end, 44 percent feel overwhelmed. In research at three universities, underclassmen were most vulnerable to negative life events, perhaps because they lacked experience in coping with stressful situations. Freshmen had the highest levels of depression; sophomores had the most anger and hostility. Seniors may handle life's challenges better because they have developed better coping mechanisms. In the study, more seniors reported that they faced problems squarely and took action to resolve them, while younger students were more likely to respond passively, for instance, by trying not to let things bother them.

6 First-generation college students—those whose parents never experienced at least one full year of college—encounter more difficulties with social adjustment than freshmen whose parents attended college. Second-generation students may have several advantages: more knowledge of college life, greater social support, more preparation for college in high school, a greater focus on college activities, and more financial resources.

7   The percentage of students seeking psychological help because of stress or anxiety has risen dramatically in the last 15 years. Students say they react to stress in various ways: physiologically (by sweating, stuttering, trembling, or developing physical symptoms); emotionally (by becoming anxious, fearful, angry, guilty, or depressed); behaviorally (by crying, eating, smoking, being irritable or abusive); or cognitively (by thinking about and analyzing stressful situations and strategies that might be useful in dealing with them).

8   A supportive network of friends and family makes a difference. Undergraduates with higher levels of social support and self-efficacy reported feeling less stressed and more satisfied with life than others.

9   Does stress increase drinking among college students? Many assume so, since life stress is a recognized risk for alcohol use in general. In a recent study of 137 undergraduates, however, the relationship between drinking and stress turned out to be more complex. For some, drinking occasions were times to discuss problems with friends, regardless of the day's stress. On average, students tended to drink more on days when they were feeling good—possibly because of what the researchers called the "celebratory and social" nature of college drinking. Drinking—and positive emotions—also peaked on weekends.

10   Campuses are providing more frontline services than they have in the past, including career-guidance workshops, telephone hot lines, and special social programs for lonely, homesick freshmen. In one study of 128 undergraduates, those who learned relaxation and stress-reduction techniques in a six-week program reported less stress, anxiety, and psychological distress than a control group of students. The participants—who had described themselves as "extremely stressed" before the intervention—also began to increase health-promoting behaviors.

How Can I Cope With Test Stress?

11   For many students, midterms and final exams are the most stressful times of the year. Students at various colleges and universities found that the incidence of colds and flu soared during finals. Some students feel the impact of test stress in other ways—headaches, upset stomachs, skin flare-ups, or insomnia.

12   Because of stress's impact on memory, students with advanced skills may perform worse under exam pressure than their less skilled peers. Sometimes students become so preoccupied with the

possibility of failing that they can't concentrate on studying. Others, including many of the best and brightest students, freeze up during tests and can't comprehend multiple-choice questions or write essay answers, even if they know the material.

13   The students most susceptible to exam stress are those who believe they'll do poorly and who see tests as extremely threatening. Unfortunately, such negative thoughts often become a self-fulfilling prophecy. As they study, these students keep wondering: What good will studying do? I never do well on tests. As their fear increases, they try harder, pulling all-nighters. Fueled by caffeine, munching on sugary snacks, they become edgy and find it harder and harder to concentrate. By the time of the test, they're nervous wrecks, scarcely able to sit still and focus on the exam.

14   Can you do anything to reduce test stress and feel more in control? Absolutely. One way is to defuse stress through relaxation. Students taught relaxation techniques—such as controlled breathing, meditation, progressive relaxation, and guided imagery (visualization)—a month before finals tend to have higher levels of immune cells during the exam period and feel in better control during their tests.

Strategies for Prevention   DEFUSING TEST STRESS

- **Plan ahead.** A month before finals, map out a study schedule for each course. Set aside a small amount of time every day or every other day to review the course materials.

- **Be positive.** Picture yourself taking your final exam. Imagine yourself walking into the exam room feeling confident, opening up the test booklet, and seeing questions for which you know the answers.

- **Take regular breaks.** Get up from your desk, breathe deeply, stretch, and visualize a pleasant scene. You'll feel more refreshed than you would if you chugged another cup of coffee.

- **Practice.** Some teachers are willing to give practice finals to prepare students for test situations, or you and your friends can test each other.

- **Talk to other students.** Chances are that many of them share your fears about test taking and may have discovered some helpful techniques of their own. Sometimes talking to your adviser or a counselor can also help.

- **Be satisfied with doing your best.** You can't expect to ace every test; all you can and should expect is your best effort. Once you've completed the exam, allow yourself the sweet pleasure of relief that it's over.

—From HALES. *An Invitation to Health*, 12e (pp. 86–88)
Copyright © 2007 Cengage Learning.

● Comprehension Questions

Write the letter of the answer on the line. Then explain your thinking.

Vocabulary

____ 5. Which of the following best defines the word *lingering* as used in paragraph 3 of this selection?

   a. Leaving

   b. Remaining

   c. Revealing

   d. Harmless

WHY? What information in the selection leads you to give that answer? _____

_____

_____

_____

_____ 6. Which of the following best defines *squarely* as used in paragraph 5?

    a. Directly

    b. By thinking inside the box

    c. About a location

    d. Unimaginatively

WHY? What information in the selection leads you to give that answer? _____

_____

_____

_____

_____ 7. Which words below have the same general meaning as *chugged,* which appears in the "Strategies for Prevention" box?

    a. Sipped, nipped, tasted

    b. Bought, purchased, paid for

    c. Gulped, guzzled, swigged

    d. Avoided, evaded, dodged

WHY? What information in the selection leads you to give that answer? _____

_____

_____

_____

_____ 8. Based on the way the word *cognitively* is used in paragraph 7, which of the following is its dictionary definition?

    a. Of or relating to the way one acts or conducts oneself, especially in public.

    b. Of or relating to the mental process of acquiring knowledge and understanding to solve a problem or issue.

    c. Of or relating to how one feels.

    d. Of or relating to the inability to grasp or understand complex problems or situations.

WHY? What information in the selection leads you to give that answer? _____

_____

_____

_____

_____ 9. In paragraph 11, what does *incidence* mean?

    a. Accident

    b. Fluke

    c. Stress

    d. Occurrence

WHY? What information in the selection leads you to give that answer? _____

_____

_____

_____

Topics and Main Ideas

_____ 10. Which of the following best expresses the main idea of the selection?

    a. Stress is the number-one problem that all students face.

    b. Students need to learn how to cope with stress to successfully navigate school.

    c. The stress of students increases as the semester progresses.

    d. Many students experience school-related stress for a variety of reasons, but there are tactics that can be learned to help manage it.

WHY? What information in the selection leads you to give that answer? _____

_____

_____

_____

____ 11. Which of the following sentences best summarizes the bulleted list in the second paragraph?

    a. The common stressors that affect students on college campuses seem to be universal.

    b. American students find that many things cause stress.

    c. There are only nine stressors that students experience.

    d. Frustrations, friendships, pressures, changes, and losses cause more stress than the other items listed.

WHY? What information in the selection leads you to give that answer? _____

_____

_____

_____

____ 12. Which of the following statements is the best topic sentence of paragraph 3?

    a. "Students arrive with the underpinnings of problems that are brought out by the stress of campus life," says one counselor.

    b. Others fall into the same patterns of alcohol abuse that they observed for years in their families or suffer lingering emotional scars from childhood physical or sexual abuse.

    c. Many students bring complex psychological problems with them to campus, including learning disabilities and mood disorders like depression and anxiety.

    d. Some have grown up in broken homes and bear the scars of family troubles.

WHY? What information in the selection leads you to give that answer? _____

_____

_____

_____

____ 13. Which of the following best expresses the main idea of the box "Strategies for Prevention"?

    a. The best way to deal with test anxiety is to do your best every time.

    b. There are several strategies for getting a handle on the stress caused by tests.

    c. To prevent test stress you should plan ahead, be positive, take breaks, and collaborate with other students when taking tests.

    d. Despite strategies, there is really no way to prevent test stress.

WHY? What information in the selection leads you to give that answer? _____

_____

_____

_____

____ 14. Which statement best summarizes the section "Students Under Stress"?

    a. Seniors are under less stress than freshmen and sophomores.

    b. Underclassmen are more vulnerable to stress.

    c. A supportive network of friends can help decrease stress levels in undergraduates.

    d. The reasons students are under stress and how they cope with their stress varies.

WHY? What information in the selection leads you to give that answer? _____

_____

_____

_____

Patterns of Supporting Details

____ 15. What pattern organizes this reading selection?

    a. Cause and effect

    b. Example

    c. Time order

    d. Contrast

WHY? What information in the selection leads you to give that answer? _____

_____

_____

_____

____ 16. What is the pattern of the first two sentences of paragraph 4?

      a. Definition

      b. Classification

      c. Example

      d. Comparison

WHY? What information in the selection leads you to give that answer? _____

_____

_____

_____

____ 17. Paragraph 13 has two patterns. What are they?

      a. Cause and effect; process

      b. Classification; description

      c. Cause and effect; space order

      d. Comparison and contrast; time order

WHY? What information in the selection leads you to give that answer? _____

_____

_____

_____

____ 18. What relationship is primarily demonstrated in paragraph 7?

      a. Classification

      b. Example

      c. Definition

      d. Cause and effect

WHY? What information in the selection leads you to give that answer? _____

_____

_____

_____

____ 19. What relationship is represented in this sentence in paragraph 1? *You've probably heard that these are the best years of your life, but being a student—full-time or part-time, in your late teens, early twenties, or later in life—can be extremely stressful.*

    a. Cause and effect

    b. Contrast

    c. Definition

    d. Example

WHY? What information in the selection leads you to give that answer? _____

_____

_____

_____

Note Taking

____ 20. Which of the following lists of topics best organizes the information in the reading selection?

    a. The misnomer of the unstressed student

       Studies of increased stress on campus

       First-generation college students

       Coping strategies

    b. Common campus stressors

       Which students are more susceptible to stress

       Stress management tips

    c. Strategies for prevention

       Coping with stress

       Stress and the college student

    d. Test pressures and other stressors

       Freshmen, sophomores, and seniors

       First-generation and second-generation students

       Psychological help on the rise

WHY? What information in the selection leads you to give that answer? _____

_____

_____

_____

21–24. Change paragraph 7 into an outline.

Topic: _____

Main idea: _____

Inferences

_____ 25. Based on the information in this passage, which of the following would the author agree is a common stressor among college students?

a. Time management issues

b. Not getting along with the teacher

c. Taking morning classes but not being a morning person

d. Not owning a personal computer

WHY? What information in the selection leads you to give that answer? _____

_____

_____

_____

____ 26. According to the reading selection, which of the following students probably has the best coping strategy for dealing with stress?

    a. A student whose aunt went to college but whose parents did not.

    b. A student who has completed ninety college credit hours.

    c. A student who comes from a home with a history of alcoholism.

    d. An out-of-state student with no family or friends close by.

WHY? What information in the selection leads you to give that answer? _____

_____

_____

_____

____ 27. Which of the following is _not_ an example of a common stressor?

    a. Juggling a full class schedule and a full-time job

    b. Four scheduled finals in two days

    c. Losing one's mother to cancer during the semester

    d. Feedback from an instructor on how to rewrite a C paper for a higher grade

WHY? What information in the selection leads you to give that answer? _____

_____

_____

_____

____ 28. If you are stuck in a traffic jam, which of the following actions would best help reduce your stress level?

a. Honking your horn and yelling

b. Berating yourself because you did not have the foresight to take a different route

c. Breathing slowly and deeply

d. Calling, texting, or sending e-mails from your smart phone to reschedule the day's appointments

WHY? What information in the selection leads you to give that answer? _____

_____

_____

_____

____ 29. Which of the following is an effect of stress?

a. It can rob you of energy.

b. It can distract you from fun.

c. It can interfere with achieving success.

d. All of the above.

WHY? What information in the selection leads you to give that answer? _____

_____

_____

_____

Purpose and Tone

____ 30. Which statement best characterizes the purpose of this selection?

a. To inform readers about the major causes of stress on American college and university campuses

b. To persuade readers that they can deal with stress effectively by following nine simple steps

c. To help readers identify with students who are stressed

d. To inform readers of the types of stress students experience, factors that increase their risk of stress, and how they can overcome it

WHY? What information in the selection leads you to give that answer? _____

_____

_____

_____

____ 31. The tone of the box "Strategies for Prevention" could be described as:

   a. Snide

   b. Instructional

   c. Persuasive

   d. New age

WHY? What information in the selection leads you to give that answer? _____

_____

_____

_____

____ 32. Which word best describes the tone of paragraph 14?

   a. Preachy

   b. Ambivalent

   c. Critical

   d. Encouraging

WHY? What information in the selection leads you to give that answer? _____

_____

_____

_____

_____ 33. Which word best characterizes the tone of the following sentences? *Some campuses have provided counseling services to help students manage stress. Some critics say that students need to learn how to cope with stress on their own. Should colleges reach out and help or should students be left to learn this skill on their own?*

    a. Paradoxical

    b. Disparaging

    c. Inquiring

    d. Argumentative

WHY? What information leads you to give that answer? _____

_____

_____

_____

_____ 34. What tone is conveyed in the following sentence? *You can take control of your own stress responses to testing by practicing relaxation techniques, not cramming, and having a positive attitude.*

    a. Empowering

    b. Hyperbolic

    c. Resentful

    d. Lethargic

WHY? What information leads you to give that answer? _____

_____

_____

_____

Points of View

_____ 35. Which of the following statements from the selection is presented as a fact and an opinion?

    a. In research at three universities, underclassmen were most vulnerable to negative life events, perhaps because they lacked experience in coping with stressful situations. (paragraph 5)

    b. According to surveys of students at colleges and universities around the country and the world, stressors are remarkably similar. (paragraph 2)

c. First-generation college students—those whose parents never experienced at least one full year of college—encounter more difficulties with social adjustment than freshmen whose parents attended college. (paragraph 6)

d. The students most susceptible to exam stress are those who believe they'll do poorly and who see tests as extremely threatening. (paragraph 13)

WHY? What information in the selection leads you to give that answer? _____

_____

_____

_____

_____ 36. Which description best characterizes this reading?

   a. Mostly factual from expert sources of information

   b. Mostly opinion from an informed source

   c. Full of biased opinions from a person on the street

   d. Full of statements of fact from an informed source

WHY? What information in the selection leads you to give that answer? _____

_____

_____

_____

_____ 37. Which statement best describes what the adjective *older* in the following sentence does? *If you're an older student, you may have children, housework, and homework to balance.*

   a. It points to a bias.

   b. It points to an insult.

   c. It points to an opinion.

   d. It points to a descriptive fact.

WHY? What information in the selection leads you to give that answer? _____

_____

_____

_____

_____ 38. Which of the following lends the most credibility to the author?

    a. She has a doctorate in health sciences

    b. Her concise, clear writing style, filled with factual details

    c. Her distinction between first- and second-generation students

    d. Her inclusion of a box giving extra information for dealing with test stress

WHY? What information in the selection leads you to give that answer? _____

_____

_____

_____

_____ 39. What bias does the author of this reading have?

    a. A belief that stress cannot be overcome

    b. A bias toward overanalyzing the issues surrounding stress on campus and its effects on college and university students

    c. A positive (though mostly factual) bias toward overcoming or at least managing stress

    d. A bias against college

WHY? What information in the selection leads you to give that answer? _____

_____

_____

_____

● Critical Thinking

CRITICAL THINKING LEVEL 1: REMEMBER

40. List at least five common stressors.

   ● _____

   ● _____

   ● _____

   ● _____

   ● _____

CRITICAL THINKING LEVEL 2: UNDERSTAND

41–44. Create Cornell notes, including a summary, based on the three sections of this reading.

CRITICAL THINKING LEVEL 3: APPLY

45. What social, cultural, or economic factors might play a role in the high levels of stress found among college students?

_____

_____

_____

_____

CRITICAL THINKING LEVEL 4: ANALYZE

46–48. There are two basic kinds of stress: **eustress,** which is moderate or normal stress that is considered beneficial, and **distress,** which is extreme or unhealthy stress. Identify at least three stressful situations in your life, and decide if they are eustress or distress.

_____

_____

_____

_____

CRITICAL THINKING LEVEL 5: EVALUATE

49. What techniques (either referred to in this reading selection or from your own experience) seem to be the most helpful ways for you to deal with stress? Think of a recent stressful experience, and evaluate whether you handled the stress in the best way. Did you do everything you could, or could you have coped better?

_____

_____

_____

_____

CRITICAL THINKING LEVEL 6: CREATE

50. Now that you have read this reading selection, think of some ways you could advise an incoming first-year student to deal with his or her stress.

_____

_____

_____

_____

Reading B

BUSINESS COMMUNICATION

● Pre-Reading the Selection

The excerpt that begins on page 654 comes from the business communication textbook *Contemporary Business Communication*. The excerpt is titled "Communicating in a Diverse Environment."

Surveying the Reading

1. Survey the textbook selection that follows. Then check the elements that are included in this reading.

_____ Title

_____ Headings

_____ First sentences of paragraphs

_____ Words in bold or italic type

_____ Images and captions

Guessing the Purpose

2. Based on the source and the title of the reading selection, do you think the author's purpose is mostly to persuade, inform, or express? _____

Predicting the Content

3. Based on your survey, what are three things you expect the reading selection to discuss?

- _____
- _____
- _____

Activating Your Knowledge

4. What do you know about other cultures' customs, based on people you know or cultures you have been exposed to on TV or in the movies? List a few cultures and give an example of one of their customs.

- _____
- _____
- _____

● Reading with Pen in Hand

Students who annotate as they read are more successful than students who do not annotate. That's why you will annotate each reading in *Engage* as you read. In the reading that follows, use the following symbols:

★ or (Point)   to indicate a main idea

① ② ③   to indicate major details

Access the Reading CourseMate via www.cengagebrain.com to hear vocabulary words from this selection and view a video about this topic.

Communicating in a Diverse Environment

1   Paying attention to the needs of others means that we recognize and accept diversity. When we talk about diversity, we mean cultural differences not only within the U.S. and Canadian work force but also in the worldwide marketplace. The dominant role that the United States plays in the global economy does not mean that international business matters are handled "the American way."

2   Some years ago a book called *The Ugly Americans* condemned Americans abroad for their "Let 'em do it our way or not at all" attitude. As Al Ries, chairman of Trout & Ries Advertising Inc., once pointed out, "A company that keeps its eye on Tom, Dick, and Harry is going to miss Pierre, Hans, and Yoshiko."

3   When we talk about culture, we mean the customary traits, attitudes, and behaviors of a group of people. **Ethnocentrism** is the belief that one's own cultural group is superior. Such an attitude hinders communication, understanding, and goodwill between trading partners. An attitude of arrogance is not only counterproductive but also unrealistic, considering that the U.S. population represents less than 5 percent of the world population. Moreover, of the world's countries, the United States is currently fourth in population and is expected to drop to eighth place by the year 2050.

4   Another fact of life in international business is that comparatively few Americans speak a foreign language. Although English is the major language for conducting business worldwide, it would be naive to assume that it is the other person's responsibility to learn English.

5   Diversity will have profound effects on our lives and will pose a growing challenge for managers. The following discussion provides useful guidance for communicating with people from different cultures—both internationally as well as domestically. Although it is helpful to be aware of cultural differences, competent communicators recognize that each member of a culture is an individual, with individual needs, perceptions, and experiences, and should be treated as such.

Cultural Differences

6   Cultures differ widely in the traits they value. For example, as shown in Table B.1, international cultures differ widely in their emphasis on individualism, long-term orientation, time orientation, power distance, uncertainty avoidance, formality, materialism, and context-sensitivity. (You should be aware, of course, that just as you are learning the international way of communicating, other cultures are learning the American way of communicating. At some point, perhaps one universal way of communicating will emerge—but don't hold your breath!)

7   Each person interprets events through his or her mental filter, and that filter is based on the receiver's unique knowledge, experiences, and viewpoints. For example, the language of time is as different among cultures as the language of words. Americans, Canadians, Germans, and Japanese are very time-conscious and very precise about appointments; Latin American and Middle Eastern cultures tend to be more casual about time. For example, if your

Mexican host tells you that he or she will meet with you at three, it's most likely *más o menos* (Spanish for "more or less").

8   Businesspeople in both Asian and Latin American countries tend to favor long negotiations and slow deliberations. They exchange pleasantries at some length before getting down to business. Likewise, many non-Western cultures use the silent intervals for contemplation, whereas businesspeople from the United States and Canada tend to have little tolerance for silence in business negotiations. As a result, Americans and Canadians may rush in and offer compromises and counterproposals that would have been unnecessary if they had shown more patience.

9   Body language, especially gestures and eye contact, also varies among cultures. For example, our sign for "okay"—forming a circle with our forefinger and thumb—means "zero" in France, "money" in Japan, and a vulgarity in Brazil. Americans and Canadians consider eye contact important. In Asia and many Latin American countries, however, looking a partner full in the eye is considered an irritating sign of ill breeding.

10 Touching behavior is very culture-specific. Many Asians do not like to be touched, except for a brief handshake in greeting. However, handshakes in much of Europe tend to last much longer than in the United States and Canada, and Europeans tend to shake hands every time they see each other, perhaps several times a day. Germans typically use a firm grip and one shake; Asians typically grasp the other's hand delicately and shake only briefly. In much of Europe, men often kiss each other upon greeting; unless an American or Canadian businessperson is aware of this custom, he or she might react inappropriately.

11 Our feelings about space are partly an outgrowth of our culture and partly a result of geography and economics. For example, Americans and Canadians are used to wide-open spaces and tend to move about expansively, using hand and arm motions for emphasis. But in Japan, which has much smaller living and working spaces, such abrupt and extensive body movements are not typical. Likewise, Americans and Canadians tend to sit face to face so they can maintain eye contact, whereas the Chinese and Japanese (to whom eye contact is not so important) tend to sit side by side during negotiations.

12 Also, the sense of personal space differs among cultures. In the United States and Canada, most business exchange occurs at about 5 feet, within the so-called social zone. However, both in Middle

Eastern and Latin American countries, this distance is too far. Businesspeople there tend to stand close enough to feel your breath as you speak. Most Americans and Canadians tend to back away unconsciously from such close contact.

13   Finally, social behavior is culture-dependent. For example, in the Japanese culture, the matter of who bows first upon meeting, how deeply the person bows, and how long the bow is held is dependent upon one's status.

14   Competent communicators become familiar with such role-related behavior and also learn the customs regarding giving (and accepting) gifts, exchanging business cards, the degree of formality expected, and the accepted means of entertaining and being entertained.

Group-Oriented Behavior

15   As shown in Table B.1, the business environment in a capitalistic society such as that in the United States and Canada places great value on the contributions of the individual toward the success of the organization. Individual effort is often stressed more than group effort, and a competitive atmosphere prevails. In other cultures, however, originality and independence of judgment are not valued as highly as teamwork. The Japanese say, "A nail standing out will be hammered down." Thus, the Japanese go to great lengths to reach decisions through consensus, wherein every participating member, not just a majority, is able to agree.

16   Closely related to the concept of group-oriented behavior is the notion of "saving face." The desire to save face simply means that neither party in a given interaction should suffer embarrassment. Human relationships are highly valued in Japanese cultures and are embodied in the concept of *wa*, or the Japanese pursuit of harmony. This concept makes it difficult for the Japanese to say "no" to a request because it would be impolite. They are very reluctant to offend others—even if they unintentionally mislead them instead. Thus, a "yes" to a Japanese might mean "Yes, I understand you" rather than "Yes, I agree."

17   Latin Americans also tend to avoid an outright "no" in their business dealings, preferring instead a milder, less explicit, response. In intercultural communications, one has to read between the lines, because what is left unsaid or unwritten may be just as important as what *is* said or written.

Table B.1 Cultural Values

Value	High	Low
Individualism: Cultures in which people see themselves first as individuals and believe that their own interests take priority.	United States Canada Great Britain Australia Netherlands	Japan Taiwan Mexico Greece Hong Kong
Long-Term Orientation: Cultures that maintain a long-term perspective.	Pacific Rim countries	United States Canada
Time Orientation: Cultures that perceive time as a scarce resource and that tend to be impatient.	United States	Pacific Rim and Middle Eastern countries
Power Distance: Cultures in which management decisions are made by the boss simply because he or she is the boss.	France Spain Japan Mexico Brazil	United States Israel Germany Ireland

Value	High	Low
Uncertainty Avoidance: Cultures in which people want predictable and certain futures.	Israel Japan Italy Argentina	United States Canada Australia Singapore
Formality: Cultures that attach considerable importance to tradition, ceremony, social rules, and rank.	Latin American countries	United States Canada Scandinavian countries
Materialism: Cultures that emphasize assertiveness and the acquisition of money and material objects.	Japan Austria Italy	Scandinavian countries
Context Sensitivity: Cultures that emphasize the surrounding circumstances (or context), make extensive use of body language, and take the time to build relationships and establish trust.	Asian, Hispanic, and African countries	Northern European countries

Source: From *Human Relations* by A. J. DuBrin. Copyright © 1997. Adapted by permission of Prentice-Hall, Inc. Upper Saddle River, NJ.

—From OBER. *Contemporary Business Communication,* 7e (pp. 45–49)
Copyright © 2009 Cengage Learning.

● Comprehension Questions

Write the letter of the answer on the line. Then explain your thinking.

Vocabulary

_____ 5. Which of the following best defines the word *culture* as used in paragraph 3 of this reading selection?

  a. How a group of people think and act

  b. Bacterial growth

c. Excellence in the arts

d. Care for others

WHY? What information in the selection leads you to give that answer? _____

_____

_____

_____

_____ 6. An example of *ethnocentrism* is:

a. One neighbor hating another

b. A Nazi's attitude toward a Jewish person

c. A man in a remote jungle tribe slapping his wife

d. A Chinese mother raising her children to excel

WHY? What information in the selection leads you to give that answer? _____

_____

_____

_____

_____ 7. What does *consensus* mean?

a. A minority of a group's members agree

b. The majority of the group agrees

c. All the members of the group agree

d. No one can agree on a solution

WHY? What information in the selection leads you to give that answer? _____

_____

_____

_____

_____ 8. What synonym for the word *expansive* is used in paragraph 11?

a. Outgrowth

b. Extensive

c. Emphasis

d. Economics

WHY? What information in the selection leads you to give that answer? _____

_____

_____

_____

____ 9. In paragraph 17, what clue is given to the meaning of the word *explicit*?

    a. An example: *business dealings*

    b. An antonym: *milder*

    c. A synonym: *outright*

    d. A root: *plic,* meaning "put"

WHY? What information in the selection leads you to give that answer? _____

_____

_____

_____

Topics and Main Ideas

____ 10. Which of the following best expresses the main idea of the reading selection?

    a. Business managers need to understand how people from different cultures think and act so they can communicate in a way that shows respect for others' way of life.

    b. Unless Americans learn to value cultural diversity, they will be perceived as arrogant—as they often have been.

    c. Business negotiators from Asia and Latin America tend to get more of what they want than Americans and Canadians because of their ability to wait out silences.

    d. The amount of eye contact that is considered appropriate varies from culture to culture.

WHY? What information in the selection leads you to give that answer? _____

_____

_____

_____

_____ 11. Which of the following statements from the selection best expresses the main idea of paragraph 9?

    a. Body language, especially gestures and eye contact, also varies among cultures.

    b. For example, our sign for "okay"—forming a circle with our forefinger and thumb—means "zero" in France, "money" in Japan, and a vulgarity in Brazil.

    c. Americans and Canadians consider eye contact important.

    d. In Asia and many Latin American countries, however, looking a partner full in the eye is considered an irritating sign of ill breeding.

WHY? What information in the selection leads you to give that answer? _____

_____

_____

_____

_____ 12. Which of the following statements best expresses the main idea of paragraph 10?

    a. In much of Europe, men often kiss each other upon greeting; unless an American or Canadian businessperson is aware of this custom, he or she might react inappropriately.

    b. Germans typically use a firm grip and one shake; Asians typically grasp the other's hand delicately and shake only briefly.

    c. Many Asians do not like to be touched, except for a brief handshake in greeting.

    d. Touching behavior is very culture-specific.

WHY? What information in the selection leads you to give that answer? _____

_____

_____

_____

____ 13. Which of the following best expresses the main idea of the section "Group-Oriented Behavior"?

a. "A nail standing out will be hammered down."

b. Originality and teamwork are equally valued in group-oriented cultures.

c. People from some cultures find it difficult to say "no" in meetings.

d. Cultures vary in whether they value the individual or the group more.

WHY? What information in the selection leads you to give that answer? _____

_____

_____

_____

____ 14. Which statement best summarizes the information given in the table?

a. The most important cultural value to understand is individualism.

b. Cultures value certain attitudes and approaches more than others.

c. Cultures value time, space, and material goods in varying proportions.

d. Western and Eastern cultures have opposing viewpoints on eight dimensions.

WHY? What information in the selection leads you to give that answer? _____

_____

_____

_____

Patterns of Supporting Details

____ 15. What pattern of organization is suggested by the heading "Cultural Differences"?

a. Time order

b. Contrast

c. Cause and effect

d. Space order

WHY? What information in the selection leads you to give that answer? _____

_____

_____

_____

_____ 16. What is the predominant pattern of organization in paragraph 7?

    a. Contrast

    b. Classification

    c. Example

    d. Space order

WHY? What information in the selection leads you to give that answer? _____

_____

_____

_____

_____ 17. How is paragraph 8 organized?

    a. Comparison

    b. Classification

    c. Process

    d. Definition

WHY? What information in the selection leads you to give that answer? _____

_____

_____

_____

_____ 18. What relationship is demonstrated in the following sentence? _Our feelings about space are partly an outgrowth of our culture and partly a result of geography and economics._

    a. Time order

    b. Example

    c. Definition

    d. Cause and effect

WHY? What information in the selection leads you to give that answer? _____

_____

_____

_____

____ 19. What three kinds of relationships does the following sentence include? *Thus, a "yes" to a Japanese might mean "Yes, I understand you" rather than "Yes, I agree."*

    a. Cause and effect, classification, example

    b. Cause and effect, definition, contrast

    c. Definition, example, comparison

    d. Time order, contrast, space order

WHY? What information in the selection leads you to give that answer? _____

_____

_____

_____

Note Taking

____ 20. Which of the following lists of topics best organizes the information in the selection?

    a. Americans' cultural problems

       Cultural differences in negotiations

       Competition versus teamwork orientation

    b. Cultural diversity's importance

       Cultural differences in valued traits

       Cultural differences related to working in groups

    c. The effects of ethnocentrism

       Cultural interpretations

       Business environments

    d. Communication skills

       International communications

       Agreement and disagreement

WHY? What information in the selection leads you to give that answer? _____

_____

_____

_____

21–24.   How do particular countries demonstrate their values of individualism and time orientation? Parts of Table B.1 are reprinted below. For one country in the "High" and "Low" column for each value, find the explanation in the reading selection of why the country is rated as high or low on the value. Note the specific information and the paragraph you found it in.

Value	High	Low
Individualism: Cultures in which people see themselves first as individuals and believe that their own interests take priority.	United States Canada Great Britain Australia Netherlands _____ _____ _____ _____	Japan Taiwan Mexico Greece Hong Kong _____ _____ _____ _____
Time Orientation: Cultures that perceive time as a scarce resource and that tend to be impatient.	United States _____ _____ _____ _____	Pacific Rim and Middle Eastern countries _____ _____ _____ _____

Source: From *Human Relations* by A. J. DuBrin. Copyright © 1997. Adapted by permission of Prentice-Hall, Inc. Upper Saddle River, NJ.

Inferences

_____ 25. Based on the information in paragraphs 1–4, what does the author seem to infer about the readers?

a. They are culturally sensitive businesspeople.

b. They have no interest in business.

c. They are members of the fastest growing economy in the world: China.

d. They are Americans.

WHY? What information in the selection leads you to give that answer? _____

_____

_____

_____

_____

____ 26. Which of the following assumptions most influenced the author's main point in this selection?

    a. People cannot understand others without knowing their language.

    b. Cultures may value different traits, but all cultures have equal value.

    c. The concept of harmony can be learned.

    d. Stereotypes are never useful.

WHY? What information in the selection leads you to give that answer? _____

_____

_____

_____

_____

____ 27. What does the author imply in paragraph 3?

    a. Arrogance produces goodwill.

    b. Arrogance is damaging when partners are unequal in strength.

    c. Arrogance only makes sense when a country has the most power.

    d. The mighty always fall.

WHY? What information in the selection leads you to give that answer? _____

_____

_____

_____

____ 28. Which of the following is a valid conclusion based on the information in the section "Group-Oriented Behavior"?

    a. More is known about Japanese cultures than many others.

    b. In Japan and Latin America, competition is not valued.

    c. Independence is a uniquely American trait.

    d. Japanese and Americans meeting as trading partners may need to adjust their decision-making processes.

WHY? What information in the selection leads you to give that answer? _____

_____

_____

_____

_____ 29. What can you infer from Table B.1?

    a. Individualism and long-term orientation never occur together.

    b. The United States and Japan have a lot of cultural values in common.

    c. The United States is not materialistic.

    d. Formality and power distance are probably linked.

WHY? What information in the selection leads you to give that answer? _____

_____

_____

_____

Purpose and Tone

_____ 30. In paragraph 3, the author defines _ethnocentrism_. The author most likely includes this definition to show readers that:

    a. Culture includes the idea of ethnic background.

    b. Ethnocentrism is the major stumbling block to cross-cultural communication.

    c. Americans are beautiful, not ugly.

    d. When a communicator doesn't take into account the individual within the culture, communication will suffer.

WHY? What information in the selection leads you to give that answer? _____

_____

_____

_____

_____ 31. Which of the following best characterizes the purpose and tone of this selection?

    a. Informative purpose; neutral tone

    b. Informative purpose; admiring tone

    c. Persuasive purpose; humble tone

    d. Persuasive purpose; subjective tone

WHY? What information in the selection leads you to give that answer? _____

_____

_____

_____

_____ 32. In the following sentence, which word has a degree of intensity that is not neutral? *Diversity will have profound effects on our lives and will pose a growing challenge for managers.*

   a. Diversity

   b. Profound

   c. Growing

   d. Managers

WHY? What information in the selection leads you to give that answer? _____

_____

_____

_____

_____ 33. What is the purpose of Table B.1?

   a. To provide a set of examples of how cultural values differ

   b. To demonstrate the effects of certain beliefs within a culture

   c. To classify each culture according to its degree of context sensitivity

   d. To list arguments for and against various cultural values

WHY? What information in the selection leads you to give that answer? _____

_____

_____

_____

_____ 34. What is the purpose of the following sentence from paragraph 12? *Most Americans and Canadians tend to back away unconsciously from such close contact.*

   a. To teach Latin Americans and Middle Easterners to back up when communicating with Americans and Canadians

   b. To remind businesspeople to use mouthwash before going to their meetings

c. To help Americans and Canadians become more conscious of this behavior and so avoid it

d. To entertain Americans and Canadians by discussing embarrassing moments the author has experienced

WHY? What information in the selection leads you to give that answer? _____

_____

_____

_____

Points of View

____ 35. Which of the following statements from the selection is presented as an opinion rather than a fact?

a. Although English is the major language for conducting business worldwide, it would be naive to assume that it is the other person's responsibility to learn English.

b. Our sign for "okay"—forming a circle with our forefinger and thumb—means "zero" in France, "money" in Japan, and a vulgarity in Brazil.

c. Americans and Canadians consider eye contact important.

d. Touching behavior is very culture-specific.

WHY? What information in the selection leads you to give that answer? _____

_____

_____

_____

____ 36. Which statement best characterizes the Al Ries quotation in paragraph 2?

a. This biased statement contradicts what the selection's author says.

b. This opinion is only a different way of saying he's biased toward Americans.

c. Ries uses fictitious examples to state a general truth.

d. This fact can be verified by looking up the information online.

WHY? What information in the selection leads you to give that answer? _____

_____

_____

_____

____ 37. Which statement best describes what the adjective *dominant* in the following sentence does? *The dominant role that the United States plays in the global economy does not mean that international business matters are handled "the American way."*

    a. It points to a fact.

    b. It points to a lie.

    c. It points to an opinion.

    d. It points to a bias.

WHY? What information in the selection leads you to give that answer? _____

_____

_____

____ 38. Which of the following sources of information that the author draws on can be considered an expert?

    a. Al Ries, chairman of Trout & Ries Advertising, Inc.

    b. Businesspeople

    c. A. J. DuBrin, author of *Human Relations*

    d. A. J. DuBrin and the author of this selection, Scott Ober

WHY? What information in the selection leads you to give that answer? _____

_____

_____

_____

____ 39. What can you infer about the author's bias?

    a. He is biased in favor of sensitivity toward others.

    b. He has an ethnocentric bias.

    c. He is biased against students.

    d. He is biased toward Japanese cultural values.

WHY? What information in the selection leads you to give that answer? _____

_____

_____

_____

• Critical Thinking

CRITICAL THINKING LEVEL 1: REMEMBER

40. Write down at least four general traits that cultures value differently.

_____

_____

_____

_____

41. Select one trait from your list and tell whether your culture is high or low on that trait.

_____

_____

_____

_____

CRITICAL THINKING LEVEL 2: UNDERSTAND

42. Summarize three points the author makes about Japanese values related to groups.

_____

_____

_____

_____

CRITICAL THINKING LEVEL 3: APPLY

43. The author says the sense of personal space differs among cultures. Consider your own culture. How far apart do people stand when they are talking at work?

_____

_____

_____

CRITICAL THINKING LEVEL 4: ANALYZE

44–47. Examine the definition of the cultural value "formality" in Table B.1. For each part of the definition, give one example from your life.

- A tradition: _____

- A ceremony: _____

- A social rule: _____

- Rank: _____

48. What do your examples suggest about how much your culture cares about formality: a great deal, very little, or somewhere in between? Why do you say so?

_____

_____

_____

_____

CRITICAL THINKING LEVEL 5: EVALUATE

49. Would you expect Irish people to have feelings about space that are more like those of Americans and Canadians or more like those of Japanese? Give a reason for your evaluation.

_____

_____

_____

_____

CRITICAL THINKING LEVEL 6: CREATE

50. Think of a social behavior not covered in this reading selection (see paragraph 13 for an example of social behavior). This might be something done by you and your friends, your parents or other family members, or people at work, your house of worship, or a team, club, or organization you belong to. Name the behavior, and explain why you do or do not believe it is culture dependent.

_____

_____

_____

_____

Reading C

● Pre-Reading the Selection

The excerpt that begins on page 675 comes from an online training manual by Phil Bartle. The excerpt is titled "Overcoming the Factors of Poverty: The Big Five."

Surveying the Reading

1. Survey the selection that follows. Then check the elements that are included in this reading.

_____ Title

_____ Headings

_____ First sentences of paragraphs

_____ Words in bold or italic type

_____ Images and captions

Guessing the Purpose

2. Based on the source and the title of the reading selection, do you think the author's purpose is mostly to persuade, inform, or express? _____

Predicting the Content

3. Based on your survey, what are three things you expect the reading selection to discuss?

- _____
- _____
- _____

Activating Your Knowledge

4. What do you know about poverty, based on what you have been exposed to in your home, hometown, on TV, or in the movies? How would you define poverty?

- _____
- _____
- _____

● Reading with Pen in Hand

Students who annotate as they read are more successful than students who do not annotate. That's why you will annotate each reading in *Engage* as you read. In the reading that follows, use the following symbols:

★ or (Point)   to indicate a main idea

① ② ③   to indicate major details

Access the Reading CourseMate via **www.cengagebrain.com** to hear vocabulary words from this selection and view a video about this topic.

Overcoming the Factors of Poverty: The Big Five

Phil Bartle, PhD

Poverty as a Social Problem

1   We have all felt a shortage of cash at times. That is an individual experience. It is not the same as the social problem of poverty. While money is a measure of wealth, lack of cash can be a measure of lack of wealth, but it is not the social problem of poverty.

2   Poverty as a social problem is a deeply embedded wound that permeates every dimension of culture and society. It includes sustained low levels of income for members of a community. It includes a lack of access to services like education, markets, health care, lack of decision making ability, and lack of communal facilities like water, sanitation, roads, transportation, and communications. Furthermore, it is a "poverty of spirit," that allows members of that community to believe in and share despair, hopelessness, apathy, and timidity. Poverty, especially the factors that contribute to it, is a social problem, and its solution is social.

3   The simple transfer of funds, even if it is to the victims of poverty, will not eradicate or reduce poverty. It will merely alleviate the symptoms of poverty in the short run. It is not a durable solution. Poverty as a social problem calls for a social solution. That solution is the clear, conscious and deliberate removal of the big five factors of poverty.

Factors, Causes, and History

4   A "factor" and a "cause" are not quite the same thing. A "cause" can be seen as something that contributes to the origin of a problem like poverty, while a "factor" can be seen as something that contributes to its continuation after it already exists.

5   Poverty on a world scale has many historical causes: colonialism, slavery, war and conquest. There is an important difference between those causes and what we call factors that maintain conditions of poverty. The difference is in terms of what we, today, can do about them. We can not go back into history and change the past. Poverty exists. Poverty was caused. What we potentially can do something about are the factors that perpetuate poverty.

6   It is well known that many nations of Europe, faced by devastating wars, such as World Wars I and II, were reduced to bare poverty, where people were reduced to living on handouts and charity, barely surviving. Within decades they had brought themselves up in terms of real domestic income, to become thriving and influential modern nations of prosperous people. We know also that many other nations have remained among the least developed of the planet, even though billions of dollars of so-called "aid" money was spent on them. Why? Because the factors of poverty were not attacked, only the symptoms. At the macro or national level, a low GDP (gross domestic product) is not the poverty itself; it is the symptom of poverty, as a social problem.

7   The factors of poverty (as a social problem) that are listed here, ignorance, disease, apathy, dishonesty and dependency, are to be seen simply as conditions. No moral judgment is intended. They are not good or bad, they just are. If it is the decision of a group of people, as in a society or in a community, to reduce and remove poverty, they will have to, without value judgment, observe and identify these factors, and take action to remove them as the way to eradicate poverty.

8   The big five, in turn, contribute to secondary factors such as lack of markets, poor infrastructure, poor leadership, bad governance, under-employment, lack of skills, absenteeism, lack of capital, and others. Each of these are social problems, each of them are caused by one or more of the big five, and each of them contribute to the perpetuation of poverty, and their eradication is necessary for the removal of poverty.

Factors of Poverty

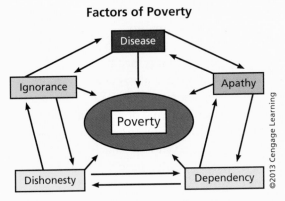

©2013 Cengage Learning

9   Let us look briefly at each of the big five in turn.

Ignorance:

10   Ignorance means having a lack of information, or lack of knowledge. It is different from stupidity which is lack of intelligence, and different from foolishness which is lack of wisdom. The three are often mixed up and assumed to be the same by some people.

11   "Knowledge is power," goes the old saying. Unfortunately, some people, knowing this, try to keep knowledge to themselves (as a strategy of obtaining an unfair advantage), and hinder others from obtaining knowledge. Do not expect that if you train someone in a particular skill, or provide some information, that the information or skill will naturally trickle or leak into the rest of a community.

12   It is important to determine what the information is that is missing. Many planners and good minded persons who want to help a community become stronger, think that the solution is education. But education means many things. Some information is not important to the situation. It will not help a farmer to know that Romeo and Juliet both died in Shakespeare's play, but it would be more useful to know which kind of seed would survive in the local soil, and which would not.

Disease:

13   When a community has a high disease rate, absenteeism is high, productivity is low, and less wealth is created. Apart from the misery, discomfort and death that results from disease, it is also a major factor in poverty in a community. Being well (well-being) not only

helps the individuals who are healthy, it contributes to the eradication of poverty in the community.

14   Here, as elsewhere, prevention is better than cure. It is one of the basic tenets of PHC (primary health care). The economy is much healthier if the population is always healthy; more so than if people get sick and have to be treated. Health contributes to the eradication of poverty more in terms of access to safe and clean drinking water, separation of sanitation from the water supply, knowledge of hygiene and disease prevention—much more than clinics, doctors and drugs, which are costly curative solutions rather than prevention against disease.

15   Remember, we are concerned with factors, not causes. It does not matter if tuberculosis was introduced by foreigners who first came to trade, or if it were autochthonic. It does not matter if HIV that carries AIDS was a CIA plot to develop a biological warfare weapon, or if it came from green monkeys in the soup. Those are possible causes. Knowing the causes will not remove disease. Knowing the factors can lead to better hygiene and preventive behavior, for their ultimate eradication.

16   Many people see access to health care as a question of human rights, the reduction of pain and misery and the quality of life of the people. These are all valid reasons to contribute to a healthy population. What is argued here, further than those reasons, is that a healthy population contributes to the eradication of poverty, and it is also argued that poverty is not only measured by high rates of morbidity and mortality, but also that disease contributes to other forms and aspects of poverty.

Apathy:

17   Apathy is when people do not care, or when they feel so powerless that they do not try to change things, to right a wrong, to fix a mistake, or to improve conditions.

18   Sometimes, some people feel so unable to achieve something, they are jealous of their family relatives or fellow members of their community who attempt to do so. Then they seek to bring the attempting achiever down to their own level of poverty. Apathy breeds apathy.

19   Sometimes apathy is justified by religious precepts, "Accept what exists because God has decided your fate." That fatalism may be

misused as an excuse. It is OK to believe God decides our fate, if we accept that God may decide that we should be motivated to improve ourselves. "Pray to God, but also row to shore," a Russian proverb, demonstrates that we are in God's hands, but we also have a responsibility to help ourselves.

20   We were created with many abilities: to choose, to cooperate, to organize in improving the quality of our lives; we should not let God or Allah be used as an excuse to do nothing. That is as bad as a curse upon God. We must praise God and use our God-given talents. In the fight against poverty, the mobilizer uses encouragement and praise, so that people (1) will want to and (2) learn how to take charge of their own lives.

Dishonesty:

21   When resources that are intended to be used for community services or facilities, are diverted into the private pockets of someone in a position of power, there is more than morality at stake here. In this training series, we are not making a value judgment that it is good or bad. We are pointing out, however, that it is a major cause of poverty. Dishonesty among persons of trust and power. The amount stolen from the public, that is received and enjoyed by the individual, is far less than the decrease in wealth that was intended for the public.

22   The amount of money that is extorted or embezzled is not the amount of lowering of wealth to the community. Economists tell of the "multiplier effect." Where new wealth is invested, the positive effect on the economy is more than the amount created. When investment money is taken out of circulation, the amount of wealth by which the community is deprived is greater than the amount gained by the embezzler. When a Government official takes a $100 bribe, social investment is decreased by as much as a $400 decrease in the wealth of the society.

23   It is ironic that we get very upset when a petty thief steals ten dollars' worth of something in the market, yet an official may steal a thousand dollars from the public purse, which does four thousand dollars worth of damage to the society as a whole, yet we do not punish the second thief. We respect the second thief for her or his apparent wealth, and praise that person for helping all her or his

relatives and neighbors. In contrast, we need the police to protect the first thief from being beaten by people on the street.

24   The second thief is a major cause of poverty, while the first thief may very well be a victim of poverty that is caused by the second. Our attitude, as described in the paragraph above, is more than ironic; it is a factor that perpetuates poverty. If we reward the one who causes the major damage, and punish only the ones who are really victims, then our misplaced attitudes also contribute to poverty. When embezzled money is then taken out of the country and put in a foreign (e.g., Swiss) bank, then it does not contribute anything to the national economy; it only helps the country of the offshore or foreign bank.

Dependency:

25   Dependency results from being on the receiving end of charity. In the short run, as after a disaster, that charity may be essential for survival. In the long run, that charity can contribute to the possible demise of the recipient, and certainly to ongoing poverty.

26   It is an attitude, a belief, that one is so poor, so helpless, that one can not help one's self, that a group cannot help itself, and that it must depend on assistance from outside. The attitude, and shared belief is the biggest self justifying factor in perpetuating the condition where the self or group must depend on outside help.

27   The community empowerment methodology is an alternative to giving charity (which weakens), but provides assistance, capital and training aimed at low income communities identifying their own resources and taking control of their own development—becoming empowered. All too often, when a project is aimed at promoting self reliance, the recipients, until their awareness is raised, expect, assume and hope that the project is coming just to provide resources for installing a facility or service in the community.

28   Among the five major factors of poverty, the dependency syndrome is the one closest to the concerns of the community mobilizer.

Conclusion

29   These five factors are not independent of one another. Disease contributes to ignorance and apathy. Dishonesty contributes to disease and dependency. And so on. They each contribute to each other.

30   In any social change process, we are encouraged to "think globally, act locally." The Big Five factors of poverty appear to be wide-

spread and deeply embedded in cultural values and practices. We may mistakenly believe that any of us, at our small level of life, can do nothing about them.

31 Do not despair. If each of us make a personal commitment to fight the factors of poverty at whatever station in life we occupy, then the sum total of all of us doing it, and the multiplier effect of our actions on others, will contribute to the decay of those factors, and the ultimate victory over poverty.

—Copyright © 2011 by Phil Bartle, PhD. Reprinted by permission of the author.

Vocabulary

_____ 5. Which of the following best defines the word *permeates* as used in paragraph 2 of this selection?

   a. Penetrates

   b. Avoids

   c. Harms

   d. Creates

WHY? What information in the selection leads you to give that answer? _____

_____

_____

_____

_____ 6. Which of the following words best defines *eradicate* as used in paragraph 7?

   a. Propagate

   b. Decrease

   c. Eliminate

   d. Condone

WHY? What information in the selection leads you to give that answer? _____

_____

_____

_____

____ 7. Which words below have the same general meaning as *diverted*, which appears in paragraph 21?

   a. Mean, cruel, cherished

   b. Rerouted, redirected, deflected

   c. Unnecessary, dispensable, optional

   d. Entertained, engrossed, delighted

WHY? What information in the selection leads you to give that answer? _____

_____

_____

_____

____ 8. Based on the use of the word *transfer* in paragraph 3, which dictionary definition seems most applicable?

   a. Convey from one surface to another

   b. To change by extension or metaphor

   c. The act of moving something from one place to another

   d. To change employment, typically from one department to another within the same organization

WHY? What information in the selection leads you to give that answer? _____

_____

_____

_____

____ 9. In paragraph 14, what does *tenet* mean?

   a. Problem

   b. Expedient

   c. Renter

   d. Principle

WHY? What information in the selection leads you to give that answer? _____

_____

_____

_____

Topics and Main Ideas

____ 10. Which of the following best expresses the main idea of the selection?

    a. There are many causes of poverty.

    b. Though poverty is an overwhelming global issue, it can be overcome by thinking globally and acting locally.

    c. To eliminate poverty, each of the five factors must be addressed.

    d. The five factors of poverty are not independent of each other.

WHY? What information leads you to give that answer? _____

_____

_____

____ 11. Which paragraphs does the following thesis statement control? *Being well (well-being) not only helps the individuals who are healthy, it contributes to the eradication of poverty in the community.*

    a. Paragraph 13 only

    b. Paragraphs 13–14

    c. Paragraphs 13–15

    d. Paragraphs 13–16

WHY? What information in the selection leads you to give that answer? _____

_____

_____

____ 12. Which of the following statements best expresses the main idea of paragraph 2?

    a. Poverty as a social problem is a deeply embedded wound that permeates every dimension of culture and society.

    b. It includes sustained low levels of income for members of a community.

    c. Furthermore, it is a "poverty of spirit," that allows members of that community to believe in and share despair, hopelessness, apathy, and timidity.

    d. Poverty, especially the factors that contribute to it, is a social problem, and its solution is social.

WHY? What information in the selection leads you to give that answer? _____

_____

_____

_____

_____ 13. Which of the following best expresses the main idea of paragraph 5?

    a. Poverty on a world scale has many historical causes: colonialism, slavery, war and conquest.

    b. There is an important difference between those causes and what we call factors that maintain conditions of poverty.

    c. The difference is in terms of what we, today, can do about them.

    d. What we potentially can do something about are the factors that perpetuate poverty.

WHY? What information in the selection leads you to give that answer? _____

_____

_____

_____

_____ 14. Which statement best summarizes the section "Ignorance"?

    a. Ignorance means having a lack of information, or lack of knowledge.

    b. All knowledge is power and therefore, people must be informed of practical as well as academic information, so they are well informed.

    c. It is important to supply those in poverty with the missing information that will help them to overcome their ignorance and their poverty.

    d. Do not expect that if you train someone in a particular skill, or provide some information, that the information or skill will naturally trickle or leak into the rest of a community.

WHY? What information in the selection leads you to give that answer? _____

_____

_____

_____

Patterns of Supporting Details

_____ 15. What pattern organizes this reading selection?

a. Cause and effect

b. Examples

c. Time order

d. Space order

WHY? What information in the selection leads you to give that answer? _____

_____

_____

_____

_____ 16. What is the predominant pattern of organization within paragraph 4?

a. Definition

b. Classification

c. Example

d. Contrast

WHY? What information in the selection leads you to give that answer? _____

_____

_____

_____

_____ 17. What two patterns are present in paragraph 27?

a. Process and definition

b. Classification and cause and effect

c. Contrast and cause and effect

d. Definition and comparison

WHY? What information in the selection leads you to give that answer? _____

_____

_____

_____

____ 18. What relationship is demonstrated in the following sentence? *Apathy is when people do not care, or when they feel so powerless that they do not try to change things, to right a wrong, to fix a mistake, or to improve conditions.*

  a. Classification

  b. Example

  c. Definition

  d. Cause and effect

WHY? What information in the selection leads you to give that answer? _____

_____

_____

_____

____ 19. What relationship is represented through the role of this sentence in paragraph 22? *When a Government official takes a $100 bribe, social investment is decreased by as much as a $400 decrease in the wealth of the society.*

  a. Cause and effect

  b. Contrast

  c. Definition

  d. Example

WHY? What information in the selection leads you to give that answer? _____

_____

_____

_____

Note Taking

____ 20. Which of the following lists of topics best organizes the information in the selection?

  a. Poverty as a Social Problem

    Factors, Causes, and History

  b. Poverty as a Social Problem

    Factors, Causes, and History

    The Big Five

    Conclusion

   c. Ignorance
      Disease
      Apathy
      Dishonesty
      Dependency
   d. The Effect of the Five Factors of Poverty
      How Poverty Is a Social Factor
      The Differences between Factors and Causes
      Conclusion

WHY? What information in the selection leads you to give that answer? _____

_____

_____

_____

21–25. Name and give an example of each of the five factors of poverty.

• _____

_____

• _____

_____

• _____

_____

• _____

_____

• _____

_____

Inferences

___ 26. Based on the information in this passage, which of the following Chinese proverbs would the author agree with?

   a. Give a man a fish and you feed him for a day. Teach a man to fish and you feed him for a lifetime.

   b. A bird does not sing because it has an answer. It sings because it has a song.

   c. Do not remove a fly from your friend's forehead with a hatchet.

   d. A book holds a house of gold.

WHY? What information in the selection leads you to give that answer? _____

_____

_____

_____

___ 27. Which of the following products would the author agree are most effective for helping overcome disease?

   a. Water purification tablets

   b. Mosquito netting

   c. HIV/AIDS medicine

   d. Flu vaccinations

WHY? What information in the selection leads you to give that answer? _____

_____

_____

_____

___ 28. Which of the following is *not* an example of apathy?

   a. Students who do not attempt to study for a test because they do not understand the material

   b. A young mother who does not take her daughter to the doctor for an infection because she is unaware of it

   c. A child who does not try to fight a bully because nobody believes his or her side of the story

   d. A husband and wife who stop communicating because when they communicate, they always seem to fight

WHY? What information in the selection leads you to give that answer? _____

_____

_____

_____

_____ 29. In paragraph 20, who is the "mobilizer"?

    a. This is another name for God

    b. The author of the reading

    c. The person who feels apathetic

    d. Anyone who is fighting poverty

WHY? What information in the selection leads you to give that answer? _____

_____

_____

_____

_____ 30. What action is connoted or implied by the quotation marks around *aid* in paragraph 6?

    a. That the aid given did not achieve its intended result

    b. That aid was never given

    c. That *aid* is a quotation from someone

    d. That the author is defining *aid*, just as he defined *factor* and *cause* in paragraph 4

WHY? What information in the selection leads you to give that answer? _____

_____

_____

_____

Purpose and Tone

_____ 31. Which statement best characterizes the purpose of this selection?

    a. To inform readers about the major and minor factors of poverty

    b. To persuade readers that they can do something to help overcome poverty by informing them of the factors that cause it.

    c. To move readers emotionally with the stark realities of poverty around the world

    d. To convince readers that poverty and its factors have a hold in the core societal values of the cultures that bear its weight, and there is not much to be done except hope change will come

WHY? What information in the selection leads you to give that answer? _____

_____

_____

_____

_____ 32. The tone of paragraph 7 could be described as:

    a. Moral

    b. Instructional

    c. Inflammatory

    d. Critical

WHY? What information in the selection leads you to give that answer? _____

_____

_____

_____

_____ 33. Which word best describes the tone of the "Conclusion" section?

    a. Hopeless

    b. Ambivalent

    c. Judgmental

    d. Encouraging

WHY? What information in the selection leads you to give that answer? _____

_____

_____

_____

____ 34. Which word best characterizes the tone of the following sentence? *Dependency results from being on the receiving end of charity.*

    a. Ironic

    b. Cynical

    c. Wry

    d. Sympathetic

WHY? What information in the selection leads you to give that answer? _____

_____

_____

_____

____ 35. What tone is conveyed in the following sentence? *Poverty as a social problem is a deeply embedded wound that permeates every dimension of culture and society.*

    a. Indignant

    b. Hyperbolic

    c. Concerned

    d. Apathetic

WHY? What information in the selection leads you to give that answer? _____

_____

_____

_____

Points of View

_____ 36. Which of the following statements from the selection is presented as a fact rather than an opinion?

  a. We have all felt a shortage of cash at times. (paragraph 1)

  b. We can not go back into history and change the past. (paragraph 5)

  c. It is OK to believe God decides our fate, if we accept that God may decide that we should be motivated to improve ourselves. (paragraph 19)

  d. If each of us make a personal commitment to fight the factors of poverty at whatever station in life we occupy, then the sum total of all of us doing it, and the multiplier effect of our actions on others, will contribute to the decay of those factors, and the ultimate victory over poverty. (paragraph 31)

WHY? What information in the selection leads you to give that answer? _____

_____

_____

_____

_____ 37. Which description best characterizes this reading?

  a. Mostly factual, from an expert source of information

  b. Mostly opinion, from an informed source

  c. Full of biased opinions, from a person on the street

  d. Full of statements of fact, from an informed source

WHY? What information in the selection leads you to give that answer? _____

_____

_____

_____

_____ 38. Which statement best describes what the adjective _deeply_ does in the following sentence? _The Big Five factors of poverty appear to be widespread and deeply embedded in cultural values and practices._

  a. It points to a fact.

  b. It points to a lie.

  c. It points to an opinion.

  d. It points to a bias.

WHY? What information in the selection leads you to give that answer? _____

_____

_____

_____

____ 39. Which of the following lends the most credibility to the author?

    a. He has earned his doctorate.

    b. His concise and clear writing style

    c. His distinction between factors and causes of poverty

    d. The example of irony given in the section titled "Dishonesty"

WHY? What information in the selection leads you to give that answer? _____

_____

_____

_____

____ 40. What bias does the author of this reading have?

    a. A bias toward overcoming poverty

    b. A bias toward pointing fingers

    c. A belief that poverty may not be overcome

    d. A bias against the causes of poverty

WHY? What information in the selection leads you to give that answer? _____

_____

_____

_____

● Critical Thinking

CRITICAL THINKING LEVEL 1: REMEMBER

41. Explain the difference between a factor and a cause of poverty.

_____

_____

_____

_____

CRITICAL THINKING LEVEL 2: UNDERSTAND

42–44. Create an "APP" for the above reading selection.

About: _____

  Point: _____

    Proof: _____

_____

_____

_____

_____

_____

_____

_____

_____

_____

CRITICAL THINKING LEVEL 3: APPLY

45. Paraphrase in your own words the following quote by Mahatma Gandhi: _Poverty is the worst form of violence._

_____

_____

_____

_____

Once you paraphrase the quote, give an example from the reading selection that supports the ideas behind the quote.

_____

_____

_____

_____

CRITICAL THINKING LEVEL 4: ANALYZE

46–48. Analyze the Gandhi quote. Use three factors of poverty to explain how they support the quote.

● _____

● _____

● _____

CRITICAL THINKING LEVEL 5: EVALUATE

49. Examine the following photograph. Explain the tone of the image and the feelings it evokes in you.

AP Photo/Adil Bradlow

_____

_____

_____

_____

CRITICAL THINKING LEVEL 6: CREATE

50. Now that you have read this selection, think of some ways you could personally help fight poverty.

_____

_____

_____

_____

Credits

Chapter 1

12–13: From DOWNING. *On Course: Strategies for Creating Success in College and in Life* (pp. 3–4). Copyright © 2011 Wadsworth, a part of Cengage Learning, Inc. Reproduced by permission. www.cengage.com/permissions. 31: Anthony Balderrama, "Using the Right Keywords in Your Job Search." Used with permission from Careerbuilder. www.careerbuilder.com. 32: Anthony Balderrama, "Using the Right Keywords in Your Job Search." Used with permission from Careerbuilder. www.careerbuilder.com. 36–37: Linda Cook, "Wahlberg, ensemble provide a win in 'Fighter.'" Copyright © 2011 *The Quad-City Times*. All rights reserved. This material may not be published, broadcast, rewritten or redistributed. Reprinted by permission. www.qctimes.com. 39–41: From STARR. *Biology: Today and Tomorrow*, 8e (pp. 378–379). Copyright © 2008 Brooks/Cole, a part of Cengage Learning, Inc. Reproduced by permission. www.cengage.com/permissions. 45–49: Adapted from DREWNIANY/JEWLER. *Creative Strategy in Advertising*, 10e (pp. 12–16). Copyright © 2011 Wadsworth, a part of Cengage Learning, Inc. Reproduced by permission. www.cengage.com/permissions. 56–59: Denise Kersten, "Today's Generations Face New Communication Gaps." Copyright © 2002 by USA Today. Reprinted by permission.

Chapter 2

67–69: Kathryn Blaze Carlson, "CNN Reporter Sanjay Gupta Becomes Part of the Story in Haiti." Material reprinted with the express permission of National Post Inc. 72: From KIDNER. *Making Europe*, 1e (p. 512). Copyright © 2009 Wadsworth, a part of Cengage Learning, Inc. Reproduced by permission. www.cengage.com/permissions. 74: From BRYM/LIE. *Sociology*, 3e (p. 352). Copyright © 2010 Brooks/Cole, a part of Cengage Learning, Inc. Reproduced by permission. www.cengage.com/permissions. 76: From FERRARO. *Cultural Anthropology*, 6e (p. 152). Copyright © 2006 Wadsworth, a part of Cengage Learning, Inc. Reproduced by permission. www.cengage.com/permissions. 78: From BRYM/LIE. *Sociology*, 3e (p. 26). Copyright © 2010 Brooks/Cole, a part of Cengage Learning, Inc. Reproduced by permission. www.cengage.com/permissions. 79: From FERRARO. *Cultural Anthropology*, 6e (p. 227). Copyright © 2006 Wadsworth, a part of Cengage Learning, Inc. Reproduced by permission. www.cengage.com/permissions. 80: From WEITEN. *Psychology*, 7e (p. 315). Copyright © 2008 Wadsworth, a part of Cengage Learning, Inc. Reproduced by permission. www.cengage.com/permissions. 81: From COOPER. *Those Who Can, Teach*, 12e (p. 155). Copyright © 2009 Wadsworth, a part of Cengage Learning, Inc. Reproduced by permission. www.cengage.com/permissions. 82: From FERRARO. *Cultural Anthropology*, 6e (p. 102). Copyright © 2006 Wadsworth, a part of Cengage Learning, Inc. Reproduced by permission. www.cengage.com/permissions. 82: From WELCH. *Understanding American Government: The Essentials* (p. 174). Copyright © 2009 Brooks/Cole, a part of Cengage Learning, Inc. Reproduced by permission. www.cengage.com/permissions. 83: From WELCH. *Understanding American Government: The Essentials* (p. 11). Copyright © 2009 Brooks/Cole, a part of Cengage Learning, Inc. Reproduced by permission. www.cengage.com/permissions. 84: From WEEKS. *Population*, 10e (p. 48). Copyright © 2008 Wadsworth, a part of Cengage Learning, Inc. Reproduced by permission. www.cengage.com/permissions. 85: From KALAT. *Introduction to Psychology*, 9e (p. 480). Copyright © 2011 Brooks/Cole, a part of Cengage Learning, Inc. Reproduced by permission. www.cengage.com/permissions. 85: From RYAN/CONOVER. *Graphic Communication Today*, 4e (p. 25). Copyright © 2004 Brooks/Cole, a part of Cengage Learning, Inc. Reproduced by permission. www.cengage.com/permissions. 85: From CILETTI. *Marketing Yourself*, 2e (p. 88). Copyright © 2004 Brooks/Cole, a part of Cengage Learning, Inc. Reproduced by permission. www.cengage.com/permissions. 86: From BULLIET. *The Earth and Its Peoples, Brief Edition, Complete*, 5e (p. 16). Copyright © 2012 Wadsworth, a part of Cengage Learning, Inc. Reproduced by permission. www.cengage.com/permissions. 86: From RIZZO. *Fundamentals of Anatomy and Physiology*, 3e (pp. 13–14). Copyright © 2010 Brooks/Cole, a part of Cengage Learning, Inc. Reproduced by permission. www.cengage.com/permissions. 87: From SHAW. *Cengage Advantage Books: Business Ethics*, 7e (p. 6). Copyright © 2011 Wadsworth, a part of Cengage Learning, Inc. Reproduced by permission. www.cengage.com/permissions. 87: From KAIL/CAVANAUGH. *Cengage Advantage Books: Human Development*, 5e (p. 45). Copyright © 2010 Brooks/Cole, a part of Cengage Learning, Inc. Reproduced by permission. www.cengage.com/permissions. 100: From DEMPSEY/FORST. *An Introduction to Policing*, 5e (p. 142). Copyright © 2010 Delmar Learning, a part of Cengage Learning, Inc. Reproduced by permission. www.cengage.com/permissions. 108: From KALAT. *Introduction to Psychology*, 9e (p. 84). Copyright © 2011 Brooks/Cole, a part of Cengage Learning, Inc. Reproduced by permission. www.cengage.com/permissions. 108: From CILETTI. *Marketing Yourself*, 2e (p. 36). Copyright © 2004 Brooks/Cole, a part of Cengage Learning, Inc. Reproduced by permission. www.cengage.com/permissions. 109: From HESS/HESS ORTHMANN. *Criminal Investigation*, 9e (p. 685). Copyright © 2010 Brooks/Cole, a part of Cengage Learning, Inc. Reproduced by permission. www.cengage.com/permissions. 110: From SIMMERS. *Diversified Health Occupations*, 7e (p. 129). Copyright © 2009 Brooks/Cole, a part of Cengage Learning, Inc. Reproduced by permission. www.cengage.com/permissions. 113–114: From BERNSTEIN. *Essentials of Psychology*, 5e (pp. 316–317). Copyright © 2011 Wadsworth, a part of Cengage Learning, Inc. Reproduced by permission. www.cengage.com/permissions. 115–116: From FERRARO. *Cultural Anthropology*, 6e (p. 264). Copyright © 2006 Wadsworth, a part of Cengage Learning, Inc. Reproduced by permission. www.cengage.com/permissions.

116: From HUERTA. *Educational Foundations* (p. 180). Copyright © 2008 Wadsworth, a part of Cengage Learning, Inc. Reproduced by permission. www.cengage.com/permissions. 117: From HESS/HESS ORTHMANN. *Criminal Investigation*, 9e (pp. 501–502). Copyright © 2010 Brooks/Cole, a part of Cengage Learning, Inc. Reproduced by permission. www.cengage.com/permissions. 118–119: From BRYM/LIE. *Sociology*, 3e (p. 220). Copyright © 2010 Brooks/Cole, a part of Cengage Learning, Inc. Reproduced by permission. www.cengage .com/permissions. 124–125: From HALES. *An Invitation to Health* (with CengageNOW and InfoTrac 1-Semester Printed Access Card), 12e (pp. 37–38). Copyright © 2007 Brooks/Cole, a part of Cengage Learning, Inc. Reproduced by permission. www.cengage.com/ permissions. 125 (Table 2.1): Reprinted by permission of the author Judd Allen, Ph.D. www.healthyculture.com. 132–134: From www .unicef.org. Reproduced by permission.

Chapter 3

140–141: From Lisa Fine, "Cracking the Shell," *Education Week,* November 21, 2001, pp. 22–29. Excerpted by permission of Editorial Projects in Education. 149: From SHAW. *Cengage Advantage Books: Business Ethics,* 7e (p. 232). Copyright © 2011 Wadsworth, a part of Cengage Learning, Inc. Reproduced by permission. www.cengage.com/permissions. 149: From DURAND/BARLOW. *Essentials of Abnormal Psychology,* 5e (p. 35). Copyright © 2010 Brooks/Cole, a part of Cengage Learning, Inc. Reproduced by permission. www .cengage.com/permissions. 150: From THROOP/CASTELLUCCI. *Reaching Your Potential,* 4e (p. 41). Copyright © 2011 Brooks/Cole, a part of Cengage Learning, Inc. Reproduced by permission. www.cengage.com/permissions. 150: From ROBINSON/MCCORMICK. *Concepts in Health and Wellness,* 1e (p. 324). Copyright © 2011 Delmar Learning, a part of Cengage Learning, Inc. Reproduced by permission. www.cengage.com/permissions. 151: From WEEKS. *Population,* 10e (pp. 3–4). Copyright © 2008 Wadsworth, a part of Cengage Learning, Inc. Reproduced by permission. www.cengage.com/permissions. 157: From KAIL/CAVANAUGH. *Cengage Advantage Books: Human Development,* 5e (p. 306). Copyright © 2010 Brooks/Cole, a part of Cengage Learning, Inc. Reproduced by permission. www.cengage.com/permissions. 157: Adapted from ANDERSON/FERRO/HILTON. *Connecting with Computer Science,* 2e (p. 267). Copyright © 2011 Brooks/Cole, a part of Cengage Learning, Inc. Reproduced by permission. www.cengage.com/permissions. 157: From BRYANT/COURTNEY/DEWALT/SCHWARTZ. *The Cultural Feast: An Introduction to Food and Society,* 2e (pp. 6–7). Copyright © 2004 Brooks/Cole, a part of Cengage Learning, Inc. Reproduced by permission. www.cengage.com/permissions. 158: From DEMPSEY/FORST. *An Introduction to Policing,* 5e (p. 422). Copyright © 2010 Delmar Learning, a part of Cengage Learning, Inc. Reproduced by permission. www.cengage.com/permissions. 158: From POLLACK. *Creative Nonfiction* (p. 11). Copyright © 2010 Brooks/Cole, a part of Cengage Learning, Inc. Reproduced by permission. www.cengage.com/permissions. 159: Adapted from CILETTI. *Marketing Yourself,* 2e (pp. 316–317). Copyright © 2004 Brooks/Cole, a part of Cengage Learning, Inc. Reproduced by permission. www .cengage.com/permissions. 159: From PRICE/CRAPO. *Cross-Cultural Perspectives,* 4e (p. 30). Copyright © 2002 Brooks/Cole, a part of Cengage Learning, Inc. Reproduced by permission. www.cengage.com/permissions. 159: Adapted from KAIL/CAVANAUGH. *Cengage Advantage Books: Human Development,* 5e (p. 406). Copyright © 2010 Brooks/Cole, a part of Cengage Learning, Inc. Reproduced by permission. www.cengage.com/permissions. 160: From HALES. *An Invitation to Health* (with CengageNOW and InfoTrac 1-Semester Printed Access Card), 12e (p. 84). Copyright © 2007 Brooks/Cole, a part of Cengage Learning, Inc. Reproduced by permission. www .cengage.com/permissions. 160: From BESSETTE/PITNEY. *American Government and Politics* (p. 370). Copyright © 2012 Brooks/Cole, a part of Cengage Learning, Inc. Reproduced by permission. www.cengage.com/permissions. 161: From MILLER/SPOOLMAN. *Living in the Environment,* 17e (p. 44). Copyright © 2012 Brooks/Cole, a part of Cengage Learning, Inc. Reproduced by permission. www .cengage.com/permissions. 161: From WILLIAMS. *Management,* 4e (p. 215). Copyright © 2004 Brooks/Cole, a part of Cengage Learning, Inc. Reproduced by permission. www.cengage.com/permissions. 162: From SHAFFER. *Social and Personality Development,* 6e (pp. 370–371). Copyright © 2009 Wadsworth, a part of Cengage Learning, Inc. Reproduced by permission. www.cengage.com/permissions. 165: From KAIL/CAVANAUGH. *Cengage Advantage Books: Human Development,* 5e (p. 350). Copyright © 2010 Brooks/Cole, a part of Cengage Learning, Inc. Reproduced by permission. www.cengage.com/permissions. 165: From MANCINI. *Selling Destinations,* 4e (p. 253). Copyright © 2010 Wadsworth, a part of Cengage Learning, Inc. Reproduced by permission. www.cengage.com/permissions. 166: From STARR/MCMILLAN. *Human Biology,* 8e (p. 8). Copyright © 2010 Brooks/Cole, a part of Cengage Learning, Inc. Reproduced by permission. www.cengage.com/permissions. 167: From CARBAUGH. *International Economics,* 12e (p. 256). Copyright © 2008 Brooks/Cole, a part of Cengage Learning, Inc. Reproduced by permission. www.cengage.com/permissions. 167: From BRYANT/COURTNEY/DEWALT/SCHWARTZ. *The Cultural Feast: An Introduction to Food and Society,* 2e (p. 236). Copyright © 2004 Brooks/Cole, a part of Cengage Learning, Inc. Reproduced by permission. www.cengage.com/permissions. 168: From BRYM/LIE. *Sociology,* 3e (p. 178). Copyright © 2010 Brooks/Cole, a part of Cengage Learning, Inc. Reproduced by permission. www.cengage.com/permissions. 168: From BERTINO. *Forensic Science: Fundamentals and Investigations* (pp. 4–5). Copyright © 2010 Brooks/Cole, a part of Cengage Learning, Inc. Reproduced by permission. www.cengage.com/permissions. 168: From ROBINSON/MCCORMICK. *Concepts in Health and Wellness,* 1e (p. 148). Copyright © 2011 Delmar Learning, a part of Cengage Learning, Inc. Reproduced by permission. www.cengage.com/permissions. 169–171: From DEMPSEY/FORST. *An Introduction to Policing,* 5e (pp. 322–323). Copyright © 2010 Delmar Learning, a part of Cengage Learning, Inc. Reproduced by permission. www.cengage.com/permissions. 172–174: From MILLER/SPOOLMAN. *Essentials of Ecology,* 6e (pp. 118–119). Copyright © 2012 Brooks/Cole, a part of Cengage Learning, Inc. Reproduced by permission. www.cengage.com/permissions. 177: From MAVILLE/HUERTA. *Health Promotion in Nursing,* 2e (p. 328). Copyright © 2008 Brooks/Cole, a part of Cengage Learning, Inc. Reproduced by permission. www.cengage.com/permissions. 177: From MAVILLE/HUERTA. *Health Promotion in Nursing,* 2e (p. 328). Copyright © 2008 Brooks/Cole, a part of Cengage Learning, Inc. Reproduced by permission. www.cengage.com/permissions. 177–179: From COOPER. *Those Who Can, Teach,* 12e (pp. 104–106). Copyright © 2009 Wadsworth, a part of Cengage Learning, Inc. Reproduced by permission. www.cengage.com/permissions. 179–180: From HESS/HESS ORTHMANN. *Criminal Investigation,* 9e (p. 78). Copyright © 2010 Brooks/Cole, a part of Cengage Learning, Inc. Reproduced by permission. www .cengage.com/permissions. 180–181: From BRYM/LIE. *Sociology,* 3e (p. 373). Copyright © 2010 Brooks/Cole, a part of Cengage Learning, Inc. Reproduced by permission. www.cengage.com/permissions. 181: From SHAFFER. *Social and Personality Development,* 6e

(p. 121). Copyright © 2009 Wadsworth, a part of Cengage Learning, Inc. Reproduced by permission. www.cengage.com/permissions. 181: From WILLIAMS. *Management,* 4e (pp. 384–385). Copyright © 2004 Brooks/Cole, a part of Cengage Learning, Inc. Reproduced by permission. www.cengage.com/permissions. 182: From WILLIAMS. *Management,* 4e (p. 385). Copyright © 2004 Brooks/Cole, a part of Cengage Learning, Inc. Reproduced by permission. www.cengage.com/permissions. 182: From WILLIAMS. *Management,* 4e (p. 385). Copyright © 2004 Brooks/Cole, a part of Cengage Learning, Inc. Reproduced by permission. www.cengage.com/permissions. 183: From FERRARO. *Cultural Anthropology,* 6e (pp. 213–214). Copyright © 2006 Wadsworth, a part of Cengage Learning, Inc. Reproduced by permission. www.cengage.com/permissions. 185–189: From KOCH. *So You Want to Be a Teacher?* (pp. 204–207). Copyright © 2009 Brooks/Cole, a part of Cengage Learning, Inc. Reproduced by permission. www.cengage.com/permissions. 196–199: From Joanie Baker, "School Texts :(Educators Differ on How to Handel Cell Phones in Classrooms." Bowling Green Daily News. Copyright © 2009 by MCCLATCHY-TRIBUNE REGIONAL NEWS. Reproduced with permission of MCCLATCHY-TRIBUNE REGIONAL NEWS.

Chapter 4

206–207: From GAINES/MILLER. *Criminal Justice in Action,* 5e (p. 4). Copyright © 2011 Brooks/Cole, a part of Cengage Learning, Inc. Reproduced by permission. www.cengage.com/permissions. 209: From HESS/HESS ORTHMANN. *Criminal Investigation,* 9e (p. 379). Copyright © 2010 Brooks/Cole, a part of Cengage Learning, Inc. Reproduced by permission. www.cengage.com/permissions. 212: From HUERTA. *Educational Foundations* (p. 201). Copyright © 2008 Wadsworth, a part of Cengage Learning, Inc. Reproduced by permission. www.cengage.com/permissions. 214: From SHAW. *Cengage Advantage Books: Business Ethics,* 7e (p. 226). Copyright © 2011 Wadsworth, a part of Cengage Learning, Inc. Reproduced by permission. www.cengage.com/permissions. 216–217: Jenny Everett, "Zumba Secrets: How to Get a Workout at Da Club This Weekend." Reprinted by permission of Condé Nast Publications. 219: From FERRARO. *Cultural Anthropology,* 6e (p. 322). Copyright © 2006 Wadsworth, a part of Cengage Learning, Inc. Reproduced by permission. www.cengage.com/permissions. 224: From KOCH. *So You Want to Be a Teacher?* (pp. 94, 102). Copyright © 2009 Brooks/Cole, a part of Cengage Learning, Inc. Reproduced by permission. www.cengage.com/permissions. 226: From LAUER/PENTAK. *Design Basics,* 8e (p. 5). Copyright © 2012 Brooks/Cole, a part of Cengage Learning, Inc. Reproduced by permission. www.cengage.com/permissions. 228: From KALAT. *Introduction to Psychology,* 9e (p. 128). Copyright © 2011 Brooks/Cole, a part of Cengage Learning, Inc. Reproduced by permission. www.cengage.com/permissions. 229: From HUERTA. *Educational Foundations* (p. 193). Copyright © 2008 Wadsworth, a part of Cengage Learning, Inc. Reproduced by permission. www.cengage.com/permissions. 232: From HALES. *An Invitation to Health* (with CengageNOW and InfoTrac 1-Semester Printed Access Card), 12e (p. 323). Copyright © 2007 Brooks/Cole, a part of Cengage Learning, Inc. Reproduced by permission. www.cengage.com/permissions. 233: From CASHINGHINO. *Moving Images: Making Movies, Understanding Media* (p. 121). Copyright © 2010 Delmar, a part of Cengage Learning, Inc. Reproduced by permission. www.cengage.com/permissions. 235: From HALES. *An Invitation to Health* (with CengageNOW and InfoTrac 1-Semester Printed Access Card), 12e (p. 120). Copyright © 2007 Brooks/Cole, a part of Cengage Learning, Inc. Reproduced by permission. www.cengage.com/permissions. 236: From BRYM/LIE. *Sociology,* 3e (p. 143). Copyright © 2010 Brooks/Cole, a part of Cengage Learning, Inc. Reproduced by permission. www.cengage.com/permissions. 237: From HALES. *An Invitation to Health* (with CengageNOW and InfoTrac 1-Semester Printed Access Card), 12e (pp. 348–349). Copyright © 2007 Brooks/Cole, a part of Cengage Learning, Inc. Reproduced by permission. www.cengage.com/permissions. 238: From BULLIET. *The Earth and Its Peoples, Brief Edition, Complete,* 5e (p. 224). Copyright © 2012 Wadsworth, a part of Cengage Learning, Inc. Reproduced by permission. www.cengage.com/permissions. 238: From WILLIAMS. *Management,* 4e (p. 451). Copyright © 2004 Brooks/Cole, a part of Cengage Learning, Inc. Reproduced by permission. www.cengage.com/permissions. 239: From CASHINGHINO. *Moving Images: Making Movies, Understanding Media* (pp. 135–136). Copyright © 2010 Delmar, a part of Cengage Learning, Inc. Reproduced by permission. www.cengage.com/permissions. 239–242: From WILLIAMS. *Management,* 4e (pp. 108–109). Copyright © 2004 Brooks/Cole, a part of Cengage Learning, Inc. Reproduced by permission. www.cengage.com/permissions. 246–247: From WEITEN. *Psychology,* 7e (pp. 327–328). Copyright © 2008 Wadsworth, a part of Cengage Learning, Inc. Reproduced by permission. www.cengage.com/permissions. 249: From MILLER/SPOOLMAN. *Living in the Environment,* 17e (p. 614). Copyright © 2012 Brooks/Cole, a part of Cengage Learning, Inc. Reproduced by permission. www.cengage.com/permissions. 250: From WEITEN. *Psychology,* 7e (p. 491). Copyright © 2008 Wadsworth, a part of Cengage Learning, Inc. Reproduced by permission. www.cengage.com/permissions. 251: From KENDALL. *Sociology in Our Times,* 6e (p. 112). Copyright © 2008 Brooks/Cole, a part of Cengage Learning, Inc. Reproduced by permission. www.cengage.com/permissions. 253: From HALES. *An Invitation to Health* (with CengageNOW and InfoTrac 1-Semester Printed Access Card), 12e (p. 129). Copyright © 2007 Brooks/Cole, a part of Cengage Learning, Inc. Reproduced by permission. www.cengage.com/permissions. 257–259: From GAINES/MILLER. *Criminal Justice in Action,* 5e (pp. 300–302). Copyright © 2011 Brooks/Cole, a part of Cengage Learning, Inc. Reproduced by permission. www.cengage.com/permissions. 266–268: Reprinted by permission of Gasaway Long & Associates, PLLC.

Chapter 5

279: From ROBINSON/MCCORMICK. *Concepts in Health and Wellness,* 1e (pp. 89–90). Copyright © 2011 Delmar Learning, a part of Cengage Learning, Inc. Reproduced by permission. www.cengage.com/permissions. 280: From ROBINSON/MCCORMICK. *Concepts in Health and Wellness,* 1e (pp. 89–90). Copyright © 2011 Delmar Learning, a part of Cengage Learning, Inc. Reproduced by permission. www.cengage.com/permissions. 281–283: From GAINES/MILLER. *Criminal Justice in Action,* 5e (pp. 80–81). Copyright © 2011 Brooks/Cole, a part of Cengage Learning, Inc. Reproduced by permission. www.cengage.com/permissions. 285–286: From BRYANT/COURTNEY/DEWALT/SCHWARTZ. *The Cultural Feast: An Introduction to Food and Society,* 2e (p. 363). Copyright © 2004 Brooks/Cole, a part of Cengage Learning, Inc. Reproduced by permission. www.cengage.com/permissions. 288: From BRYANT/COURTNEY/DEWALT/SCHWARTZ. *The Cultural Feast: An Introduction to Food and Society,* 2e (p. 363). Copyright © 2004 Brooks/Cole, a part of Cengage Learning, Inc. Reproduced by permission. www.cengage.com/permissions. 290–294: From GRIFFIN. *Invitation to Public Speaking,* 3e (pp. 23–28). Copyright © 2009 Wadsworth, a part of Cengage Learning, Inc. Reproduced by permission. www.cengage.com/permissions.

295–301: From ANDERSEN/TAYLOR. *Sociology: The Essentials*, 4e (pp. 36–40) Copyright © 2007 Cengage Learning. 305–306: From BERNSTEIN. *Essentials of Psychology*, 5e (pp. 258–259). Copyright © 2011 Wadsworth, a part of Cengage Learning, Inc. Reproduced by permission. www.cengage.com/permissions. 307: From BERNSTEIN. *Essentials of Psychology*, 5e (p. 369). Copyright © 2011 Wadsworth, a part of Cengage Learning, Inc. Reproduced by permission. www.cengage.com/permissions. 308–309: From BERNSTEIN. *Essentials of Psychology*, 5e (p. 427). Copyright © 2011 Wadsworth, a part of Cengage Learning, Inc. Reproduced by permission. www.cengage.com/permissions. 309–311: From BERNSTEIN. *Essentials of Psychology*, 5e (pp. 428–430). Copyright © 2011 Wadsworth, a part of Cengage Learning, Inc. Reproduced by permission. www.cengage.com/permissions.

Chapter 6

346–347: From ANDERSEN/TAYLOR. *Sociology: The Essentials*, 4e (pp. 601–603). Copyright © 2007 Wadsworth, a part of Cengage Learning, Inc. Reproduced by permission. www.cengage.com/permissions. 350: Reproduced from sierraclub.org with permission of the Sierra Club. 350: Reprinted by permission of Greenpeace. 351: From ANDERSEN/TAYLOR. *Sociology: The Essentials*, 4e (p. 601). Copyright © 2007 Wadsworth, a part of Cengage Learning, Inc. Reproduced by permission. www.cengage.com/permissions. 355: From BRYANT/COURTNEY/DEWALT/SCHWARTZ. *The Cultural Feast: An Introduction to Food and Society*, 2e (p. 80). Copyright © 2004 Brooks/Cole, a part of Cengage Learning, Inc. Reproduced by permission. www.cengage.com/permissions. 356–358: From BRYANT/COURTNEY/DEWALT/SCHWARTZ. *The Cultural Feast: An Introduction to Food and Society*, 2e (pp. 74–76). Copyright © 2004 Brooks/Cole, a part of Cengage Learning, Inc. Reproduced by permission. www.cengage.com/permissions. 364–369: From KLEINER. *Gardner's Art Through the Ages*, 13e (pp. 20–23). Copyright © 2011 Wadsworth, a part of Cengage Learning, Inc. Reproduced by permission. www.cengage.com/permissions. 377–380: Charles Fowler, D.M.A. "Every Child Needs the Arts" in *Creating the Future: Perspectives on Educational Change*. Copyright © 1991, 1996, 1998, 2002 New Horizons for Learning, all rights reserved. Reprinted by permission.

Chapter 7

389–390: Alisa Opar, "Illegal Fireworks Likely Cause of Massive Arkansas Blackbird Deaths." Copyright © 2011 Audubon Magazine. Reprinted by permission. 407: From ELLER. *Violence and Culture* (p. 1). Copyright © 2006 Brooks/Cole, a part of Cengage Learning, Inc. Reproduced by permission. www.cengage.com/permissions. 408: From KAIL/CAVANAUGH. *Cengage Advantage Books: Human Development*, 4e (p. 64). Copyright © 2010 Brooks/Cole, a part of Cengage Learning, Inc. Reproduced by permission. www.cengage.com/permissions. 409: From DEMPSEY/FORST. *An Introduction to Policing*, 5e (p. 286). Copyright © 2010 Delmar Learning, a part of Cengage Learning, Inc. Reproduced by permission. www.cengage.com/permissions. 410–411: From MILLER/SPOOLMAN. *Living in the Environment*, 17e (p. 481). Copyright © 2012 Brooks/Cole, a part of Cengage Learning, Inc. Reproduced by permission. www.cengage.com/permissions. 411: From HALES. *An Invitation to Health* (with CengageNOW and InfoTrac 1-Semester Printed Access Card), 12e (p. 89). Copyright © 2007 Brooks/Cole, a part of Cengage Learning, Inc. Reproduced by permission. www.cengage.com/permissions. 411–412: From WEITEN. *Psychology*, 7e (pp. 380–381). Copyright © 2008 Wadsworth, a part of Cengage Learning, Inc. Reproduced by permission. www.cengage.com/permissions. 412: From KAIL/CAVANAUGH. *Cengage Advantage Books: Human Development*, 4e (p. 587). Copyright © 2007 Brooks/Cole, a part of Cengage Learning, Inc. Reproduced by permission. www.cengage.com/permissions. 412: From KOCH. *So You Want to Be a Teacher?* (p. 67) Copyright © 2009 Brooks/Cole, a part of Cengage Learning, Inc. Reproduced by permission. www.cengage.com/permissions. 415: From VERDERBER/VERDERBER/SELLNOW. *COMM*, 1e (p. 25). Copyright © 2009 Brooks/Cole, a part of Cengage Learning, Inc. Reproduced by permission. www.cengage.com/permissions. 416: From KAIL/CAVANAUGH. *Cengage Advantage Books: Human Development*, 4e (pp. 456–457). Copyright © 2007 Brooks/Cole, a part of Cengage Learning, Inc. Reproduced by permission. www.cengage.com/permissions. 418: From BOYES/MELVIN. *Economics*, 8e (p. 550). Copyright © 2011 Cengage Learning, Inc. Reproduced by permission. www.cengage.com/permissions. 418: From DEMPSEY/FORST. *An Introduction to Policing*, 5e (p. 118). Copyright © 2010 Delmar Learning, a part of Cengage Learning, Inc. Reproduced by permission. www.cengage.com/permissions. 419: From SKLAR. *Principles of Web Design*, 4e (pp. 83–84). Copyright © 2009 Cengage Learning, Inc. Reproduced by permission. www.cengage.com/permissions. 419: From ROBINSON/MCCORMICK. *Concepts in Health and Wellness*, 1e (p. 162). Copyright © 2011 Delmar Learning, a part of Cengage Learning, Inc. Reproduced by permission. www.cengage.com/permissions. 420: From GRIGSBY. *Analyzing Politics*, 4e (p. 11). Copyright © 2009 Brooks/Cole, a part of Cengage Learning, Inc. Reproduced by permission. www.cengage.com/permissions. 421–423: From THE GRAND DESIGN by Stephen W. Hawking and Leonard Mlodinow, copyright © 2010 by Stephen W. Hawking and Leonard Mlodinow. Used by permission of Bantam Books, a division of Random House, Inc. 424–425: Jenna Goudreau, "Job Outlook: Careers Headed for the Trash Pile." Copyright © 2011. Reprinted by permission of Forbes Media LLC. 427: From KENDALL. *Sociology in Our Times*, 6e (p. 429). Copyright © 2008 Brooks/Cole, a part of Cengage Learning, Inc. Reproduced by permission. www.cengage.com/permissions. 427: From GRIGSBY. *Analyzing Politics*, 4e (p. 128). Copyright © 2009 Brooks/Cole, a part of Cengage Learning, Inc. Reproduced by permission. www.cengage.com/permissions. 428: From WEITEN. *Psychology*, 7e (p. 183). Copyright © 2008 Wadsworth, a part of Cengage Learning, Inc. Reproduced by permission. www.cengage.com/permissions. 429–430: From BULLIET. *The Earth and Its Peoples, Brief Edition, Complete*, 5e (p. 263). Copyright © 2012 Wadsworth, a part of Cengage Learning, Inc. Reproduced by permission. www.cengage.com/permissions. 431 (Table 7.1): From BRYM/LIE. *Sociology*, 3e (p. 533). Copyright © 2010 Brooks/Cole, a part of Cengage Learning, Inc. Reproduced by permission. www.cengage.com/permissions. 431–432: From GRIGSBY. *Analyzing Politics*, 4e (p. 8). Copyright © 2009 Brooks/Cole, a part of Cengage Learning, Inc. Reproduced by permission. www.cengage.com/permissions. 432: From FERRARO. *Cultural Anthropology*, 6e (p. 352). Copyright © 2006 Wadsworth, a part of Cengage Learning, Inc. Reproduced by permission. www.cengage.com/permissions. 433: From MILLER/SPOOLMAN. *Living in the Environment*, 17e (p. 264). Copyright © 2012 Brooks/Cole, a part of Cengage Learning, Inc. Reproduced by permission. www.cengage.com/permissions. 434: From VERDERBER/VERDERBER/SELLNOW. *COMM*, 1e

(p. 92). Copyright © 2009 Brooks/Cole, a part of Cengage Learning, Inc. Reproduced by permission. www.cengage.com/permissions. 437–439: From MILLER/SPOOLMAN. *Essentials of Ecology*, 6e (p. 35). Copyright © 2012 Brooks/Cole, a part of Cengage Learning, Inc. Reproduced by permission. www.cengage.com/permissions. 446–452: "A New World" from the book *Eaarth: Making Life on a Tough New Planet* by Bill McKibben. Copyright © 2010 by Bill McKibben. Reprinted by permission of Henry Holt and Company, LLC.

Chapter 8

461–462: From ANDERSON/FERRO/HILTON. *Connecting with Computer Science*, 2e (p. 48). Copyright © 2011 Brooks/Cole, a part of Cengage Learning, Inc. Reproduced by permission. www.cengage.com/permissions. 465–466: From BERNSTEIN. *Essentials of Psychology*, 5e (p. 299). Copyright © 2011 Wadsworth, a part of Cengage Learning, Inc. Reproduced by permission. www.cengage.com/permissions. 467–468: Mills, "Got Milk? For Many People, There Are Reasons To Get Rid Of It," *San Jose Mercury News*, March 27, 2000. Copyright © 2000 San Jose Mercury News. Reprinted by permission. 476: From WEEKS. *Population*, 10e (pp. 2–3). Copyright © 2008 Wadsworth, a part of Cengage Learning, Inc. Reproduced by permission. www.cengage.com/permissions. 476–477: Donna Bryson, "1st Dinosaur Fossil Discovered in Angola." Copyright © 2011 by The Associated Press. Reprinted by permission. 482: Copyright © Women for Women International. www.womenforwomen.org. Reprinted by permission. 487: Carl Sandburg, "The Fog" from CHICAGO POEMS. Copyright 1916 by Holt, Rinehart and Winston, renewed 1944 by Carl Sandburg. Reprinted by permission of Houghton Mifflin Harcourt Publishing Company. 493: Gwendolyn Brooks, from BLACKS. Copyright © 1991 by Gwendolyn Brooks Blakely. Reprinted by consent of Brooks Permissions. 505: "Myth: Shark Attacks Are Common" from www.sharksavers.org. Copyright © 2011 Shark Savers Inc. All rights reserved. Reprinted by permission. 507: Copyright © 2003 by Jack Prelutsky. Reprinted by permission of School Survival, www.school-survival.net. 508–509: From FERRARO. *Cultural Anthropology*, 6e (pp. 184–185). Copyright © 2006 Wadsworth, a part of Cengage Learning, Inc. Reproduced by permission. www.cengage.com/permissions. 511: Bob Hoose, "Water for Elephants," *Focus on the Family's Plugged In Online*. Copyright © 2011 Focus on the Family. Reprinted by permission. 512–513: Nikki Giovanni, "Poetry" from THE WOMEN AND THE MEN. Copyright © 1970, 1974, 1975 by Nikki Giovanni. Reprinted by permission of HarperCollins Publishers. 516–518: From ANDERSON/FERRO/HILTON. *Connecting with Computer Science*, 2e (pp. 50–52). Copyright © 2011 Brooks/Cole, a part of Cengage Learning, Inc. Reproduced by permission. www.cengage.com/permissions. 527–530: Copyright © 2011 by Jeremy Wagstaff. Reprinted by permission.

Chapter 9

539–541: "Who Are You And What Do You Think Of Me (Excerpt: Is This Person Attracted To Me?)" by Carlin Flora. *Psychology Today* (Jan/Feb 2011). Copyright © 2011 by Psychology Today. www.psychologytoday.com. Reprinted by permission. 552: Items 1–4 adapted from BRYANT/COURTNEY/DEWALT/SCHWARTZ. *The Cultural Feast: An Introduction to Food and Society*, 2e (p. 85). Copyright © 2004 Brooks/Cole, a part of Cengage Learning, Inc. Reproduced by permission. www.cengage.com/permissions. 558–559: Copyright © Jason Best/What's on TV/IPC+ Syndication. Reprinted by permission. 573: "Better Late Than Never," by Scott Barry Kaufman, *Psychology Today* (November/December 2008). Copyright © 2008 by Psychology Today. www.psychologytoday.com. Reprinted by permission. 577–579: From *The New York Times*, February 25th, 2011. Copyright © 2011 *The New York Times*. All rights reserved. Used by permission and protected by the Copyright Laws of the United States. The printing, copying, redistributing, or transmission of this Content without express written permission is prohibited. 580: Bernadine Healy, M.D., "Behind the Baby Count," *US News and World Report*, 9/24/06. Copyright © 2011 *US News and World Report* LP. All rights reserved. Reprinted by permission. 581–582: Copyright © 2011 by MADD. www.madd.org. Reprinted by permission. 583: Courtesy of www.techdirt.com. 587–590: From WEITEN. *Psychology*, 7e (pp. 291–292). Copyright © 2008 Wadsworth, a part of Cengage Learning, Inc. Reproduced by permission. www.cengage.com/permissions. 597–600: "Domestic Drama: On-Again, Off-Again," by Elizabeth Svoboda. *Psychology Today* (Mar/Apr 2008). Copyright © 2008 by Psychology Today. www.psychologytoday.com. Reprinted by permission.

Chapter 10

610–613: From HALES. *An Invitation to Health* (with CengageNOW and InfoTrac 1-Semester Printed Access Card), 12e (pp. 152–153). Copyright © 2007 Brooks/Cole, a part of Cengage Learning, Inc. Reproduced by permission. www.cengage.com/permissions. 617–619: Jeffrey M. Jones, "Americans Still Perceive Crime as on the Rise." Copyright © 2011 by the Gallup Organization. Reprinted by permission. 621–622: From BRYM/LIE. *Sociology: Your Compass For A New World*, Brief Edition (p. 149). Copyright © 2010 Wadsworth, a part of Cengage Learning, Inc. Reproduced by permission. www.cengage.com/permissions. 623–624: From WEEKS. *Population*, 10e (pp. 213, 215). Copyright © 2008 Wadsworth, a part of Cengage Learning, Inc. Reproduced by permission. www.cengage.com/permissions. 626–627: From BRYANT/COURTNEY/DEWALT/SCHWARTZ. *The Cultural Feast: An Introduction to Food and Society*, 2e (pp. 282–284). Copyright © 2004 Brooks/Cole, a part of Cengage Learning, Inc. Reproduced by permission. www.cengage.com/permissions.

Part 3

633–637: From HALES. *An Invitation to Health* (with CengageNOW and InfoTrac 1-Semester Printed Access Card), 12e (pp. 86–88). Copyright © 2007 Brooks/Cole, a part of Cengage Learning, Inc. Reproduced by permission. www.cengage.com/permissions. 654–659: From OBER. *Contemporary Business Communication*, 7e (pp. 45–49). Copyright © 2009 Brooks/Cole, a part of Cengage Learning, Inc. Reproduced by permission. www.cengage.com/permissions. 658–659 (Table B.1): From *Human Relations* by A. J. DuBrin. Copyright © 1997. Adapted by permission of Prentice-Hall, Inc. Upper Saddle River, NJ. 675–681: Copyright © 2011 by Phil Bartle, PhD. Reprinted by permission of the author.

Index

Absolute qualifiers, 554–555
Adjectives
  author's tone and, 478
  used to express facts, 551
  used to express opinions, 549–552
Analyze (critical thinking level), 328, 329–330, 331, 334, 341
Anderson, Lorin W., 328
Annotating, 284–285, 286–288
  defined, 284
  example, 287–288
  outline formed from, 288–289
  purpose of, 284–285
  symbols and abbreviations for, 286–287
Antonyms, as context clue, 77–78
Apply (critical thinking level), 328, 329, 331, 334, 340
Author's purpose. See Purpose
Author's tone. See Tone
Average reading rate, 33

Bar graphs, 620–623
Bias, 567–573
  defined, 542, 543, 567
  identifying, 573–575
  investigating author's, 570–573
  investigating your own, 569–570
  opinion and, 567–568
Bloom, Benjamin, 328
Bloom's Taxonomy, 328, 334
  applied to test questions, 340–343
  applied to The Scream (Munch), 331
  explained, 329–330
  summary, 334
Body, used for reading, 15–16
Bureau of Labor Statistics, 6, 7
Business communication reading, 653–673

Career, income potential of a, 6–7
Career readings
  "Dogs Trained to Smell Cell Phones Will Fight Prison Drug Crimes" (Gasaway Long), 265–274
  "Domestic Drama: On-Again, Off-Again" (Svoboda), 596–606
  "Every Child Needs the Arts" (Fowler), 376–387

"Join Our Fight Against AIDS" (UNICEF), 130–138
"A New World" (McKibben), 445–459
"School Texts :(: Educators Differ on How to Handle Cell Phones in Classrooms" (Baker), 195–204
"Social Media and Politics: Truthiness and Astroturfing" (Wagstaff), 525–537
"Today's Generations Face New Communication Gaps" (Kersten), 55–65
Casual reader, dedicated reader vs., 21, 23–24
Casual reading rate, 33
Causal chain, 230
Cause and effect
  defined, 230
  questions asked by, 236
  sample paragraph, 232
  signal words for, 231
Chunking, 29–31, 33
Classification
  defined, 222
  questions asked by, 236
  sample paragraph, 223–224
  signal words for, 223
College readings
  "Celebrity Endorsements" (Drewniany/Jewler), 45–55
  "Easter Island: Some Revisions in a Popular Environmental Story" (Miller/Spoolman), 435–445
  "The Hacker" (Anderson/Ferro/Hilton), 514–525
  "Home Confinement and Electronic Monitoring" (Gaines/Miller), 255–265
  "How Can I Change a Bad Health Habit?" (Hales), 122–130
  "Improving Everyday Memory" (Weiten), 585–596
  "Paleolithic Cave Painting" (Kleiner), 362–375
  "Technology and Learning" (Koch), 184–194
College, vocabulary of, 106–111
Communications readings, 43–65

Comparatives, 556
Comparison
  defined, 224
  finding proof for, 556–557
  questions asked by, 236
  sample paragraph, 225–226
  signal words for, 225
Computer and information sciences readings, 514–537
Connotation of words
  defined, 91, 471
  denotation vs., 470–471
  inference and, 472
  objective tone in, 475
  subjective tone in, 474
  tone and, 470
  vocabulary development through, 91–92
Context clues, 71–87
  antonyms, 77–78
  examples, 73–74, 73–77
  finding, 72–73
  four types of, 73
  punctuation note, 77
  signal words, 76
  synonyms, 80–82
  your logic, 82–83
Context, determining author's purpose, 19
Contrast
  defined, 224
  questions asked by, 236
  sample paragraph, 226
Cornell note-taking system, 303–305
Create (critical thinking level), 328, 330, 331, 334, 341
Credibility of sources, 563–566
Criminal justice readings, 255–274
Critical thinking, 323
  about The Scream (Munch), 331
  applied to visuals, 628–629
  Bloom's Taxonomy, 328–329, 334
  determining hierarchy with, 335–336
  as a learning process, 327–328
  levels of, 328–331
  reading guide for asking critical thinking questions, 352–354
  used to analyze reading passages, 345–352

used to analyze test questions, 340–345
used to determine hierarchy, 335–336
Critical thinking skills applied to visuals. See Textbook visuals

Dedicated reader, casual reader vs., 21, 23–24
Definition
  defined, 227
  questions asked by, 236
  sample paragraph, 228
  signal words for, 227
  working, 78
Denotation
  connotation vs., 470–471
  defined, 91, 470
  objective tone and, 475
Descriptions, space order pattern used for, 235
Diagrams, learning vocabulary via, 109–110
Dramatic irony, 491, 495

EASY note cards, 87–89
Education
  income and, 6–7
  readings, 184–204
Education Pays 2010 report, 6
Einstein, Albert, 15
Environmental science readings, 435–459
-est, 556
Evaluate (critical thinking level), 328, 330, 331, 334, 341
Evaluating points of view. See Points of view
Exaggeration
  hyperbole, 488–489
  with qualifiers, 554
Examples
  as context clues, 74–77
  defined, 228
  questions asked by, 237
  sample paragraph, 229–230
  signal words for, 229
Expert opinion, 561
Express (PIE), 17, 18, 463, 464–465, 466, 469
Expressive purpose, subjective tone and, 497

Fact(s)
  adjectives used to express, 551
  defined, 542, 543

702

identifying, 557–560,
573–575
opinions *vs.*, 546–547
qualifiers used to express,
553–556
sentence stems
introducing, 543
as verifiable, 543–545
Factual sentences, 547–549
Figurative language, 485–495
hyperbole, 488–489
irony, 490–494
metaphors, 485–487
personification, 487–488
similes, 485–487
"Flesh it out" paraphrasing
method, 316–319
Flowcharts, 623–625
Future, visualizing your, 8–11

General to specific hierarchy, 335
Genres, author's purpose and, 18

Habits, good reading, 17
Headings, questions formed
from, 276–277
Health readings, 122–138,
632–653
Hierarchy
critical thinking used to
determine, 335–336
defined, 335
general to specific, 335
top-to-bottom, 336
Highlighting, 284–286
defined, 284
marking the right amount
for, 285–286
outline formed from,
288–289
purpose of, 284–285
Hyperbole, 485, 488–489, 495

Imagination, used for reading, 15
Implied main idea, 413–425
of longer selections,
420–425
of paragraphs, 413–420
Income, education and, 6–7
Inferences
and details, 394–397
identifying patterns, 405–413
implied main idea, 413–425
and prior knowledge,
397–404
process, 392–393
Inform (PIE), 17, 18, 463, 464,
465–466, 469
Informative article, choosing,
25–28
Informative purpose, 496–497
Informed opinion, 562
Intensity of words, tone and,
478–479
Interactivity of reading, 15–16, 29
Interpretation of textbook
visuals
bar graphs, 620–623
flowcharts, 623–625

line graphs, 617–620
photographs, 625–627
pie charts, 614–616
tables, 609–614
Irony, 490–494
dramatic, 491, 495
situational, 490, 495
verbal, 490, 495

Krathwohl, David R., 328

Learning reading rate, 33
Learning tasks, 23–24
Line graphs, 617–620
Literal language, 485

Magazines, purpose and, 18
Main idea(s)
finding in topic sentences,
155–156
implied, 413–425
major *vs.* minor details
supporting, 212–214
in MAPPS, 144, 154–155
marking answer to question
about, 145
purpose of, 154
Major supporting detail,
212–214
MAPPS (mark, about, point,
proof, summary)
answers to questions,
marking, 144–145
explained, 143–144
finding, 208–209
highlighting (note taking)
and, 286
main idea, 154–155
major *vs.* minor details,
212–214
marking answers to
questions, 144–145
organizational patterns. *See*
Organizational patterns
outline, 288–289
supporting detail, 209
thesis statements, 169–172
topic, identifying, 145–146
topic sentence, 163–166
Marking answers to questions,
144–145
Marking the text while reading,
15–16
Metaphors, 485–487, 495
Minor supporting detail,
212–214
Most, 556
Multiple-choice questions,
342–343

Negative connotations/
denotations, 471, 480,
481, 485
Note taking
annotating for, 284–285,
286–288
asking questions and
marking answers,
276–280

Cornell system, 303–305
highlighting for, 284–286
most important ideas, 284
outline, 288–289
paraphrasing, 312–319

Objective
defined, 543
facts and, 543
Objective tone, 475
with informative purpose,
496–497
relationship between author's
tone and purpose in, 496
Opinion(s)
adjectives used to express,
549–552
bias and, 567–568
defined, 542, 543
expert, 561
facts *vs.*, 546–547
identifying, 557–560,
573–575
informed, 562
qualifiers used to express,
553–556
Opinion sentences, 547–549
Opinion words, 546, 560
Organizational patterns
cause and effect, 230–232
classification, 222–224
comparison and contrast,
224–225
definition, 227
examples, 228–230
listing, 229
questions answered by,
236–237
space order, 235–236
supporting details, 219–220
supporting details organized
by, 219–220
time order, 232–235
types of, 222
Outline, from note taking,
288–289

Paragraph, common uses of first
sentence of, 165–166
Paraphrasing, 312–319
"flesh it out" method,
316–319
"switch it, flip it, tweak it"
method, 312–315
Patterns of organization. *See*
Organizational patterns
Pauk, Walter, 303
People on the street, as source
of information,
562–563
Personification, 487–488, 495
Persuade (PIE), 17, 18, 463,
467–468, 469
Persuasive purpose, subjective
tone and, 497
Photographs, 625–627
PIE (persuade, inform, review),
17–18, 463–469
Pie charts, 614–616

Point (author's). *See* Main idea(s)
Points of view
bias, 542, 567–573
comparatives, 556
comparisons, 556–557
facts, 542, 543–545
opinions, 542, 545–551
qualifiers, 553–556
sources of information,
560–566
superlatives, 556
Positive connotation/
denotation, 471, 472,
480–481, 485
Predictions, about reading
material, 21
Prefixes, 106
adding information to the
meaning, 95–96
defined, 93
having more than one
meaning, 95
identifying, 97
Prereading habits
activating your prior
knowledge, 21
determining author's
purpose, 17–20
making predictions, 21
surveying a reading,
20–21
Prior knowledge, 631
defined, 21
as prereading habit, 21
reading knowledge and, 34
Process order, 219
Process writing, 234–235
Proof. *See also* Supporting
details
for comparisons, 556–557
in MAPPS, 144
marking answer to question
about, 145
Psychology readings, 585–606
Purpose
determining author's,
18–20, 463–469
evaluating, 503–513
more than one, 20
persuade, inform, express
(PIE), 17–18, 463, 469
of reading selection, 17–19
tone supporting, 495–502

Qualifiers, 553–556
Questions
advantages of asking, 276
critical thinking used to
analyze, 340–343
marking answers to your,
144–145
reading to answer the,
279–280
titles, headings, and
subtitles turned into,
276–277

Readers, casual *vs.* dedicated,
21, 23–24

Reading
  engaging with, 35–42
  importance of, 5
  as interaction, 15–16, 29
  learning tasks to accomplish
    while, 23–24
  motivation for, 6–7
  talking about, 14, 325–327
Reading comprehension. *See*
    Note taking
Reading material
  prior knowledge on, 21, 34
  purpose of. *See* Purpose
  surveying. *See* Surveying,
    reading material
Reading rate
  average, 33
  based on your reason for
    reading, 33–34
  casual, 33
  increasing, 29–31
  learning, 33
Reading strategies
  after you read, 24–25
  before reading, 17–21
  while you are reading,
    21–24
Remembering (critical thinking
    level), 328, 329, 331,
    334, 340
Root words, 106
  defined, 93
  for different kinds of
    movement, 95
  related to sight, hearing,
    and touch, 94

Salk, Jonas, 322
The Scream (Munch), 331
Sentence(s)
  fact, 547–549
  first in a paragraph, uses,
    165–166
  opinion, 547–549
Sentence stems, introducing
    facts, 543
Signal words
  for antonyms, 90
  for cause and effect, 231
  for classification, 223
  comparison, 80
  contrast, 77, 78
  for contrast, 226
  defined, 222
  for example context clues, 76
  for examples, 90, 229
  looking for, 86
  for process writing, 234
  for space order, 235

for synonyms, 90
  for time order, 233
Similes, 485–487, 495
Situational irony, 490, 495
Sociology reading, 674–696
Sources of information,
    560–566
  credibility, 563–566
  experts, 560, 566
  informed people, 562, 566
  people on the street,
    562–563, 566
Space (spatial) order
  defined, 235
  questions asked by, 237
  sample paragraph, 236
  signal words for pattern, 235
Spelling, word parts and, 94
Subjective
  defined, 545
  opinions and, 545
Subjective tone
  connotations suggesting, 474
  with expressive purpose, 497
  figurative language, 485
  with persuasive purpose, 497
  relationship between
    author's tone and
    purpose in, 496
Suffixes, 106
  defined, 93
  identifying, 99–100
  in word parts, 97–98
Superlatives, 556
Supporting details
  explained, 208
  finding, 208–209
  major *vs.* minor,
    212–214
  patterns organizing,
    219–220
Surveying, reading material,
    20–21
"Switch it, flip it, tweak it"
    paraphrasing method,
    312–315
Synonyms, as context clues,
    80–82

Tables, in textbooks,
    609–614
Test questions, critical thinking
    used to analyze,
    340–345
Textbooks
  thesis statements in,
    169–175
  vocabulary development
    through, 108–109

Textbook visuals
  bar graphs, 620–623
  critical thinking skills
    applied to, 628–629
  flowcharts, 623–625
  function of, 608
  interpreting, 608–609
  line graphs, 617–620
  photographs, 625–627
  pie charts, 614–616
  tables, 609–614
Thesis statement
  that organize supporting
    details, 219
  in textbook sections,
    169–175
Time order pattern, 232
  narrative writing,
    232–233
  process writing, 234–235
  questions asked by, 237
  sample paragraphs, 233,
    234
  signal words, 233, 234
Titles
  determining author's
    purpose, 19
  questions formed from,
    276–277
Tone
  connotation and, 470,
    472–478
  degree of intensity of words
    and, 478–479
  evaluating author's,
    503–513
  figurative language and,
    485–495
  objective, 474
  specific description of,
    480–485
  subjective, 474
  supporting author's
    purpose, 495–502
Topic(s)
  finding in main ideas,
    155–156
  in MAPPS, 144
  marking answer to question
    about, 145
Topic sentence, 154
  finding topics and main
    ideas in, 155–156
  location of, 163–166
  supporting detail and, 208
Top-to-bottom hierarchy, 336
Transitions, 222. *See also* Signal
    words
Twain, Mark, 6, 15, 17

Understand (critical thinking
    level), 328, 329, 331,
    334, 340
U.S. Census Bureau, 6

Verbal irony, 490, 495
Verbs, critical thinking,
    342–343
Verifiable, facts as, 543–545
Visual arts readings, 362–387
Visualization, of your future,
    8–11
Visuals. *See* Textbook visuals
Vocabulary/vocabulary
    development
  of college, 106–111
  connotation of words and,
    91–92
  with context clues, 71–87, 90
  denotation of words, 91–92
  through diagrams,
    109–110
  EASY note cards, 87–89
  expanding your, 111–113
  by learning word parts,
    93–105
  strategies, 71
  in textbooks, 108–109
  using new words, 71

Word parts, 93–105
  combining, 94, 95
  glossary, 103–105
  prefixes, 93, 95–97
  roots, 93, 94–95
  spelling changes and, 94
  suffixes, 93, 97–98
  used to make meaning of
    words, 100–101
Words
  connotations of, 470–472
  defining as you read with
    context clues, 71–77
  degree of intensity in,
    478–479
  EASY note cards to study,
    87–89
  expressing opinions, 560
  opinion, 546, 560
  showing importance of, in
    textbooks, 108–109
  signal. *See* Signal words
  using more specific tone,
    480–485
  using word parts to define.
    See Word parts
  vocabulary strategies, 71
  word parts and, 93
Working definition, 78